P9-DNH-106

HUMANS
OF NEW YORK

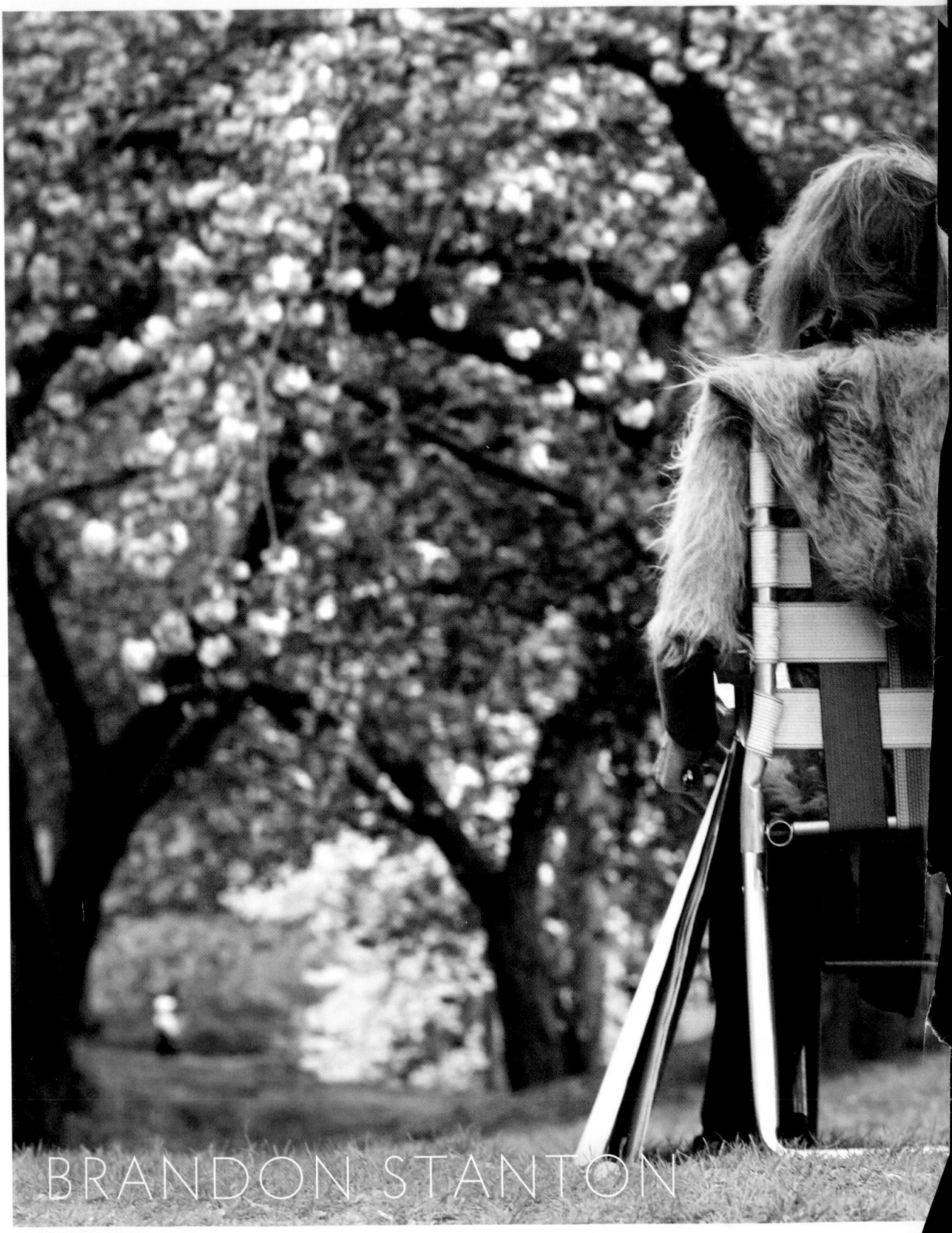
BRANDON STANTON

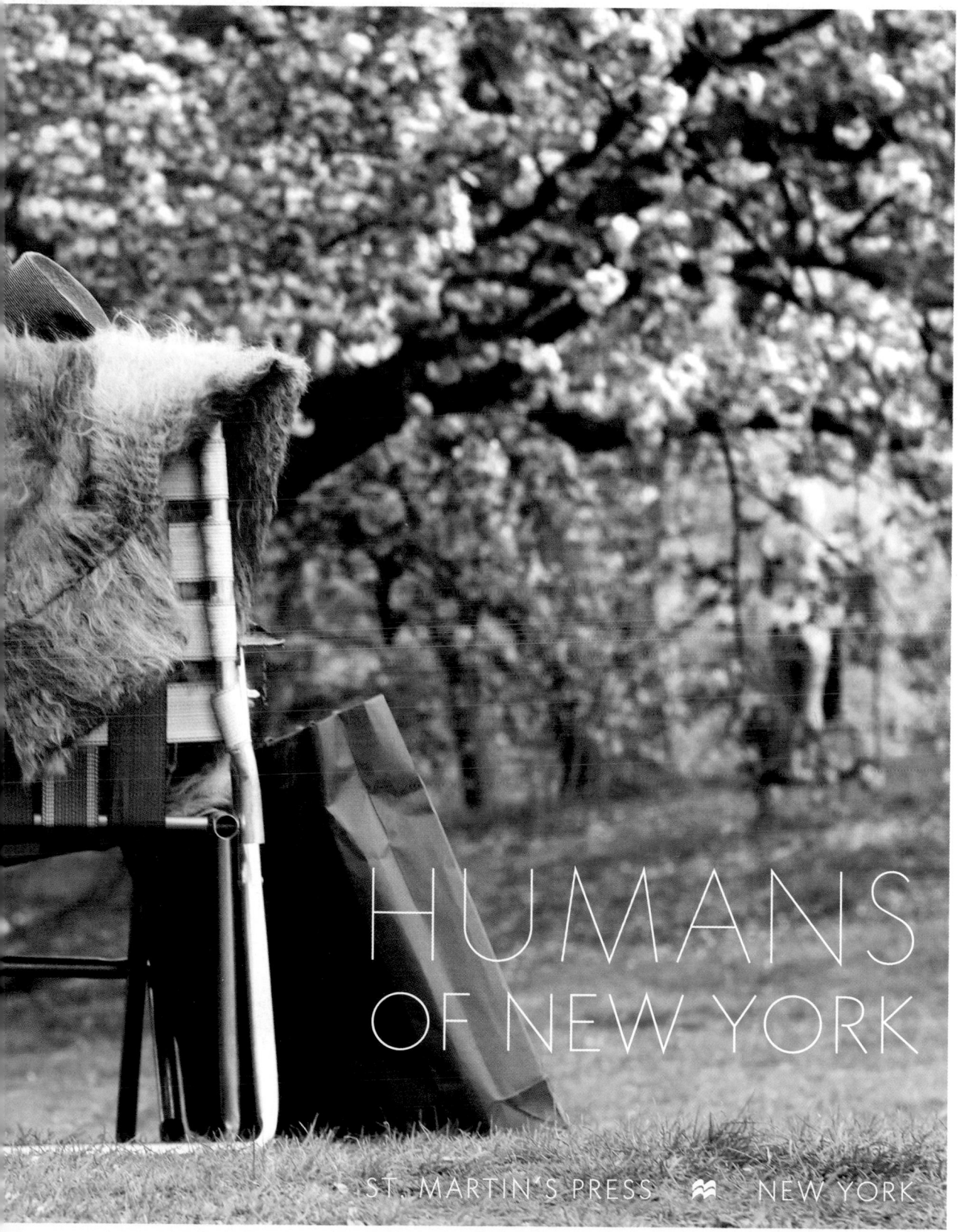

# HUMANS OF NEW YORK

ST. MARTIN'S PRESS NEW YORK

TO THE CITY OF NEW YORK.

I HAD THIS CRAZY, JUVENILE IDEA
THAT YOU WERE GOING TO MAKE ALL MY
DREAMS COME TRUE. AND YOU DID.

HUMANS OF NEW YORK. COPYRIGHT © 2013 BY BRANDON STANTON.
ALL RIGHTS RESERVED. PRINTED IN U.S.A. FOR INFORMATION, ADDRESS
ST. MARTIN'S PRESS, 175 FIFTH AVENUE, NEW YORK, N.Y. 10010.

WWW.STMARTINS.COM

BOOK DESIGN: JONATHAN BENNETT
PRODUCTION MANAGER: ERIC GLADSTONE

LIBRARY OF CONGRESS CATALOGING-IN-PUBLICATION DATA
AVAILABLE UPON REQUEST

ISBN 978-1-250-03882-1 (HARDCOVER)
ISBN 978-1-250-03881-4 (E-BOOK)

ST. MARTIN'S PRESS BOOKS MAY BE PURCHASED FOR EDUCATIONAL, BUSINESS, OR PROMOTIONAL USE. FOR INFORMATION ON BULK PURCHASES, PLEASE CONTACT MACMILLAN CORPORATE AND PREMIUM SALES DEPARTMENT AT 1-800-221-7945 EXTENSION 5442 OR WRITE SPECIALMARKETS@MACMILLAN.COM.

FIRST EDITION: OCTOBER 2013

10 9 8 7

# INTRODUCTION

I got my first camera in January 2010. I was working as a bond trader, so I only had time to use it on weekends, but I fell in love with it. Every Saturday and Sunday, I'd take my camera into downtown Chicago and photograph everything. If I found something especially beautiful, I'd photograph it from twenty different angles— just to be sure that I'd end up with one good shot. I'd return home each night with over one thousand new photos. Almost all of them were awful, but I didn't mind. I was hooked. Photography felt like a treasure hunt, and even though I sucked at it, I'd occasionally stumble upon a diamond. And that was enough to keep me wanting more.

I lost my trading job that July and immediately decided I wanted to be a photographer. I had enjoyed my time as a trader. The job was challenging and stimulating. And I'd obsessed over markets in the same way that I'd later obsess over photography. But the end goal of trading was always money. Two years of my life were spent obsessing over money, and in the end I had nothing to show for it. I wanted to spend the next phase of my life doing work that I valued as much as the reward. Photography seemed like an obvious choice. Like I said, it felt like a treasure hunt. And that seemed like a pretty good way to spend my time.

My parents thought I was crazy. There were several awkward phone calls during this time. My mother didn't try to hide her disappointment. She saw bond trading as a very prestigious profession. Photography, on the other hand, seemed like a thinly veiled attempt to avoid employment. After all, I had no experience or formal training. And it didn't help that I had no plan for making money. But I figured the best way to become a photographer was to start photographing. So I planned a photo tour through several major American cities.

I left Chicago in late July and started across the country. My first stop was Pittsburgh. I explored the city in the same way that I'd explored Chicago: I walked around aimlessly, got lost, and photographed everything. Each night I uploaded my photos to an album on my personal Facebook account. I titled the album "Yellow Steel Bridges," because that was my first impression of the city. Most of my photos were of buildings and bridges. But occasionally, I'd include a shot of an interesting person.

I repeated the process in Philadelphia. I spent my days combing the streets for interesting photographs, and each night I deposited the photos in a Facebook album. I named this album "Bricks and Flags." My photos remained similar to those I'd taken in Chicago and Pittsburgh, but with one notable exception. I was starting to take more and more pictures of people. I'd begun to move beyond candid shots, and was actually stopping strangers on the street. The resulting portraits seemed to be the most compelling of my photographs, so I focused more energy on seeking them out.

I arrived in New York in early August. I planned to spend a week in the city before hopping on a plane for the West Coast, but I ended up staying for the rest of the summer. I remember the moment my bus emerged from the Lincoln Tunnel and I saw the city for the first time. The sidewalks were covered with people. The buildings were impressive, but what struck me most were the people. There were tons of them. And they all seemed to be in a hurry. That night, I created a photo album for my New York photos. I called it "Humans of New York."

Back then I had no intention of starting a blog. I didn't even know what a blog was. But after spending some time in New York, I knew that I wanted to photograph people. I spent that entire summer stopping people on the streets. By the end of August, I'd collected over six hundred portraits. I began to sense that I was on to something special. I returned to Chicago long enough to pack my bags, and returned to New York on November 4, 2010.

I first envisioned HONY as a photographic census of New York City. I wanted to take ten thousand portraits and plot them on an interactive map of the city. That way you could click on any neighborhood in New York and scroll through the faces of people who live there. I worked for several months with that goal in mind. This effort resulted in thousands of photographs, but very few people were paying attention. During the first year of HONY, only a handful of people were coming to my Web site each day.

Then I discovered the power of social media. I've got to thank my friend Mike Schaefer, because he was the one who convinced me to start a Facebook page for Humans of New York. I'd been resisting the suggestion for some time, because I was already posting my photos to my personal account. Making a separate page seemed redundant. But one night he finally talked me into it, and I started a new page for Humans of New York. In just over a year, that haphazard decision would lead to the discovery of half a million fans.

It wasn't an immediate explosion of growth. Progress was slow at first. But after a few weeks of posting, I began to notice unfamiliar names interacting with my photography. With each new post, a few more strangers began to follow my work. I could now see a direct correlation between my work and my growth. HONY was growing every day. After months of spinning my wheels, this was a very liberating feeling.

My next big break came when I discovered Tumblr. No other platform puts a higher value on promoting its artists and creators. HONY took root on Tumblr very quickly, mainly because of the early support of Tumblr's editorial team. Soon hundreds of thousands of people were following HONY on Tumblr, and I remain very thankful for Tumblr's role in my success.

The last major evolution in HONY came when I began interviewing my subjects. Whenever possible, I started pairing my photos with a story or quotation. This mix of photography and writing caused HONY to grow even faster. Hundreds of new fans started following the site every single day. Then thousands. And as the audience began to balloon, HONY evolved from a photography project into an ongoing blog. I began to shift my priorities. I no longer aimed to complete an epic photography project. Instead, I sought to provide my audience with a few good portraits, every single day. And I hope to continue doing so for a very long time.

This book is the result of nearly three years of work. I walked several thousand miles to find these portraits. I stopped over ten thousand people on the street. It was exhausting work, but I enjoyed every minute of it. The people in these pages are very dear to me. By allowing me to take their photo, each one of them helped me to realize my dream. And I am so thankful for their participation.

Last, thanks to all of you who follow my work. You've supported me so much. It's been a dream, really. Thank you for making this happen for me. Thank you, thank you, thank you.

I hope you enjoy the Humans of New York as much as I have.

"I'M JUST FIGURING OUT
WHAT I WANT TO DO,

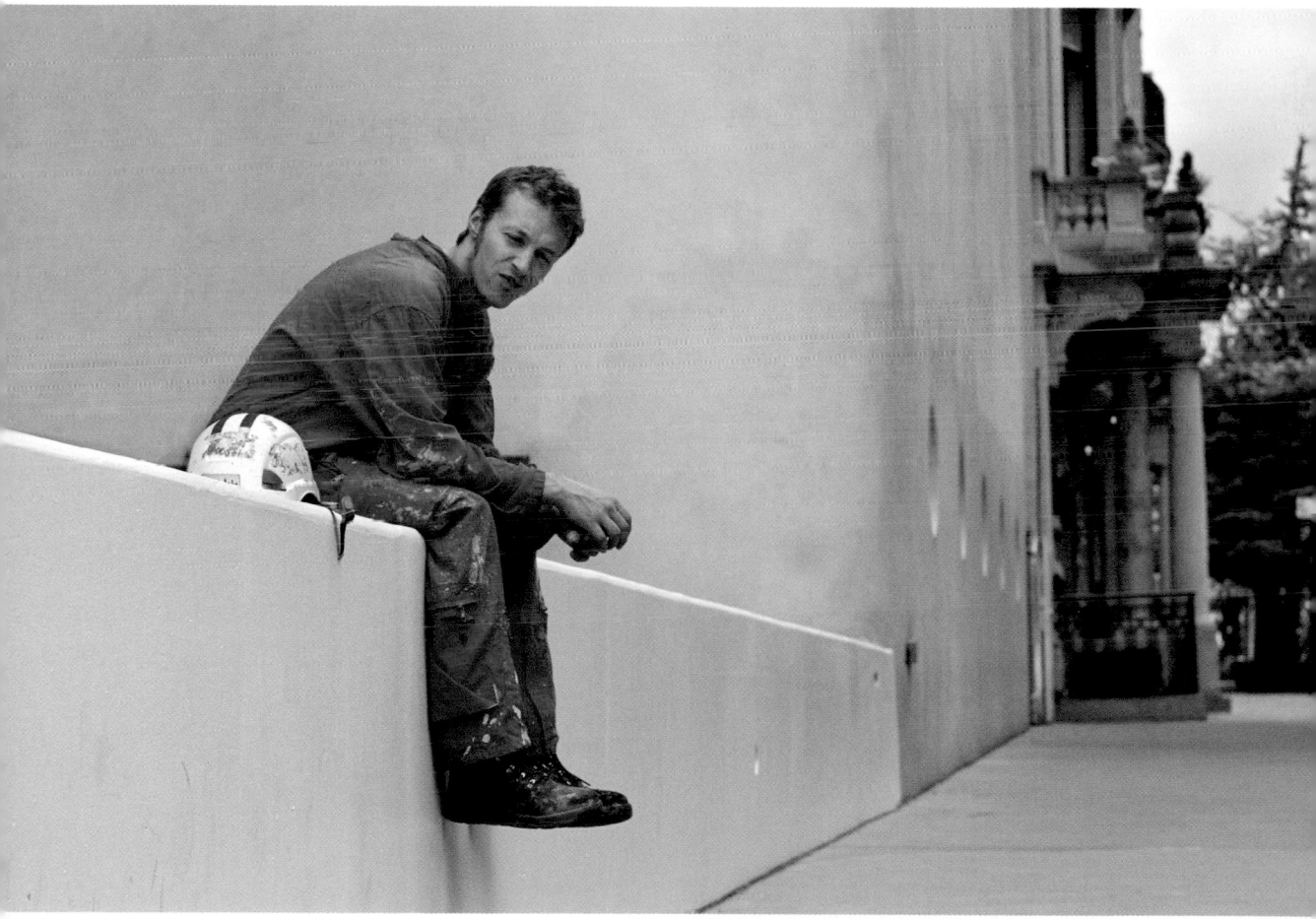

'CAUSE IT AIN'T THIS."

SEEN AT THE WEST INDIAN DAY PARADE

"WILL YOU GIVE ME A COUPLE BUCKS IF I DANCE?"

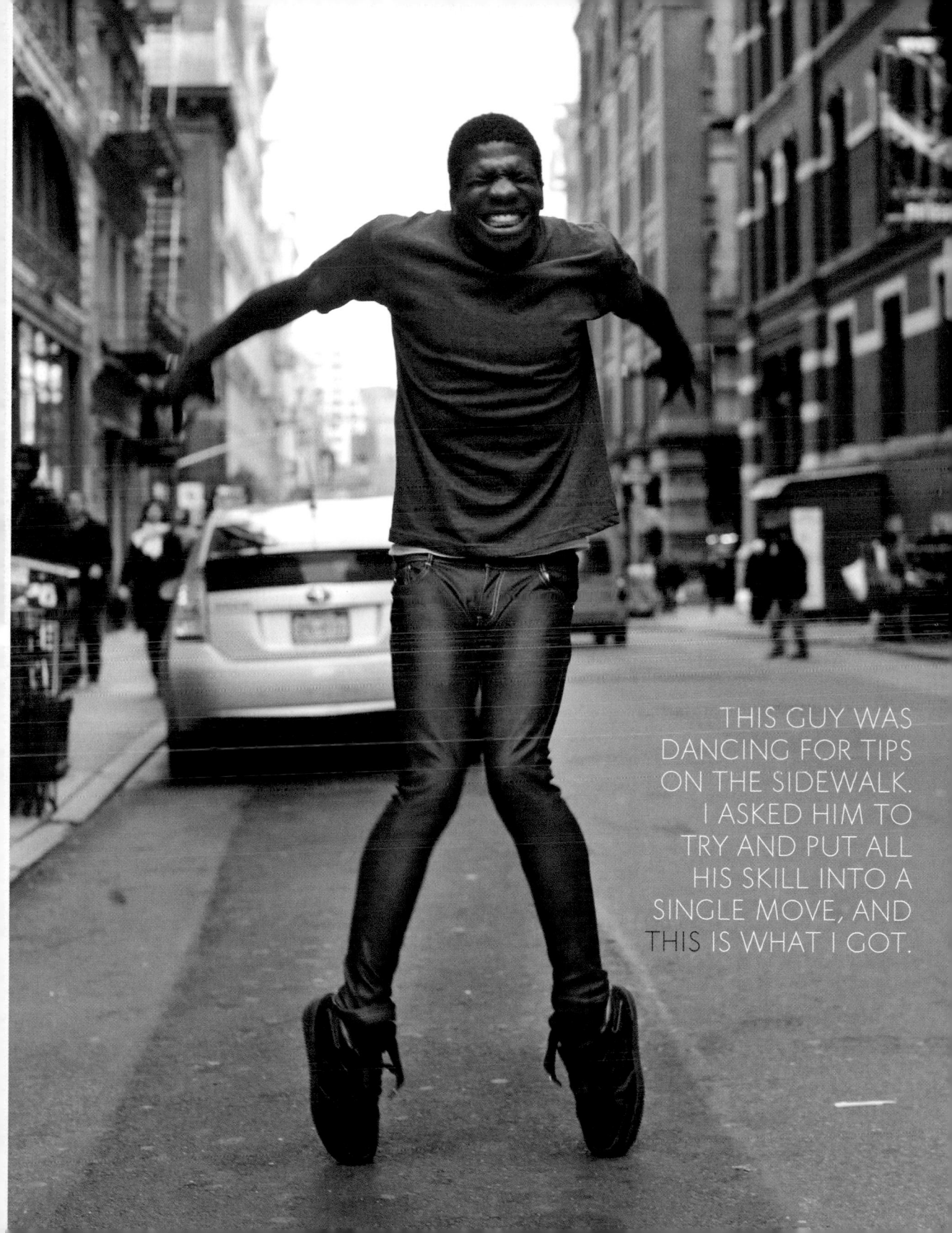

THIS GUY WAS DANCING FOR TIPS ON THE SIDEWALK. I ASKED HIM TO TRY AND PUT ALL HIS SKILL INTO A SINGLE MOVE, AND THIS IS WHAT I GOT.

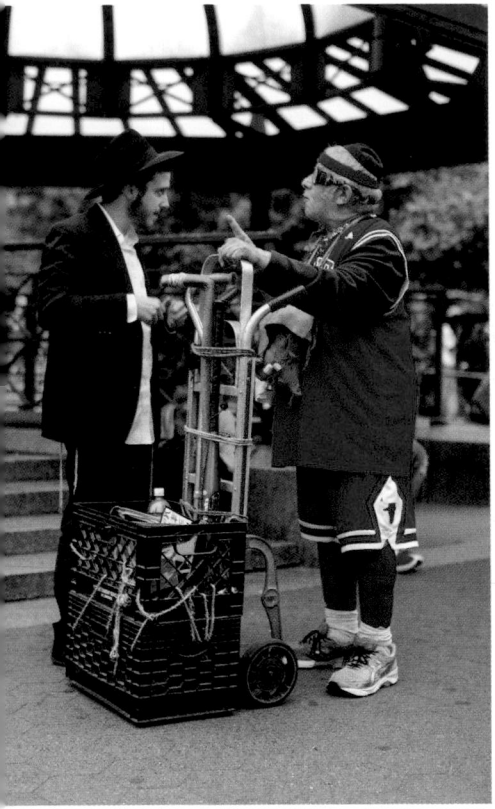

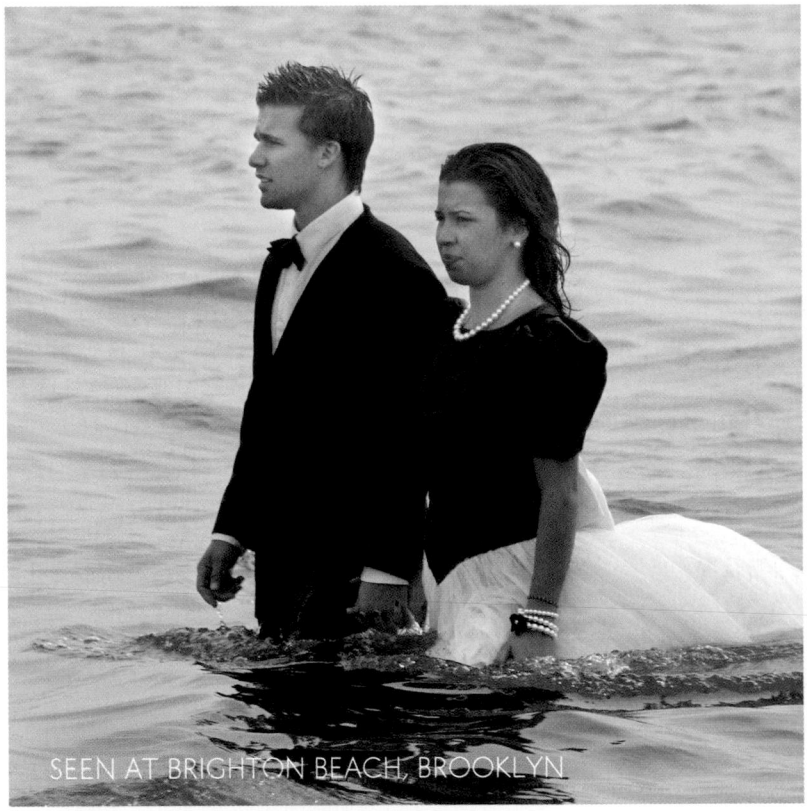

SEEN AT BRIGHTON BEACH, BROOKLYN

GOOD NEWS, EVERYONE!
ALL REMAINING MYSTERIES OF THE UNIVERSE WERE SOLVED YESTERDAY AFTERNOON.

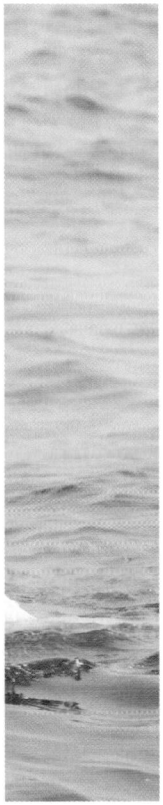

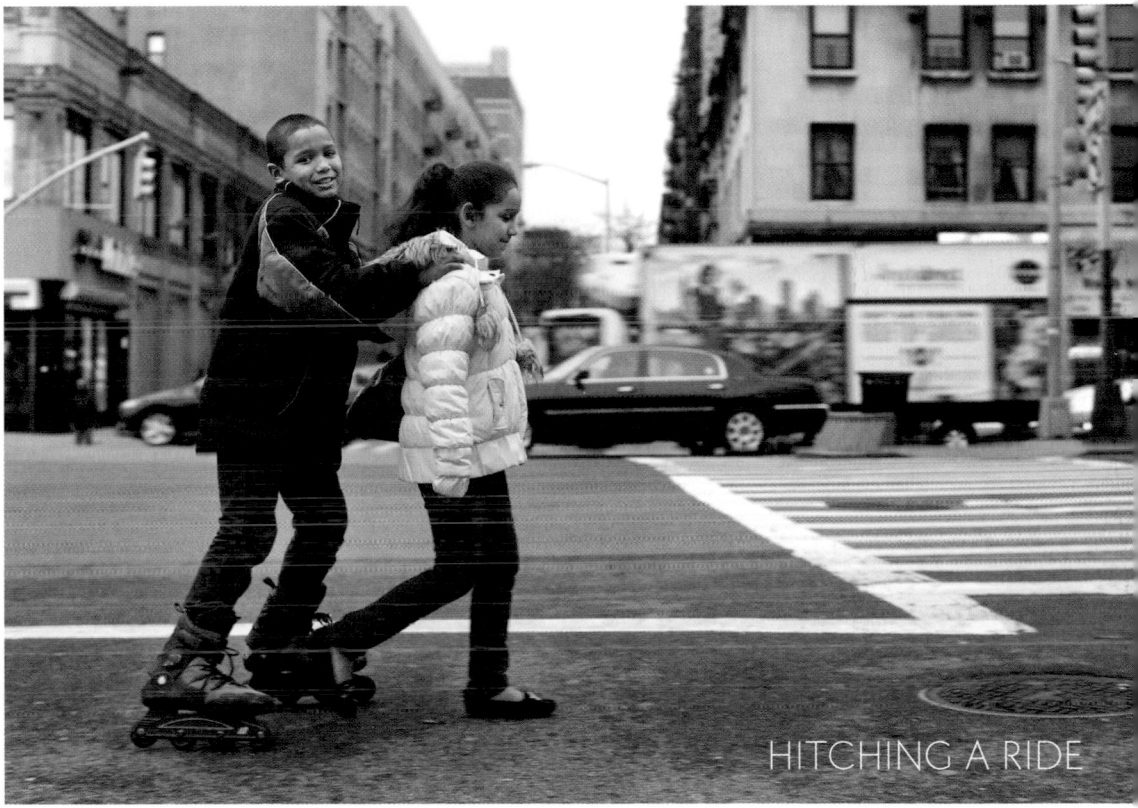
HITCHING A RIDE

SEEN IN BEDFORD-STUYVESANT, BROOKLYN

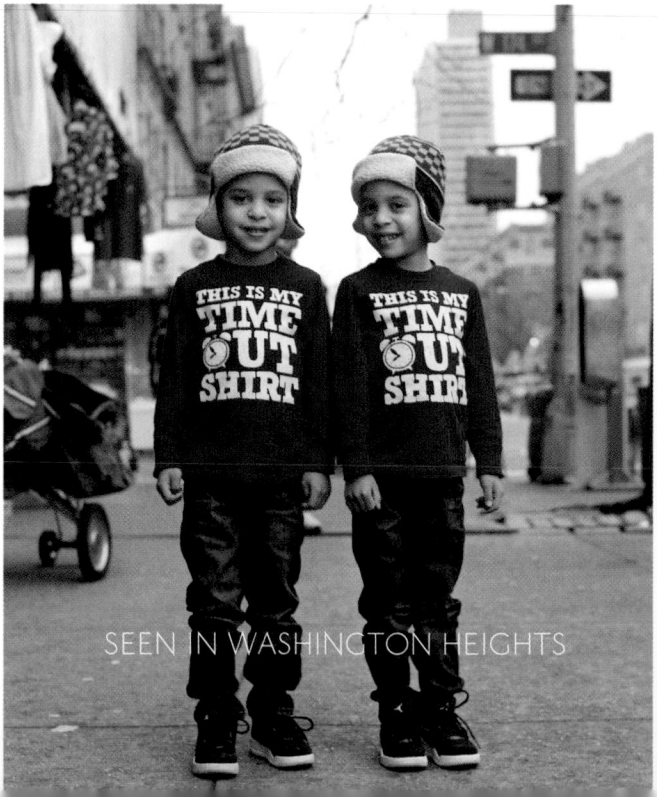


SEEN IN WASHINGTON HEIGHTS

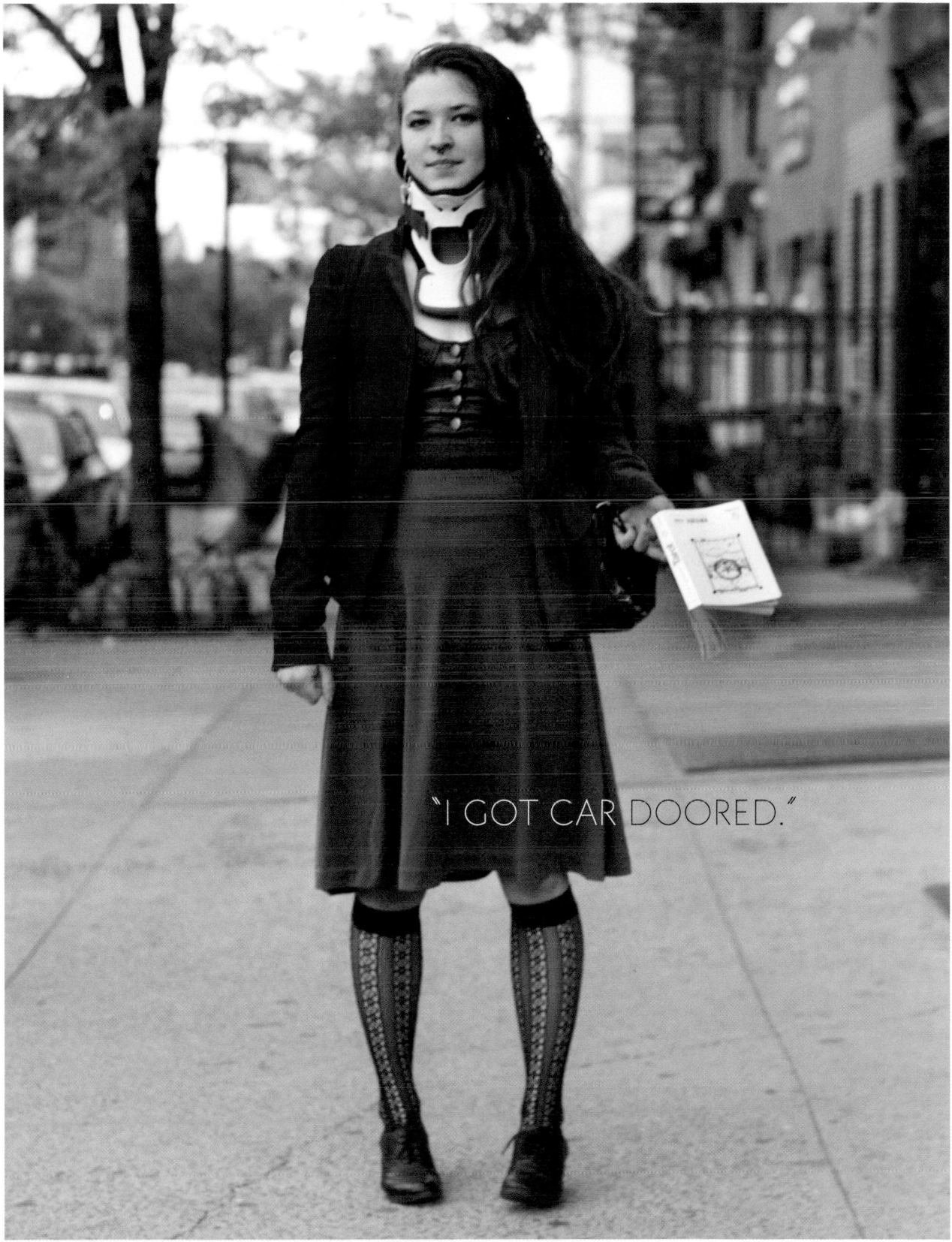
"I GOT CAR DOORED."

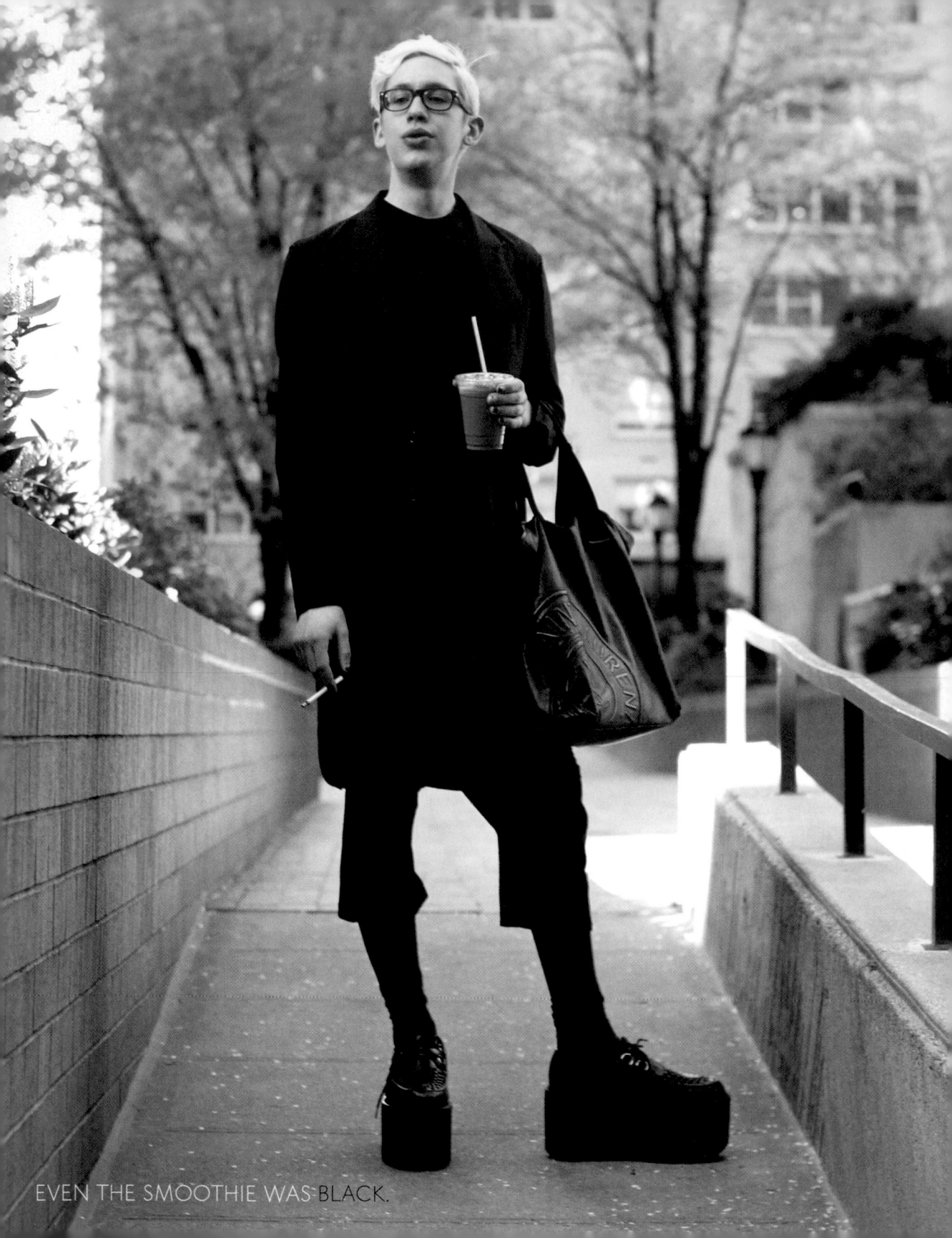

EVEN THE SMOOTHIE WAS BLACK.

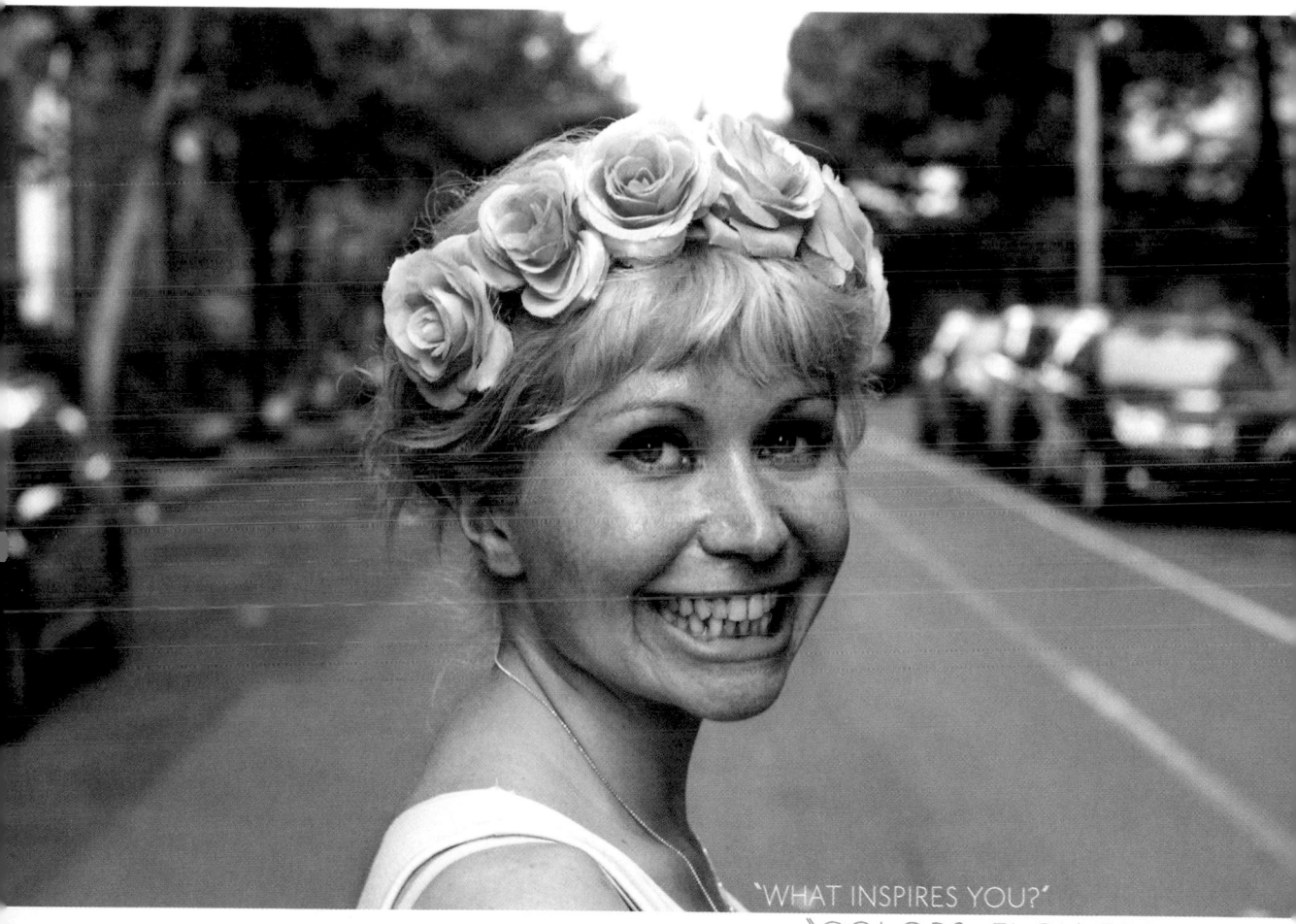

"WHAT INSPIRES YOU?"

"COLORS, FLOWERS,
AND PICNICS."

GAC FILIPAJ IS A REFUGEE FROM THE FORMER YUGOSLAVIA. FOR THE PAST TWELVE YEARS, HE HAS WORKED AS A JANITOR FOR COLUMBIA UNIVERSITY. HIS JOB TITLE IS 'HEAVY CLEANER,' WHICH INCLUDES EMPTYING THE TRASH AND CLEANING THE TOILETS.

THROUGHOUT THAT TIME, HE WORKED UNTIL 11 P.M. EVERY NIGHT DURING THE WEEK. AFTER HIS SHIFT CONCLUDED, HE WOULD START STUDYING. THIS WEEKEND, AFTER TWELVE YEARS OF STUDY, GAC GRADUATED FROM COLUMBIA UNIVERSITY WITH A CLASSICS DEGREE. RARELY HAVE I MET A PERSON WHO EXHIBITED SO MANY QUALITIES I ADMIRE.

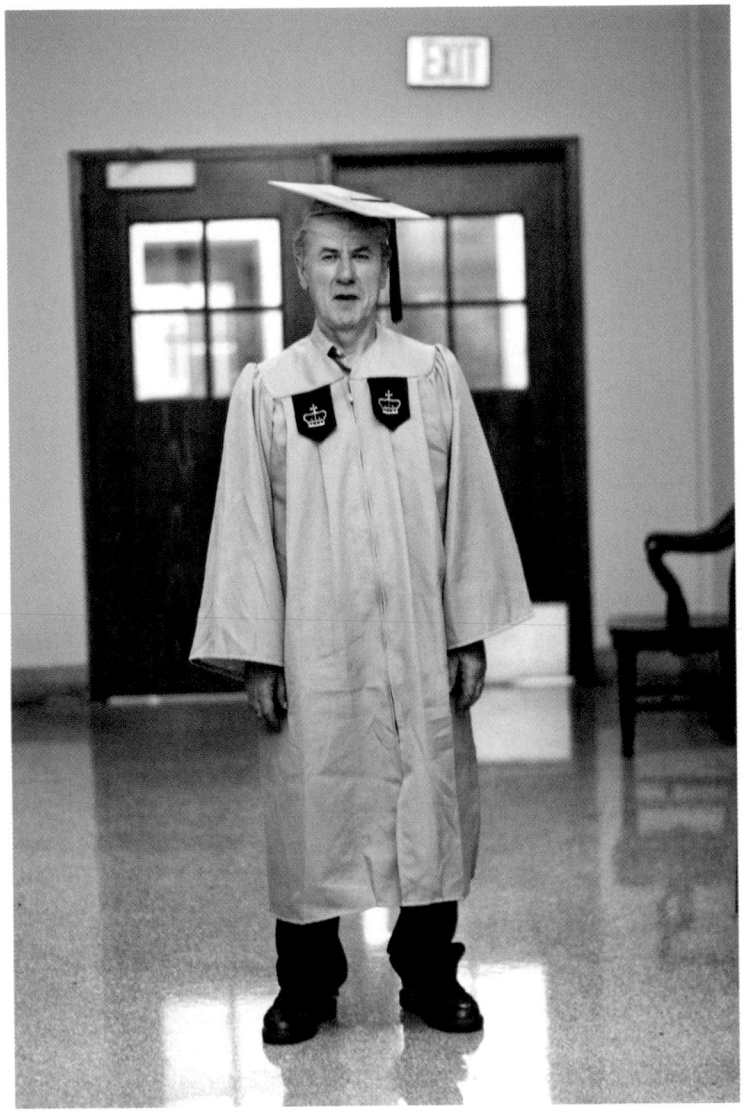

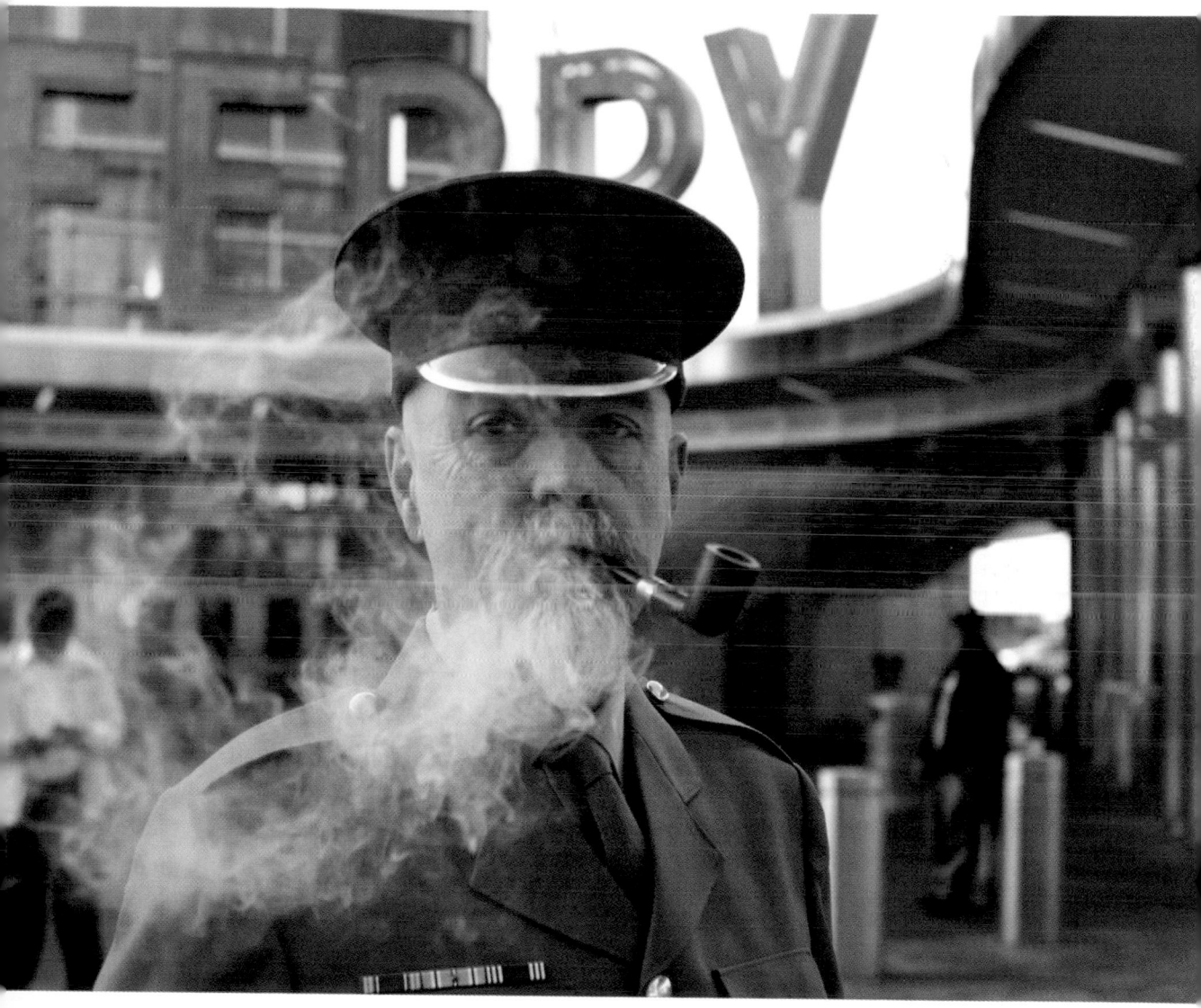


'I CAN TIE A FULL WINDSOR WHILE DRIVING DOWN THE ROAD AT SIXTY-FIVE MILES PER HOUR.'

I NOTICED A LARGE CROWD GATHERED AT WASHINGTON SQUARE PARK.
I PUSHED MY WAY TO THE CENTER, AND FOUND THIS.

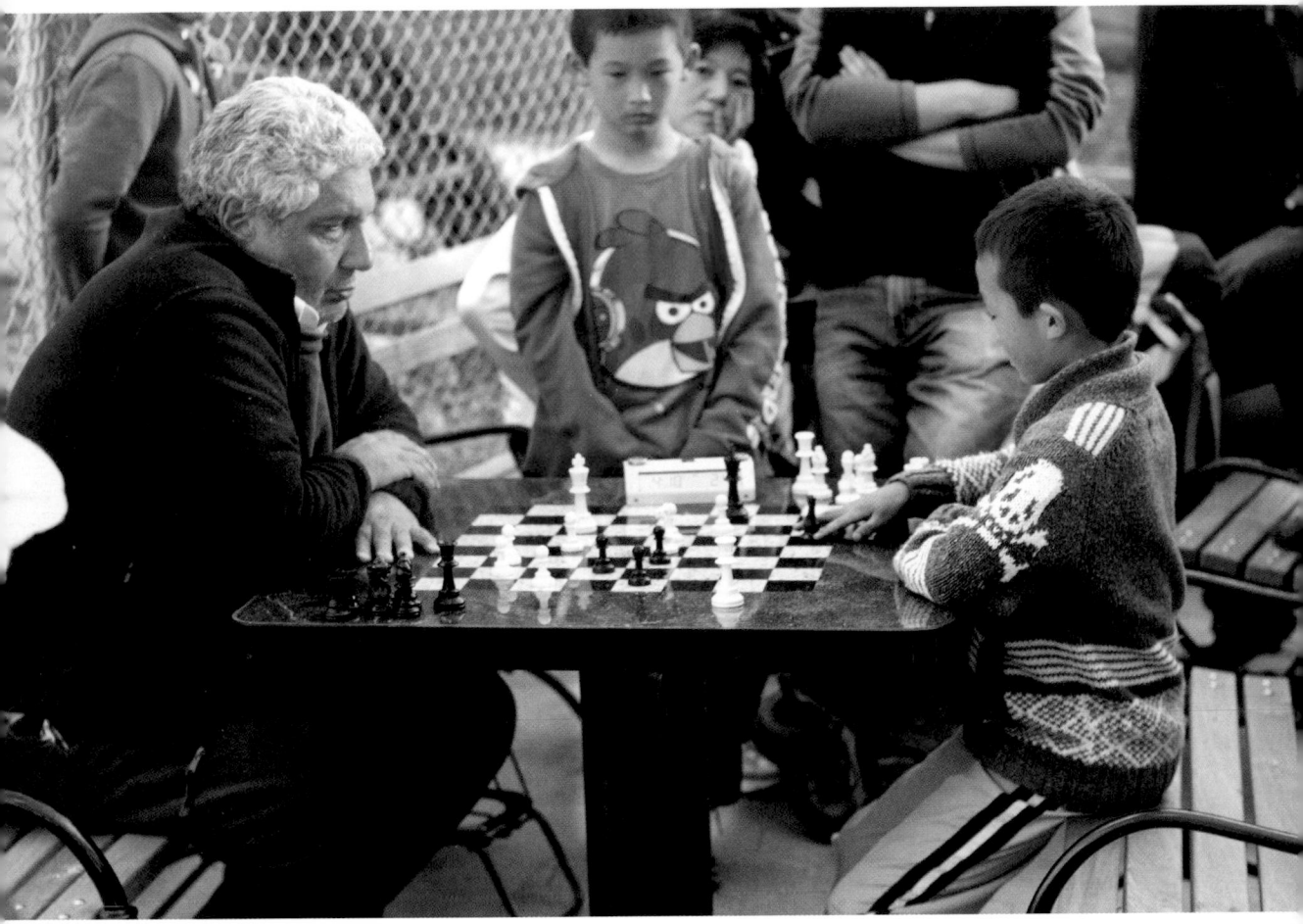

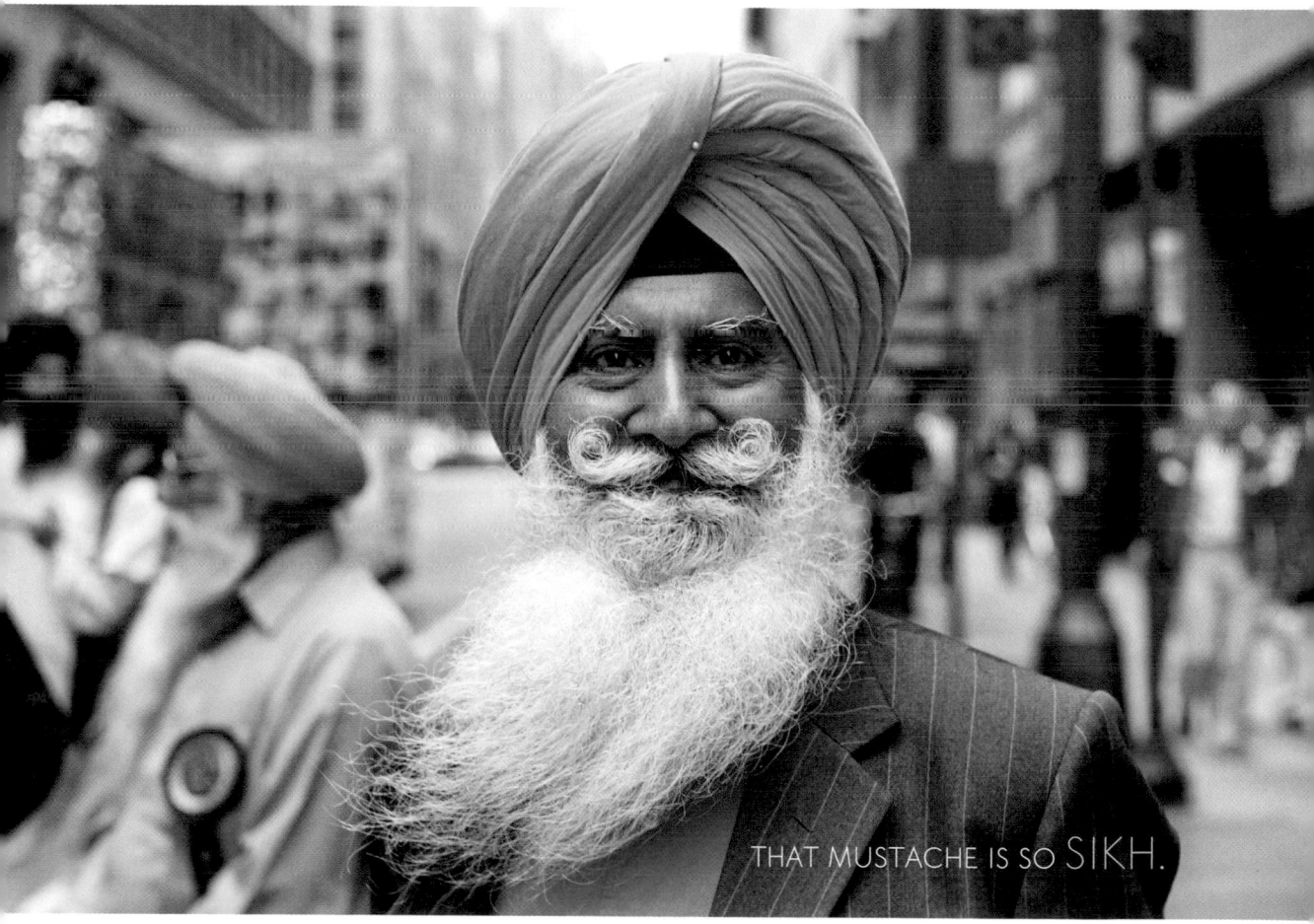


I FOUND A HUGE GEYSER OF STEAM COMING UP FROM A GRATE IN TRIBECA.
THEN I FOUND TWO BALLET STUDENTS EATING LUNCH ON A NEARBY CURB.

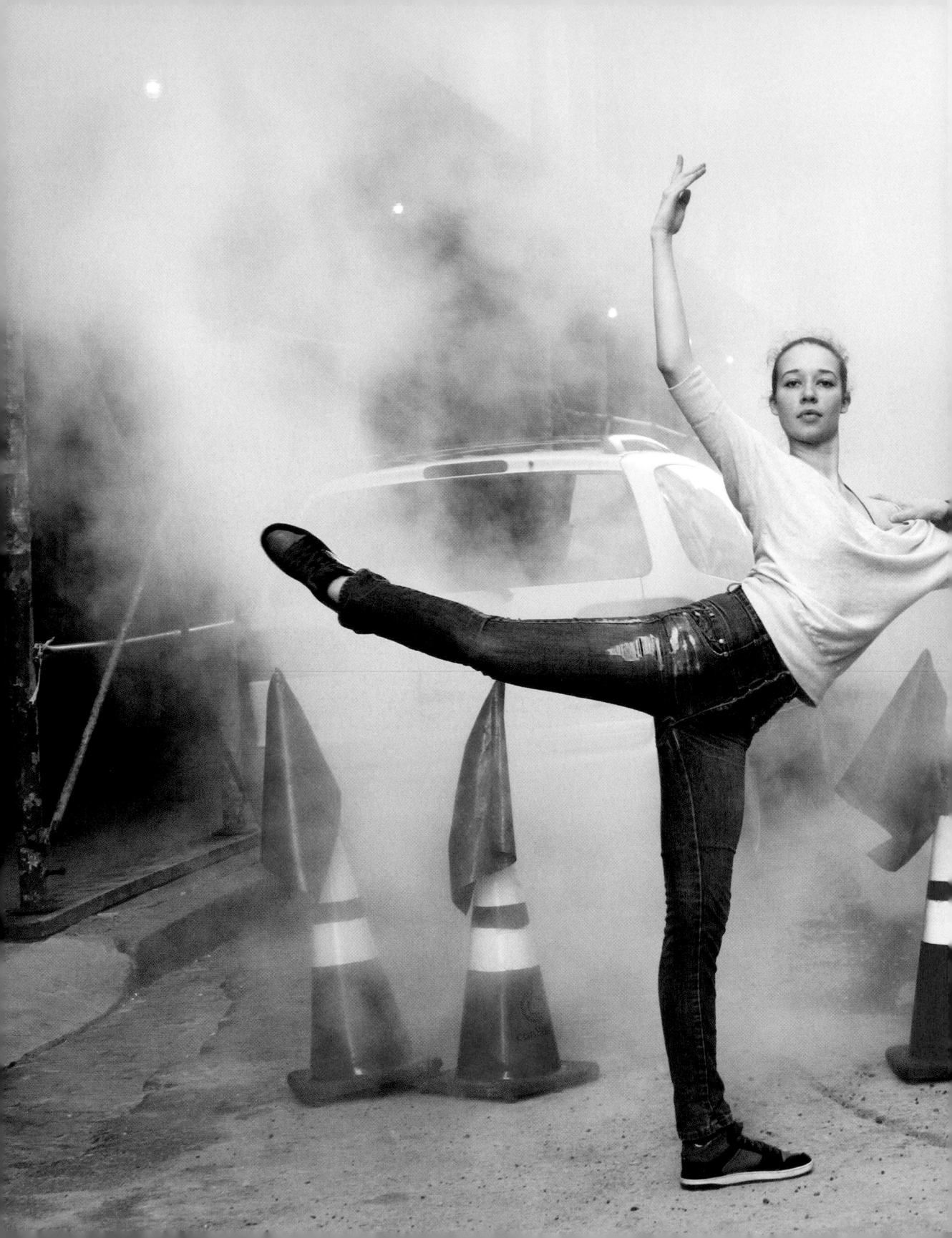

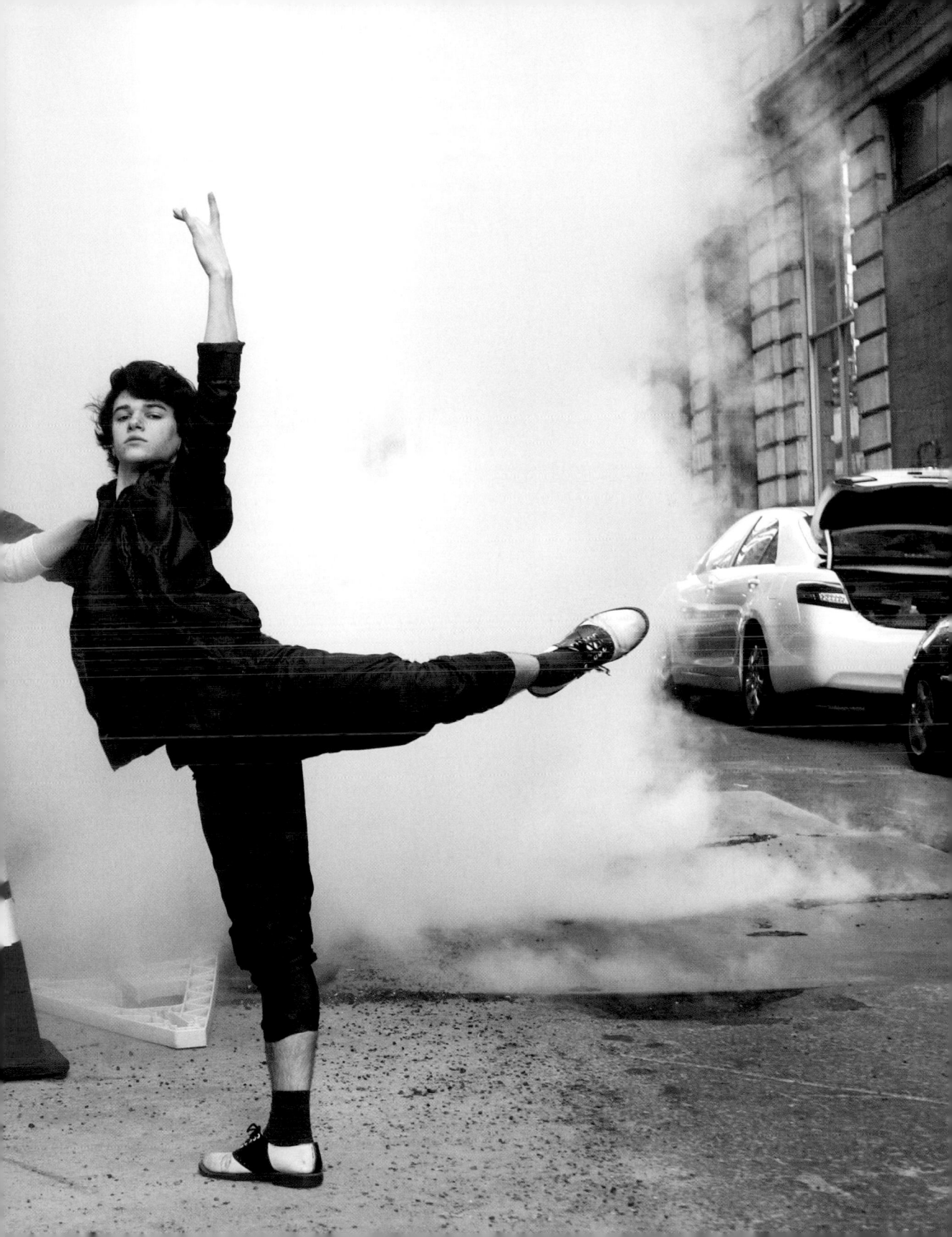

IN AN AGE OF IPHONES AND PLAYSTATIONS, IT'S GREAT TO SEE THAT SOMEBODY'S STILL ROCKING THE BUS-ON-A-STRING.

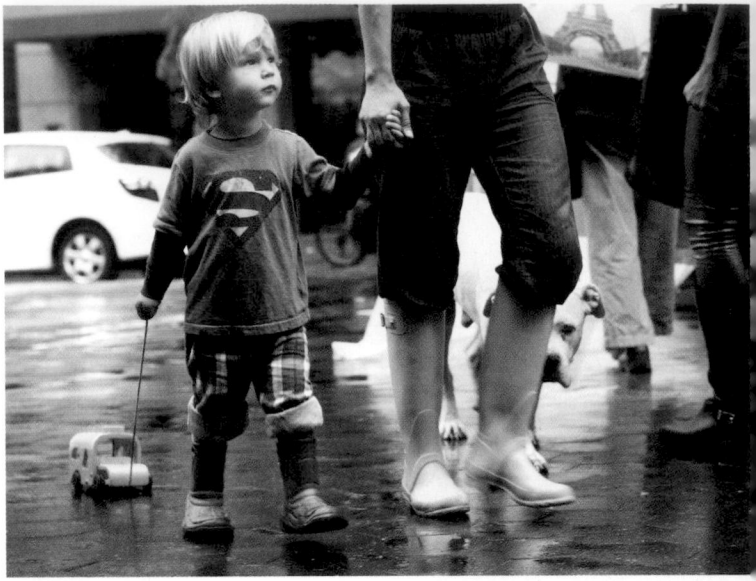

THE HONY DICTIONARY CONTAINS TWO DEFINITIONS FOR THE WORD 'CHAMPION':

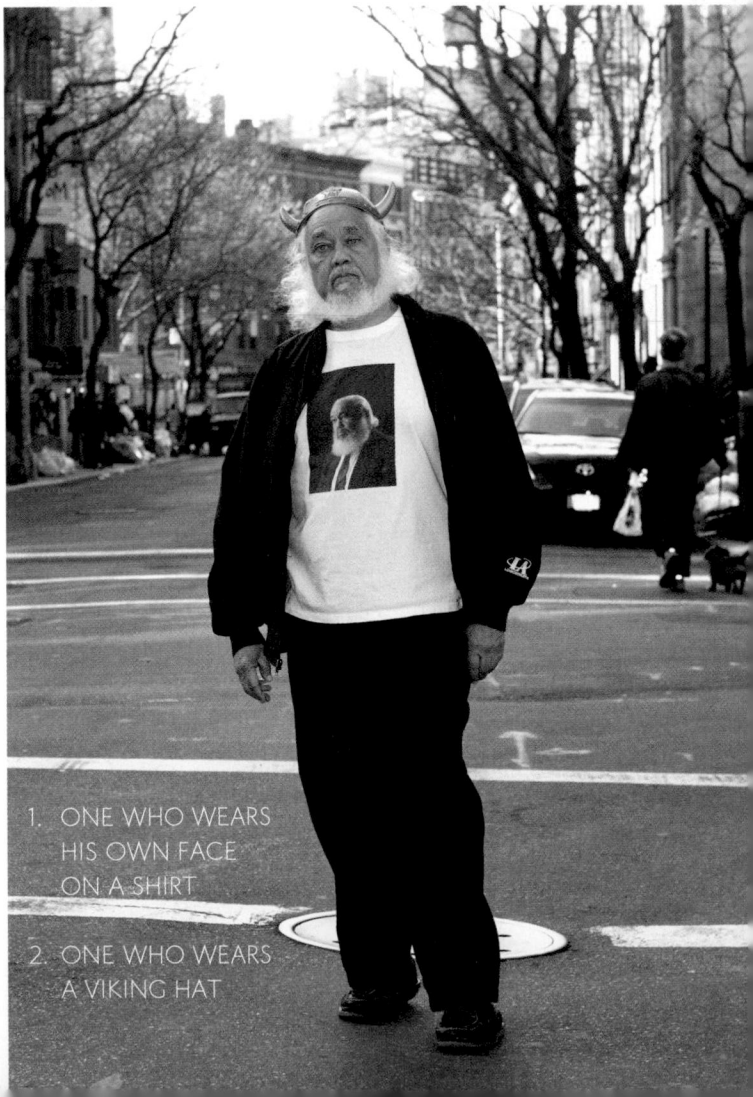

"WE'RE GONNA BE FINE."

WHILE SURVEYING HURRICANE DAMAGE ON STATEN ISLAND, I CAME ACROSS THESE VOLUNTEERS FROM THE MUSLIM-AMERICAN SOCIETY. THEY PAUSED FOR A QUICK PICTURE BEFORE HEADING BACK TO THEIR CAR FOR MORE SUPPLIES.

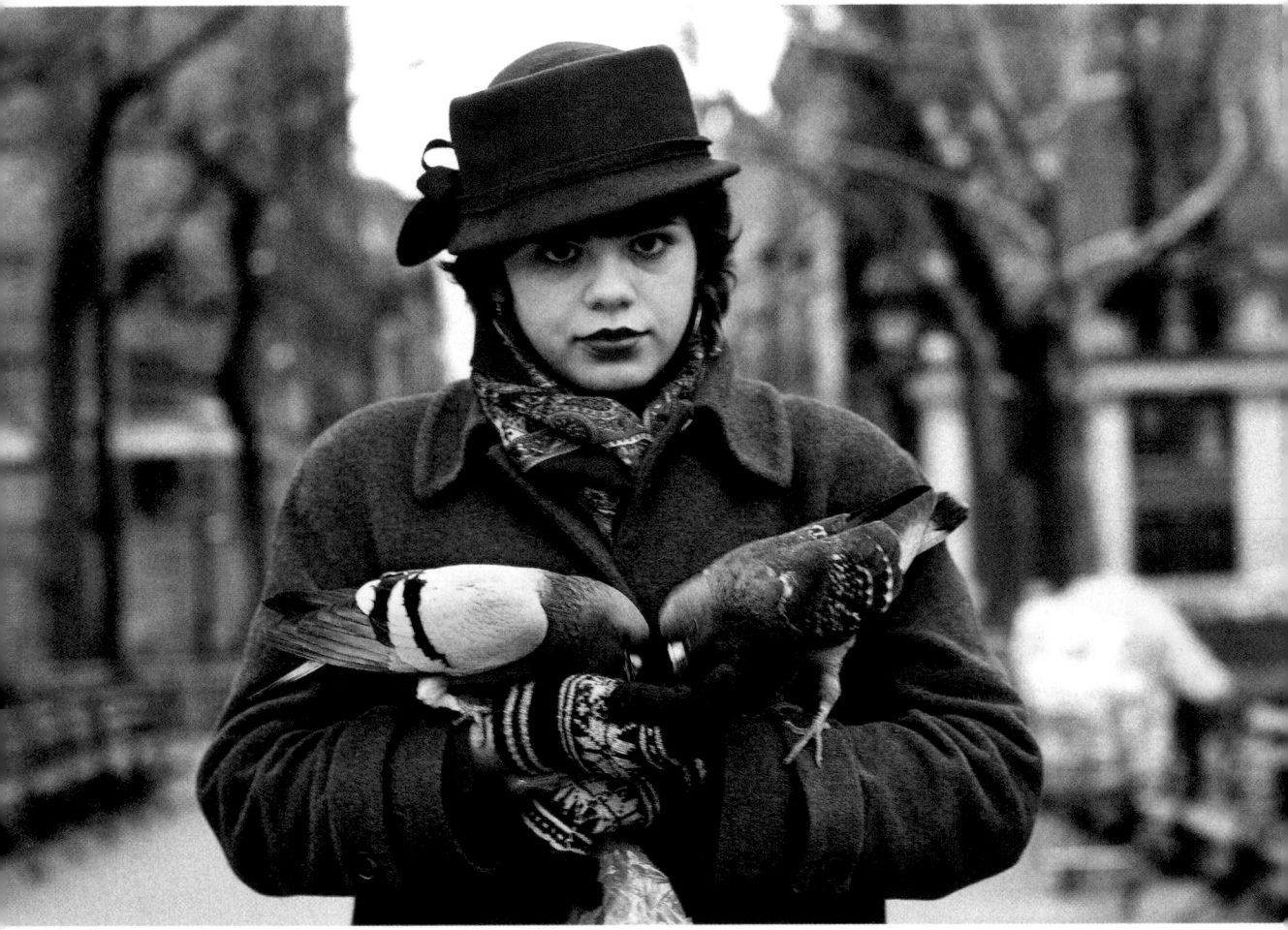

THE PIGEON WHISPERER

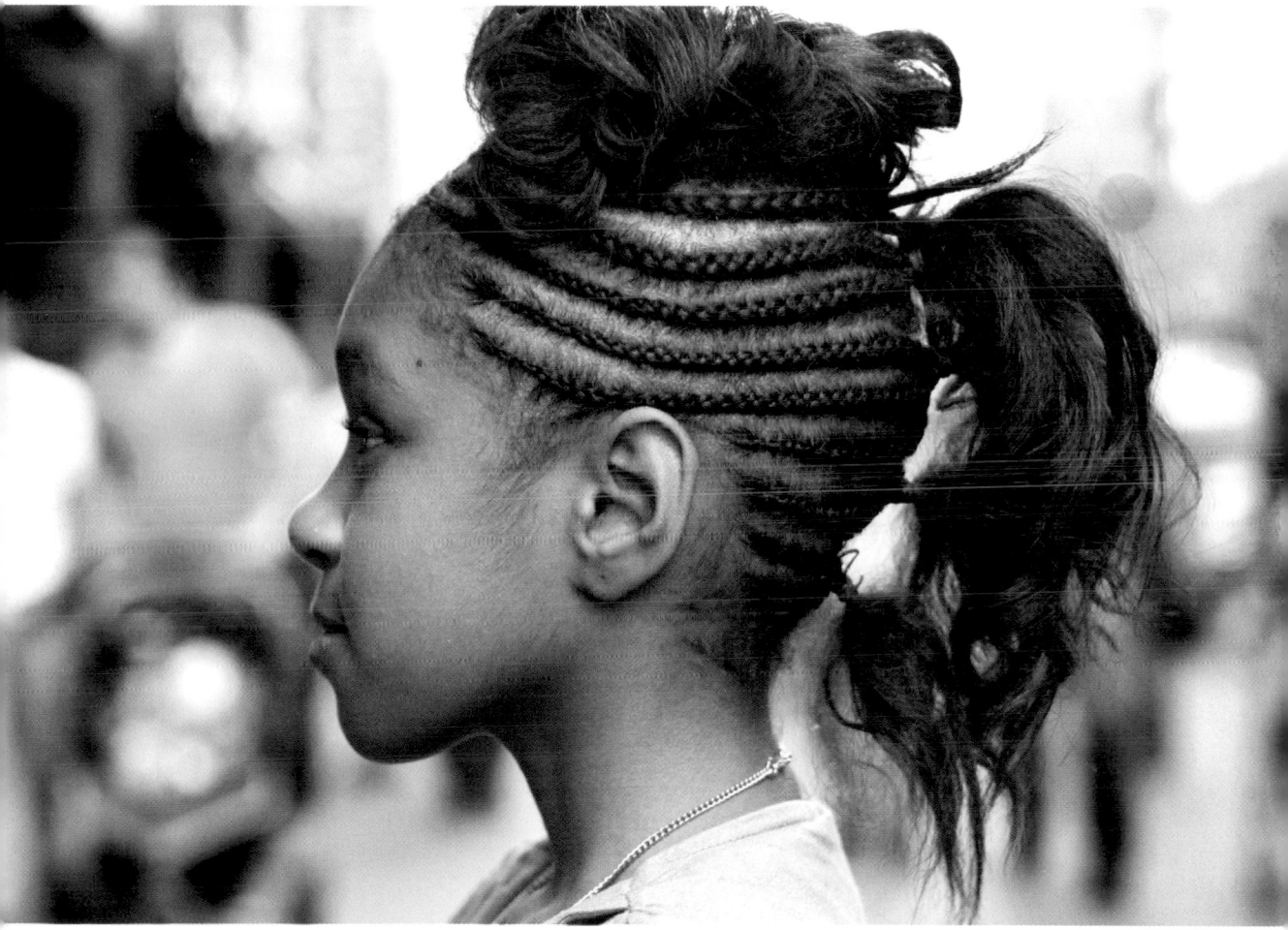

NOW THAT'S ART.

'HE WAS MY FIRST LOVE. WE DATED FOR TEN DAYS WHEN WE WERE VERY YOUNG, BUT MY MOM WOULD NOT ALLOW THE RELATIONSHIP. SHE TOLD ME: 'HE'S AN AMERICAN, AND HE'S AN ACTOR. HE'LL NEVER MAKE ANYTHING OF HIMSELF.' THEN SHE SAID: 'THERE ARE MILLIONS OF MEN, BUT I'M YOUR ONLY MOTHER.' SHE TOLD ME TO NEVER CONTACT HIM AGAIN AND I LISTENED TO HER. SHE TOOK ME TO KOREA FOR A FEW YEARS. I NEVER TRIED TO CONTACT HIM, EVEN WHEN I CAME BACK. I NEVER EVEN GAVE HIM AN EXPLANATION. THAT WAS OVER TWENTY YEARS AGO.

RECENTLY, I GOOGLED HIM AND SAW THAT HE WAS RUNNING A THEATER COMPANY. I WROTE HIM A LONG LETTER OUT OF THE BLUE, EXPLAINING EVERYTHING. WE'D BOTH BEEN MARRIED. WE BOTH HAD KIDS. BUT HERE WE ARE—FINALLY TOGETHER.'

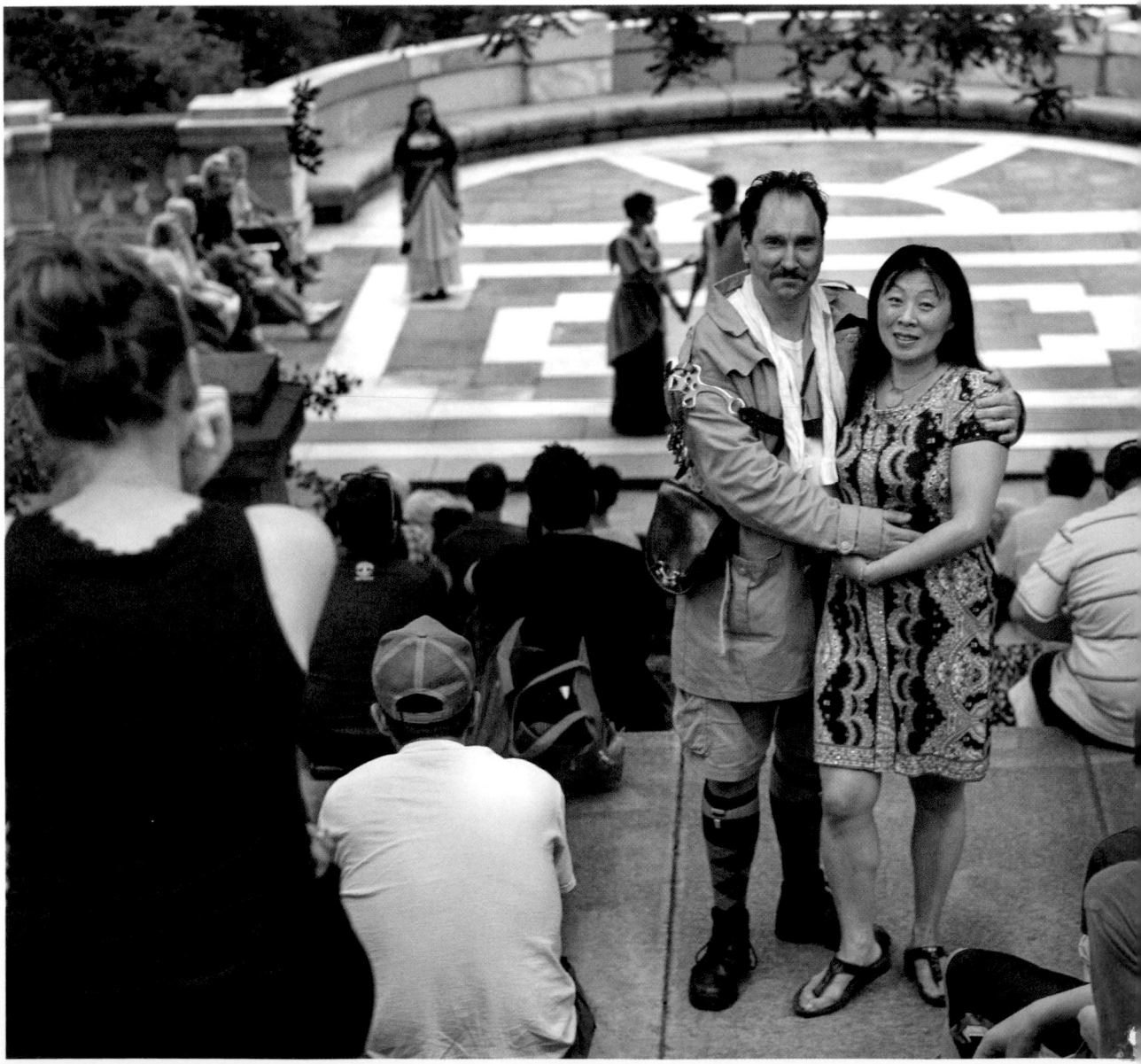

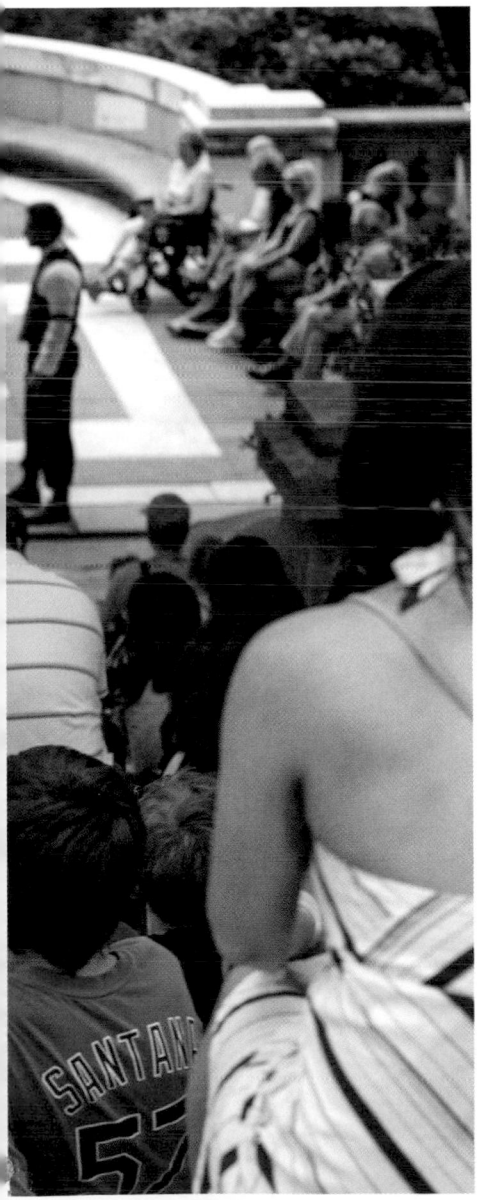


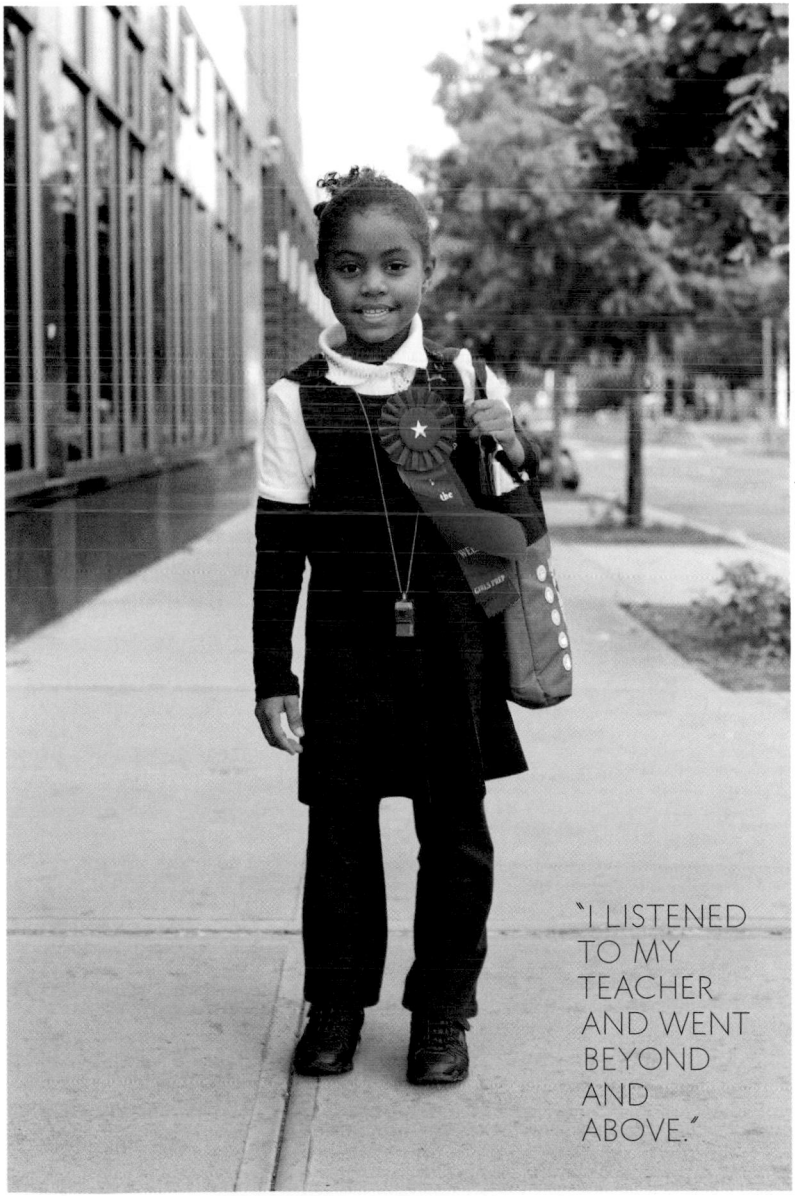

"I LISTENED TO MY TEACHER AND WENT BEYOND AND ABOVE."

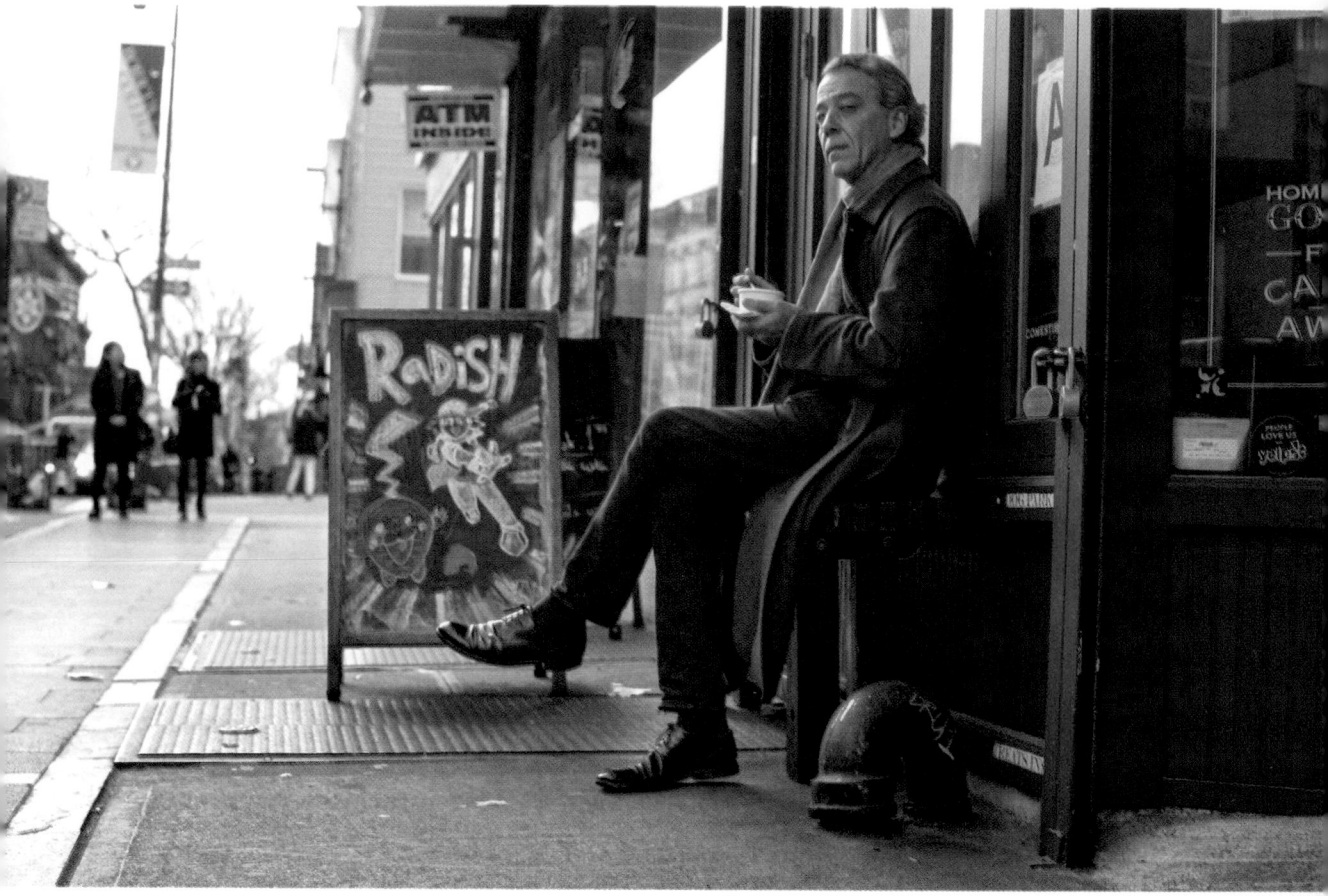


"EVERY AMERICAN SHOULD LIVE IN THE MEDITERRANEAN FOR AT LEAST A YEAR. WE HAVE A CALVINIST WORK ETHIC TRANSPORTED FROM NORTHERN EUROPE. WHEN YOU LIVE IN THE MOST BEAUTIFUL PLACE ON EARTH, THAT SEEMS LESS AND LESS IMPORTANT."

"YOU BETTER NOT MAKE IT SEEM LIKE WE WERE SITTING AROUND. . . .

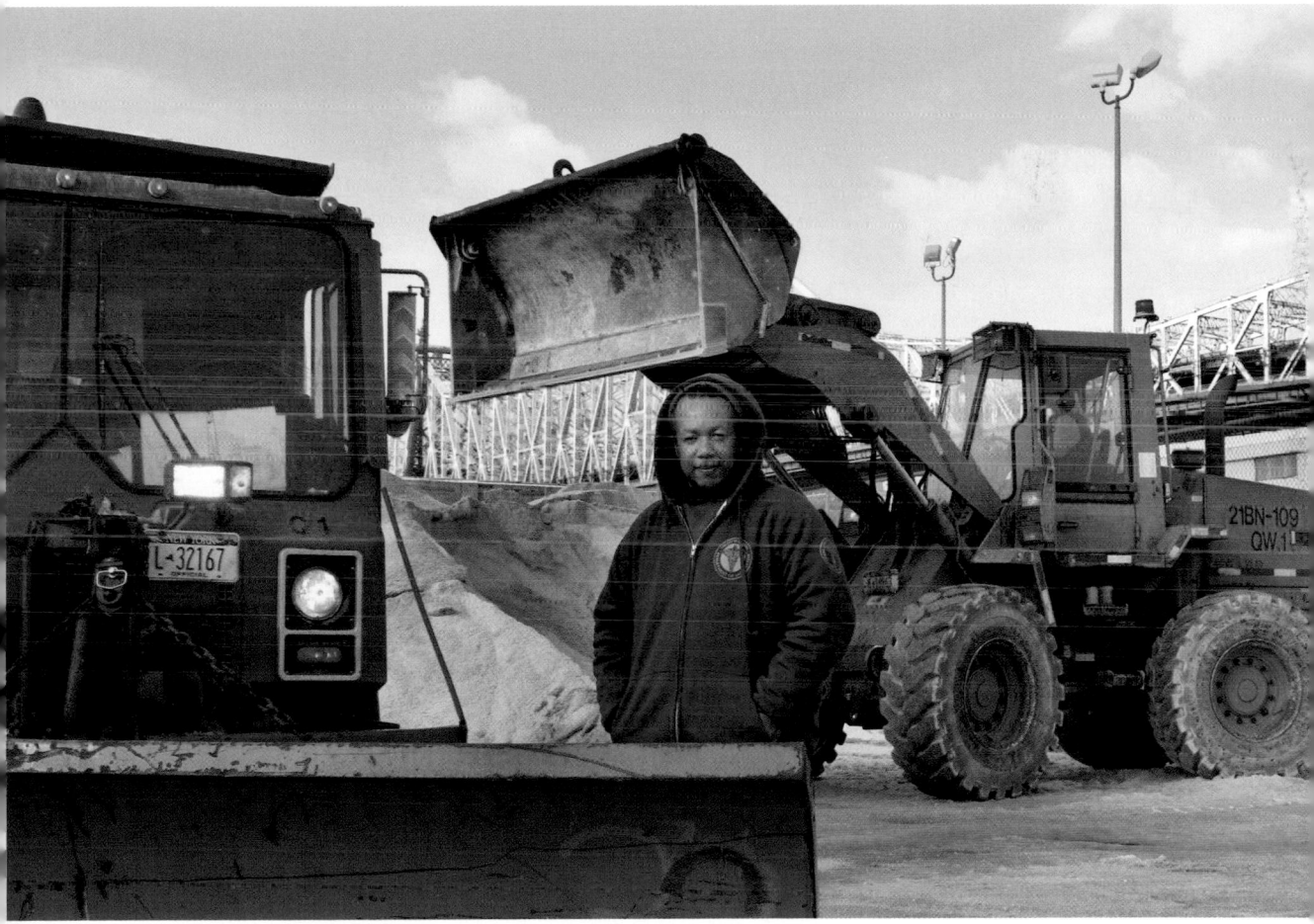


DON'T TAKE THE PICTURE UNTIL THE BULLDOZER STARTS MOVING."

"I WOKE UP, SMOKED A BOWL, GRABBED SOME RANDOM STUFF I FOUND BY THE DOOR, AND HEADED OUTSIDE."

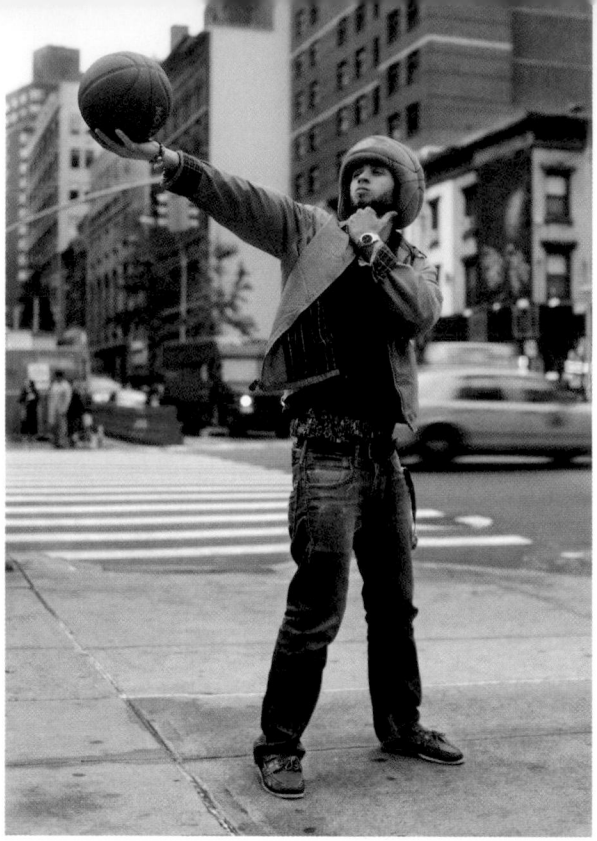

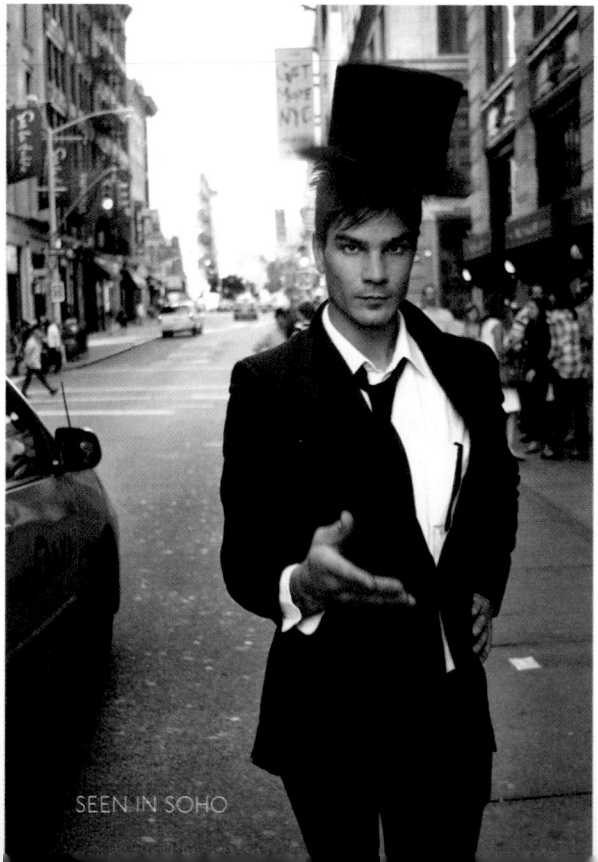

SEEN IN SOHO

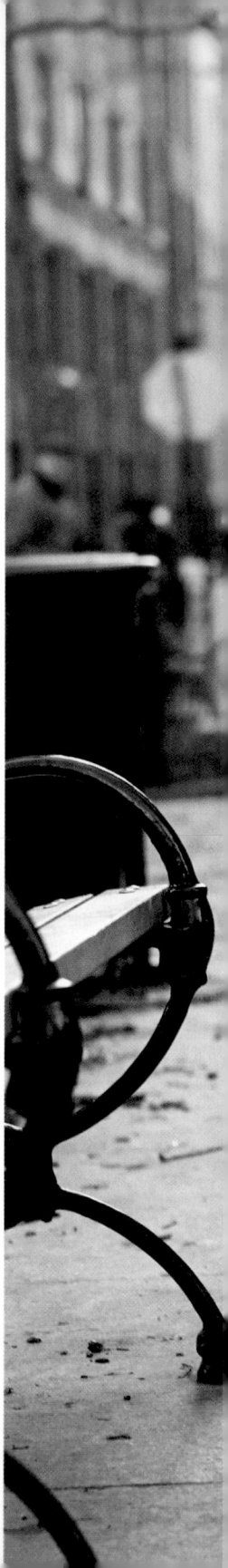

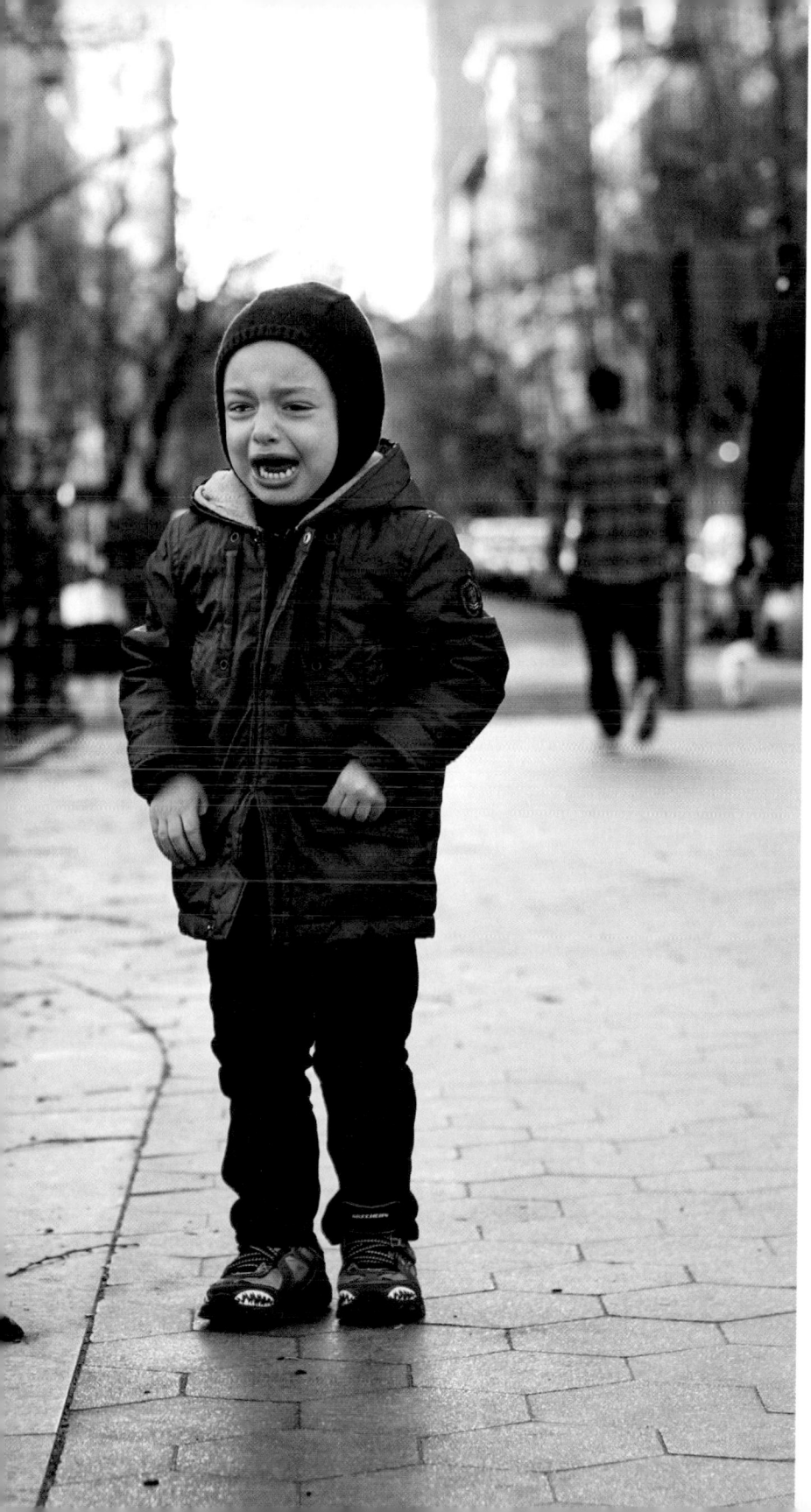

THIS LITTLE GUY WAS BOUNCING A TINY BASKETBALL WHEN IT GOT AWAY FROM HIM AND LANDED IN A BED OF PINE STRAW. TWO SQUIRRELS APPROACHED THE BALL TO INVESTIGATE. THE BOY CONCLUDED THAT THE SQUIRRELS WERE PLANNING TO STEAL HIS BALL, AND WAS OVERCOME BY DESPAIR.

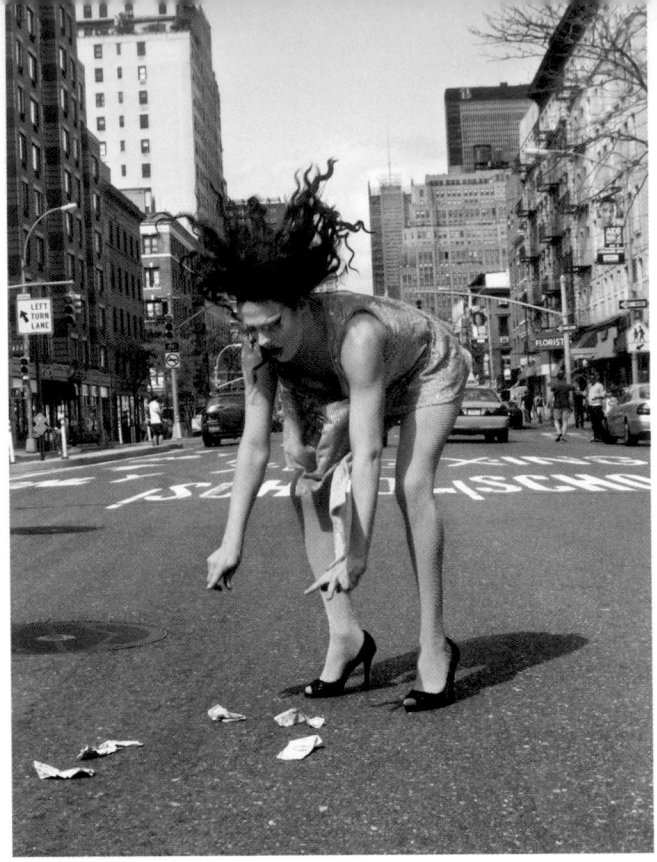


I THINK IT'D BE DIFFICULT TO BRING TOGETHER MORE ELEMENTS OF NEW YORK CITY IN A SINGLE SCENE.

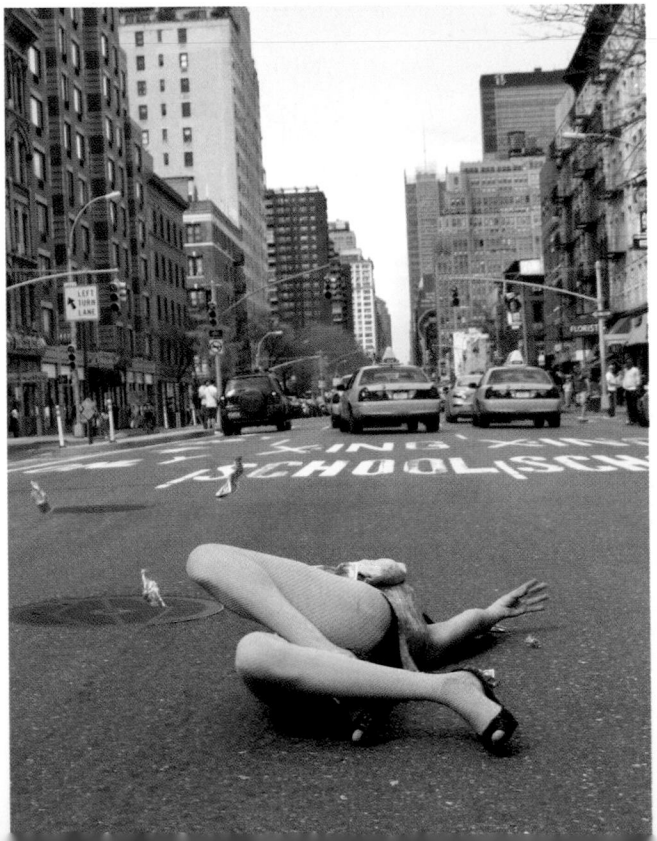


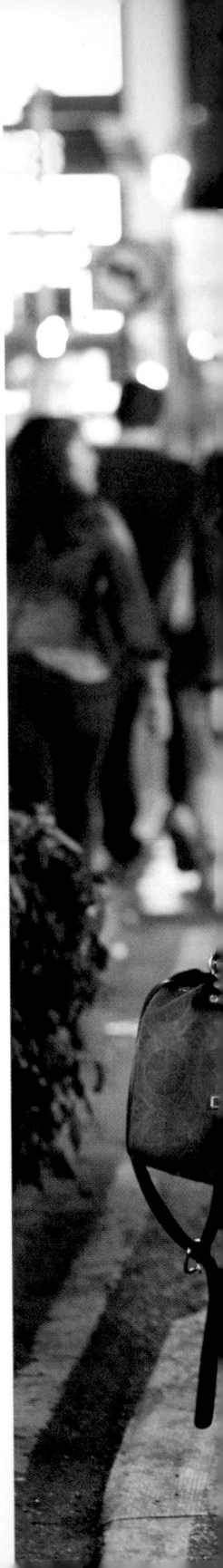

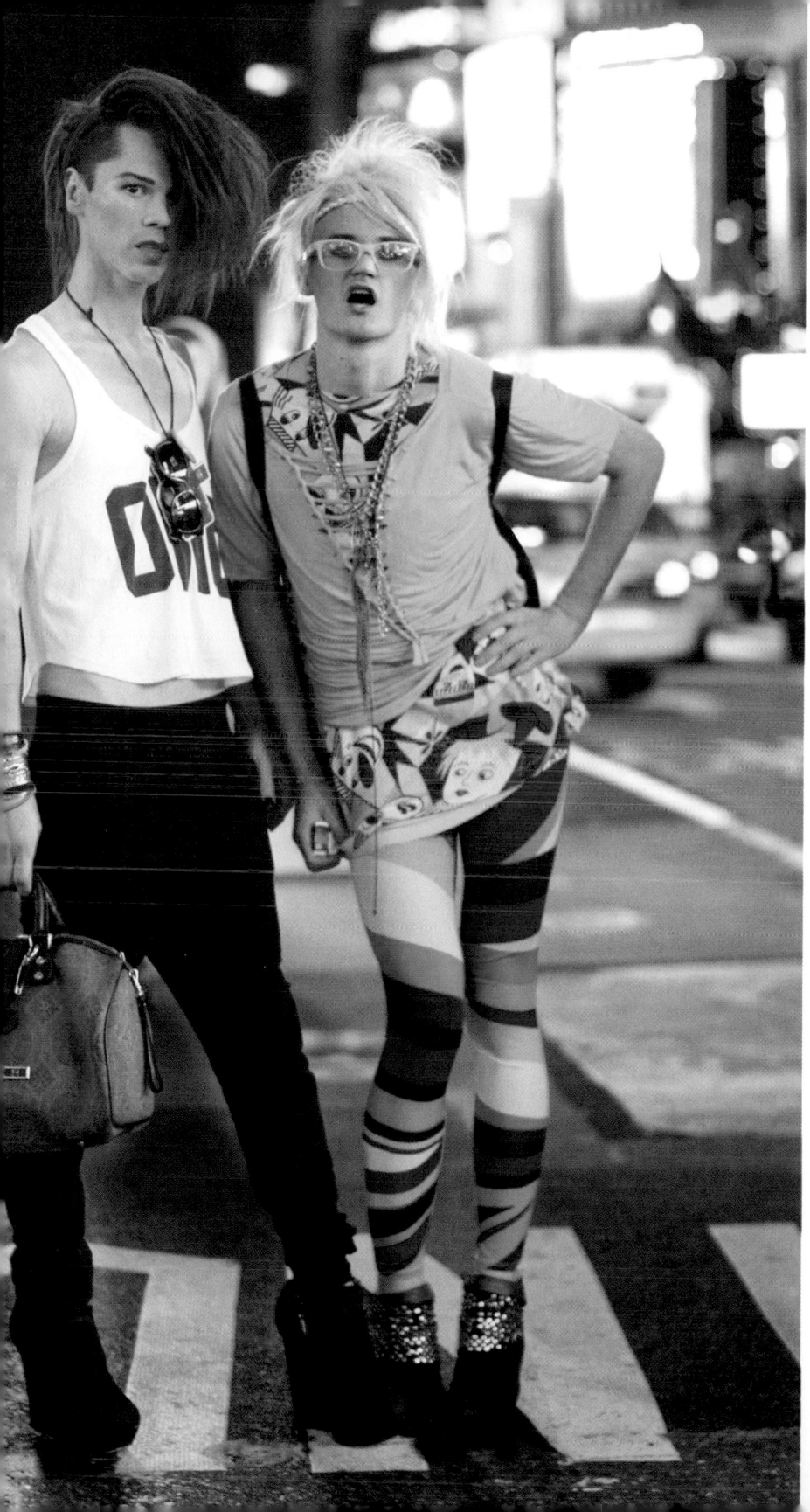

THE MAN ON THE RIGHT SPENT SEVERAL MINUTES EXPLAINING HIS PLAN TO BECOME A GENDER-BENDING ROCK STAR. IT ALL SOUNDED VERY IMPRESSIVE. THE MAN ON THE LEFT WAITED PATIENTLY WHILE HIS FRIEND HELD THE SPOTLIGHT. THEN, IN A QUIET VOICE, HE SAID: "I'M A CARD-CARRYING NATIVE AMERICAN AND THE TWILIGHT SERIES WAS BASED ON THE LEGENDS OF MY FAMILY."

BOOM.

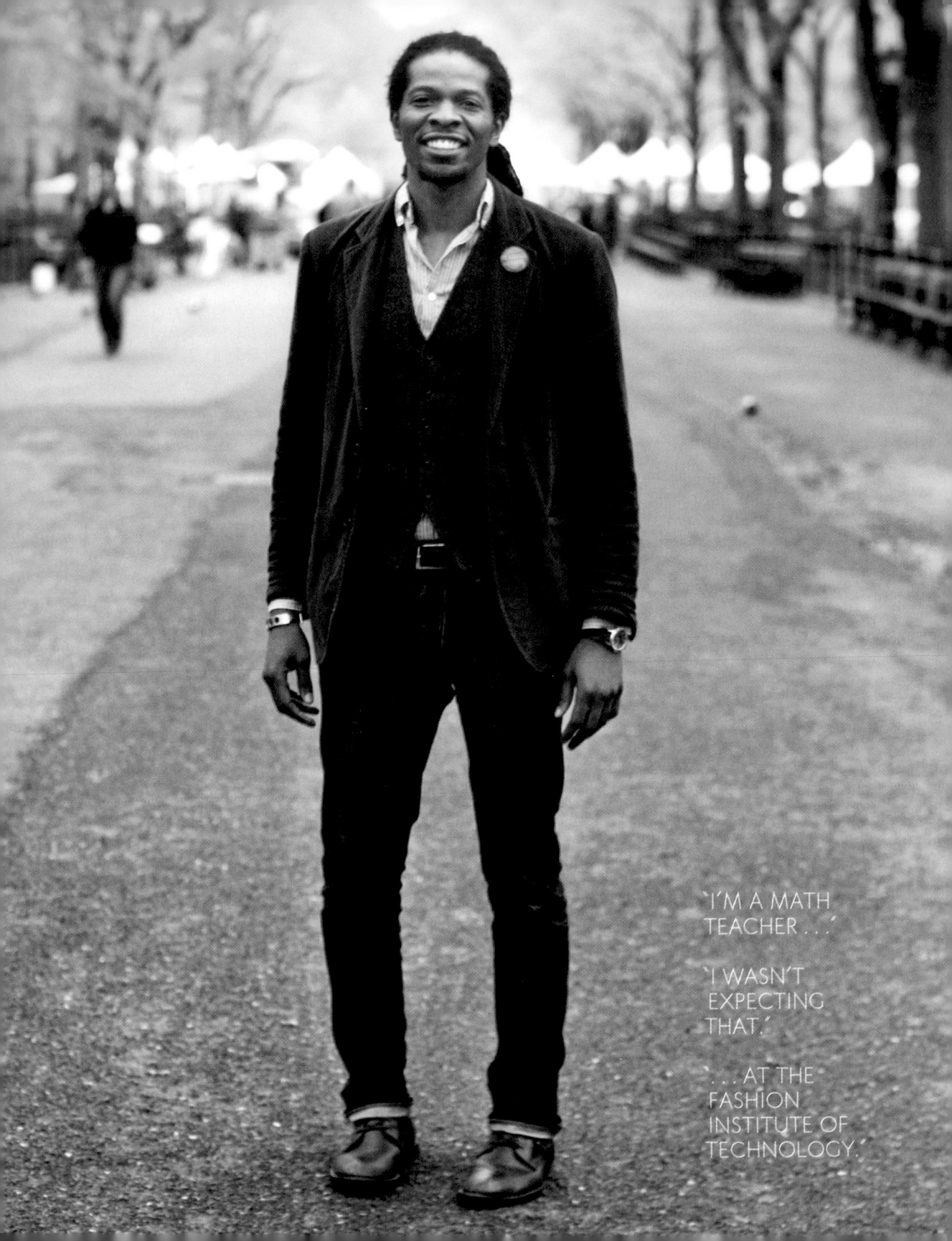

'I'M A MATH TEACHER . . .'

'I WASN'T EXPECTING THAT.'

. . . AT THE FASHION INSTITUTE OF TECHNOLOGY.'

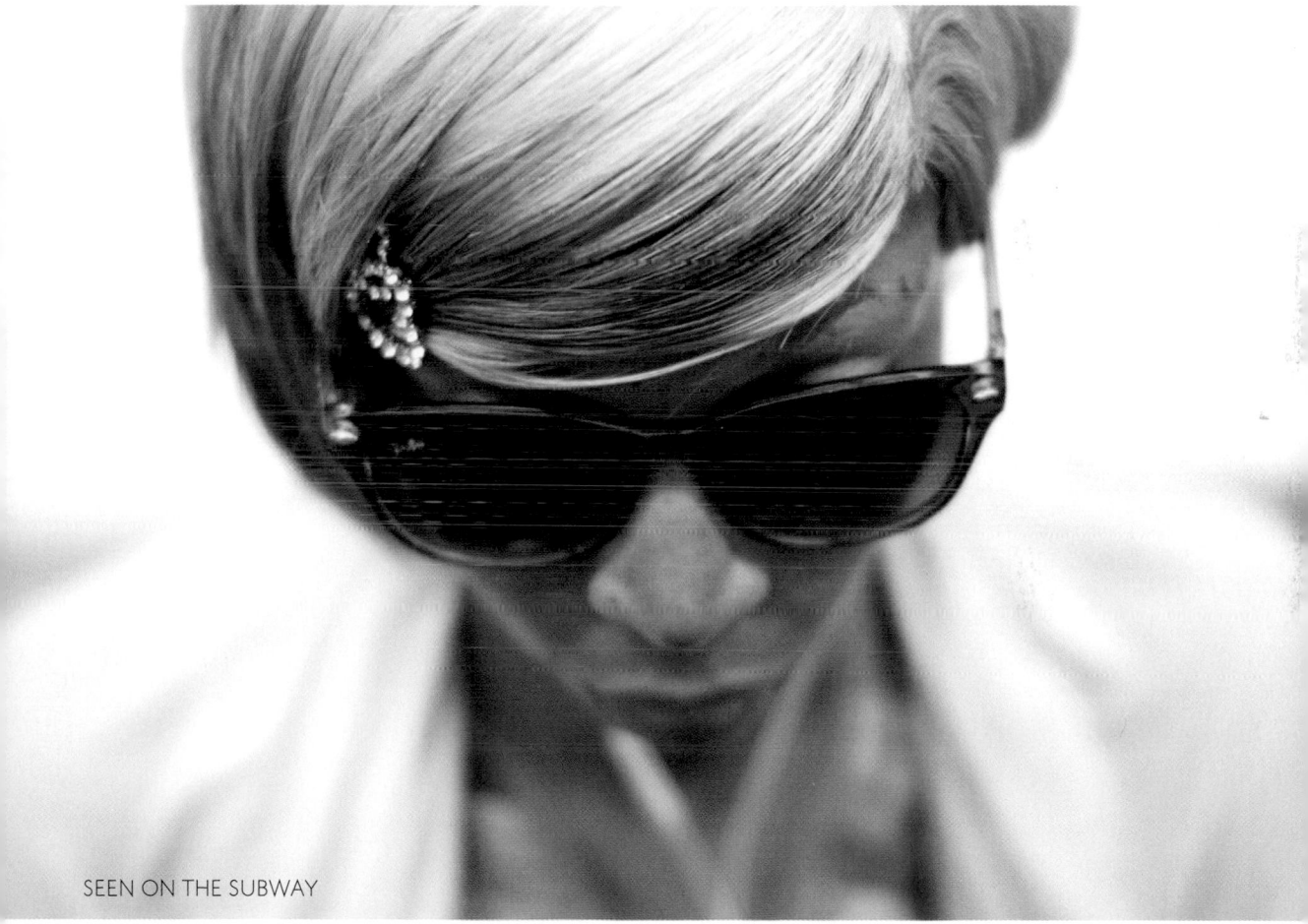

SEEN ON THE SUBWAY

A TERRIBLE CRIME HAS BEEN COMMITTED.

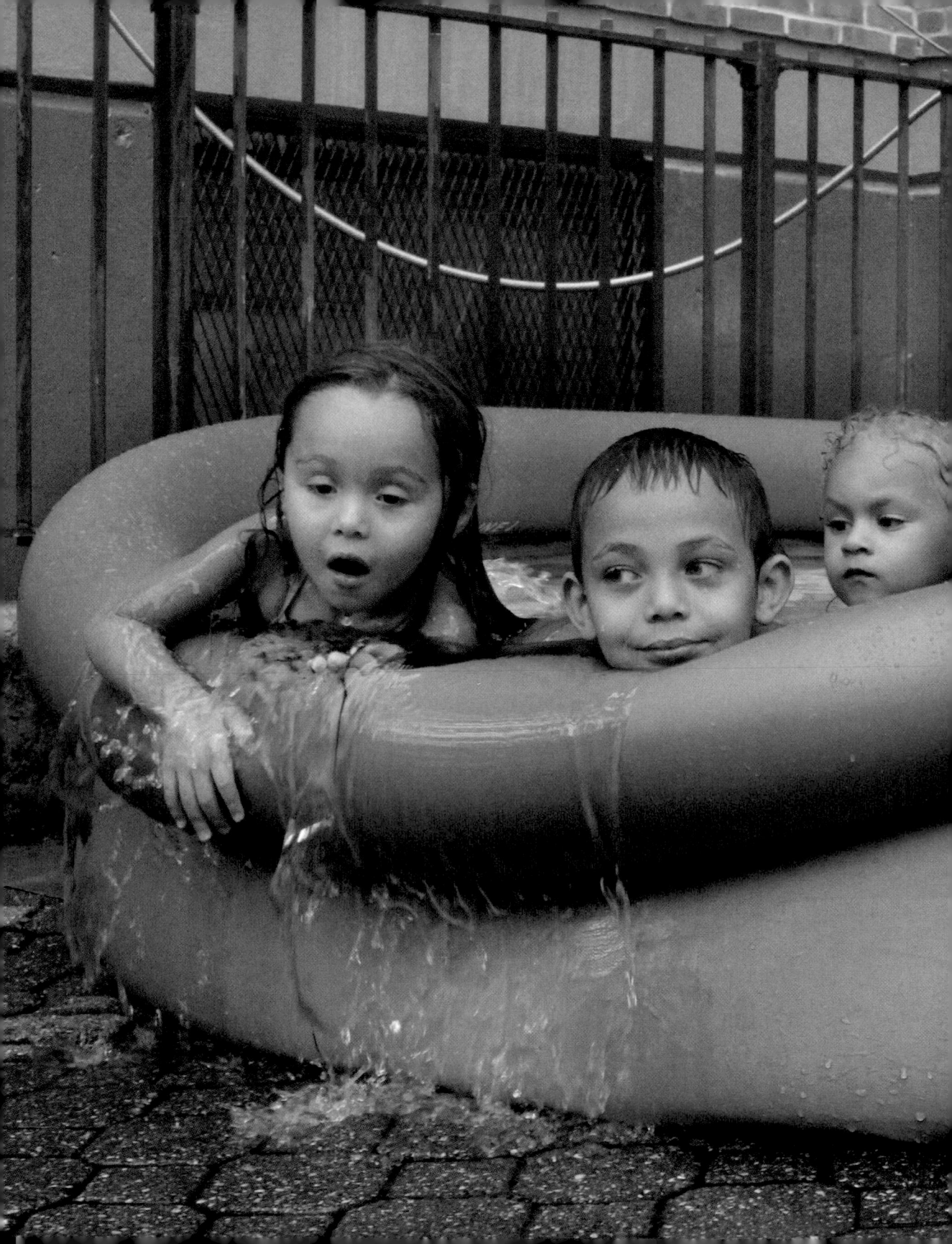

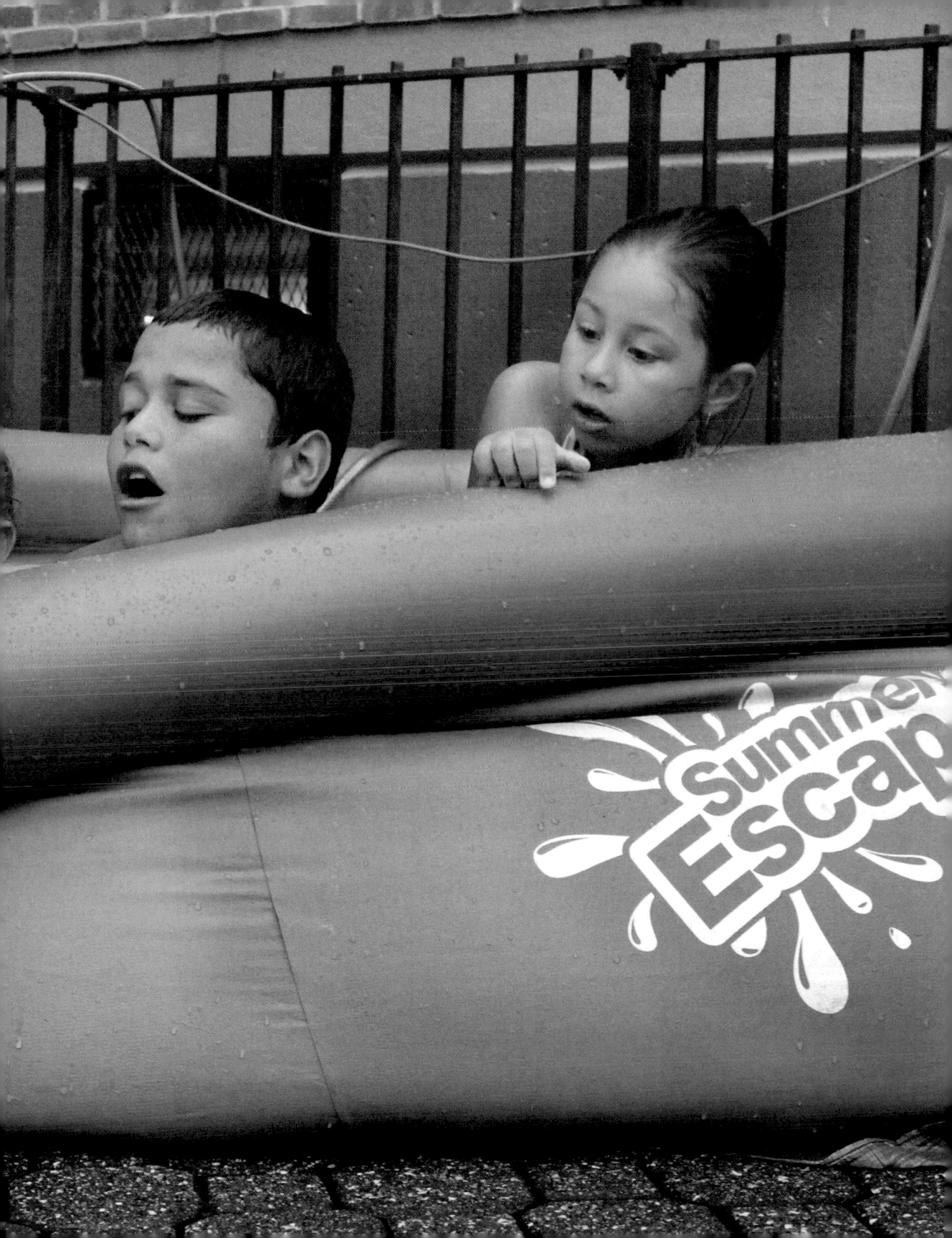
Summer
Escap

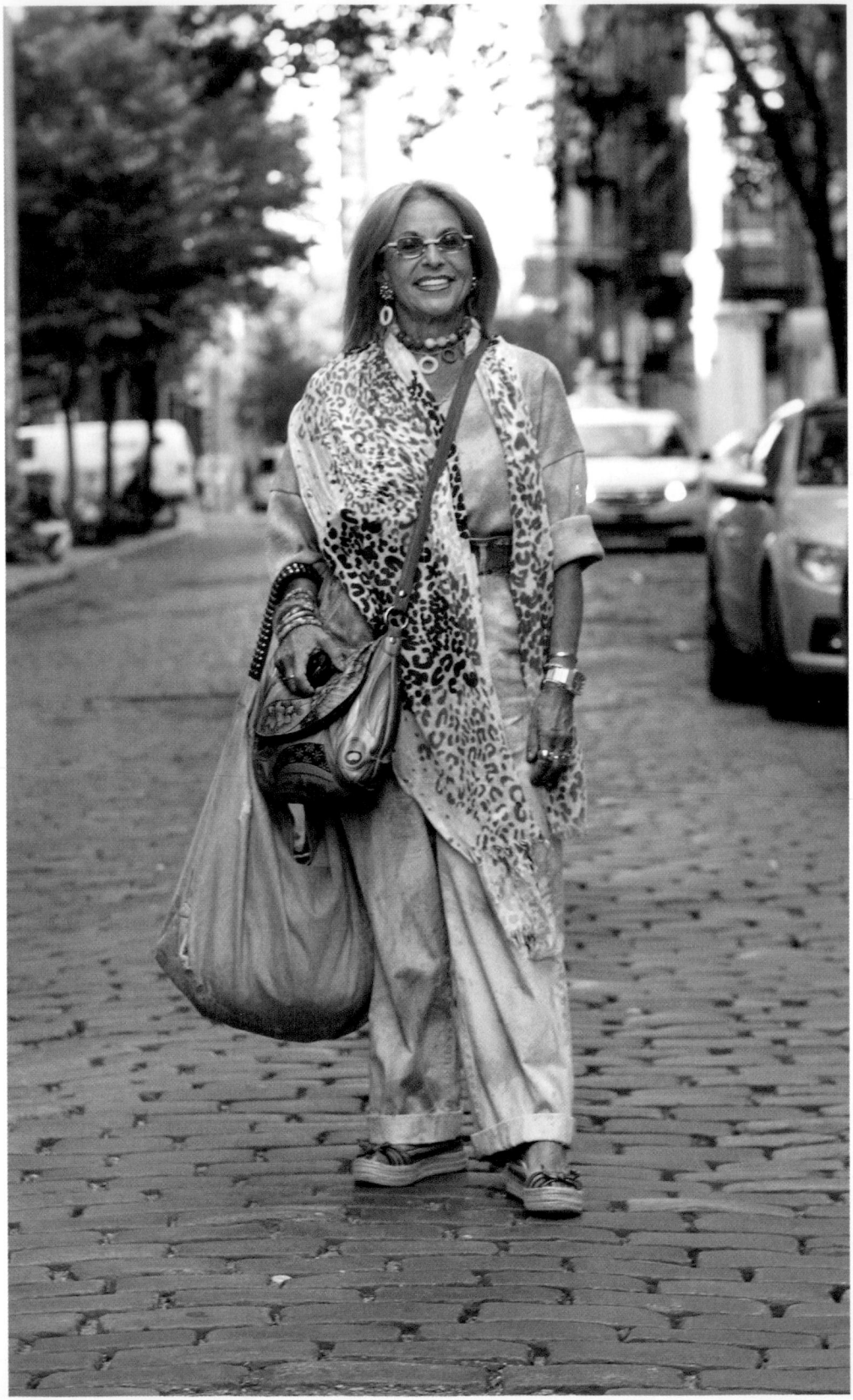

'I'VE BEEN A WIDOW FOR FIVE YEARS NOW. AND I GUESS I'M WORRIED THAT MEN LOOK AT HOW I DRESS AND JUST DON'T 'GET IT.' MY LATE HUSBAND 'GOT IT,' OF COURSE. I'D LOVE TO MEET SOMEONE, BUT I'M NOT GOING TO CHANGE ANYTHING ABOUT MYSELF TO DO IT.'

"WHATEVER'S NEEDED."

I FOUND THESE TWO SISTERS WALKING WITH THEIR MOTHER ON THE LOWER EAST SIDE. AT FIRST I ASKED FOR THE OLDER GIRL'S PHOTO, BUT THE YOUNGER GIRL RAISED HER ARM INTO THE AIR AND SCREAMED: 'MEEEEEEEEEEEEEEEEEEEEE!'

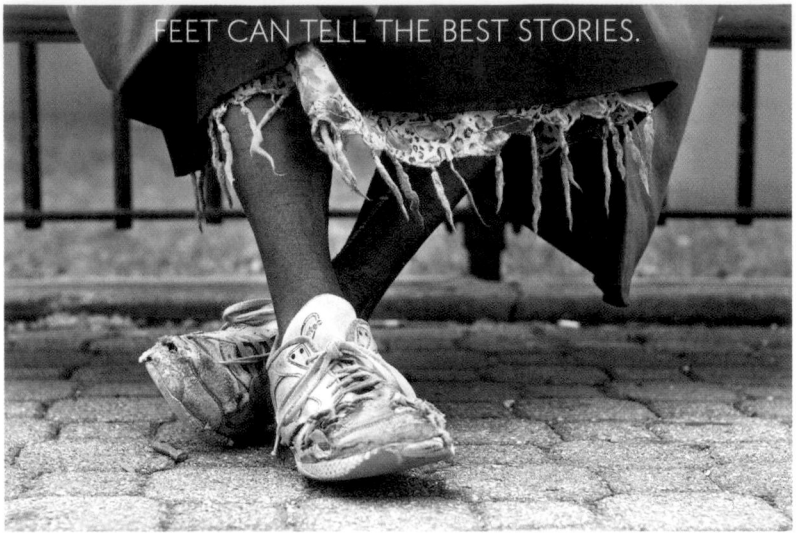
FEET CAN TELL THE BEST STORIES.

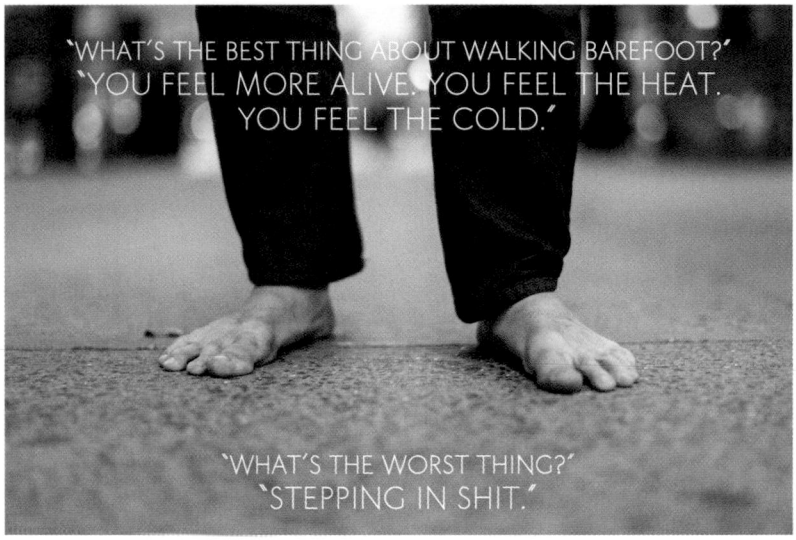
'WHAT'S THE BEST THING ABOUT WALKING BAREFOOT?'
'YOU FEEL MORE ALIVE. YOU FEEL THE HEAT.
YOU FEEL THE COLD.'
'WHAT'S THE WORST THING?'
'STEPPING IN SHIT.'

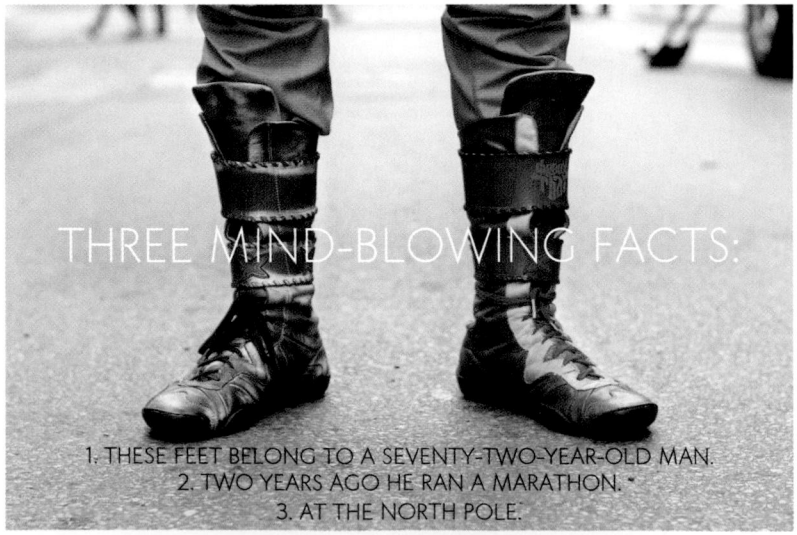
THREE MIND-BLOWING FACTS:
1. THESE FEET BELONG TO A SEVENTY-TWO-YEAR-OLD MAN.
2. TWO YEARS AGO HE RAN A MARATHON.
3. AT THE NORTH POLE.

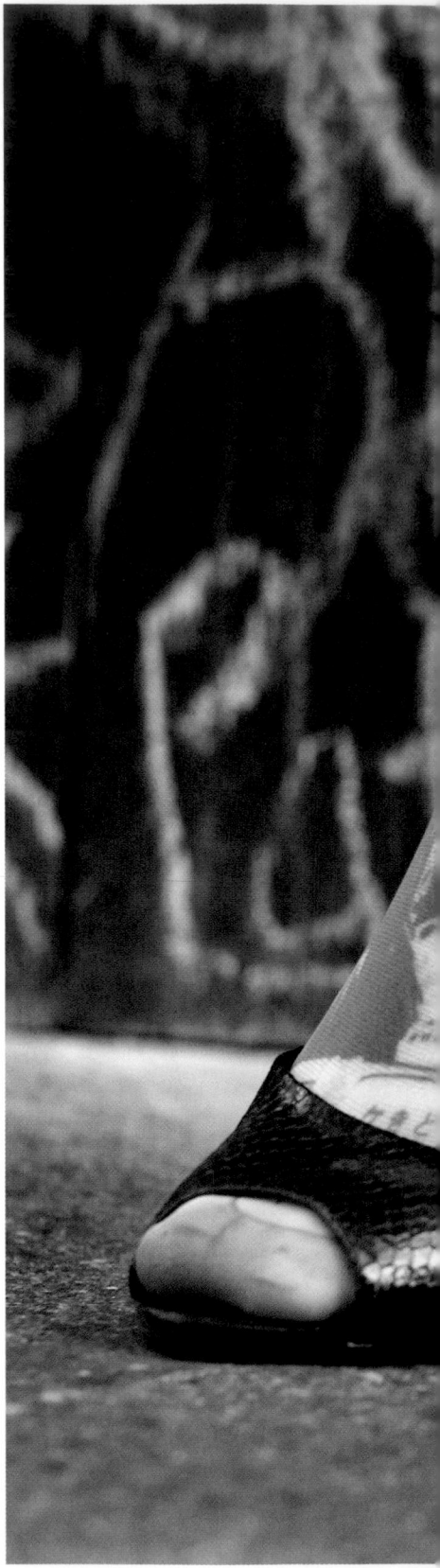

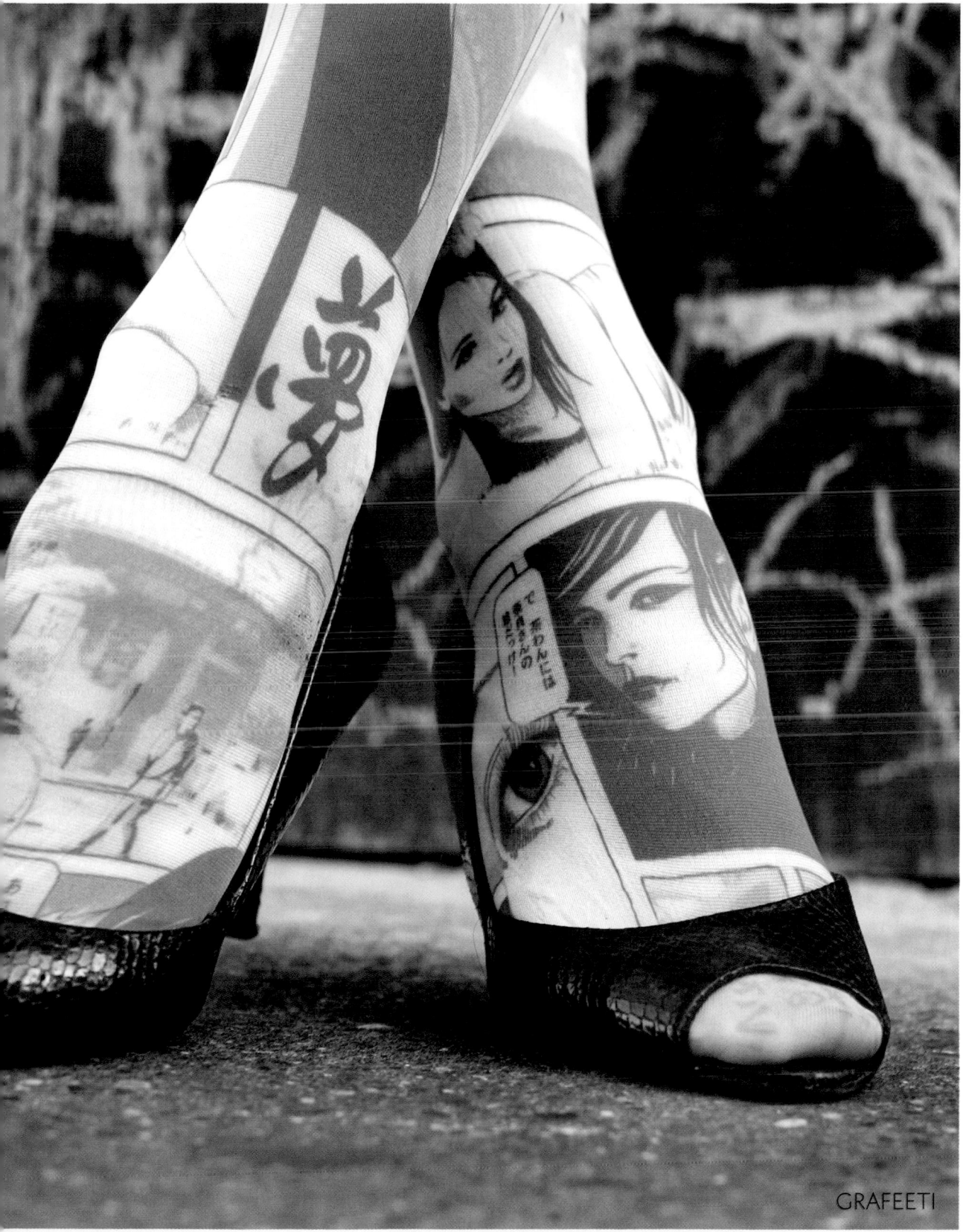
GRAFEETI

I TOLD HIM THAT I WANTED TO FEATURE THE DETAIL IN HIS HANDS AND FACE.

SO HE DID THIS.

THE GOLDEN CHILD

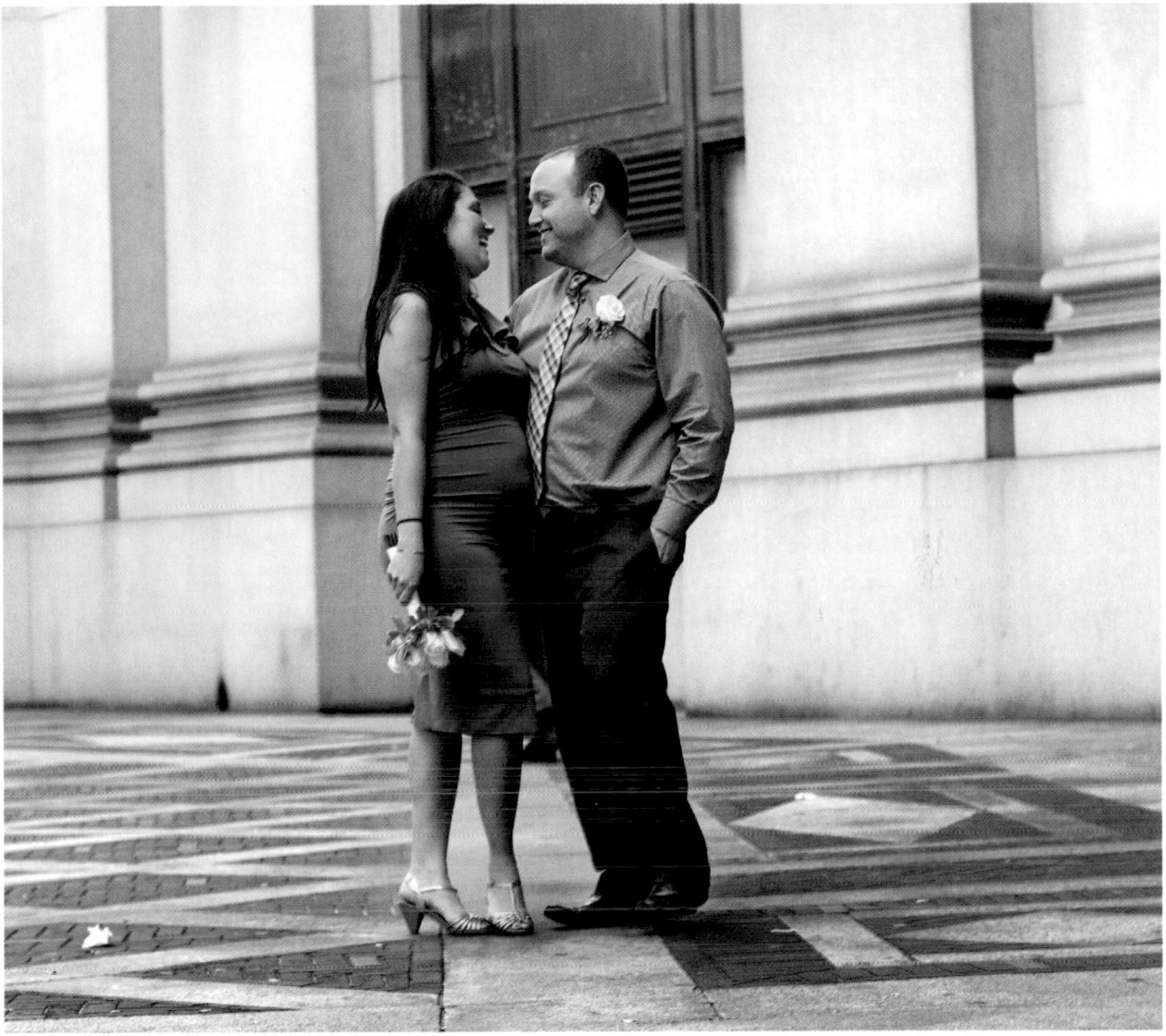

'MY FIANCÉE AND I ARE GETTING MARRIED TOMORROW AT CITY HALL. SHE IS FIVE MONTHS PREGNANT AND BEAUTIFUL.'

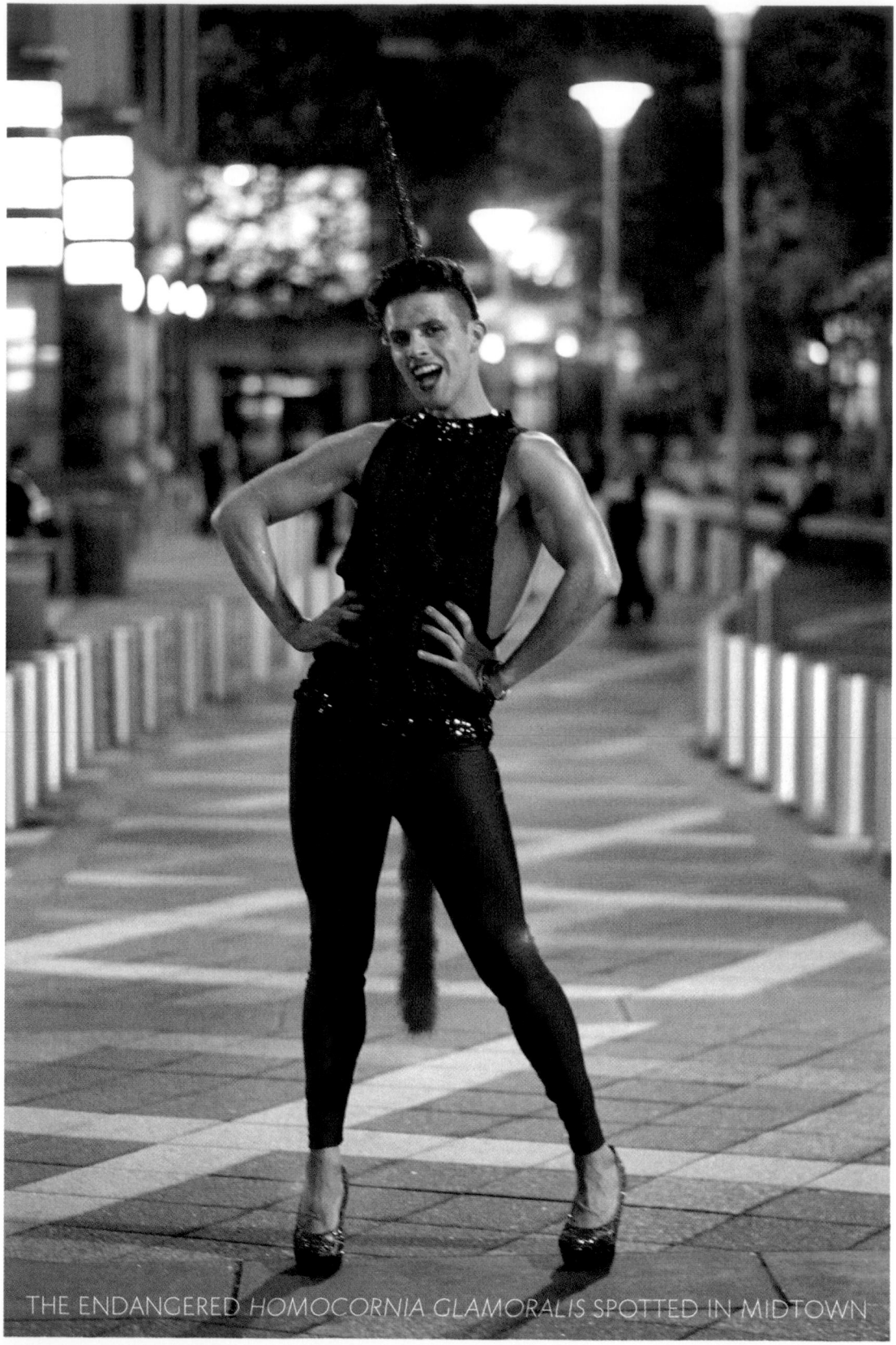

THE ENDANGERED *HOMOCORNIA GLAMORALIS* SPOTTED IN MIDTOWN

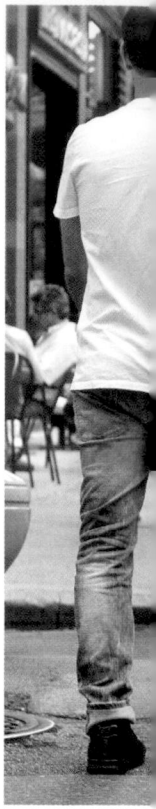

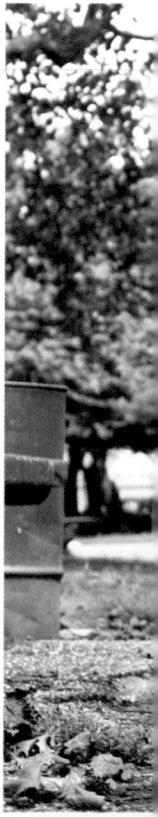

BET IT'D
BE HARD
TO HAVE
A BAD DAY
IF YOU WERE
HOLDING
HANDS WITH
THESE TWO.

ALL YOU
NEED IS
A HAND
TO HOLD
AND A
PUDDLE
TO STOMP.

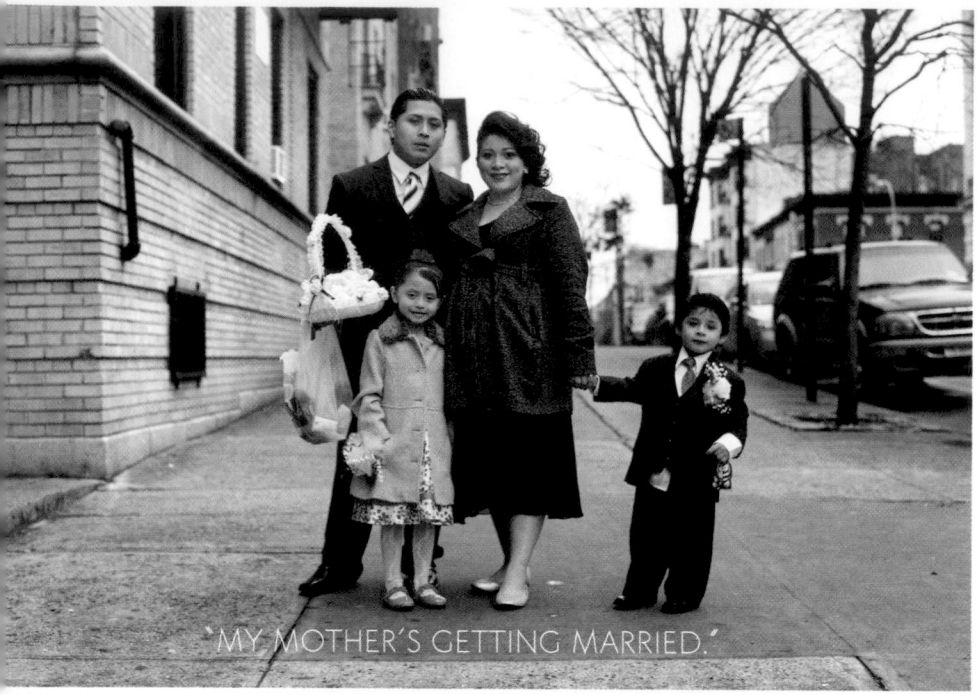

"MY MOTHER'S GETTING MARRIED."

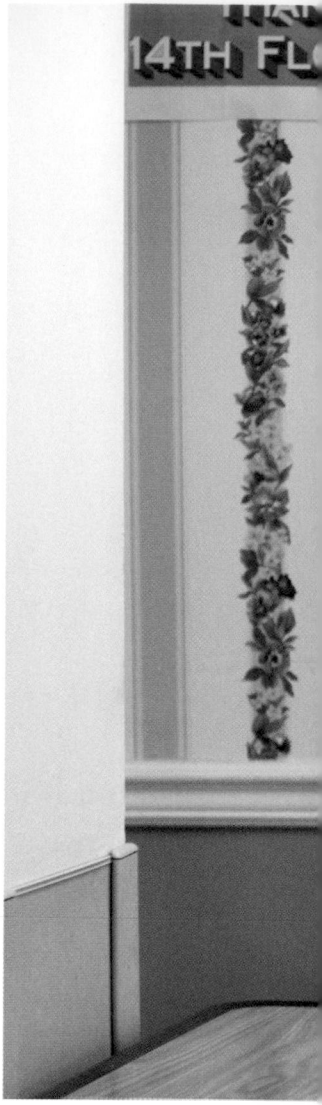


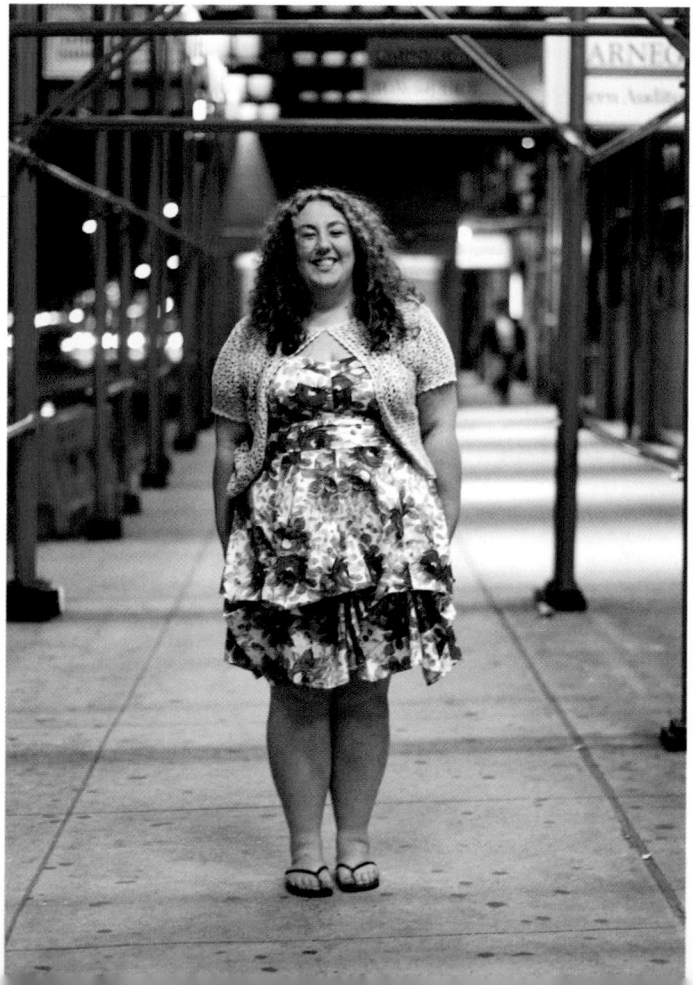

HER PARENTS WERE VERY SKEPTICAL OF THE MAN WITH THE CAMERA. LUCKILY SHE WAS FEELING BRAVE.

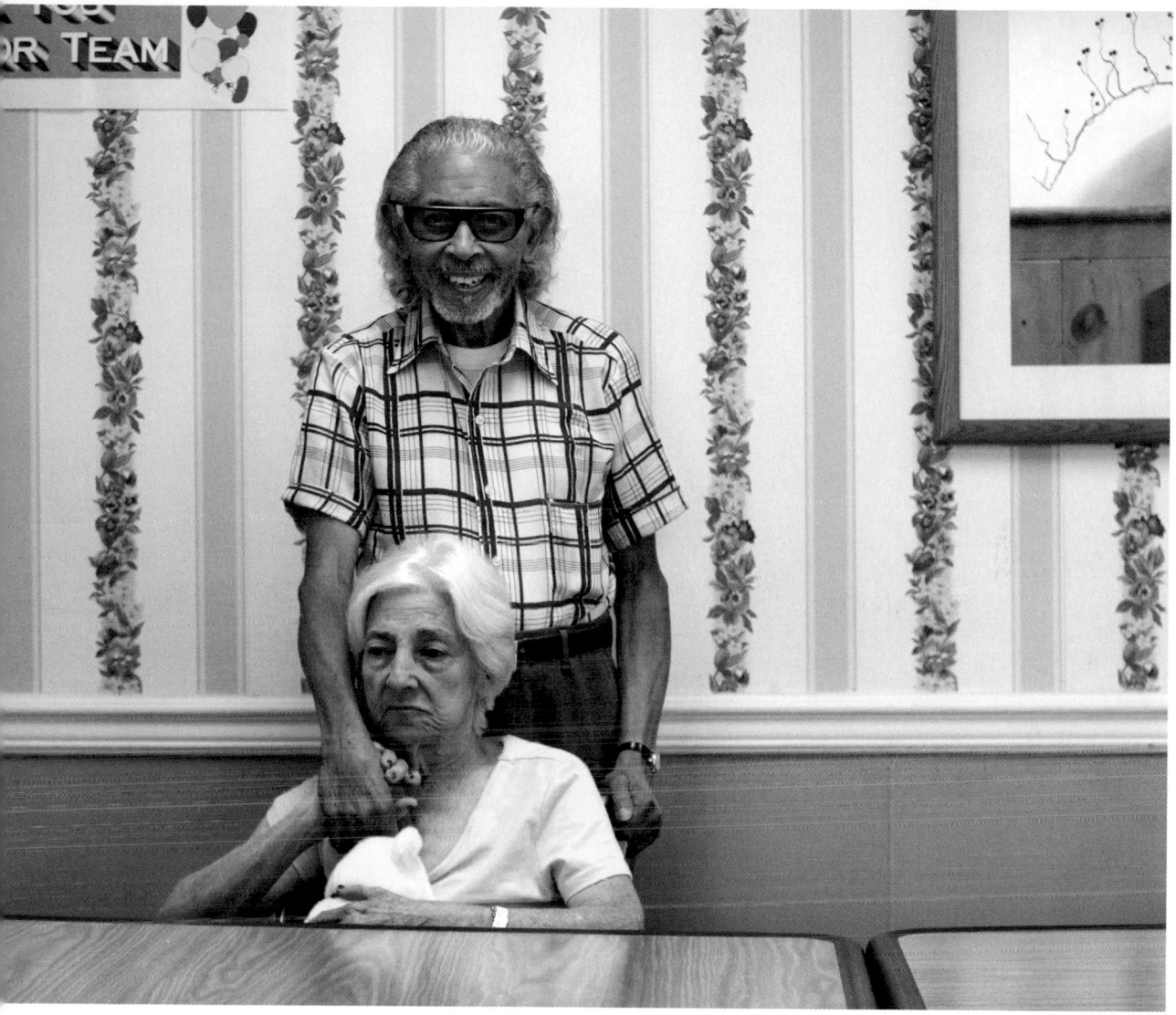


I STEPPED INSIDE AN UPPER WEST SIDE NURSING HOME, AND MET THIS MAN IN THE LOBBY. HE WAS ON HIS WAY TO DELIVER A YELLOW TEDDY BEAR TO HIS WIFE. 'I VISIT HER EVERY DAY,' HE SAID. 'EVEN WHEN THE MIND IS GONE, THE HEART SHOWS THROUGH.'

THE PAINTER HEARD ME LAUGHING, AND WITHOUT LOOKING DOWN, SAID:
'BOOGIE'S LOOKING AT YOU SIDEWAYS, ISN'T HE?'

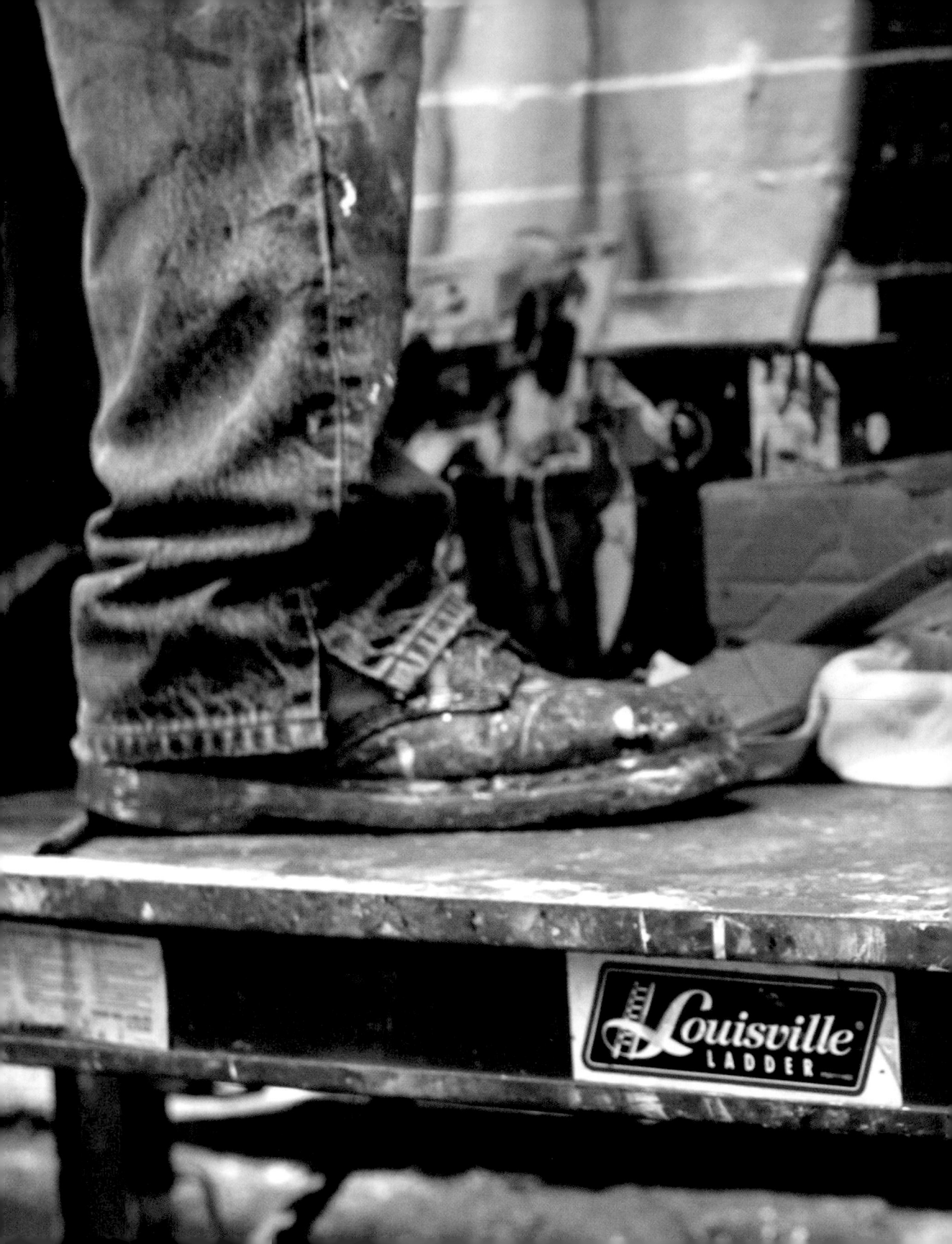
Louisville
LADDER

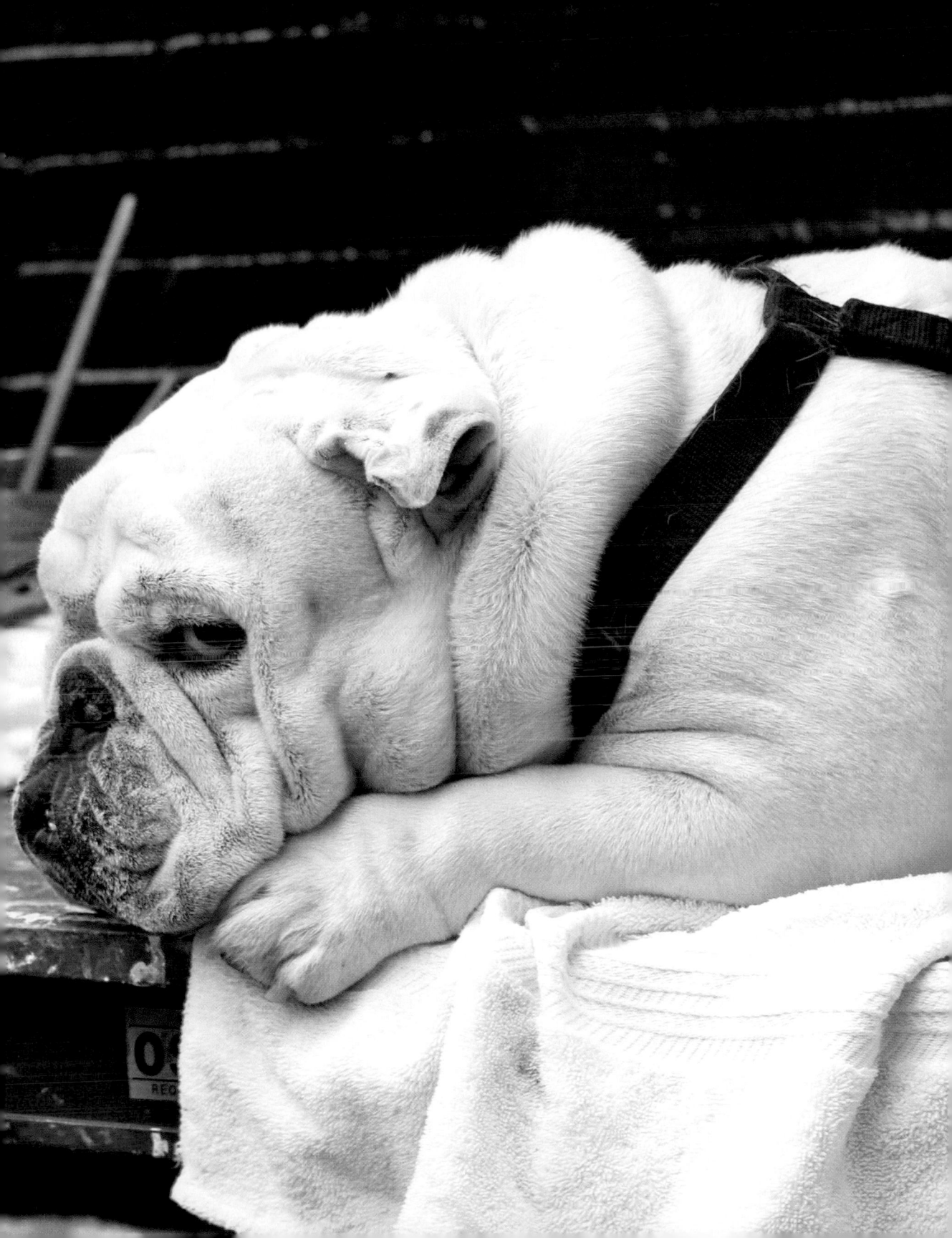

SEEN IN McCARREN PARK

"DID YOU HEAR THAT, RUBY? THE PHOTOGRAPHER JUST CALLED YOU A BOY!"

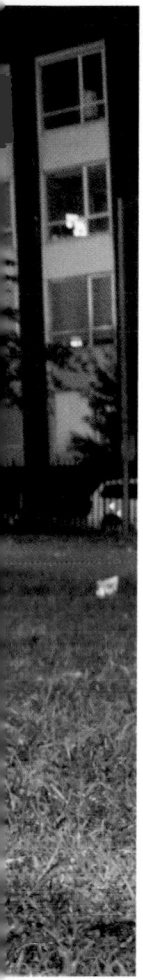

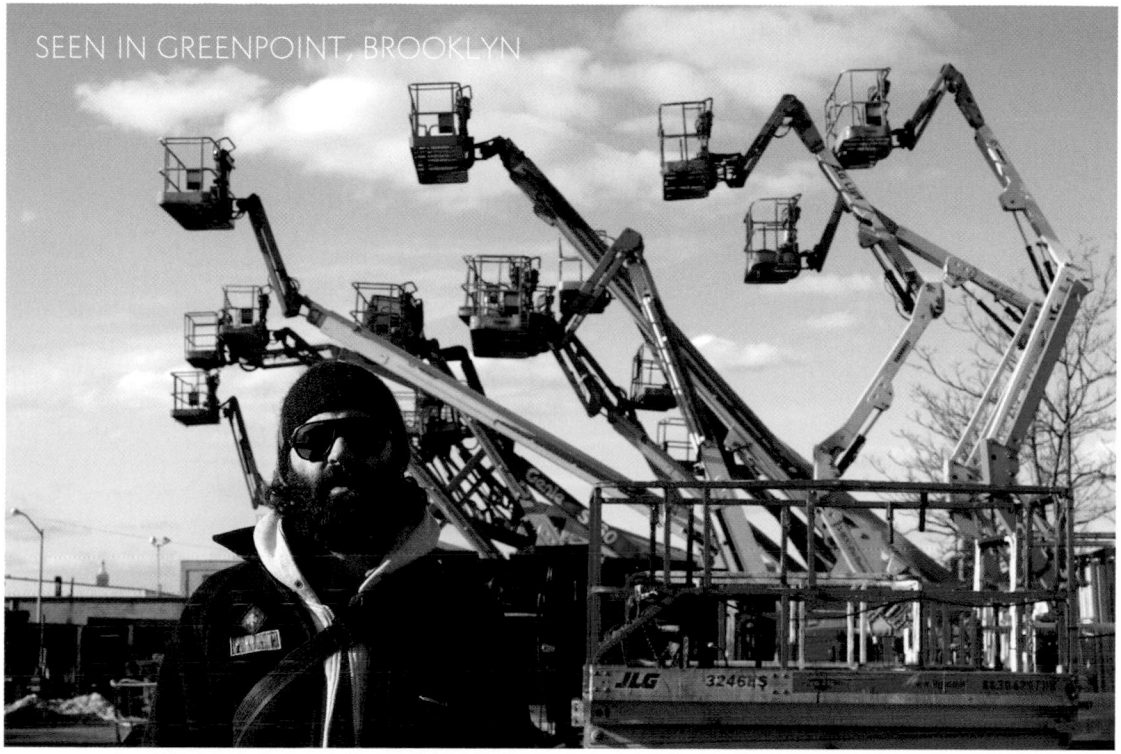


SEEN IN GREENPOINT, BROOKLYN

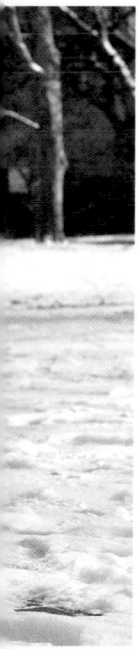

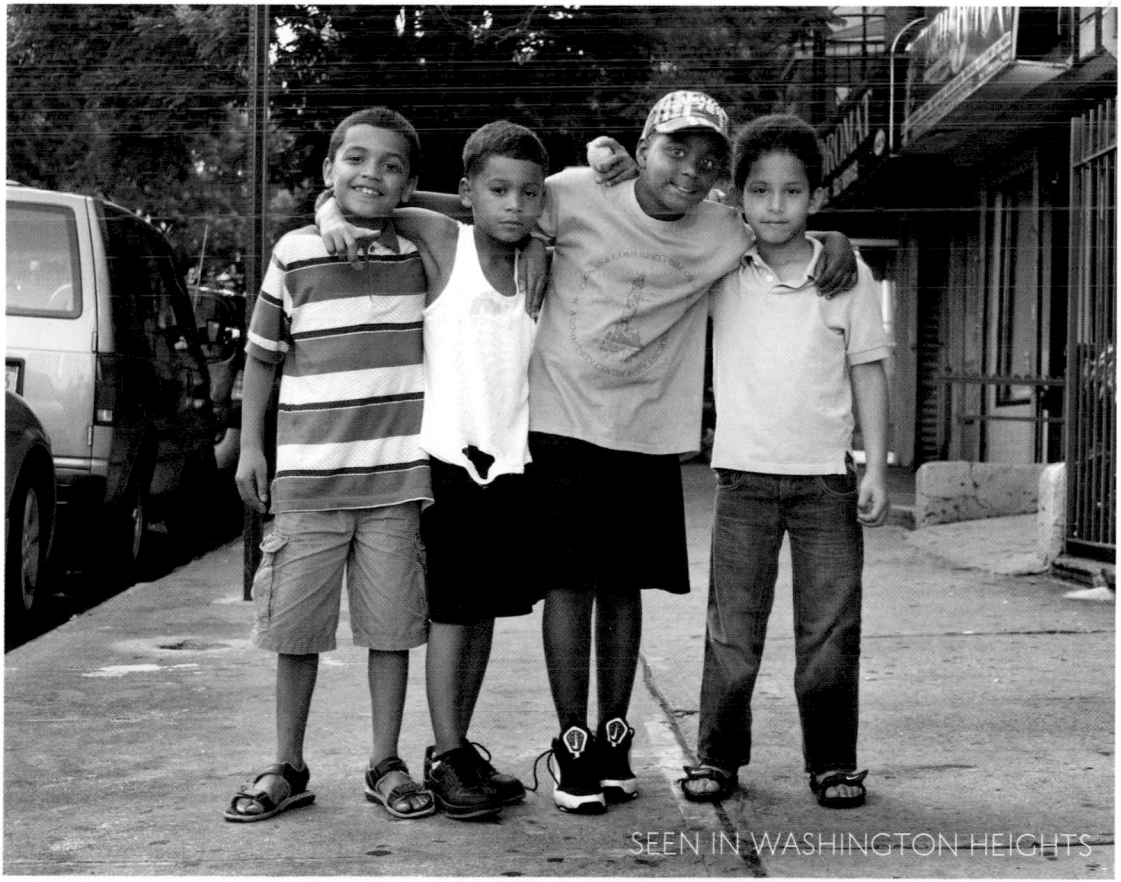

SEEN IN WASHINGTON HEIGHTS

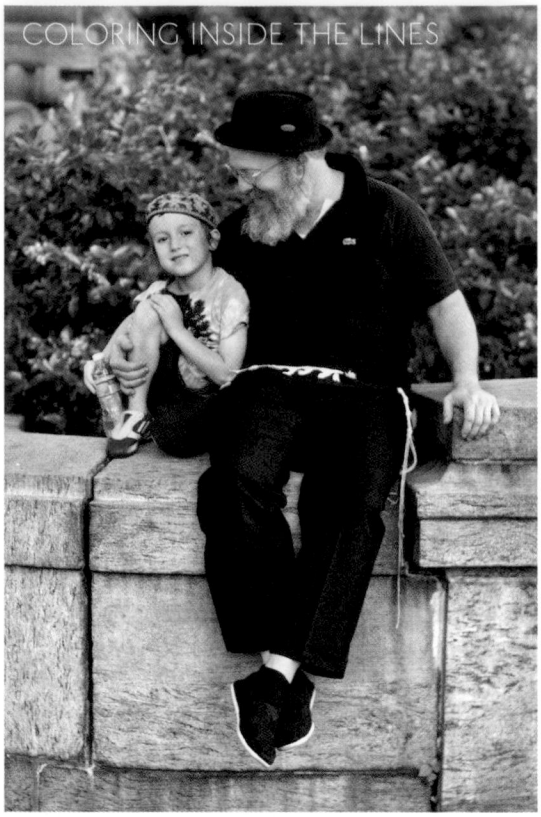

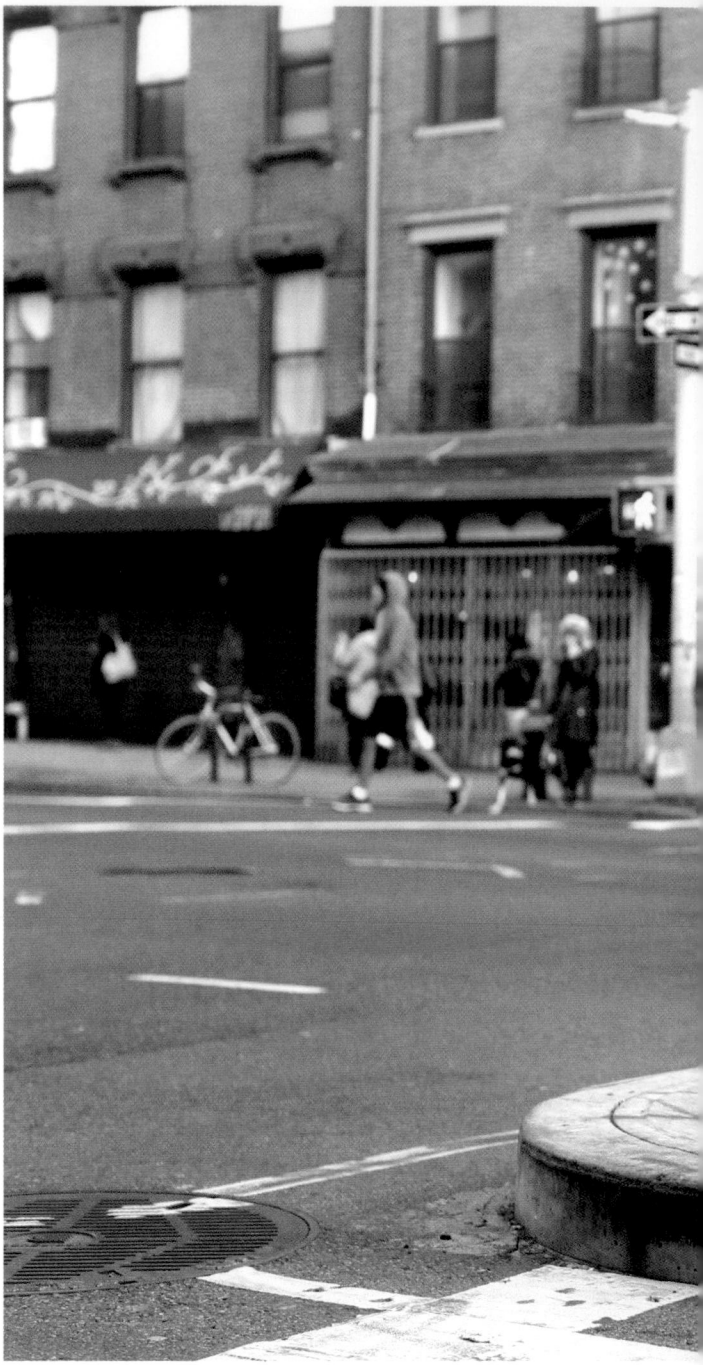

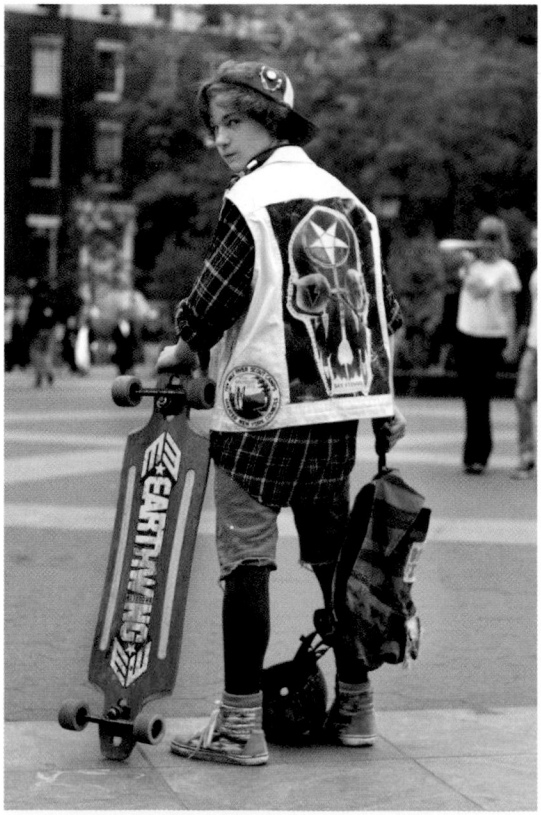


THIS KID WAS IN THE MIDDLE OF A SCAVENGER HUNT, AND HAD JUST EARNED FIVE POINTS FOR "POSING WITH A WOMAN OVER SIX FEET TALL."

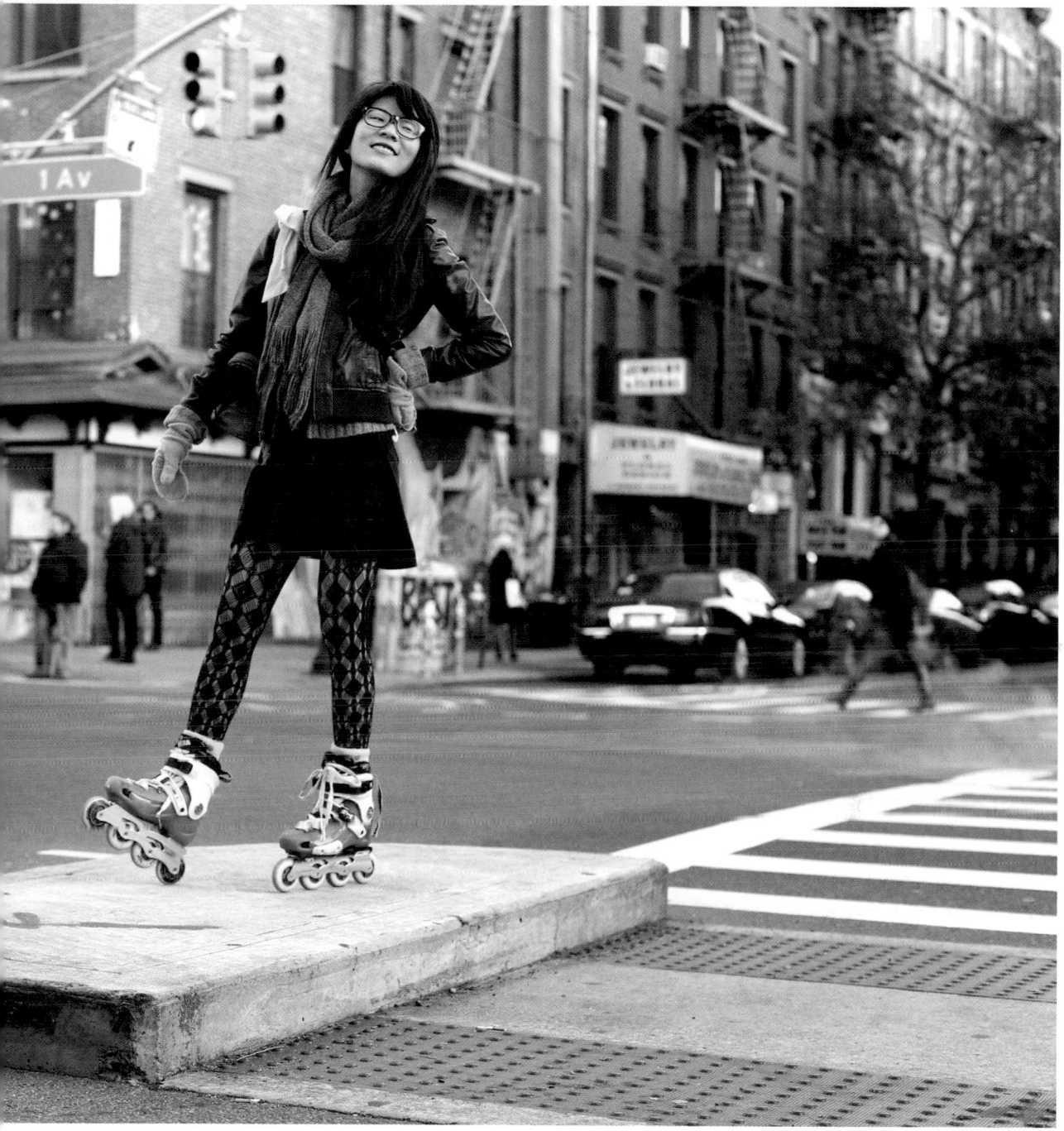


"US ROLLERBLADERS GET NO RESPECT."

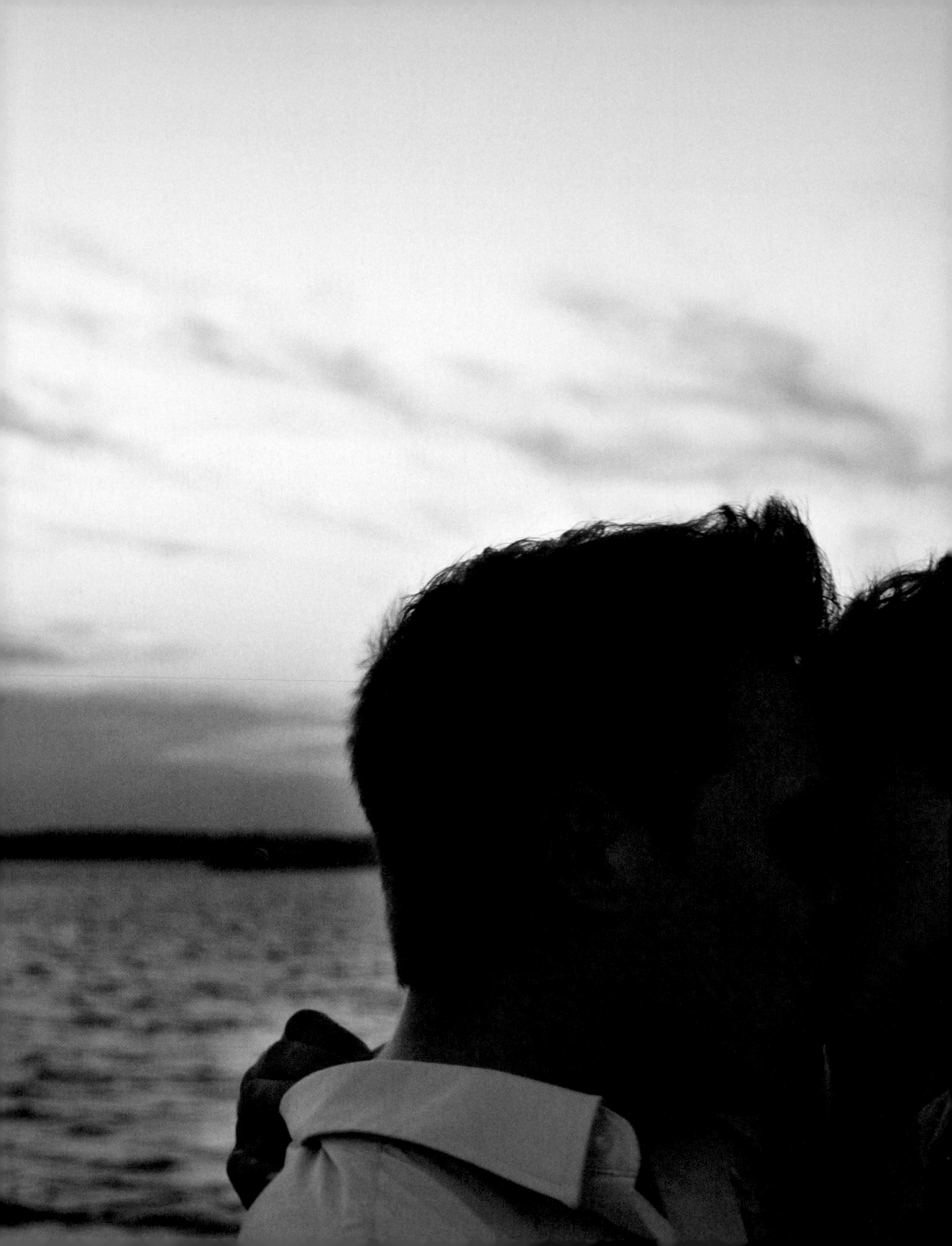

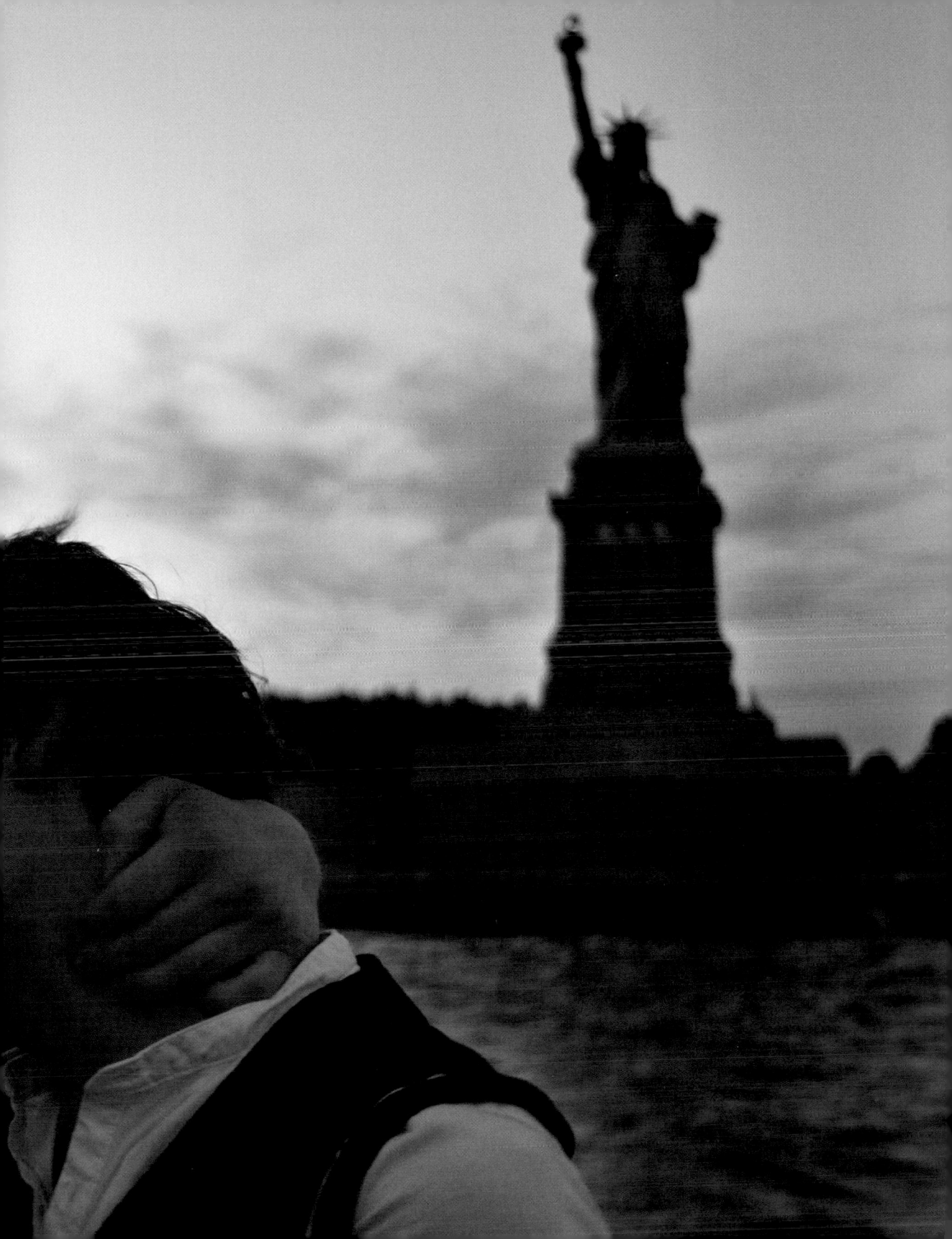

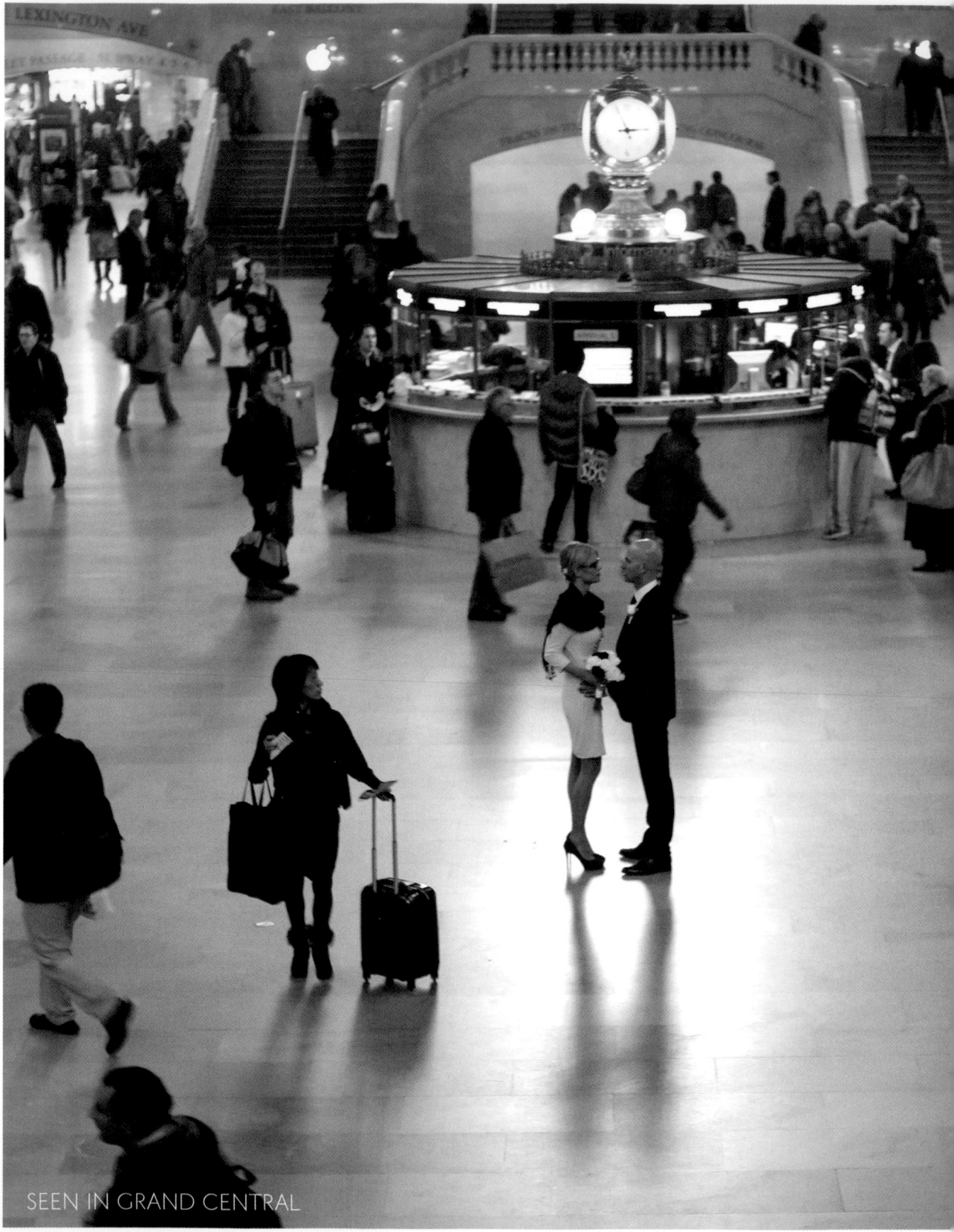


SEEN IN GRAND CENTRAL

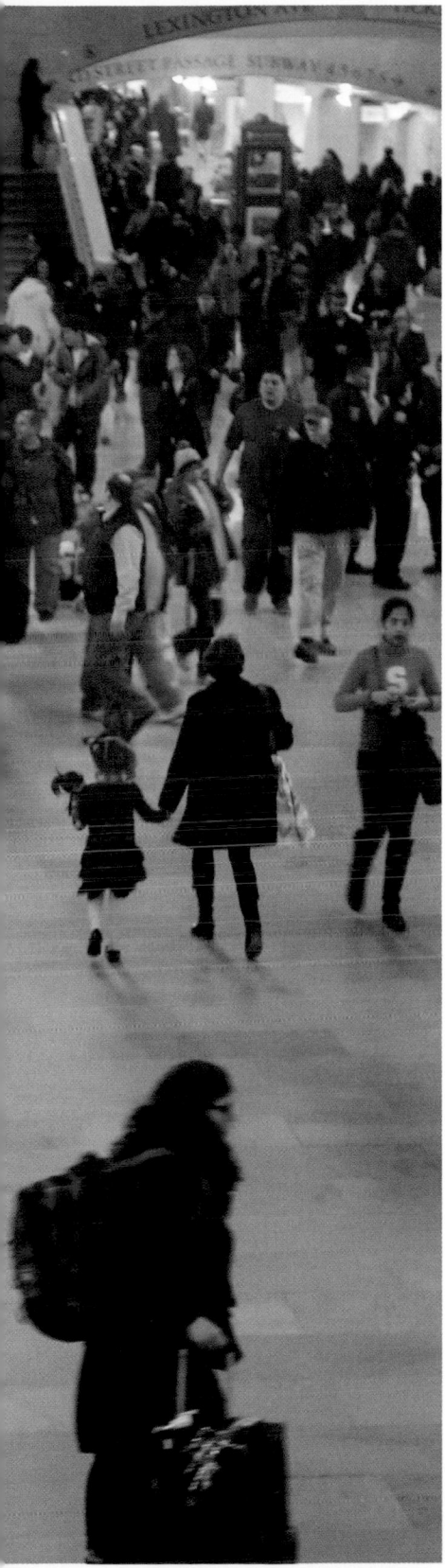

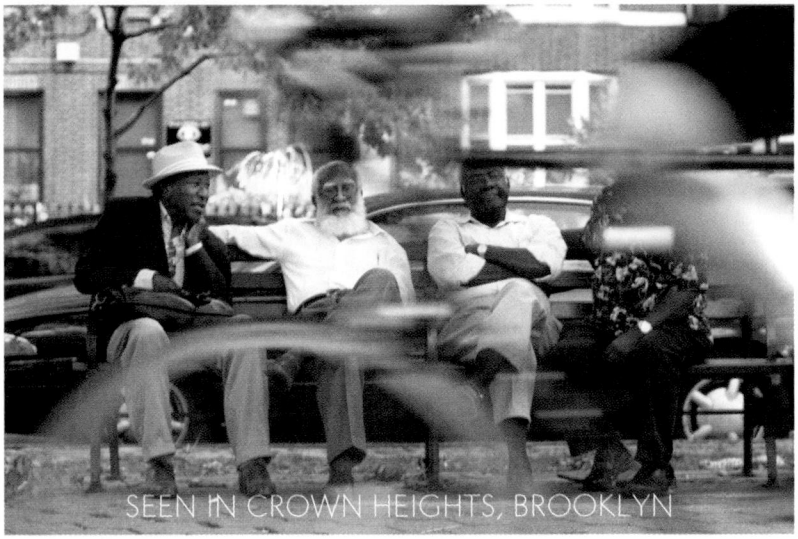

SEEN IN CROWN HEIGHTS, BROOKLYN

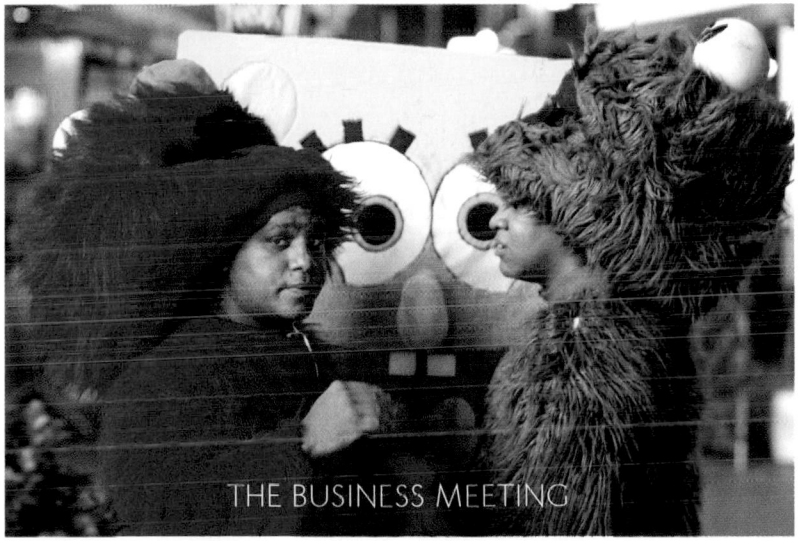

THE BUSINESS MEETING

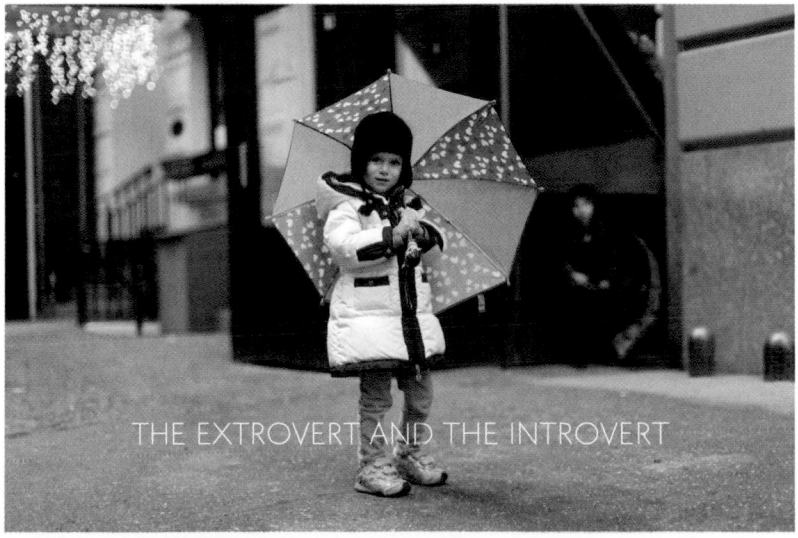

THE EXTROVERT AND THE INTROVERT

IT READS: "WHEN BIRDS LOOK INTO HOUSES, WHAT IMPOSSIBLE WORLDS THEY SEE."

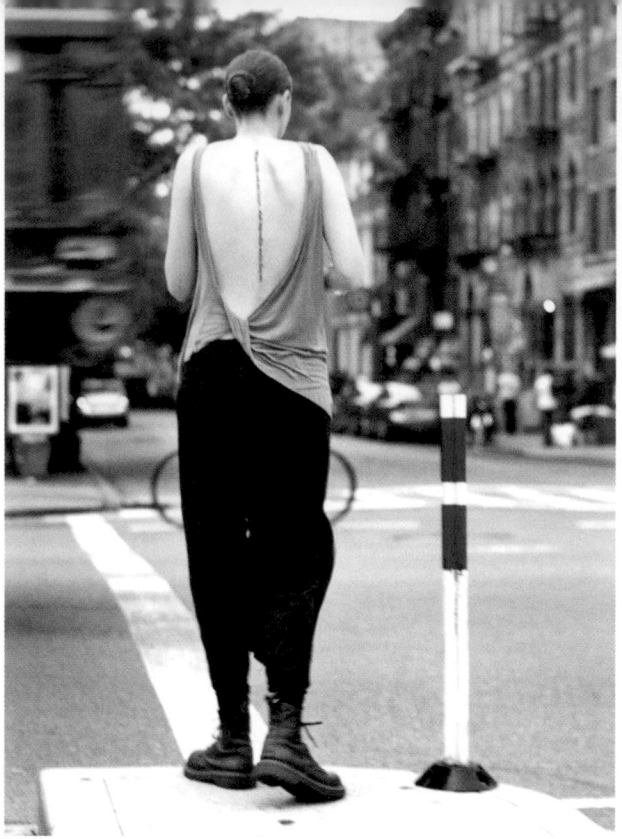

"I WAS BORN IN TRANSYLVANIA AND I WRITE BOOKS ABOUT DRACULA."

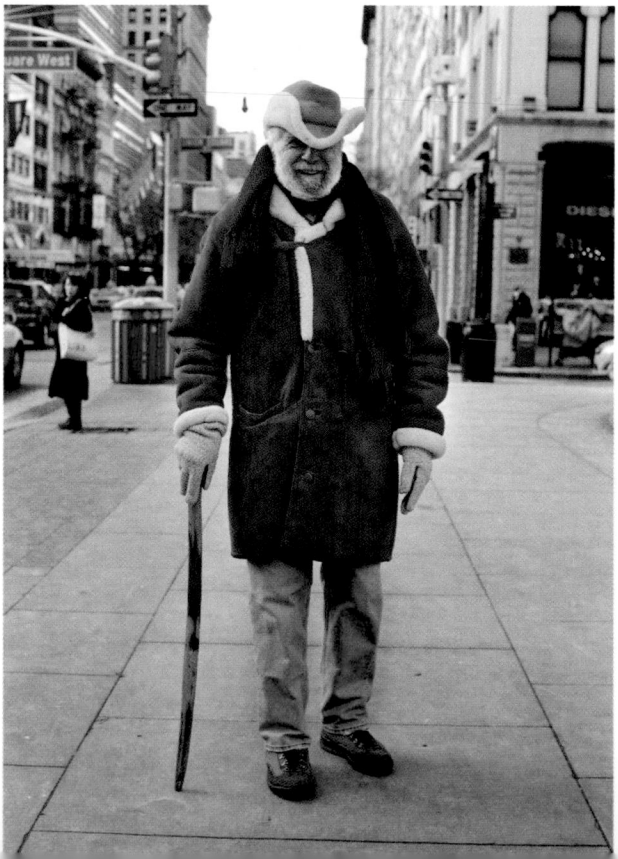

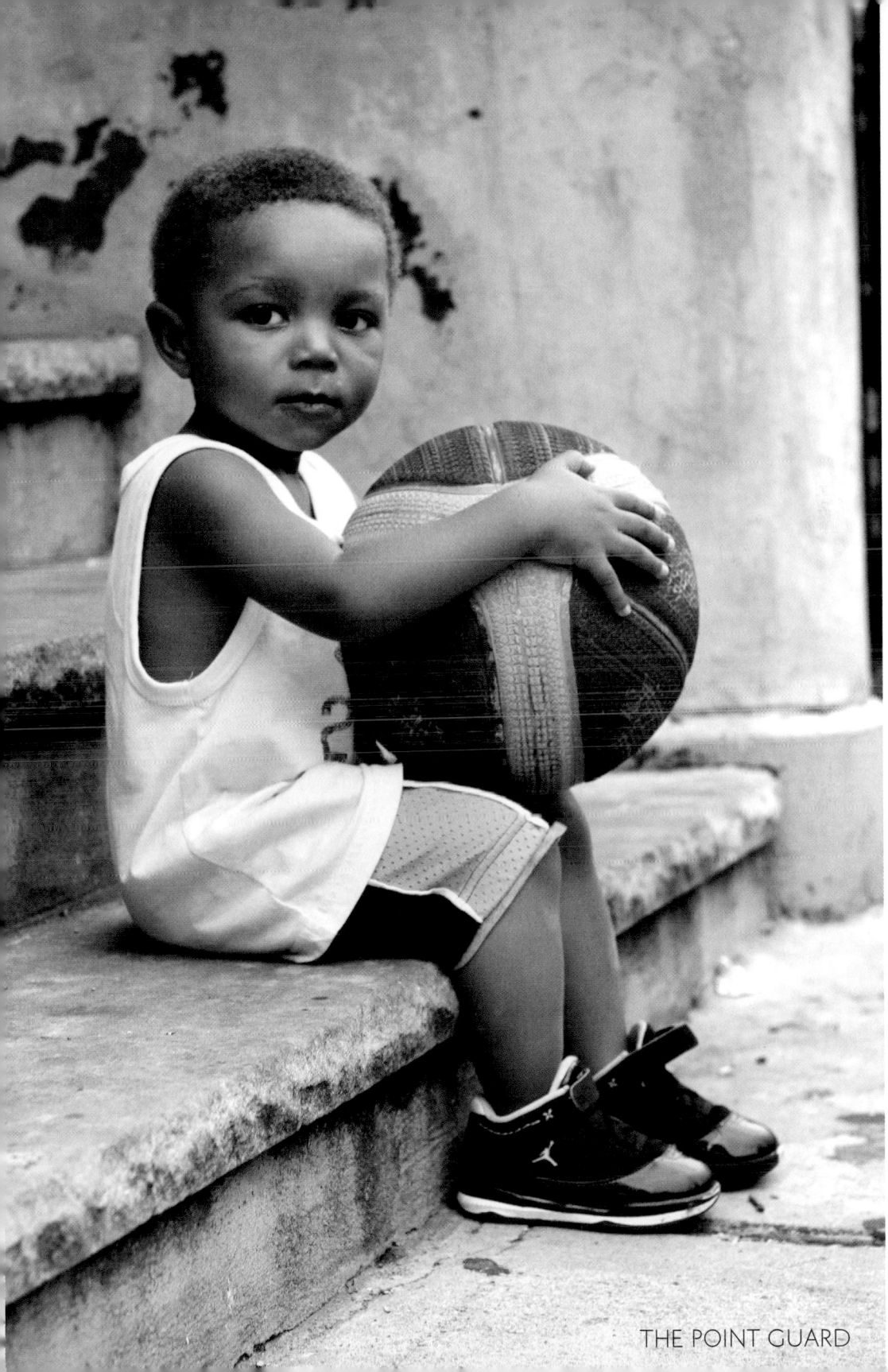

THE POINT GUARD

"HONY IS ONE OF THE ONLY THINGS KEEPING PEOPLE FROM GETTING LOST IN THE MATRIX."

THE BASH BROTHERS

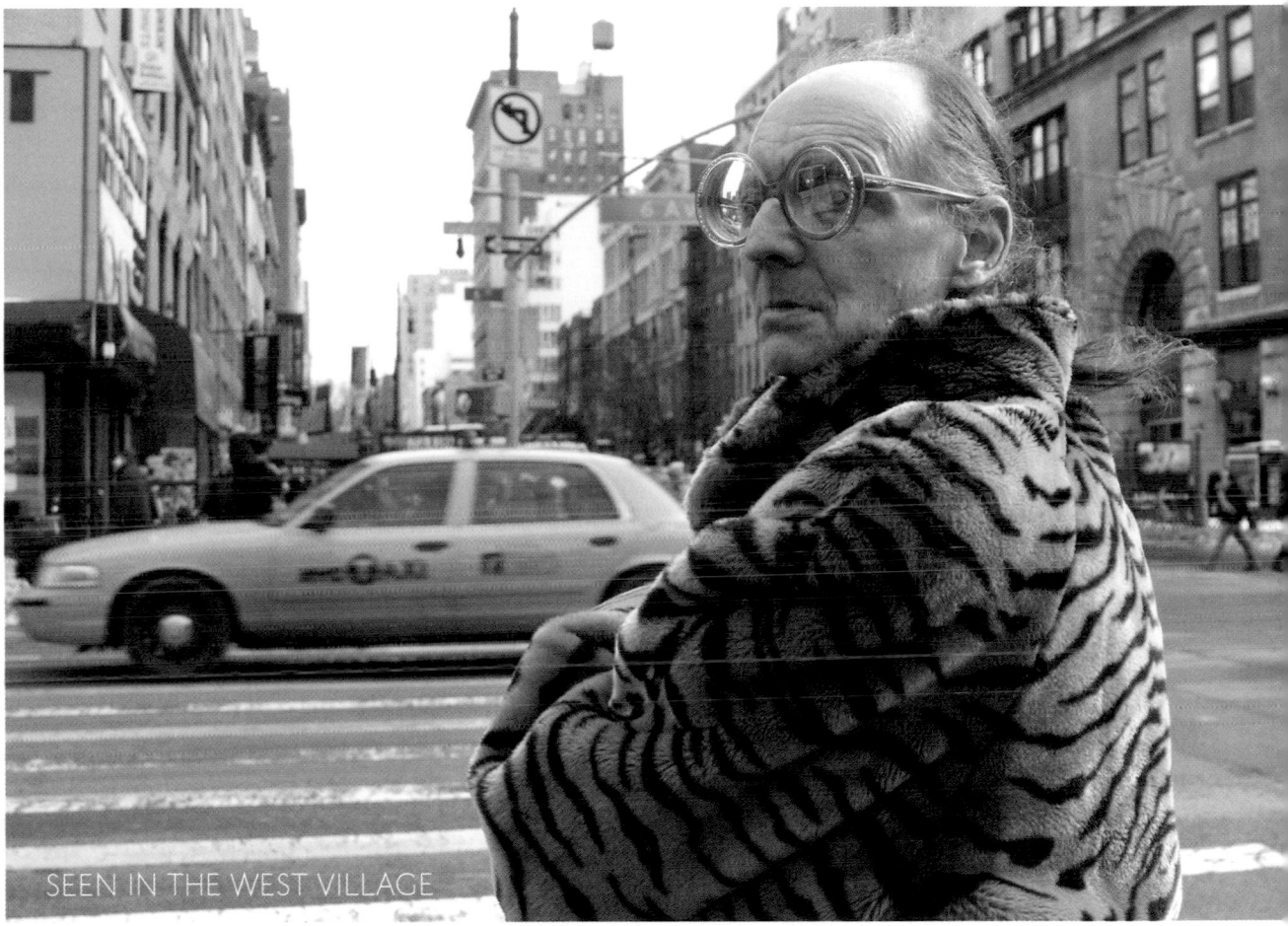
SEEN IN THE WEST VILLAGE

"I LOOK LIKE GOD. DON'T I?"

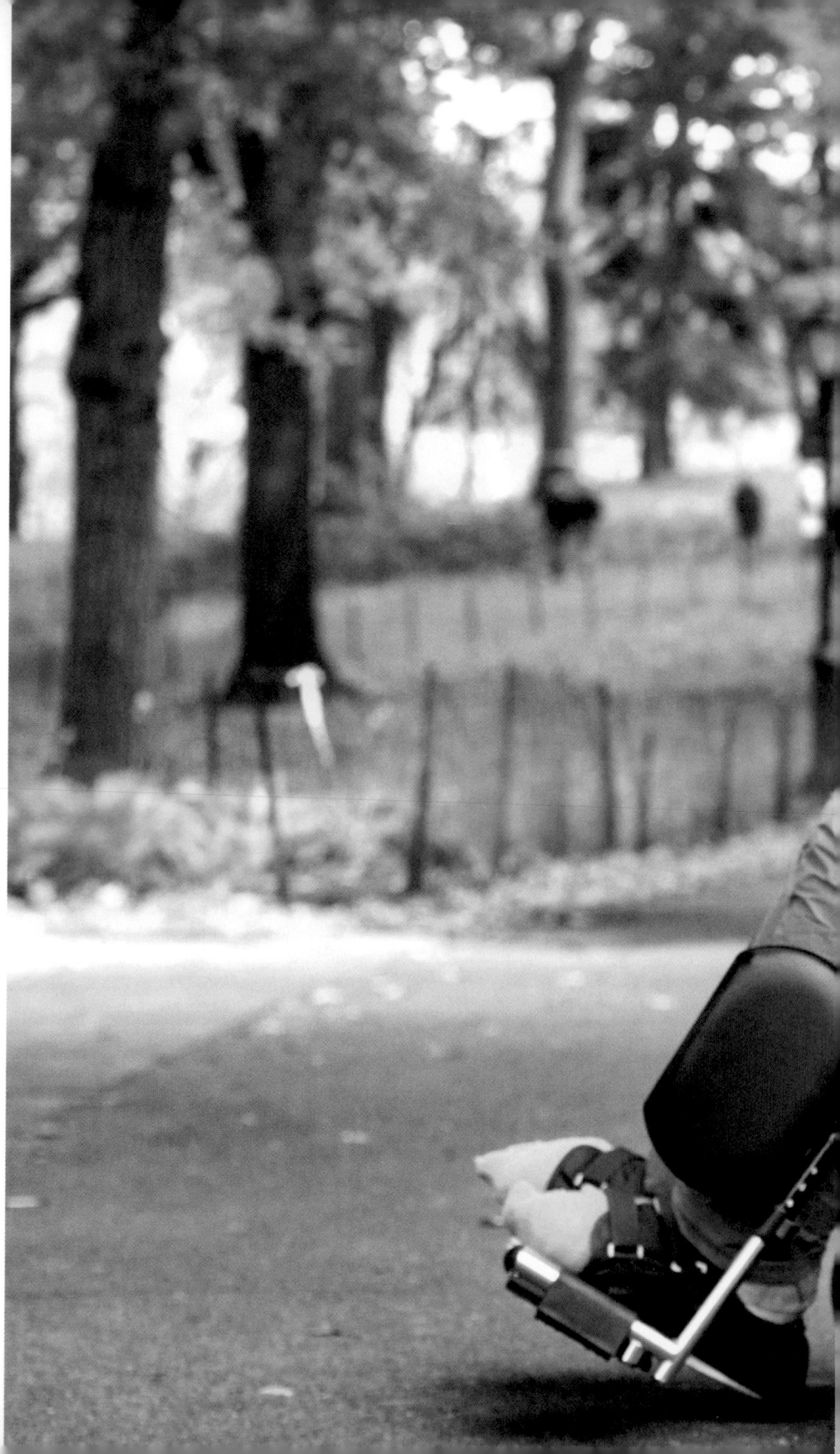

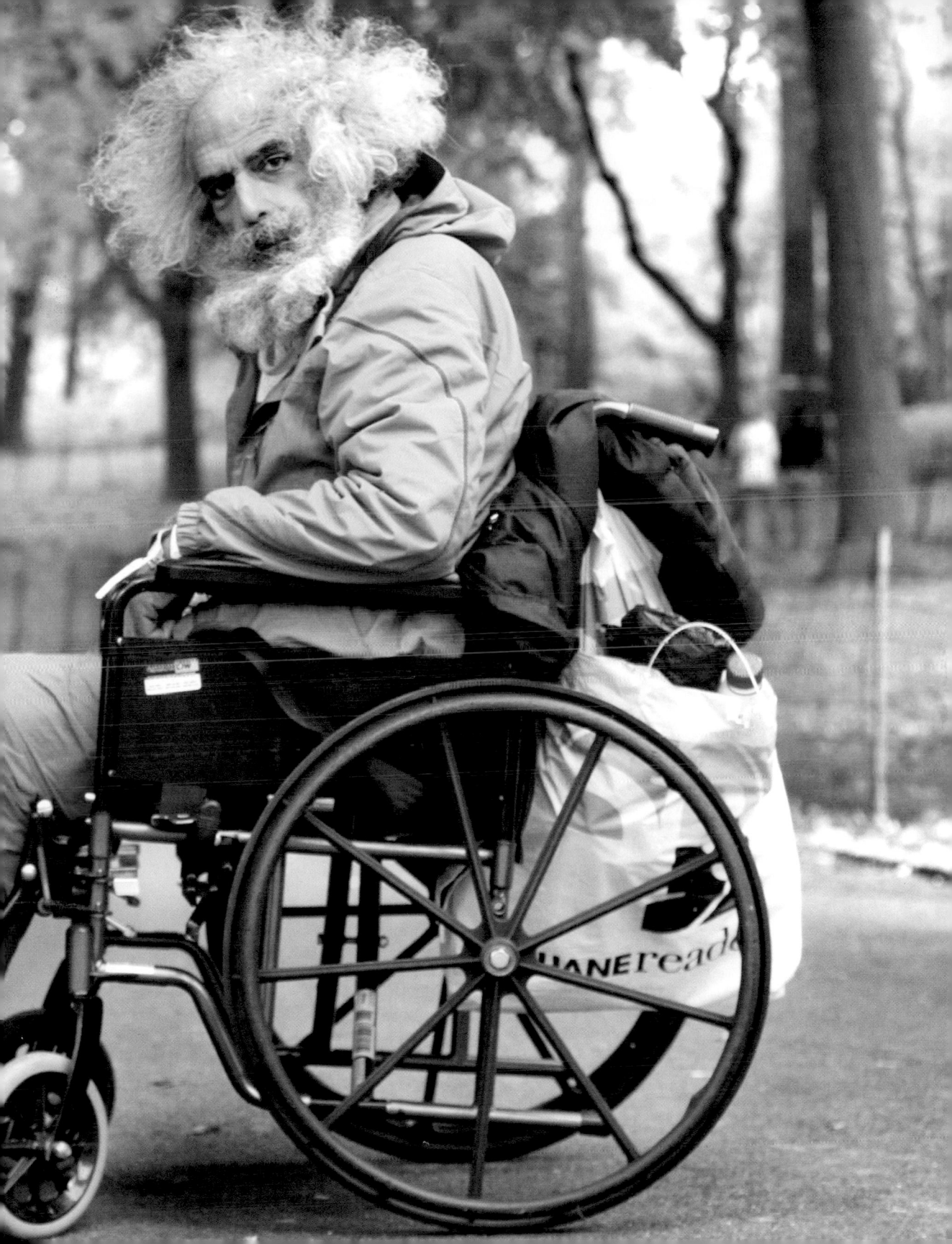
JANE read

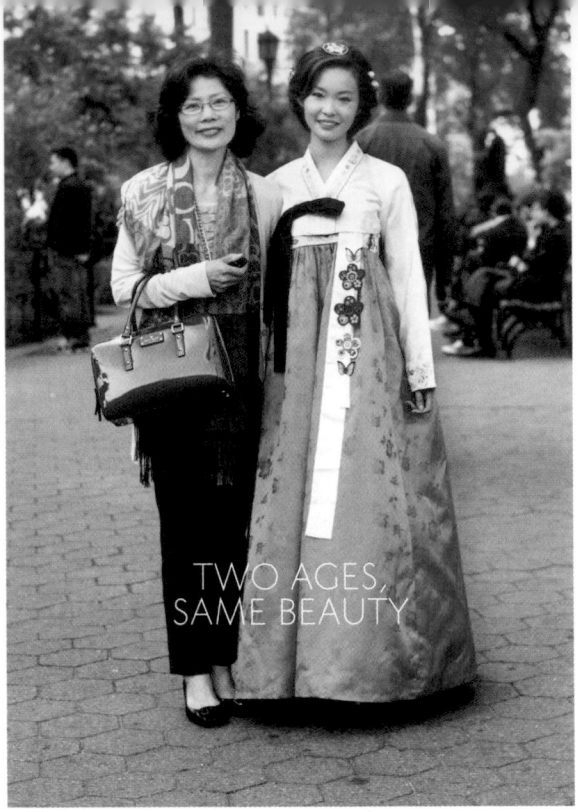

TWO AGES,
SAME BEAUTY

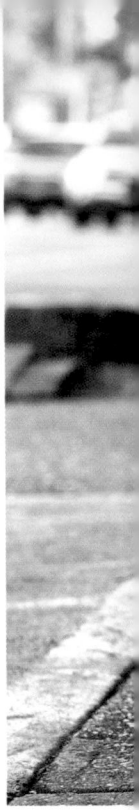

SEEN IN THE WEST VILLAGE

HE PUT HIS MOTHER, TWO GRANDMOTHERS, AND GREAT AUNT ON HIS RIGHT LEG. HE PUT HIS FATHER ON THE OTHER LEG, PROBABLY SO HE COULD HAVE A LITTLE PEACE.

SEEN IN UNION SQUARE

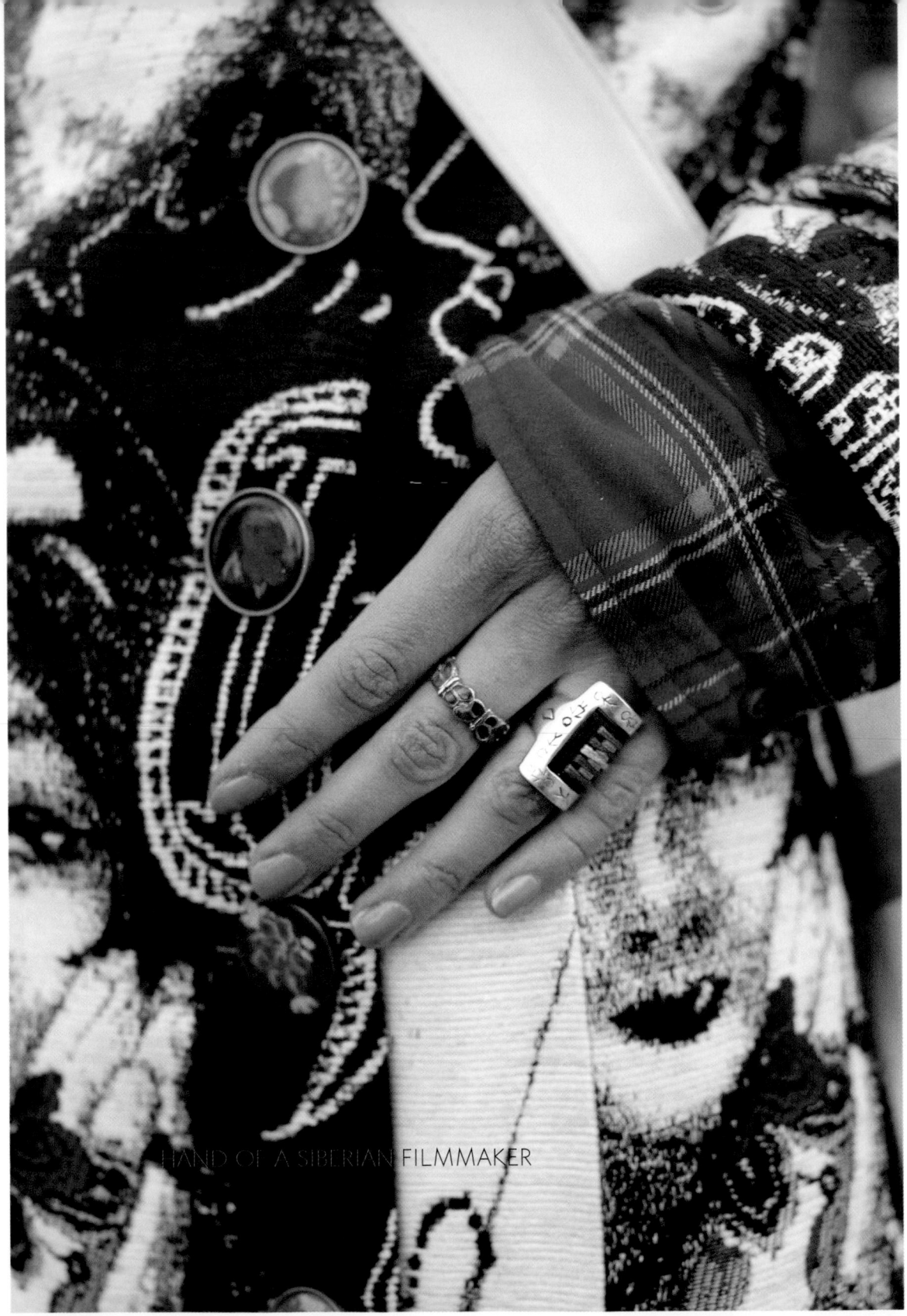

HAND OF A SIBERIAN FILMMAKER

SEEN IN COLUMBUS CIRCLE

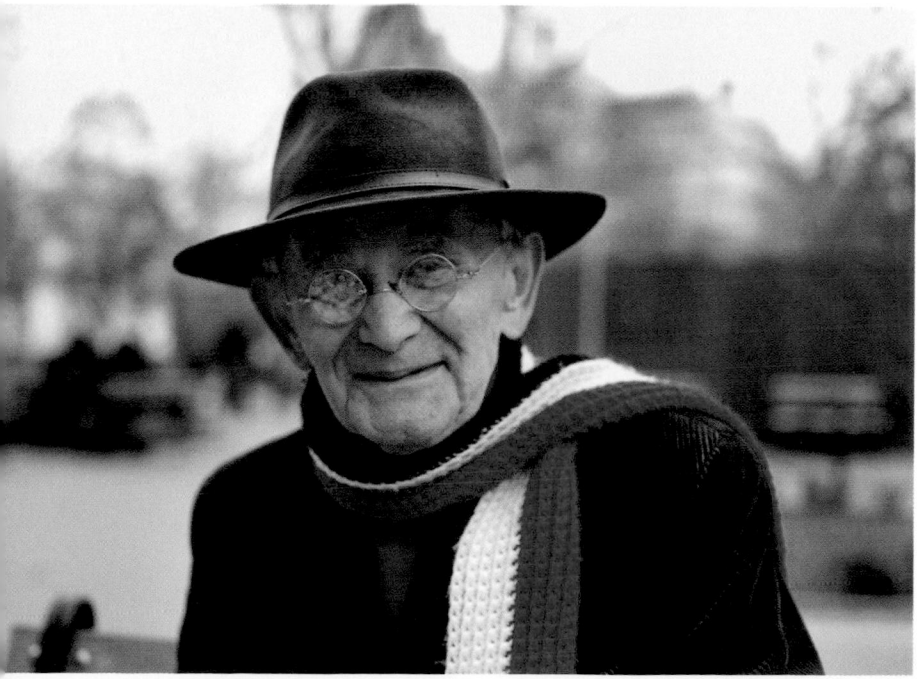

"I'M A TIME TRAVELER."

'IT BELONGS TO MY BOSS.'

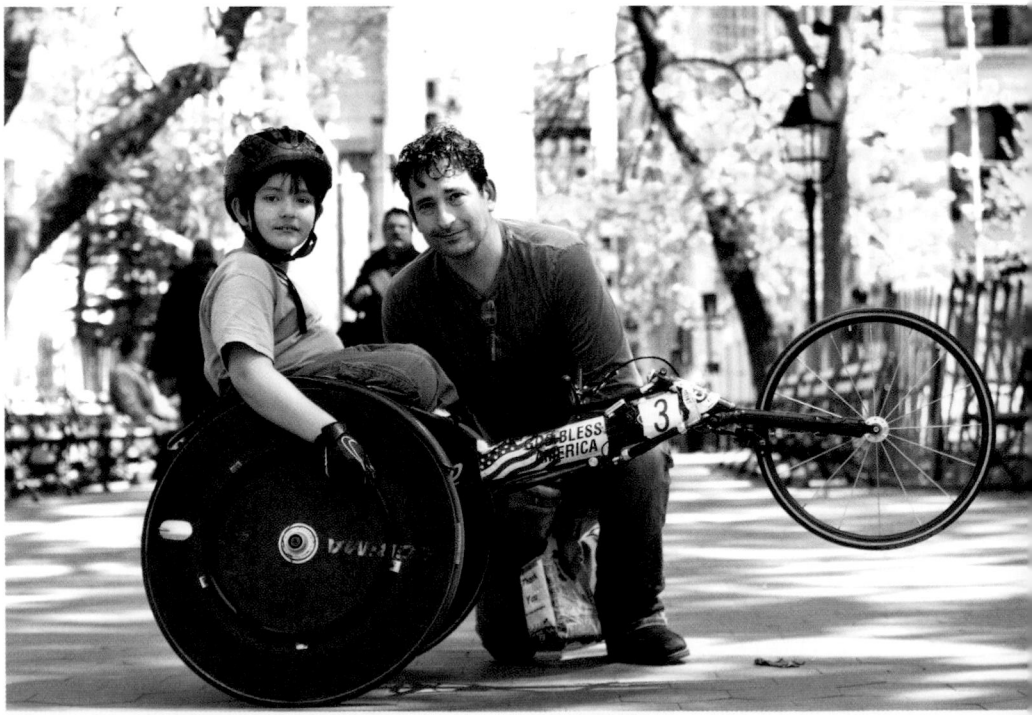


THESE TWO WERE RAISING MONEY FOR THE BOY'S ATHLETIC LEAGUE. 'IT'S A GREAT PROGRAM,' EXPLAINED THE FATHER. 'I FOUND IT WHILE SEARCHING FOR THINGS HE COULD DO.'

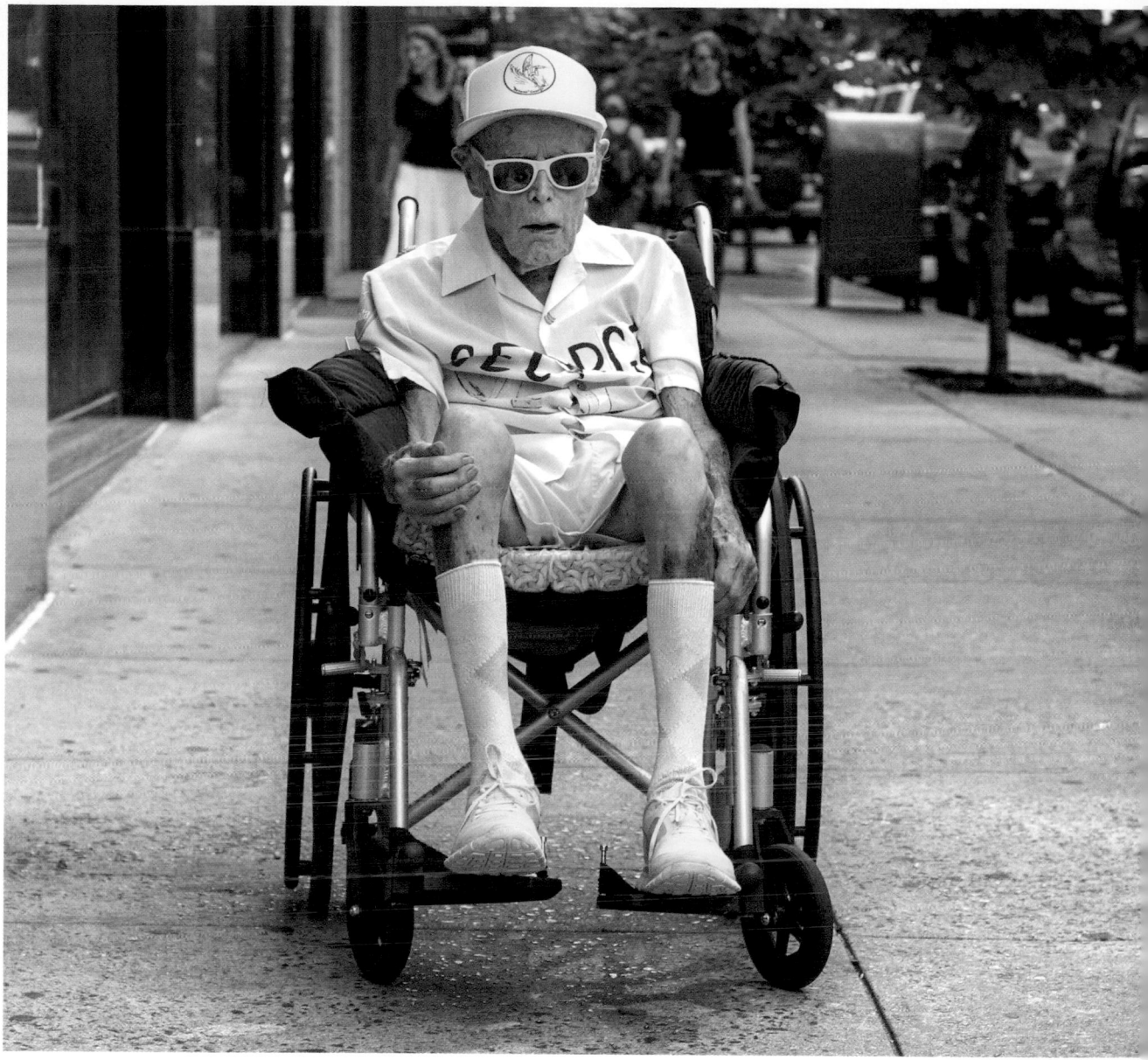

'THIS IS BANANA GEORGE,' EXPLAINED HIS CARETAKER. 'HE'S THE WORLD'S OLDEST BAREFOOT WATER-SKIER. HE'S NINETY-SEVEN NOW. WHEN HE WAS NINETY-TWO, HE SET THE WORLD RECORD FOR THE OLDEST PERSON TO WATER-SKI BAREFOOT.'

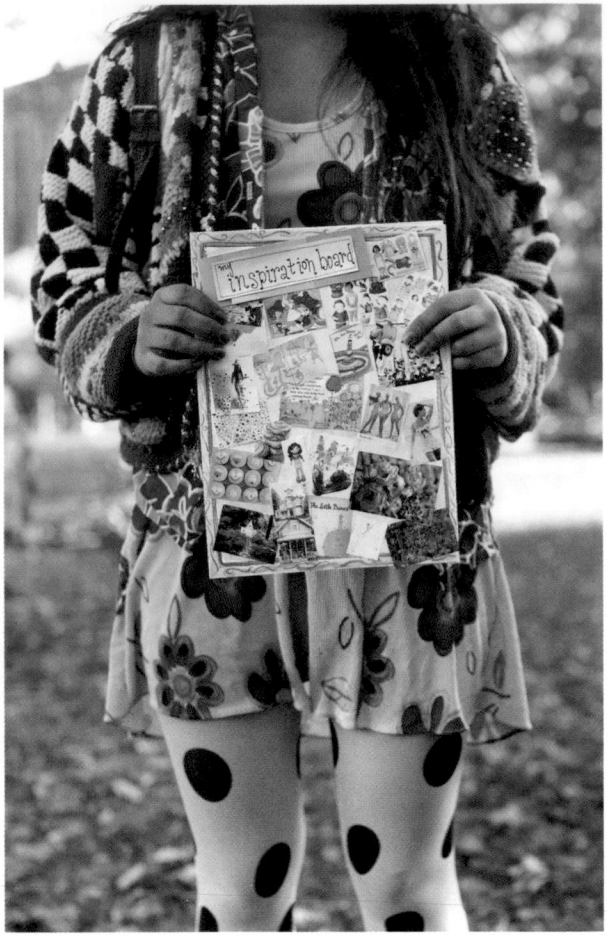


YOU KNOW SOMEBODY IS TRUE TO HERSELF WHEN HER "INSPIRATION BOARD" IS CAMOUFLAGED AGAINST HER CLOTHING.

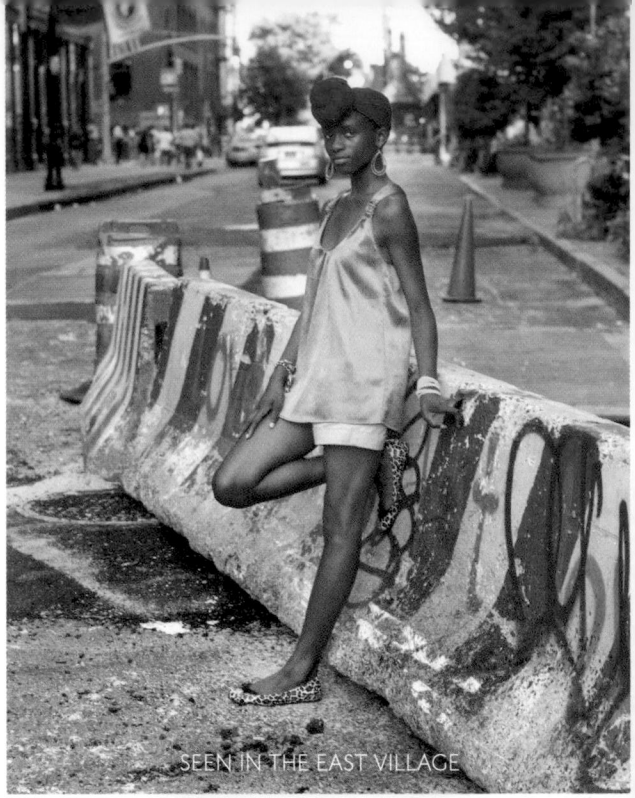

SEEN IN THE EAST VILLAGE

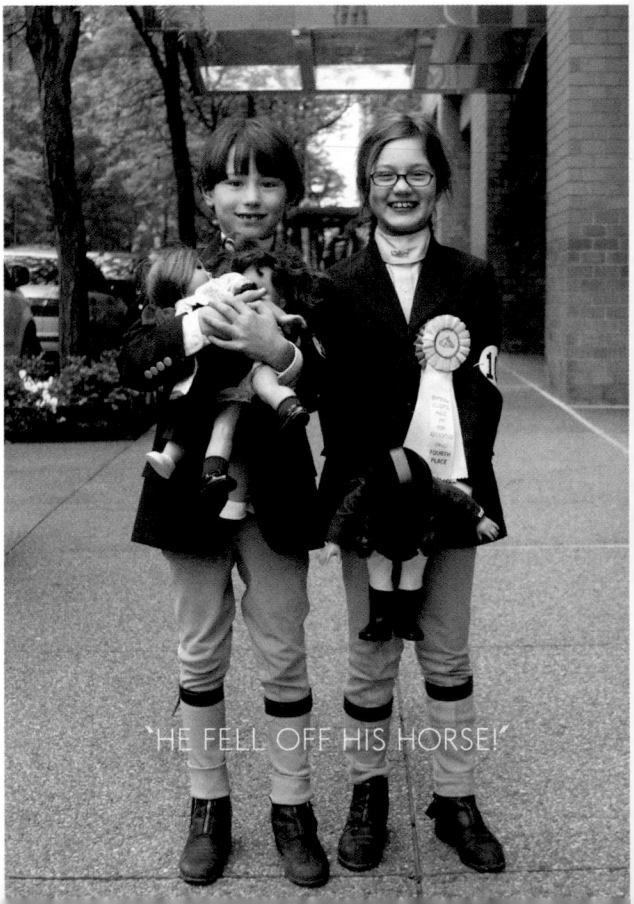

"HE FELL OFF HIS HORSE!"

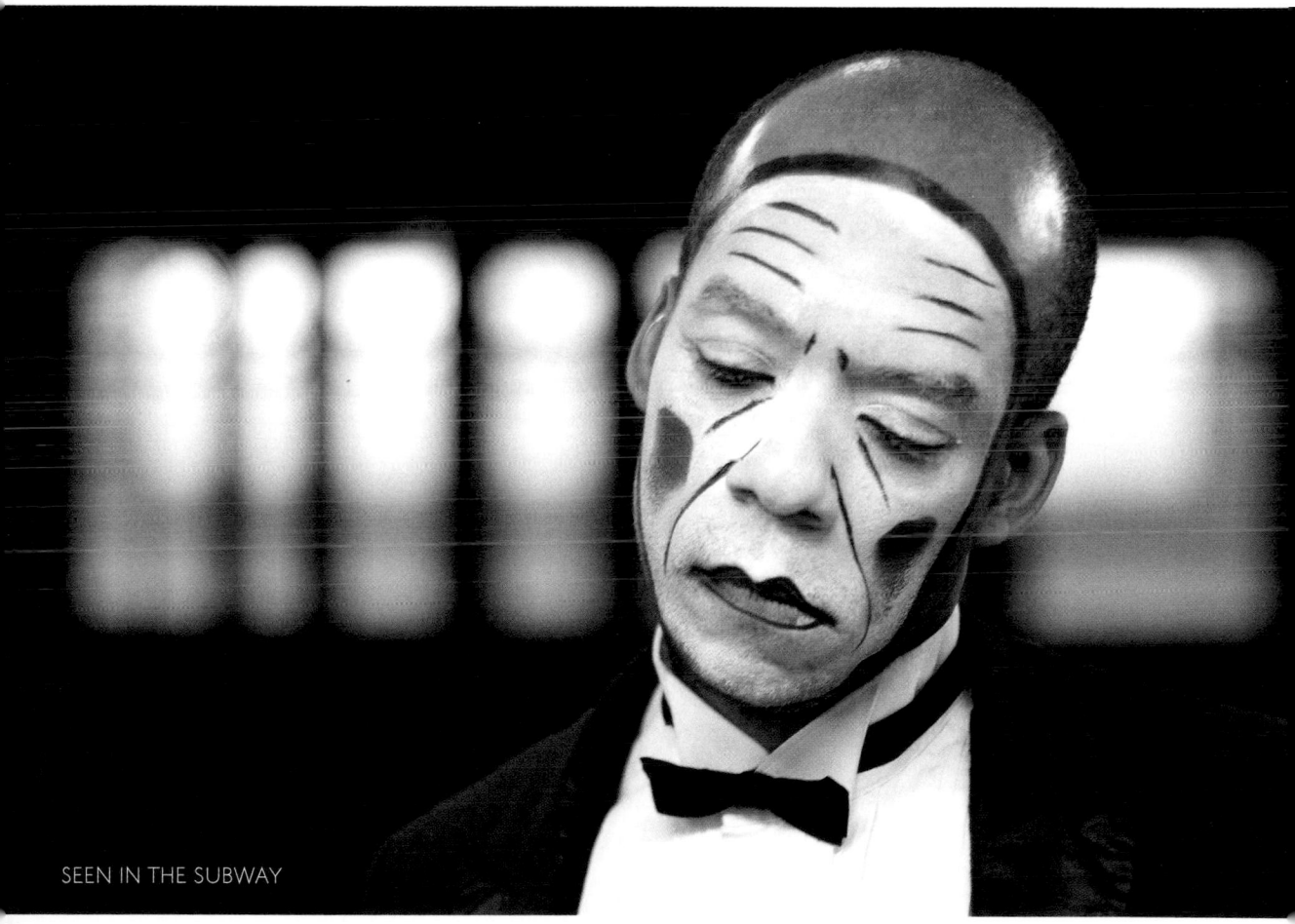

SEEN IN THE SUBWAY

DESPITE BEING HOMELESS, HE WAS GENUINELY CONCERNED ABOUT MY ABILITY TO 'MAKE IT' AS A PHOTOGRAPHER.

SEEN ON WALL STREET

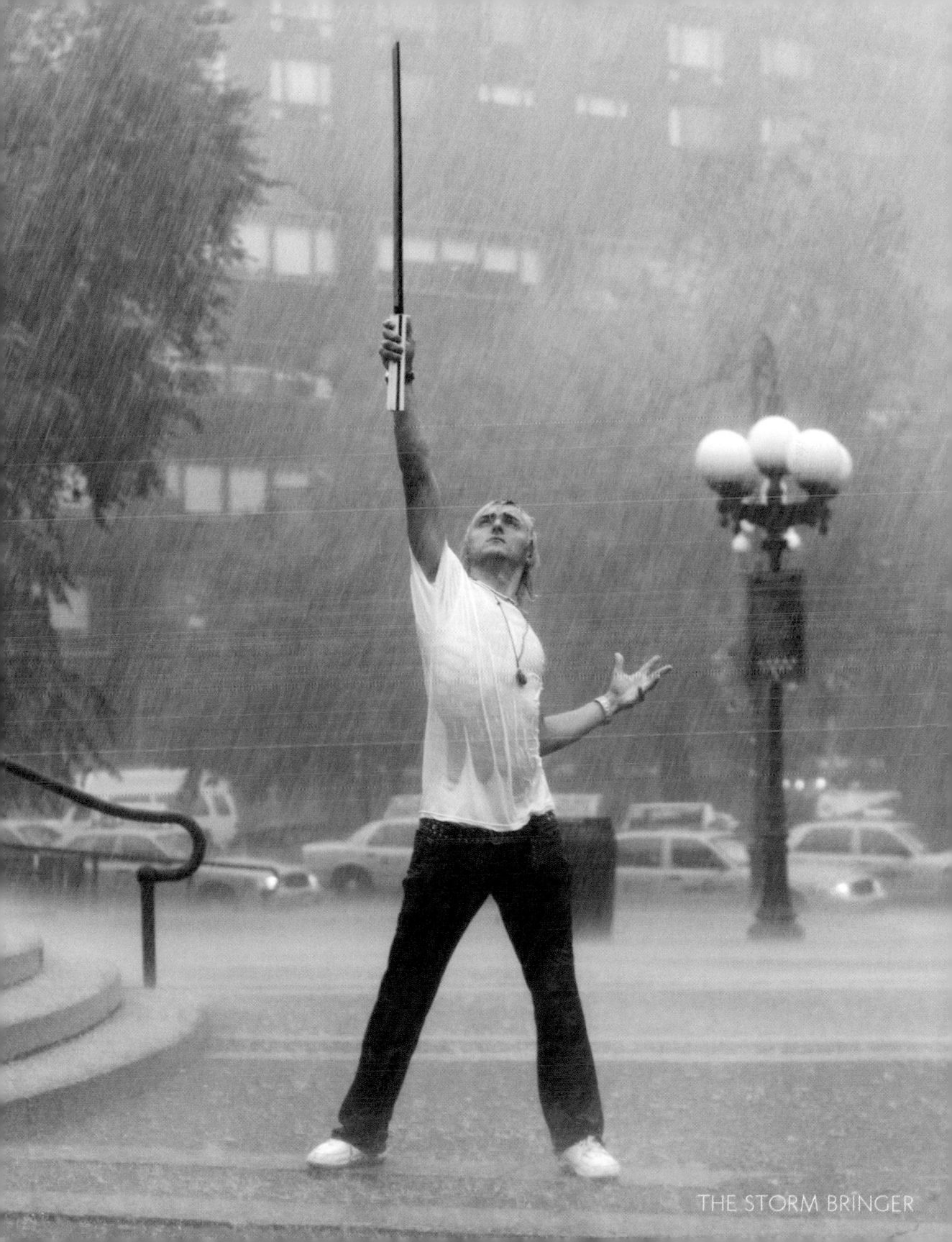

THE STORM BRINGER

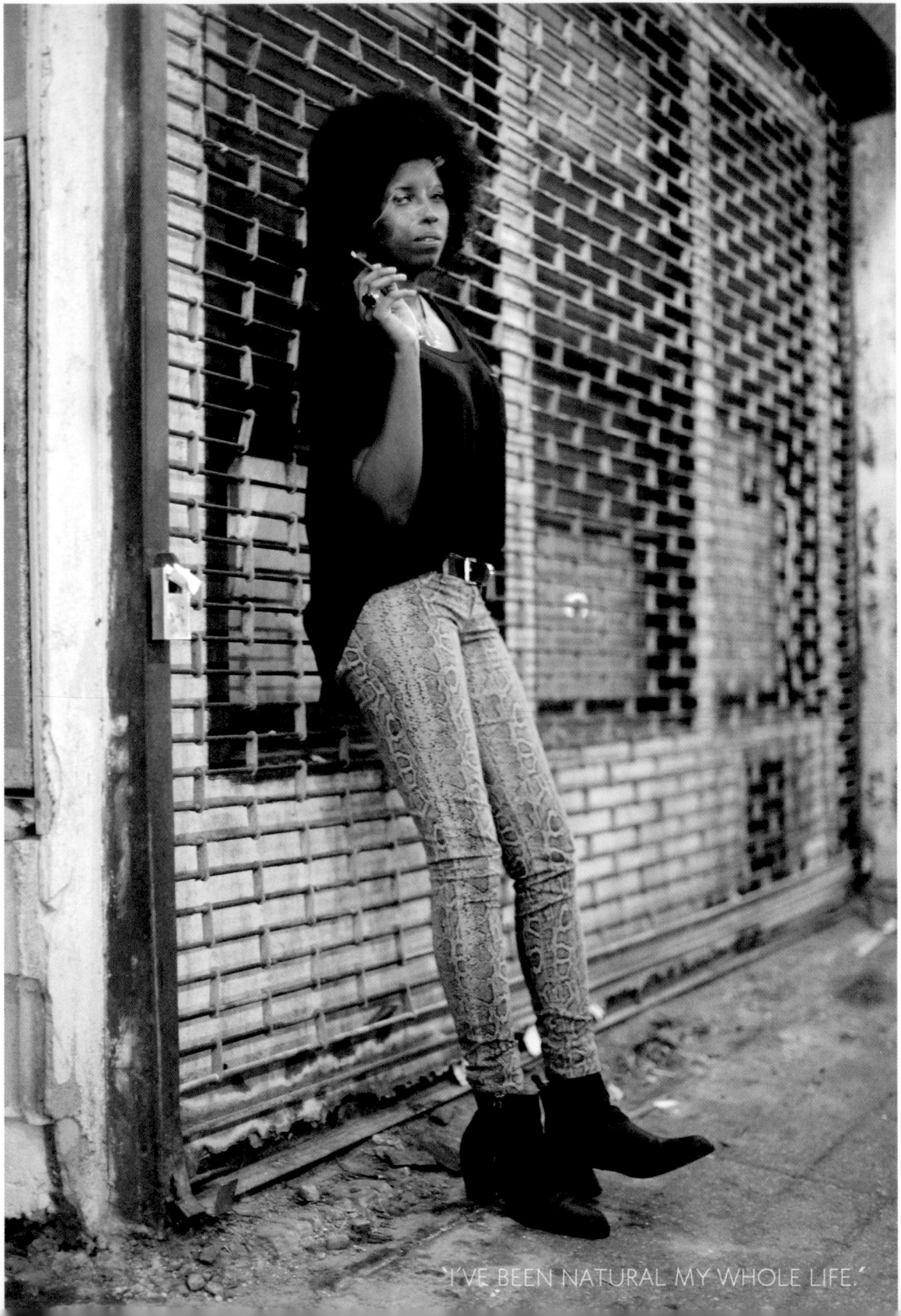

"I'VE BEEN NATURAL MY WHOLE LIFE."

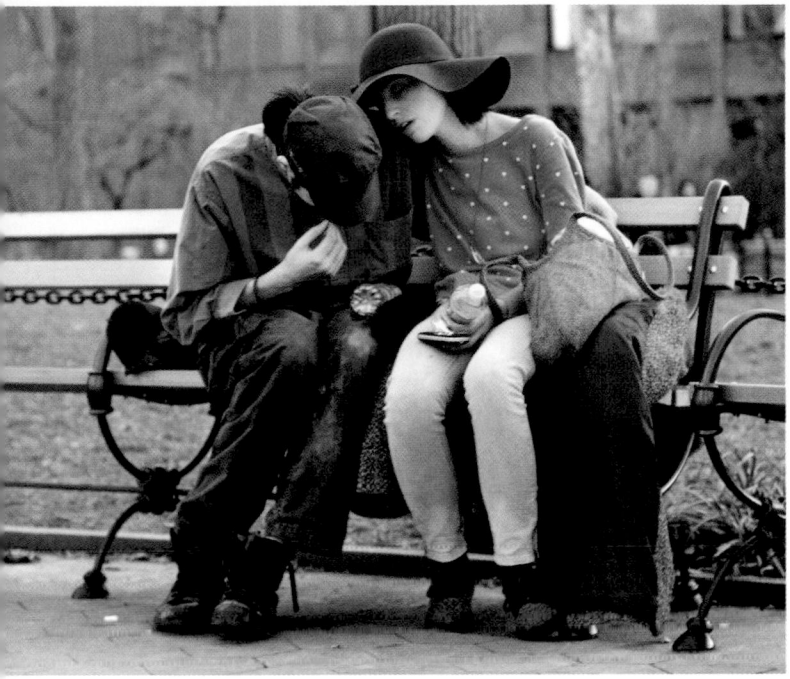

I KNEW NOTHING ABOUT THESE TWO WHEN I TOOK THEIR PHOTO IN WASHINGTON SQUARE PARK. THEY LATER BECAME A HEADLINE WHEN A CACHE OF EXPLOSIVES WAS REPORTEDLY DISCOVERED IN THEIR WEST VILLAGE APARTMENT.

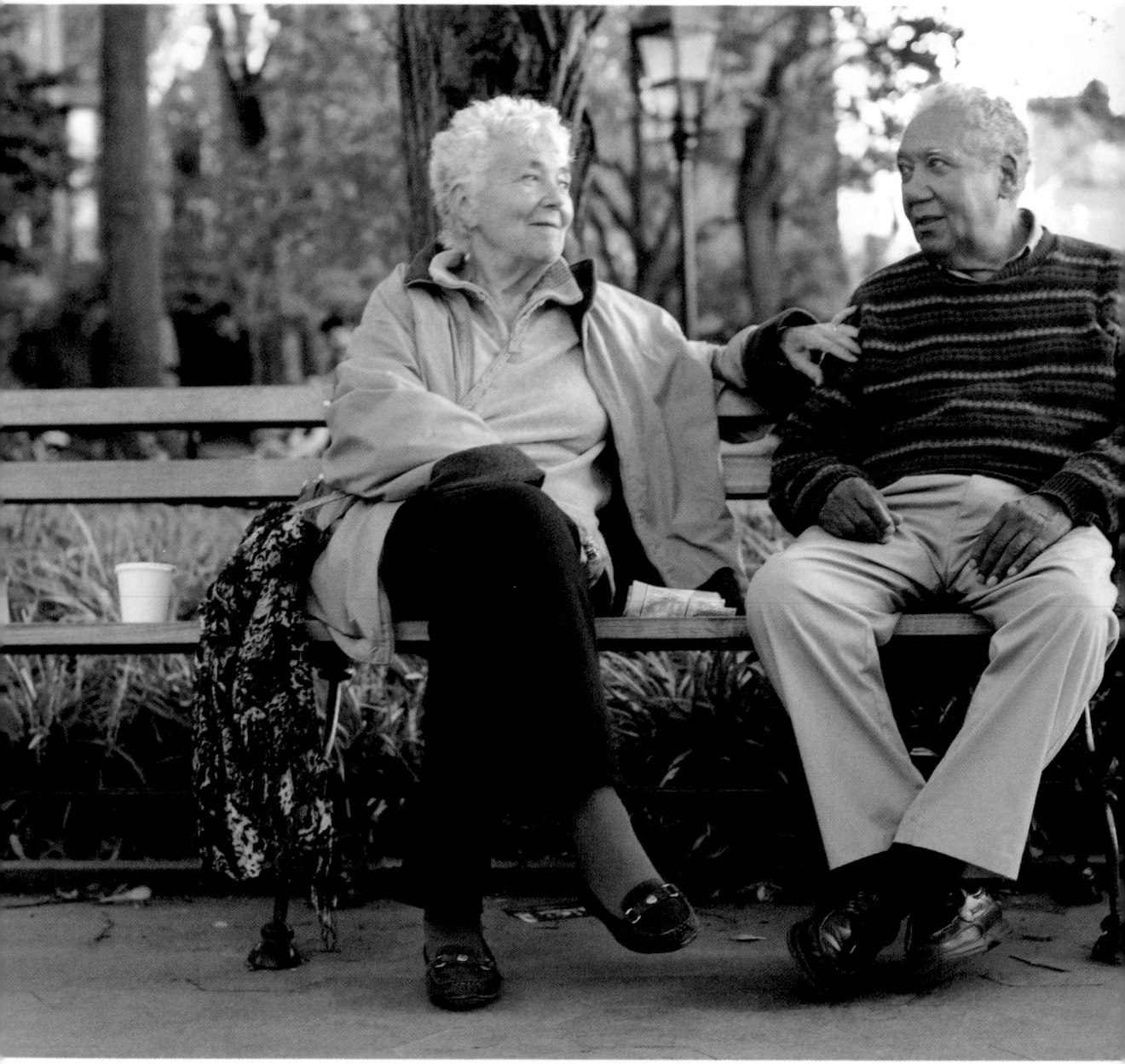

"WE WERE BOTH INVOLVED IN THE CIVIL RIGHTS MOVEMENT.
WE MET FORTY-SEVEN YEARS AGO ON A PICKET LINE."

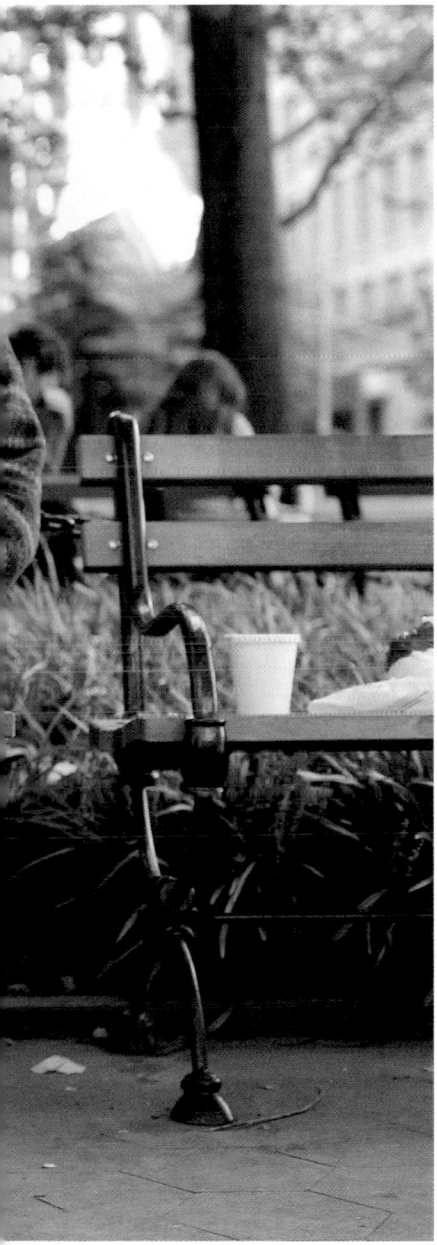

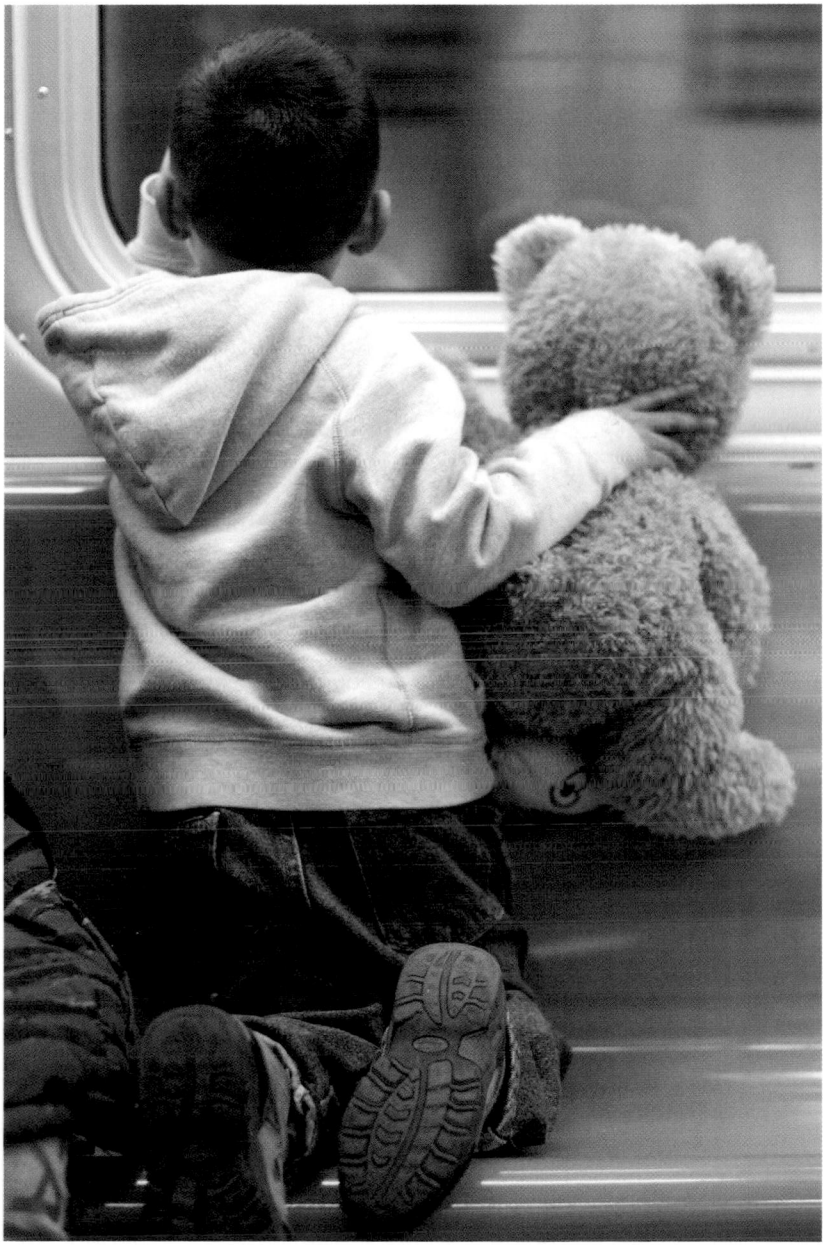

TRAVELING BUDDIES

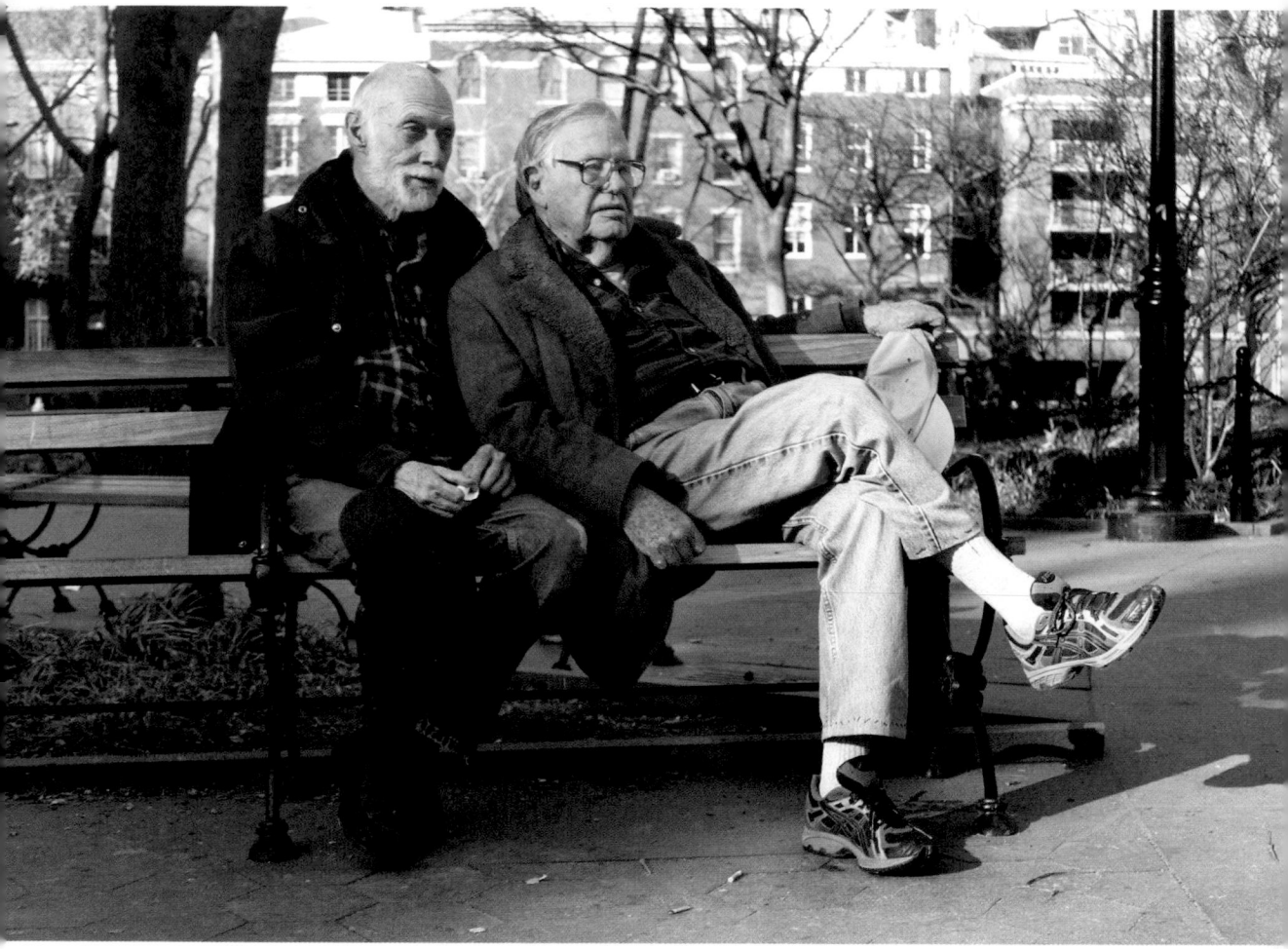

IT TAKES A LOT OF DISQUIET TO ACHIEVE THIS SORT OF QUIET COMFORT.

"MY WIFE PASSED AWAY A FEW YEARS BACK. HER NAME WAS BARBARA, I USED TO CALL HER BA. MY NAME WAS LAWRENCE, SHE USED TO CALL ME LA. WHEN SHE DIED, I CHANGED MY NAME TO BALA."

CAMERA SHY

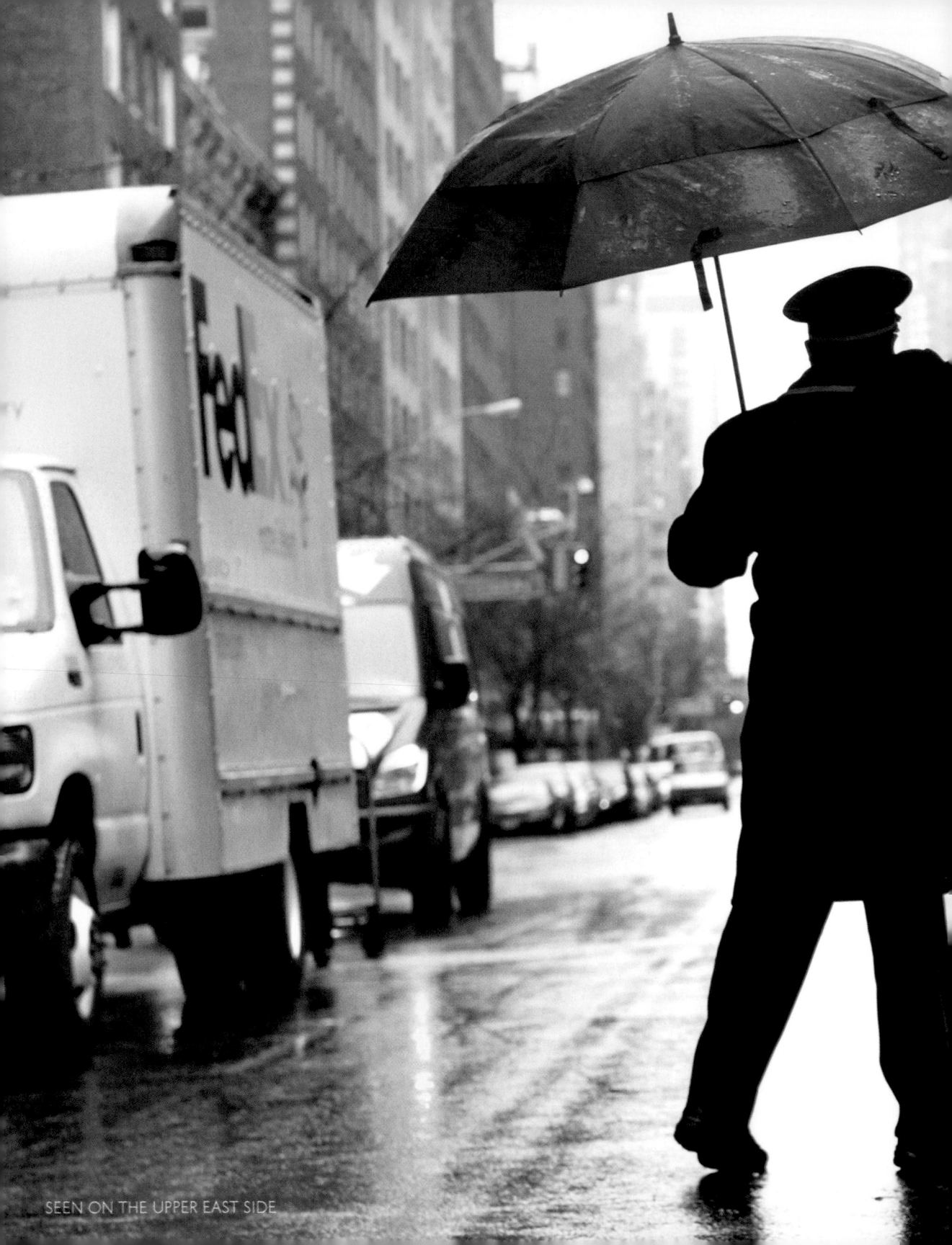


SEEN ON THE UPPER EAST SIDE

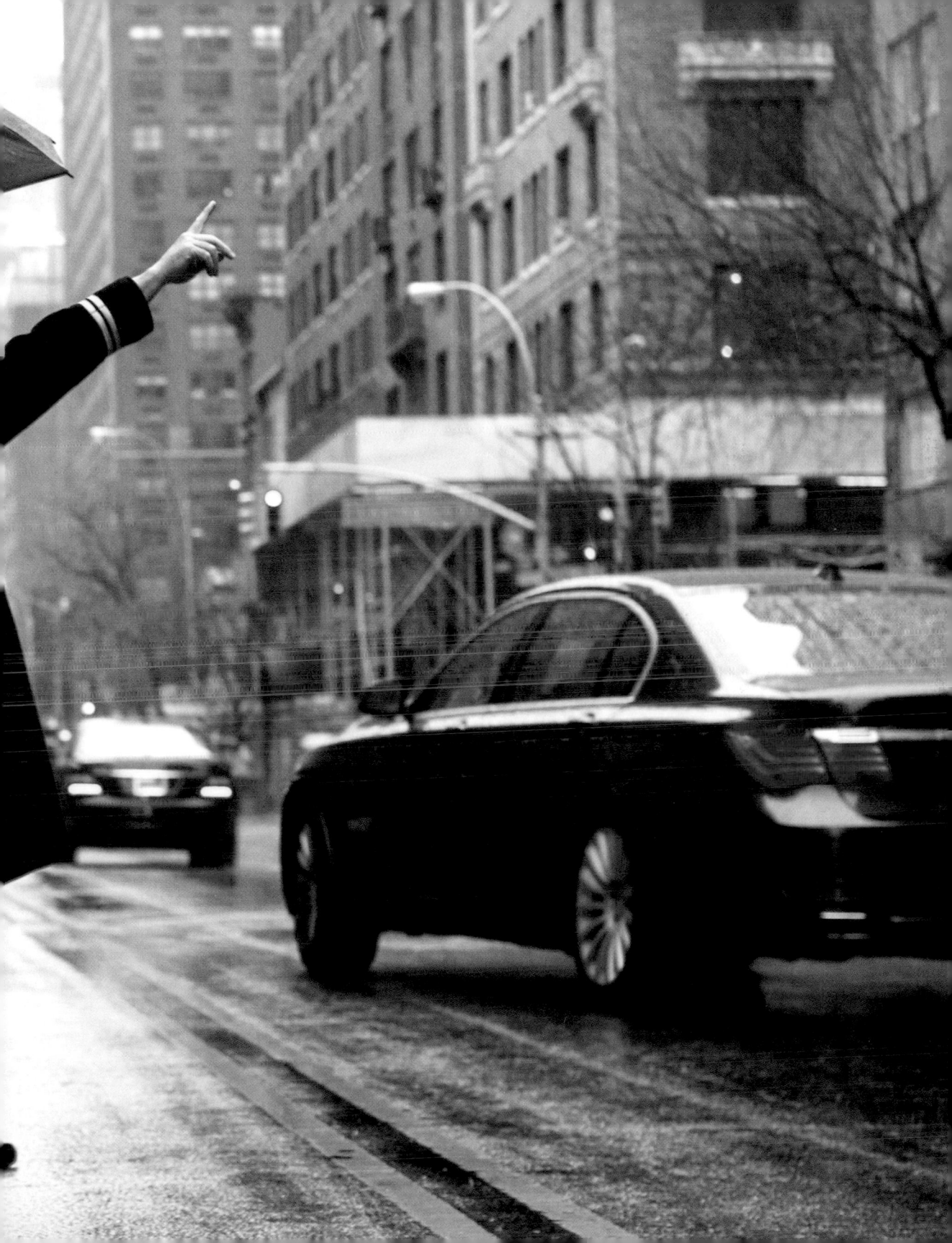

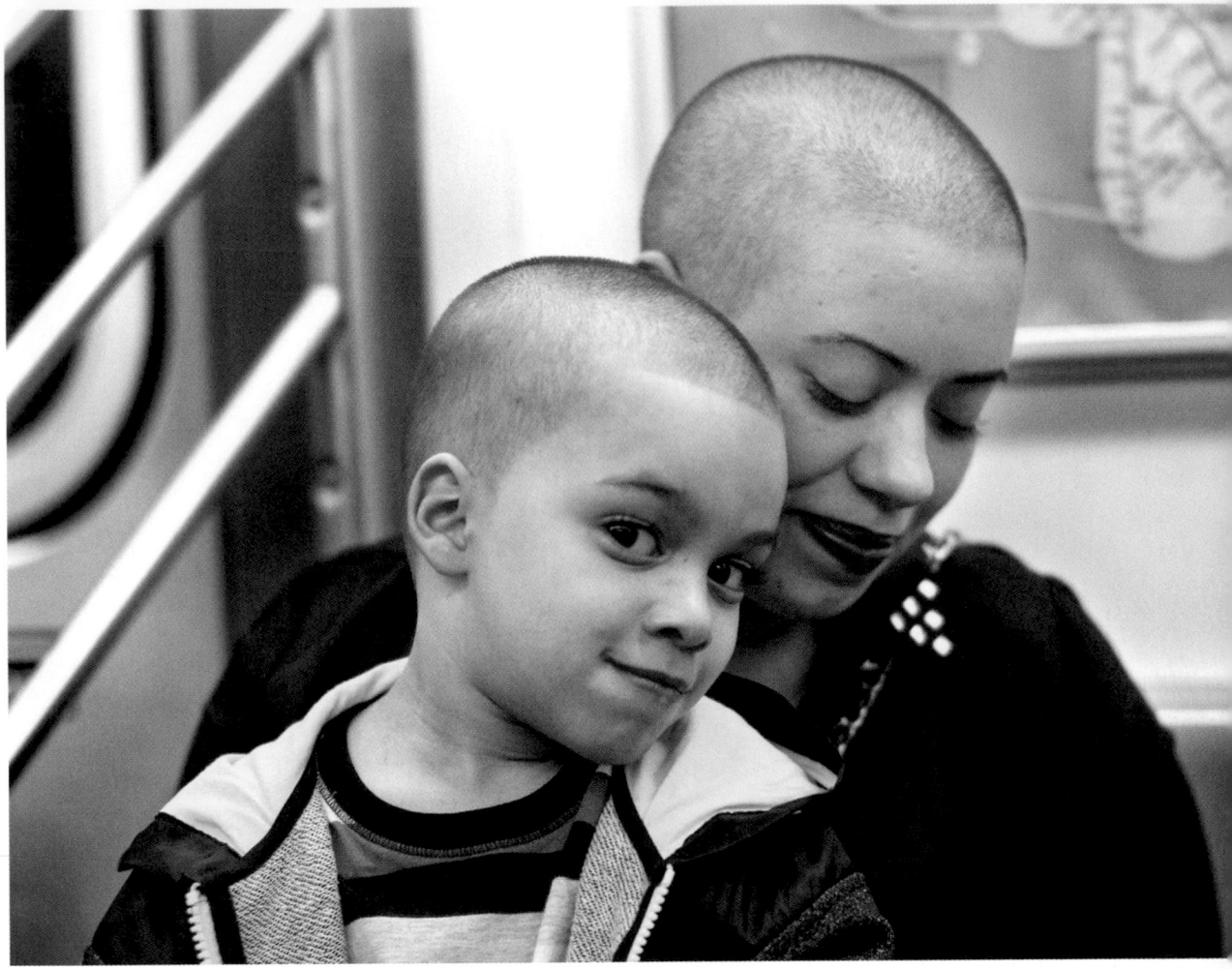

I REMEMBER TAKING AN ANTHROPOLOGY CLASS IN COLLEGE AND THE PROFESSOR WAS EXPLAINING THAT THERE IS LITTLE "SEXUAL DIMORPHISM" IN HUMANS. HE MEANT THAT THERE ARE FEW OUTWARD, OBSERVABLE DIFFERENCES BETWEEN MALES AND FEMALES. AT THE TIME I WAS CONFUSED, SO I RAISED MY HAND. "I FEEL LIKE IT'S VERY EASY TO TELL MEN AND WOMEN APART," I SAID.

"THAT'S DUE TO CULTURE," HE ANSWERED.

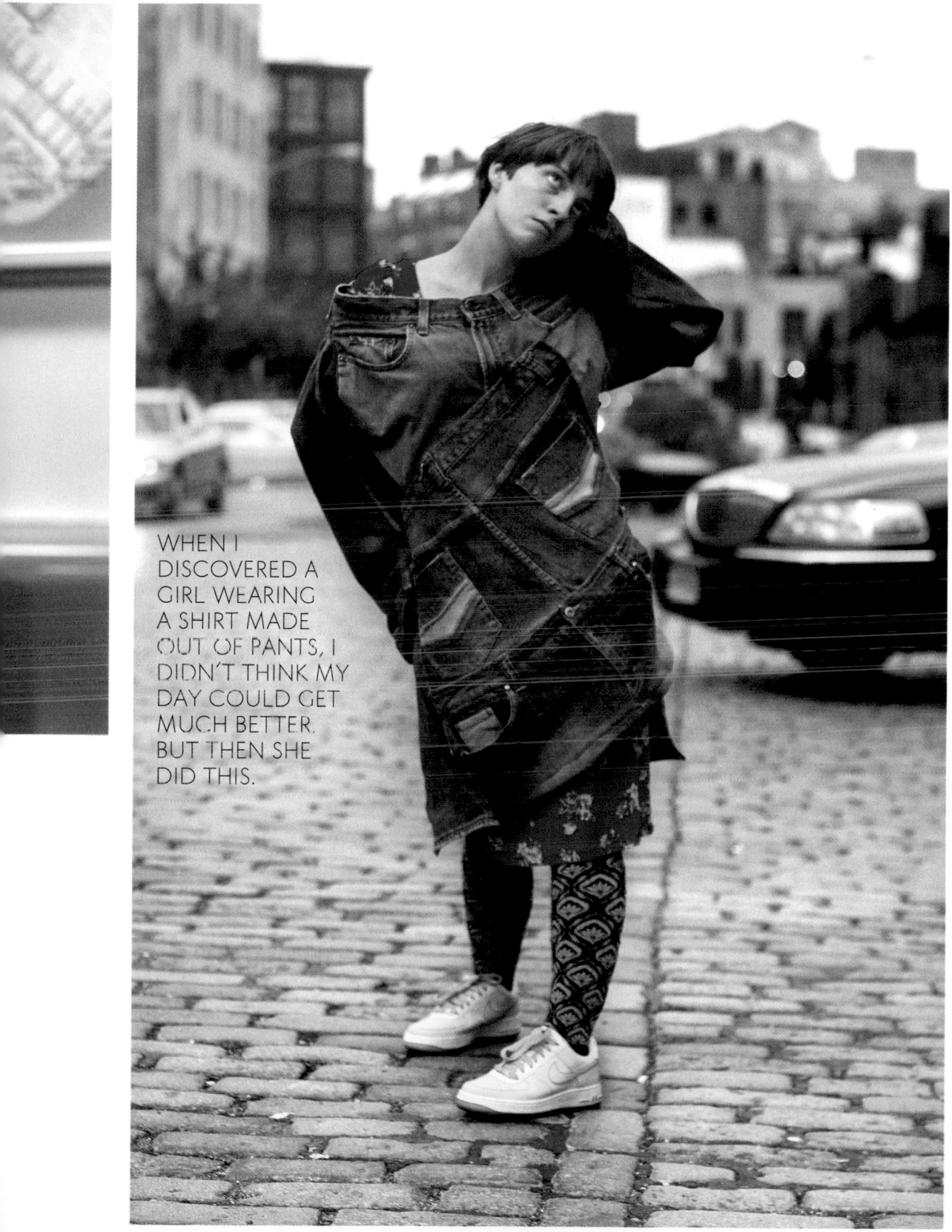
WHEN I DISCOVERED A GIRL WEARING A SHIRT MADE OUT OF PANTS, I DIDN'T THINK MY DAY COULD GET MUCH BETTER. BUT THEN SHE DID THIS.

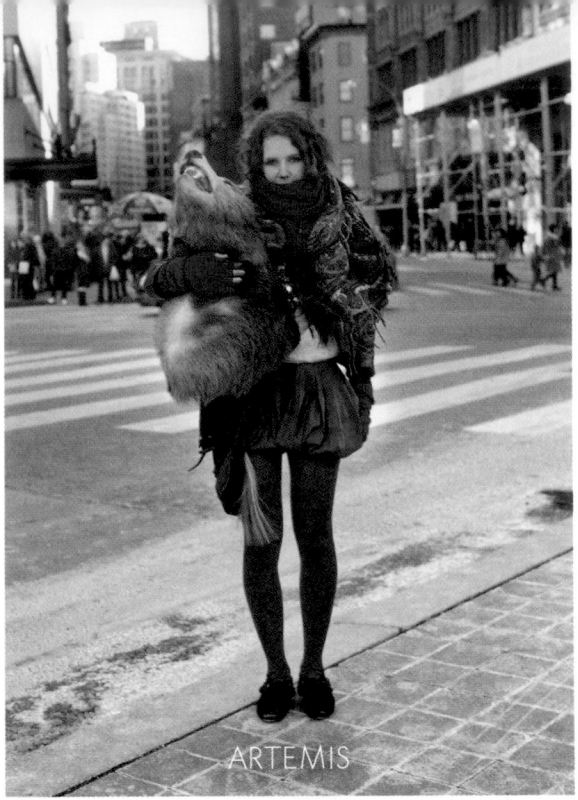

ARTEMIS

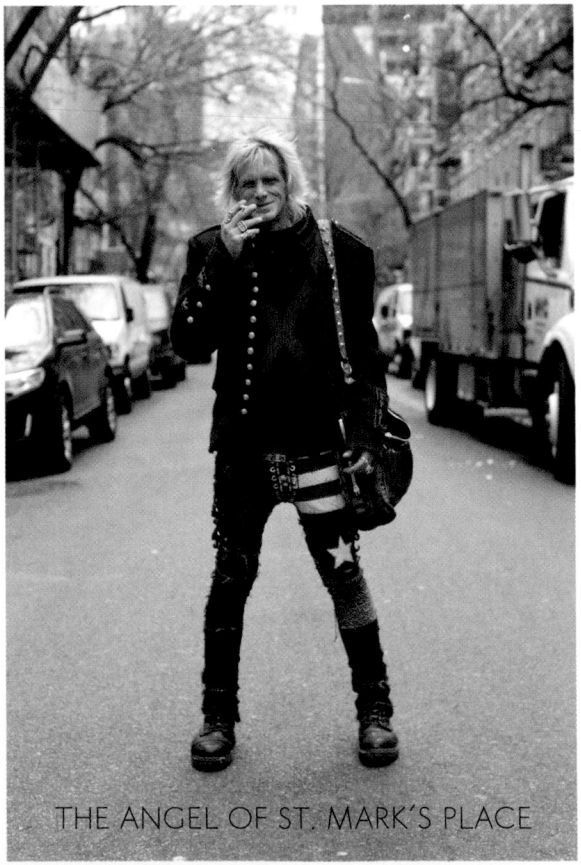

THE ANGEL OF ST. MARK'S PLACE

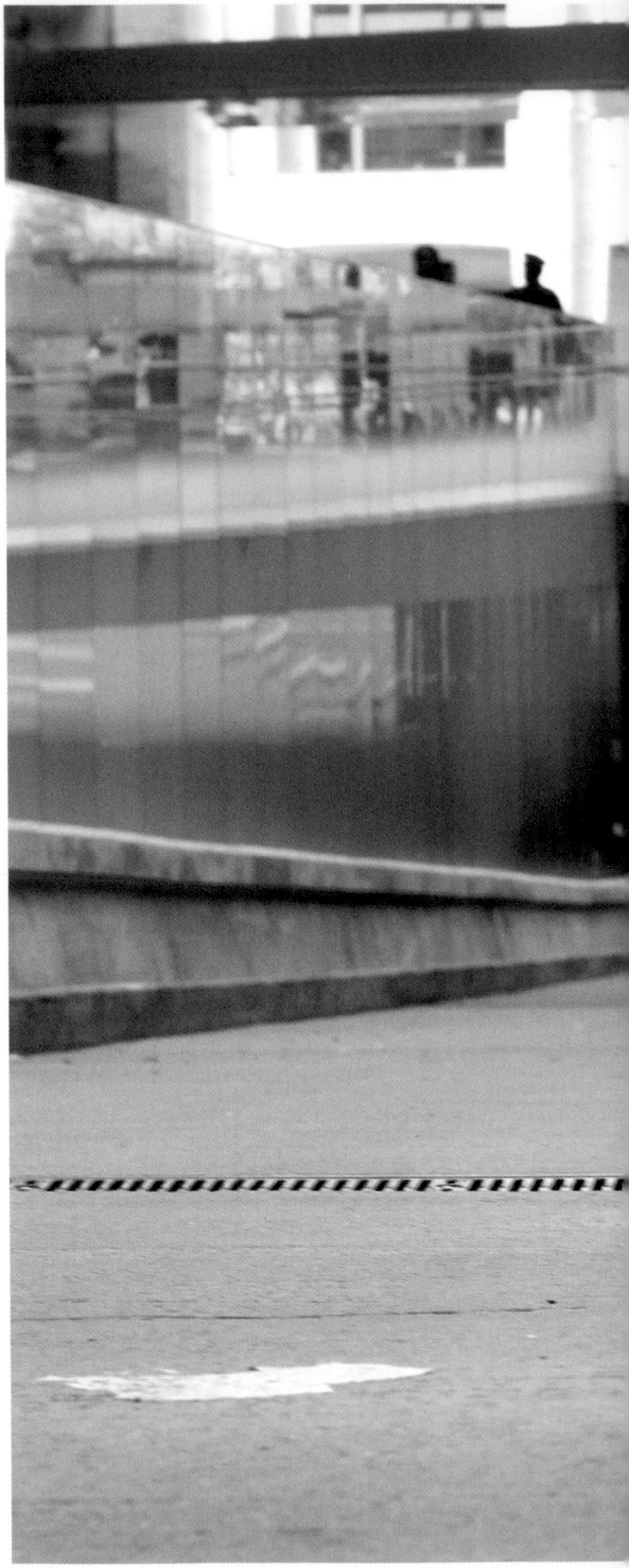

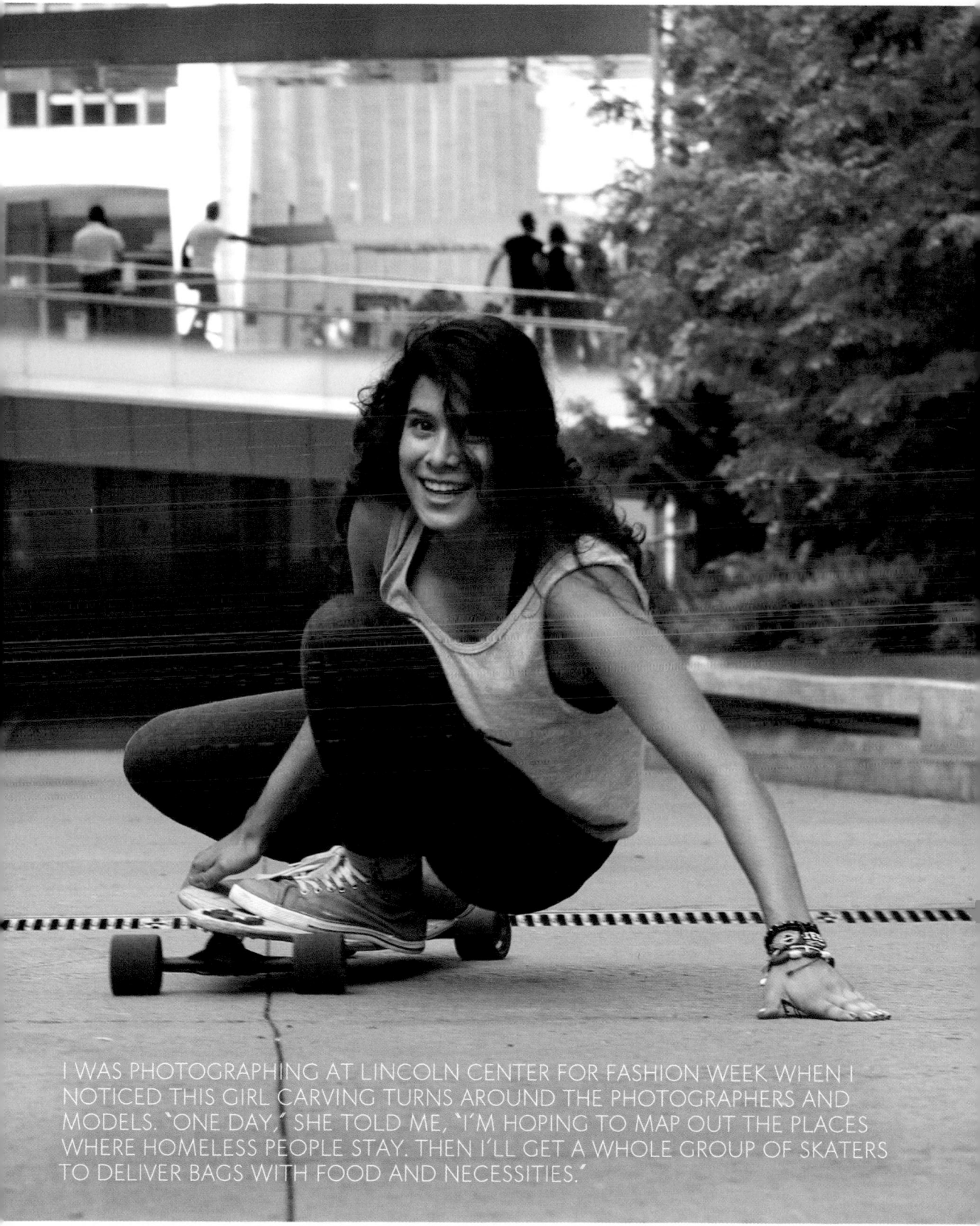

I WAS PHOTOGRAPHING AT LINCOLN CENTER FOR FASHION WEEK WHEN I NOTICED THIS GIRL CARVING TURNS AROUND THE PHOTOGRAPHERS AND MODELS. "ONE DAY," SHE TOLD ME, "I'M HOPING TO MAP OUT THE PLACES WHERE HOMELESS PEOPLE STAY. THEN I'LL GET A WHOLE GROUP OF SKATERS TO DELIVER BAGS WITH FOOD AND NECESSITIES."

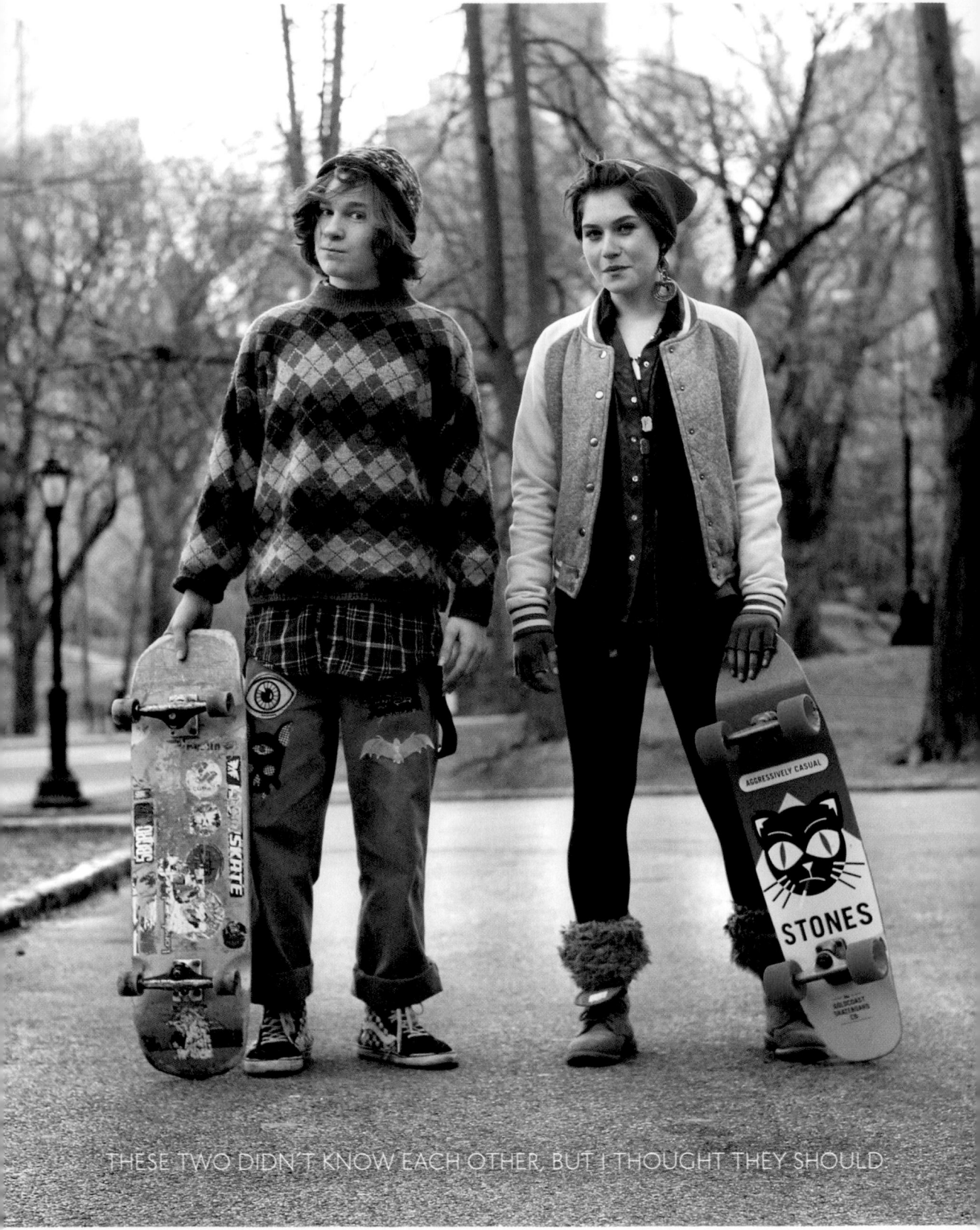


THESE TWO DIDN'T KNOW EACH OTHER, BUT I THOUGHT THEY SHOULD.

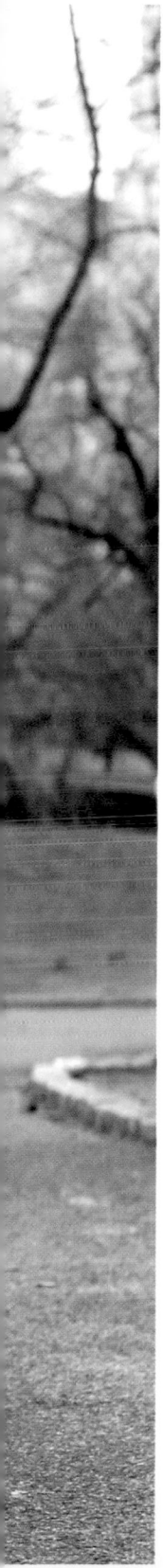

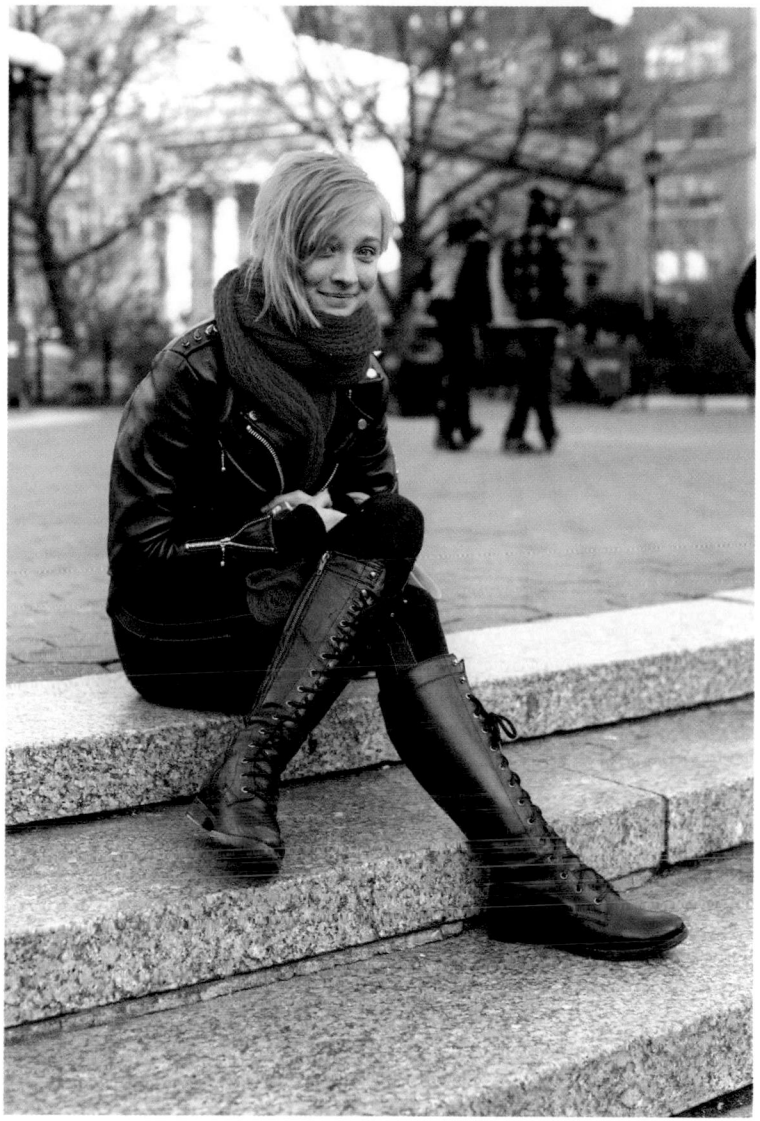

'I WAS STUDYING TO BE A BALLET DANCER, BUT NOW I'M LEARNING TO BE A TRAPEZE ARTIST.'

'WERE YOUR PARENTS UPSET ABOUT THE SWITCH?'

'NO, THEY WERE HAPPY. I FINALLY STOPPED CALLING HOME EVERY NIGHT IN TEARS.'

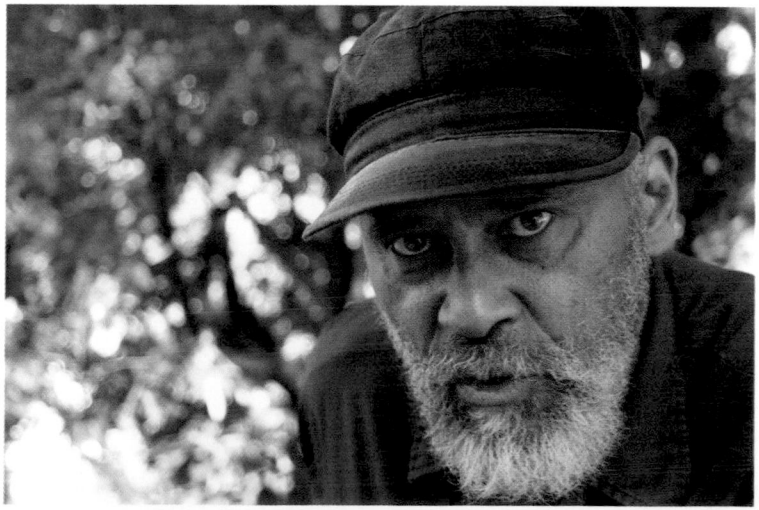

'NEW YORK HAS THE HIGHEST WASHOUT RATE OF ANY CITY IN THE COUNTRY. YOU CAN MAKE IT, BUT DON'T COME UNLESS YOU HAVE A REASON TO BE HERE.'

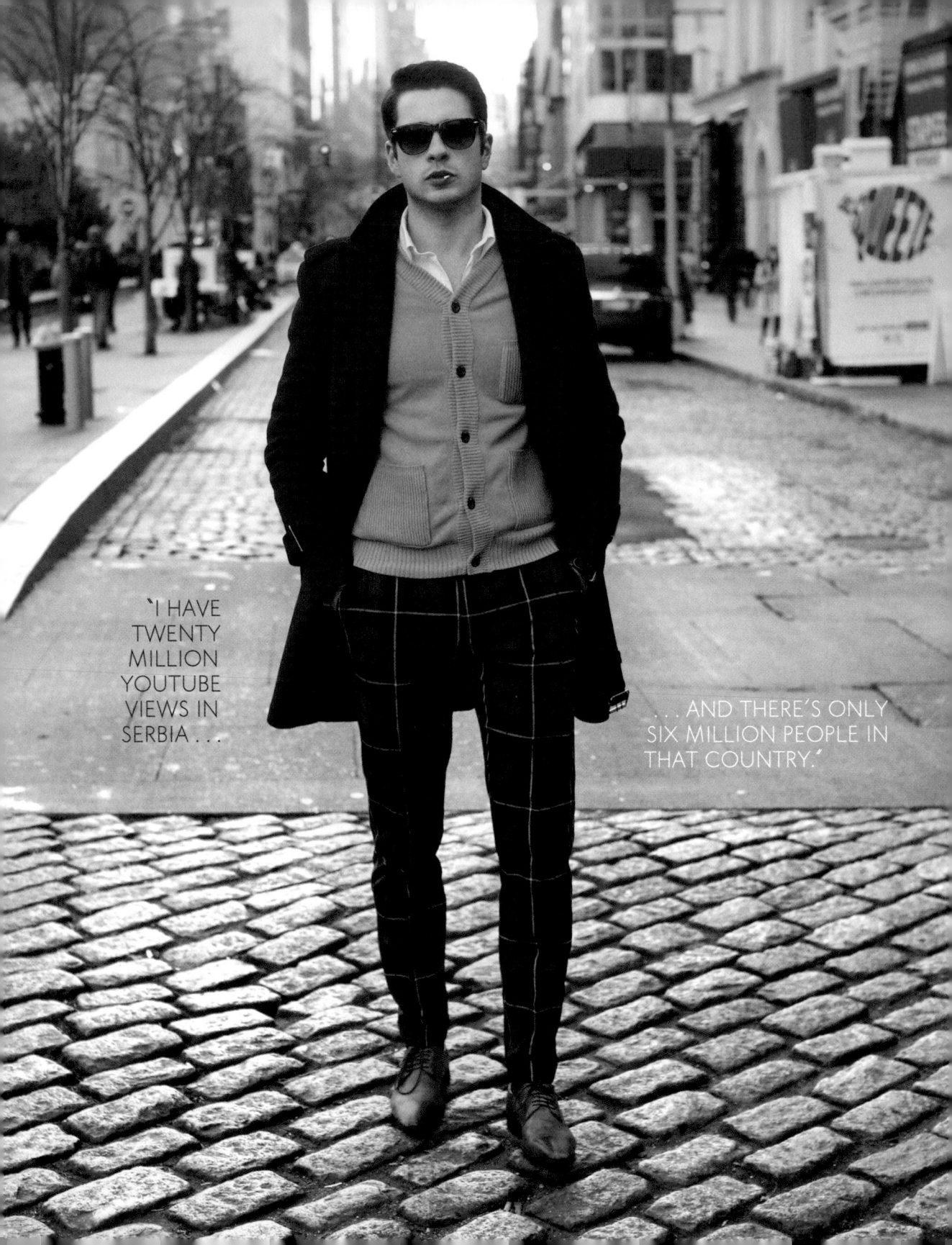

'I HAVE TWENTY MILLION YOUTUBE VIEWS IN SERBIA . . .

. . . AND THERE'S ONLY SIX MILLION PEOPLE IN THAT COUNTRY.'

SEEN IN UNION SQUARE

BE SOMEONE YOU'D WANT TO BE.

SEEN IN THE EAST VILLAGE

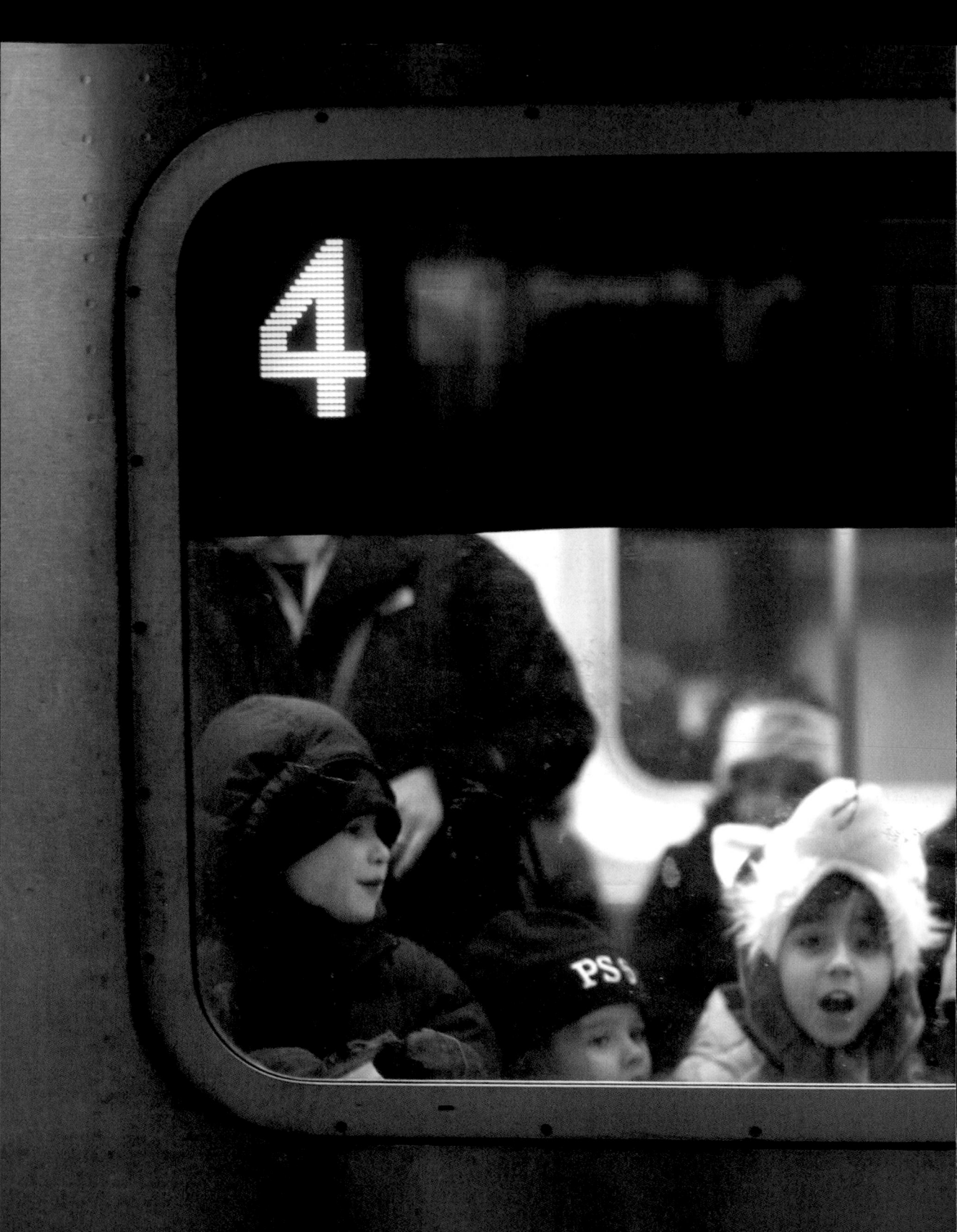
4

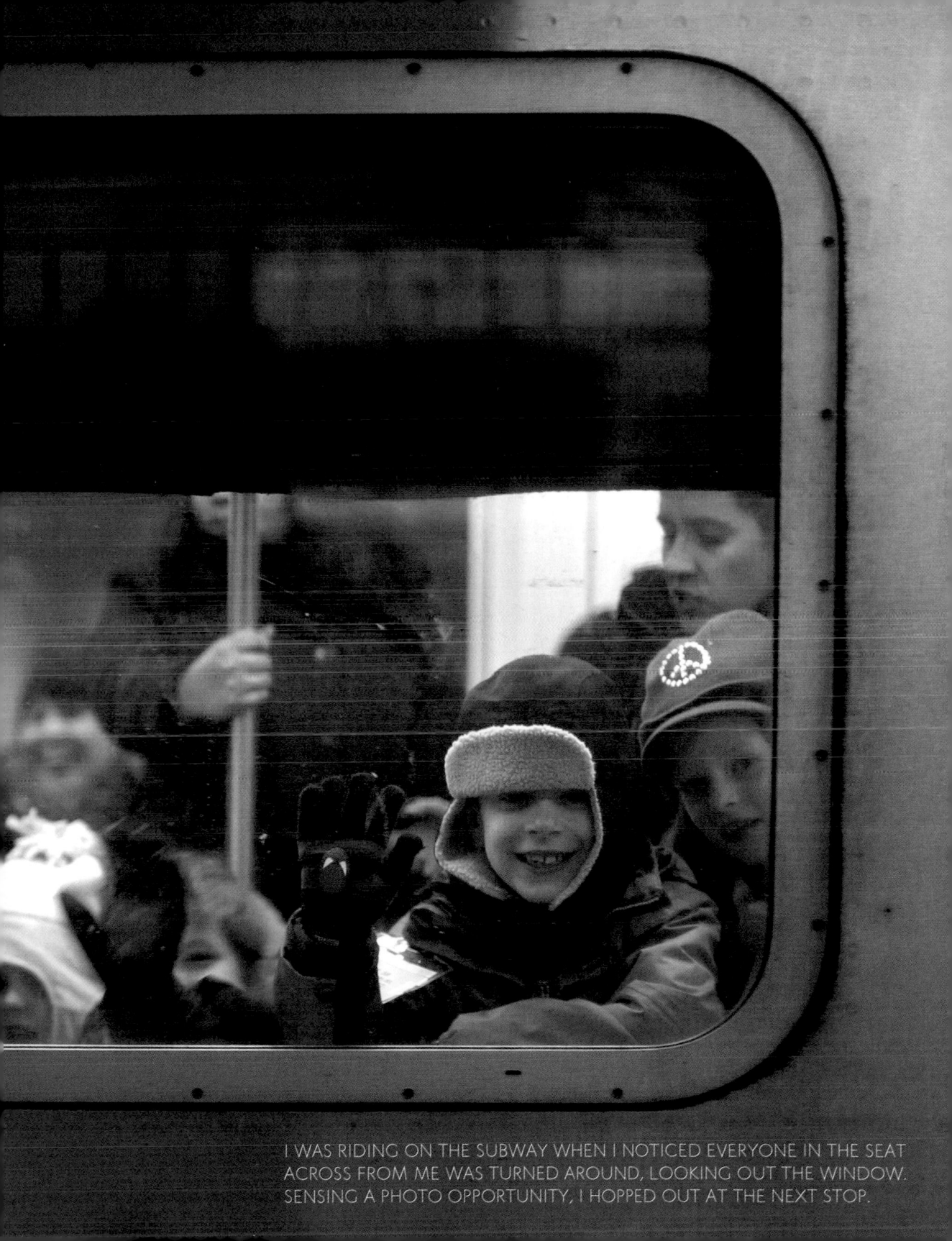

I WAS RIDING ON THE SUBWAY WHEN I NOTICED EVERYONE IN THE SEAT ACROSS FROM ME WAS TURNED AROUND, LOOKING OUT THE WINDOW. SENSING A PHOTO OPPORTUNITY, I HOPPED OUT AT THE NEXT STOP.

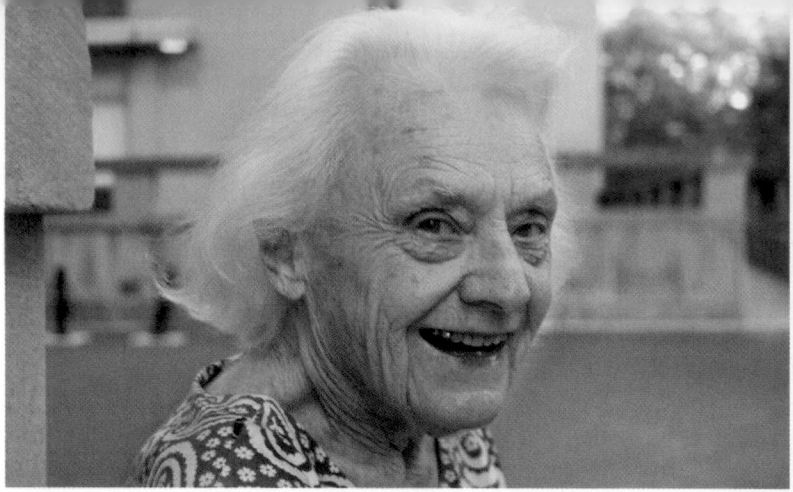

"EVERY TIME I FORCE MYSELF TO GO OUTSIDE, SOMETHING WONDERFUL HAPPENS!"

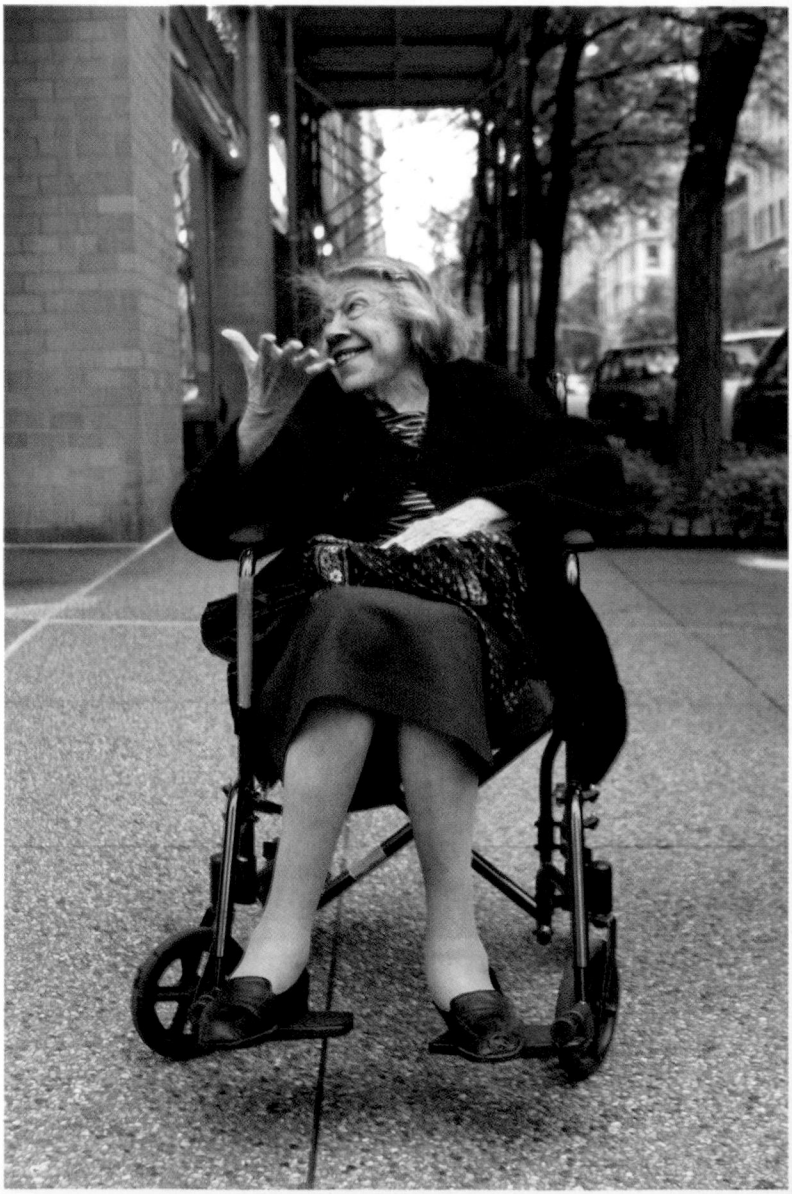

"EXCUSE ME, IS THERE ANY WAY I CAN TAKE YOUR PHOTO? I RUN A BLOG CALLED HUMANS OF NEW YORK, AND I'M TRYING TO DOCUMENT ALL THE NEIGHBORHOODS OF NEW YORK BY PHOTOGRAPHING THE PEOPLE WHO LIVE THERE."

"I DIDN'T HEAR A WORD YOU JUST SAID."

SEEN IN THE EAST VILLAGE

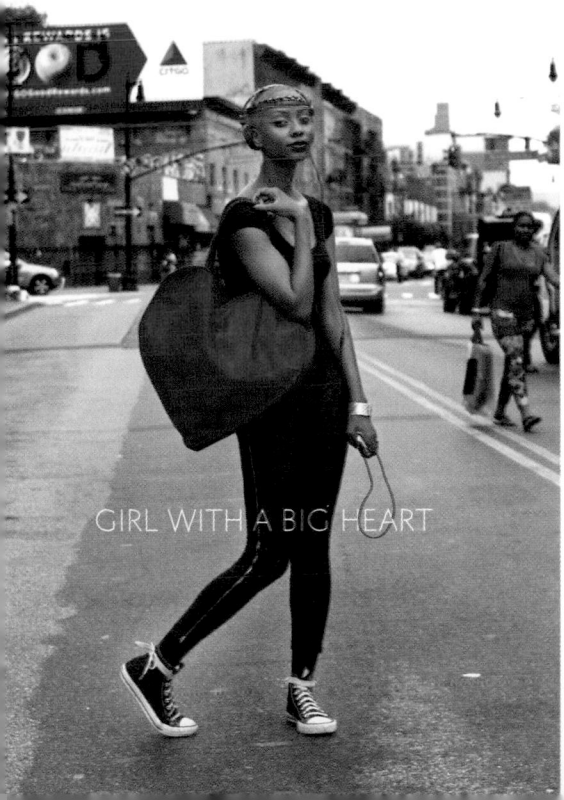

GIRL WITH A BIG HEART

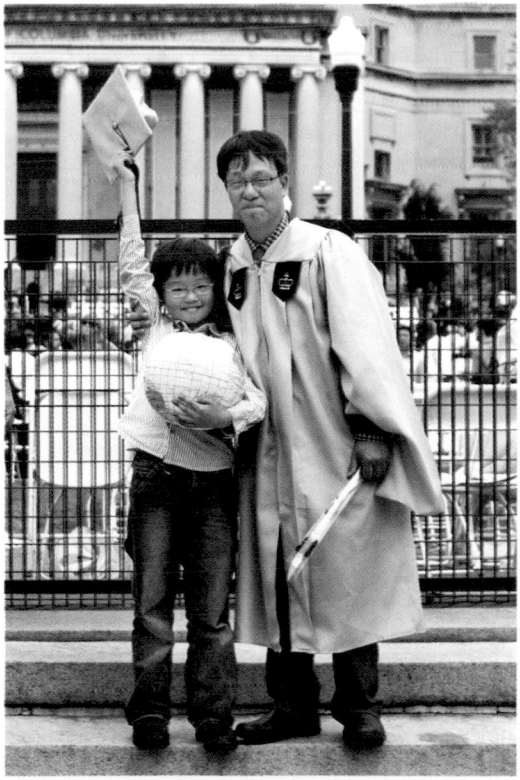

TO THE WORLD YOU MAY BE ONE PERSON, BUT TO ONE PERSON YOU MAY BE THE WORLD.

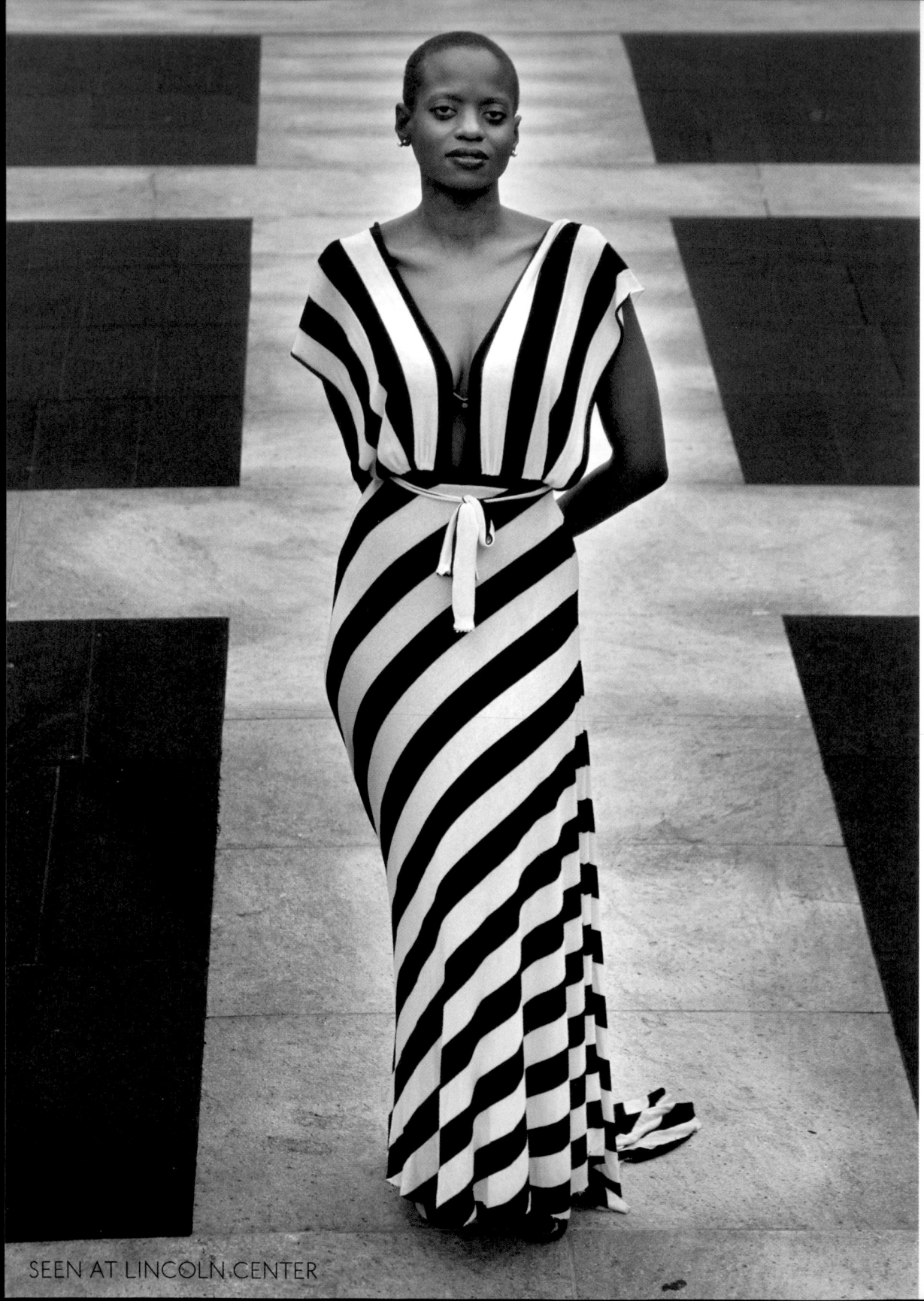

SEEN AT LINCOLN CENTER

SEEN IN BEDFORD-STUYVESANT, BROOKLYN

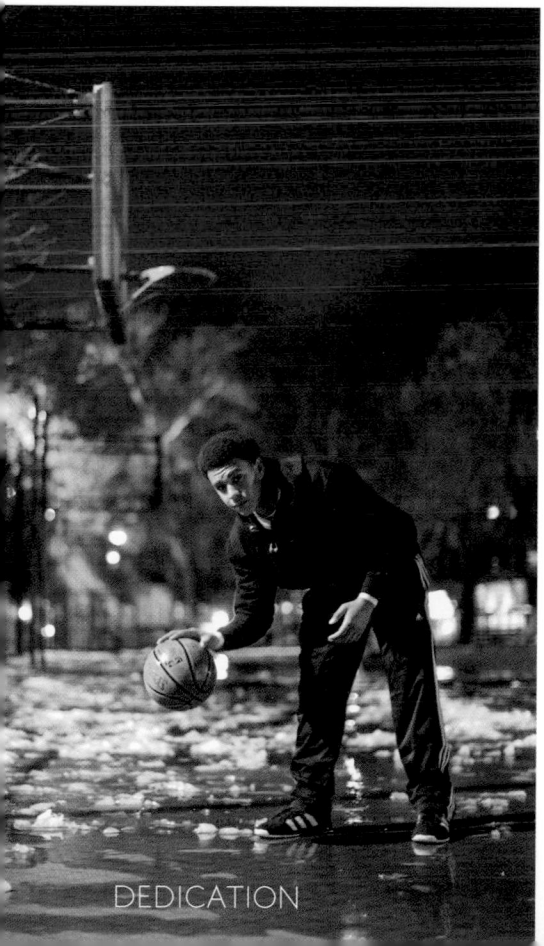


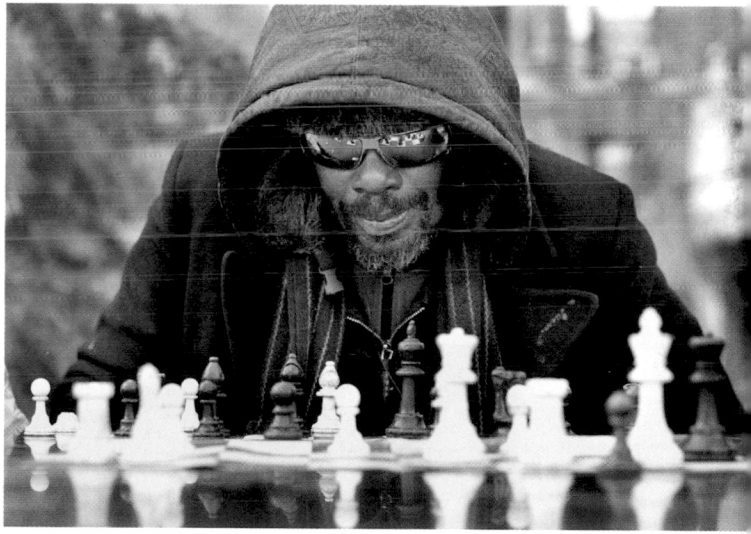

"YOU CAN PHOTOGRAPH ME COUNTING MY MONEY, IF YOU'D LIKE."

I SAW THEM WALKING ON TWO OPPOSITE ENDS OF THE PLAZA,
AND STARTED PRAYING THAT THEY'D END UP IN THE SAME PLACE.

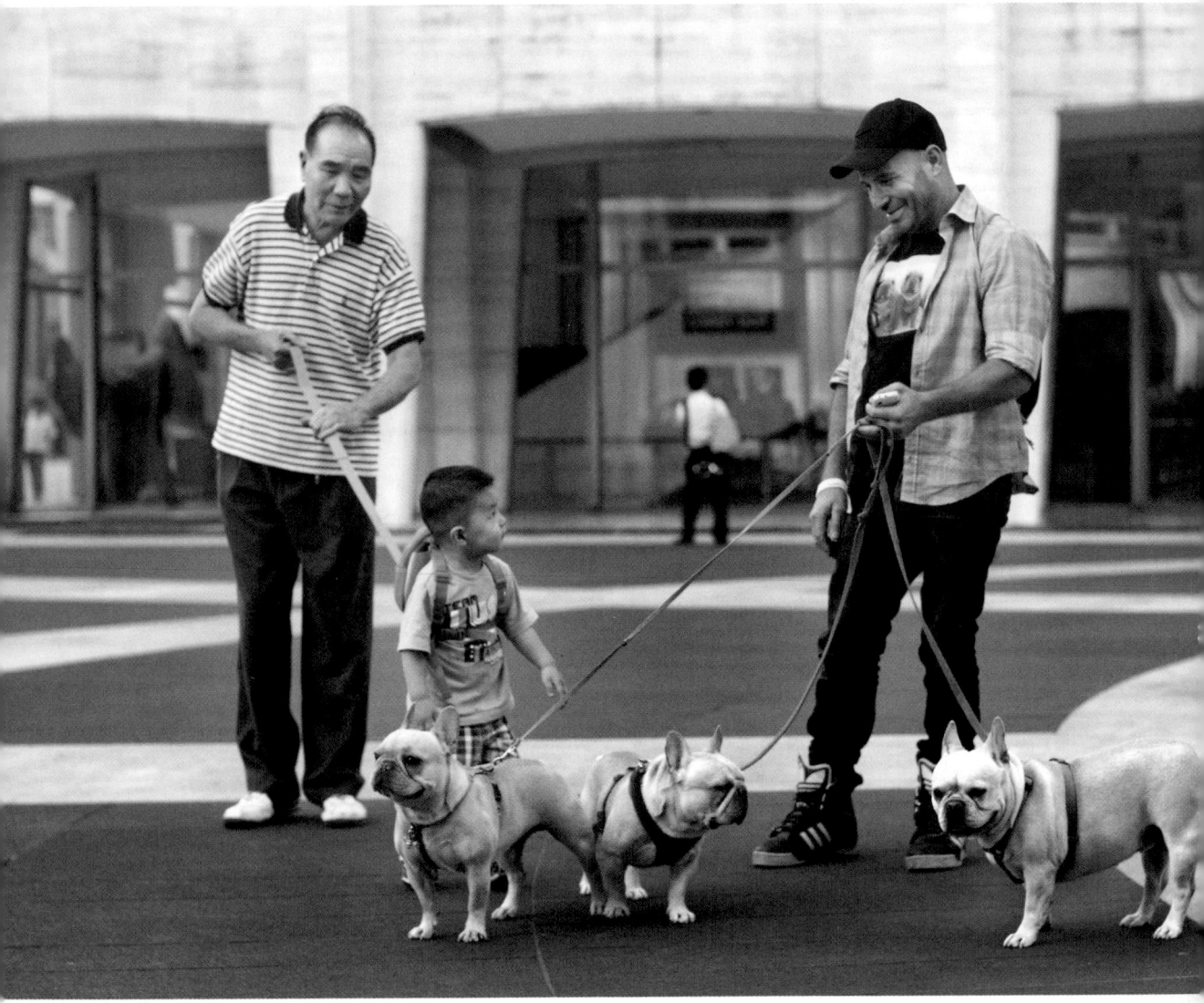

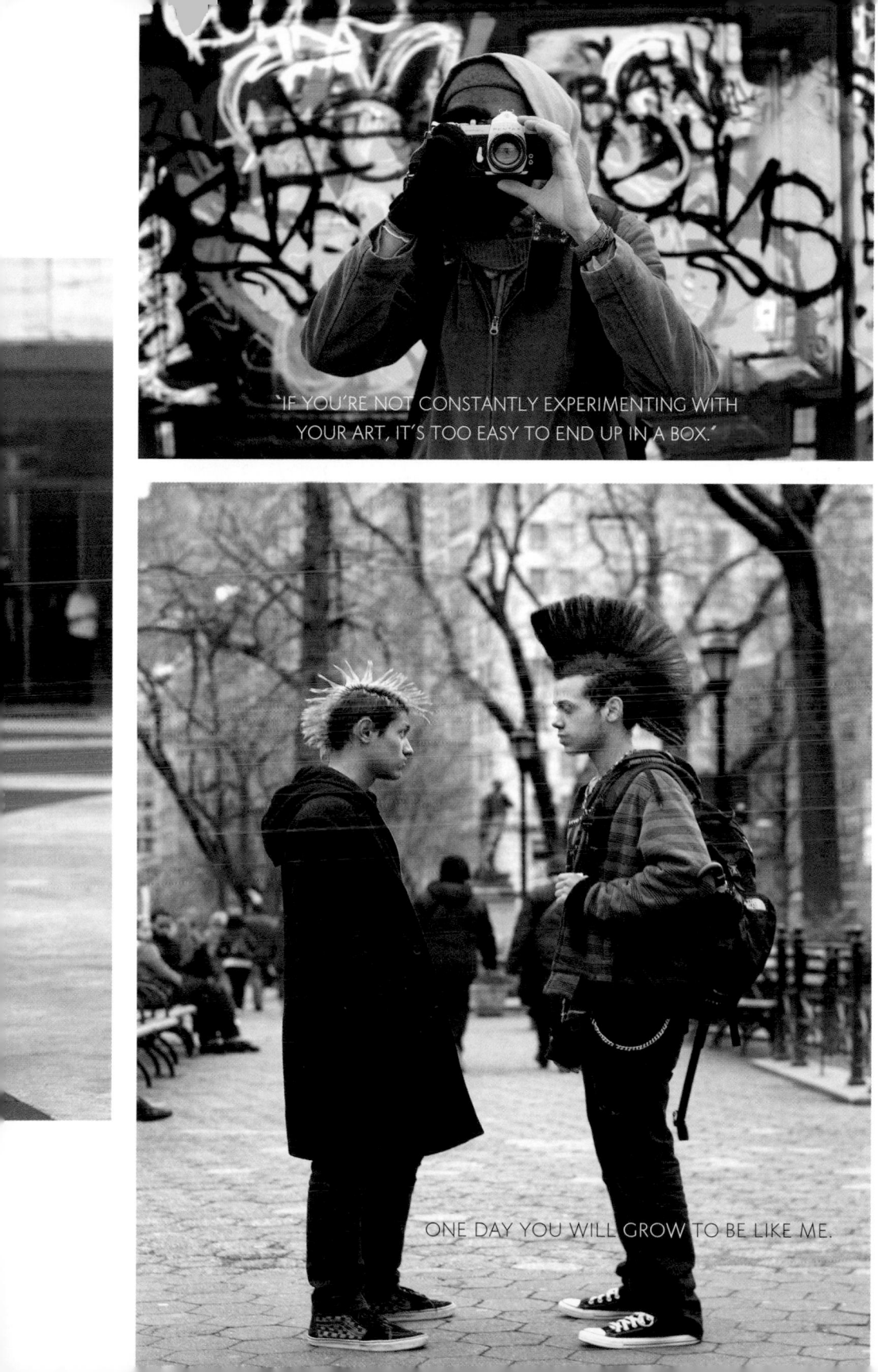
"IF YOU'RE NOT CONSTANTLY EXPERIMENTING WITH
YOUR ART, IT'S TOO EASY TO END UP IN A BOX."
"ONE DAY YOU WILL GROW TO BE LIKE ME.

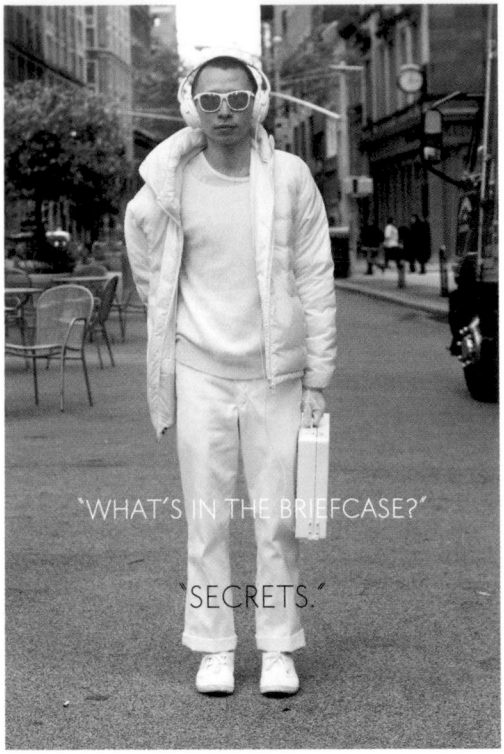

"WHAT'S IN THE BRIEFCASE?"

"SECRETS."

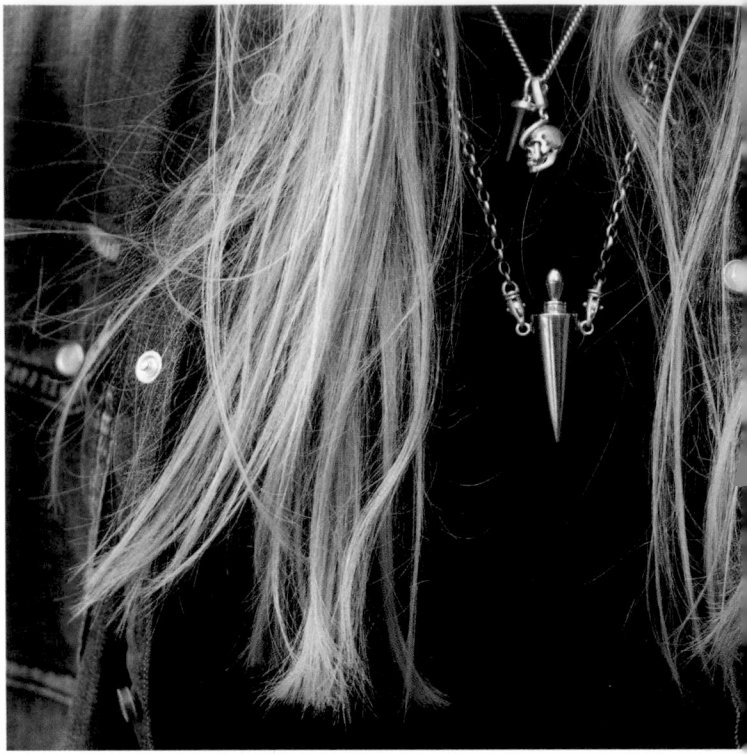

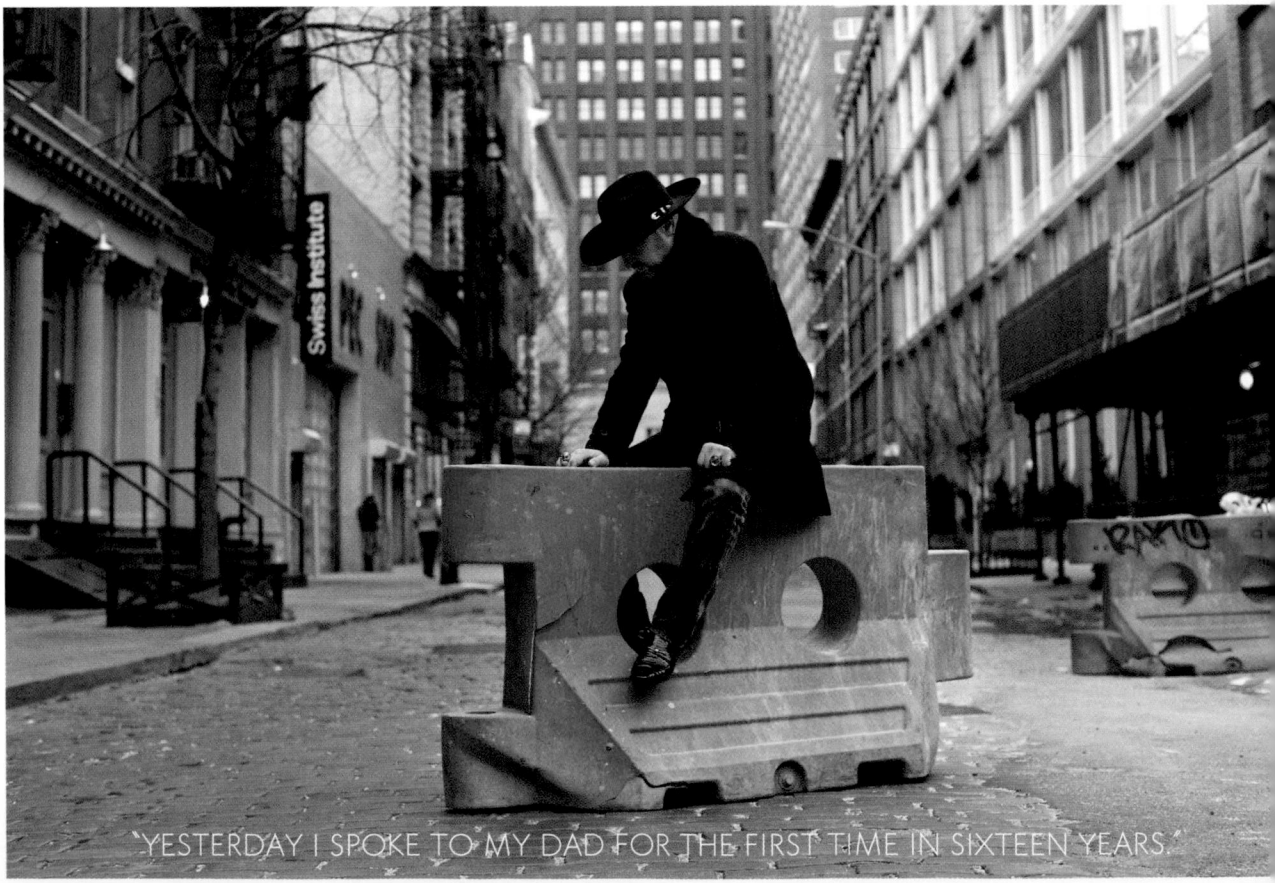


"YESTERDAY I SPOKE TO MY DAD FOR THE FIRST TIME IN SIXTEEN YEARS."

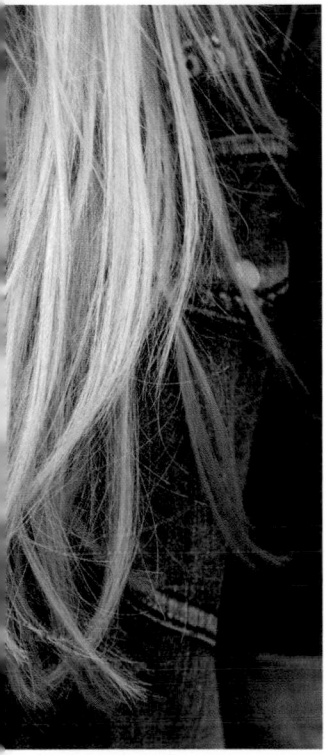

"MY MOTHER'S ASHES ARE IN THERE."

"TELL ME SOMETHING ABOUT HER."

"SHE WAS AN AMAZING POET. SHE WOULDN'T LET ANYONE READ HER POEMS, THOUGH. WE KNEW SHE WAS WRITING THEM, BUT SHE WOULDN'T LET US READ THEM. I FOUND THEM ON HER COMPUTER AFTER SHE DIED. THEY WERE SO BEAUTIFUL—I COULDN'T BELIEVE SHE WROTE THEM."

THE STARING CONTEST

FIELD OF DREAMS

"WE JUST GOT MARRIED AT BURNING MAN!"

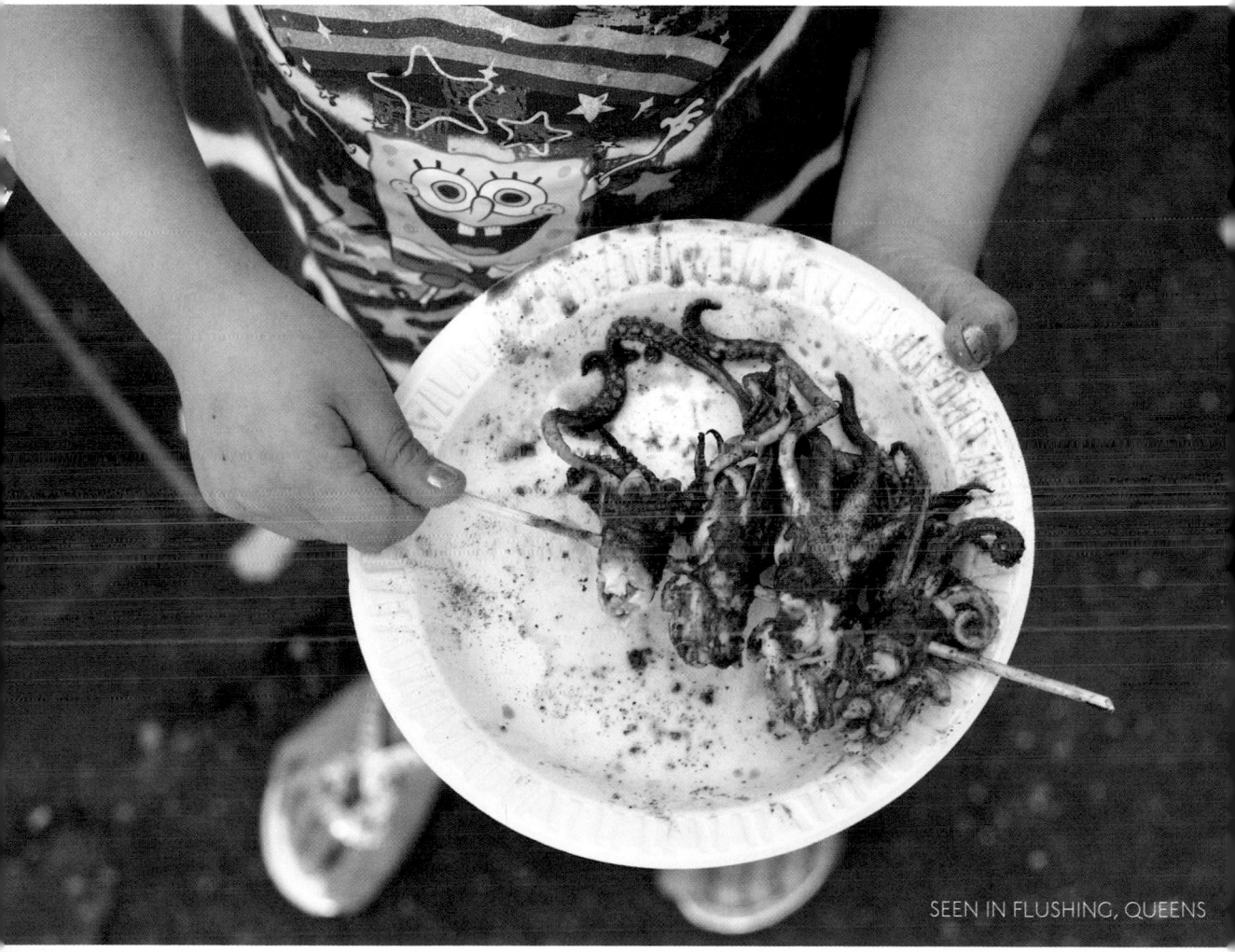

SEEN IN FLUSHING, QUEENS

I'M PRETTY SURE THAT BAG HAS A FACE.

IN SOME NEIGHBORHOODS, FACES MATURE FASTER THAN BODIES.

DATE NIGHT

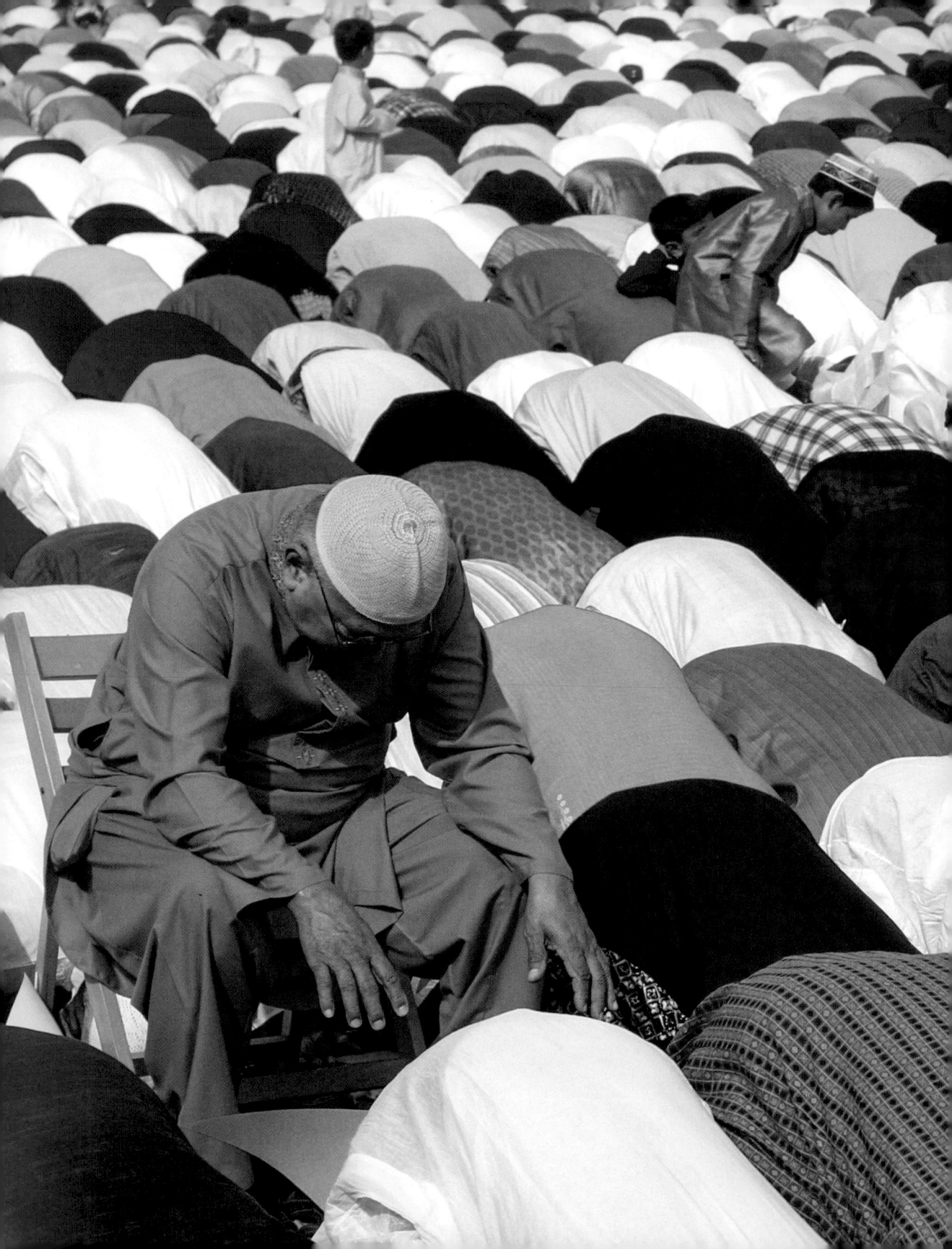

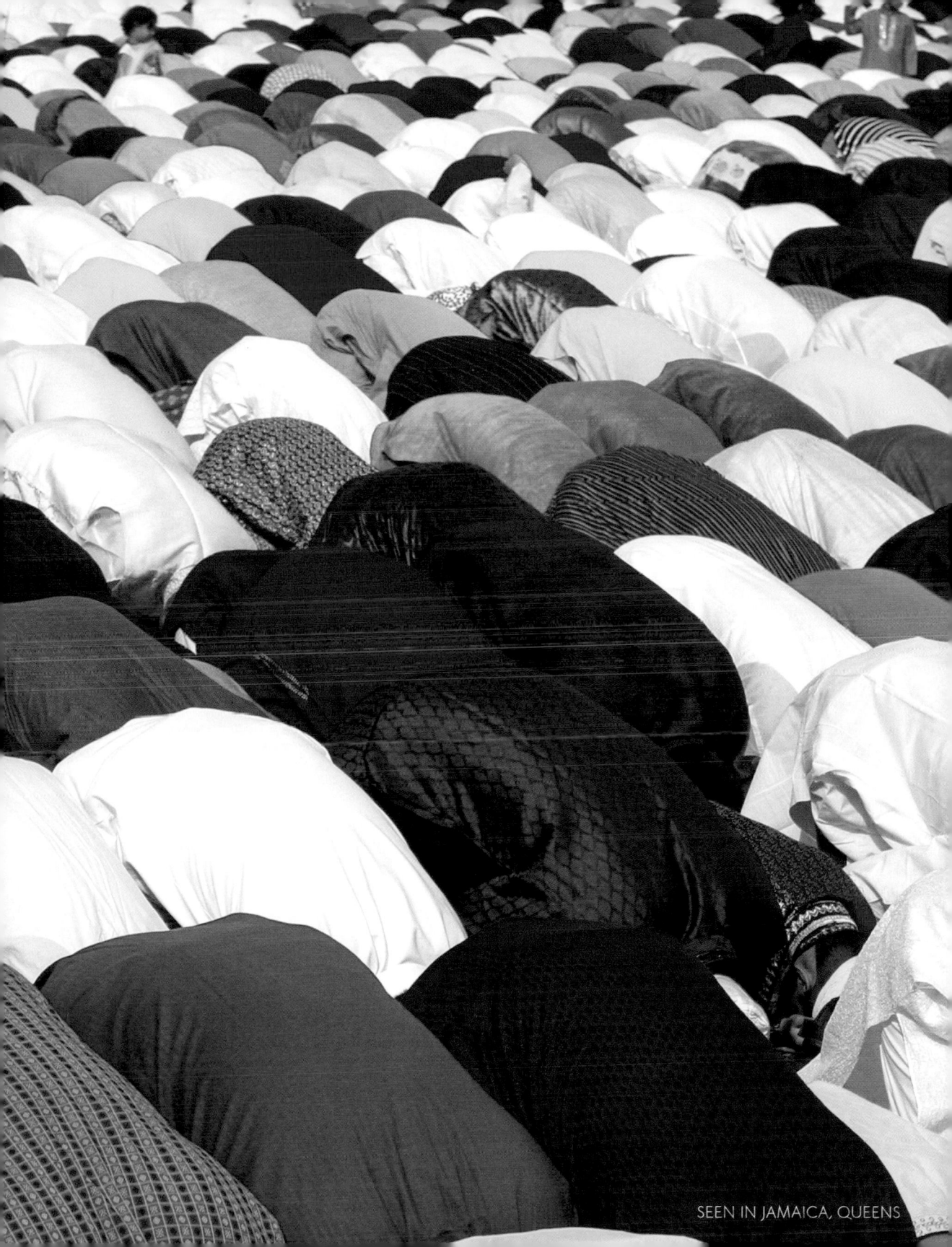

SEEN IN JAMAICA, QUEENS

PROBABLE WARLOCK HANDS, SPOTTED ON THE UPPER WEST SIDE

SEEN AT THE METROPOLITAN MUSEUM OF ART

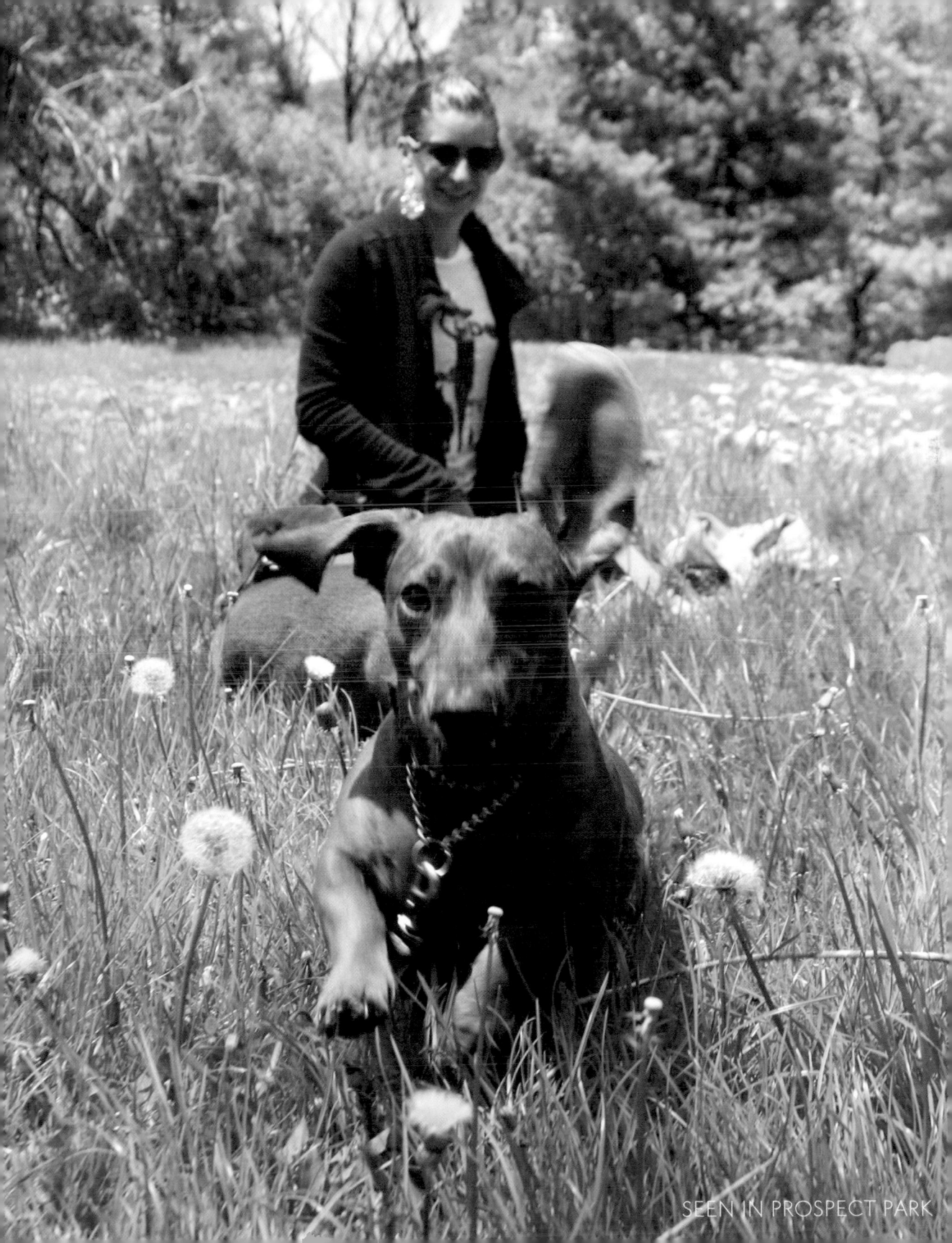

SEEN IN PROSPECT PARK

"MY HOUSE BLEW INTO THE OCEAN."

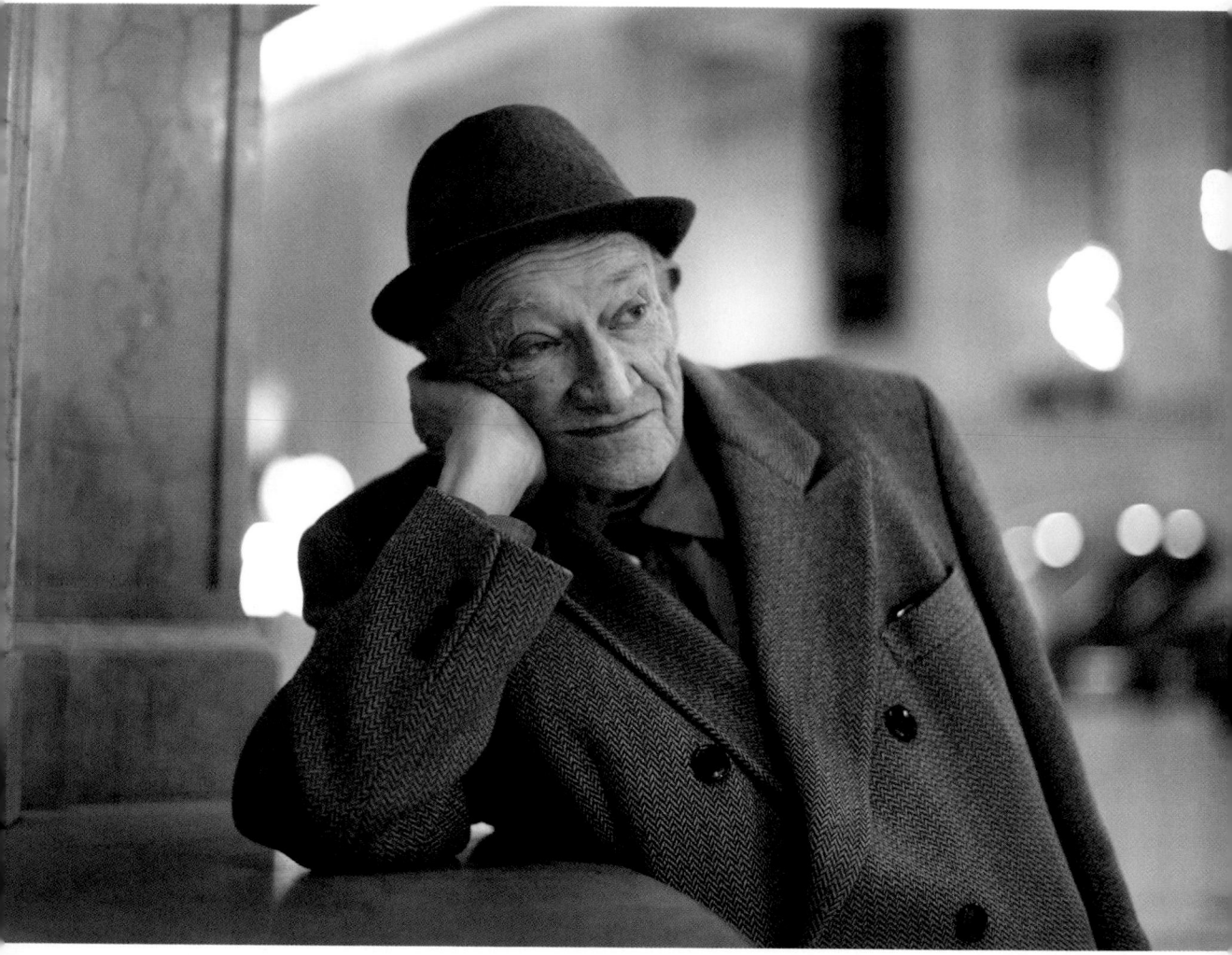

SEEN IN UNION SQUARE

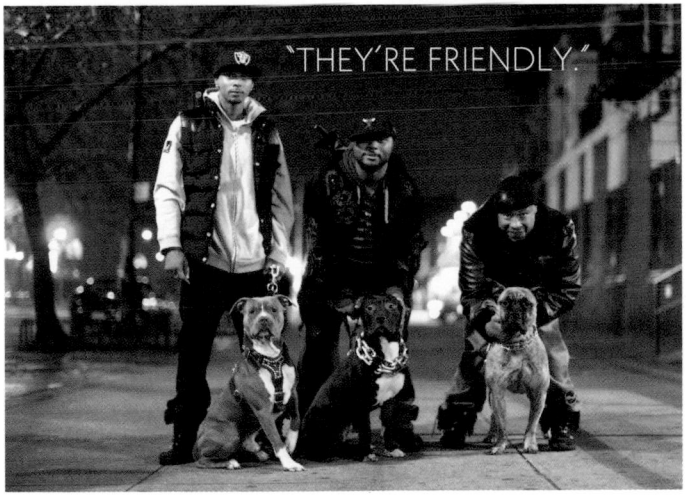


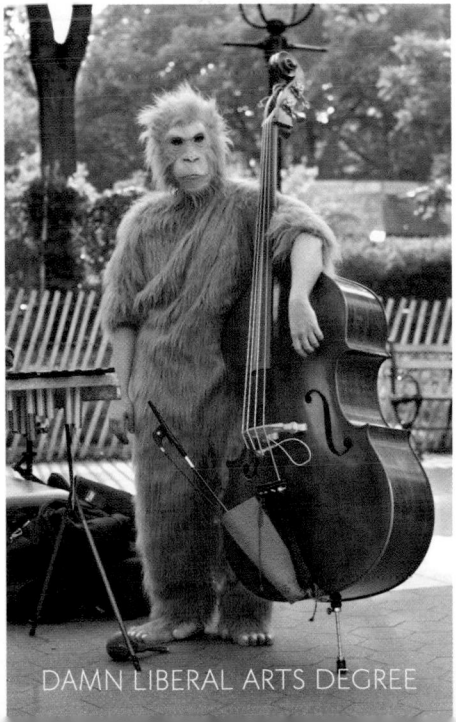

DAMN LIBERAL ARTS DEGREE

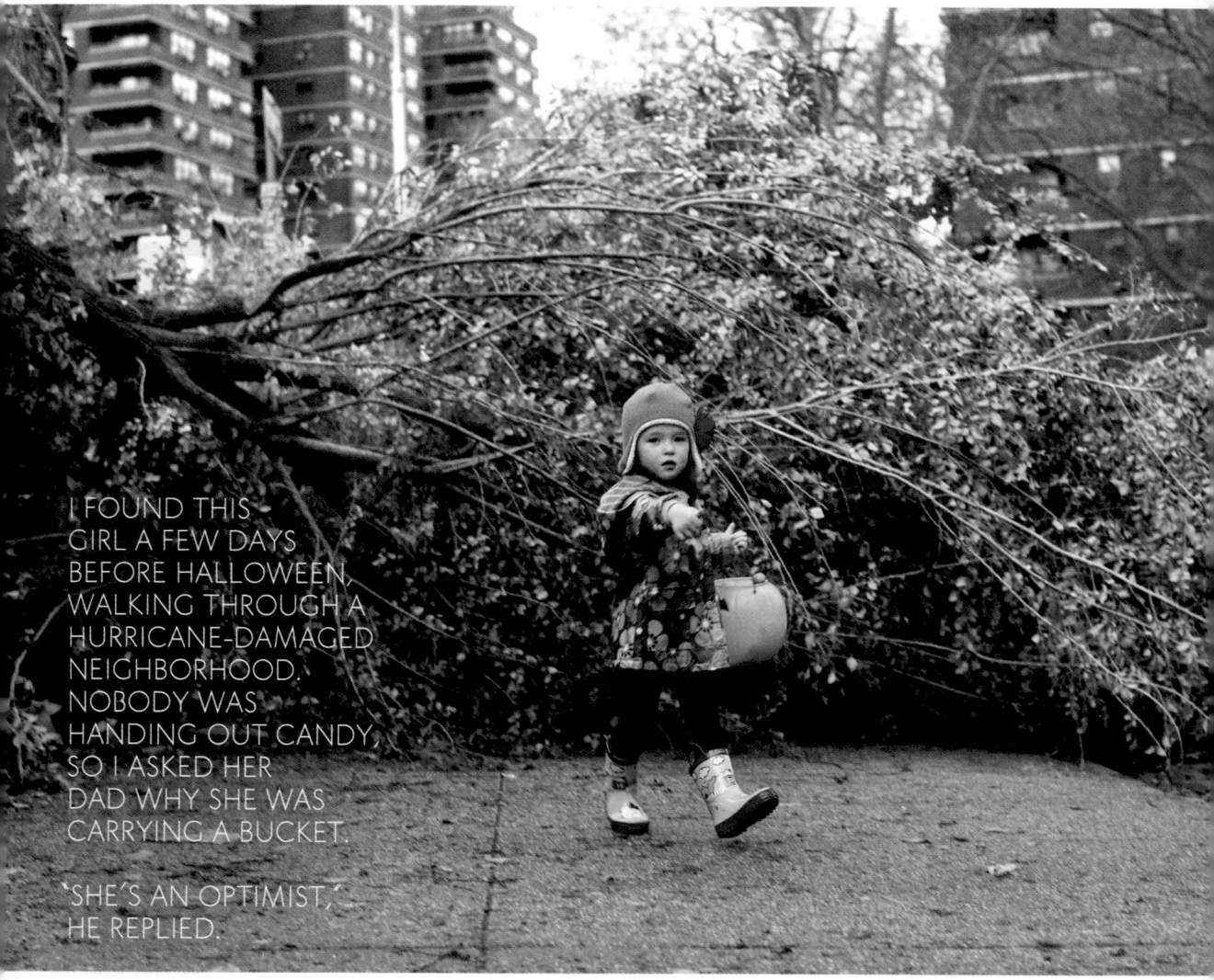

I FOUND THIS GIRL A FEW DAYS BEFORE HALLOWEEN, WALKING THROUGH A HURRICANE-DAMAGED NEIGHBORHOOD. NOBODY WAS HANDING OUT CANDY, SO I ASKED HER DAD WHY SHE WAS CARRYING A BUCKET.

'SHE'S AN OPTIMIST,' HE REPLIED.

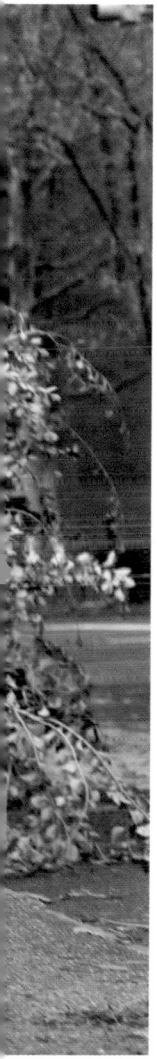

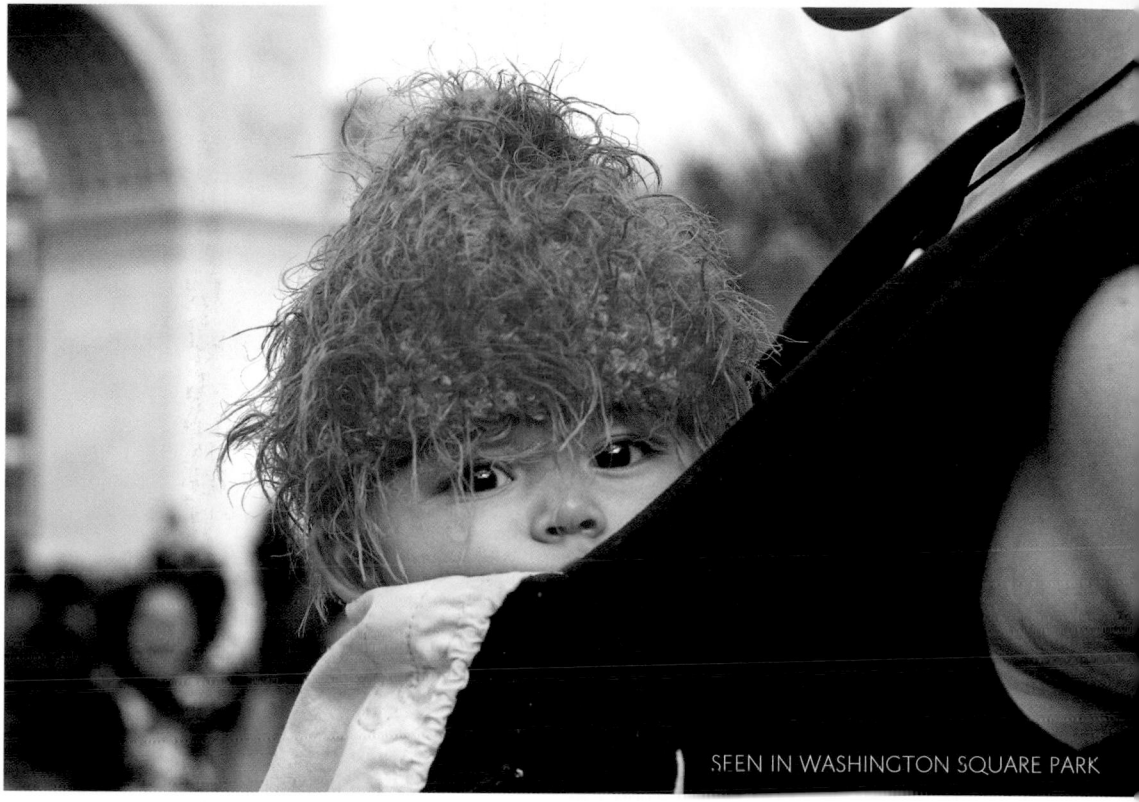

SEEN IN WASHINGTON SQUARE PARK

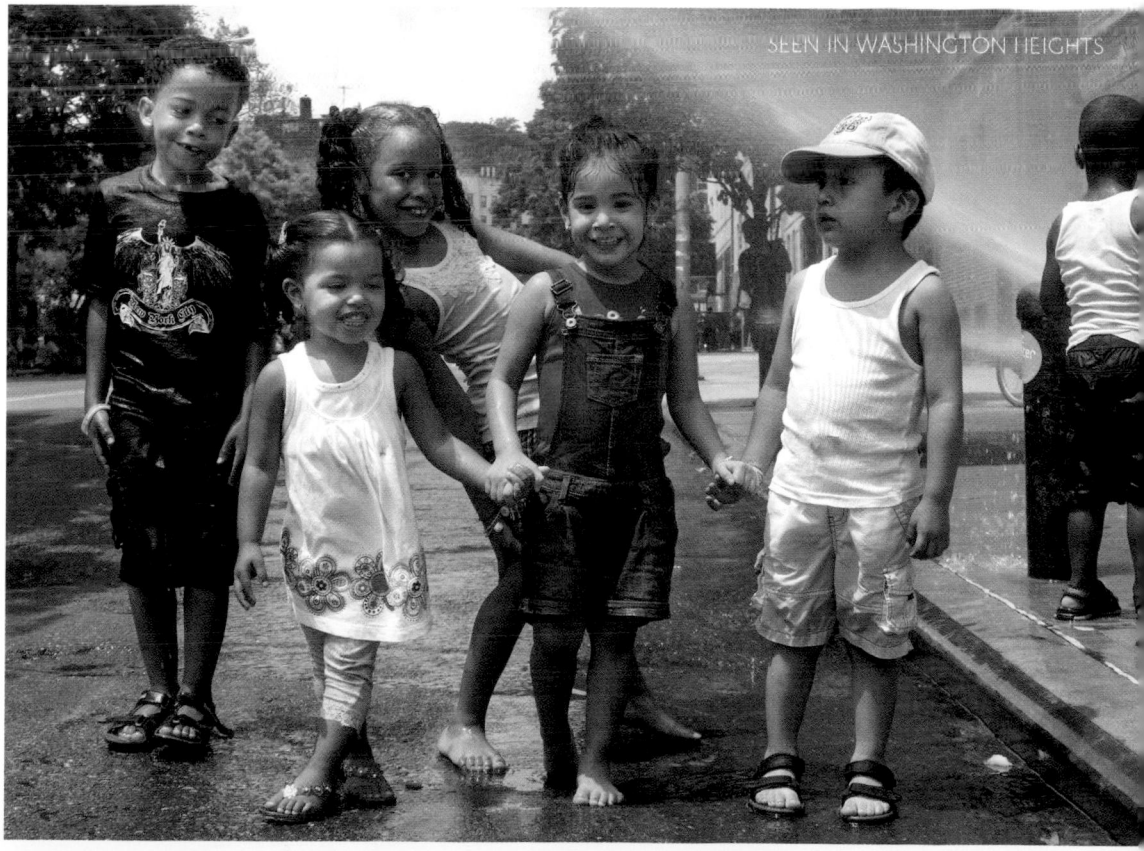

SEEN IN WASHINGTON HEIGHTS

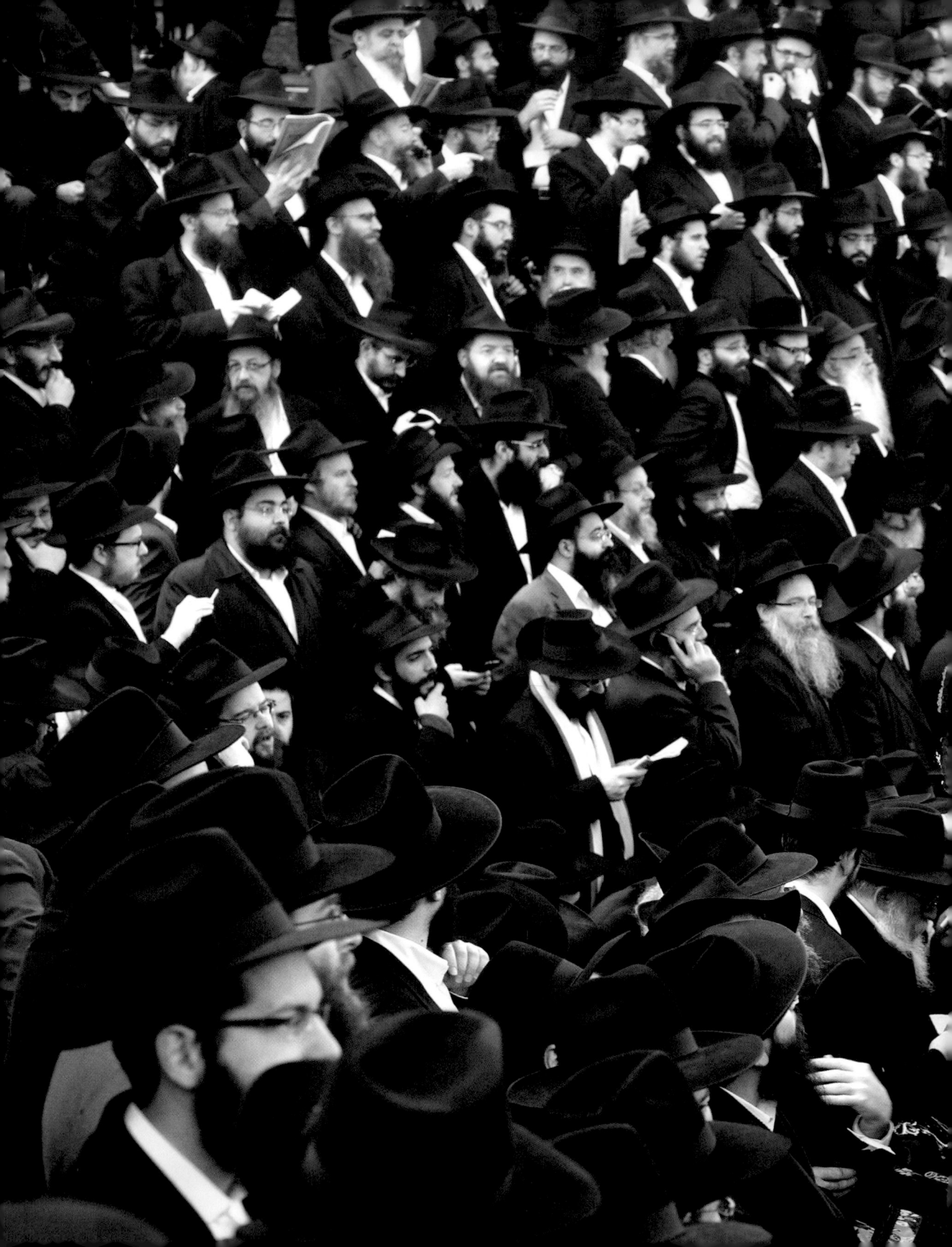

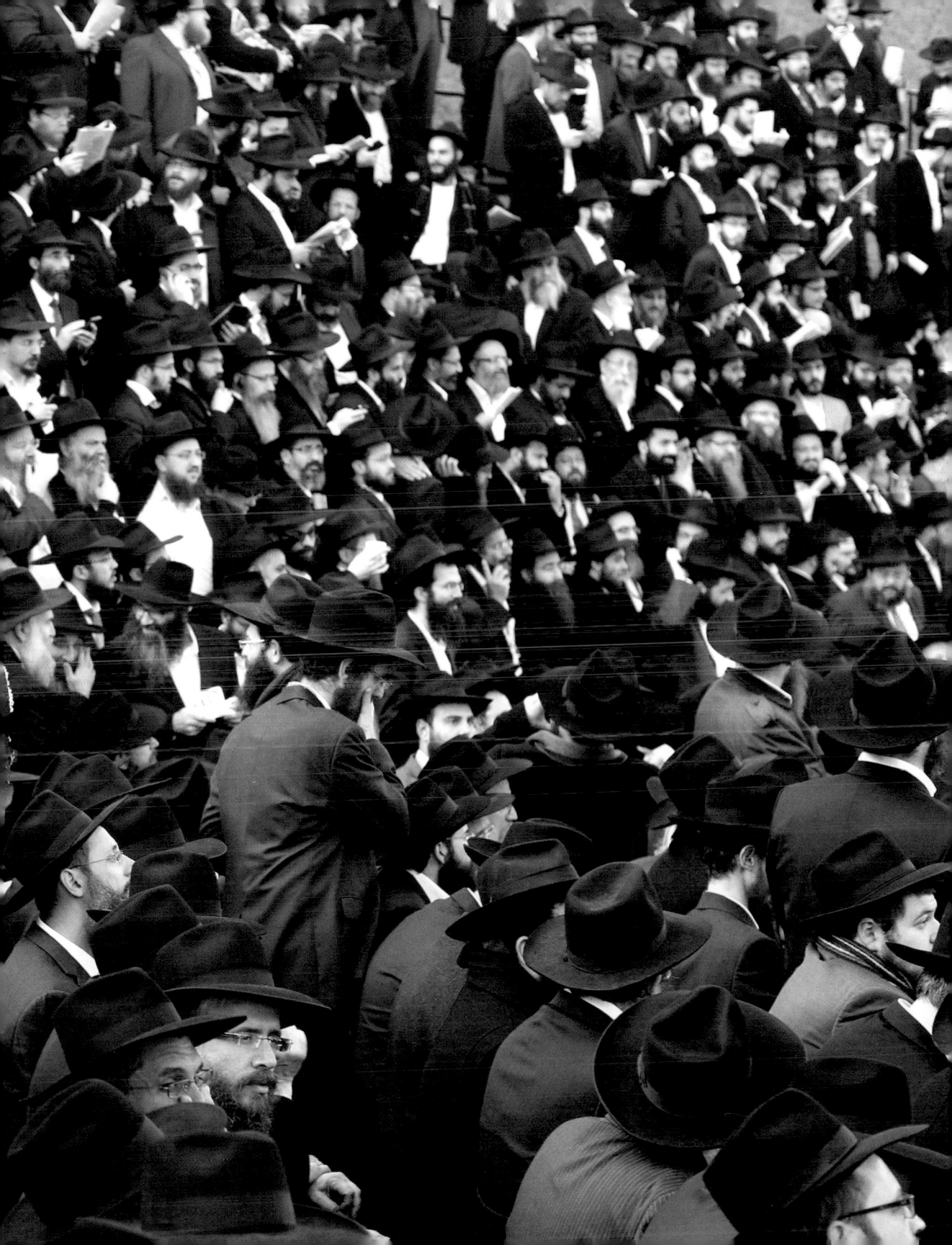

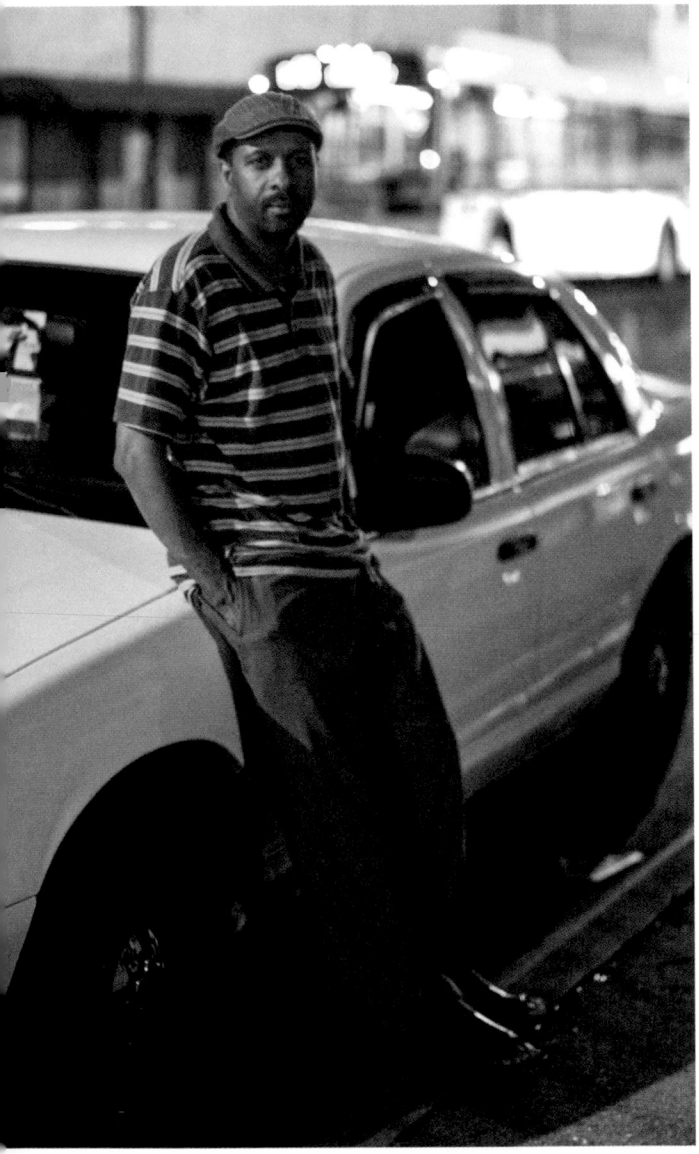

"EVERYONE WHO SEES MY RÉSUMÉ ASKS ME WHY I DRIVE A CAB. BACK IN NIGER, I WAS A FRENCH TEACHER. BUT THE GOVERNMENT STOPPED PAYING US FOR A FEW MONTHS, SO I DECIDED TO QUIT MY JOB AND MOVE TO AMERICA. THAT WAS TWELVE YEARS AGO. I THOUGHT I COULD TEACH FRENCH HERE, BUT I HAD NO IDEA HOW HARD IT WOULD BE TO GET A JOB WITHOUT PAPERS. THE ONLY PLACE I COULD FIND WORK WAS A CAR WASH. BACK IN NIGER, KIDS WOULD WASH MY CAR FOR ME. NOW ALL DAY LONG I WAS WASHING CARS FOR OTHER PEOPLE. I WAS VERY DEPRESSED. BUT I WAS TOO EMBARRASSED TO GO BACK HOME. THEN, ONE YEAR AFTER I ARRIVED, GEORGE BUSH GOT ELECTED AND EVERYONE WAS TELLING ME THAT IT MEANT VERY BAD THINGS FOR ME. THEY SAID THE REPUBLICANS WOULD MAKE TROUBLE FOR ME. SO I WAS VERY SCARED. AFTER THE CAR WASH, I BECAME A STOCK BOY. THEN, A DELIVERY DRIVER. FIVE YEARS AGO, I GOT MY PAPERS AND BECAME A CITIZEN, SO NOW I'M ABLE TO WORK AT THE AIRPORT. AT NIGHT, AND ON MY DAYS OFF, I DRIVE A CAB. JUST THIS YEAR I GRADUATED FROM BROOKLYN COLLEGE WITH A MASTER'S DEGREE IN FRENCH. I FINISHED THIRD IN MY CLASS. NOW I THINK I CAN BECOME A PROFESSOR."

DISCOVERED THESE GUYS IN BREEZY POINT, QUEENS, AFTER HURRICANE SANDY. WHEN I WALKED UP, THEY WERE IN THE PROCESS OF DISMOUNTING FROM THE BOAT. BUT THEY HELPED ME OUT BY PILING BACK IN FOR THE PHOTO OP.

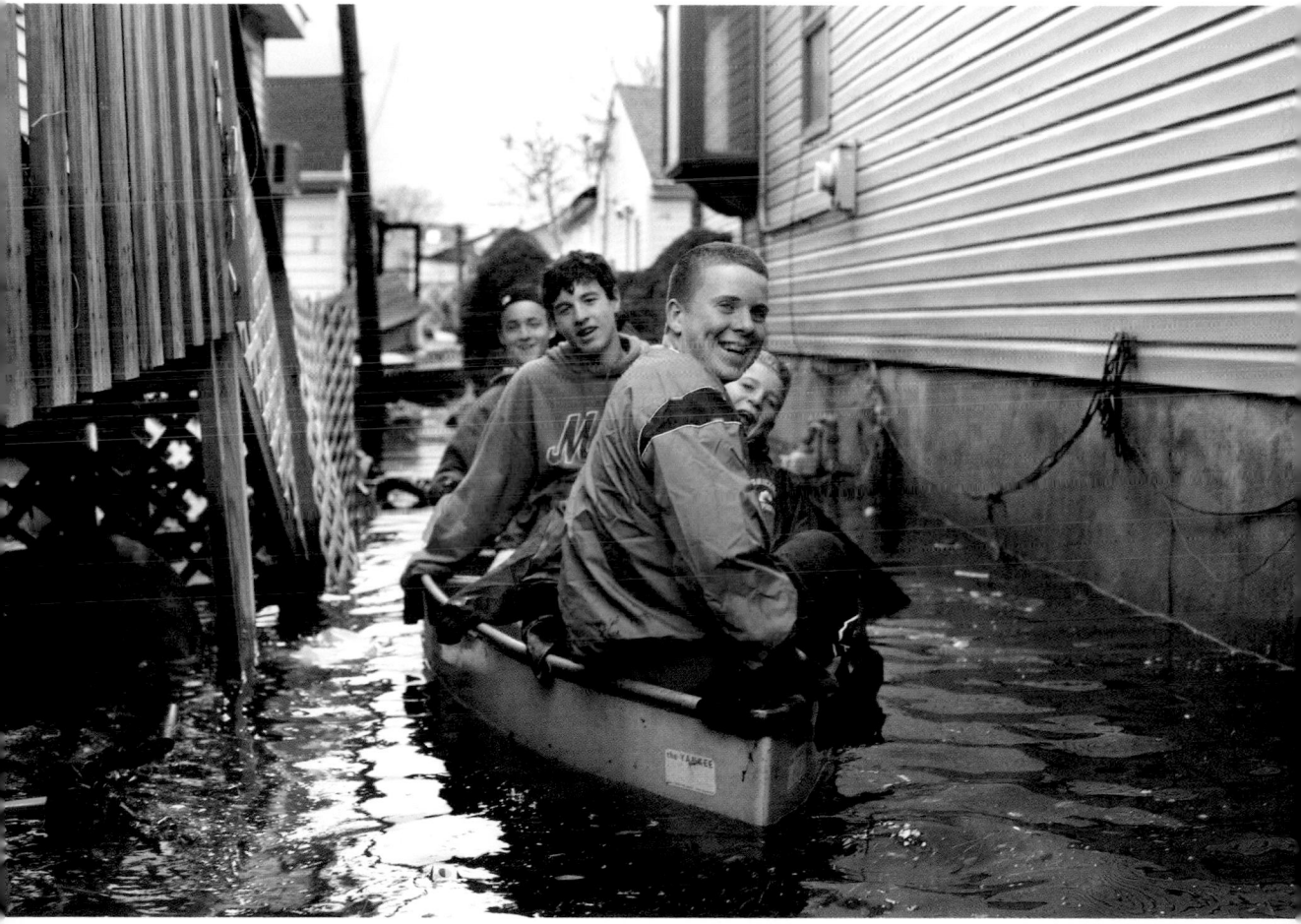

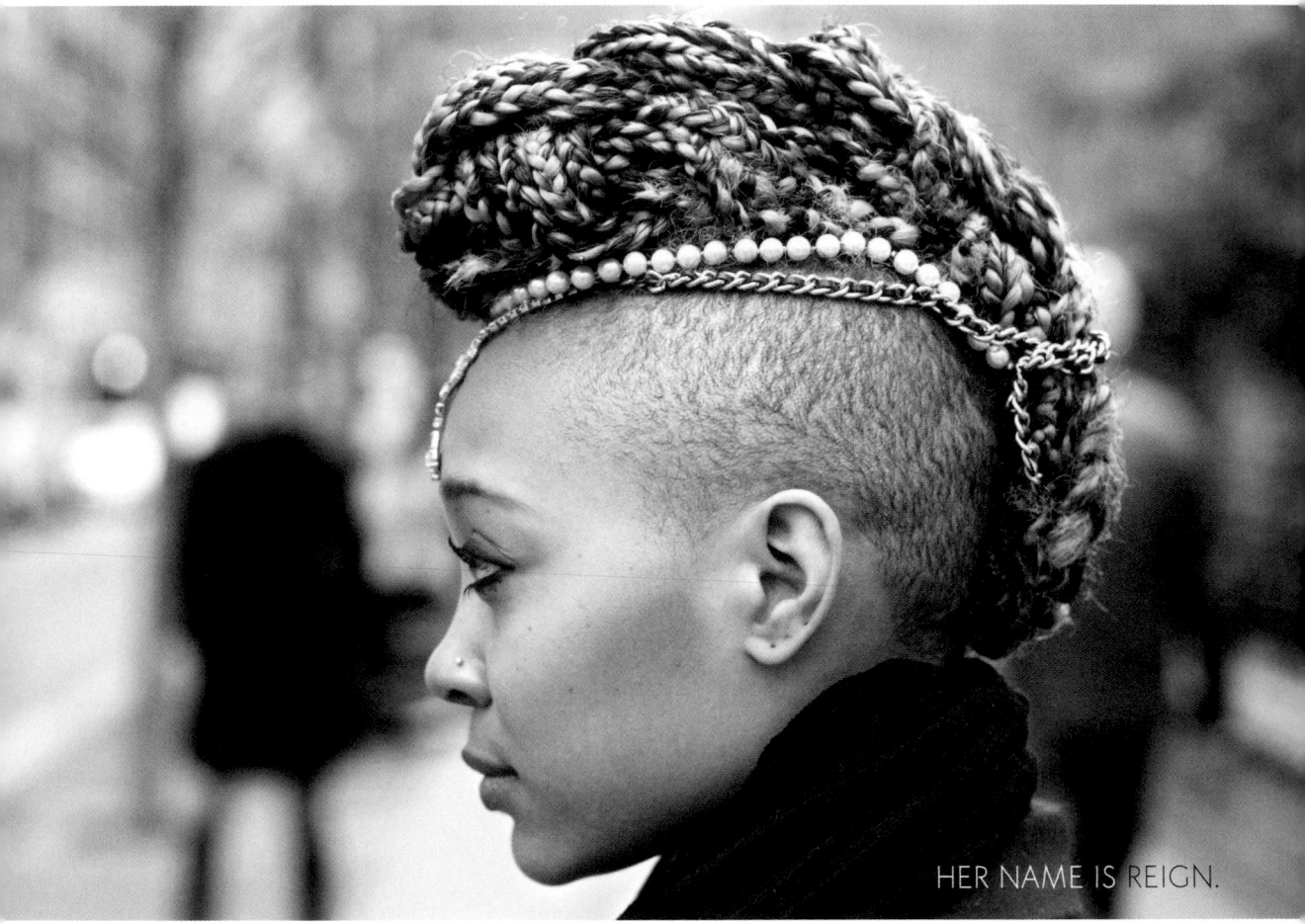
HER NAME IS REIGN.

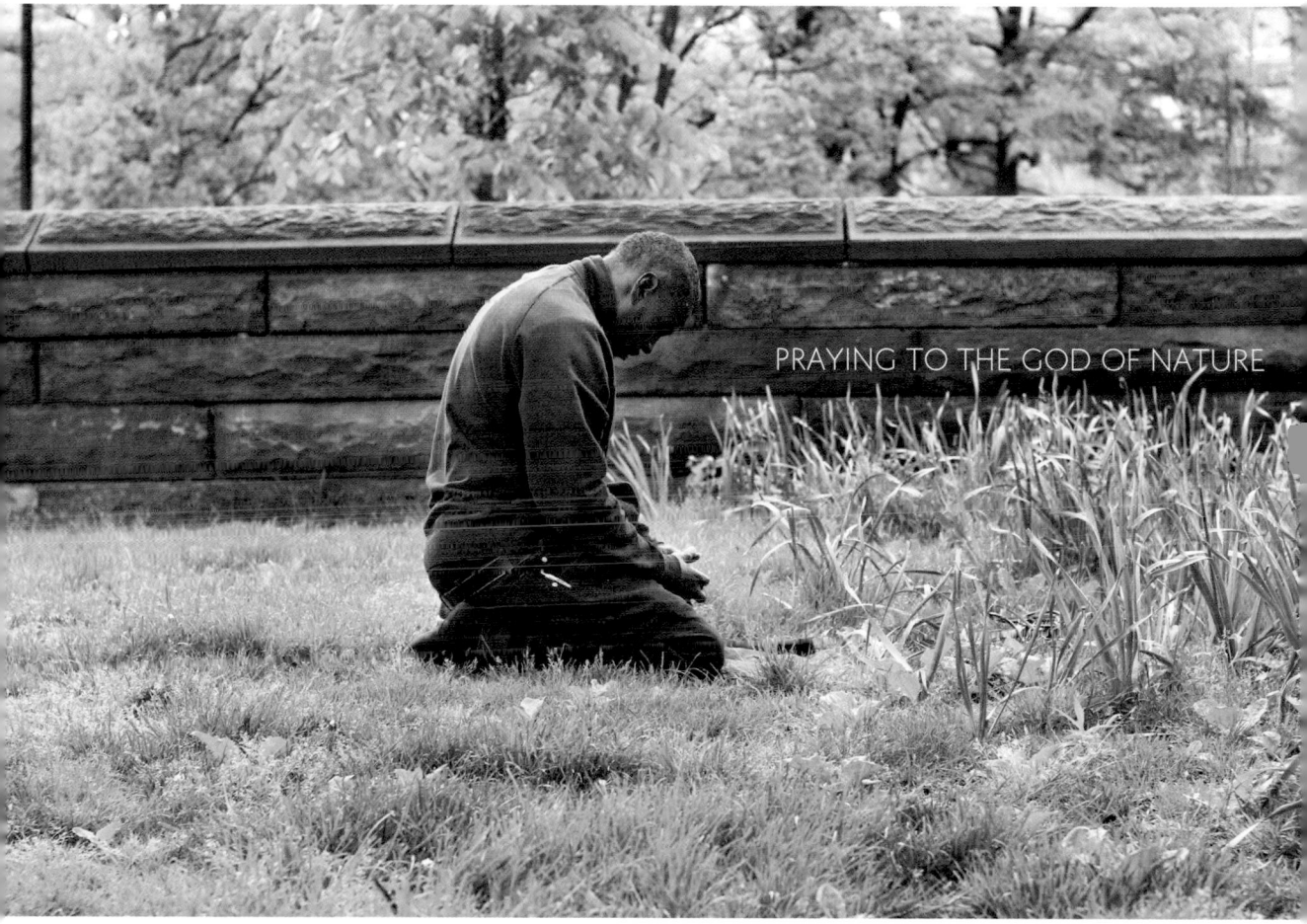
PRAYING TO THE GOD OF NATURE

SEEN IN TRIBECA

I DISCOVERED A PHOTOGENIC VACANT LOT IN SOHO, BUT WAS UNABLE TO CONVINCE ANYONE TO POSE IN IT. AFTER SEVERAL MINUTES, I FINALLY CAME ACROSS THIS FATHER AND SON FROM PARIS. THEY BARELY SPOKE ENGLISH, YET AGREED TO PARK THEIR WHEELCHAIR AND STAND FOR A PORTRAIT.

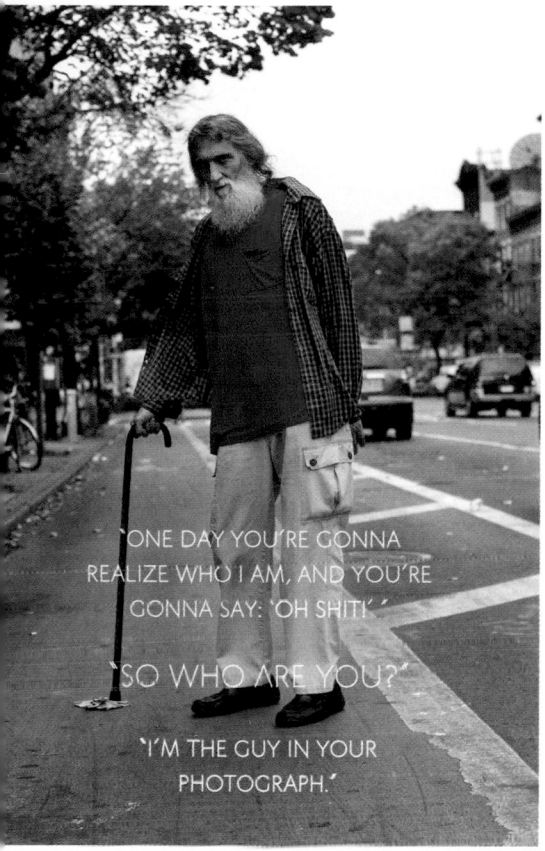

"ONE DAY YOU'RE GONNA REALIZE WHO I AM, AND YOU'RE GONNA SAY: 'OH SHIT!'"

"SO WHO ARE YOU?"

"I'M THE GUY IN YOUR PHOTOGRAPH."

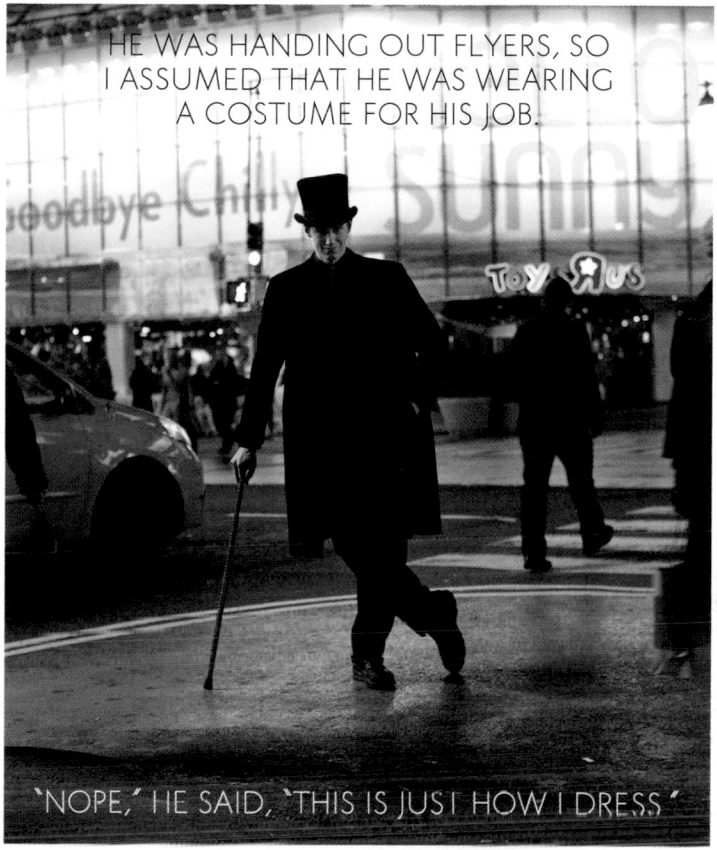


HE WAS HANDING OUT FLYERS, SO I ASSUMED THAT HE WAS WEARING A COSTUME FOR HIS JOB.

"NOPE," HE SAID, "THIS IS JUST HOW I DRESS."

SEEN IN CENTRAL PARK

"I JUST GOT BACK FROM THE EYE DOCTOR. I HOPE HE CAN SAVE THEM."

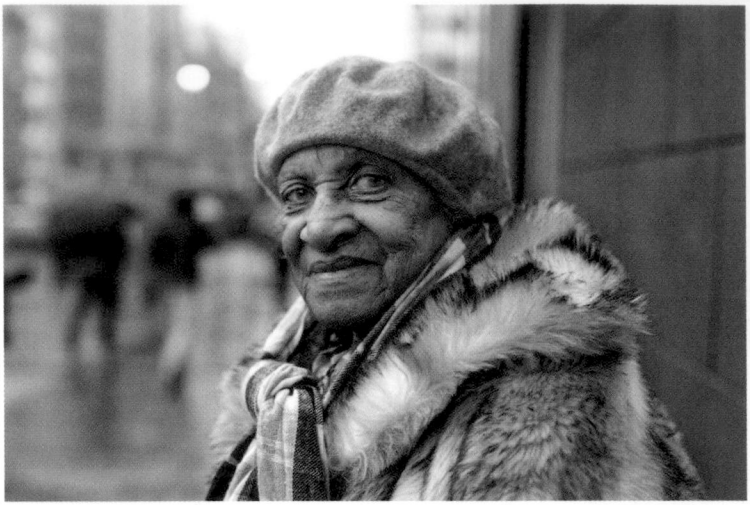

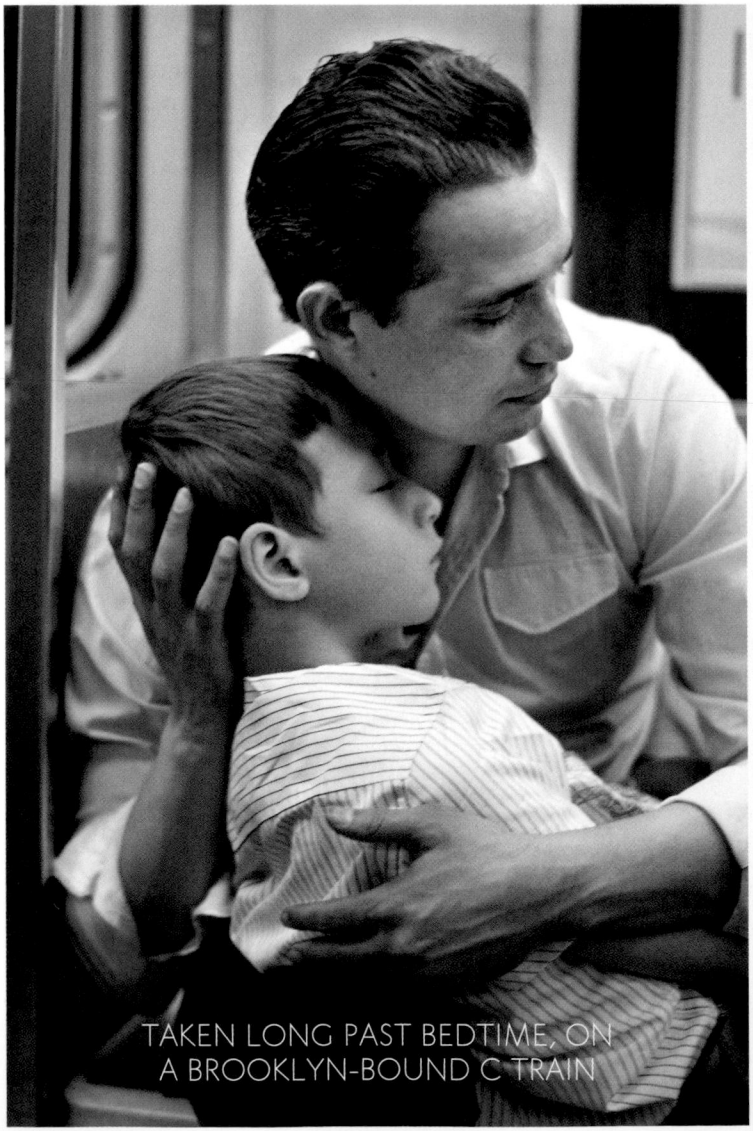

TAKEN LONG PAST BEDTIME, ON A BROOKLYN-BOUND C TRAIN

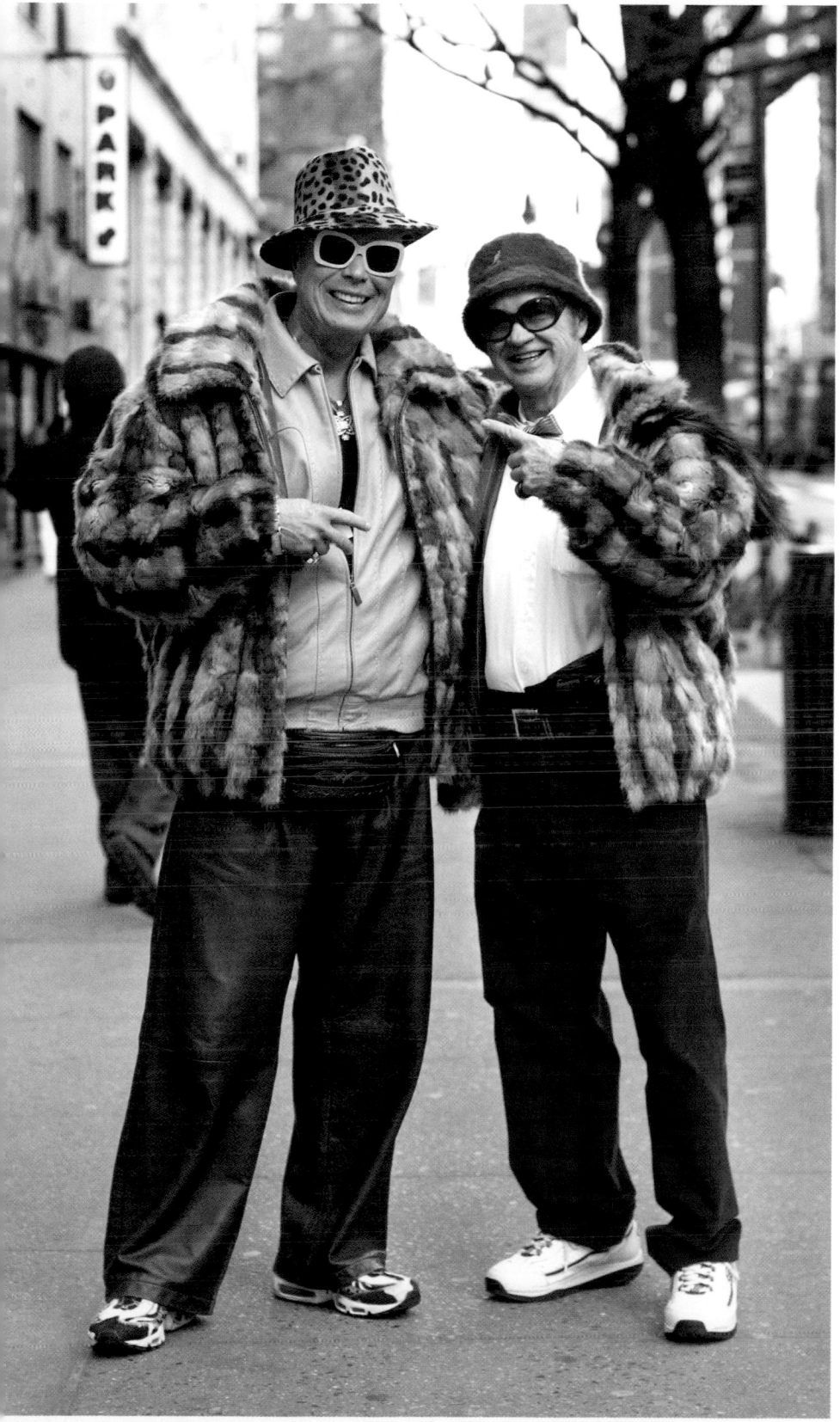


ON THE LEFT WE HAVE DONNY DIAMONDS, WORLD-CLASS BILLIARDS PLAYER. ON THE RIGHT WE HAVE DOC ASTRO, INTERNATIONAL SLINGSHOT CHAMPION. I'M NOT MAKING THIS UP.

I WAS STANDING ON A BRONX SUBWAY PLATFORM WHEN A TRAIN PULLED INTO THE STATION. I NOTICED THESE TWO PUTTING ON QUITE A SHOW IN ONE OF THE WINDOWS. I SCRAMBLED FOR MY CAMERA, AND MANAGED TO SNAP ONE SHOT BEFORE THEY PULLED AWAY.

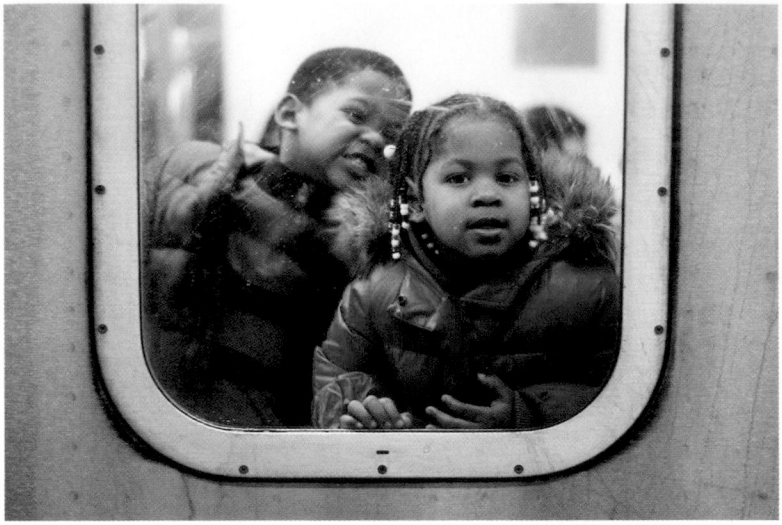

THIS KID LOOKS BETTER WALKING HOME FROM SCHOOL THAN I'VE EVER LOOKED IN MY LIFE.

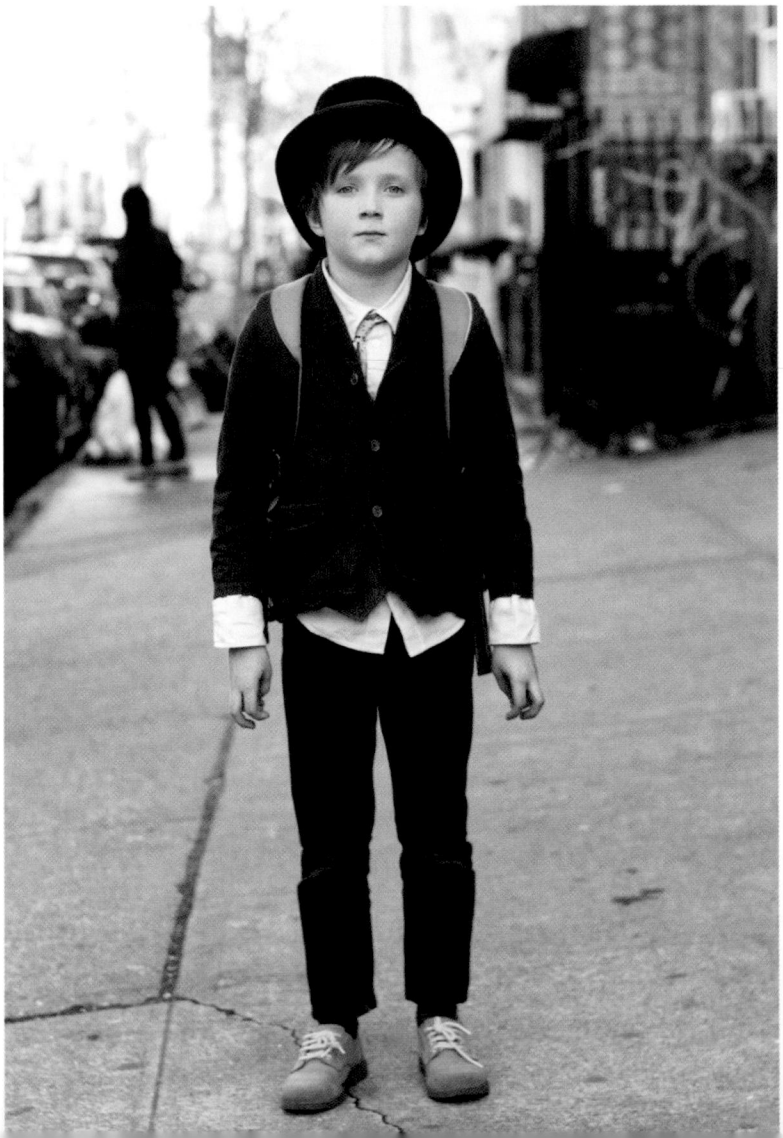

SEEN IN GREENWICH VILLAGE

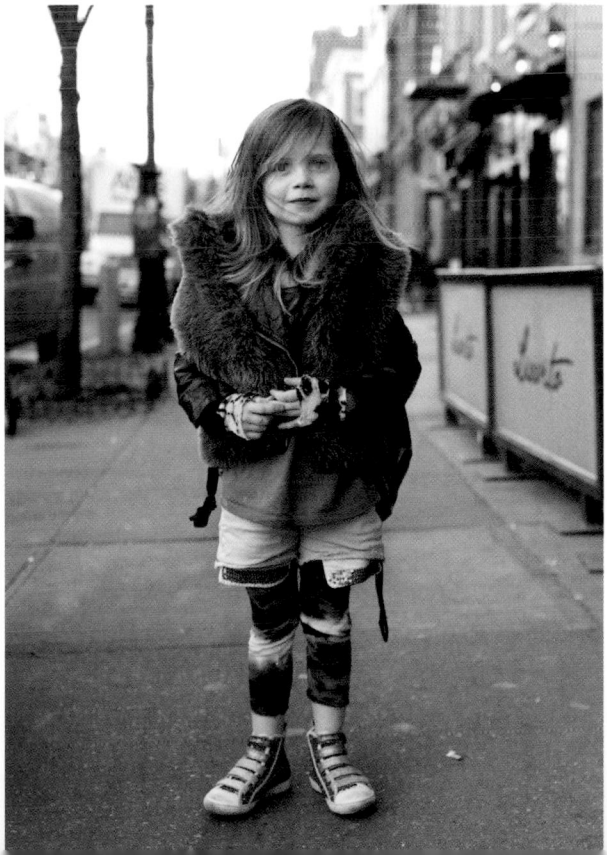

"WE ORDERED HER THOSE PANTS, AND AS SOON AS THEY ARRIVED, SHE CUT OFF THE BOTTOMS AND MADE A PAIR OF GLOVES."

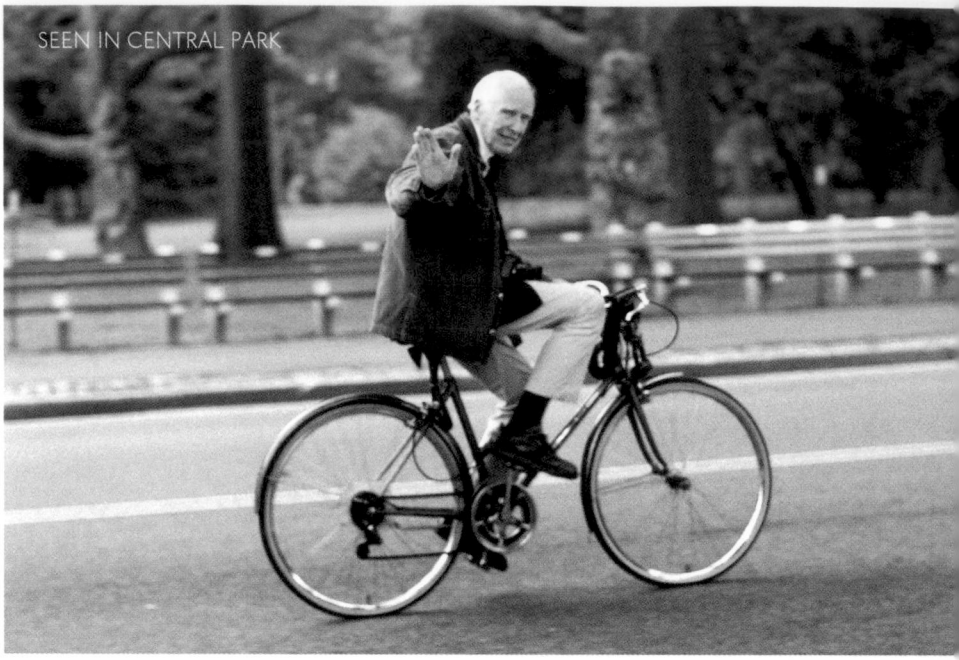


I FLAGGED THIS MAN DOWN WHILE HE WAS JOGGING ACROSS THE BROOKLYN BRIDGE. HE TURNED OUT TO BE A JAPANESE BOXER. HE THOUGHT I WAS LAUGHING AT HIM WHILE I WAS SETTING UP THE SHOT, BUT I ASSURED HIM THAT I WAS ONLY LAUGHING AT HOW AWESOME HE LOOKED.

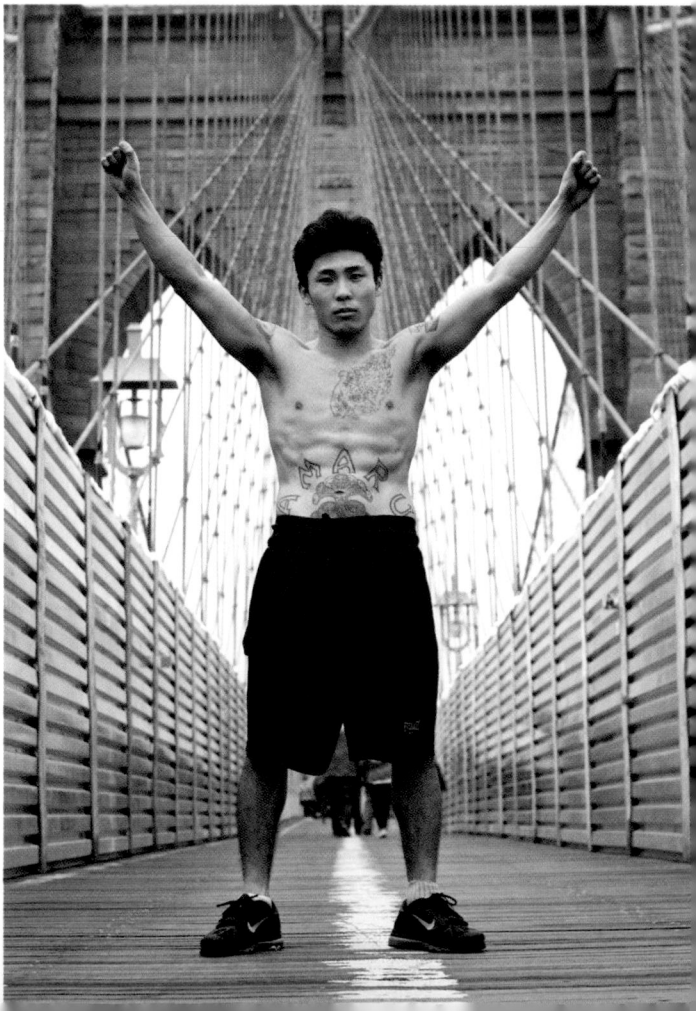

"MAKE SURE YOU CAN SEE THE BAG."

"OH, I DIDN'T REALIZE YOU WERE ADVERTISING SOMETHING."

"ISN'T EVERYTHING BEAUTIFUL ADVERTISING SOMETHING?"

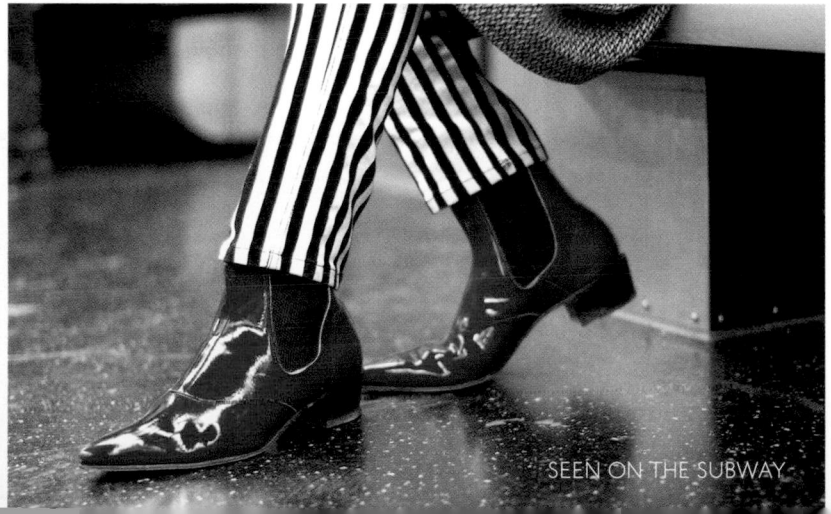

SEEN ON THE SUBWAY

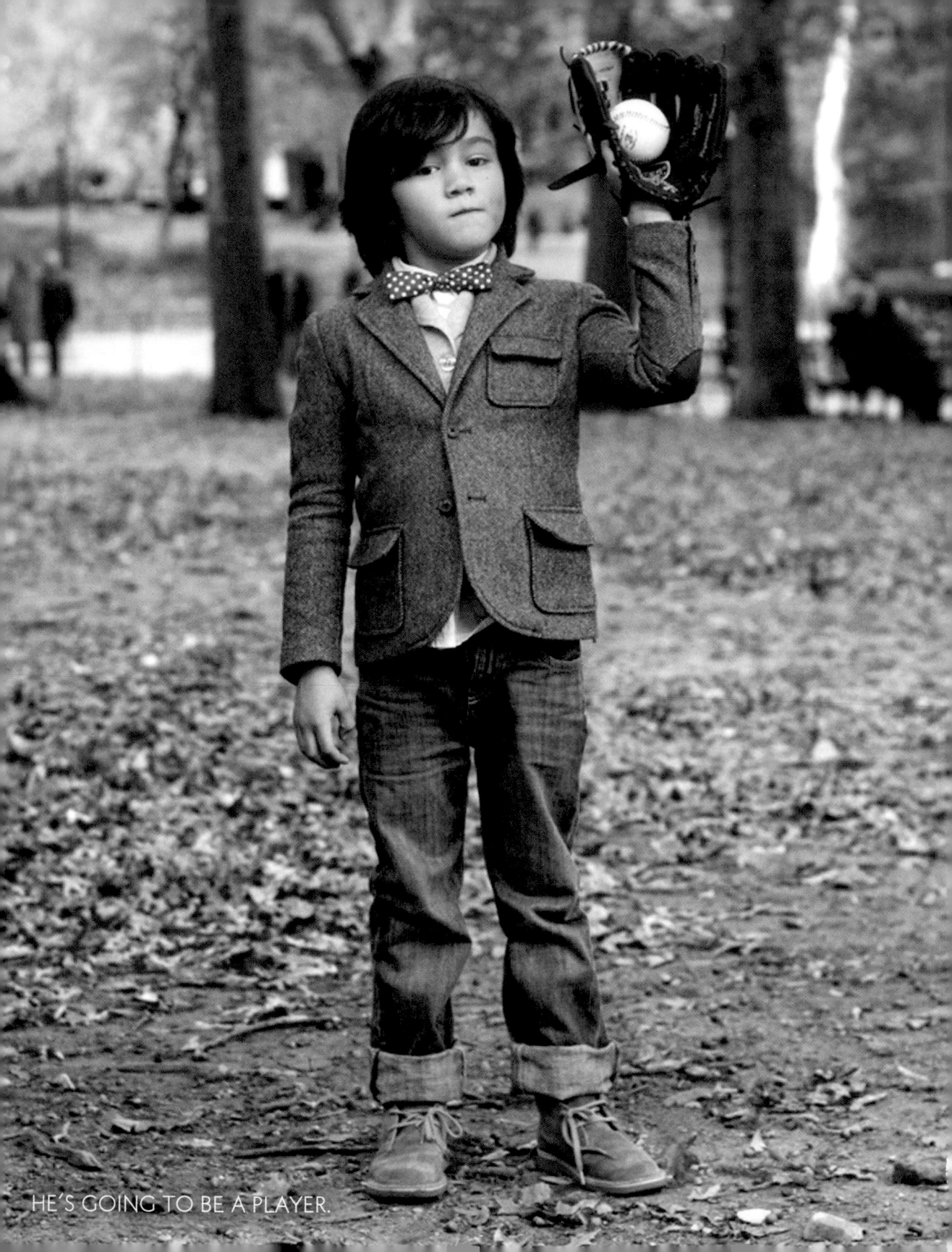

HE'S GOING TO BE A PLAYER.

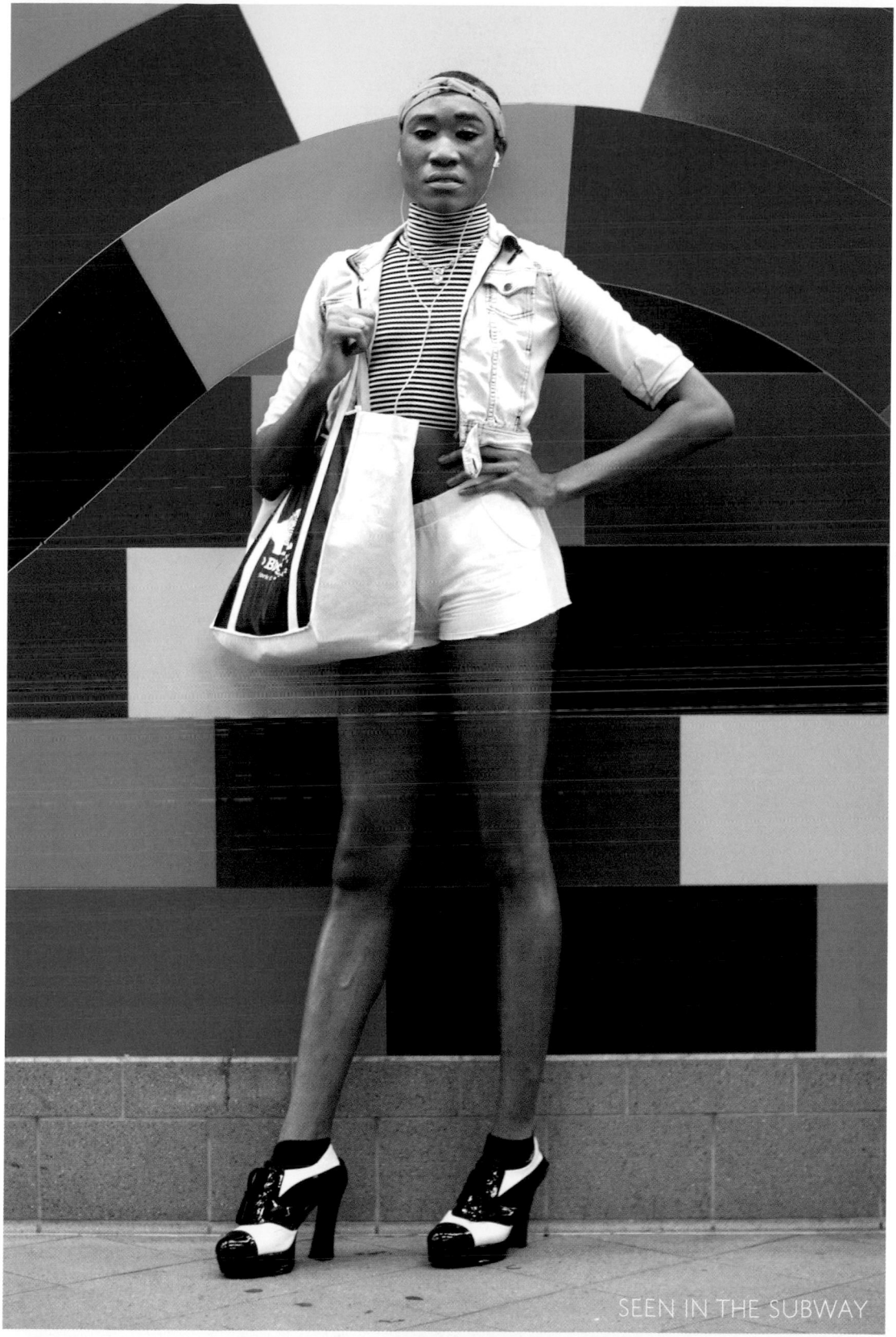
SEEN IN THE SUBWAY

I'VE SEEN THIS GUY SEVERAL TIMES. I DON'T THINK HE OWNS A SHIRT.

"I WANT TO BE AN ACTOR. I'VE GOT ALL THESE CRAZY CHARACTERS AND PERSONALITIES I CAN DO."

SEEN FROM 59TH STREET

SEEN ON CONEY ISLAND

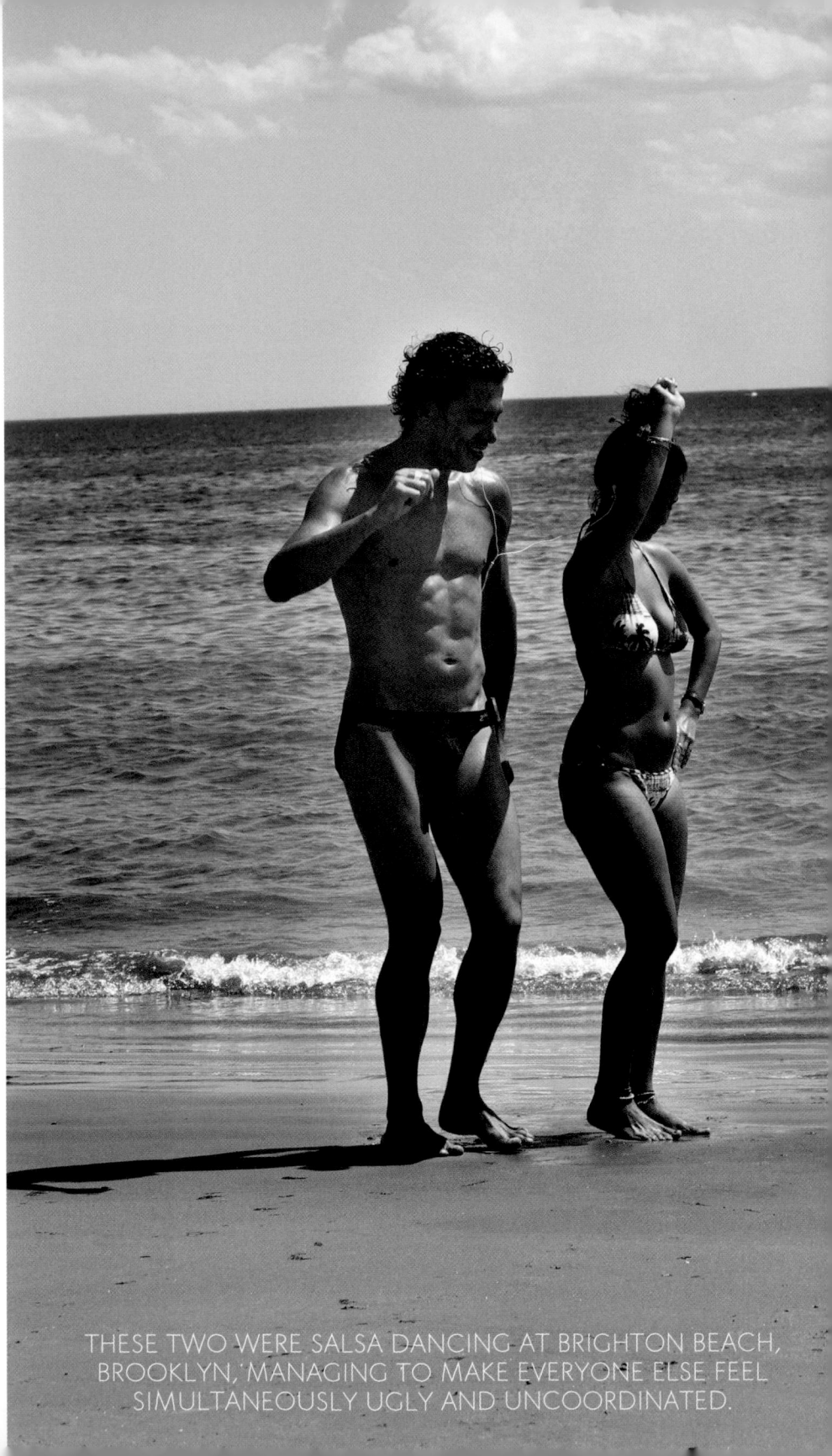

THESE TWO WERE SALSA DANCING AT BRIGHTON BEACH, BROOKLYN, MANAGING TO MAKE EVERYONE ELSE FEEL SIMULTANEOUSLY UGLY AND UNCOORDINATED.

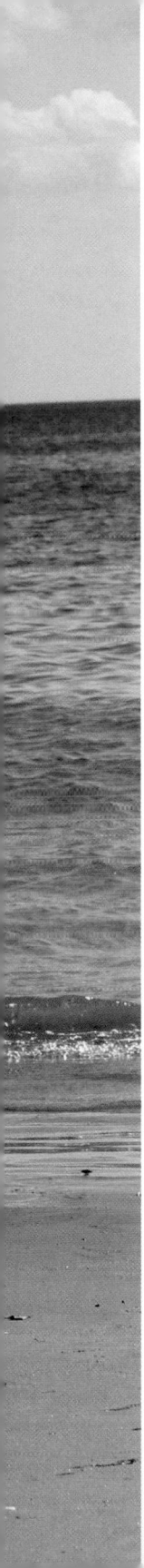

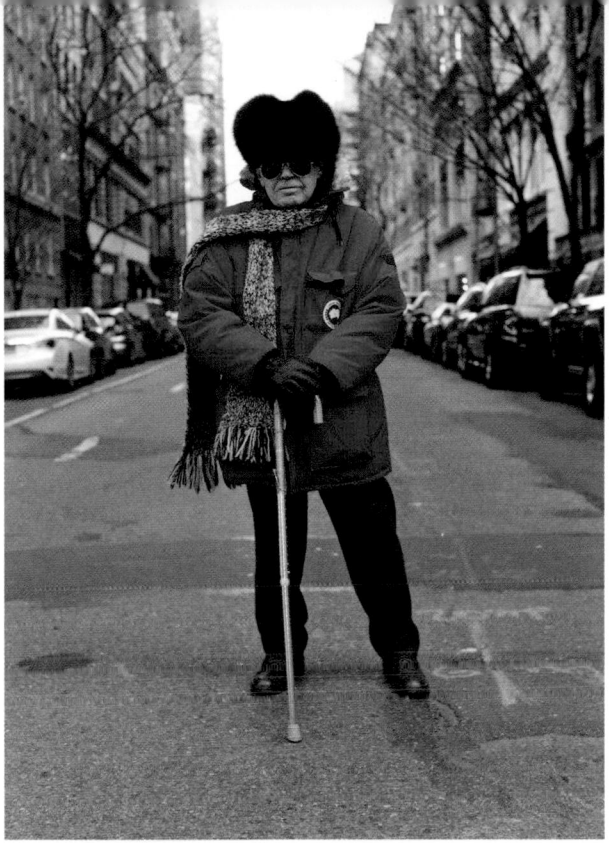

"I FOUGHT FOR TWENTY-SIX MONTHS. EIGHT COUNTRIES. THREE DIFFERENT UNITS. SIX CAMPAIGNS. ONE INVASION. THE FRENCH GAVE ME THE LEGION OF HONOR. THE U.S. GAVE ME THE BRONZE STAR. AND THE RUSSIANS GAVE ME THE ORDER OF THE GREAT PATRIOTIC WAR."

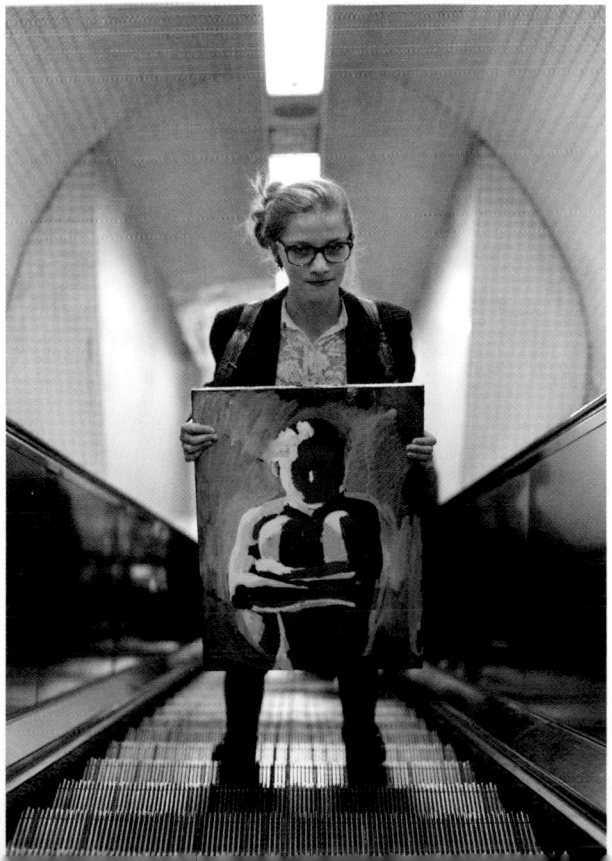

"IS THAT YOU?"

"KINDA."

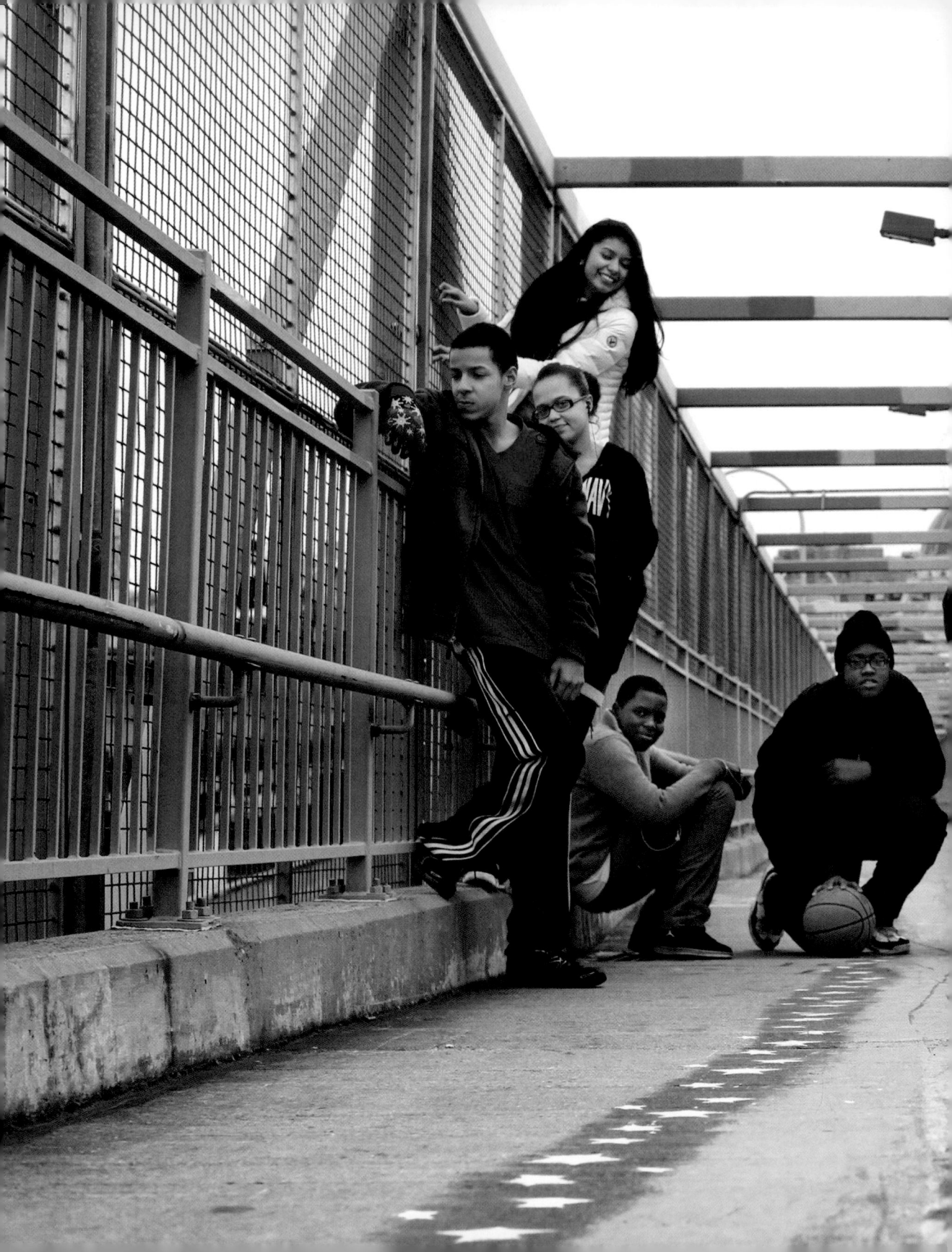

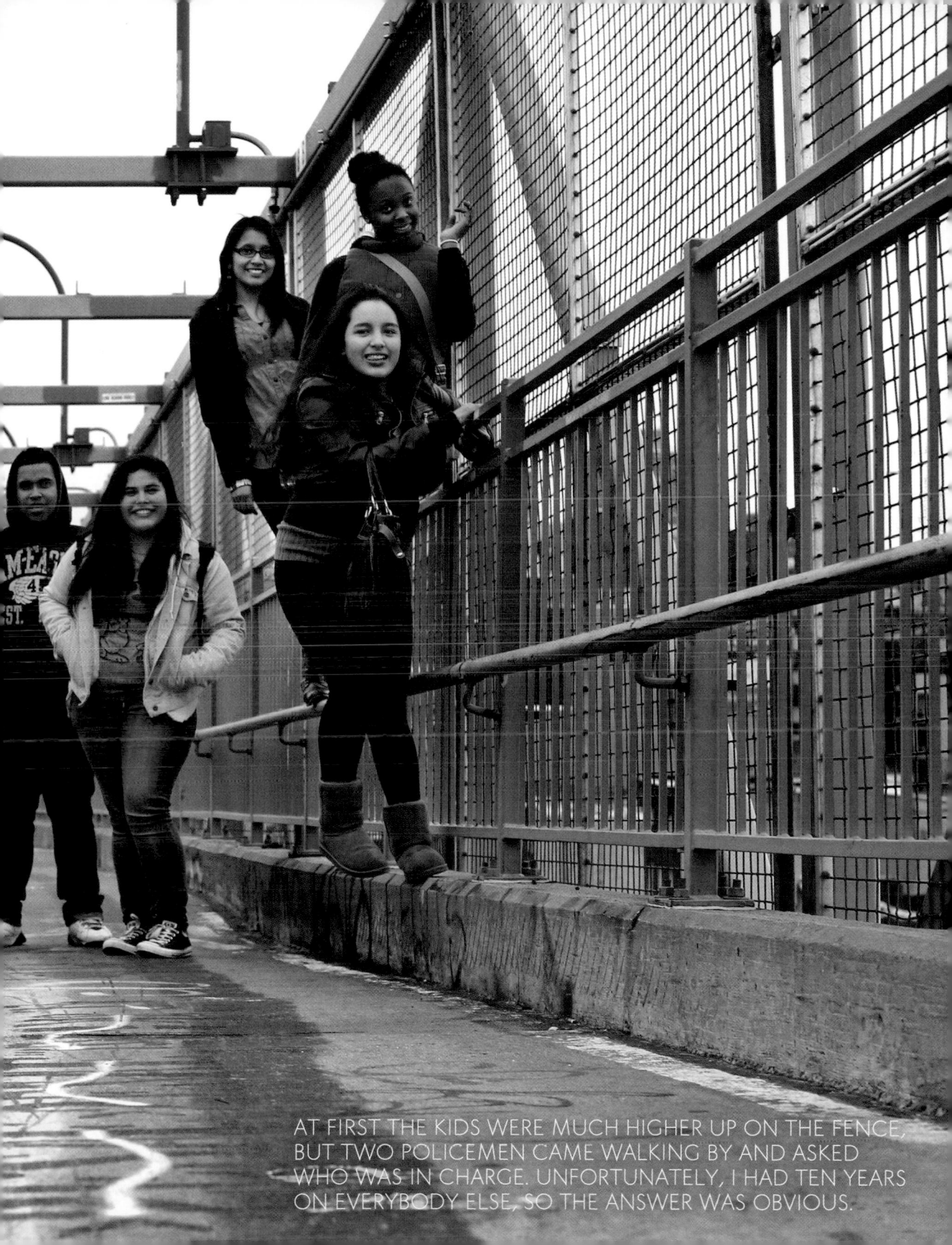

AT FIRST THE KIDS WERE MUCH HIGHER UP ON THE FENCE, BUT TWO POLICEMEN CAME WALKING BY AND ASKED WHO WAS IN CHARGE. UNFORTUNATELY, I HAD TEN YEARS ON EVERYBODY ELSE, SO THE ANSWER WAS OBVIOUS.

THIS PLACE GETS SO DEAD AT NIGHT.

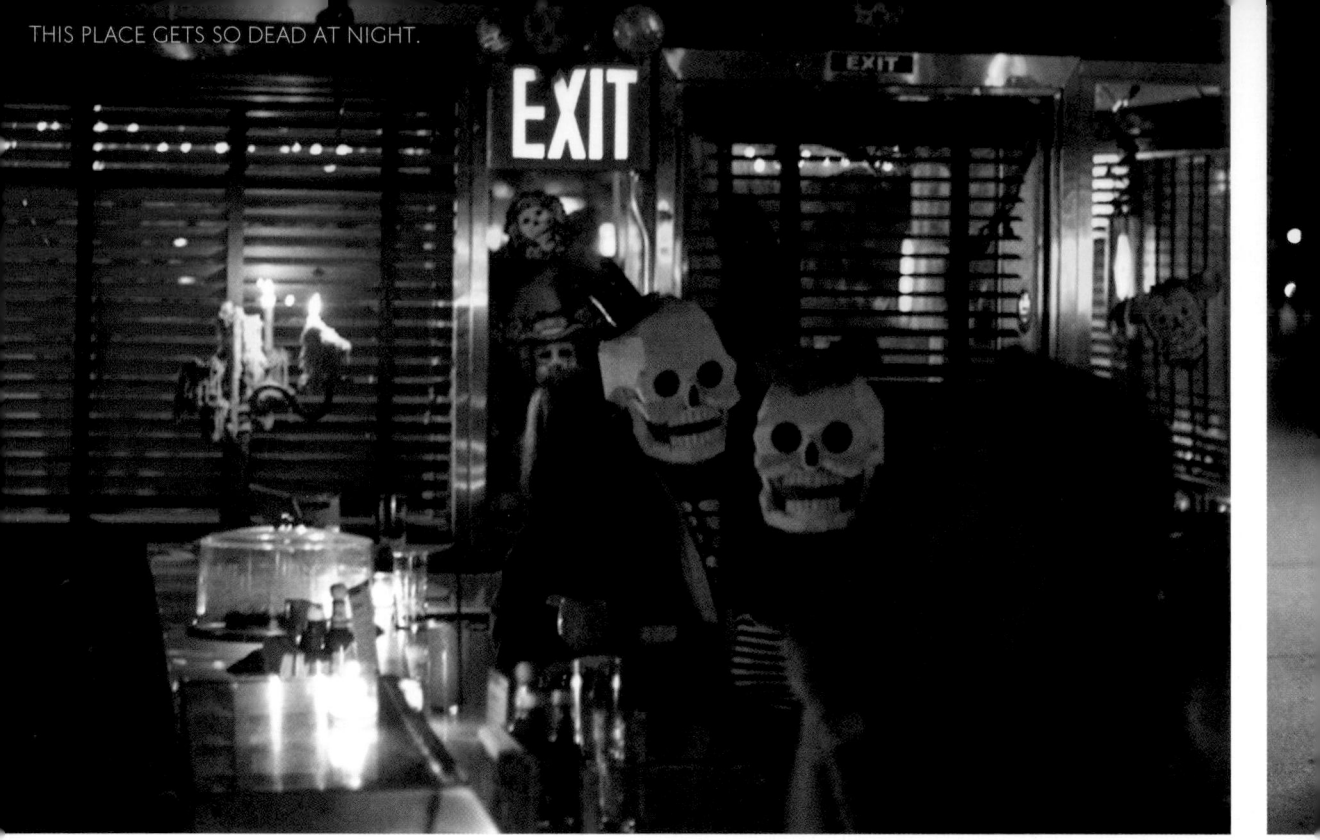


ONE AMAZING THING ABOUT NEW YORK IS THAT YOU PASS ALL THESE PEOPLE WITH ULTRA-MODERN CLOTHING AND HAIRCUTS, THEN TURN THE CORNER AND SEE SOMEONE FROM THE ANCIENT WORLD.

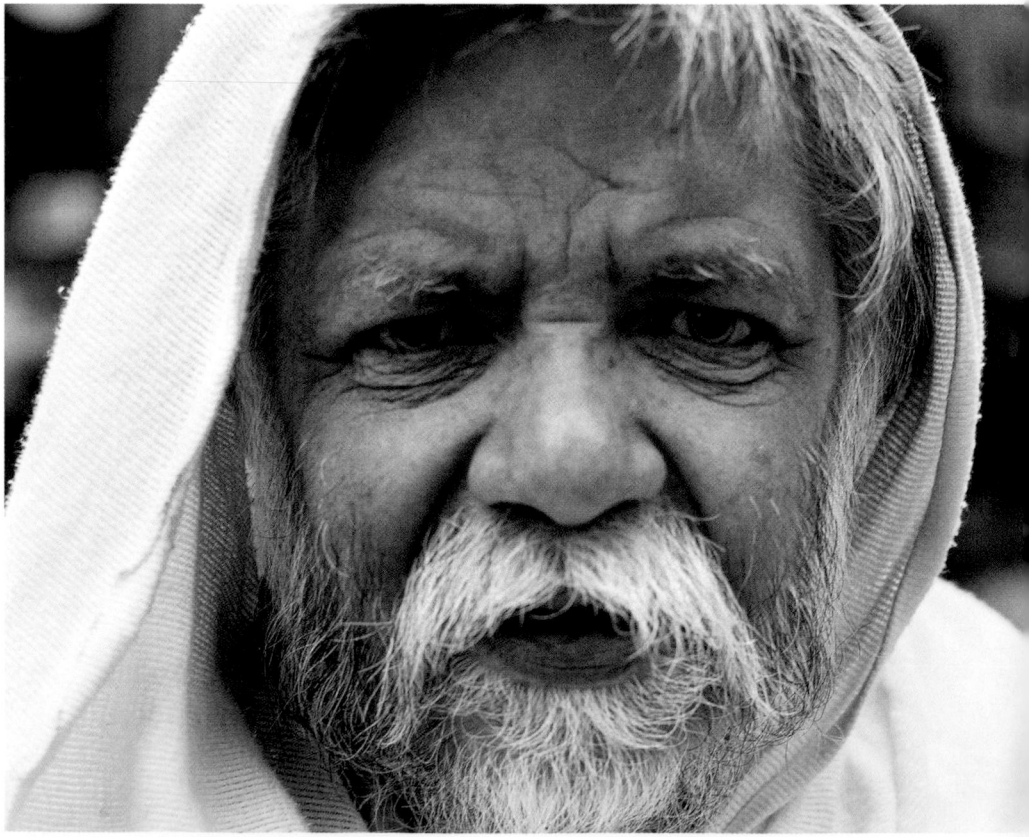

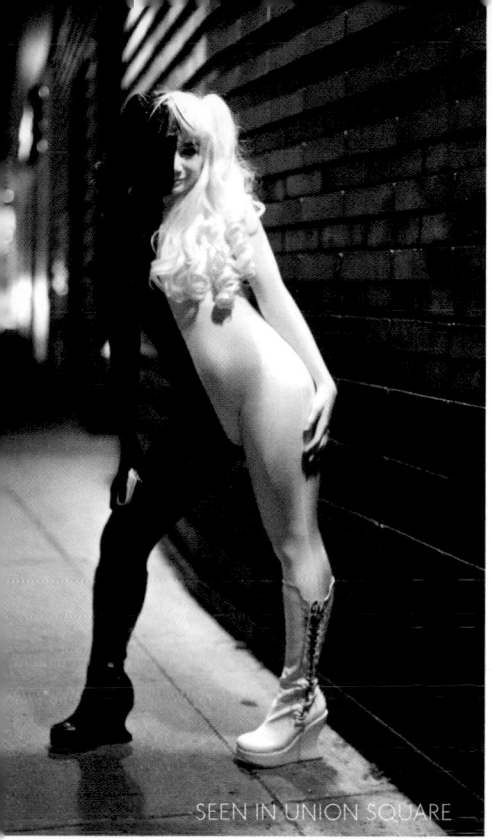

SEEN IN UNION SQUARE

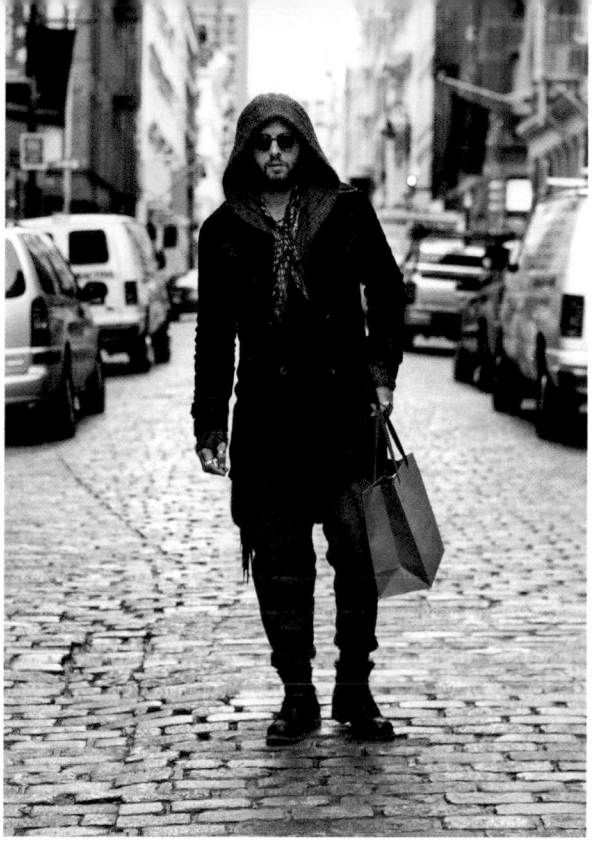

I'M NOT A FASHION EXPERT, BUT I DO KNOW WHAT "COOL AS SHIT" LOOKS LIKE.

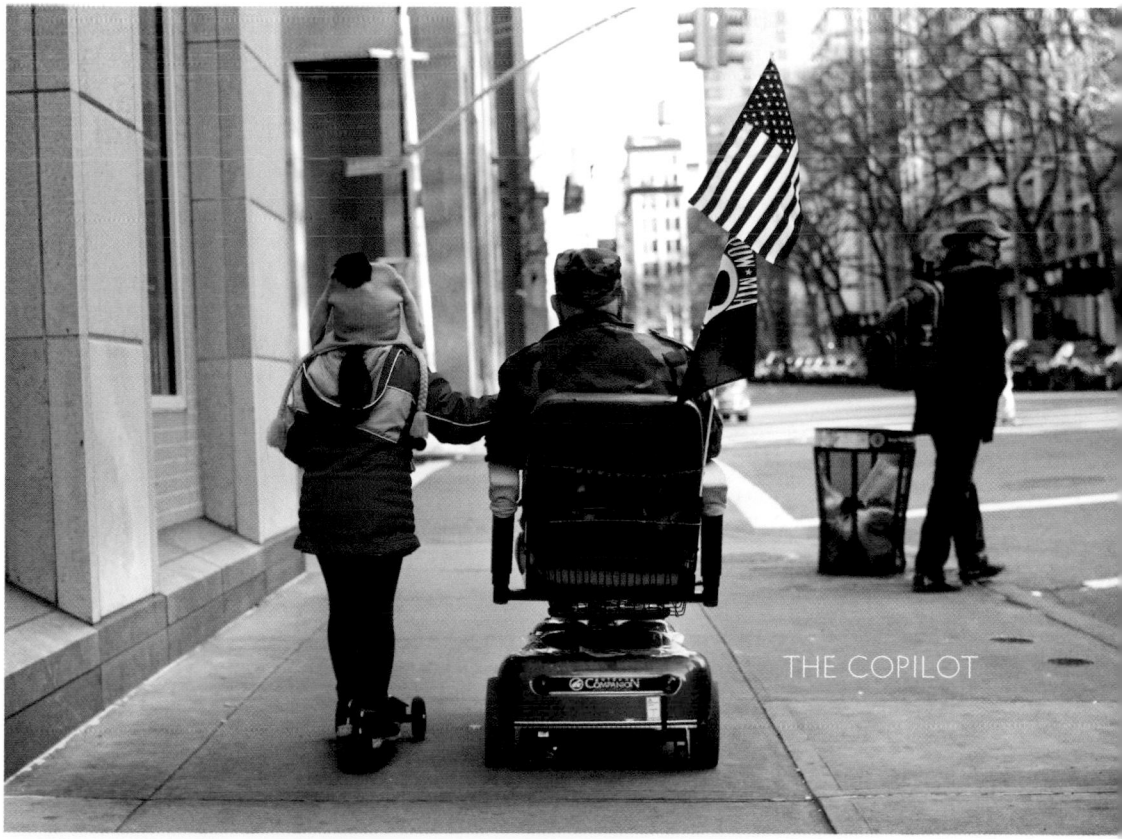


THE COPILOT

WHEN THEY CROSSED THE STREET, HE WAS CARRYING HER DRESS. JUST LIKE THIS.

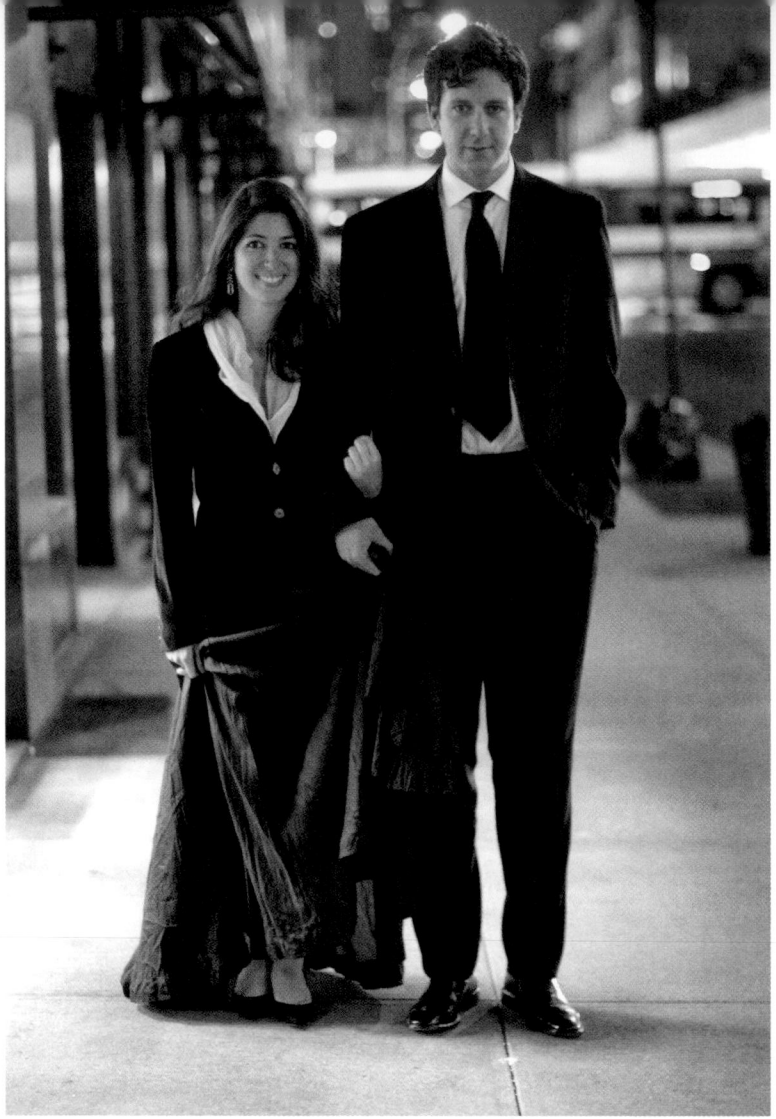

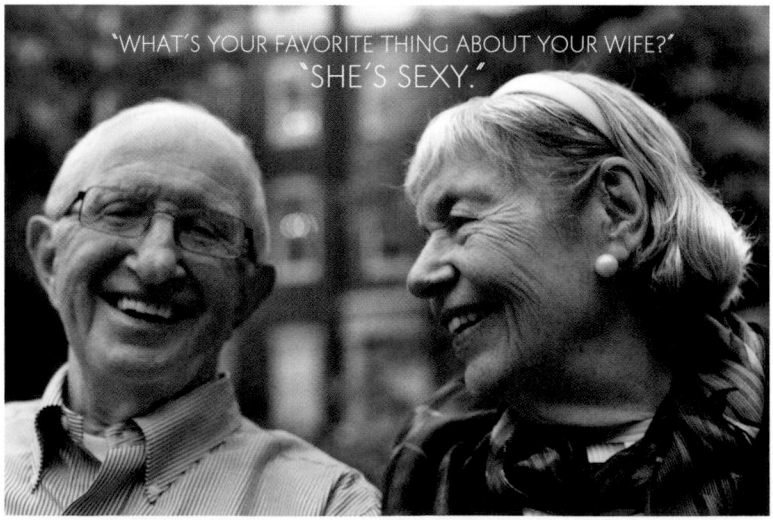

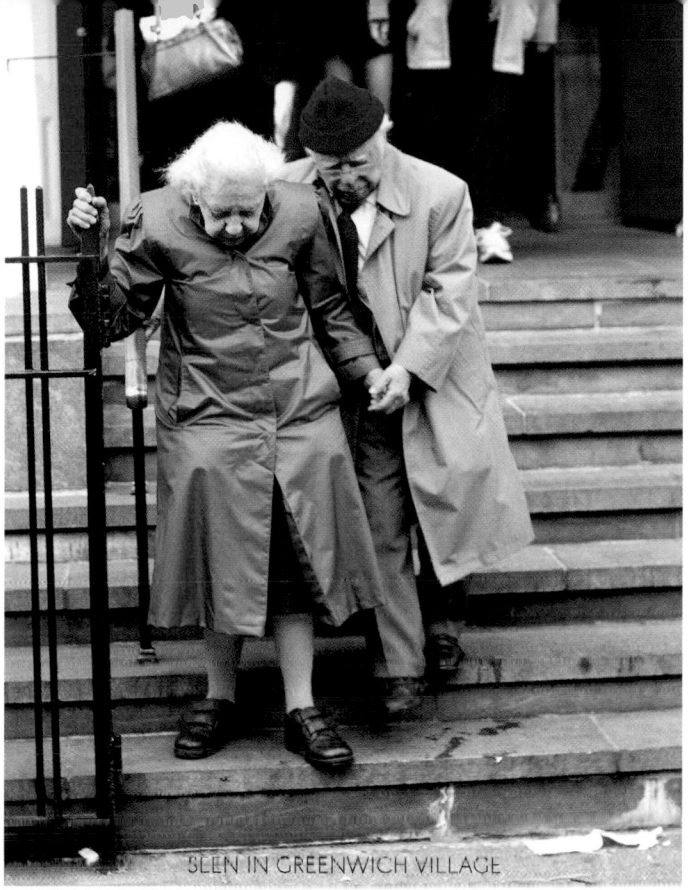

SEEN IN GREENWICH VILLAGE

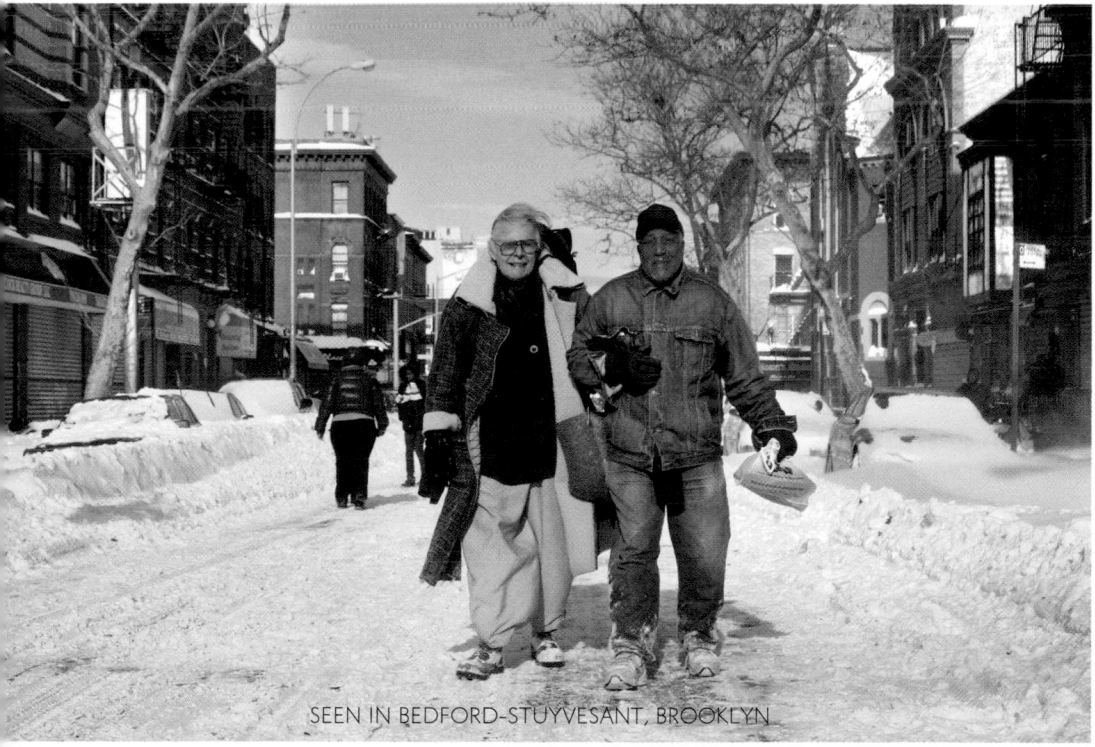

SEEN IN BEDFORD-STUYVESANT, BROOKLYN

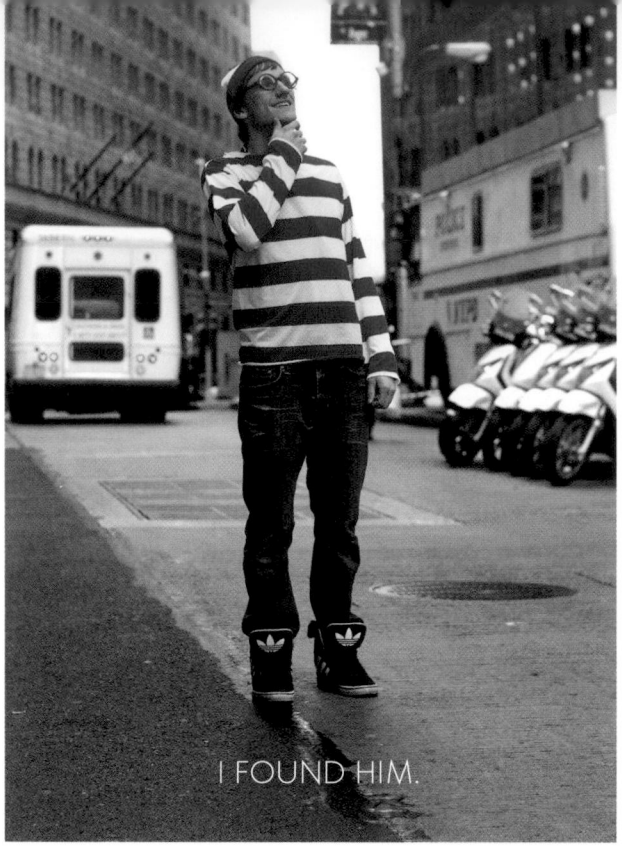
I FOUND HIM.

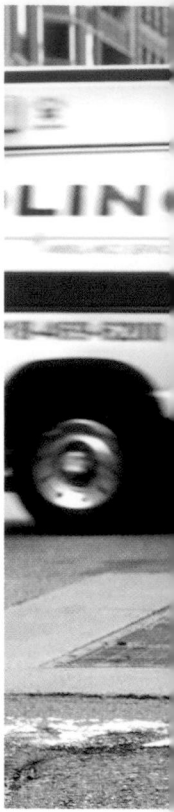

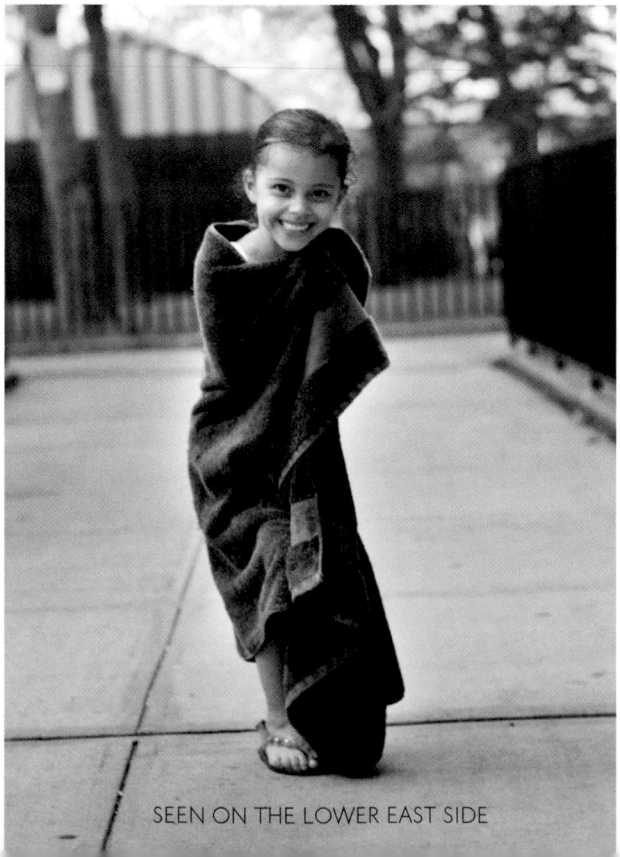
SEEN ON THE LOWER EAST SIDE

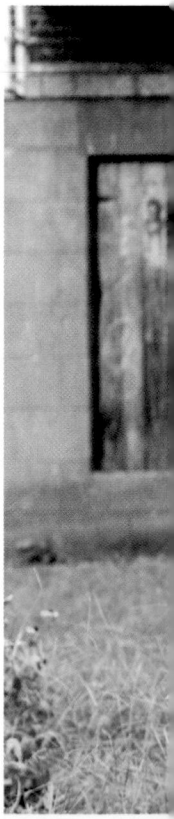

SEEN IN LOWER MIDTOWN

THIS GUY WAS A LITTLE HESITANT TO PARTICIPATE WHEN I TOLD HIM TO "JUST STAND RIGHT IN THE MIDDLE OF THE FLOWERS." LATER IN THE DAY, I PASSED HIM ON THE STREET AND HE SHOUTED: "YO! IT'S MY OFFICIAL PHOTOGRAPHER!"

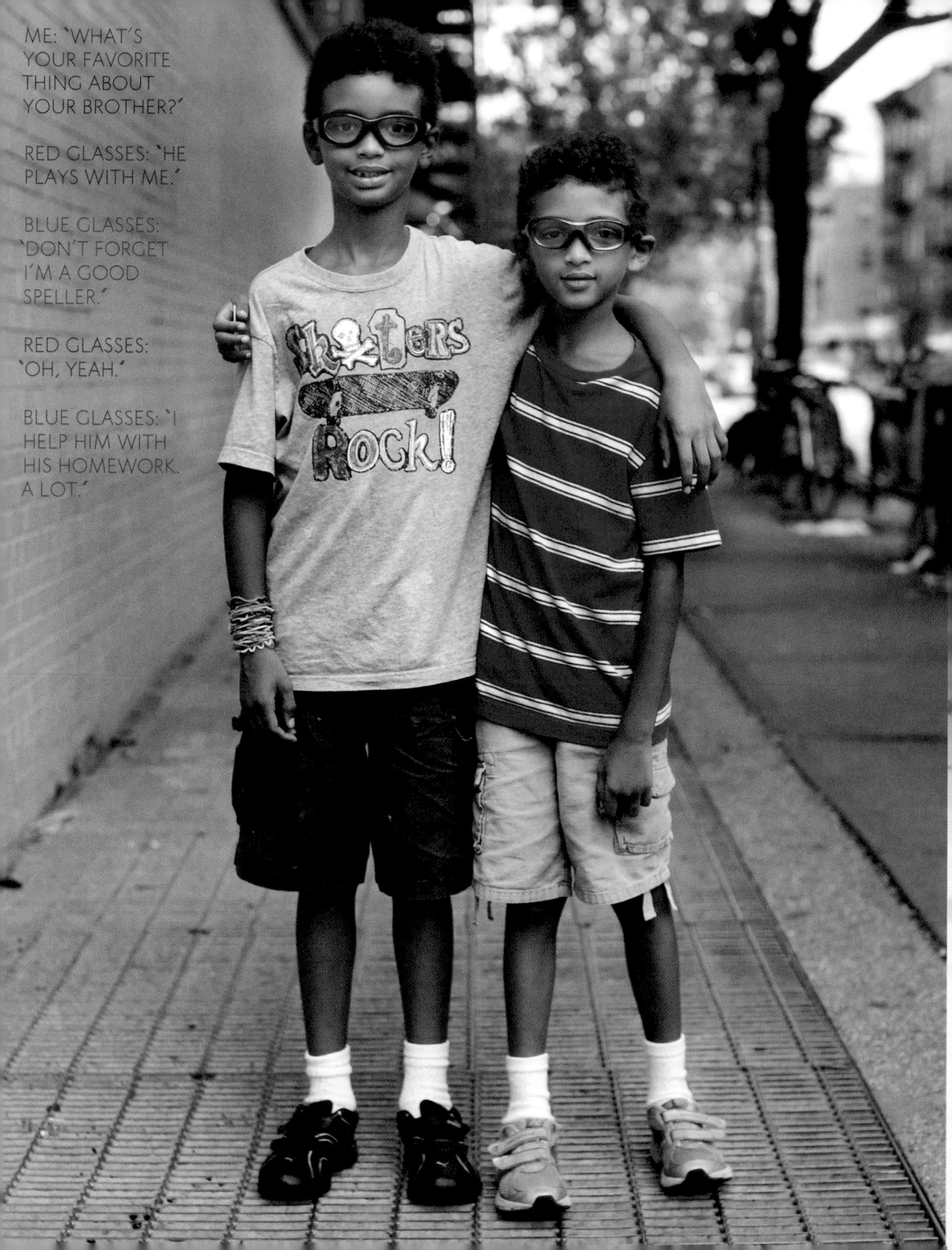


ME: 'WHAT'S YOUR FAVORITE THING ABOUT YOUR BROTHER?'

RED GLASSES: 'HE PLAYS WITH ME.'

BLUE GLASSES: 'DON'T FORGET I'M A GOOD SPELLER.'

RED GLASSES: 'OH, YEAH.'

BLUE GLASSES: 'I HELP HIM WITH HIS HOMEWORK. A LOT.'

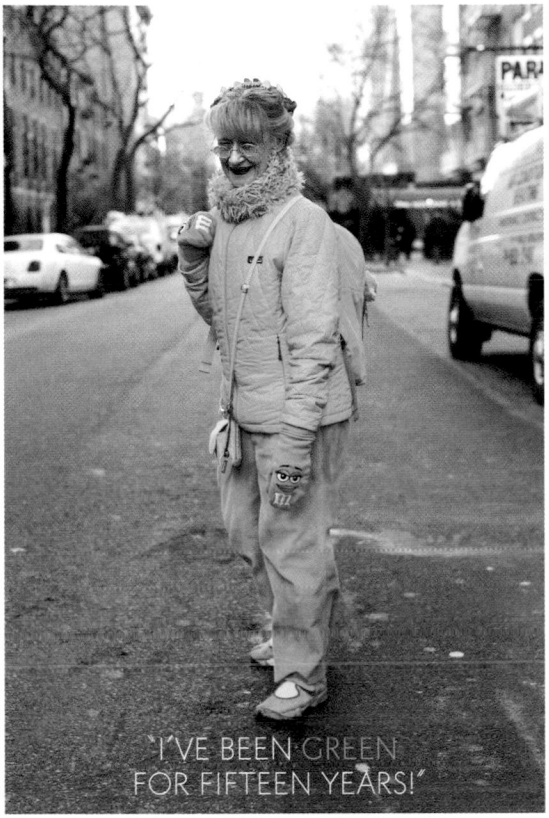

"I'VE BEEN GREEN
FOR FIFTEEN YEARS!"

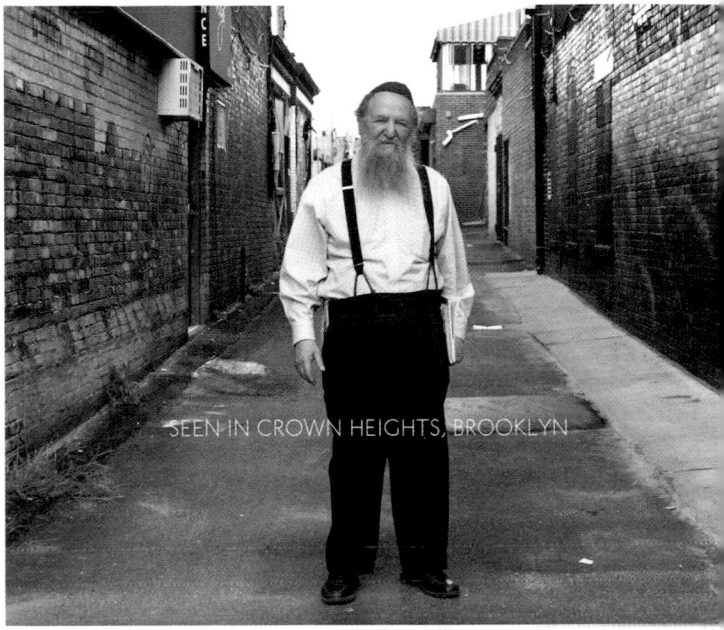

SEEN IN CROWN HEIGHTS, BROOKLYN

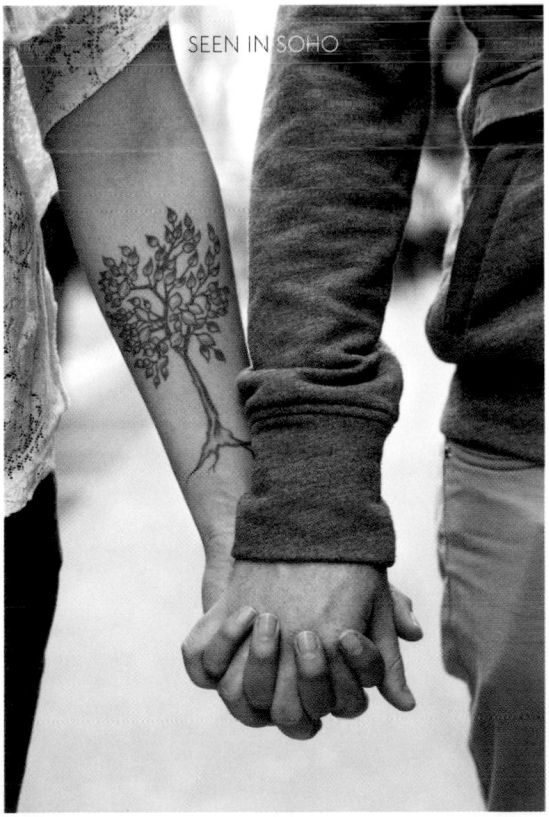

SEEN IN SOHO

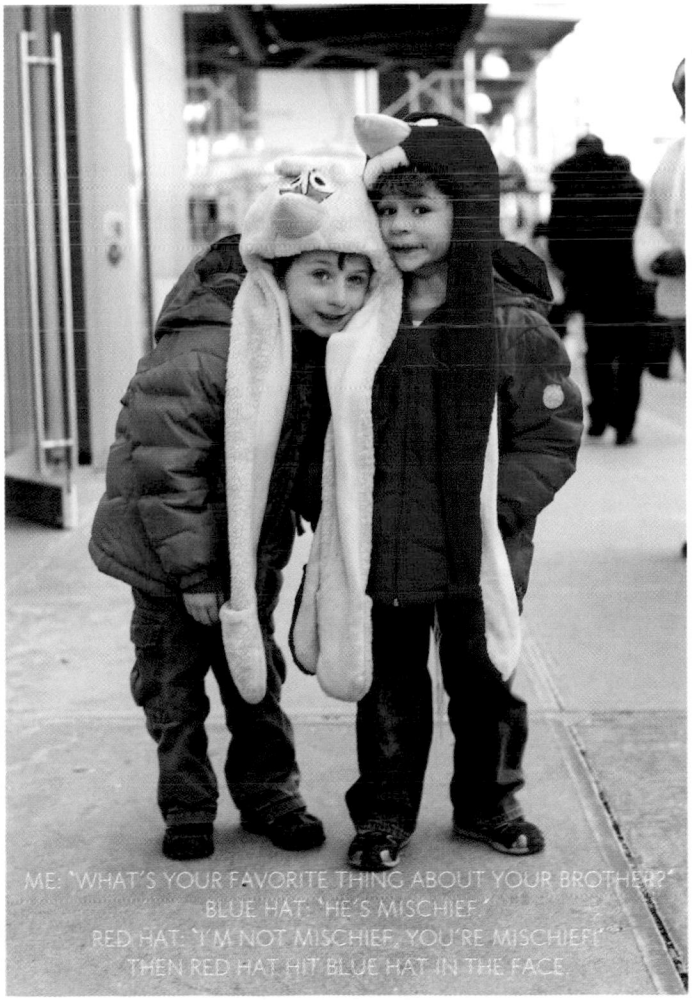

ME: "WHAT'S YOUR FAVORITE THING ABOUT YOUR BROTHER?"
BLUE HAT: "HE'S MISCHIEF."
RED HAT: "I'M NOT MISCHIEF, YOU'RE MISCHIEF!"
THEN RED HAT HIT BLUE HAT IN THE FACE.

COUNT YOUR BLESSINGS

SEEN IN LOWER MIDTOWN

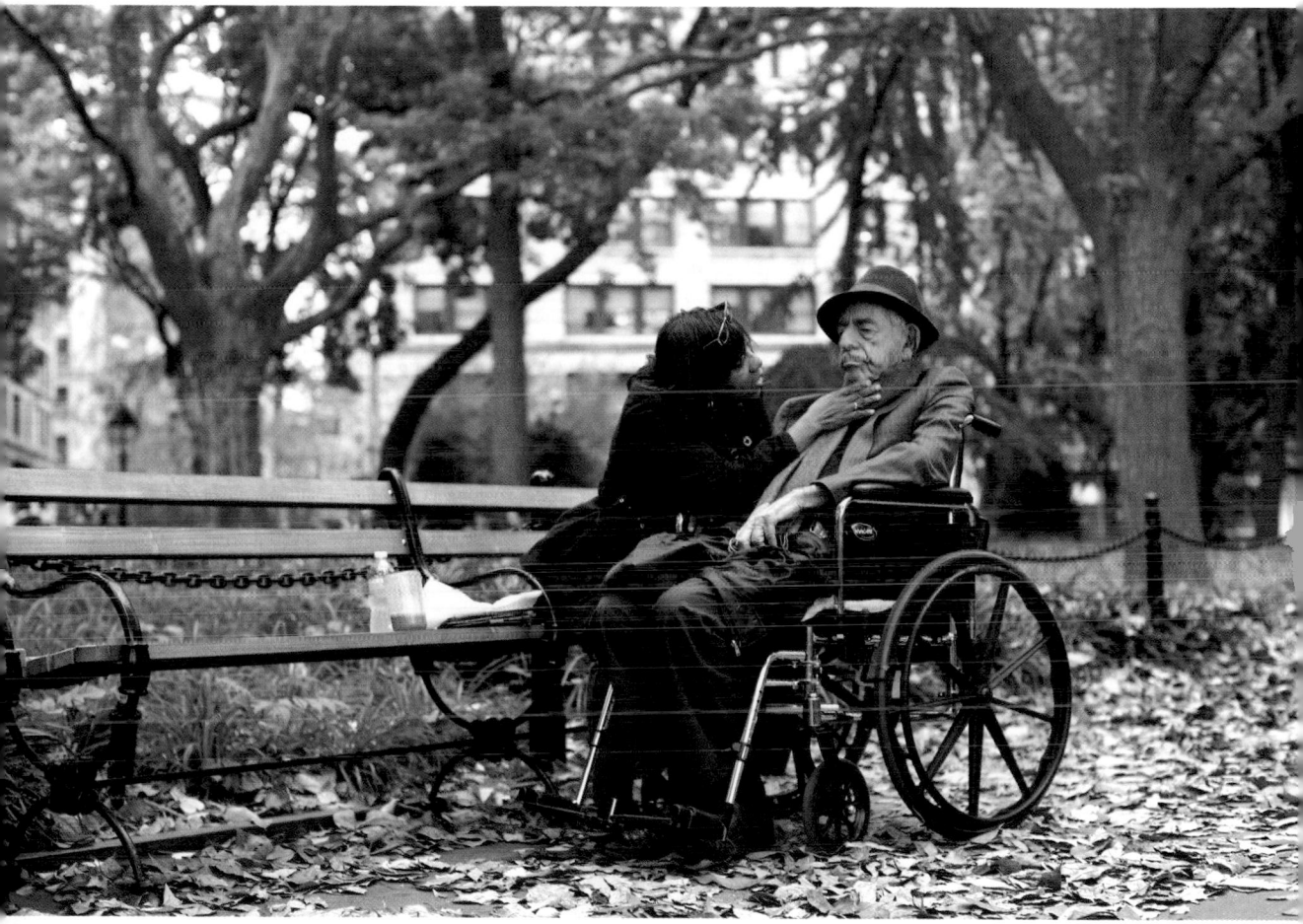

I LEANED DOWN AND ASKED THIS MAN FOR HIS PHOTOGRAPH, BUT THERE WAS NO REPLY. HIS CARETAKER WAS SITTING NEARBY. SHE SMILED AND SAID: "I'M THE ONE YOU NEED TO ASK."

"OH," I ANSWERED. "HE LOOKS WONDERFUL."

SHE SAID, FONDLY: "THAT'S HOW I LIKE HIM TO LOOK."

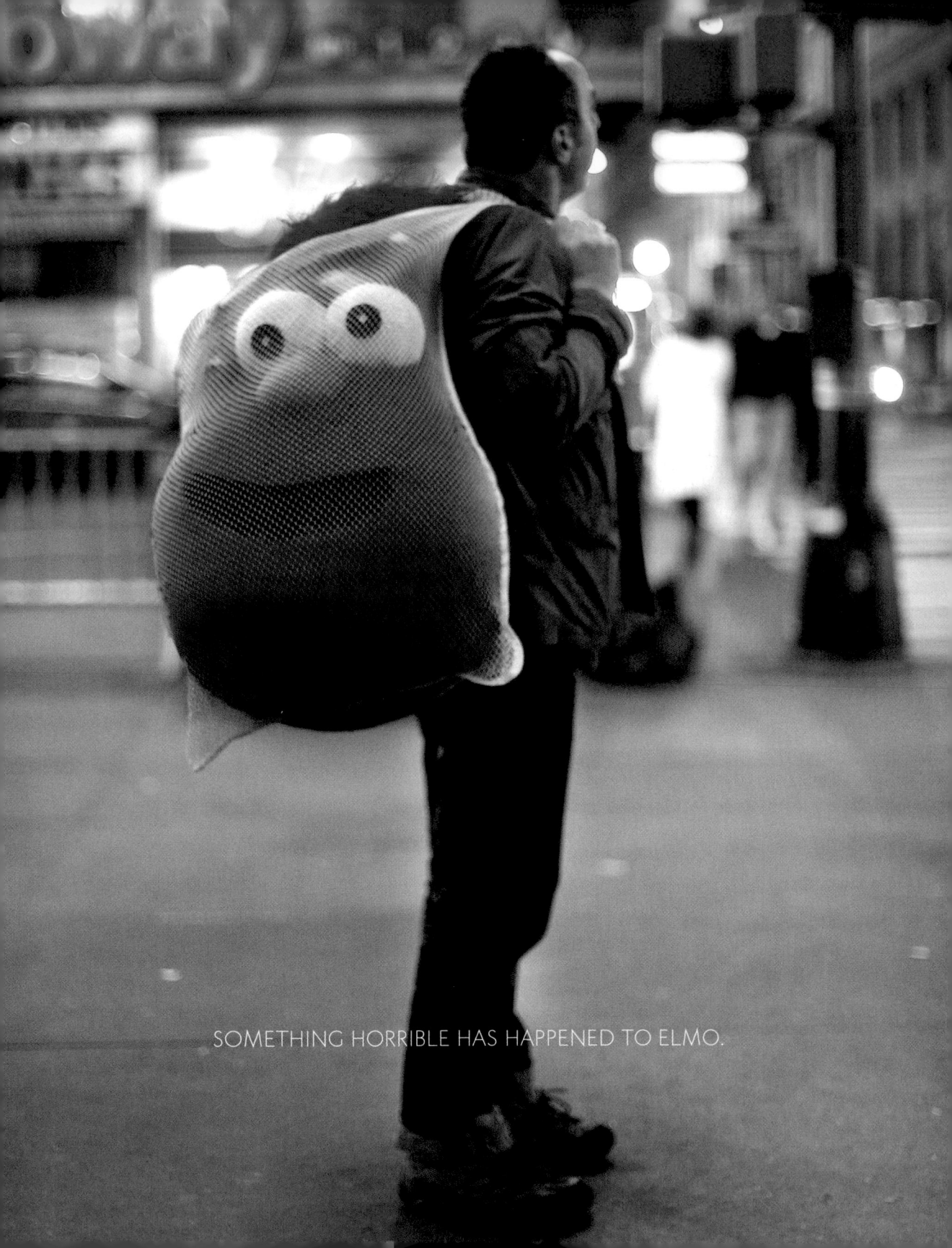
SOMETHING HORRIBLE HAS HAPPENED TO ELMO.

SEEN IN WASHINGTON HEIGHTS

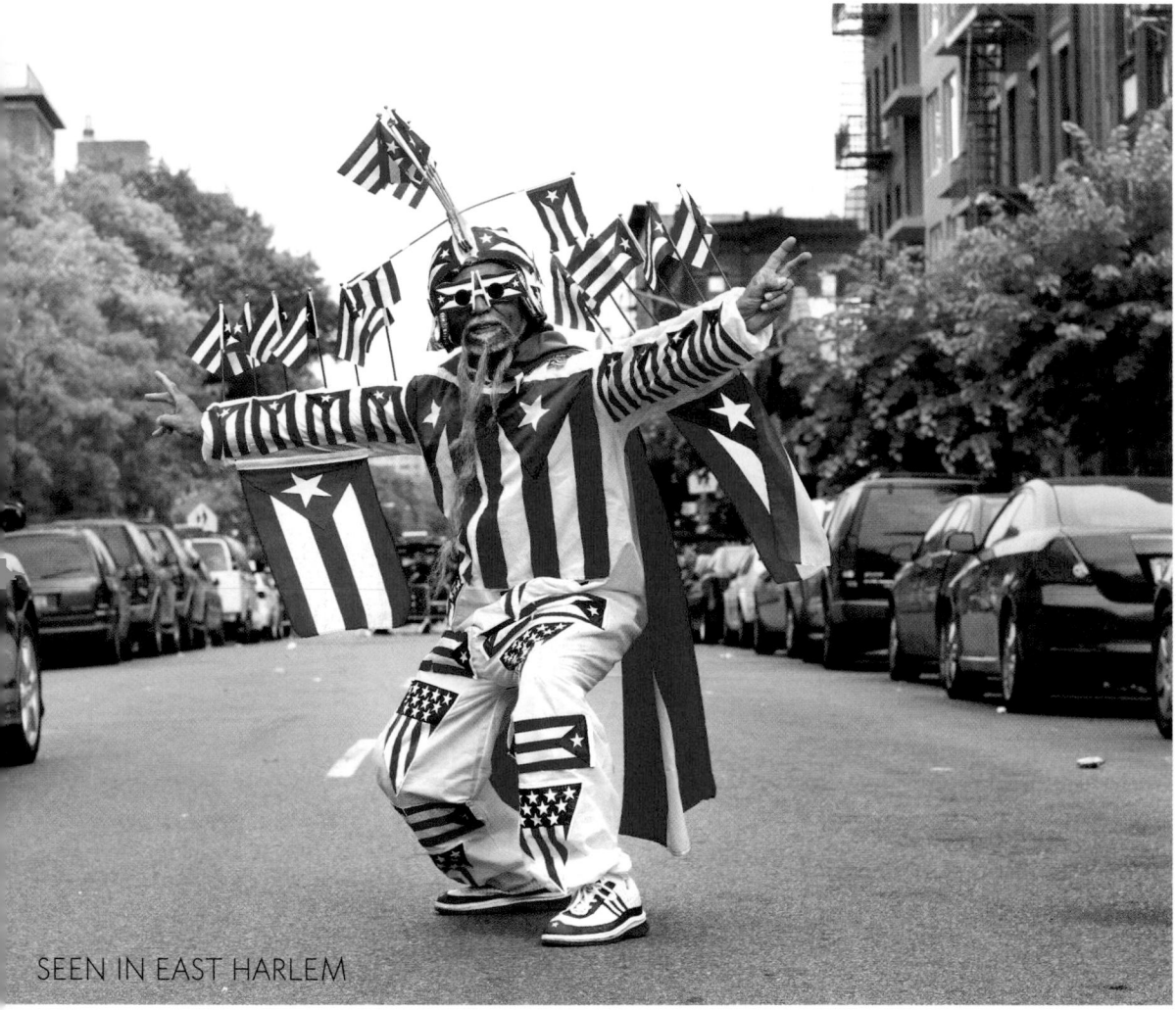

SEEN IN EAST HARLEM

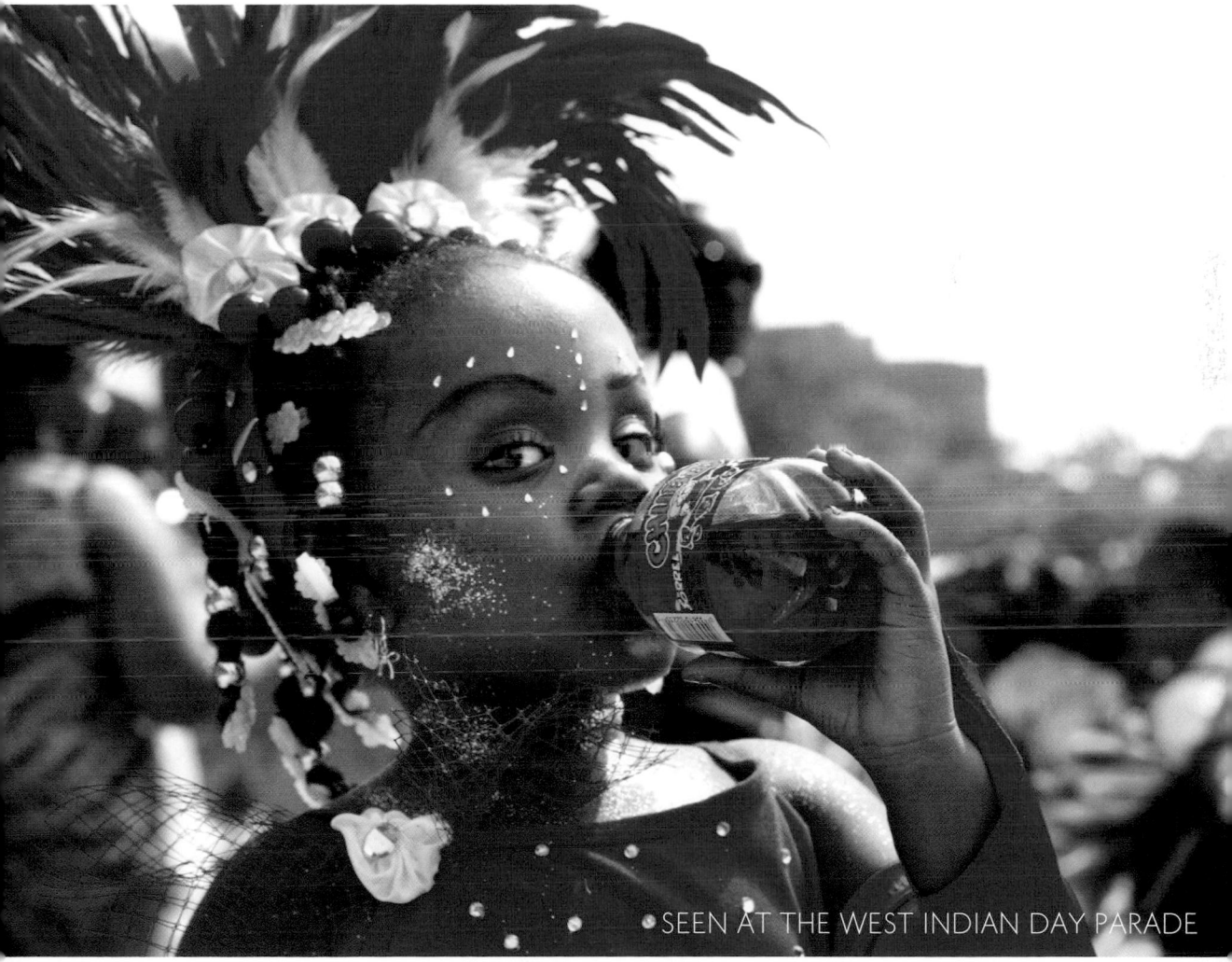

SEEN AT THE WEST INDIAN DAY PARADE

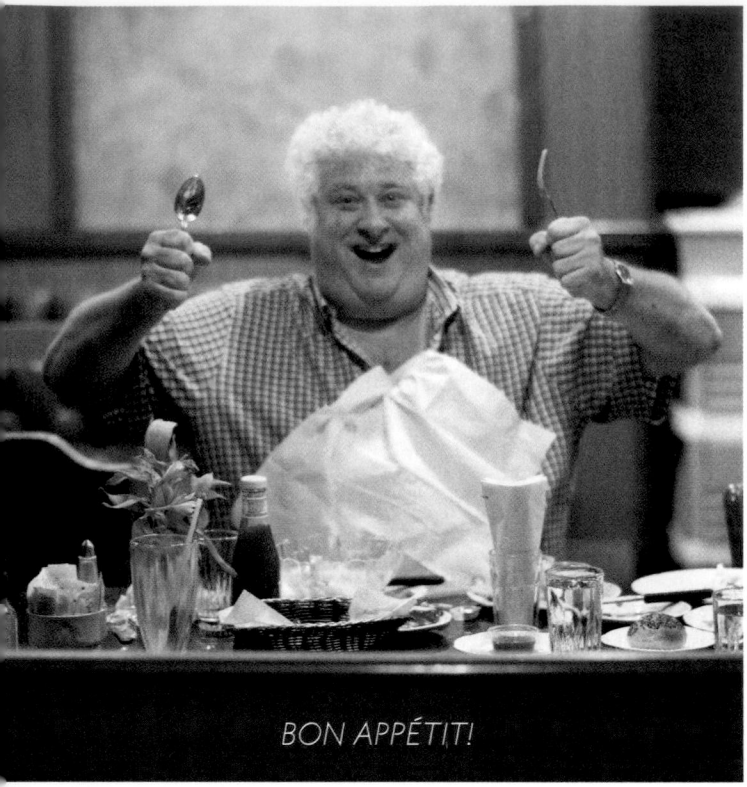

*BON APPÉTIT!*

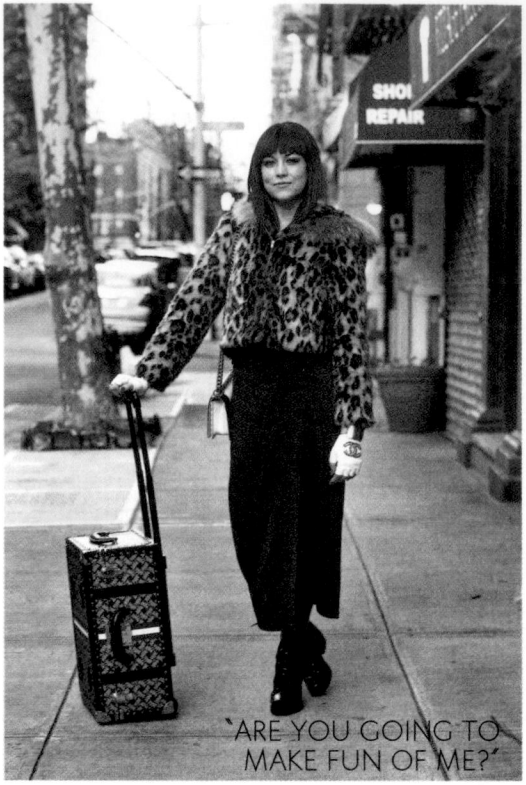


'ARE YOU GOING TO MAKE FUN OF ME?'

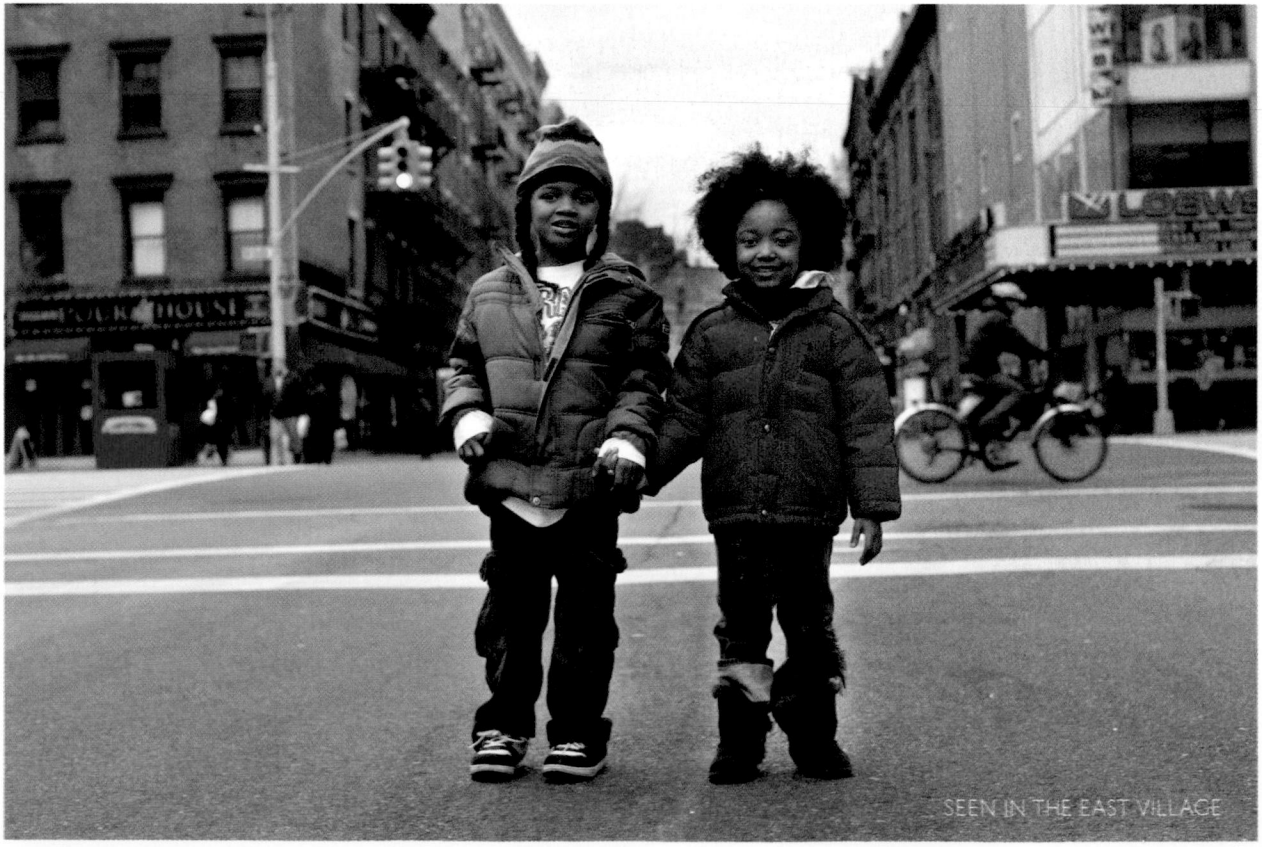


SEEN IN THE EAST VILLAGE

"DO YOU MIND IF I TAKE YOUR PHOTO, JUST LIKE THAT?"

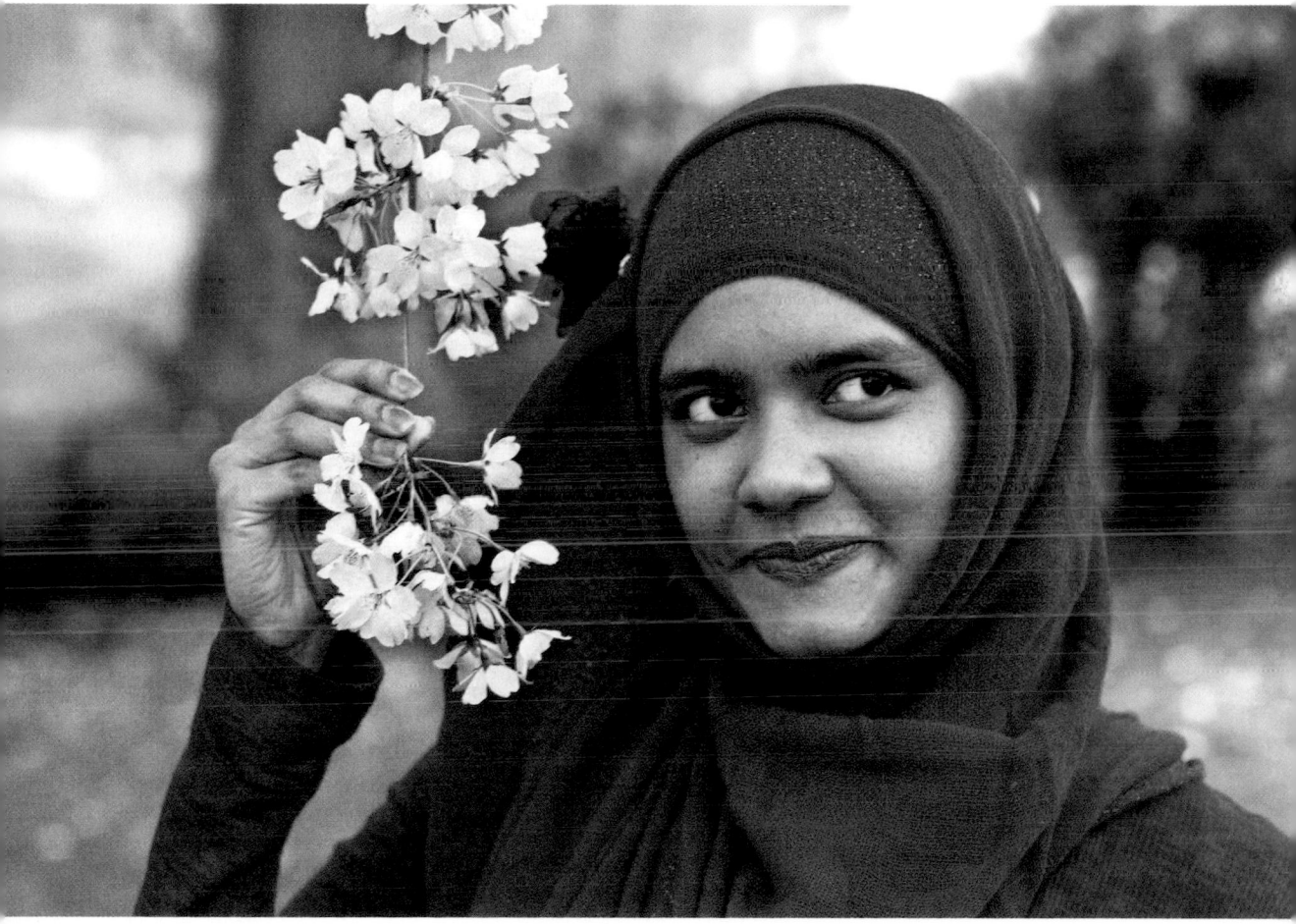

"I DON'T KNOW . . ."

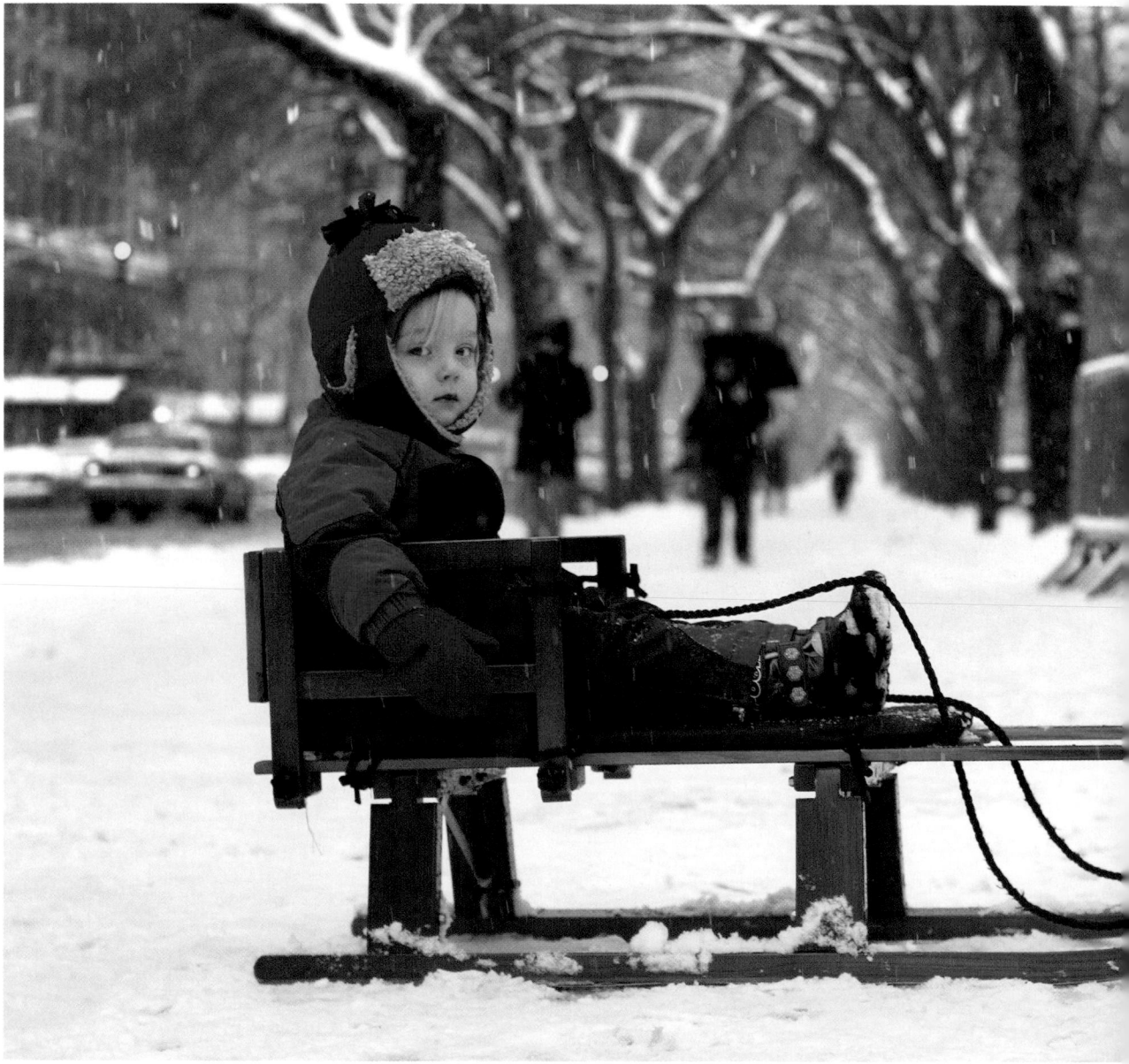

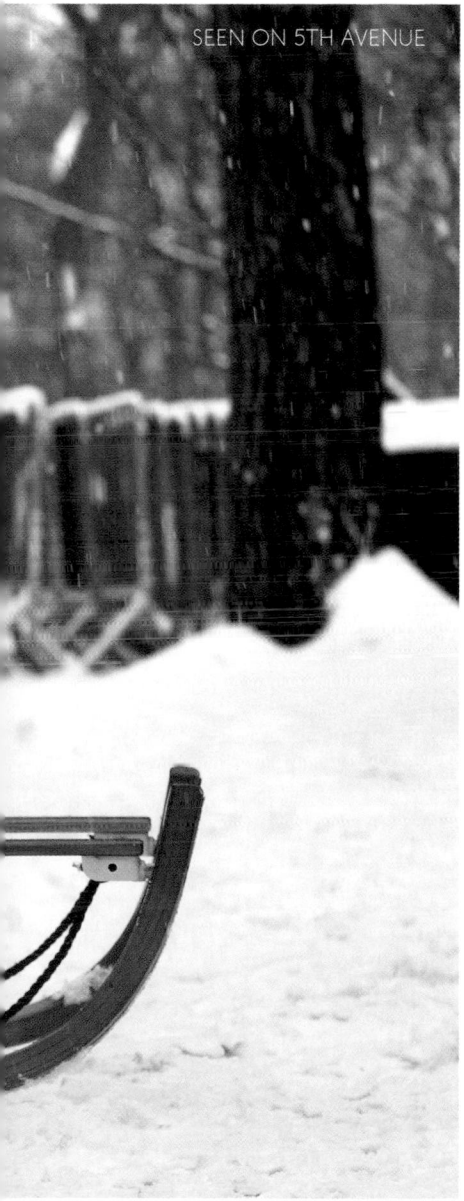


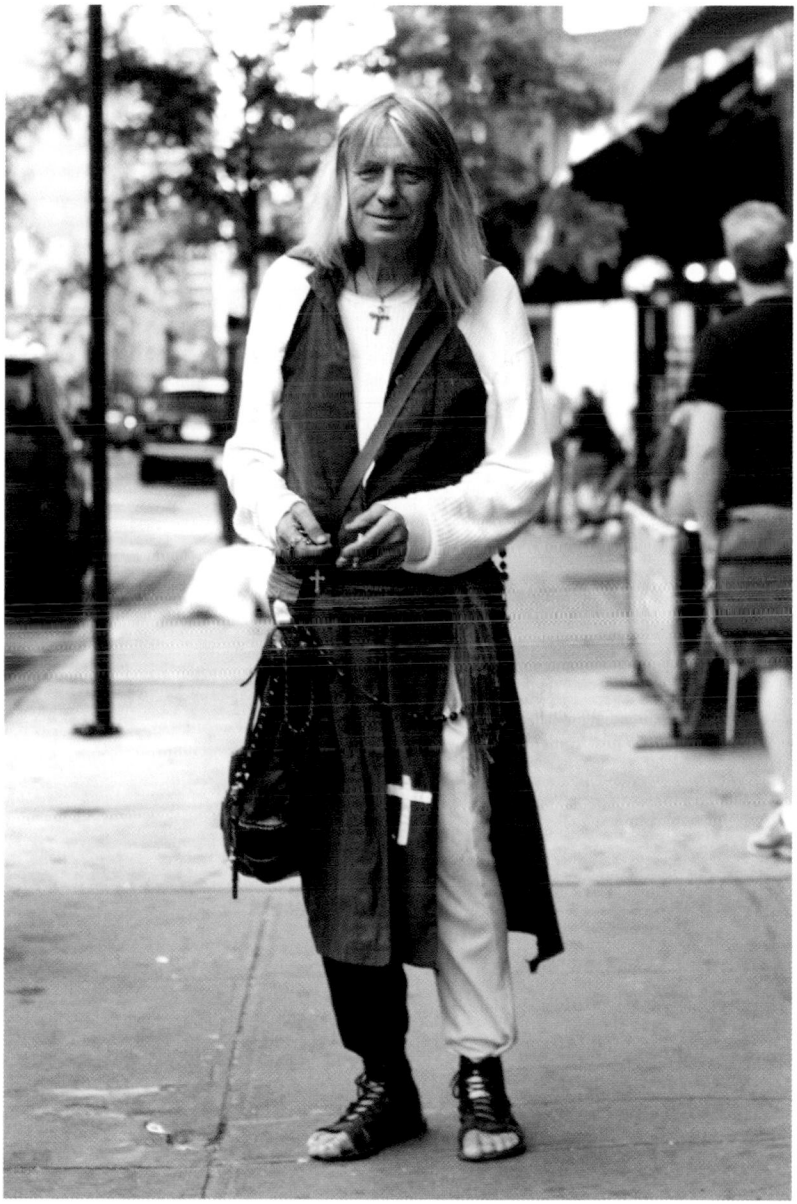

'I'M A CATHOLIC MONK. I LIVE A LIFE OF PRAYER.'
'WHAT ABOUT THE CIGARETTE?'
'SOMEBODY'S GOT TO MAKE THE CLOUDS.'

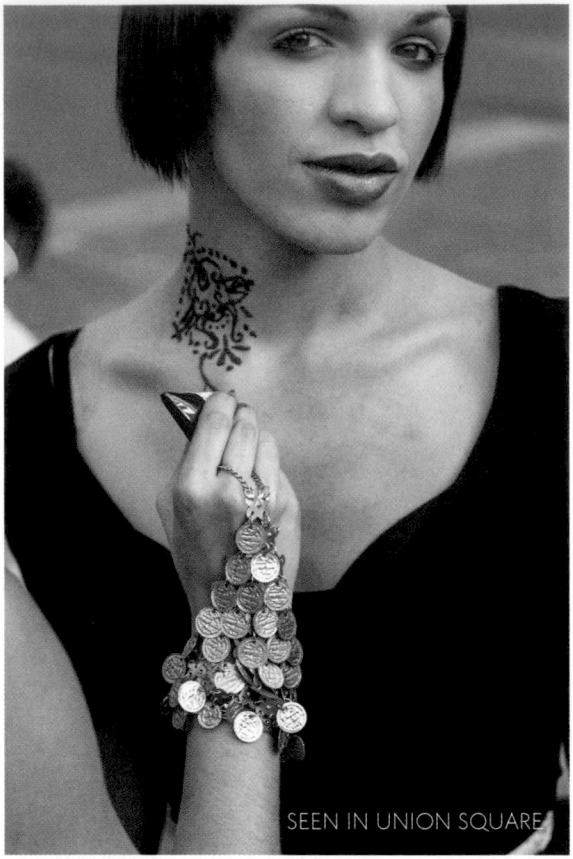

SEEN IN UNION SQUARE

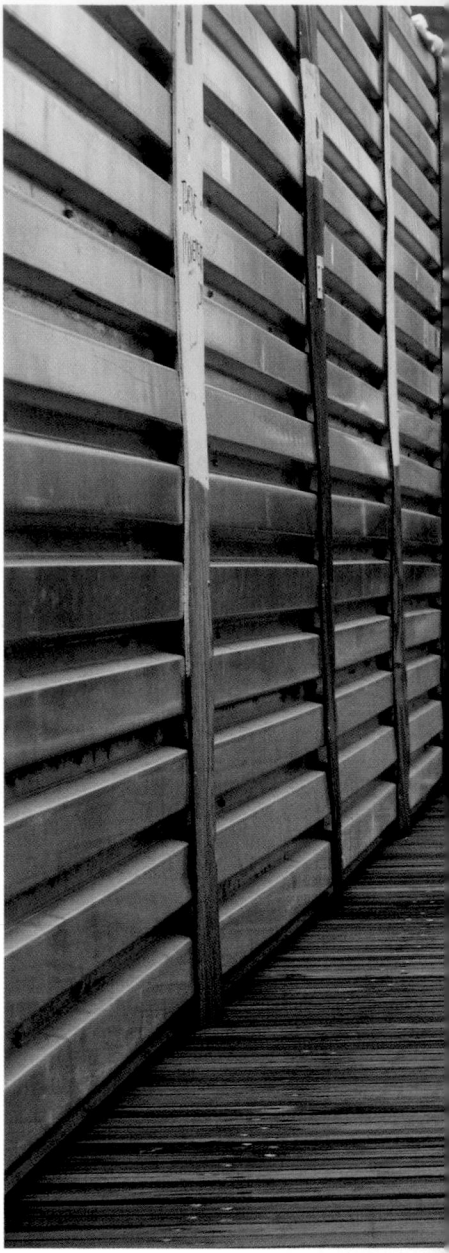

THEY MAY NOT BE WINNING ANY SAFETY AWARDS, BUT THEY MADE FOR A GREAT PHOTO.

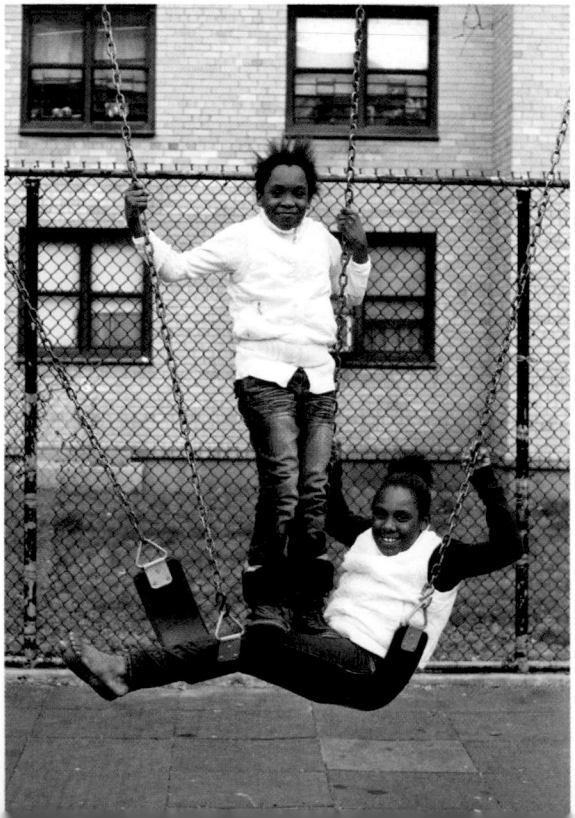

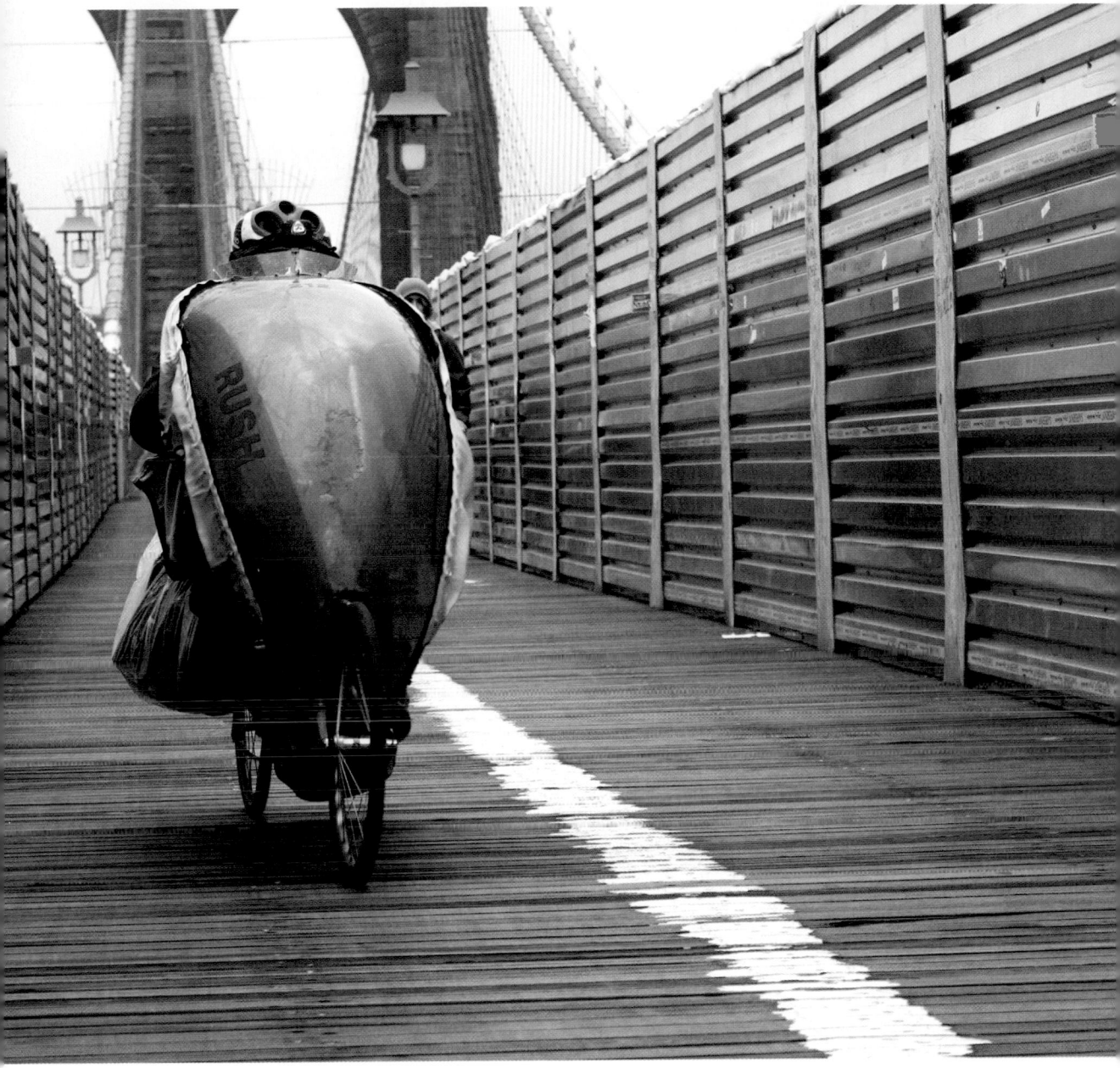


I WAS WALKING ACROSS THE BROOKLYN BRIDGE WHEN I NOTICED THIS STRANGE MISSILE COMING TOWARD ME AT A VERY HIGH SPEED. I PLANTED MYSELF DIRECTLY IN ITS PATH, HOPING TO CATCH A GREAT SHOT. THE VEHICLE VEERED AWAY AT THE LAST MOMENT, AND AS IT PASSED, THE RIDER SHOUTED THESE WORDS: "COO-COO! CAH-CAH! WOO-HOO!"

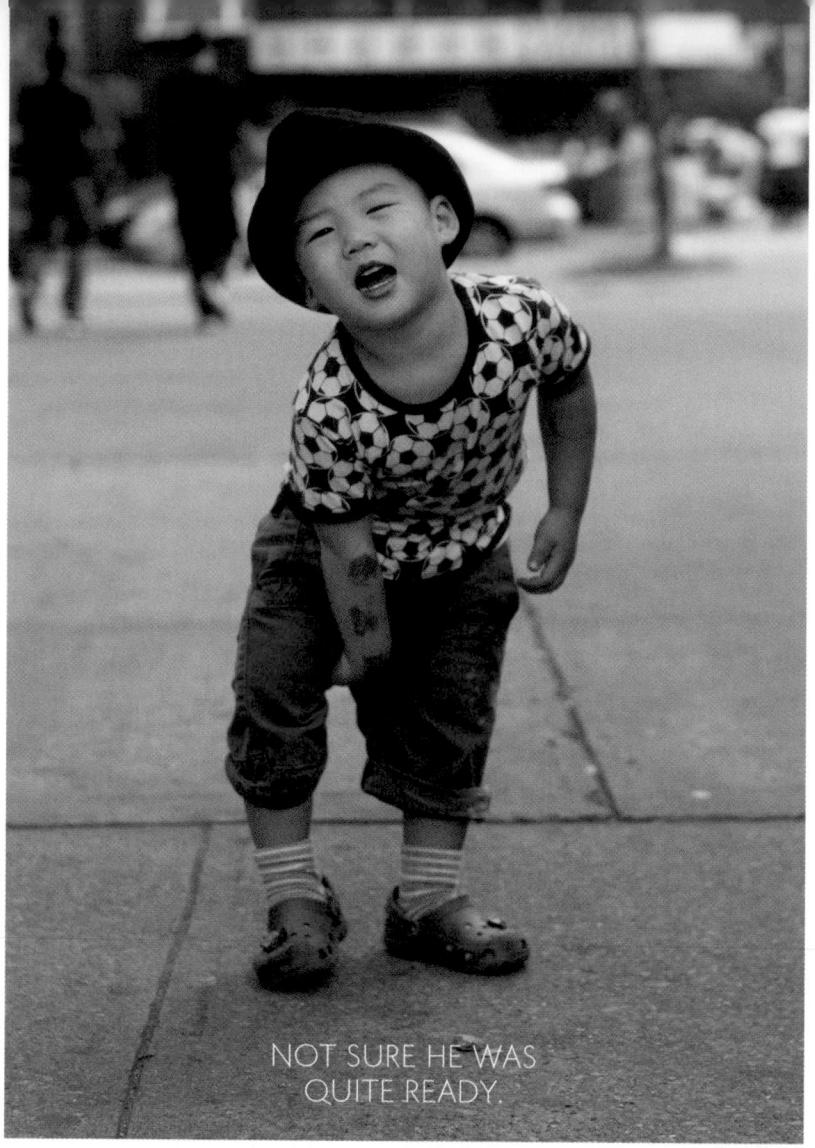

NOT SURE HE WAS
QUITE READY.

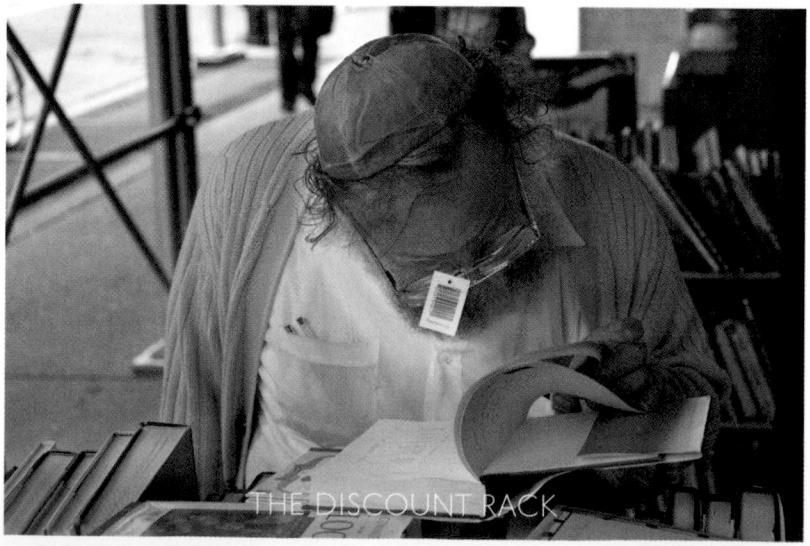

THE DISCOUNT RACK

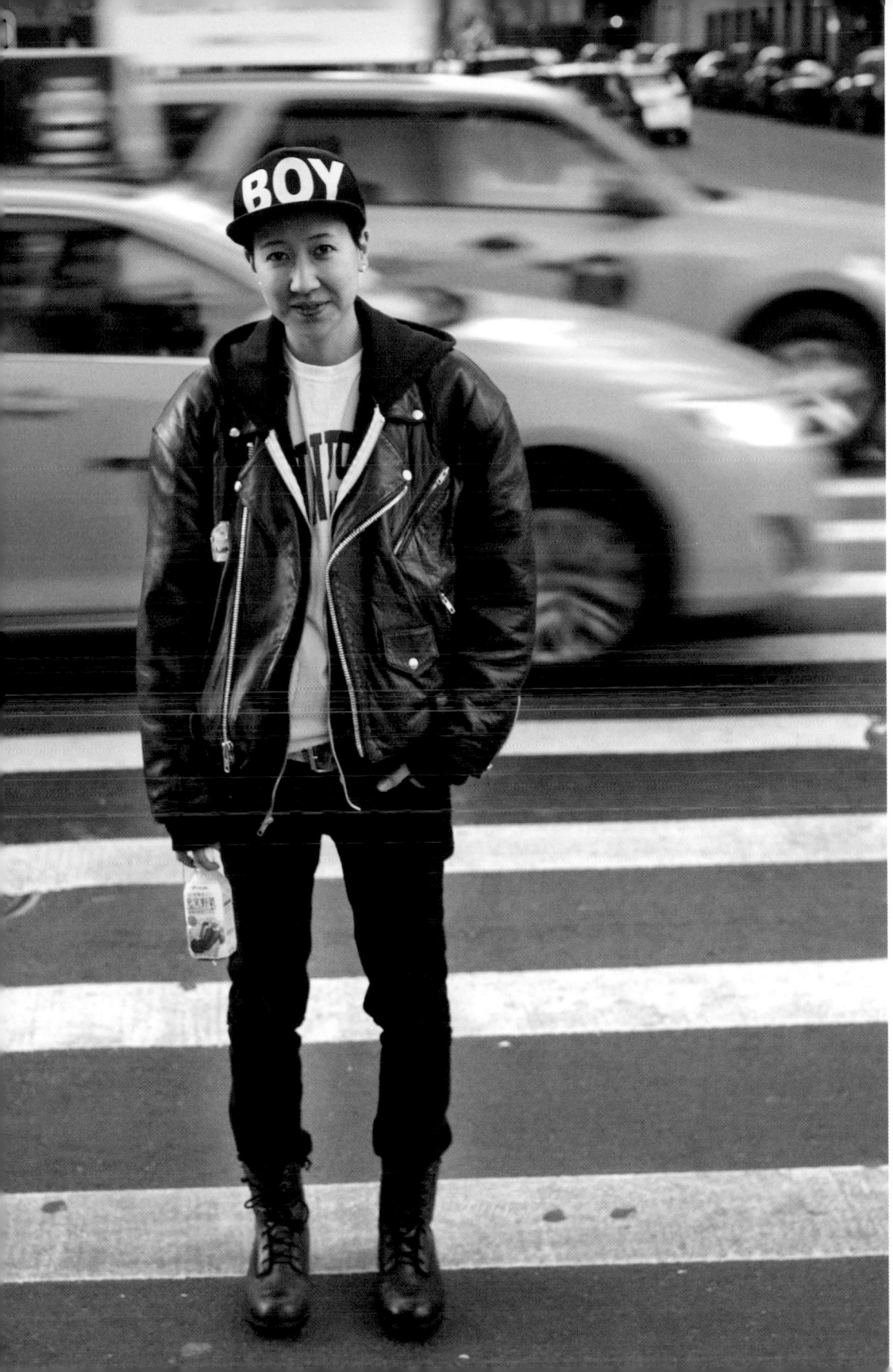


GIRL

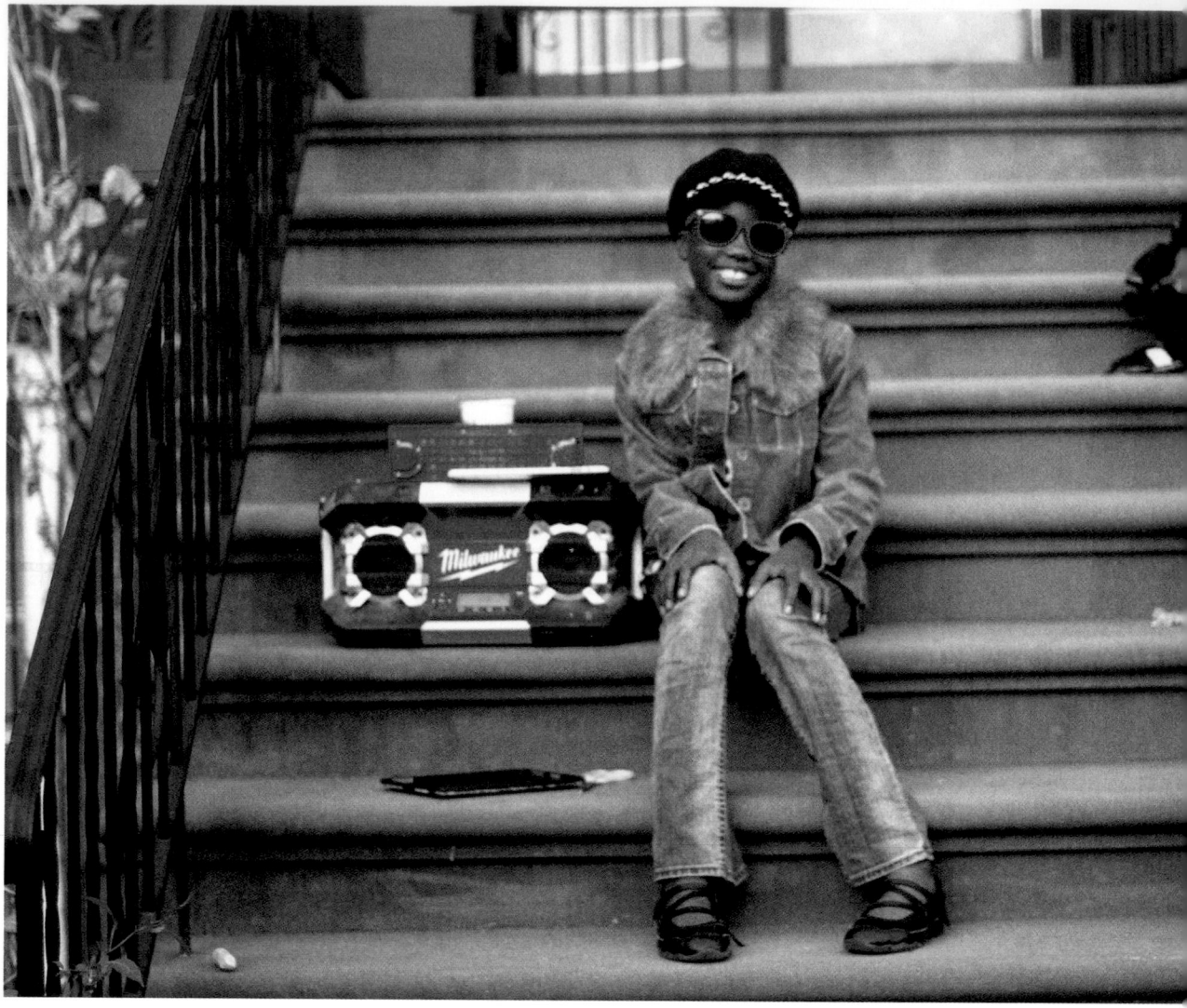


WHEN I WALKED BY, SHE WAS REALLY MOVING TO THE MUSIC—HANDS UP, HEAD NODDING, SHOULDERS SWINGING. I REALLY WANTED TO TAKE HER PHOTO, SO I WALKED UP TO THE NEAREST ADULT AND ASKED: "DOES SHE BELONG TO YOU?"

SUDDENLY THE MUSIC STOPPED, AND I HEARD: "I BELONG TO MYSELF!"

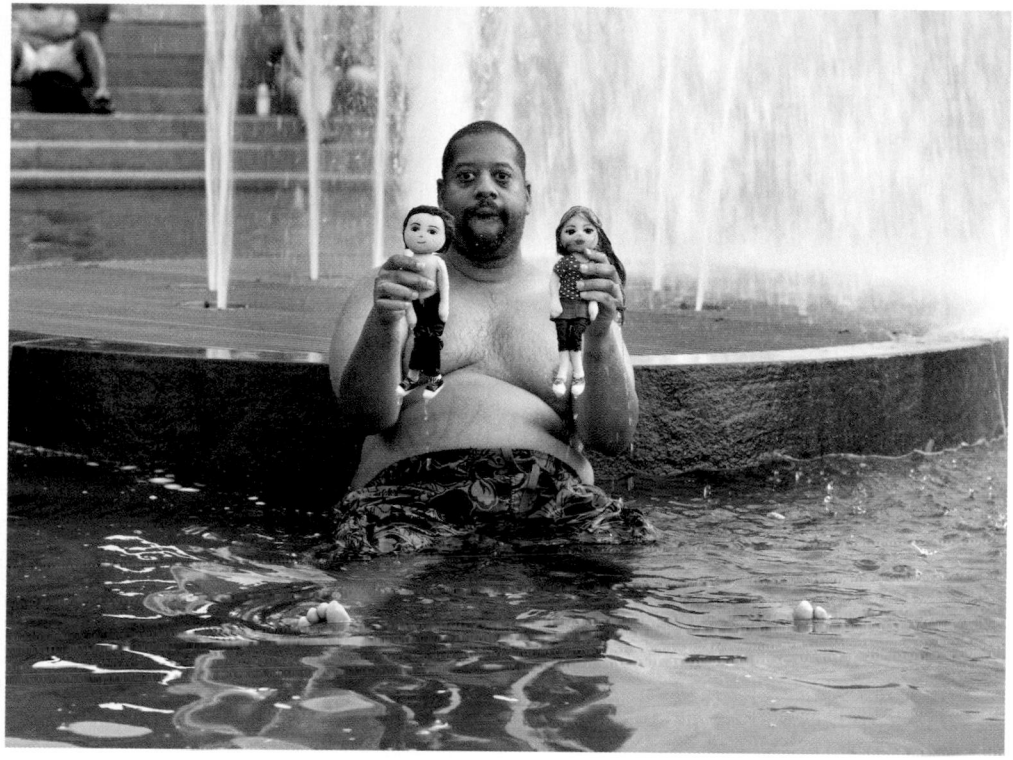

ON SUMMER DAYS, THIS MAN CAN OFTEN BE SEEN IN THE FOUNTAIN AT WASHINGTON SQUARE PARK.

"HE WAS BORN ON SAINT PATRICK'S DAY, AND EVERY YEAR THEY THROW HIM A PARADE!"

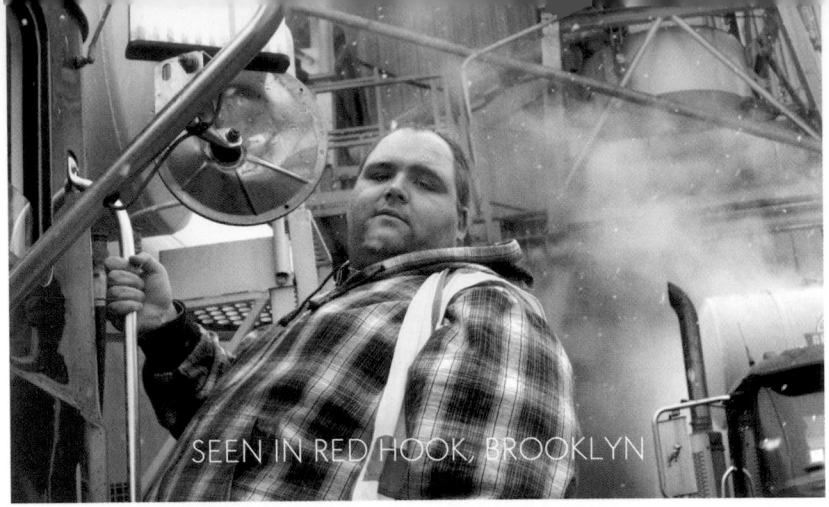

SEEN IN RED HOOK, BROOKLYN

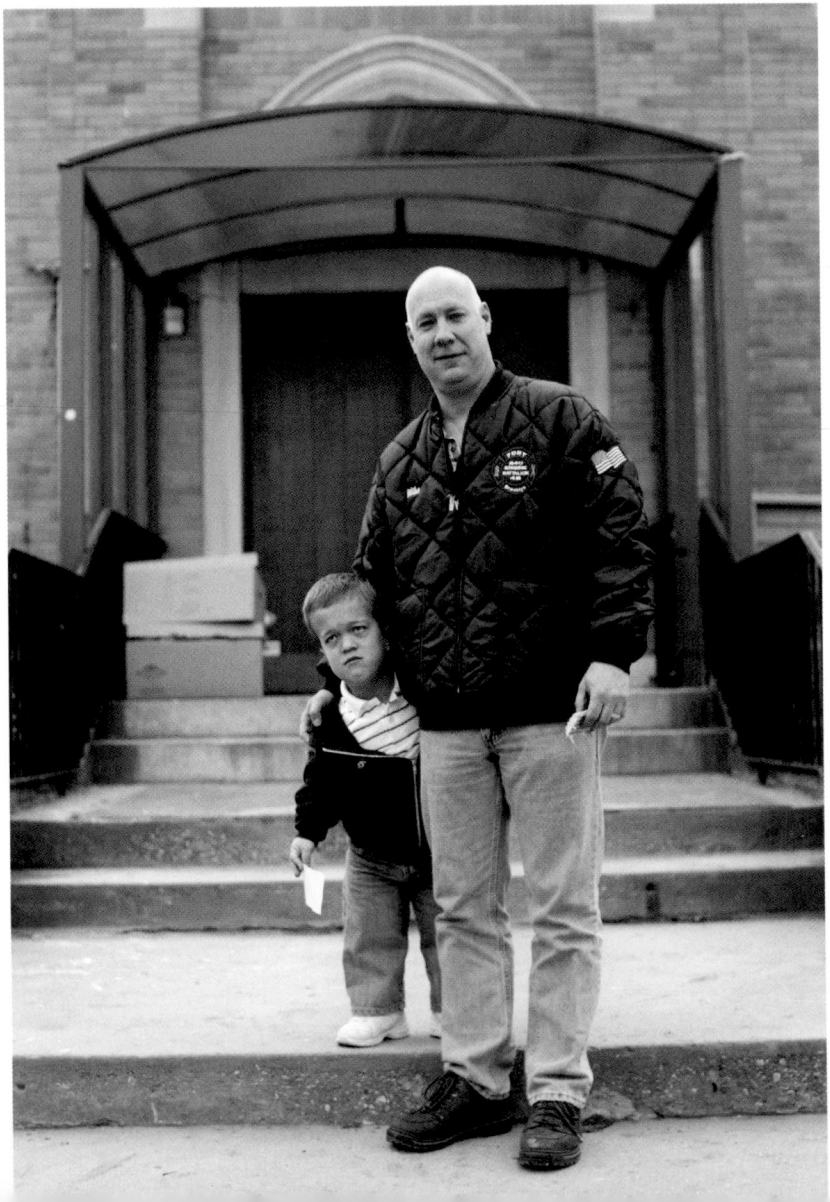

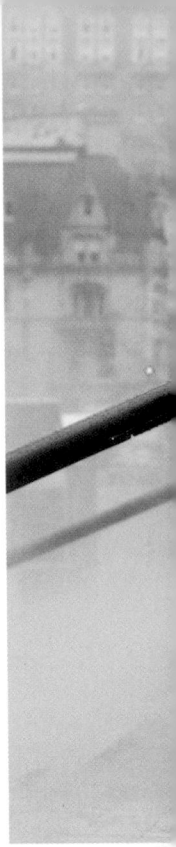

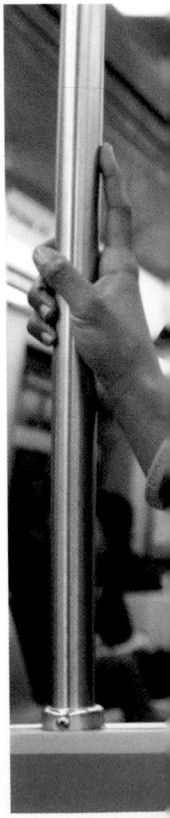

"I'M THE CHIEF OF PERSONNEL FOR THE FIRE DEPARTMENT. I'M MAKING SURE EVERYONE IS WHERE THEY NEED TO BE AND HAS WHAT THEY NEED."

"DO YOU MIND IF I TAKE YOUR PHOTO?"

"CAN MY SON BE IN THE PICTURE?"

STEAM WAS COMING OFF THE STEPS OF THE MET THAT MORNING—IT MADE FOR A VERY SURREAL SCENE. I ASKED A COUPLE OF PEOPLE FOR A PORTRAIT, BUT BOTH SAID NO. THANKFULLY I WAS BAILED OUT BY THIS ADVENTUROUS MAN WITH A FRENCH ACCENT.

SHE WAS RECITING SOME UP-TEMPO SPOKEN-WORD POETRY ON THE SUBWAY. "IT'S FREE THIS TIME," SHE ANNOUNCED. "BUT Y'ALL GONNA HAVE TO PAY WHEN I GET TO THE APOLLO!"

NOT EVERYBODY WAS INTO THE PARADE.

FOUND THESE TWO OLD FRIENDS WRESTLING ON A SIDEWALK IN BEDFORD-STUYVESANT, BROOKLYN.

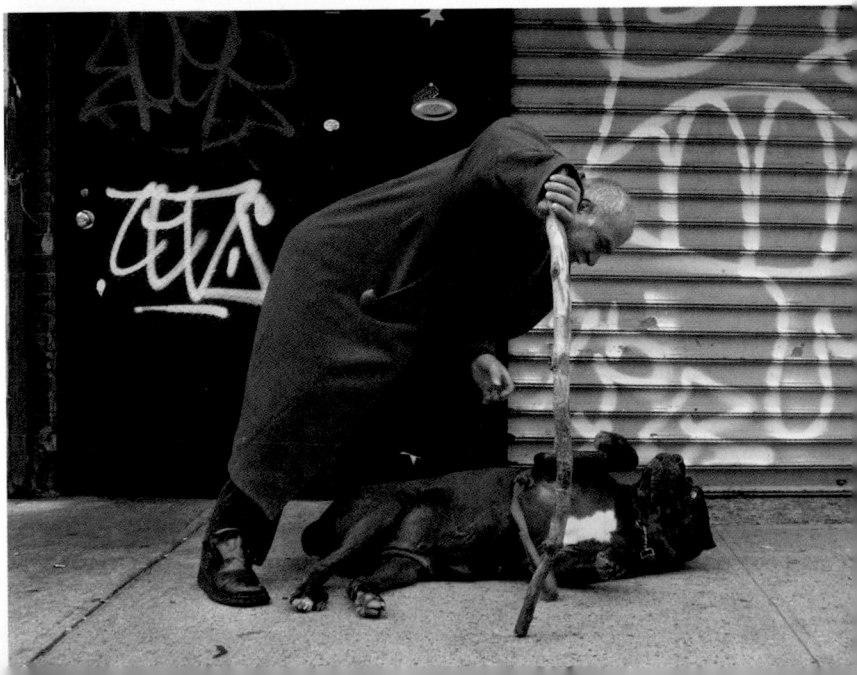

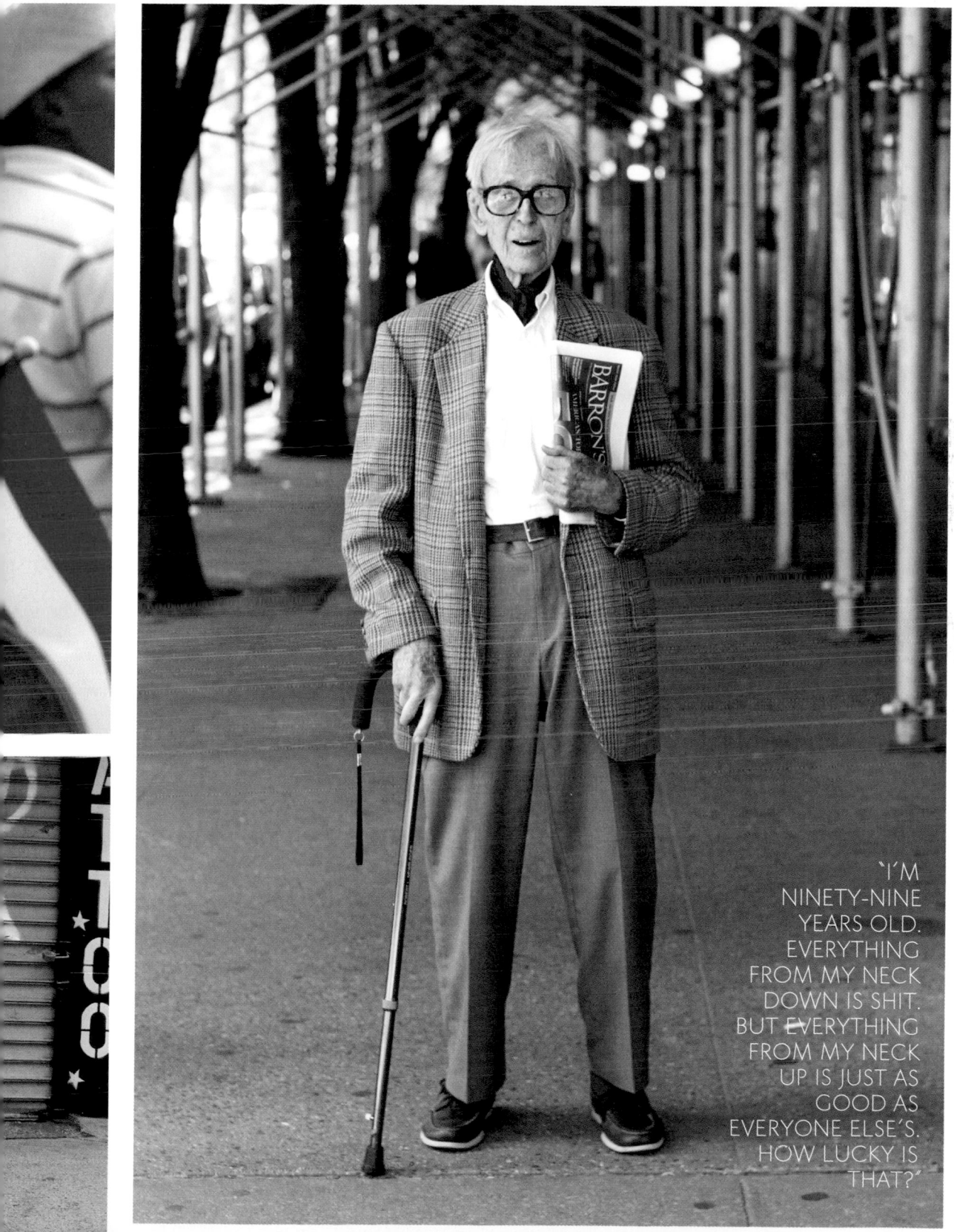


'I'M NINETY-NINE YEARS OLD. EVERYTHING FROM MY NECK DOWN IS SHIT. BUT EVERYTHING FROM MY NECK UP IS JUST AS GOOD AS EVERYONE ELSE'S. HOW LUCKY IS THAT?'

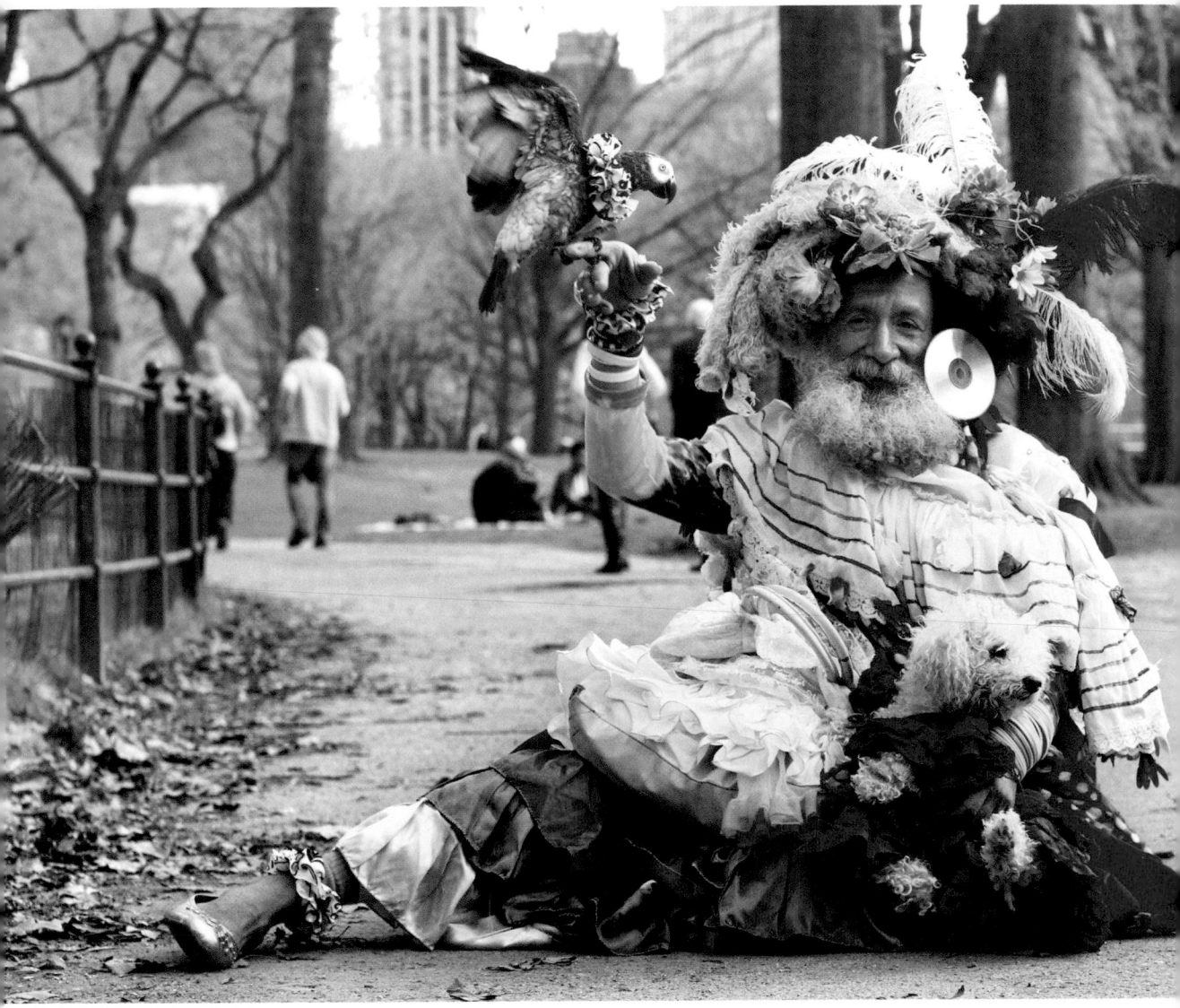

MS. COLOMBIA WAS A LAWYER,
UNTIL SHE LEARNED THAT SHE HAD HIV.

THEN SHE BECAME MS. COLOMBIA.

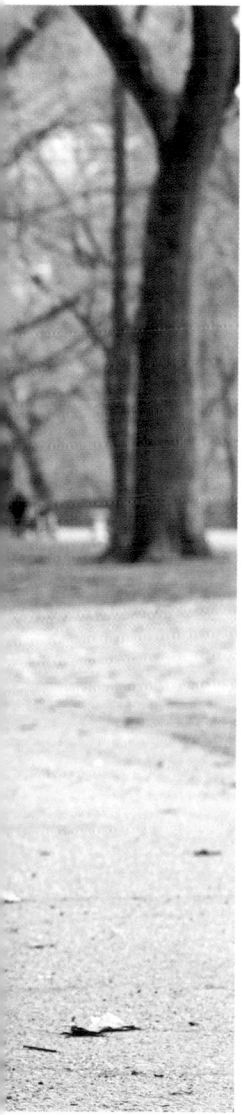

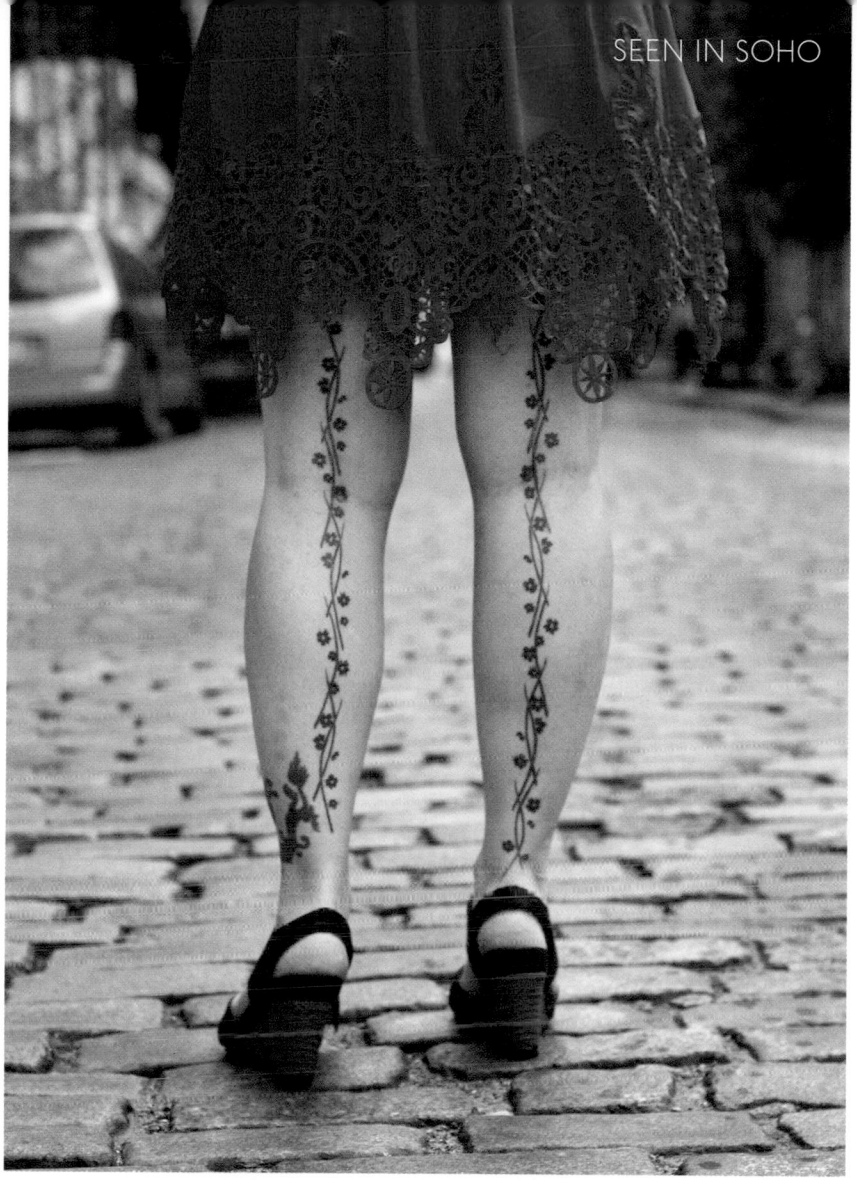
SEEN IN SOHO

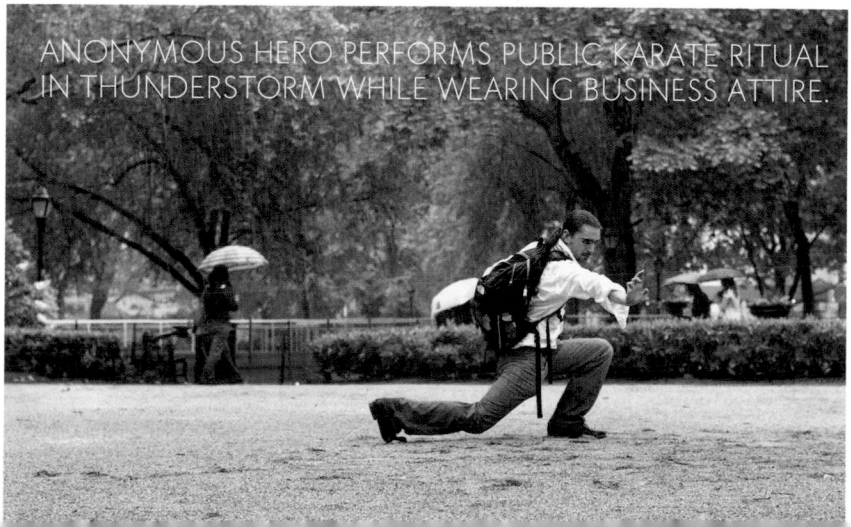
ANONYMOUS HERO PERFORMS PUBLIC KARATE RITUAL
IN THUNDERSTORM WHILE WEARING BUSINESS ATTIRE.

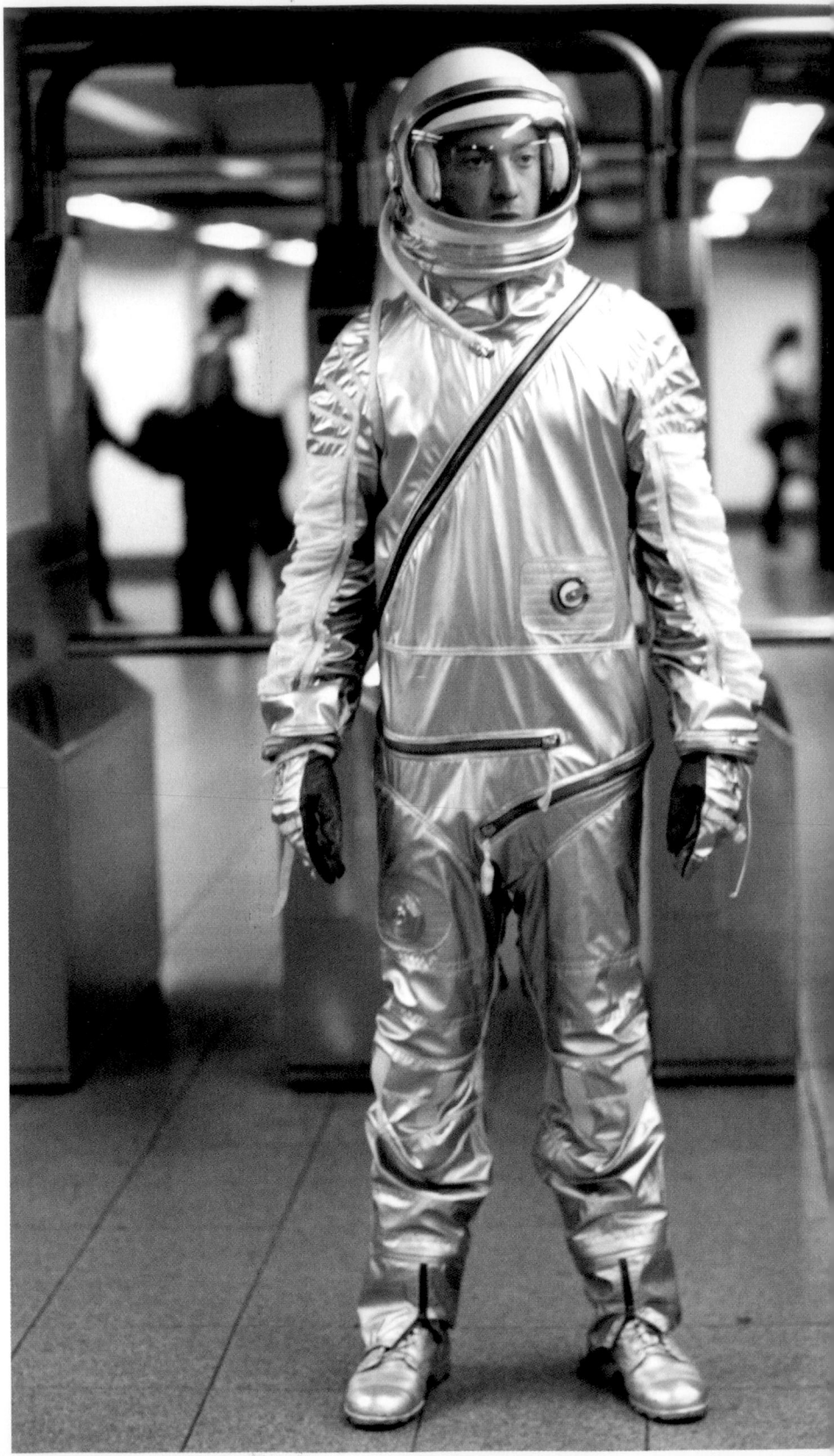

THE MORNING COMMUTE CAN BE HELL FOR A GERMOPHOBE.

"I'M THE WHOLE HAM!"

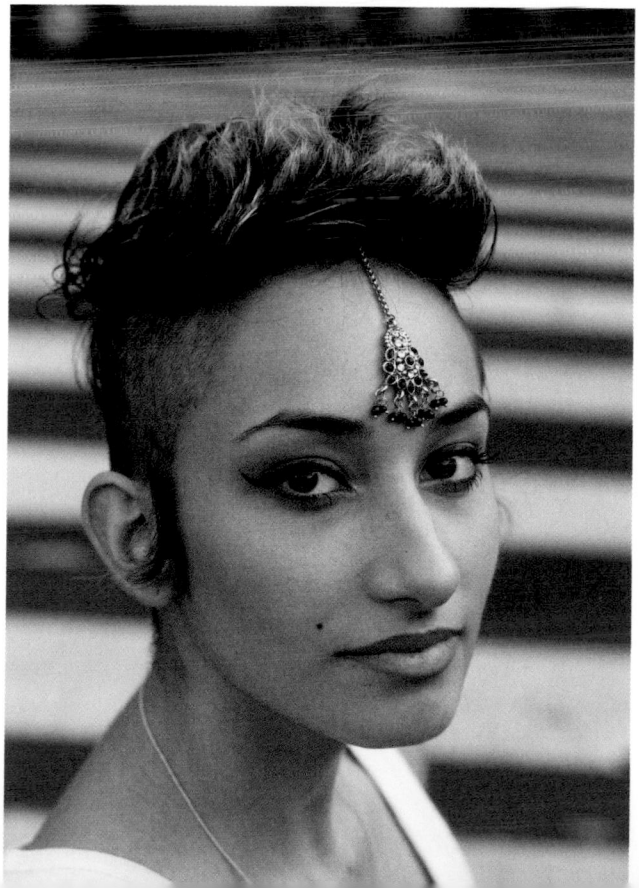

"IT SEEMS THAT A LOT OF PEOPLE MY AGE TRY TO BE INTERESTING BY HAVING PROBLEMS OR STARTING CONFLICTS. I'D RATHER BE INTERESTING BECAUSE I CREATED SOMETHING BEAUTIFUL."

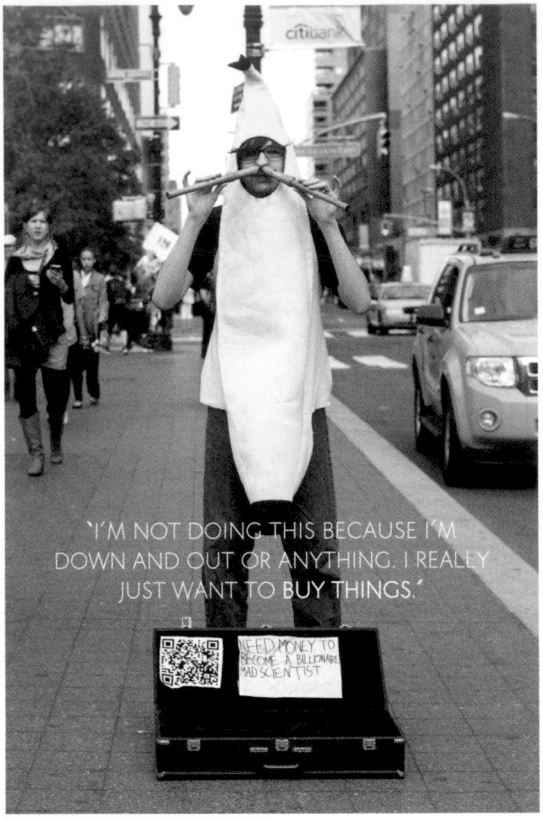


"I'M NOT DOING THIS BECAUSE I'M DOWN AND OUT OR ANYTHING. I REALLY JUST WANT TO **BUY THINGS.**"

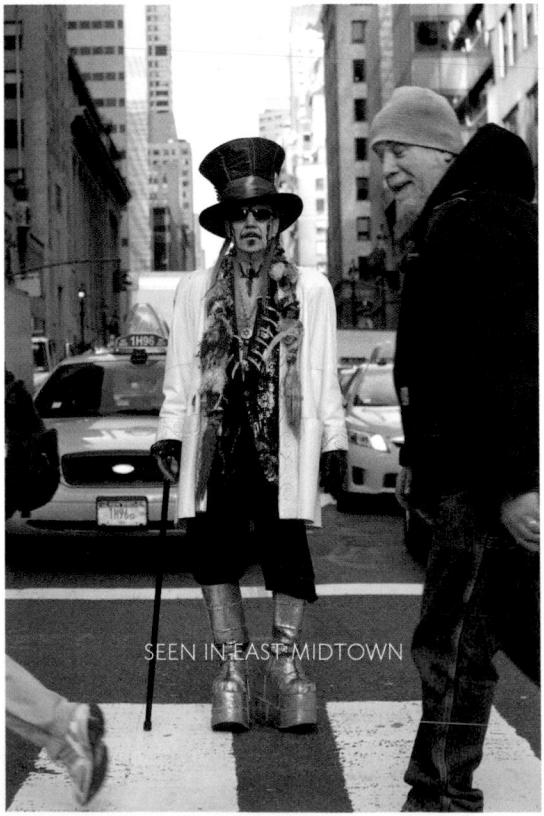

SEEN IN EAST MIDTOWN

"MY MOM DIED WHEN I WAS EIGHTEEN. I ACTED LIKE IT DIDN'T BOTHER ME 'CAUSE I WAS A PUNK ROCK KID. BUT I THINK IT CAME BACK TO ME LATER IN WEIRD WAYS."

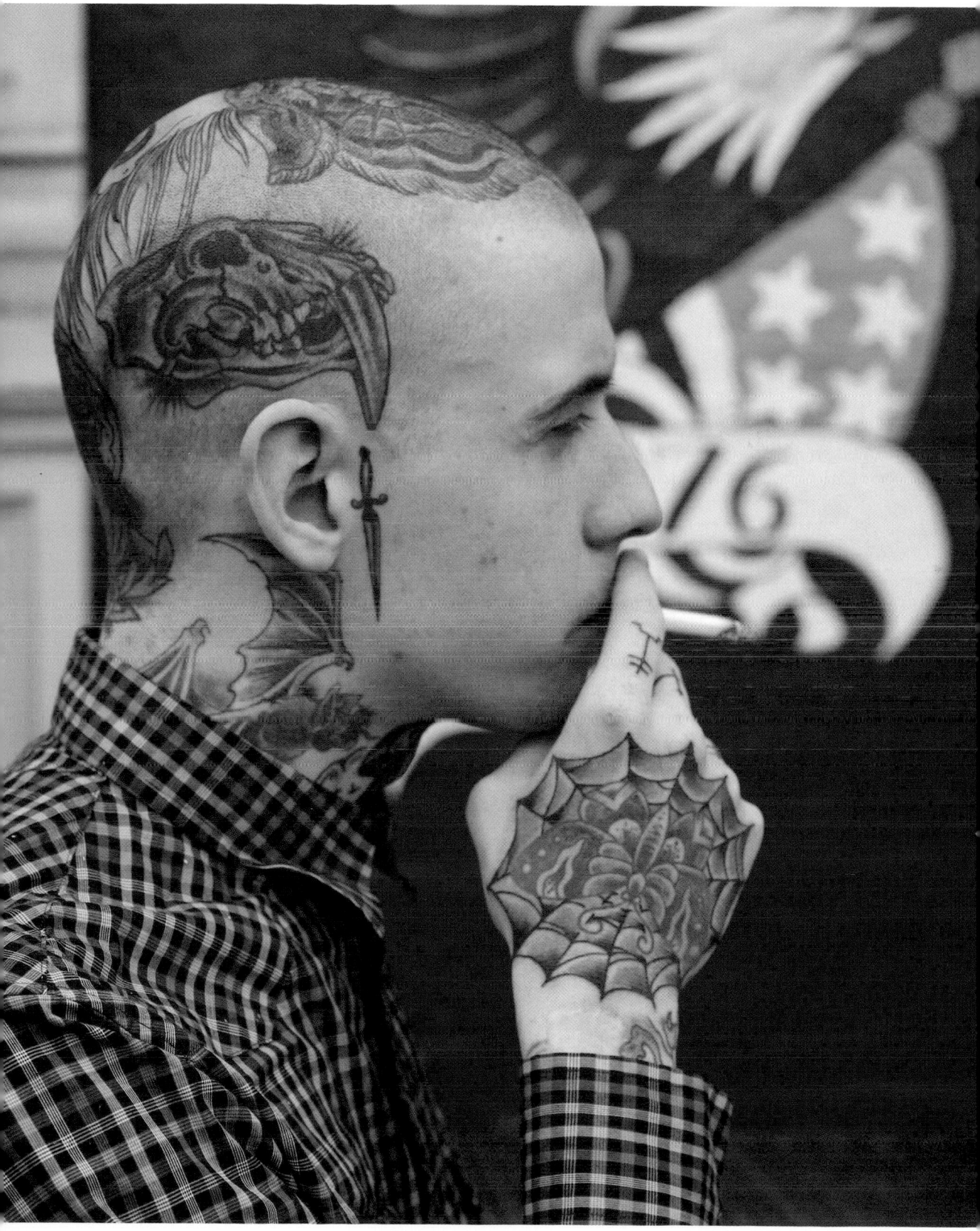

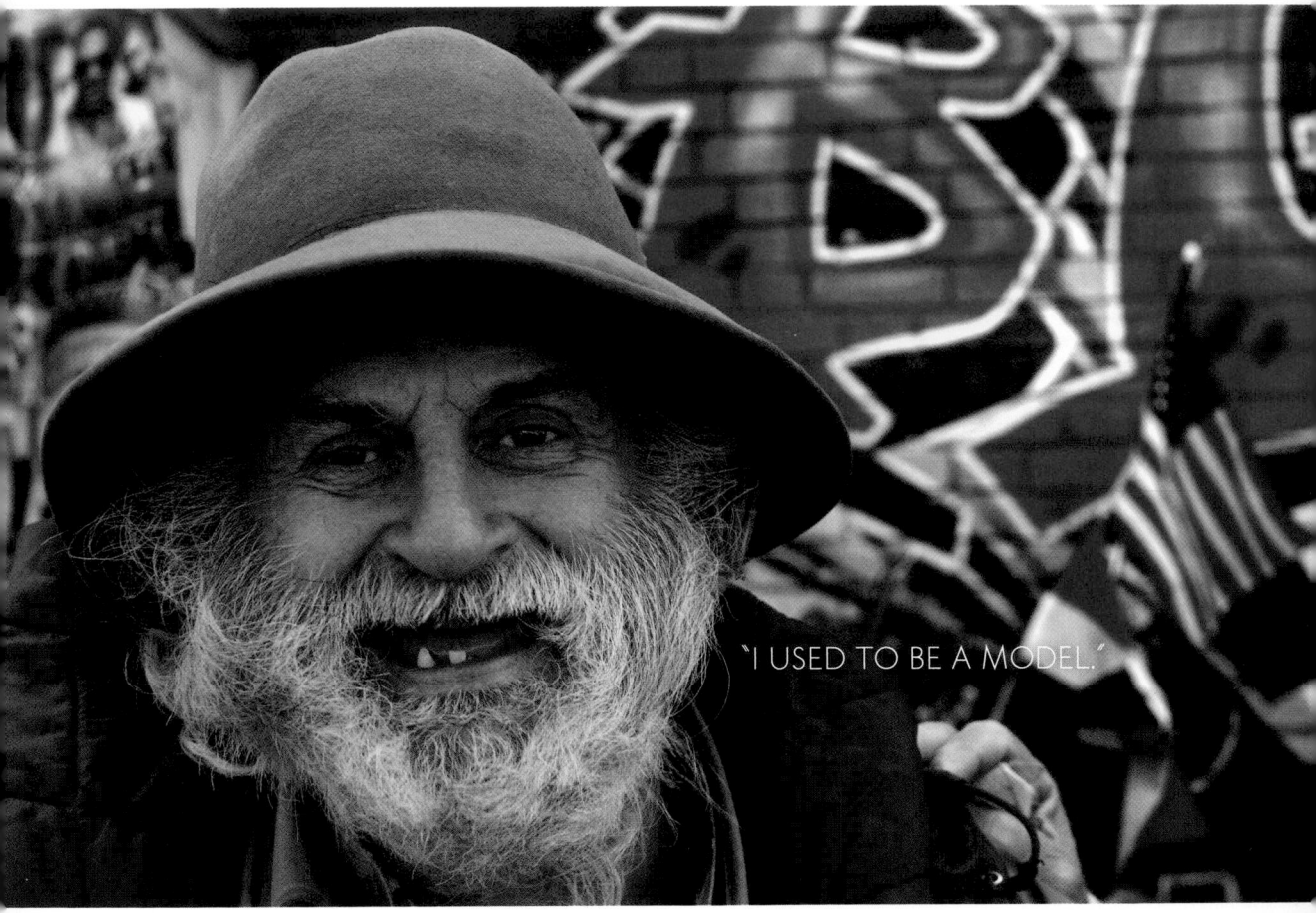
"I USED TO BE A MODEL."

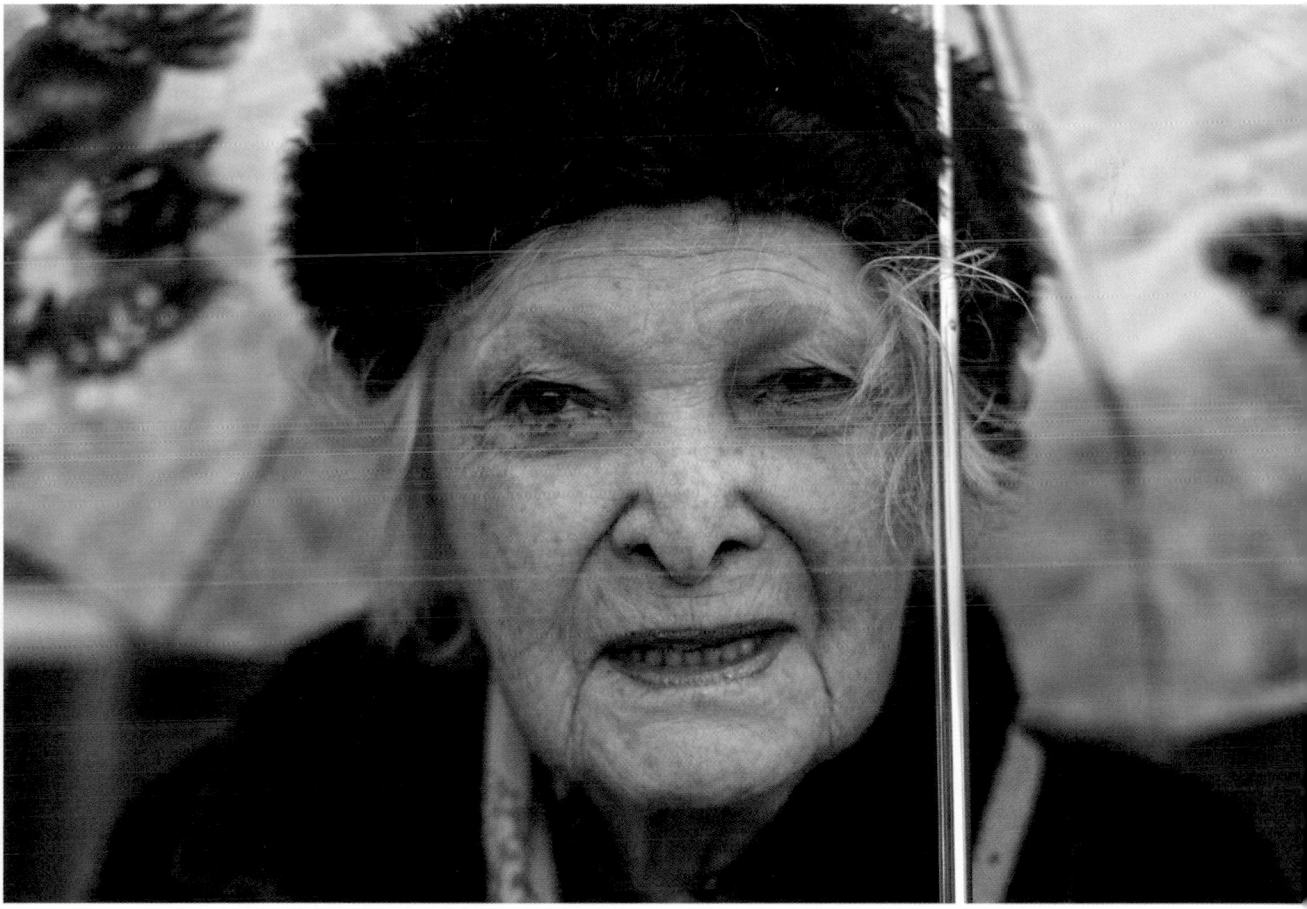

"WHEN MY HUSBAND WAS DYING, I SAID: 'MOE, HOW AM I SUPPOSED TO LIVE WITHOUT YOU?' HE TOLD ME: 'TAKE THE LOVE YOU HAVE FOR ME AND SPREAD IT AROUND.' "

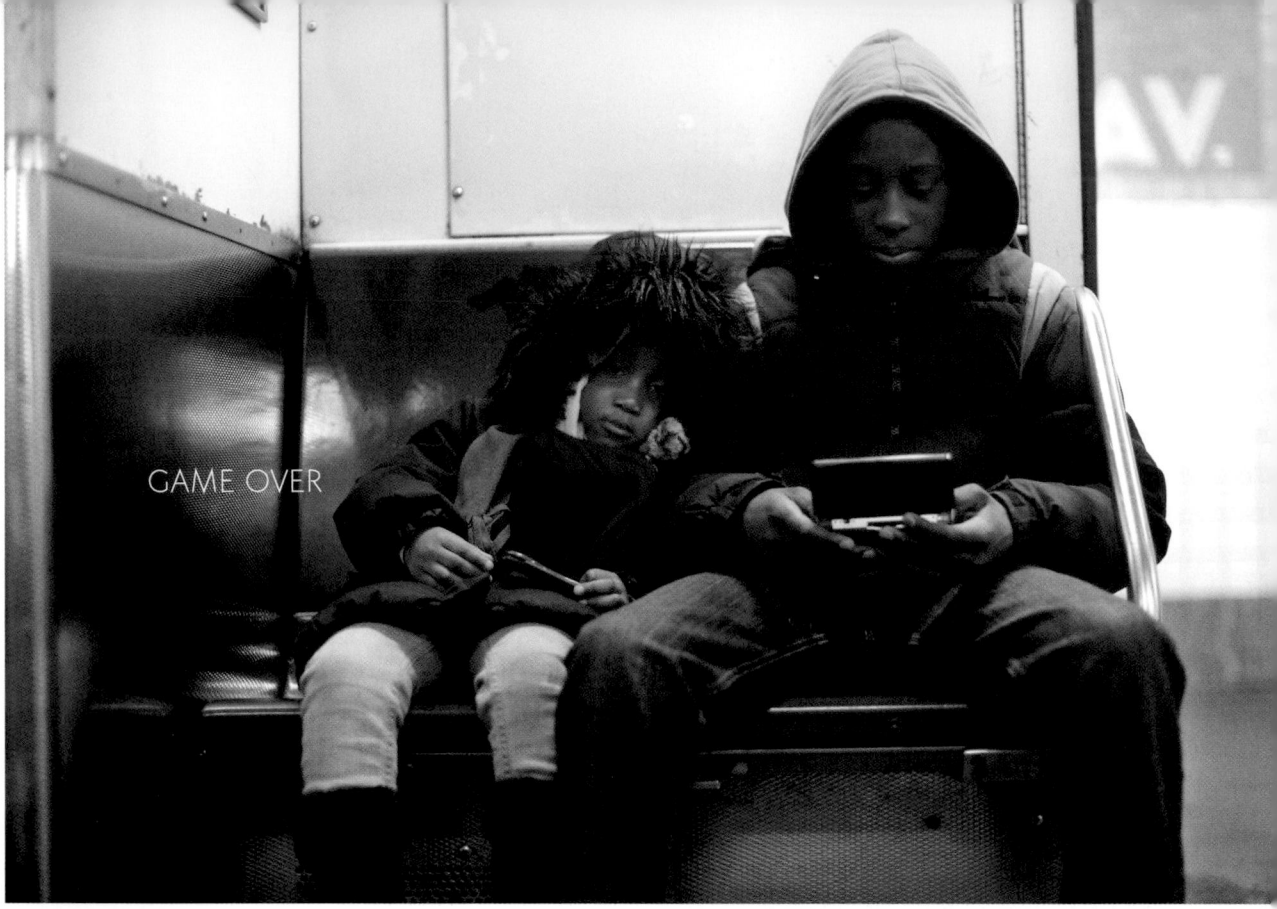
GAME OVER

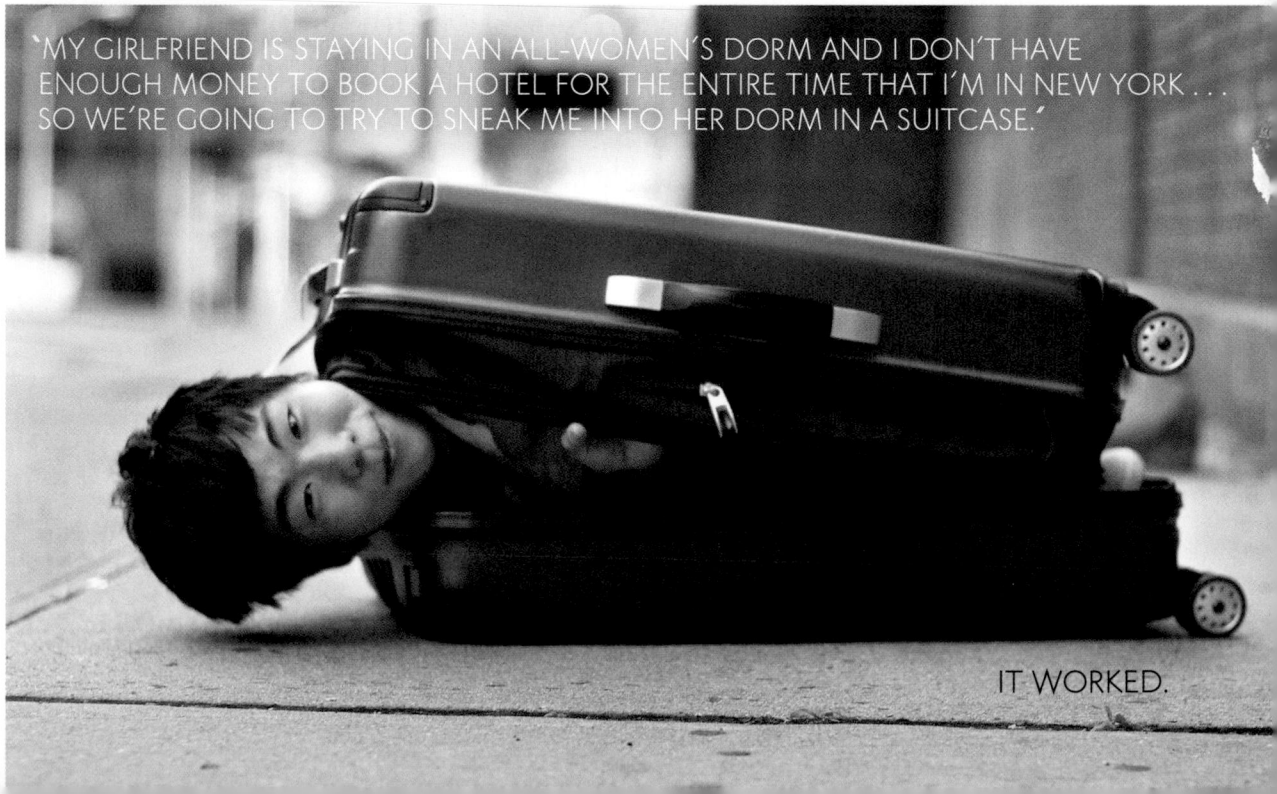
'MY GIRLFRIEND IS STAYING IN AN ALL-WOMEN'S DORM AND I DON'T HAVE ENOUGH MONEY TO BOOK A HOTEL FOR THE ENTIRE TIME THAT I'M IN NEW YORK . . . SO WE'RE GOING TO TRY TO SNEAK ME INTO HER DORM IN A SUITCASE.'
IT WORKED.

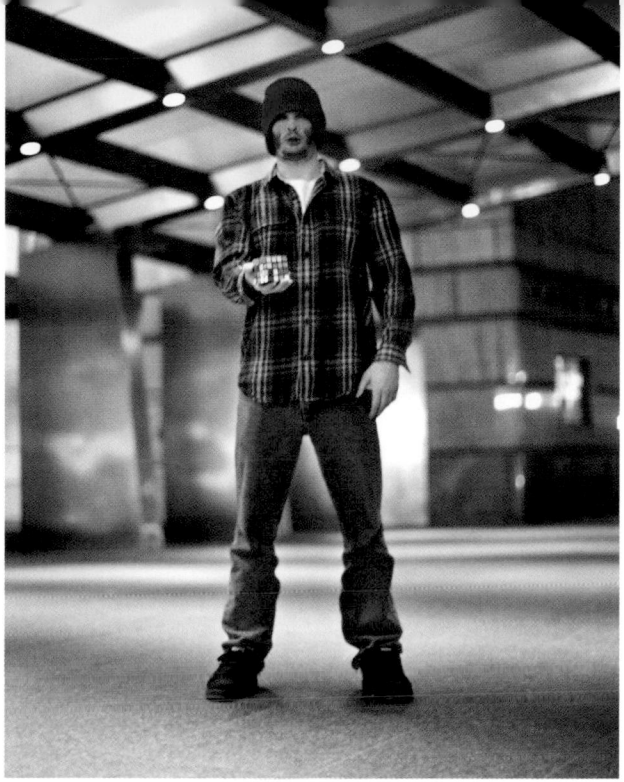

"THERE ARE MORE COMBINATIONS IN THIS CUBE THAN THERE ARE SECONDS IN THE HISTORY OF THE UNIVERSE."

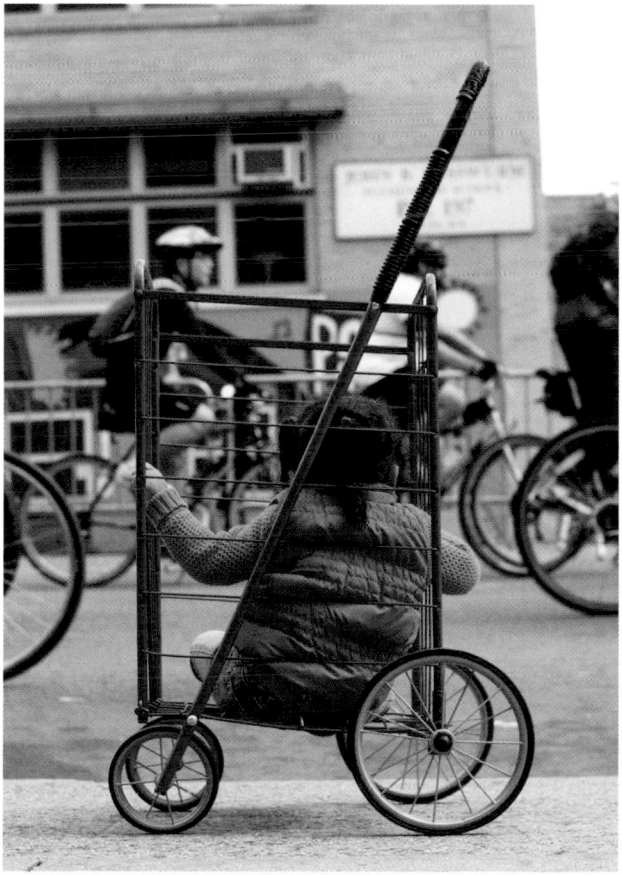

DREAM
BIG

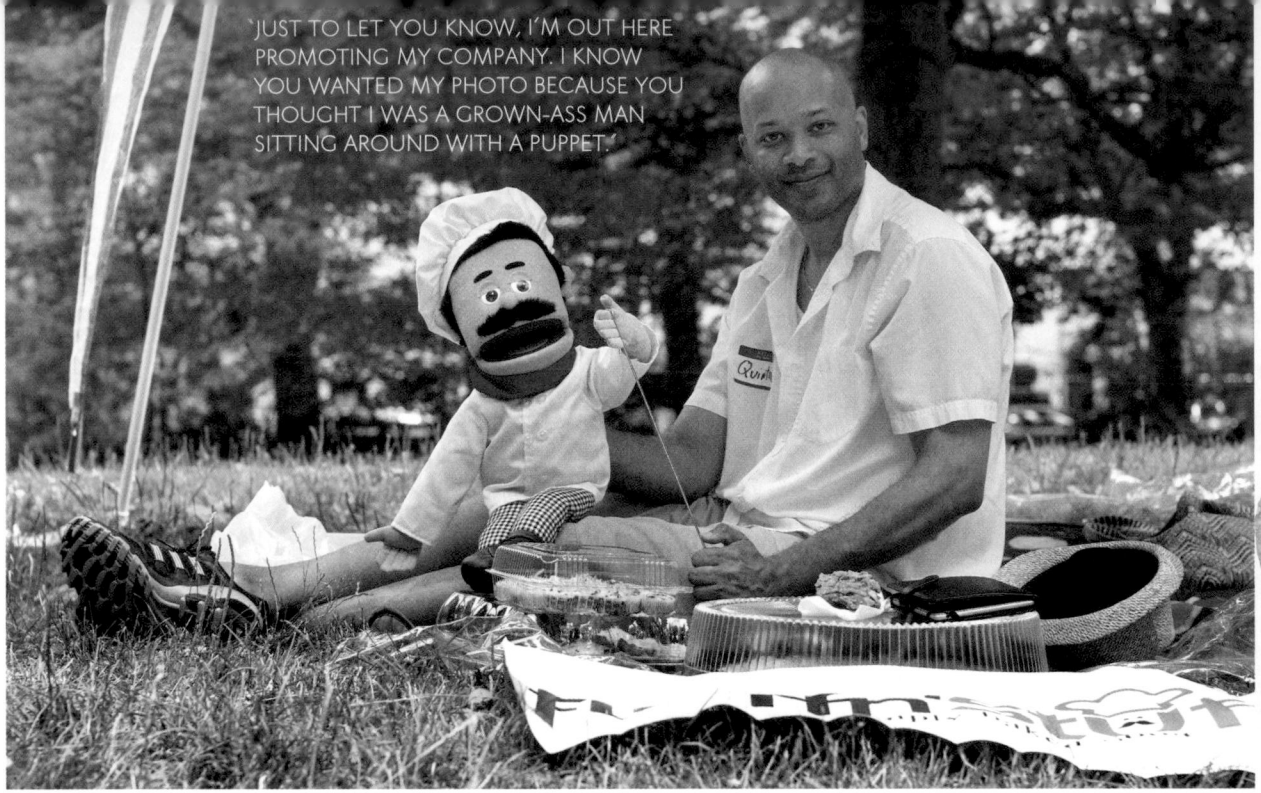

"JUST TO LET YOU KNOW, I'M OUT HERE PROMOTING MY COMPANY. I KNOW YOU WANTED MY PHOTO BECAUSE YOU THOUGHT I WAS A GROWN-ASS MAN SITTING AROUND WITH A PUPPET."

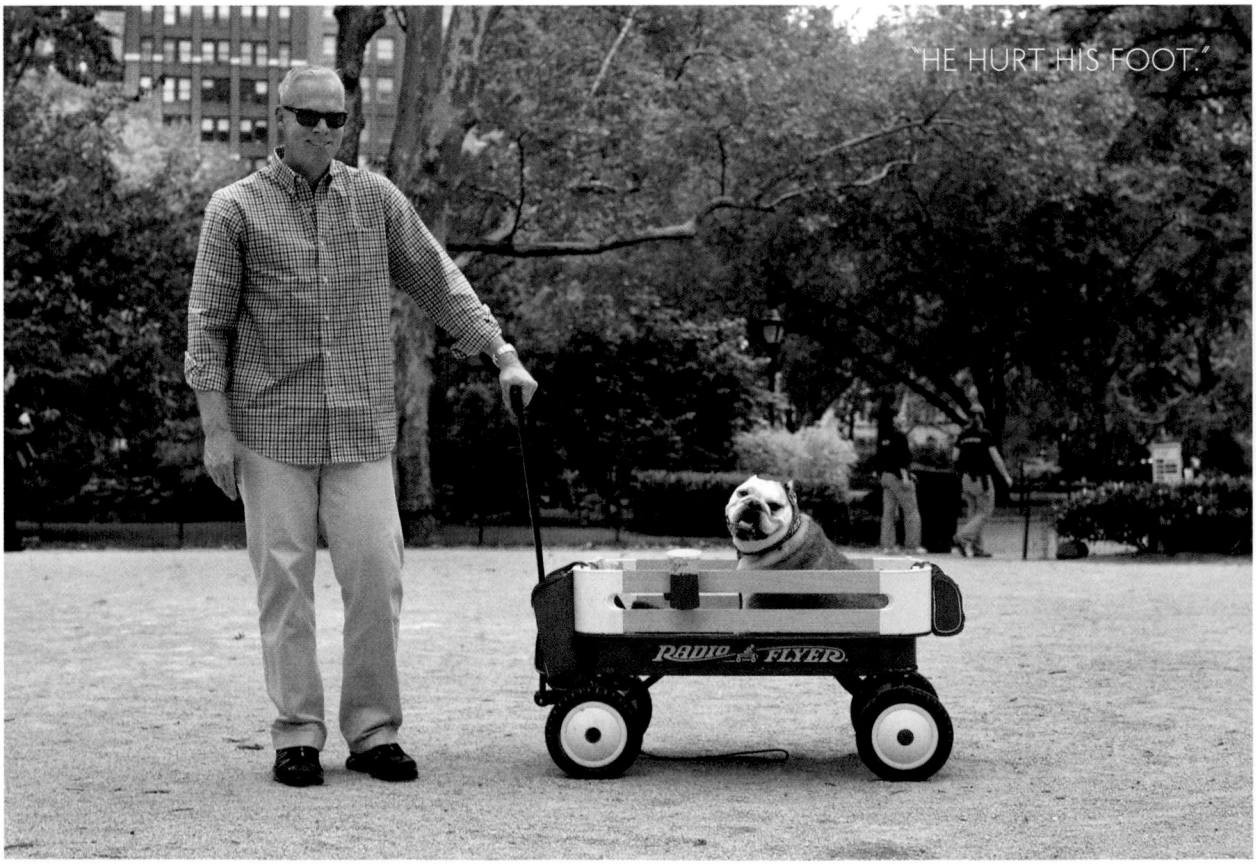


"HE HURT HIS FOOT."

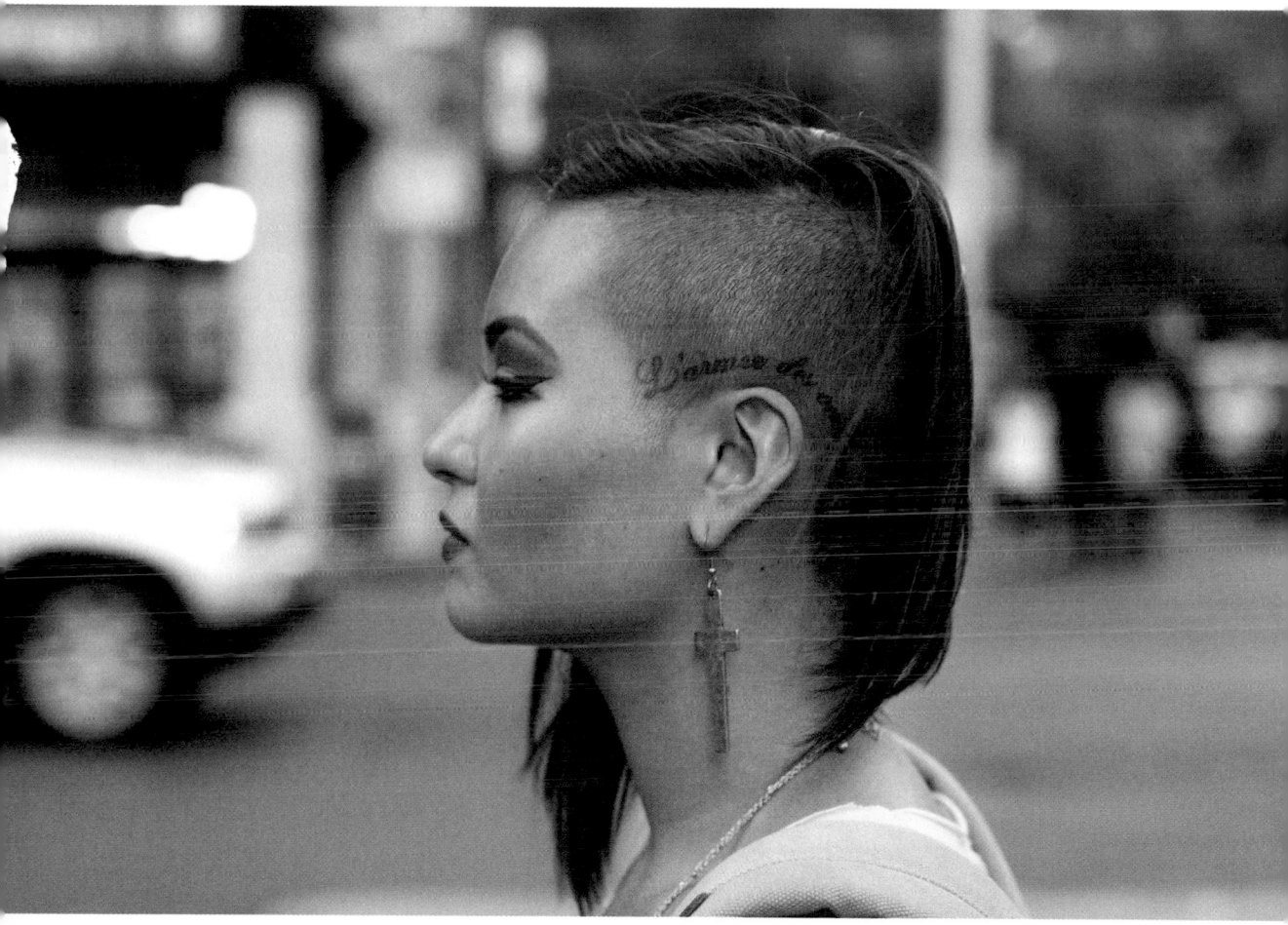

"IT'S FRENCH FOR 'ARMY OF SHADOWS.' "

"AND WHAT DOES THAT MEAN TO YOU?"

"I WAS GOING THROUGH A REALLY ROUGH TIME IN MY LIFE, AND IT FELT LIKE A WHOLE ARMY WAS AFTER ME. BUT WHEN I STARTED FEELING BETTER, I REALIZED IT WAS NOTHING BUT AN ARMY OF SHADOWS."

I DISCOVERED A YOUNG DANCE TROUPE FROM CHINA POSING FOR A PORTRAIT OUTSIDE OF LINCOLN CENTER. THE CHAPERONES NOTICED ME TAKING PHOTOS, AND BEGAN WHISPERING TO EACH OTHER. SUDDENLY ONE OF THE ADULTS BLEW A WHISTLE, THE CHILDREN LINED UP, AND A VERY PRIVATE PERFORMANCE COMMENCED.

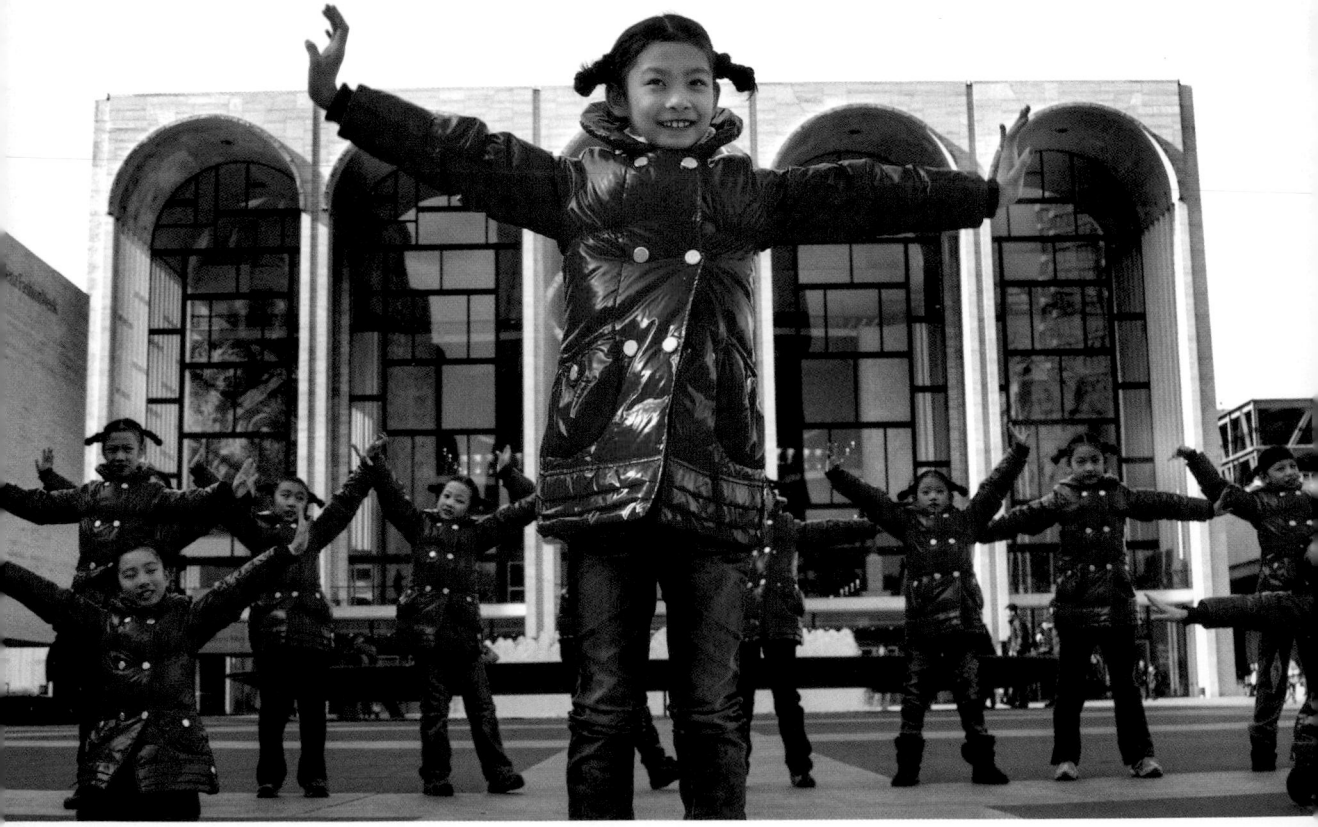

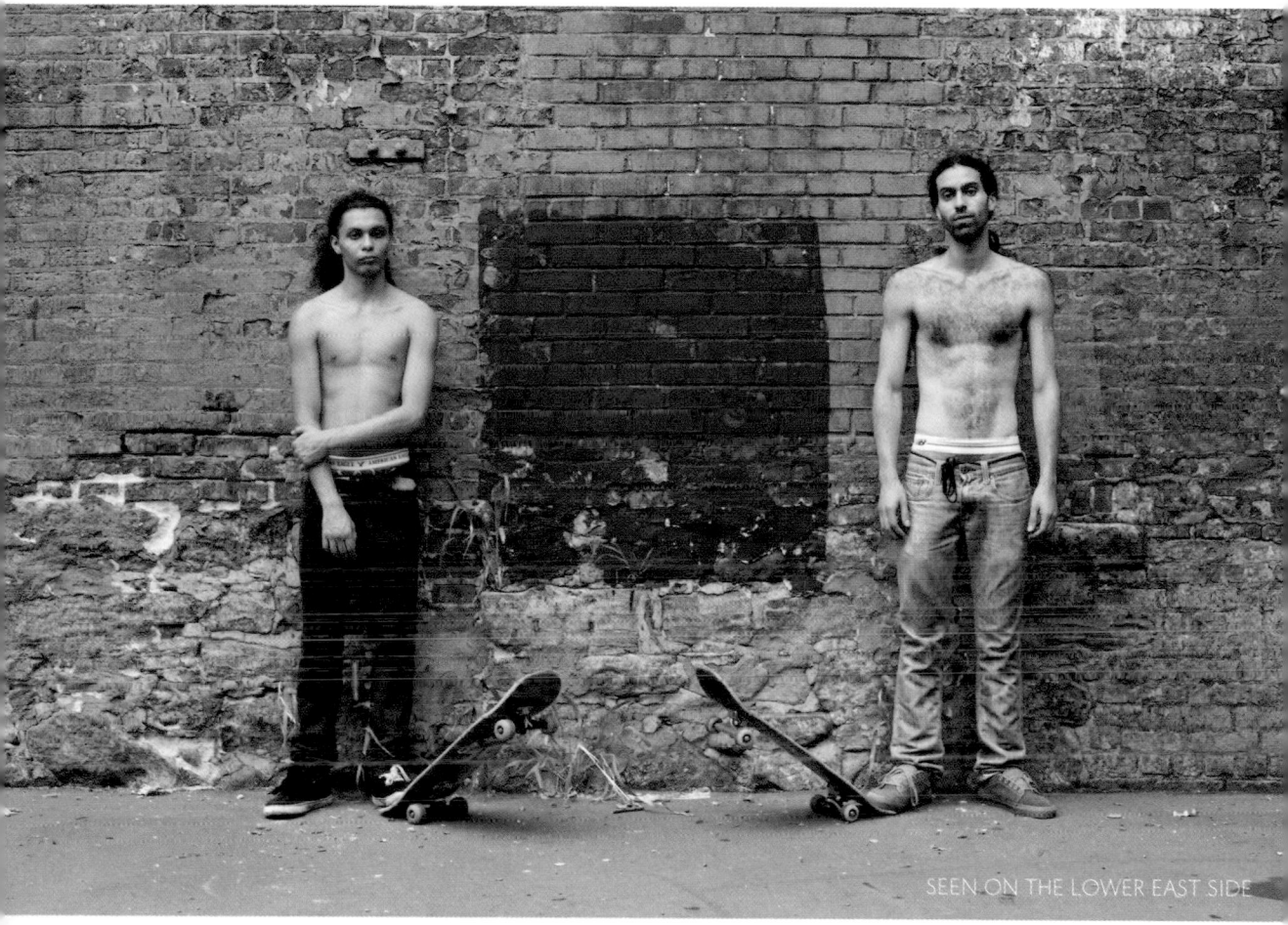
SEEN ON THE LOWER EAST SIDE

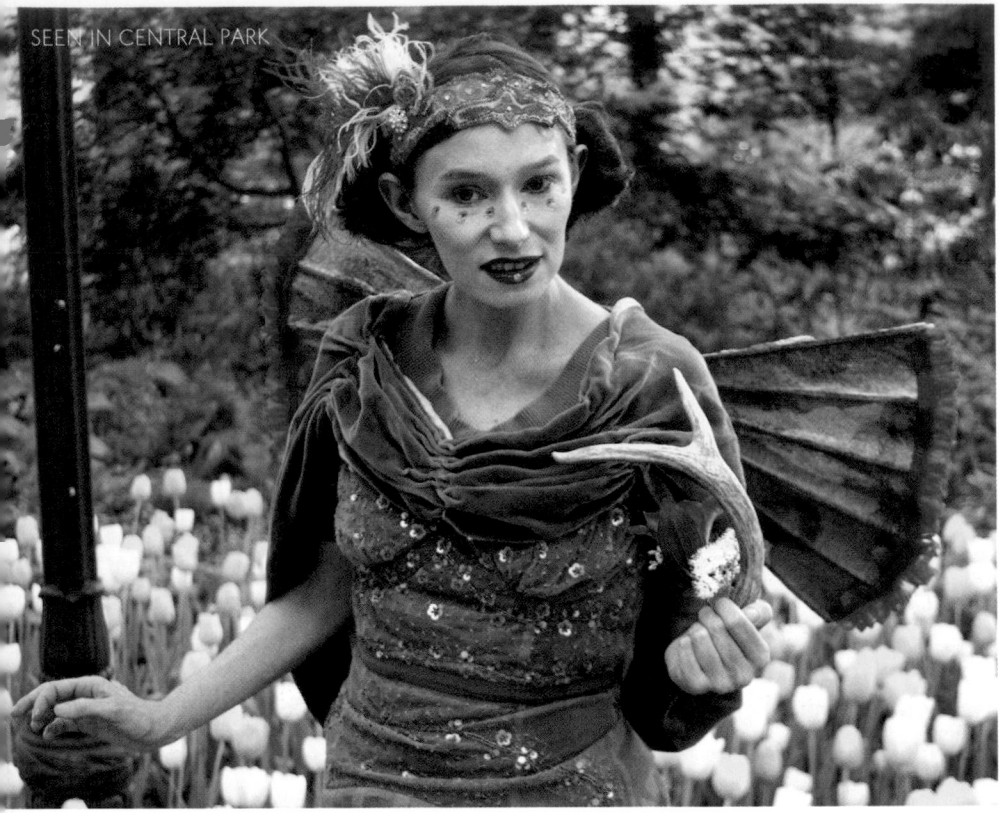

SEEN IN CENTRAL PARK

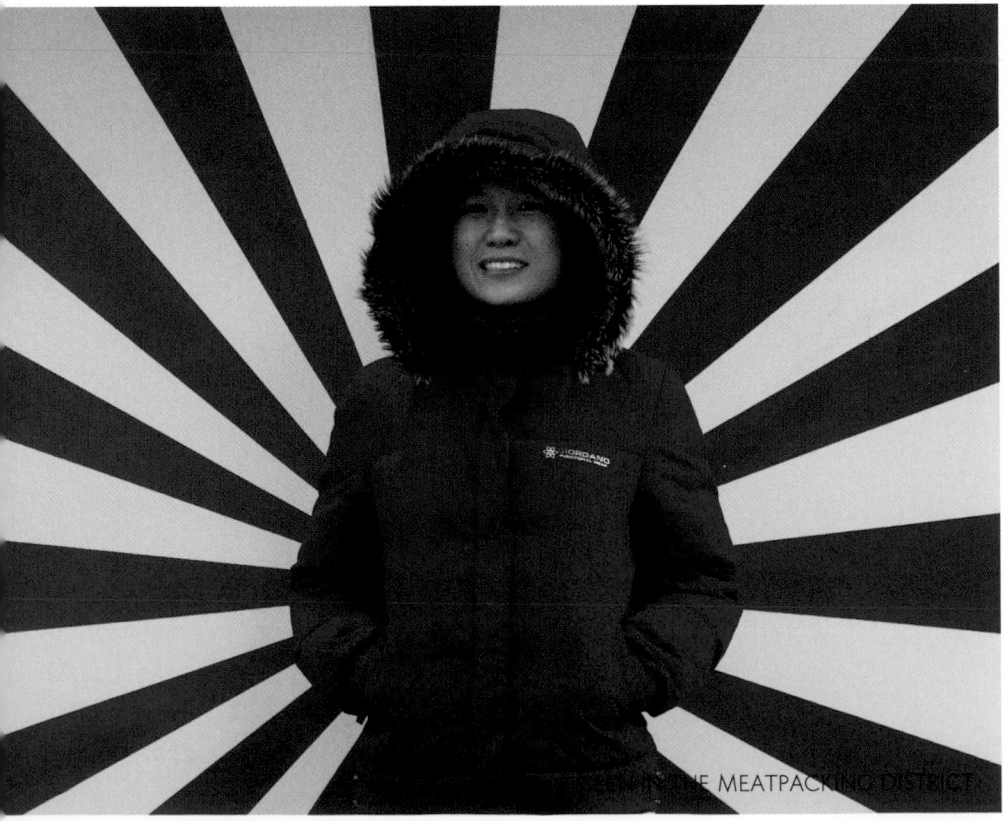


SEEN IN THE MEATPACKING DISTRICT

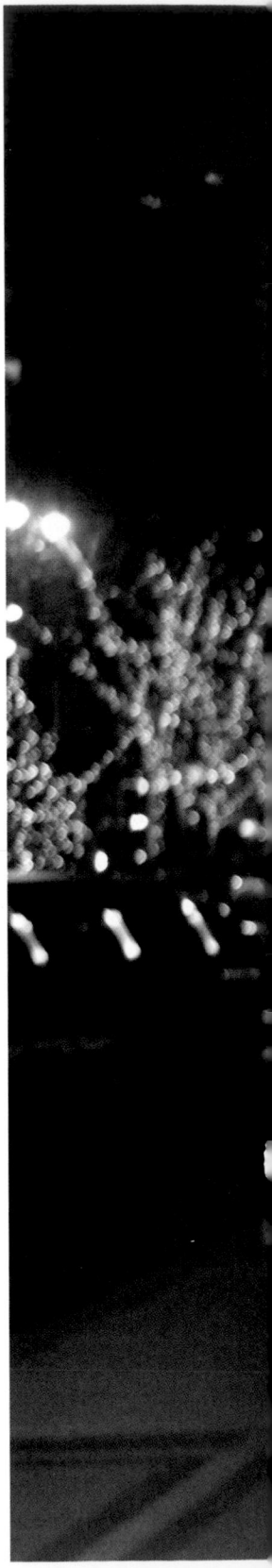

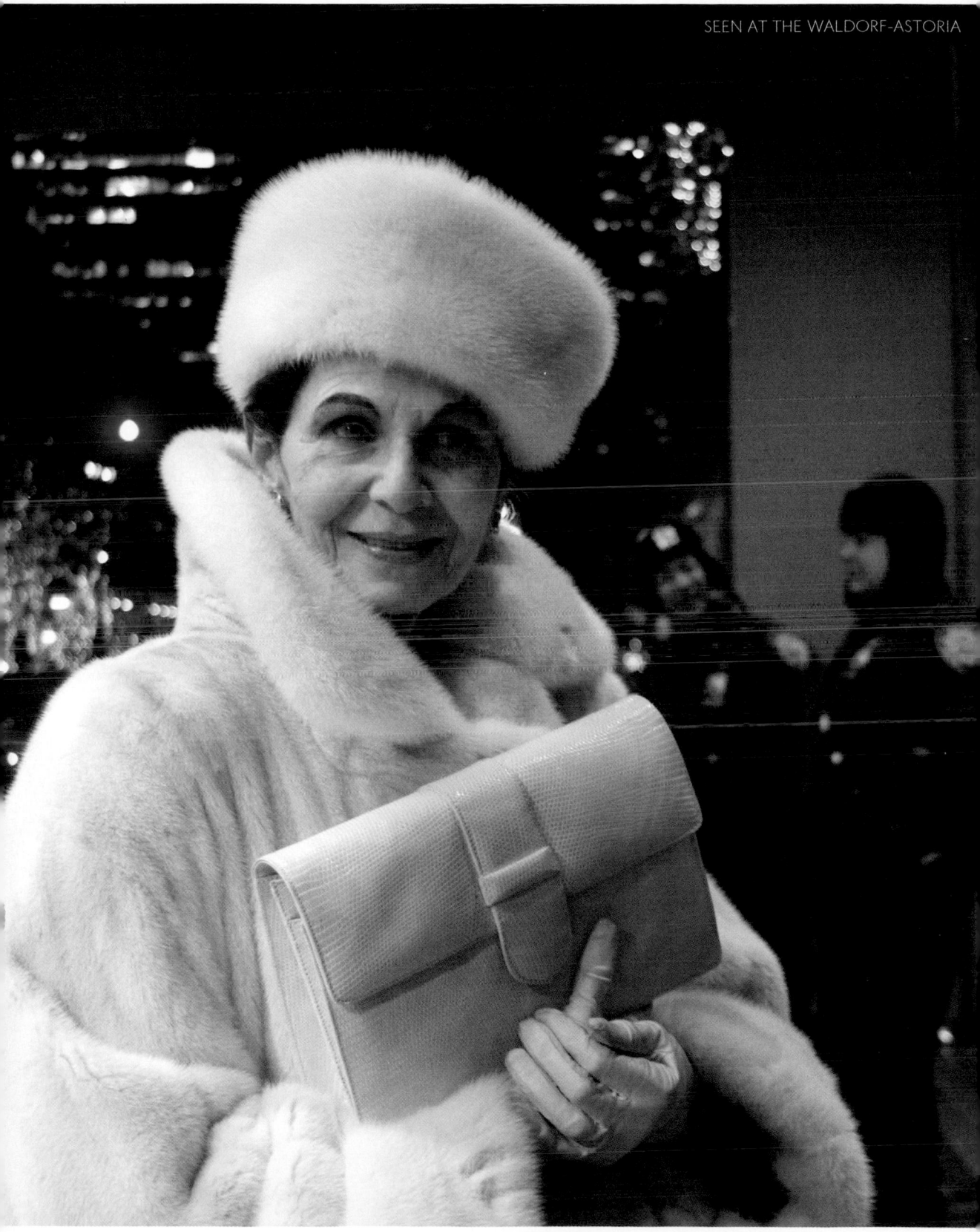

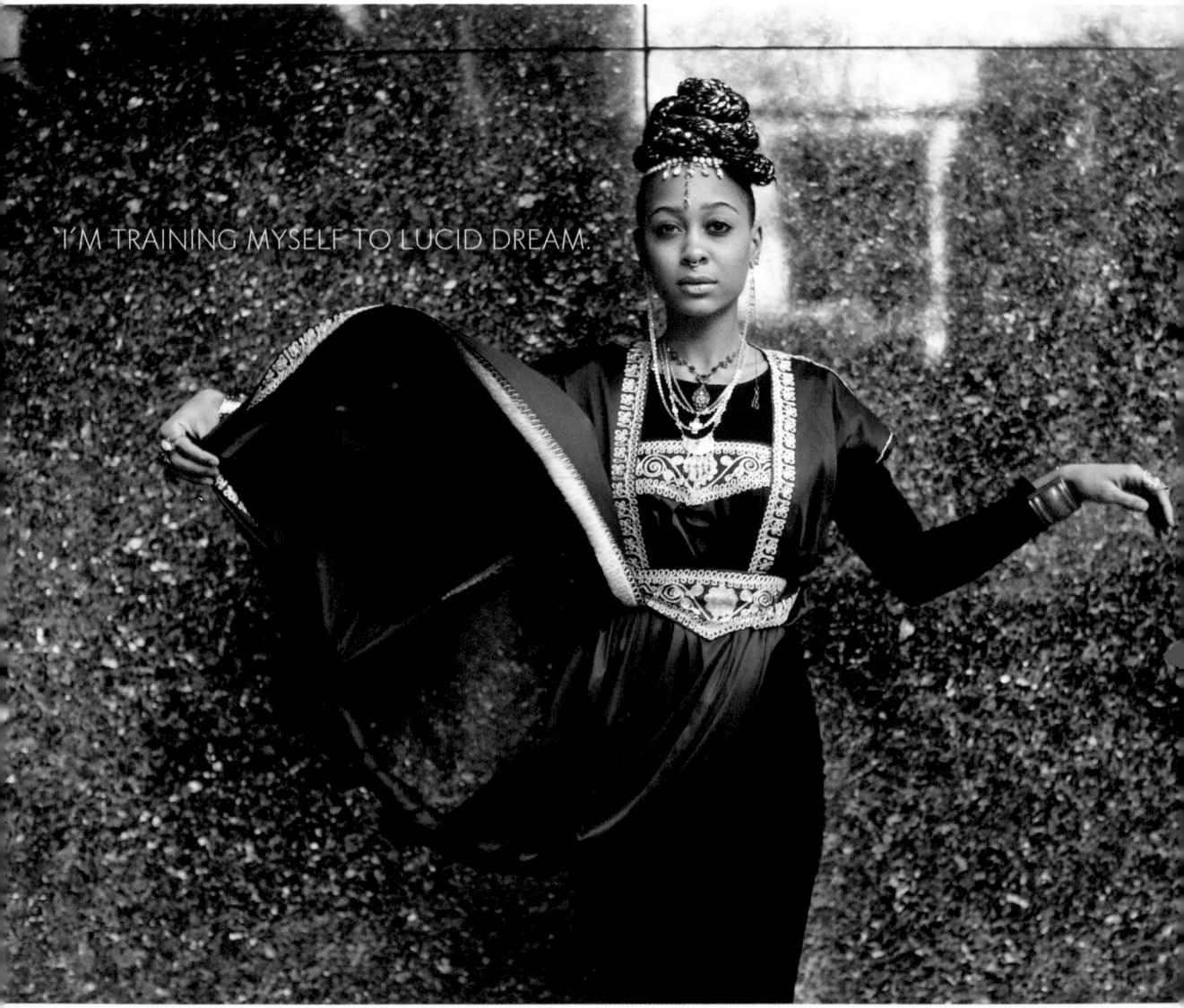
"I'M TRAINING MYSELF TO LUCID DREAM."

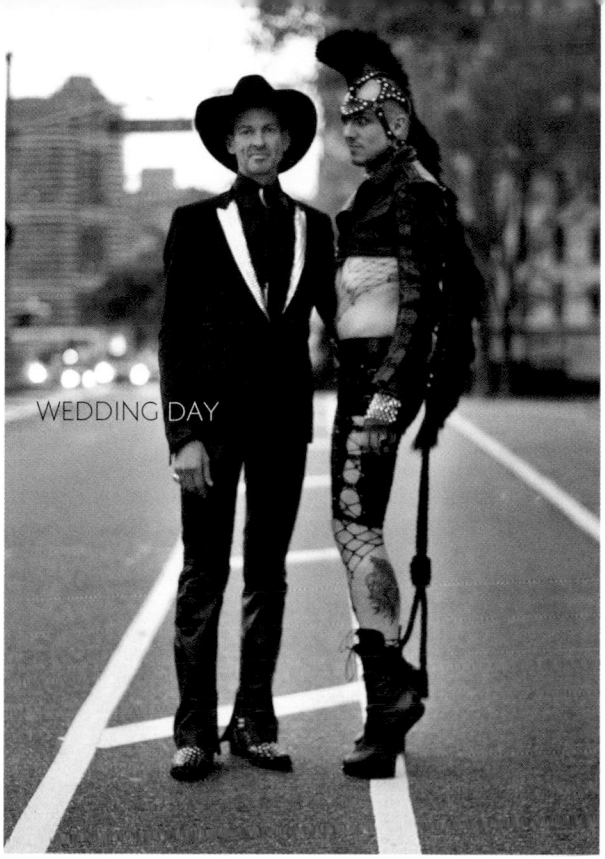


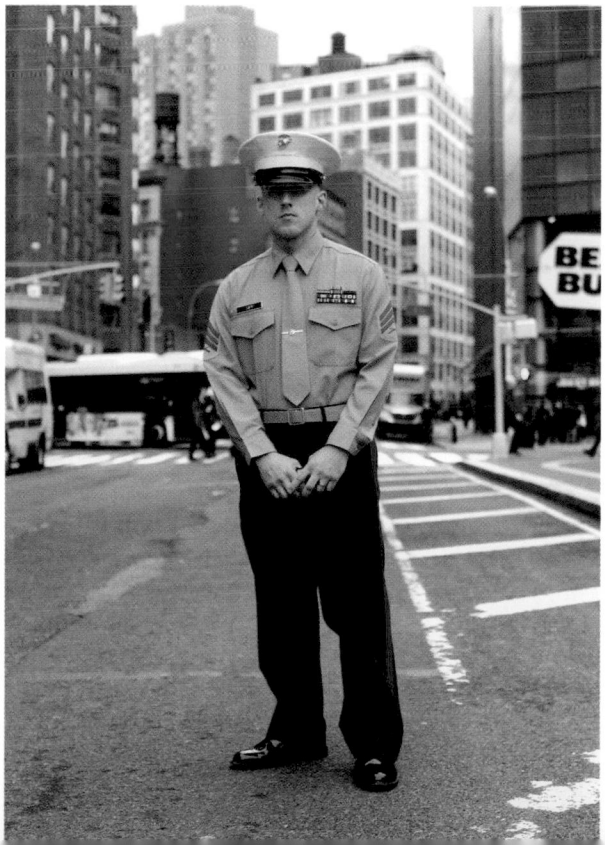

"IT'S TAUGHT ME TO BE MORE RESPECTFUL OF ALL PEOPLE. IF I MEET A MAN ON THE STREET NOW, NO MATTER HOW OLD HE IS, I'LL CALL HIM SIR."

"I'M GOING TO ISRAEL NEXT WEEK."

"ARE YOU JEWISH?"

"I AM."

"JEWISH AND WHAT?"

"JEWISH AND GERMAN, IRAQI, AFRICAN, IRISH, PORTUGUESE, FRENCH, CHEROKEE, LENAPE, AND BLACKFOOT."

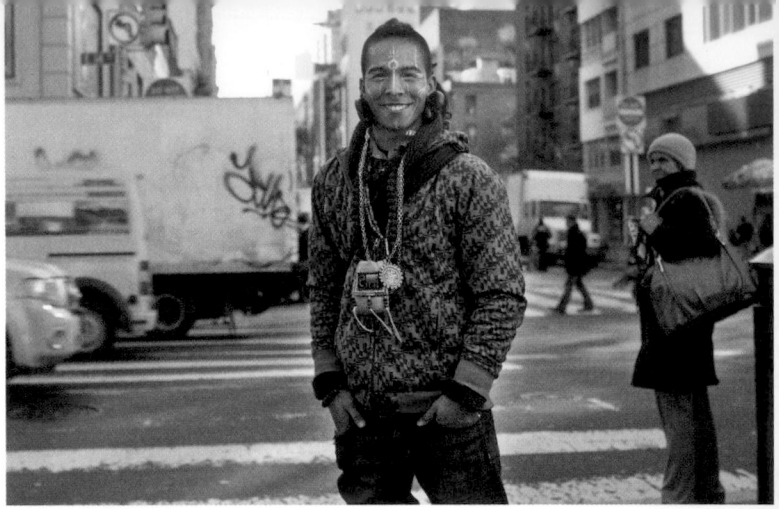

"A KID WORE SHORTS TO SCHOOL YESTERDAY AND THE HEADMASTER GOT REALLY MAD, SO TODAY THE WHOLE CLASS WORE THEM."

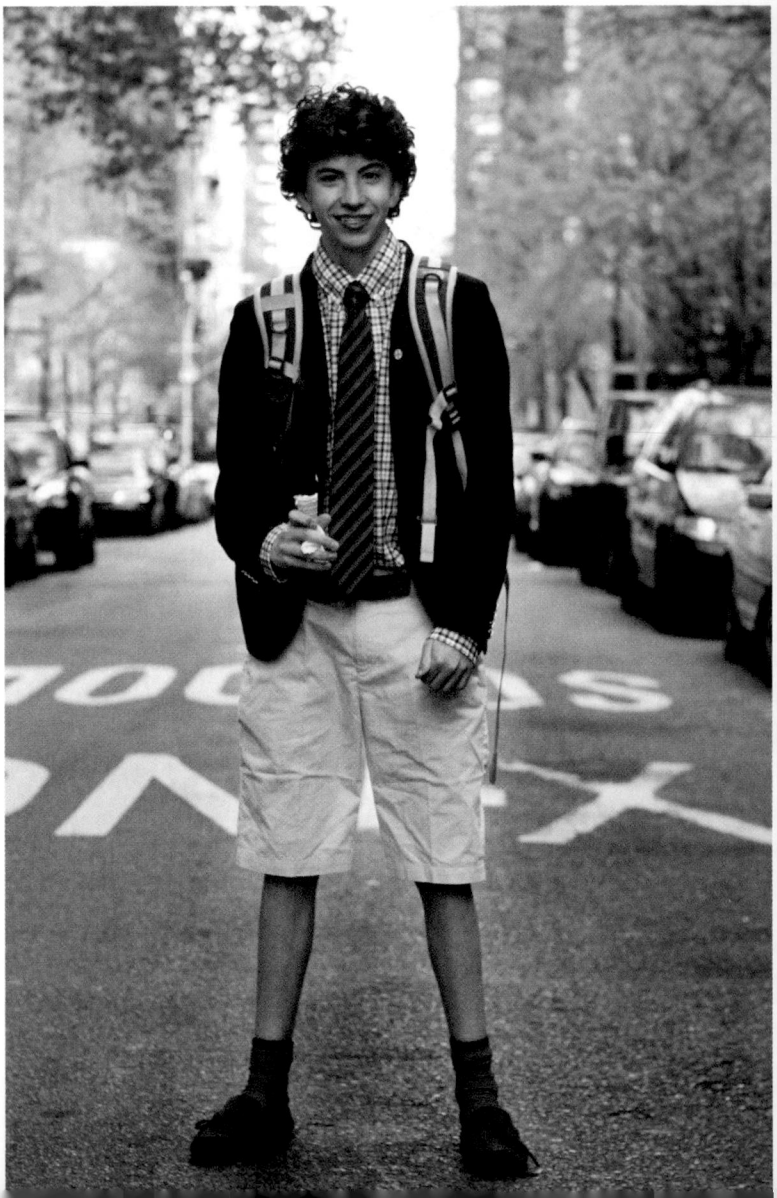

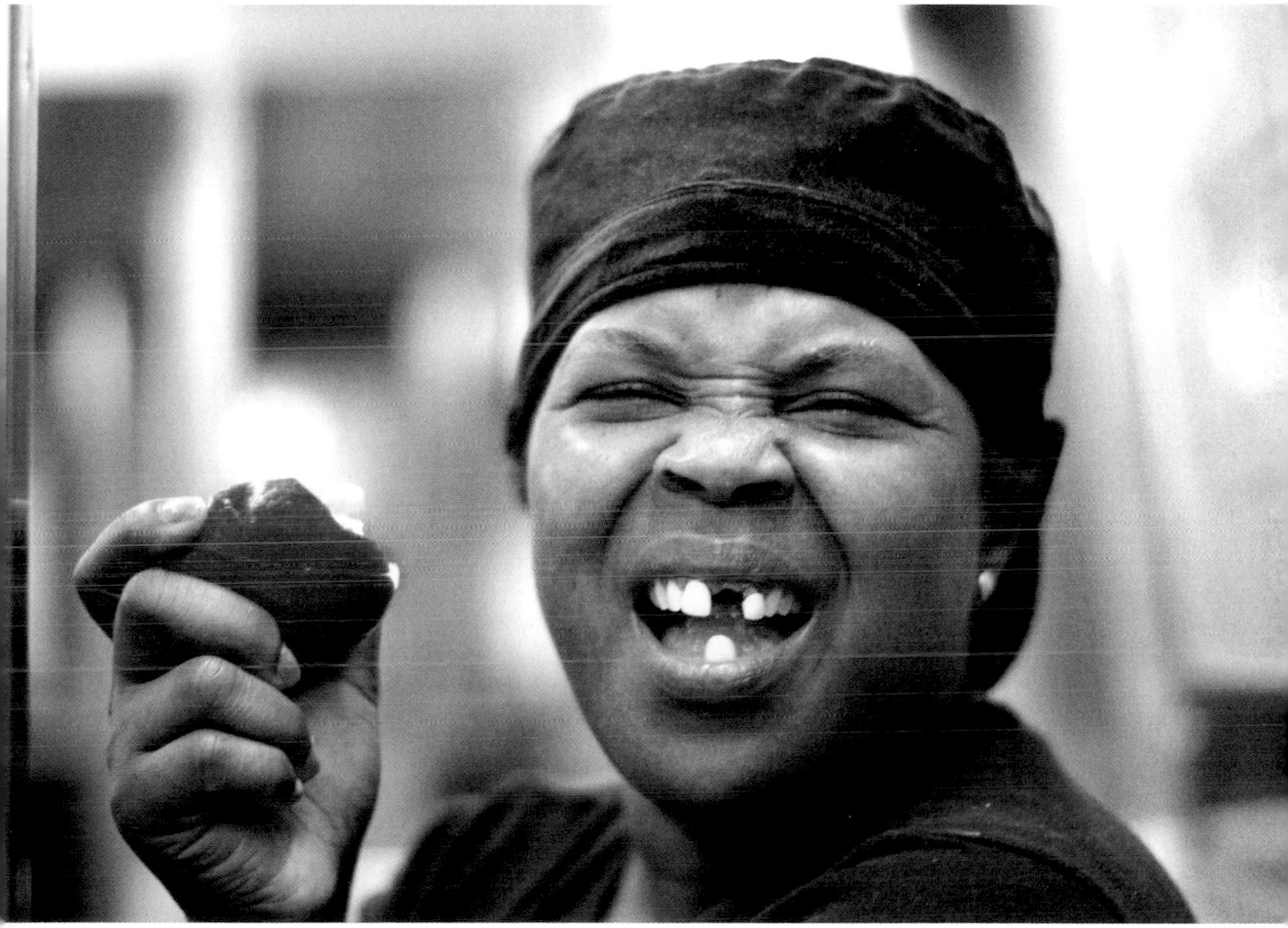

"I DON'T MIND THE WHITE PEOPLE MOVING INTO OUR NEIGHBORHOOD. THEY'RE LIKE THE INDIANS—THEY COME IN PEACE. AND THEY BROUGHT SOME WHOLE FOODS WITH 'EM. AND FLEETWOOD MAC. PLUS THE POLICE DON'T BREAK UP OUR BLOCK PARTIES ANYMORE."

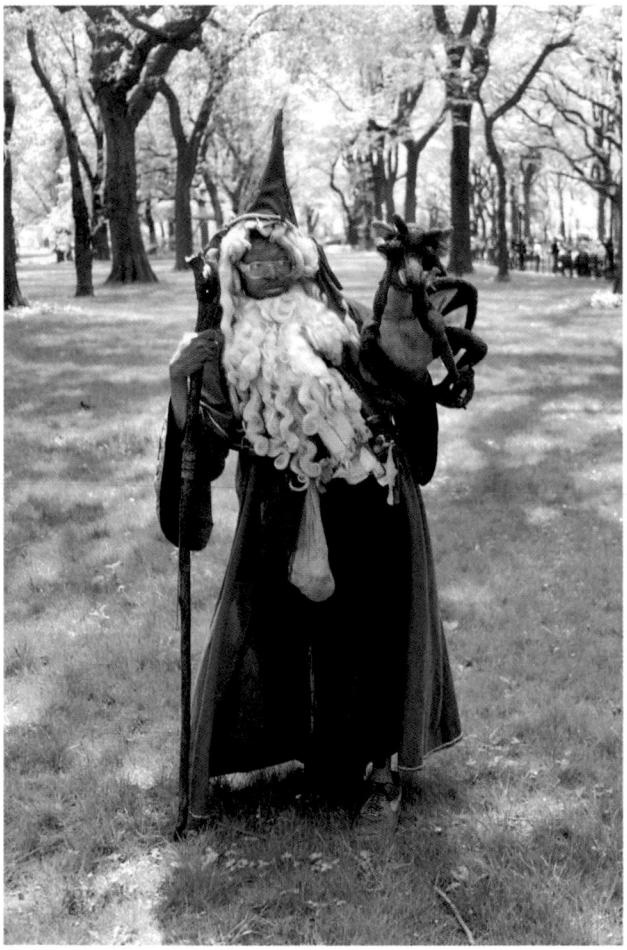

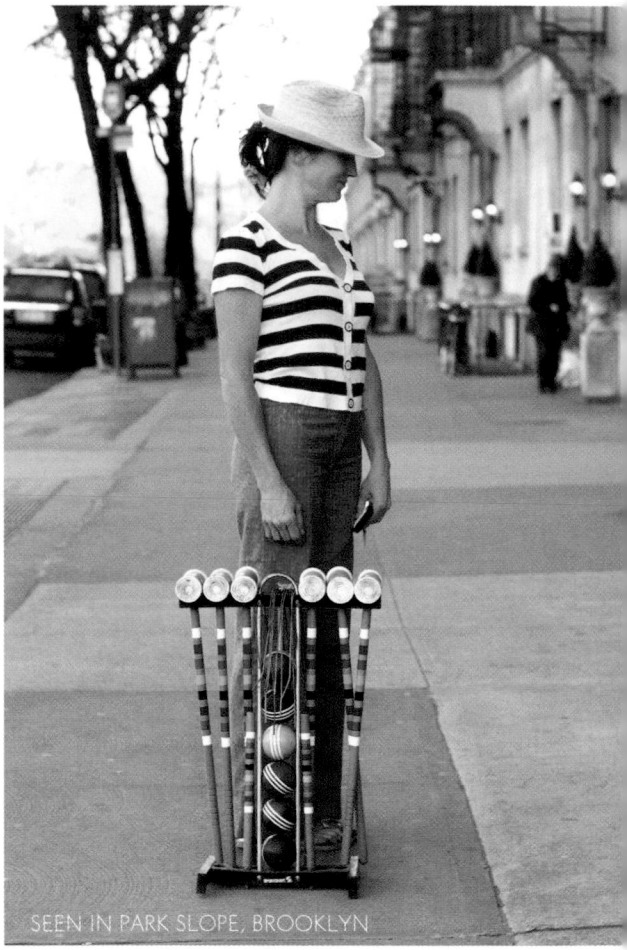

SEEN IN PARK SLOPE, BROOKLYN

SIGNS OF SPRING IN CENTRAL PARK:

1. TREES TURN GREEN.
2. FLOWERS BLOOM.
3. BLACKWOLF THE DRAGONMASTER BEGINS ASKING PEOPLE TO FEED CASH TO HIS DRAGON.

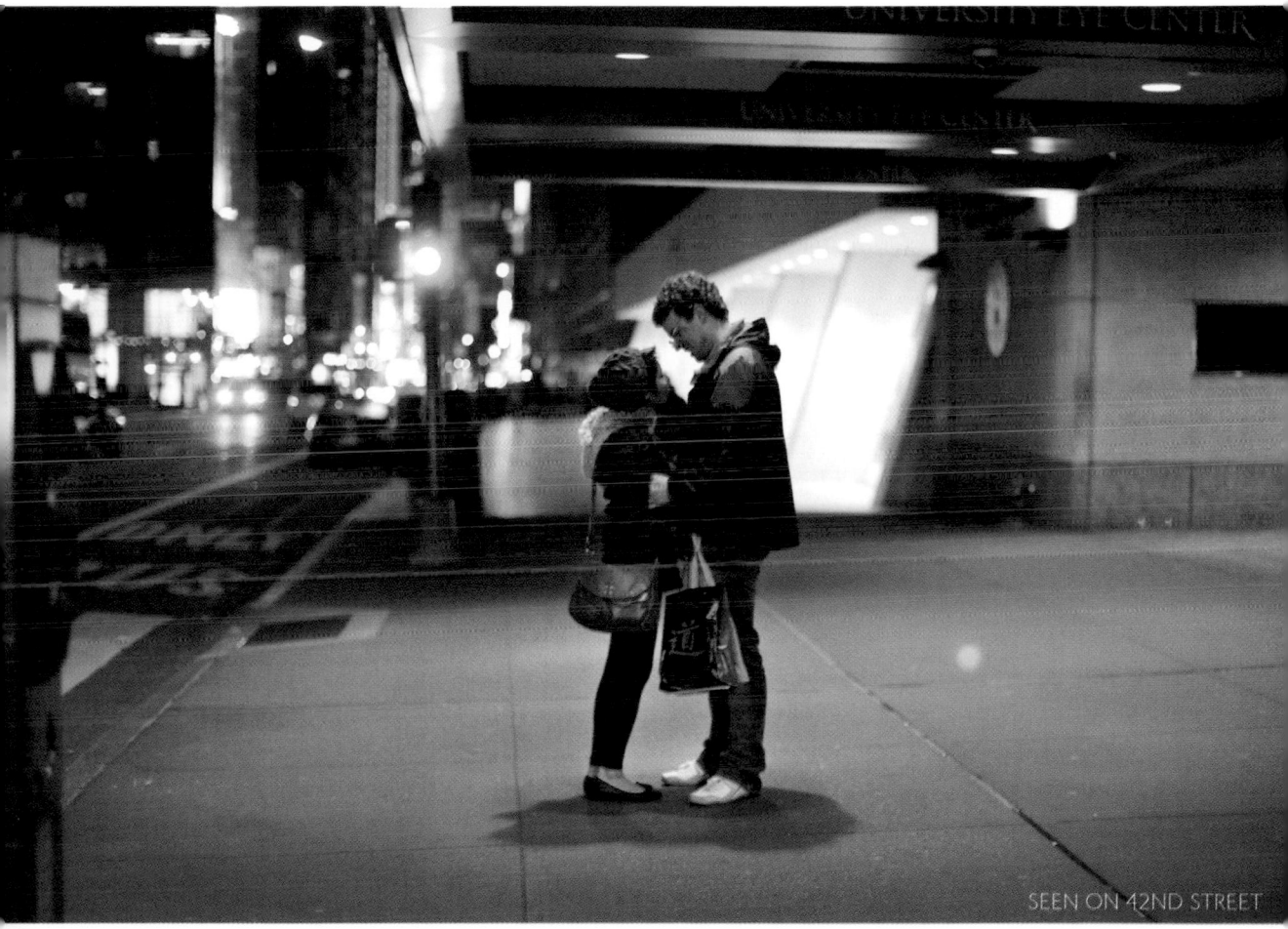


SEEN ON 42ND STREET

'JEALOUSY. DEPRESSION. LOVE. THEY PRETTY MUCH DEMONSTRATE THE WHOLE RANGE OF HUMAN EMOTION.' →

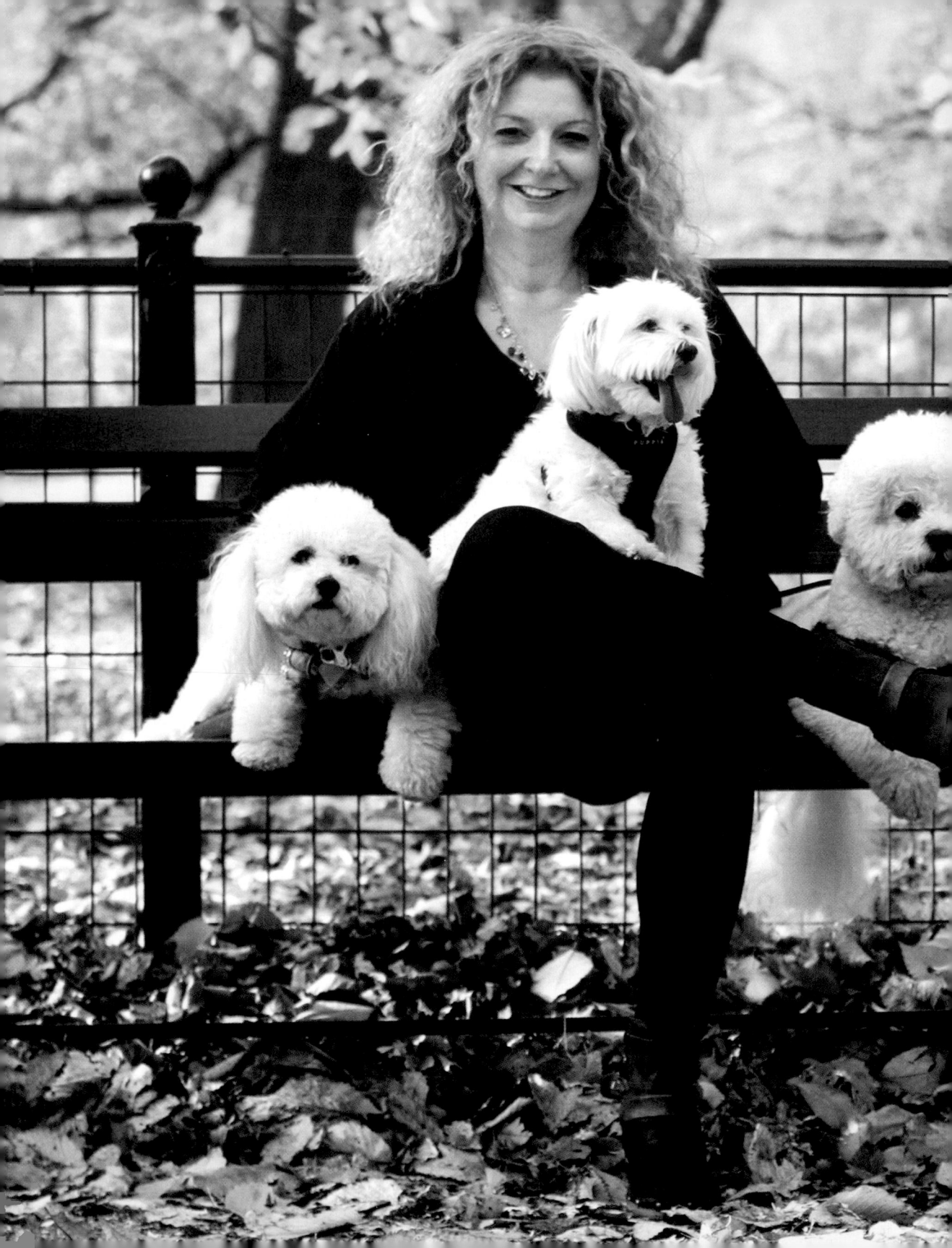

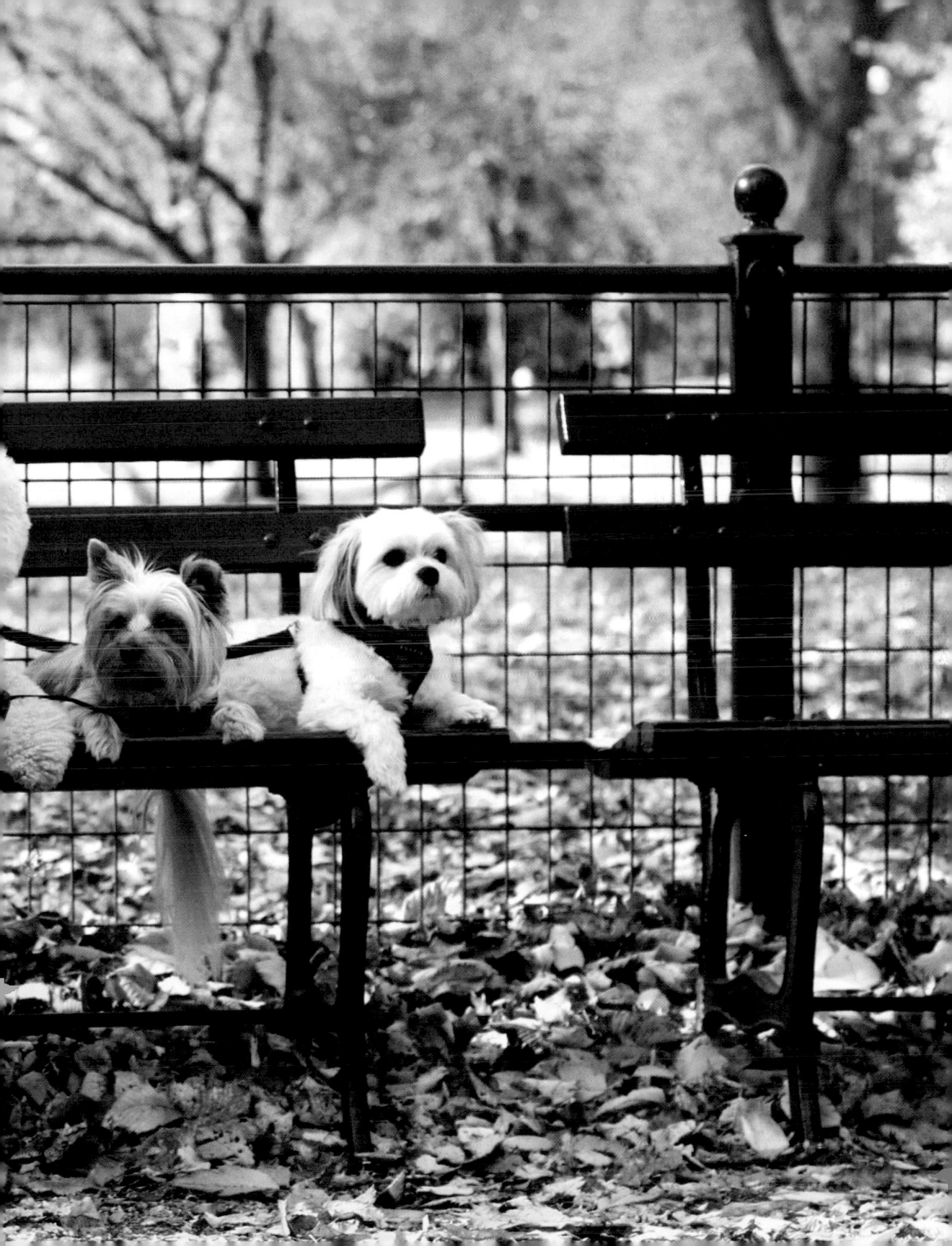

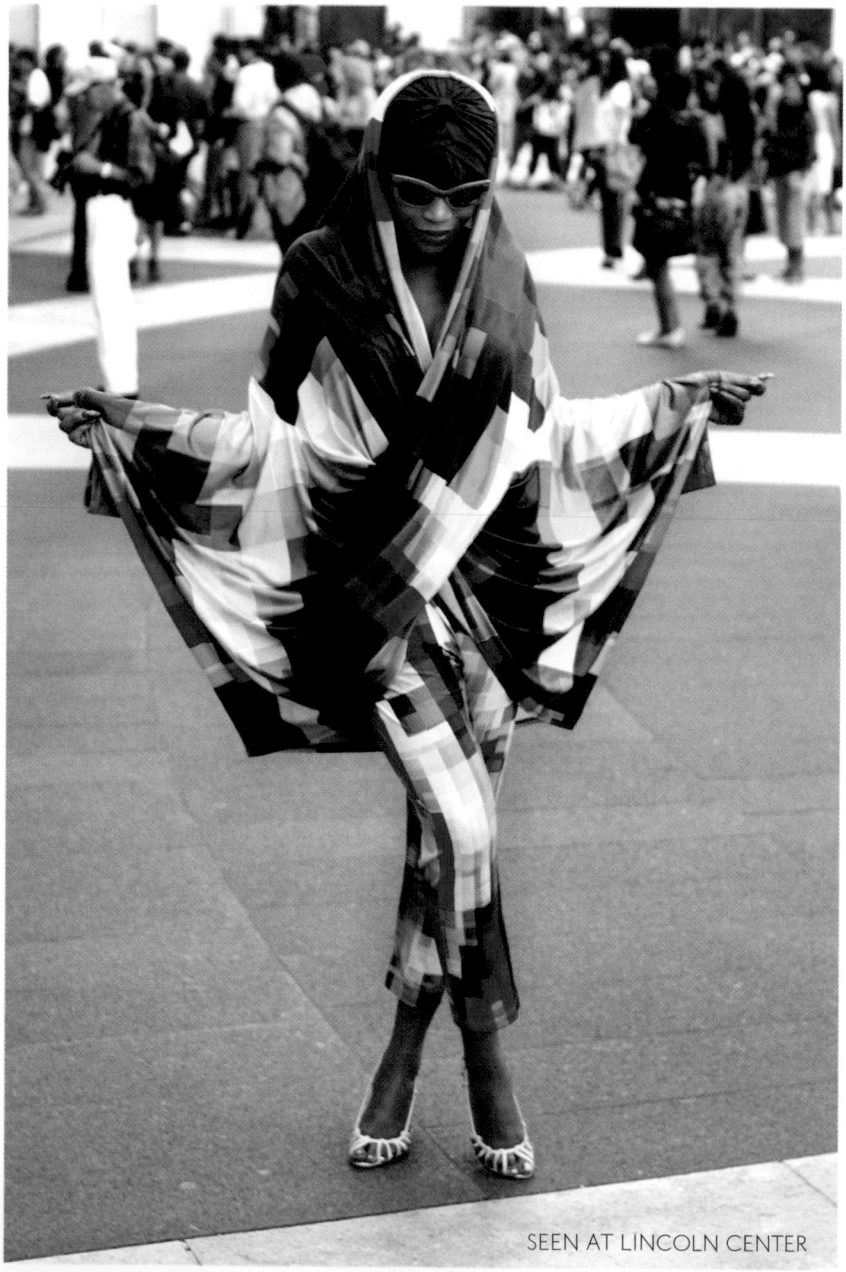

SEEN AT LINCOLN CENTER

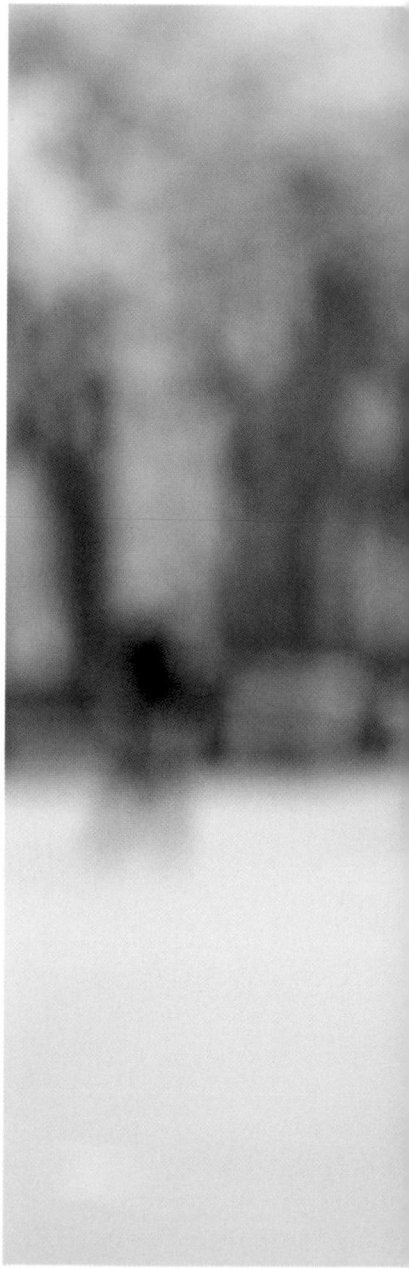

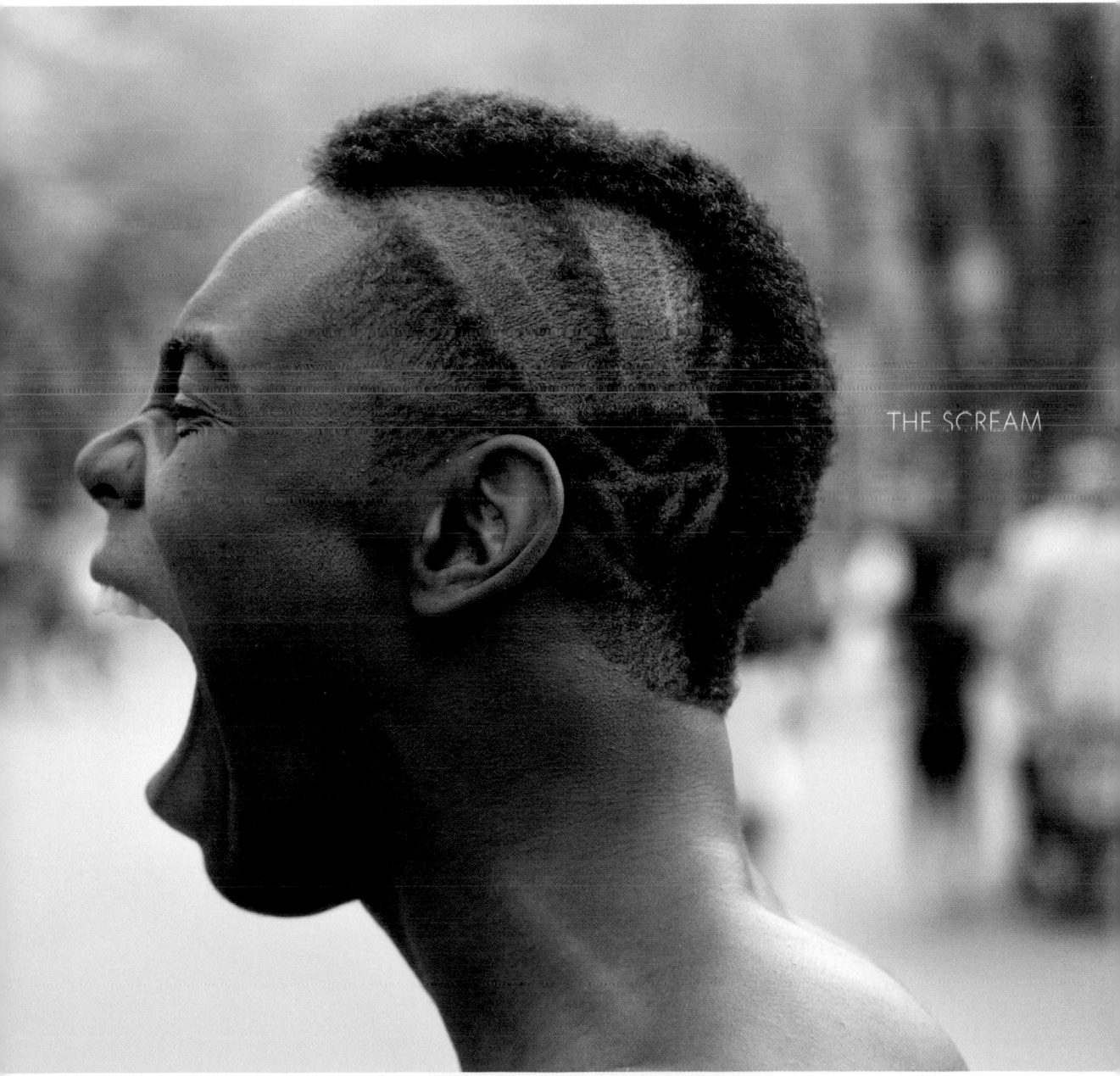
THE SCREAM

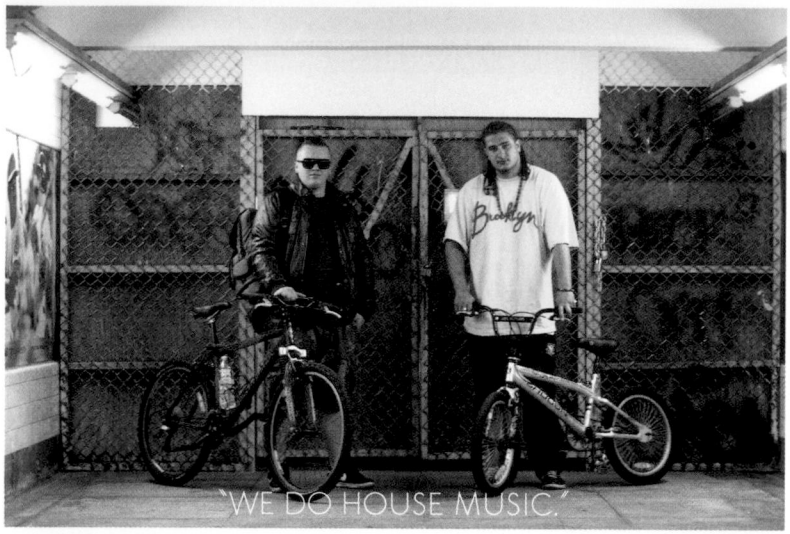


'WE DO HOUSE MUSIC.'

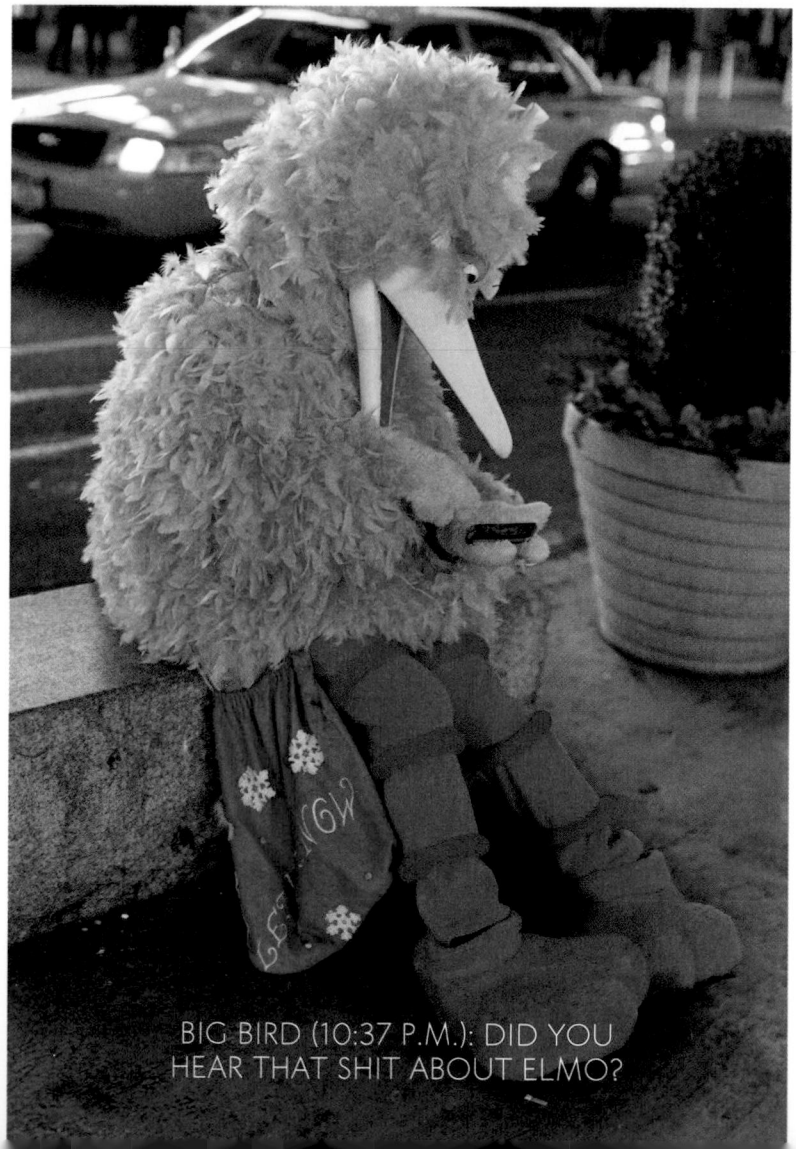

BIG BIRD (10:37 P.M.): DID YOU HEAR THAT SHIT ABOUT ELMO?

"WHERE'D YOU GROW UP?"

"ALL OVER."

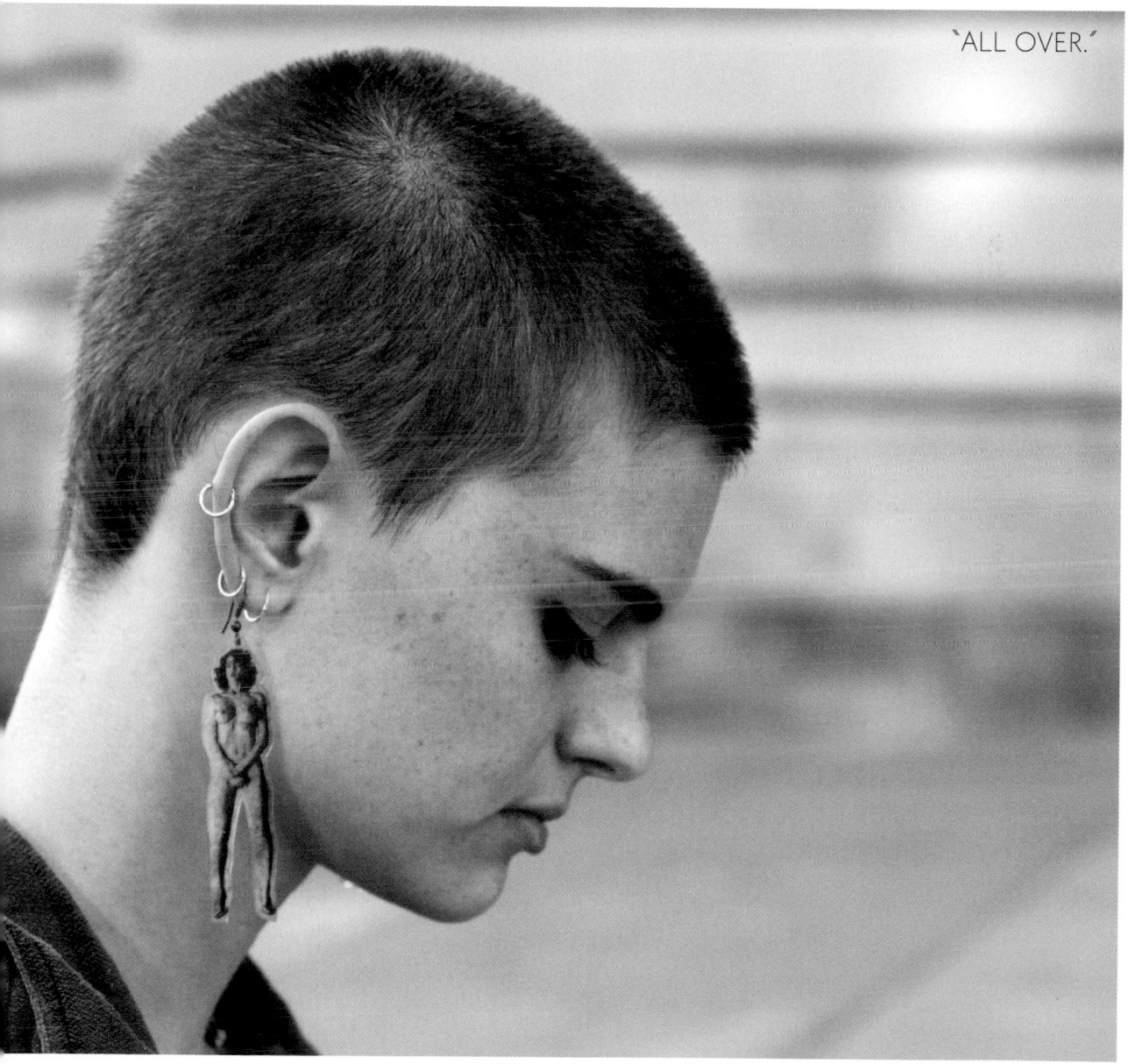

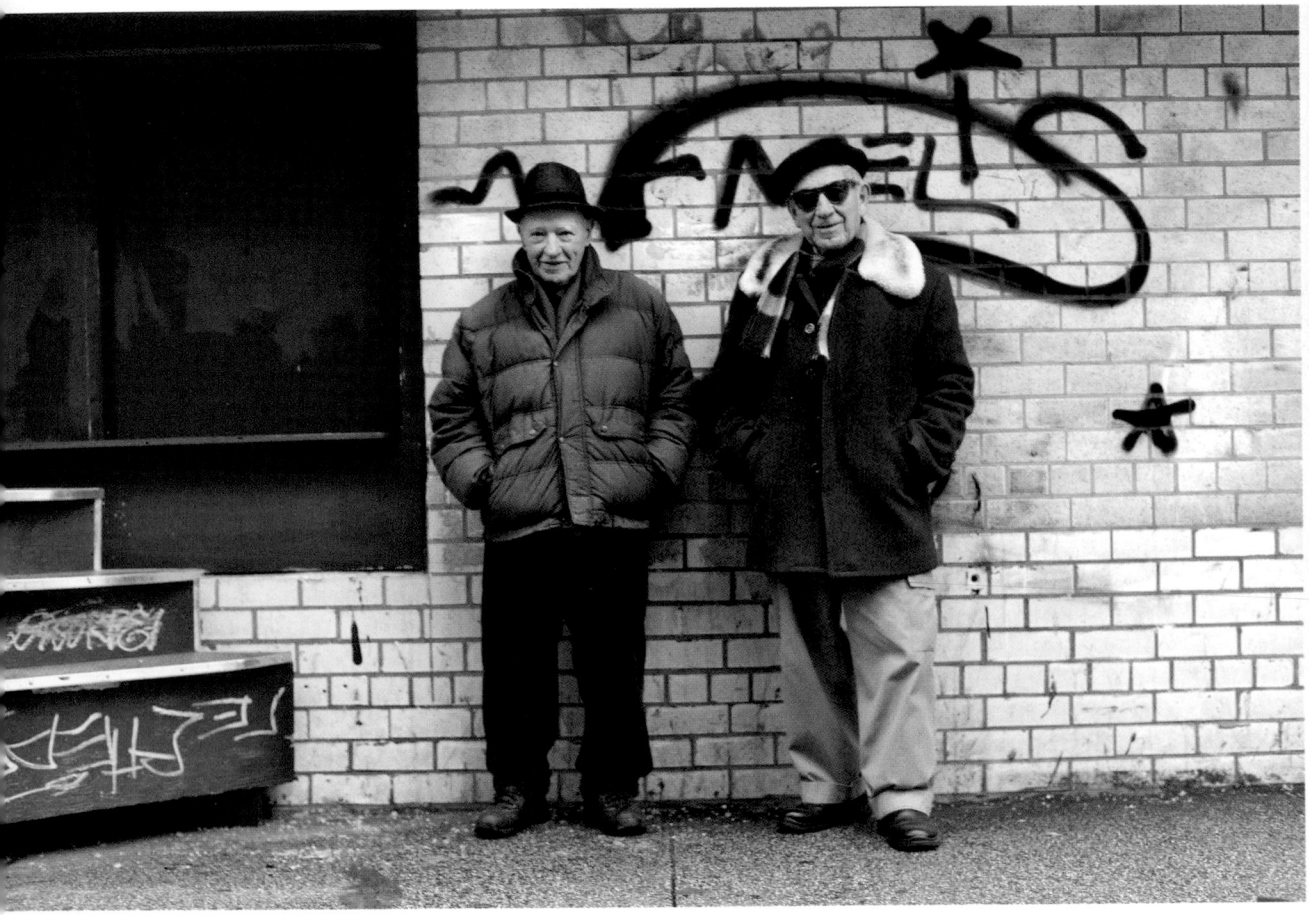

THESE MEN HAD VERY HEAVY ACCENTS, SO I COULD BARELY UNDERSTAND THEM. I TRIED MY BEST TO FOLLOW ALONG AS THE MAN ON THE RIGHT TOLD ME HIS LIFE STORY. AFTER ASKING HIM TO REPEAT SEVERAL SENTENCES, I FINALLY CONCLUDED THAT HE'D GROWN UP IN PORTUGAL AND IMMIGRATED TO AMERICA AS A YOUNG MAN. "WHAT YEAR DID YOU COME TO AMERICA?" I ASKED.

"HE WAS BORN IN RHODE ISLAND," SAID THE MAN ON THE LEFT.

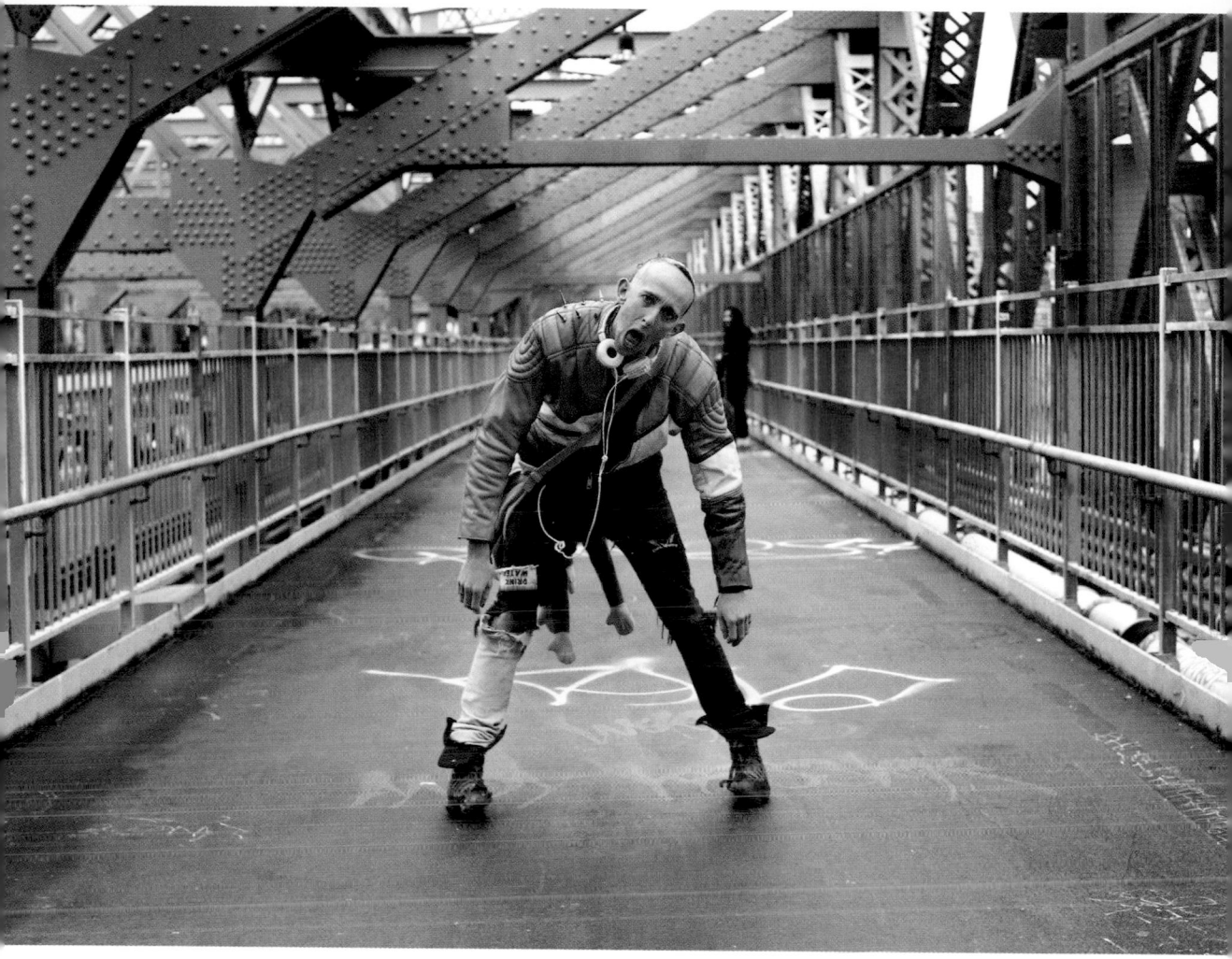

HE INTRODUCED HIMSELF AS CIRCUS, THE TRAVELING MAGICIAN. HE THEN HANDED ME A BOOK OF SPELLS. HERE ARE SOME OF THE HIGHLIGHTS:

THE SPELL TO MAKE STRANGERS WISH YOU A "HAPPY BIRTHDAY": MAKE A SIGN THAT SAYS "IT'S MY BIRTHDAY," AND HANG IT AROUND YOUR NECK.

THE CUDDLE-INDUCING SPELL: SIMPLY HANG UP A SIGN THAT SAYS "CUDDLE ZONE." PUT A FEW SOFT PILLOWS AND BLANKETS UNDER IT.

SPELL TO MAKE OBJECTS MOVE THROUGH THE AIR: MAKE SURE THERE IS A NICE PERSON IN CLOSE PROXIMITY, BOTH TO YOU AND THE OBJECT YOU DESIRE. THEN SIMPLY STRETCH YOUR ARM OUT TOWARD THE OBJECT AND, IN LESS THAN A MINUTE, IT WILL FLOAT MAGICALLY INTO YOUR HAND.

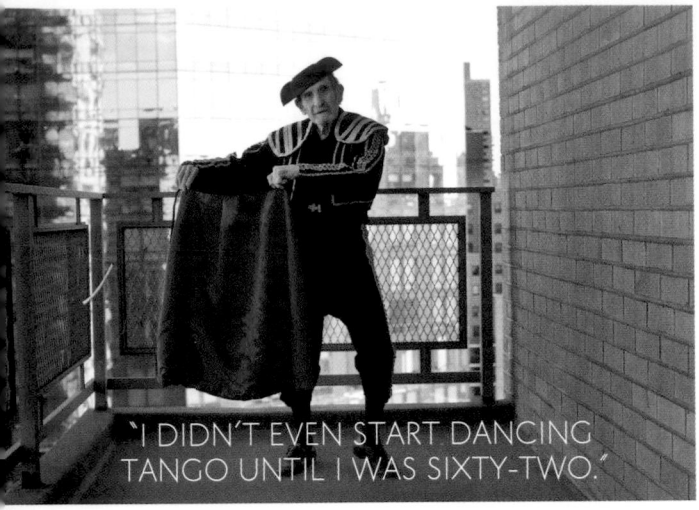

"I DIDN'T EVEN START DANCING TANGO UNTIL I WAS SIXTY-TWO."

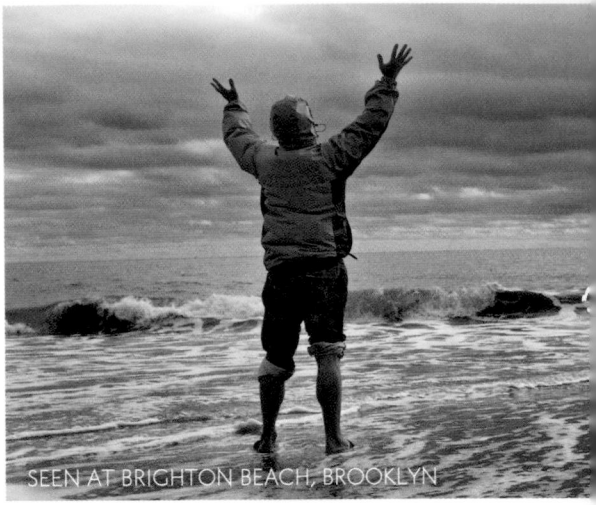

SEEN AT BRIGHTON BEACH, BROOKLYN

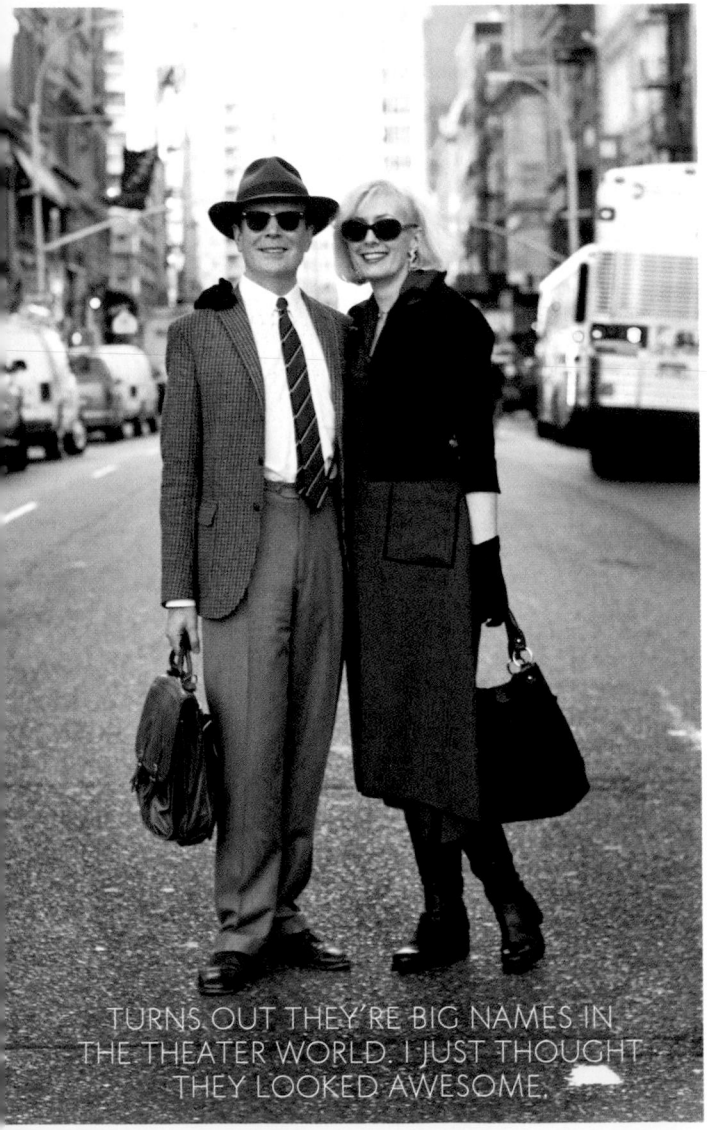

TURNS OUT THEY'RE BIG NAMES IN THE THEATER WORLD. I JUST THOUGHT THEY LOOKED AWESOME.

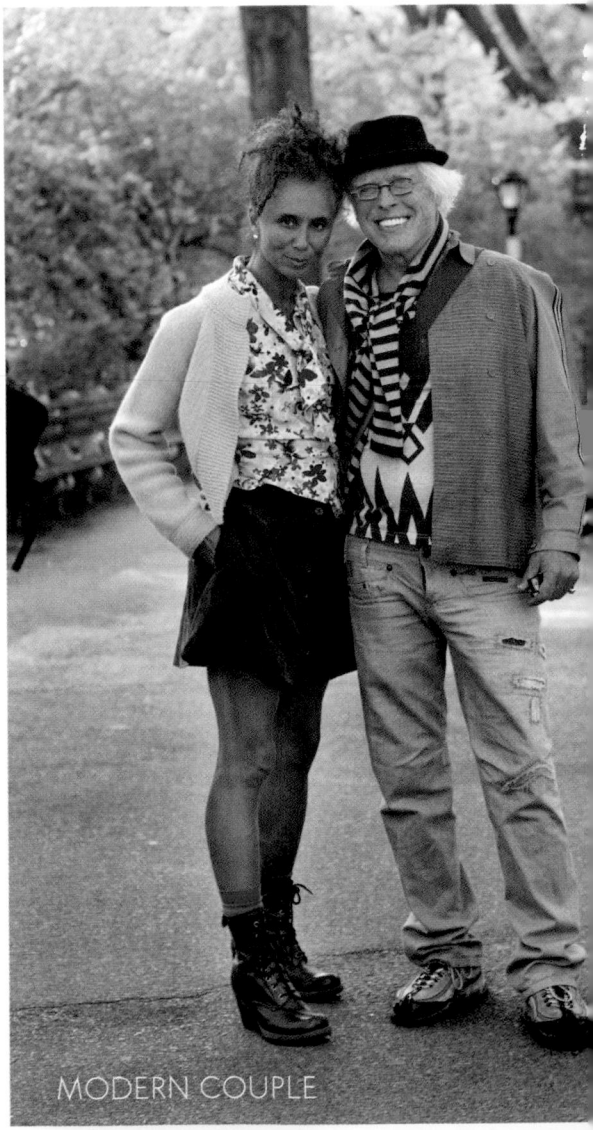

MODERN COUPLE

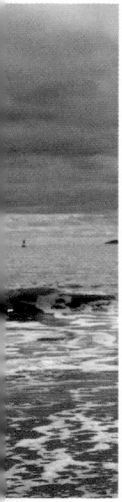

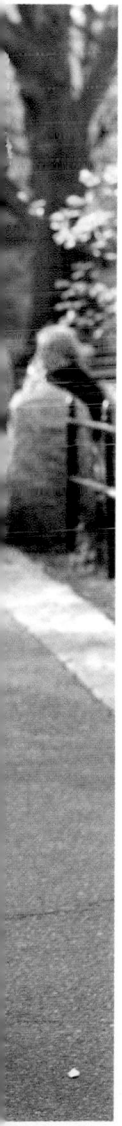

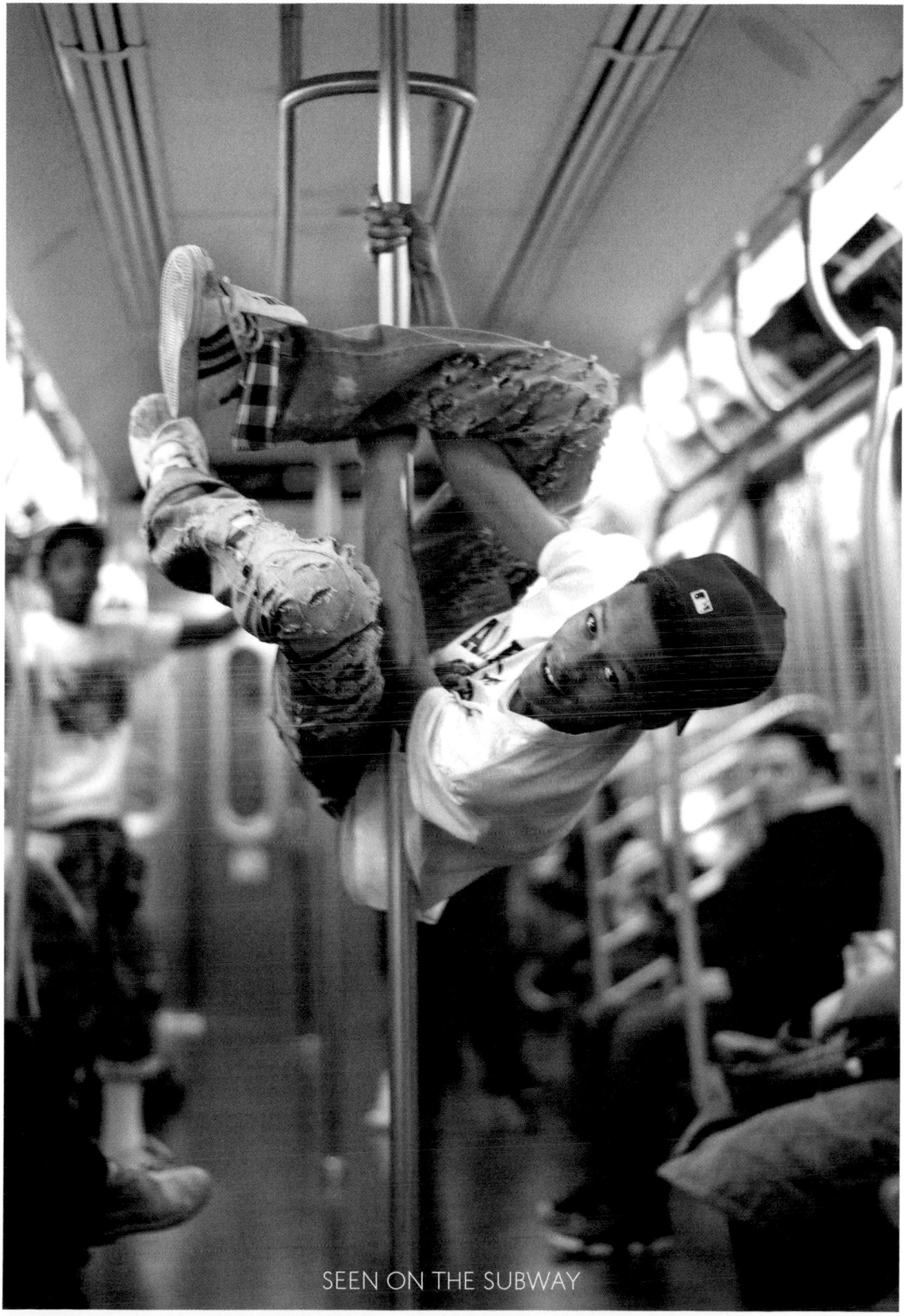

SEEN ON THE SUBWAY

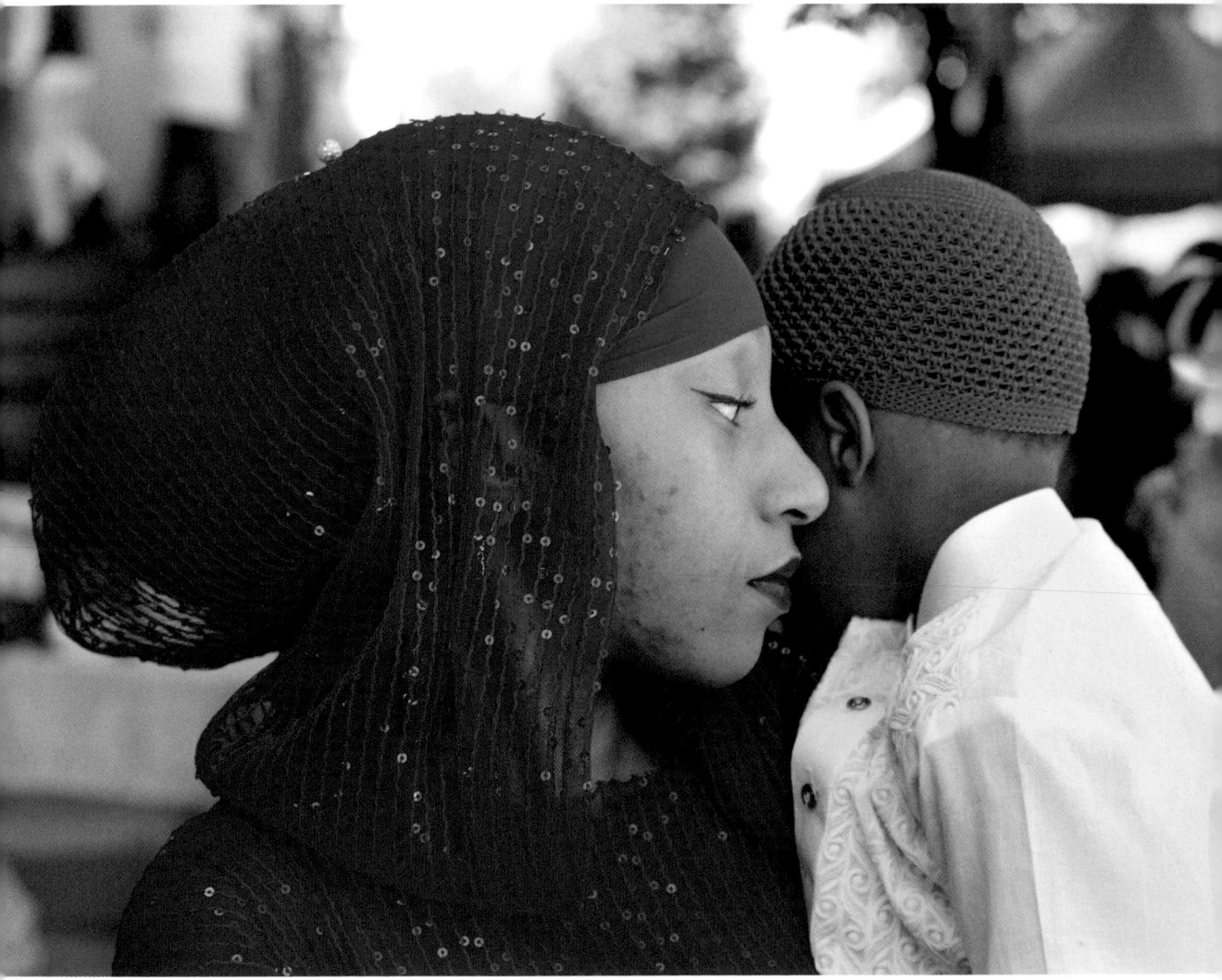

"SORRY HE'S SO SHY."

THESE TWO WERE WATCHING
CLOUDS IN WASHINGTON SQUARE
PARK, JUST LIKE THIS.

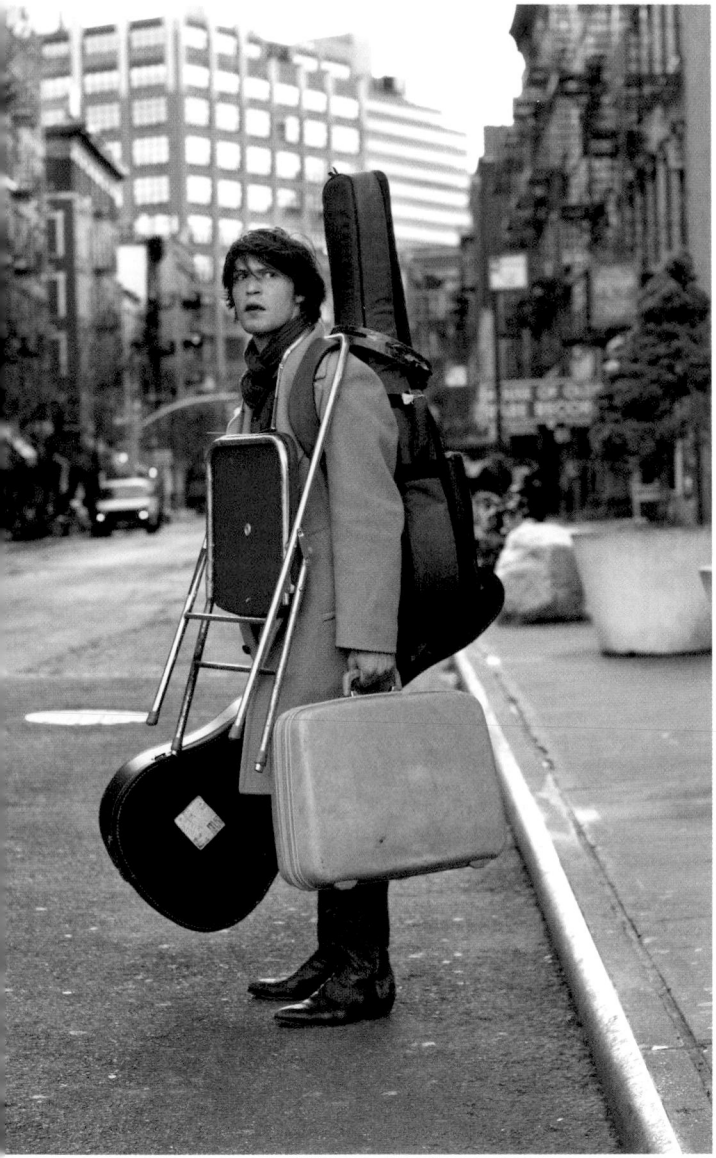

HE SAID: "I'VE GOT TO FIND A NEW SYSTEM FOR CARRYING MY STUFF."

AN OLD LADY WALKED BY, AND SAID: "CLOSE YOUR MOUTH!"

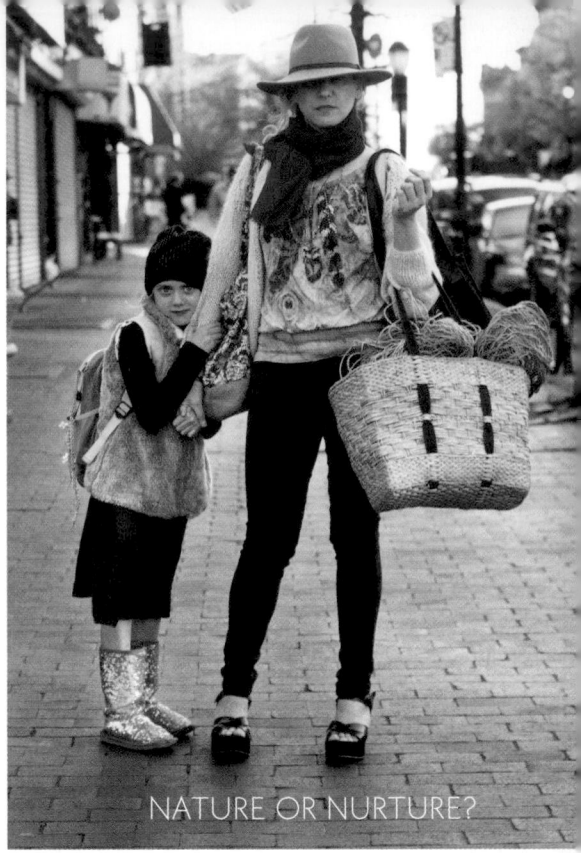

NATURE OR NURTURE?

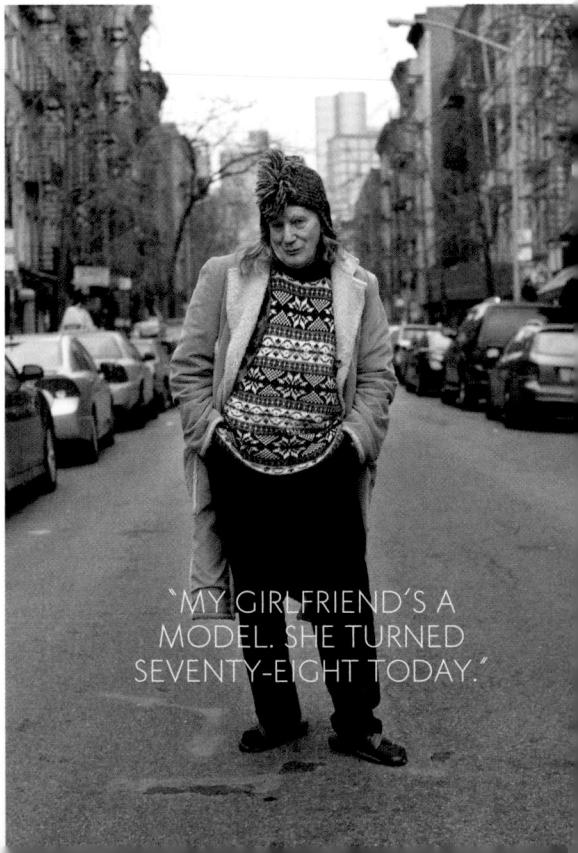

"MY GIRLFRIEND'S A MODEL. SHE TURNED SEVENTY-EIGHT TODAY."

THIS GIRL CAUGHT MY ATTENTION BECAUSE SHE WAS READING A FULL-PAGE, TIGHTLY SPACED, HANDWRITTEN LETTER. I ASKED HER IF IT WAS A HAPPY LETTER OR A SAD LETTER. "IT'S A VERY HAPPY LETTER," SHE SAID. "IT'S FROM MY BOYFRIEND IN JAIL."

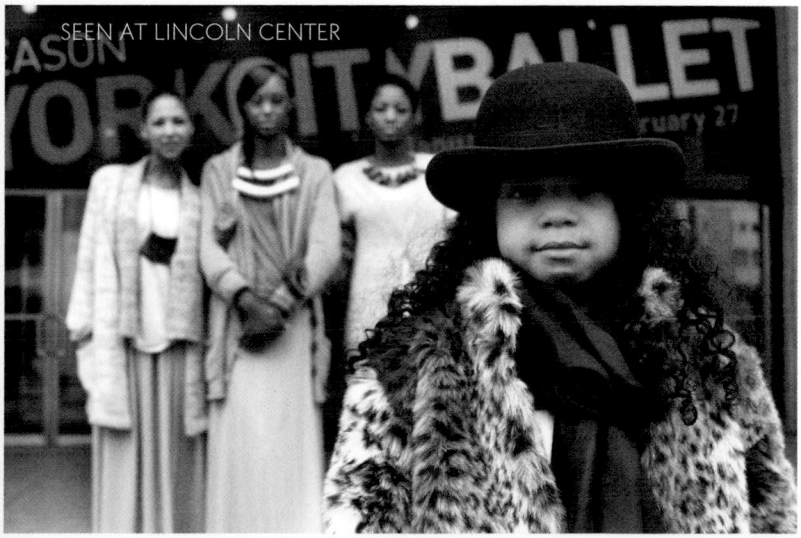


SEEN AT LINCOLN CENTER

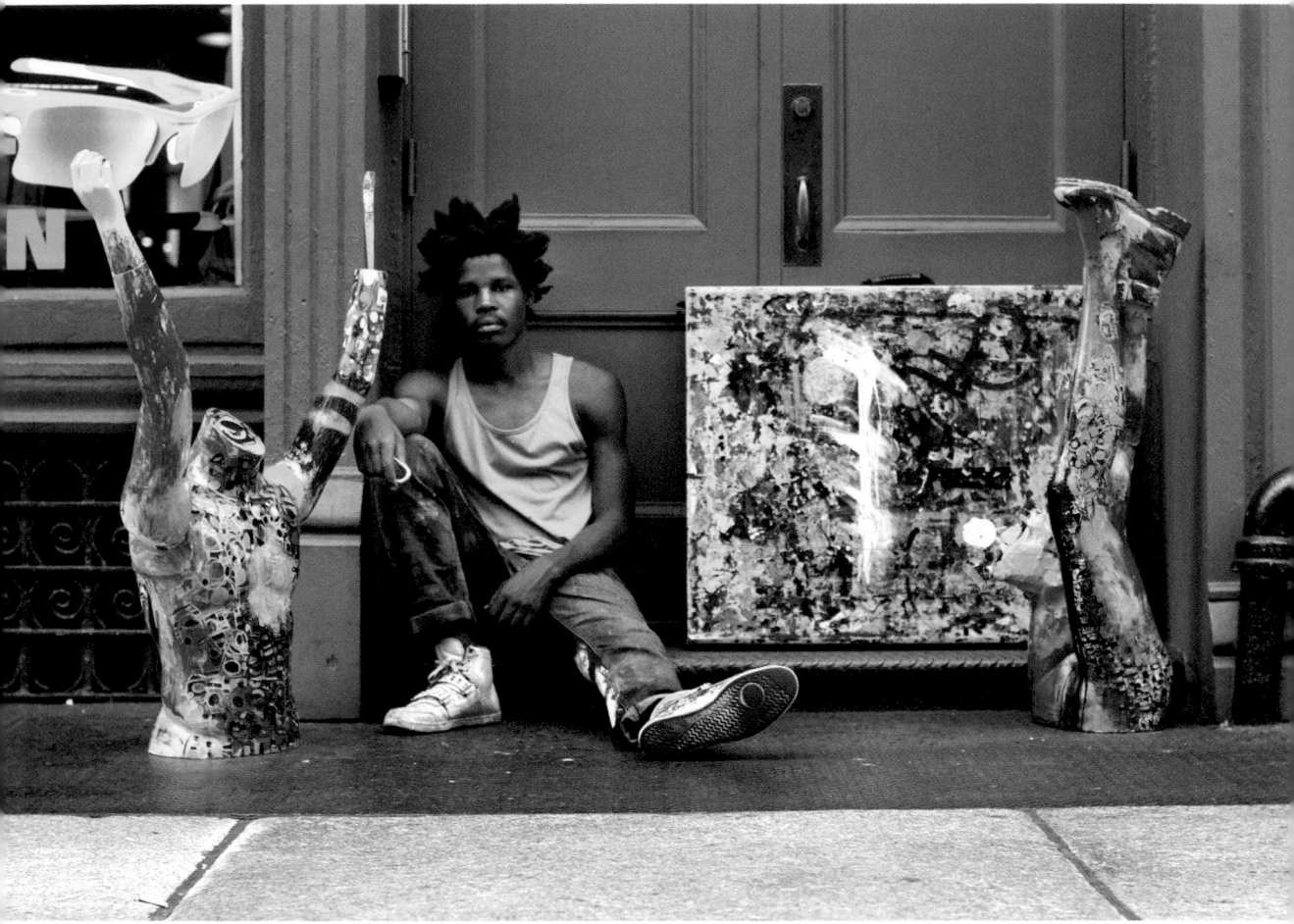

SOME ART COSTS AN ARM AND A LEG.
SOME ART IS AN ARM AND A LEG.

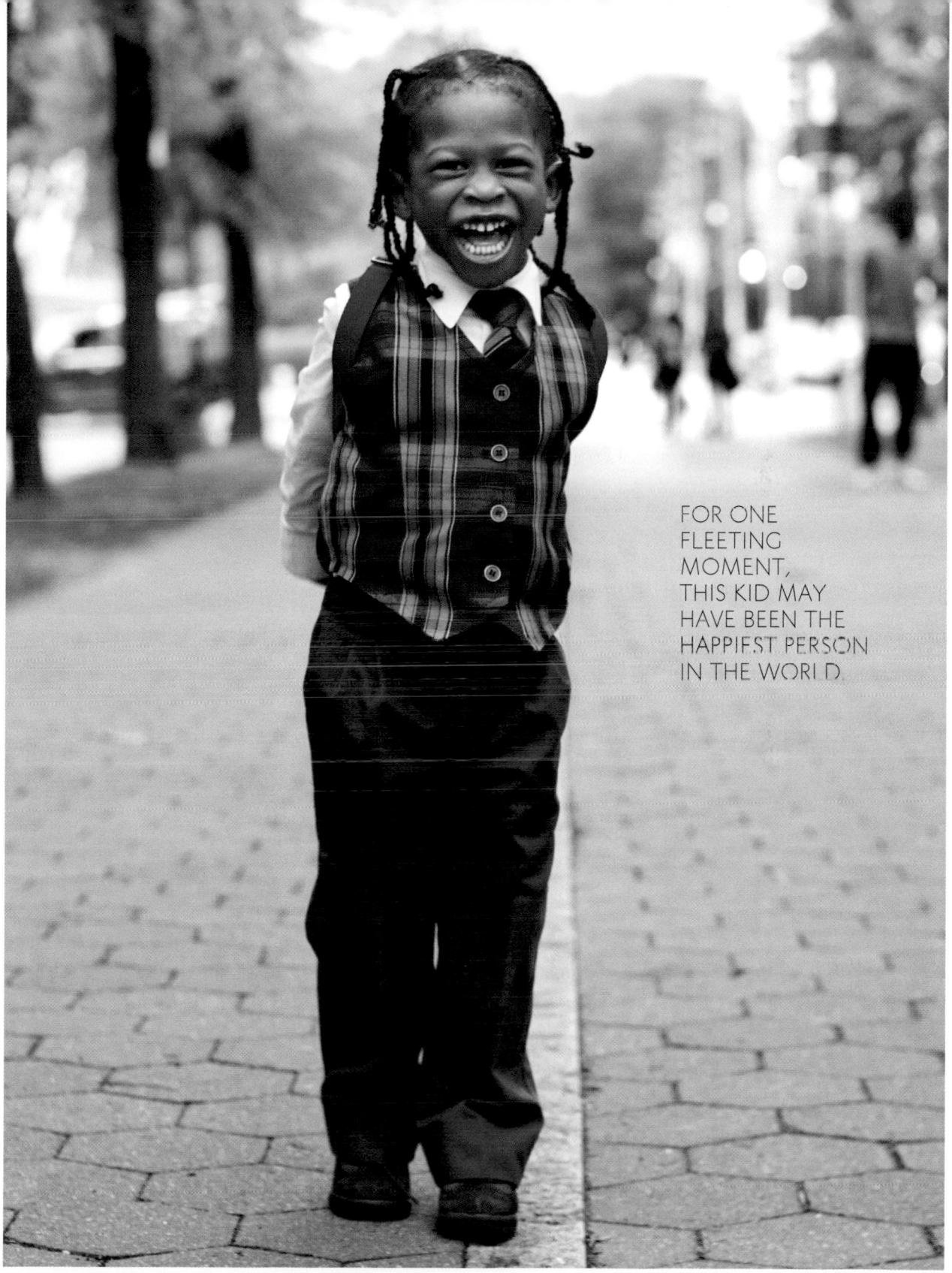
FOR ONE
FLEETING
MOMENT,
THIS KID MAY
HAVE BEEN THE
HAPPIEST PERSON
IN THE WORLD.

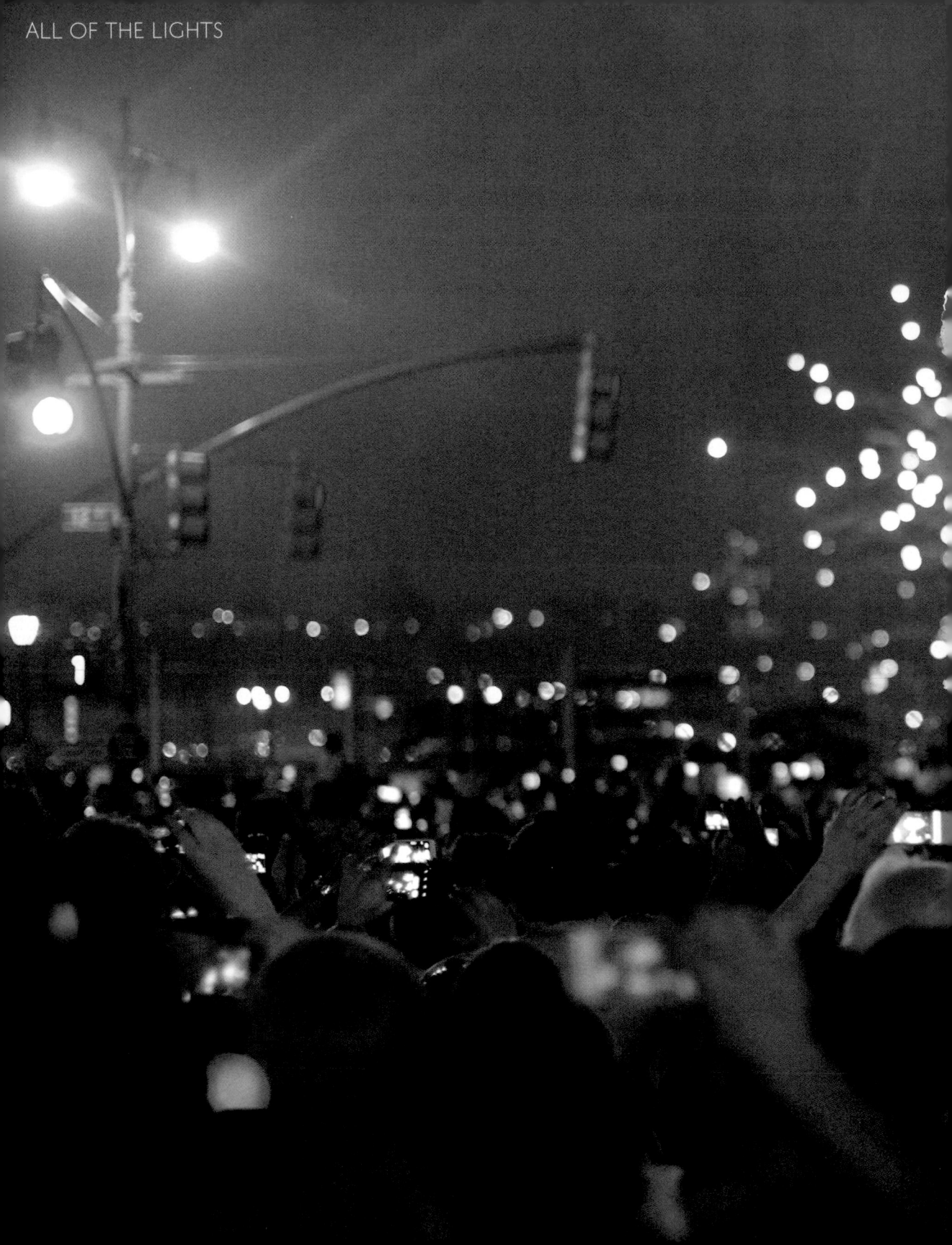

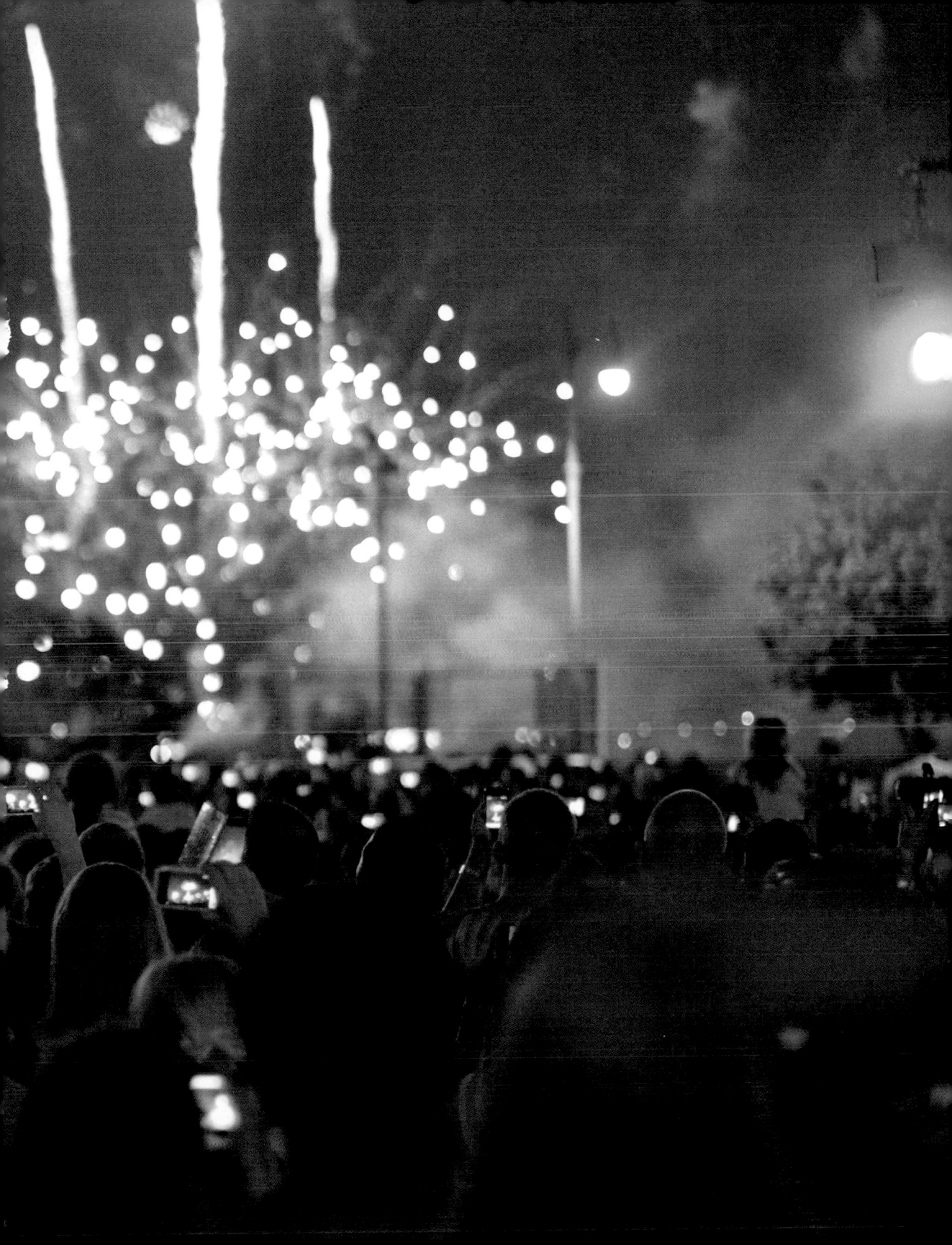

ONE OF THOSE RARE OCCASIONS WHEN DAD IS WEARING A JACKET COVERED IN CARTOONS, AND YOU'RE NOT EMBARRASSED AT ALL.

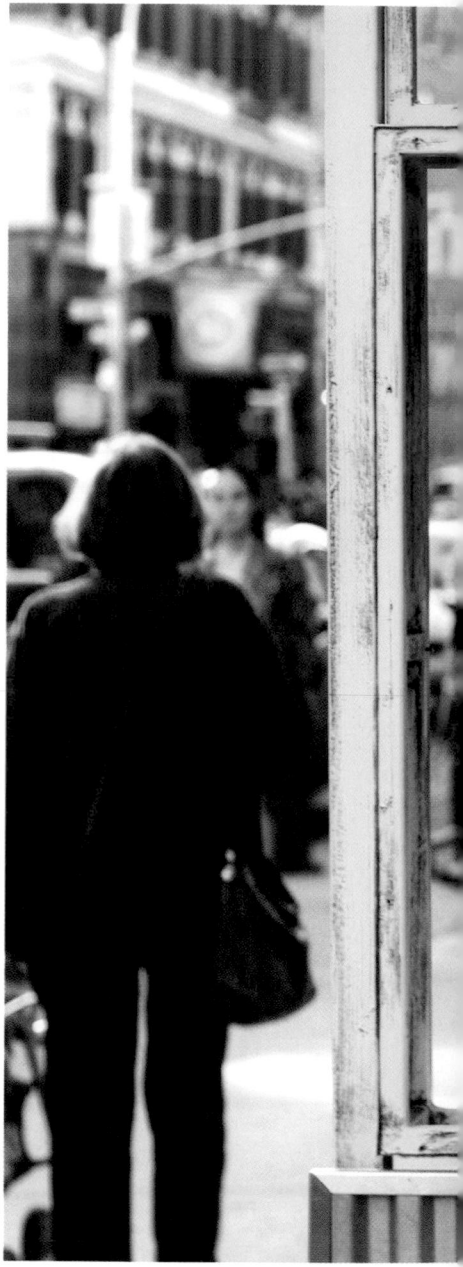

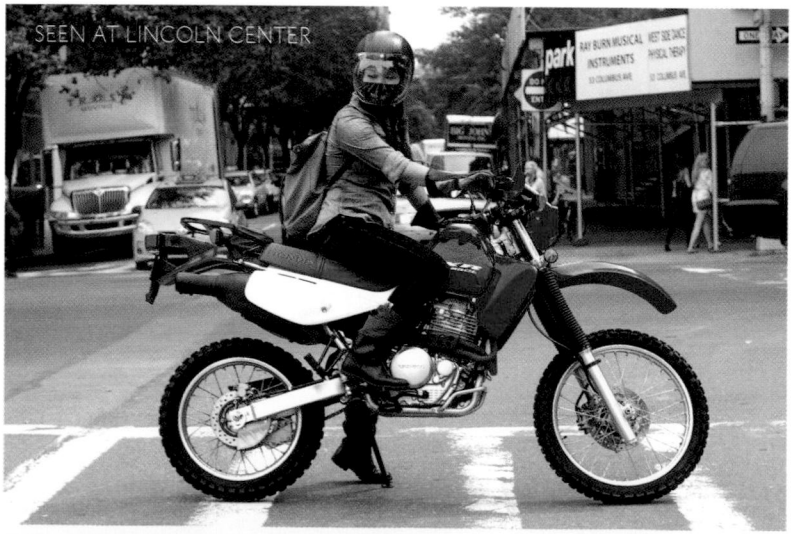


SEEN AT LINCOLN CENTER

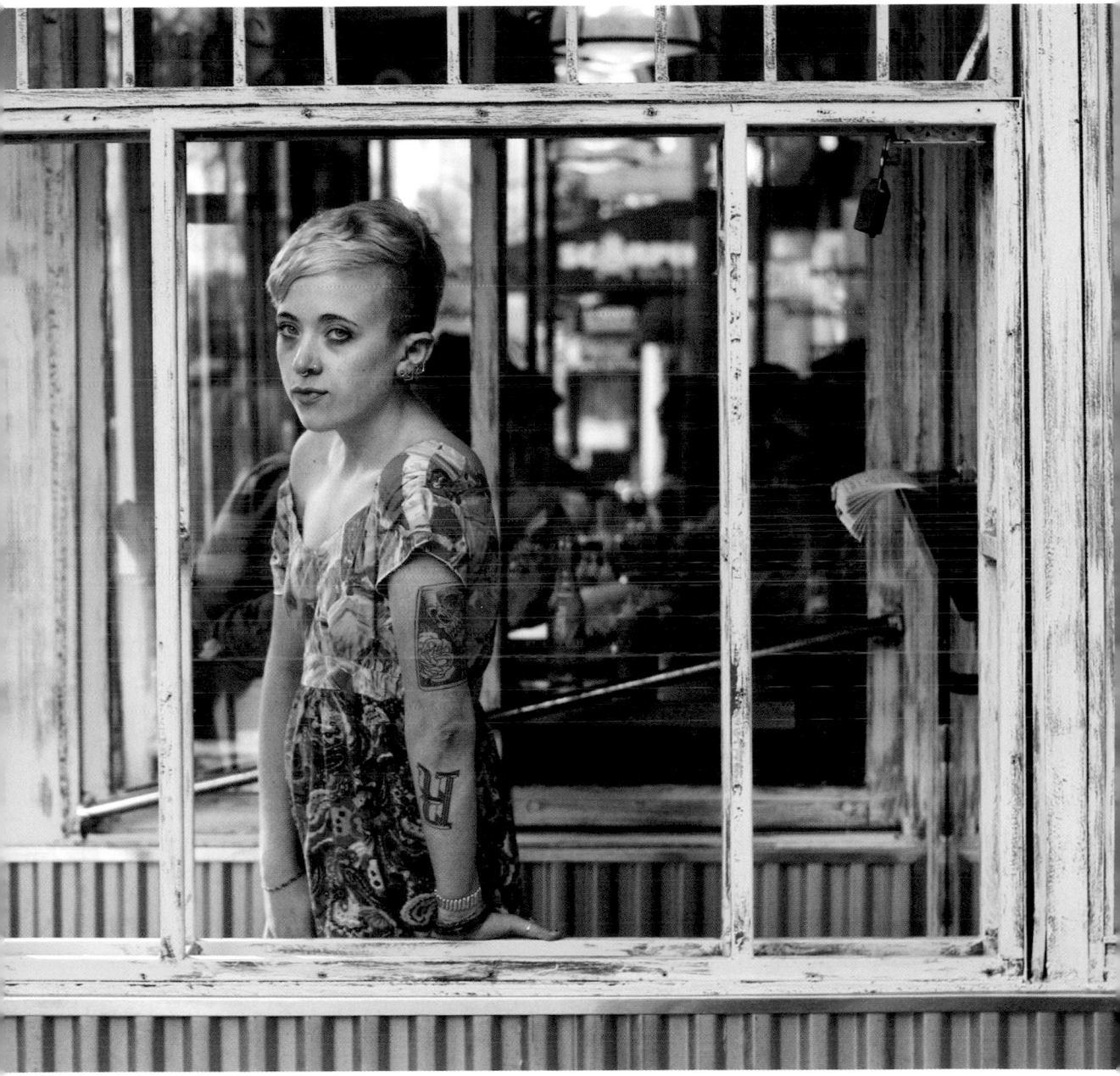

SHE HAD THE MOST BEAUTIFUL AWKWARDNESS.

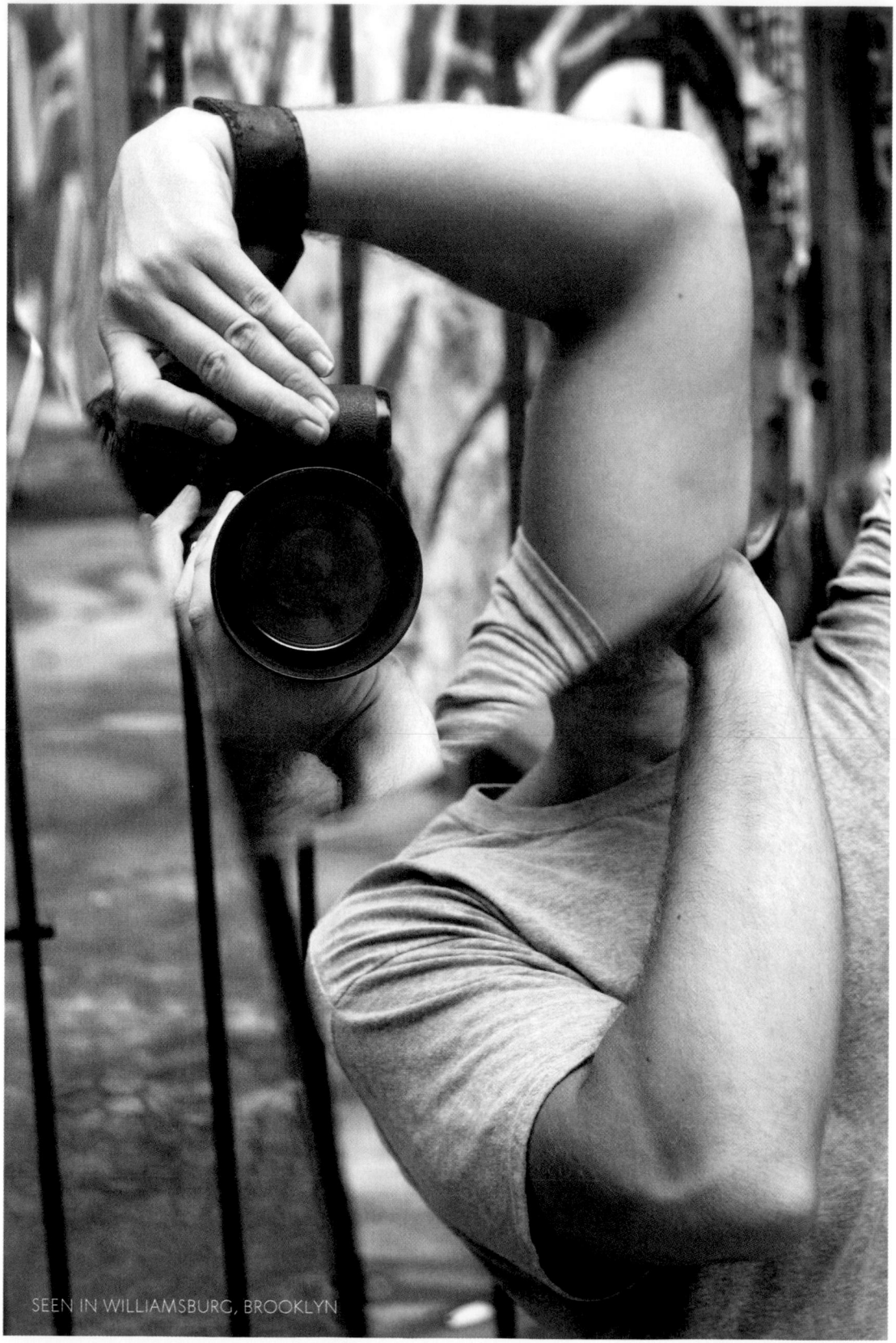

SEEN IN WILLIAMSBURG, BROOKLYN

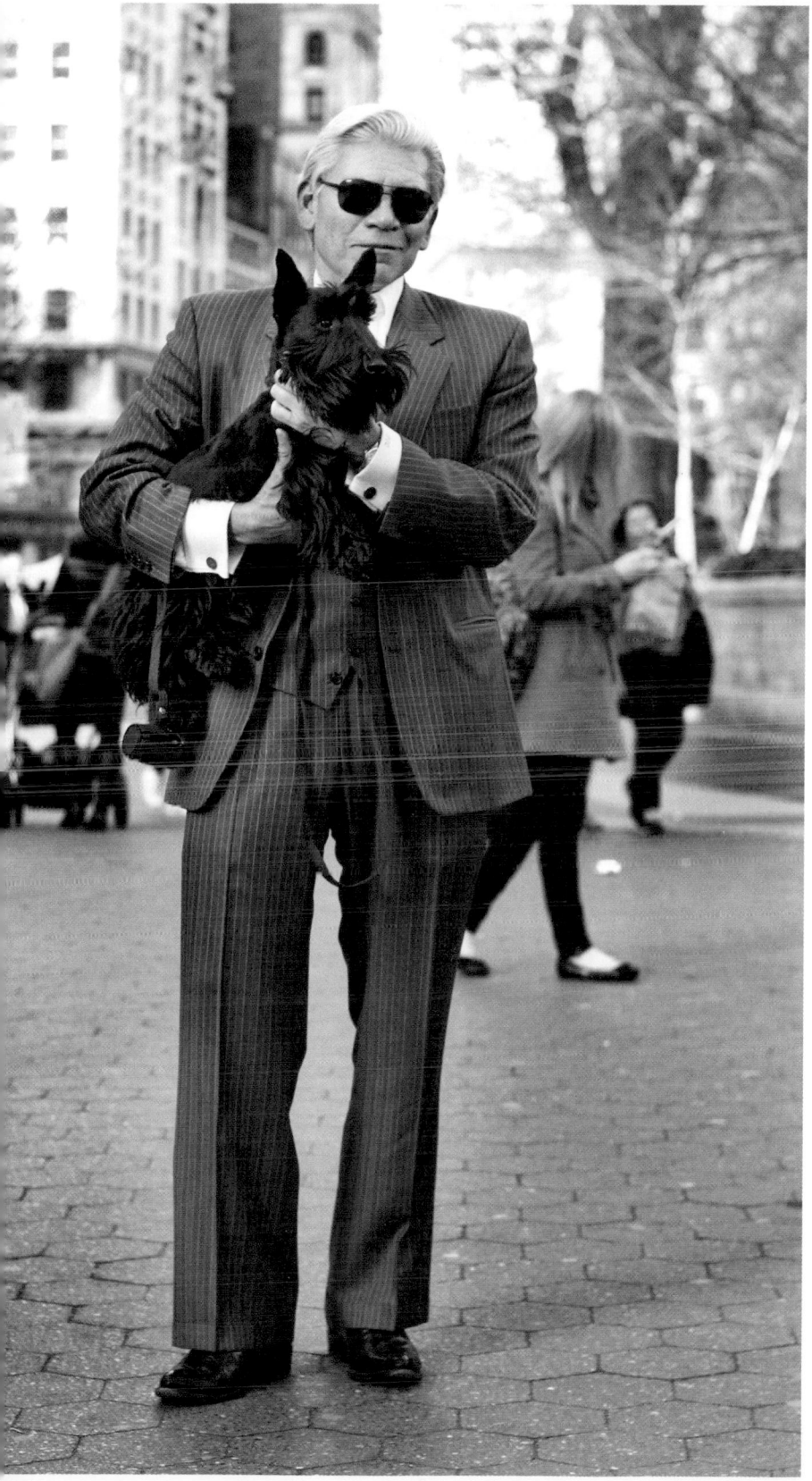

"I ALWAYS WORK MY DOG'S NAME INTO MY CLOSING ARGUMENT."

"THAT'S SO AWESOME."

"YEAH, BUT YOU NEVER WANT ME AS YOUR LAWYER."

"WHY'S THAT?"

"'CAUSE THAT MEANS YOU'RE IN DEEP, DEEP FUCKING TROUBLE."

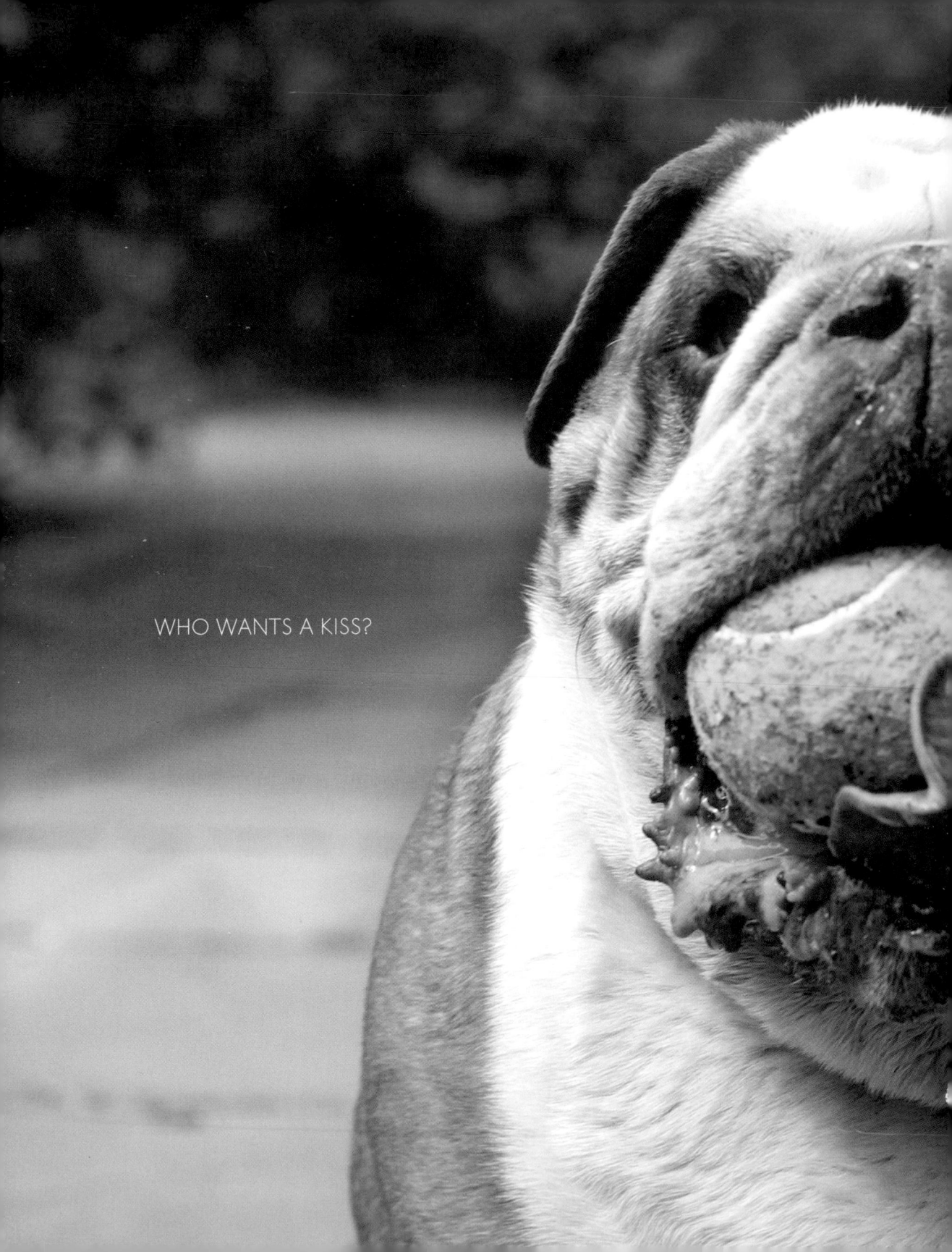
WHO WANTS A KISS?

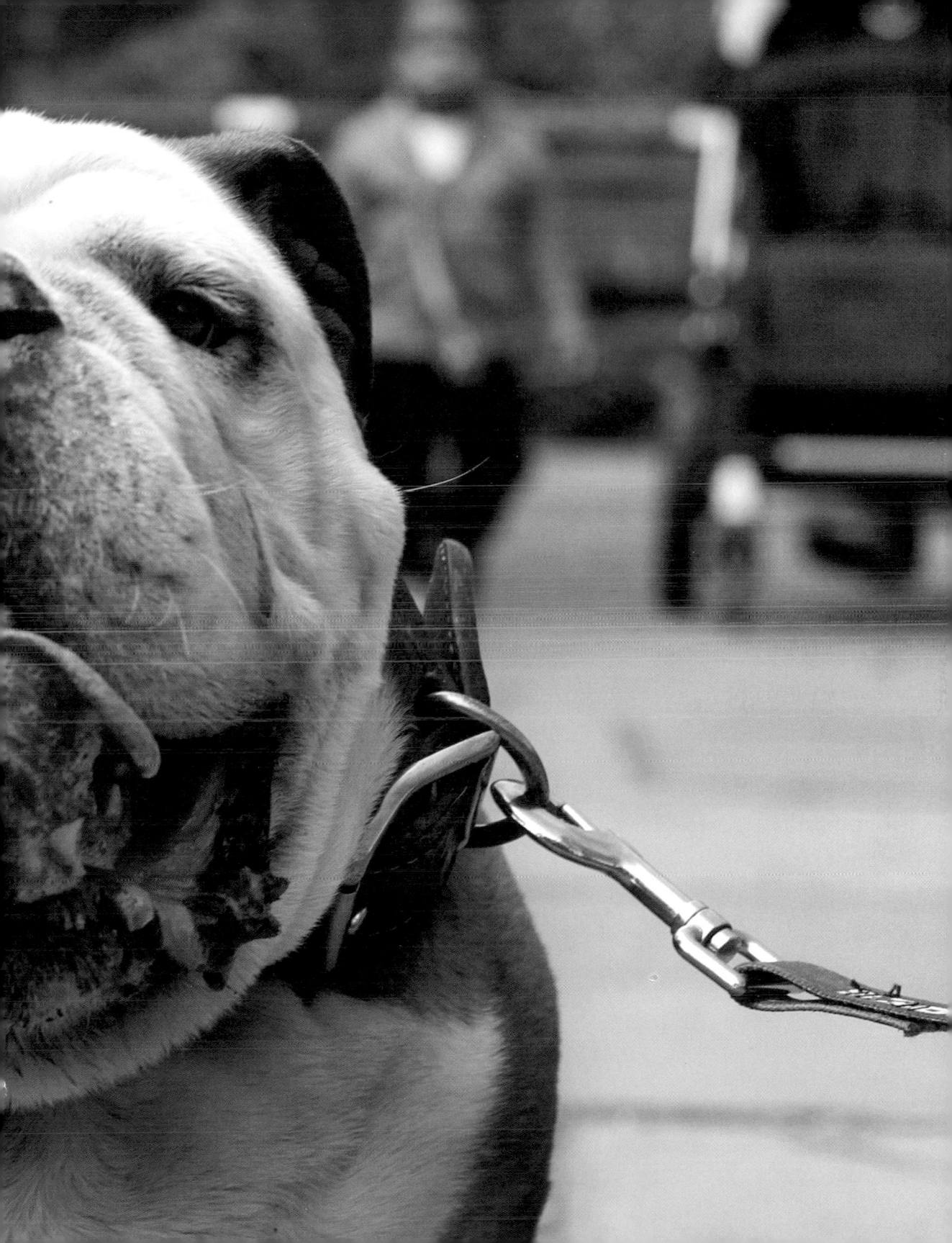

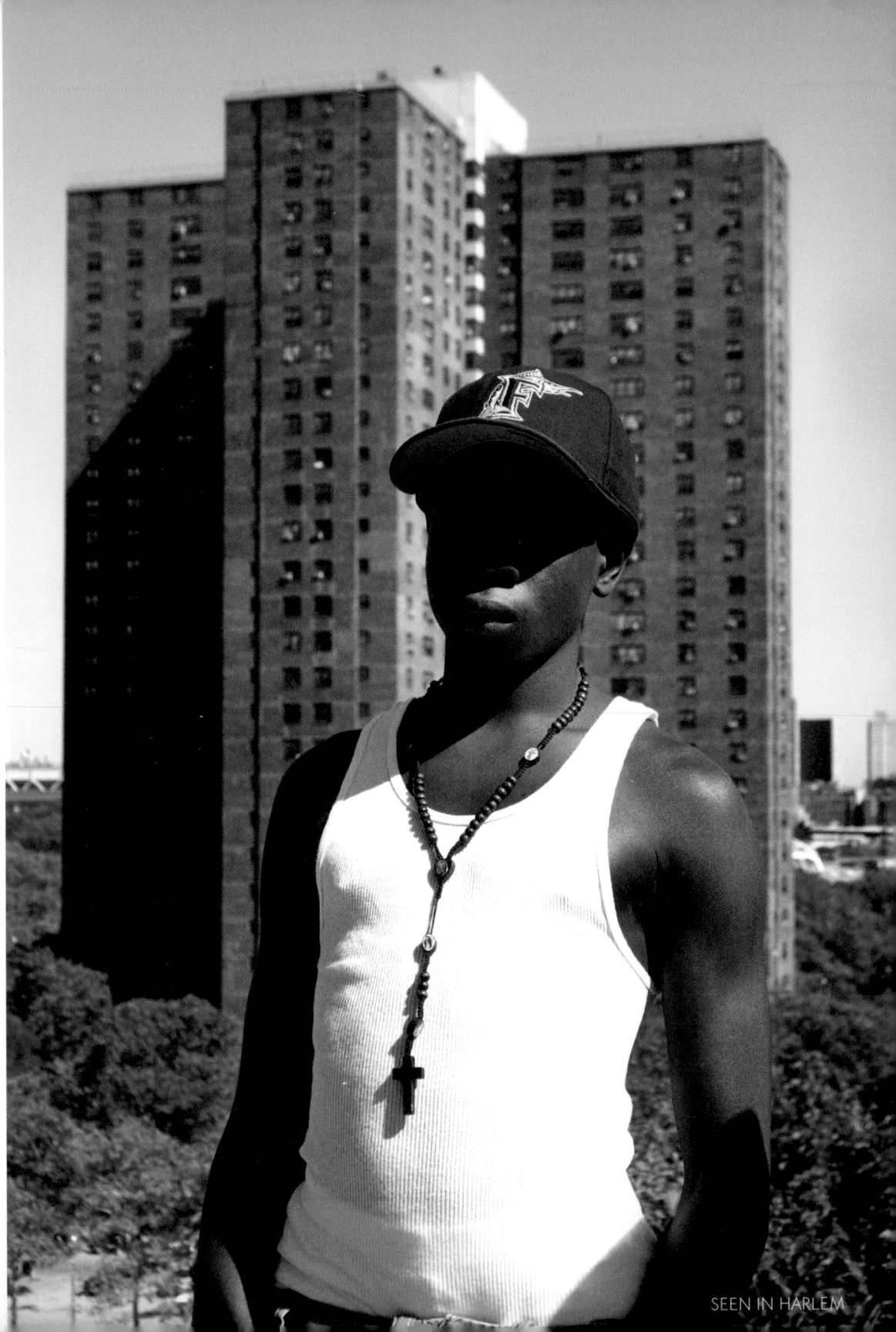

SEEN IN HARLEM

SEEN IN THE SUBWAY

SEEN IN RED HOOK, BROOKLYN

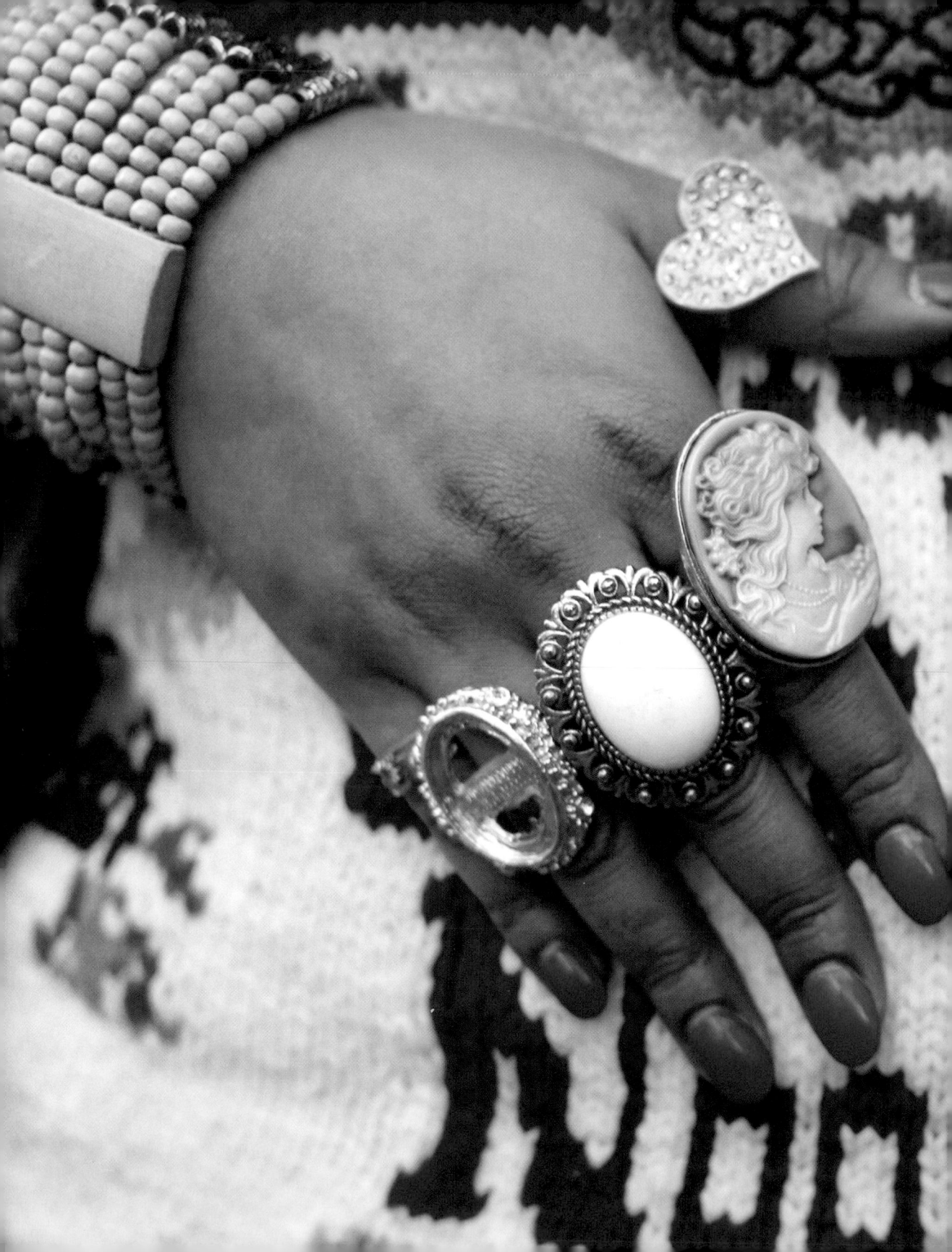

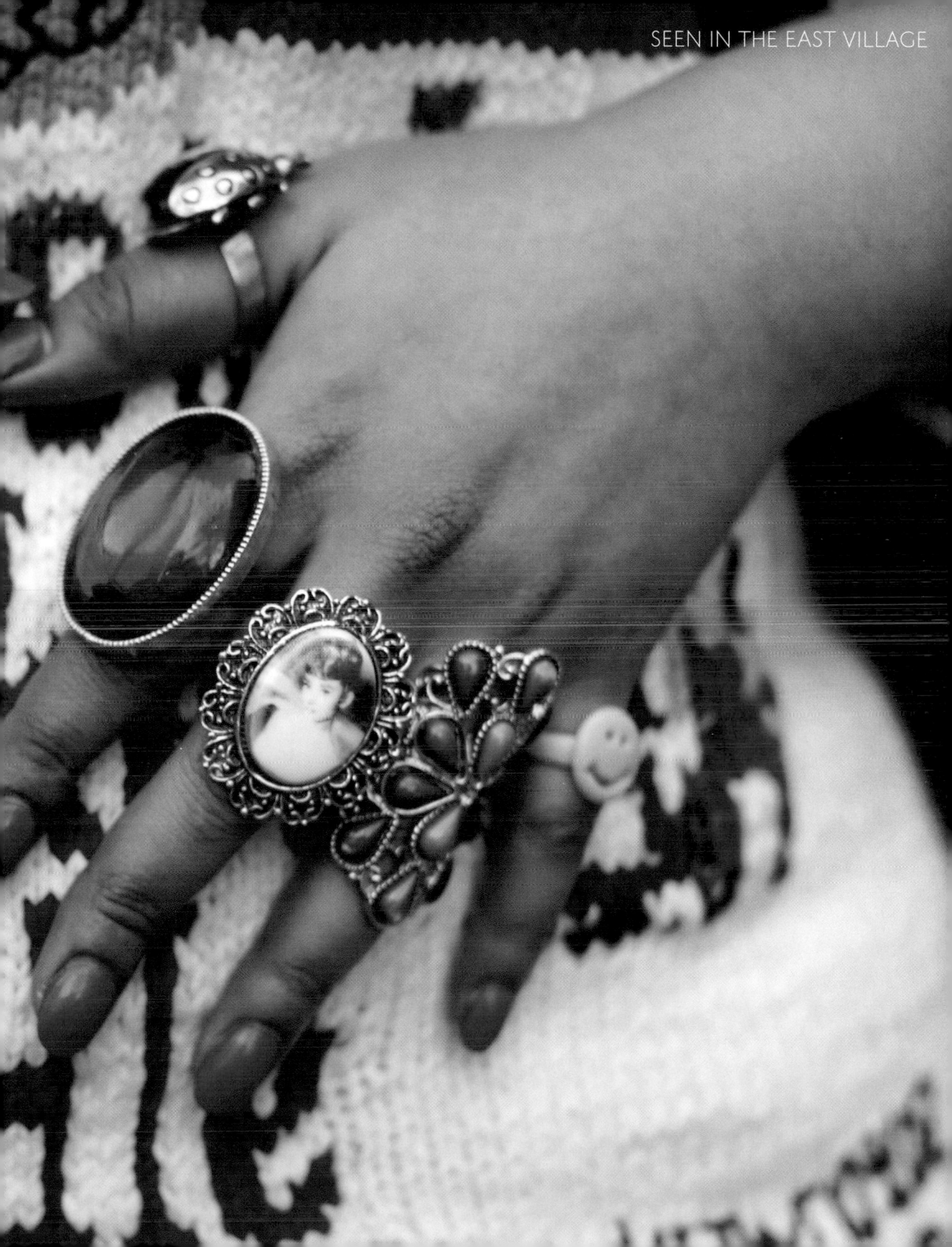

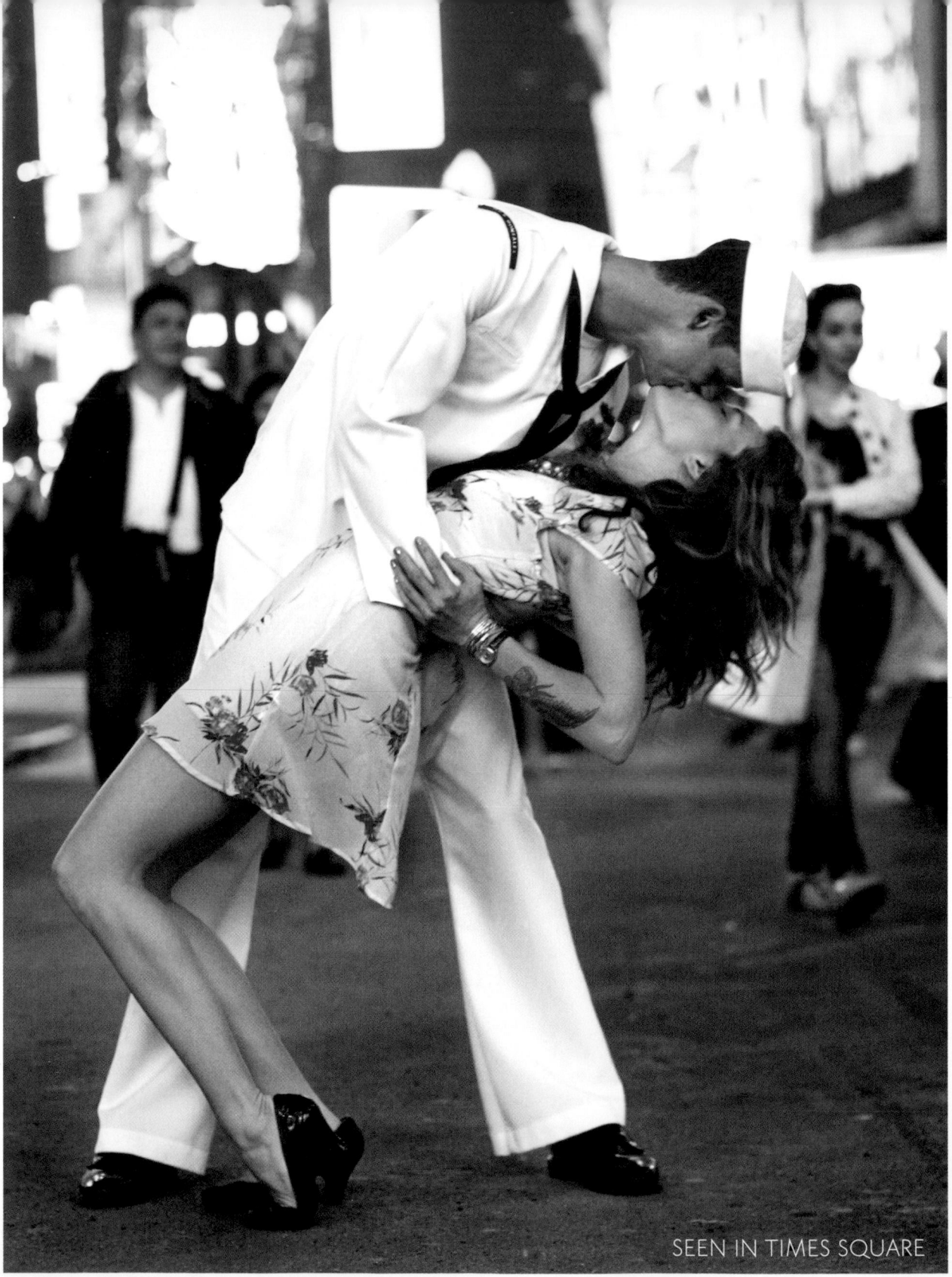

SEEN IN TIMES SQUARE

CASTING OFF

MARK TWAIN STILL COASTING OFF THOSE *HUCK FINN* ROYALTIES.

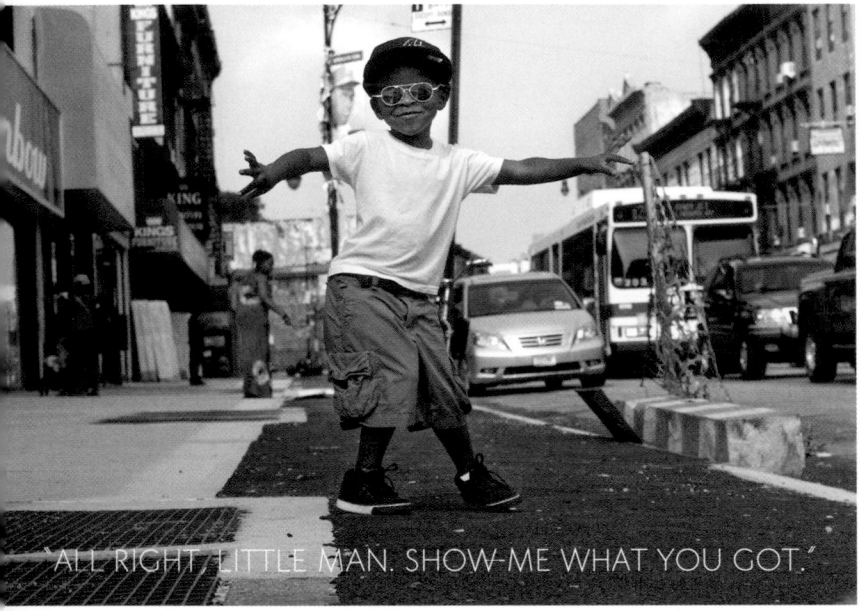

'ALL RIGHT, LITTLE MAN. SHOW ME WHAT YOU GOT.'

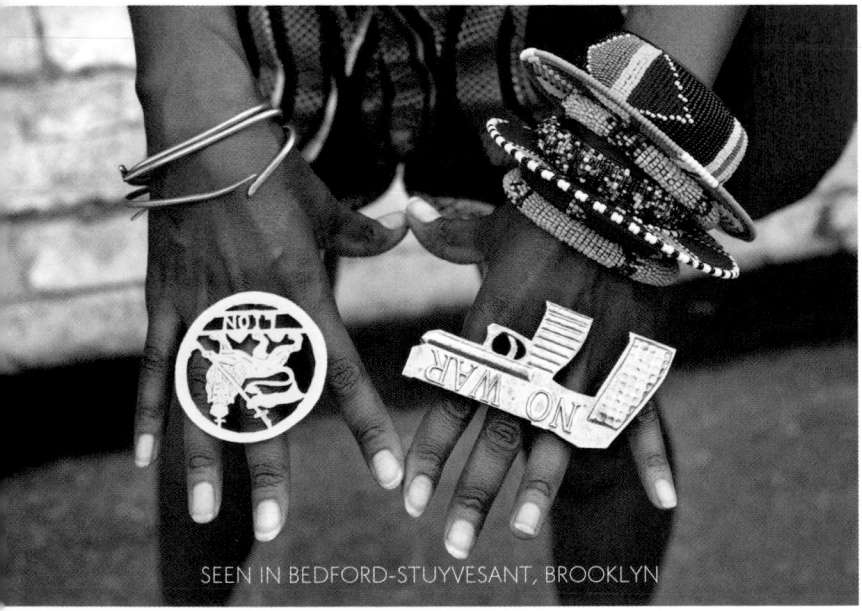


SEEN IN BEDFORD-STUYVESANT, BROOKLYN

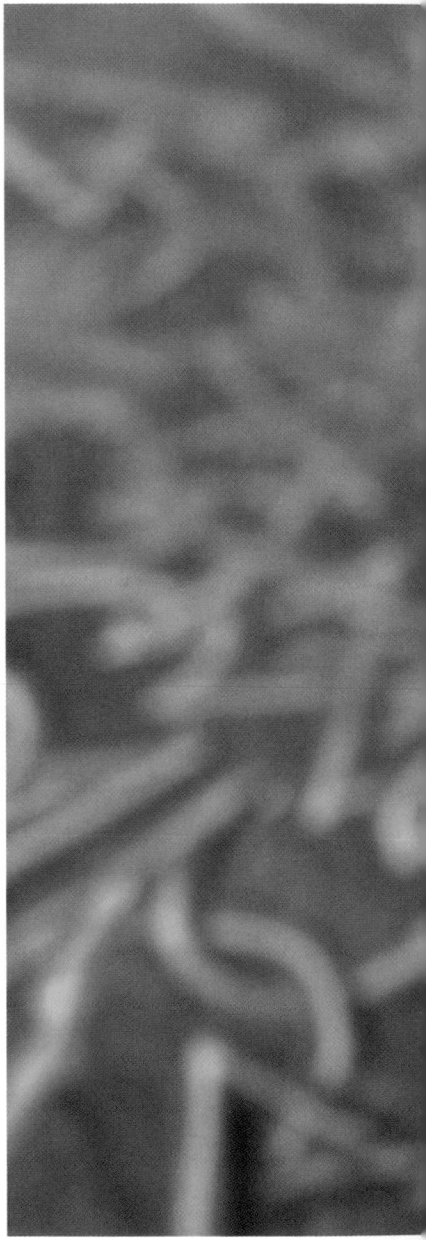

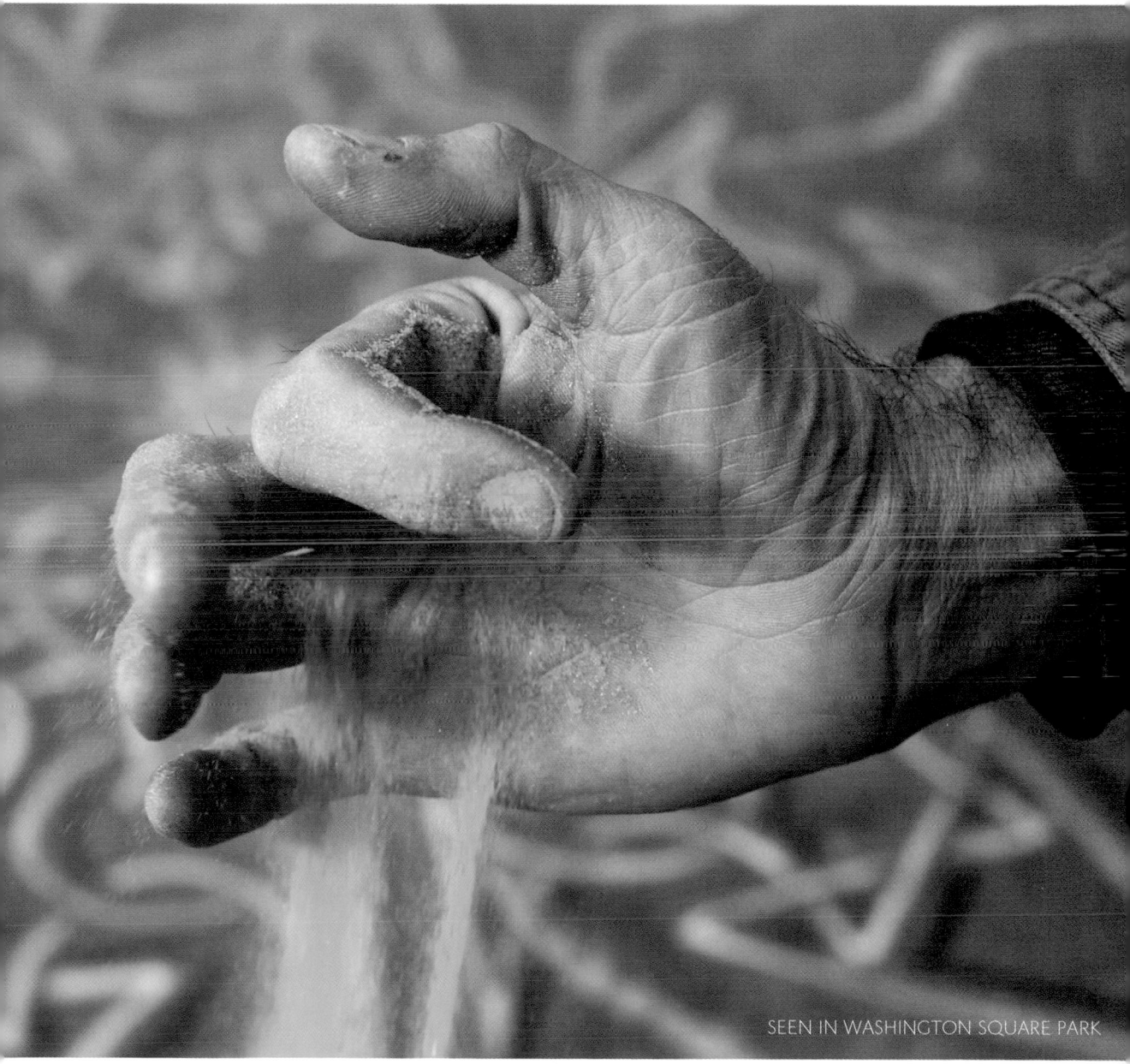

SEEN IN WASHINGTON SQUARE PARK

TESTOSTERONE REARED ITS HEAD ON AN UPTOWN 5 TRAIN LAST NIGHT.

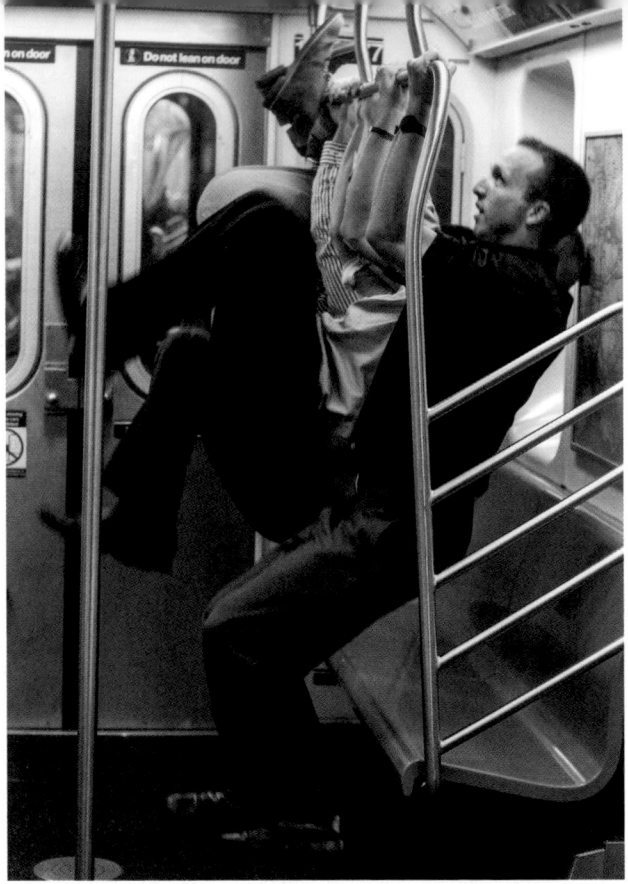


"I'M AN ILLUSTRATOR."

"WHERE CAN I SEE YOUR WORK?"

"TRUST ME, YOU'VE ALREADY SEEN IT."

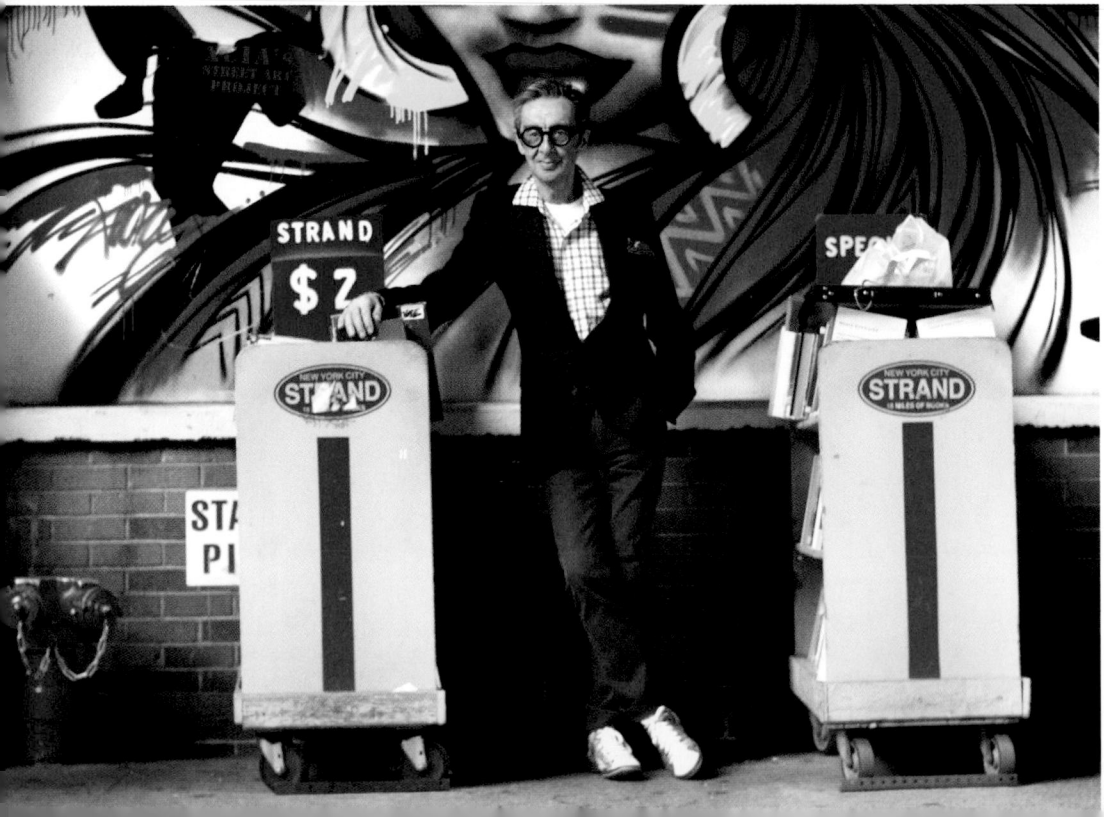

"I'M A PHOTOGRAPHER."

"WHAT DO YOU PHOTOGRAPH?"

"MYSELF."

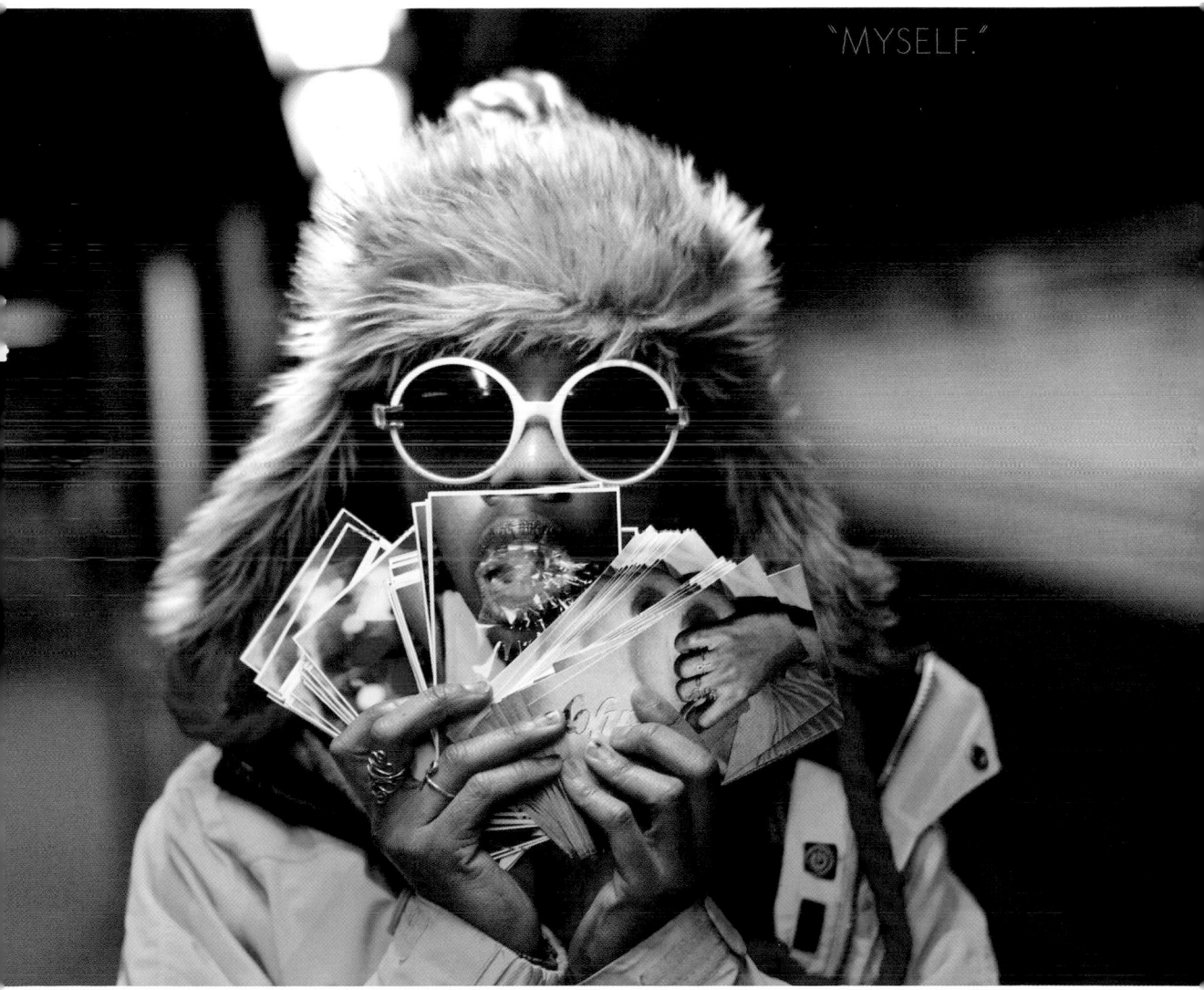

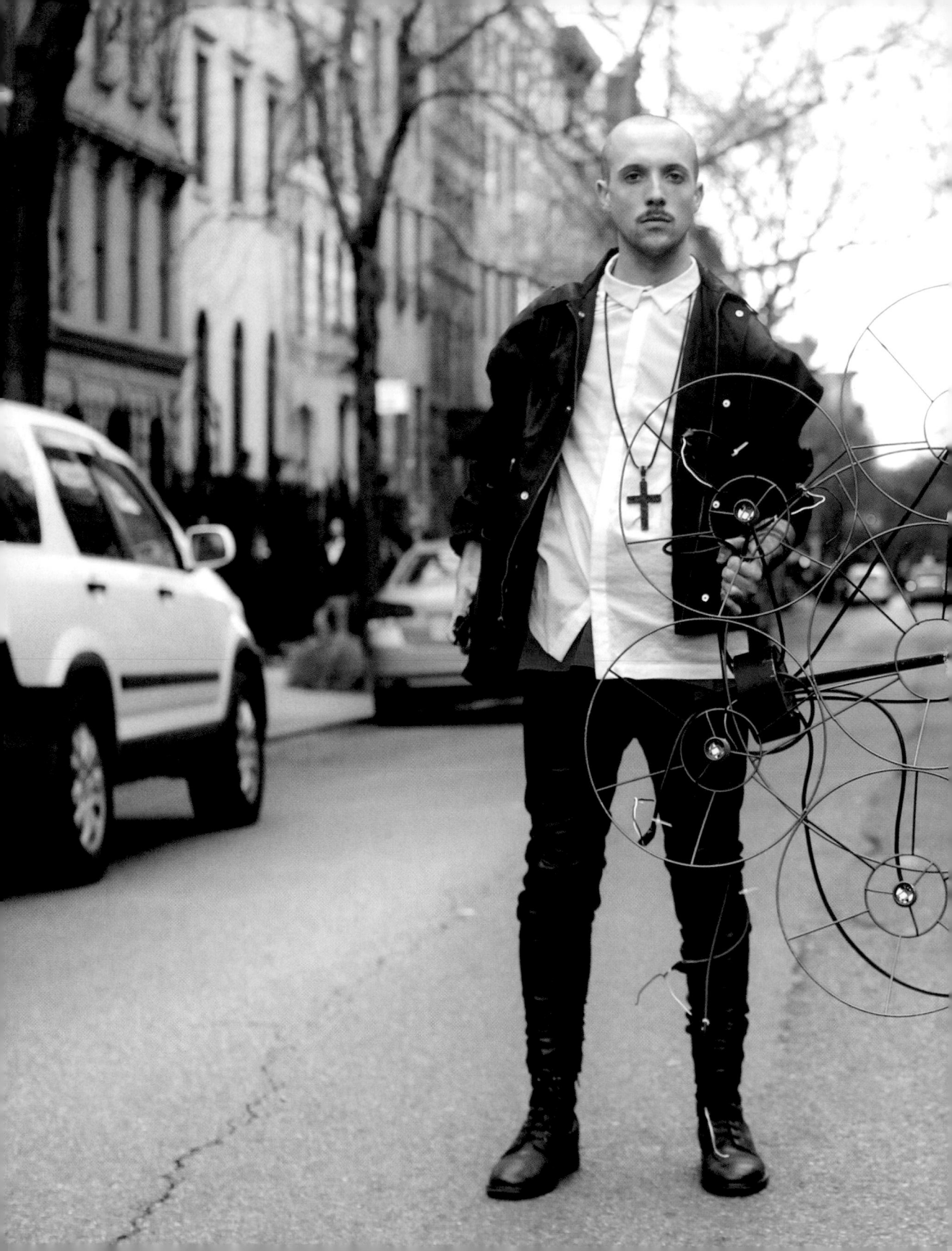

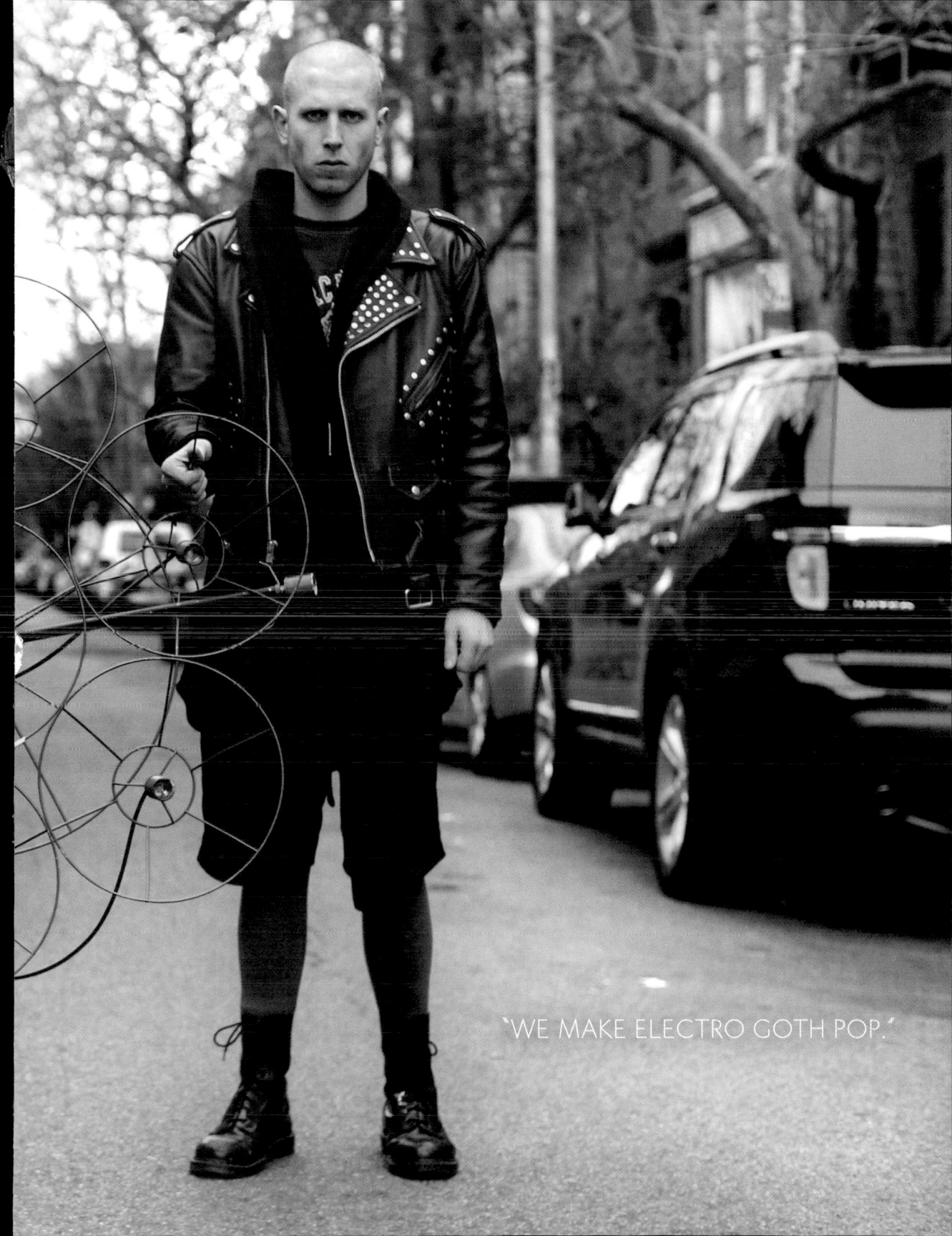

"WE MAKE ELECTRO GOTH POP."

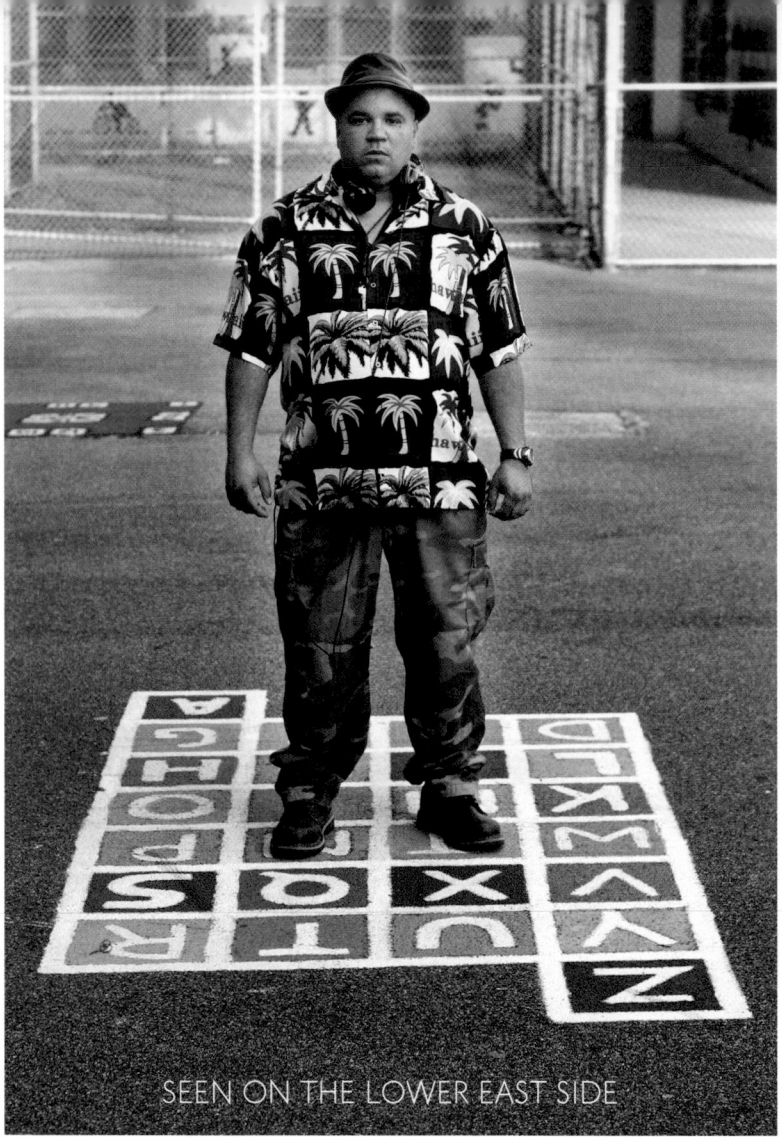


SEEN ON THE LOWER EAST SIDE

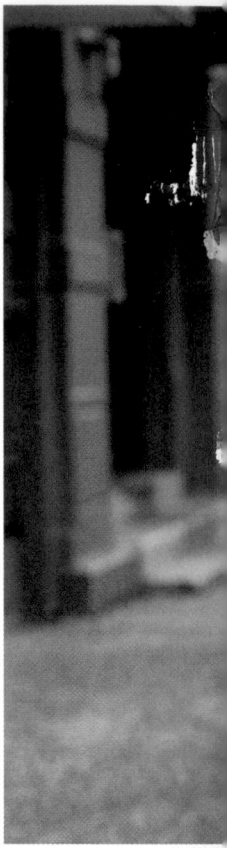

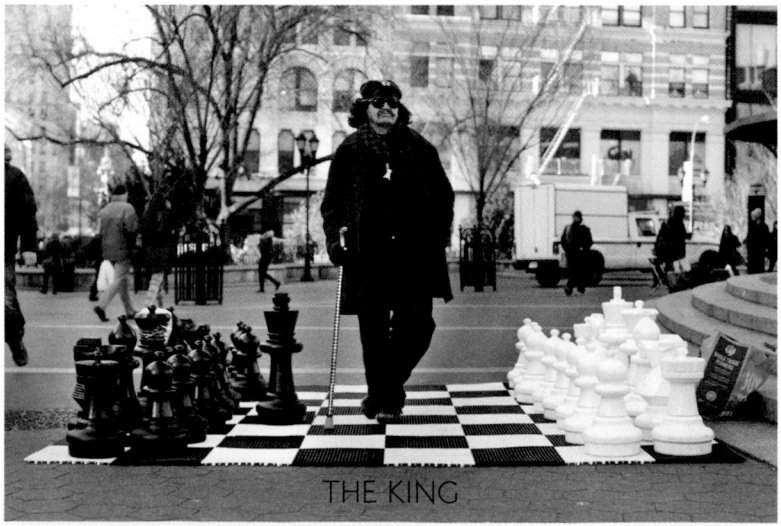

THE KING

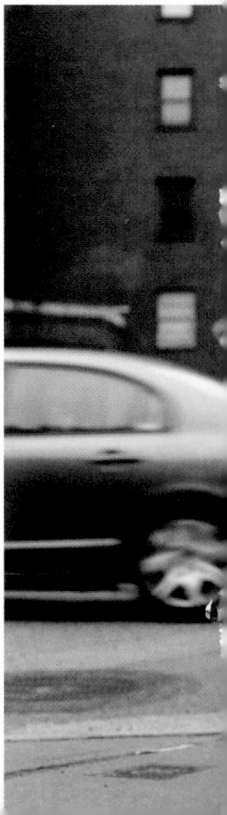

SEEN IN WASHINGTON HEIGHTS

"I'VE BEEN MARRIED FIFTY YEARS. IF I WAS TO GIVE ONE PIECE OF ADVICE TO YOUNG COUPLES, IT'D BE THIS: NEVER LOSE YOUR TEMPER AT THE SAME TIME. IF SOMEBODY'S REALLY MAD, THE OTHER ONE BETTER MAKE A RETREAT."

I FOUND THESE TWO HUNCHED OVER ON BROADWAY, JUST LIKE THIS. IT SEEMED LIKE AN INTERESTING MOMENT, SO I QUICKLY SNAPPED THE PHOTO, THEN APPROACHED THEM TO FIND OUT WHAT WAS SO INTERESTING ABOUT TODAY'S PAPER. THE MAN SEEMED SHEEPISH WHEN HE ANSWERED: "MY FILM JUST GOT REVIEWED BY *THE NEW YORK TIMES*," HE SAID, "SO I'M SHOWING MY DAUGHTER."

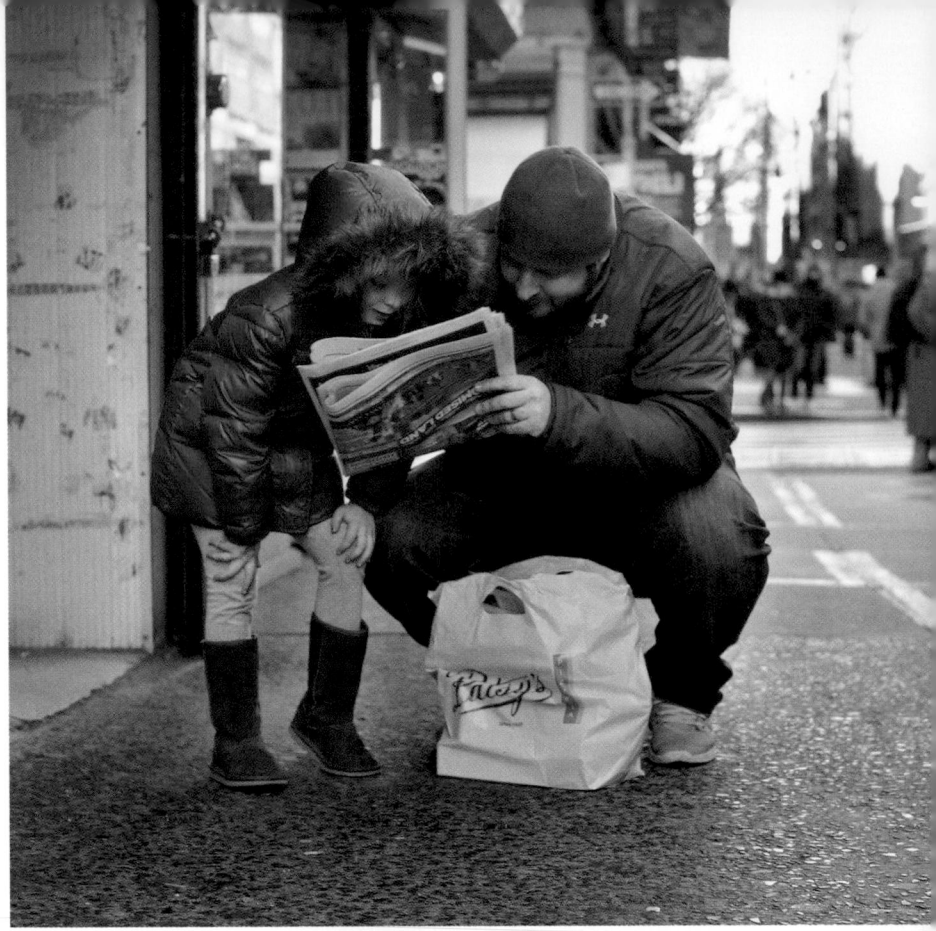

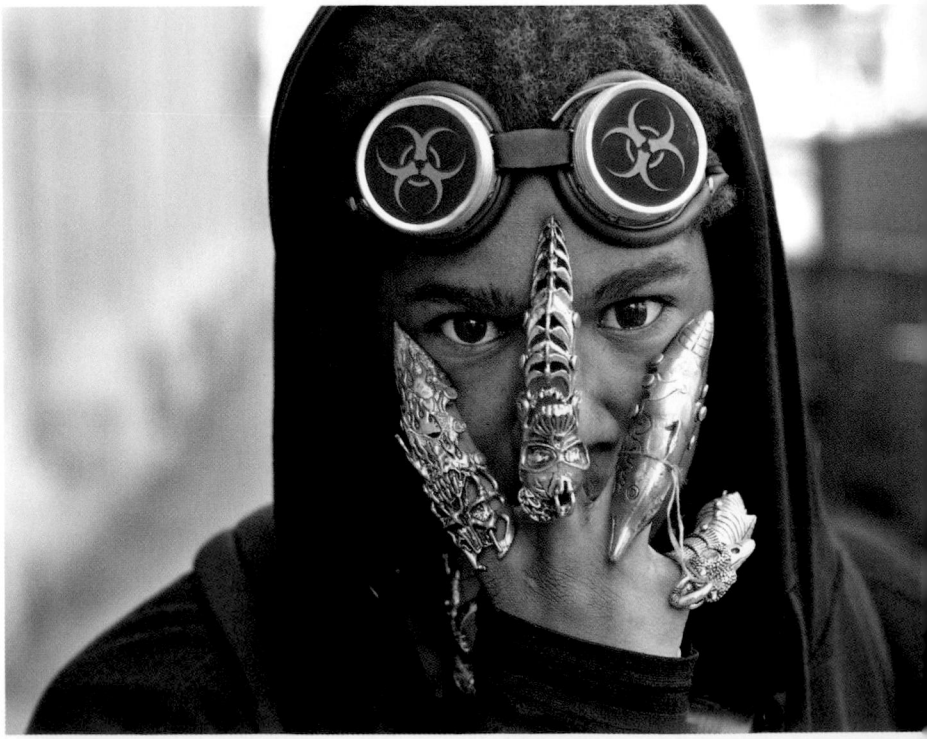

SOMETIMES THE LOUDEST PERSONAS BELONG TO THE QUIETEST PEOPLE.

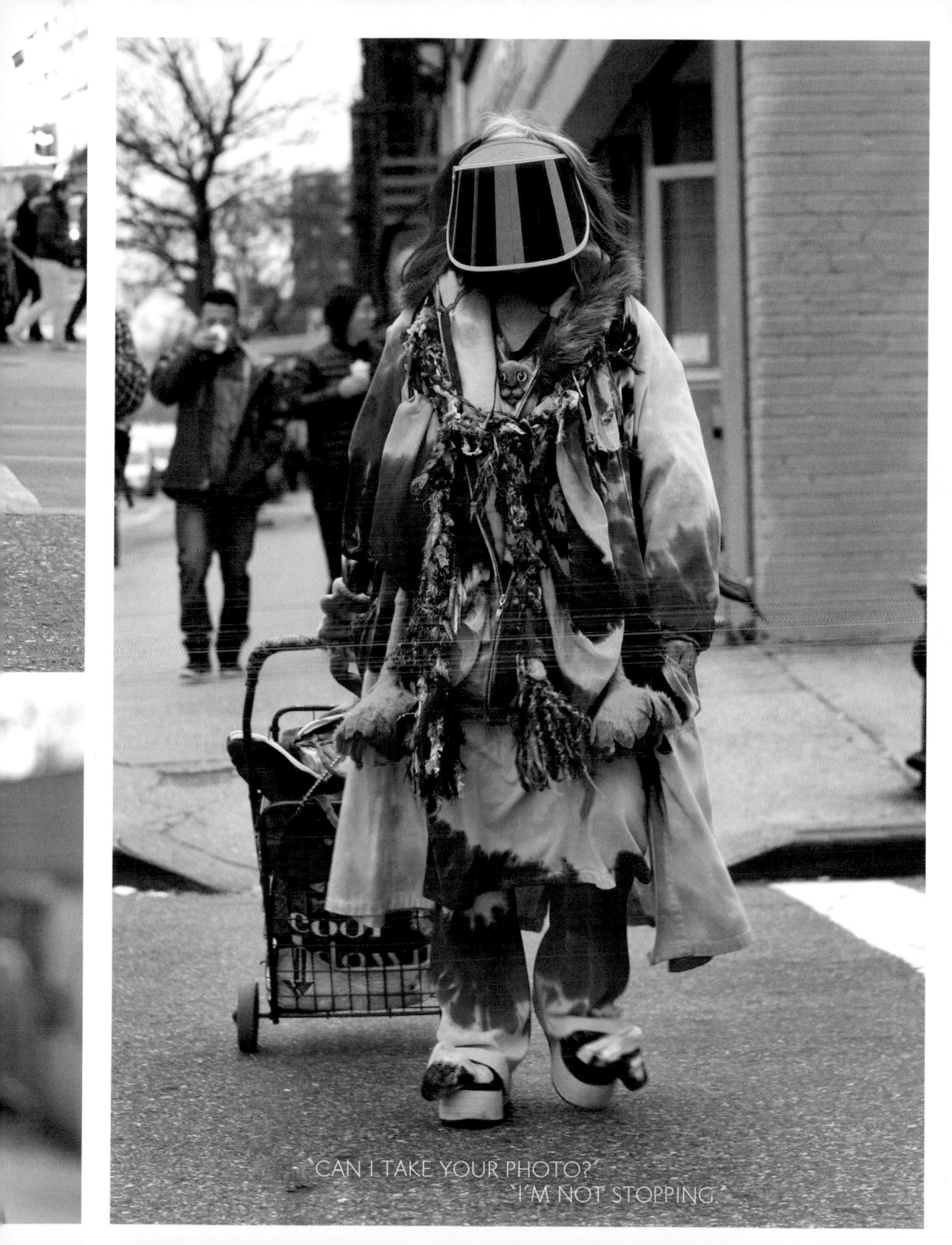

"CAN I TAKE YOUR PHOTO?"
"I'M NOT STOPPING."

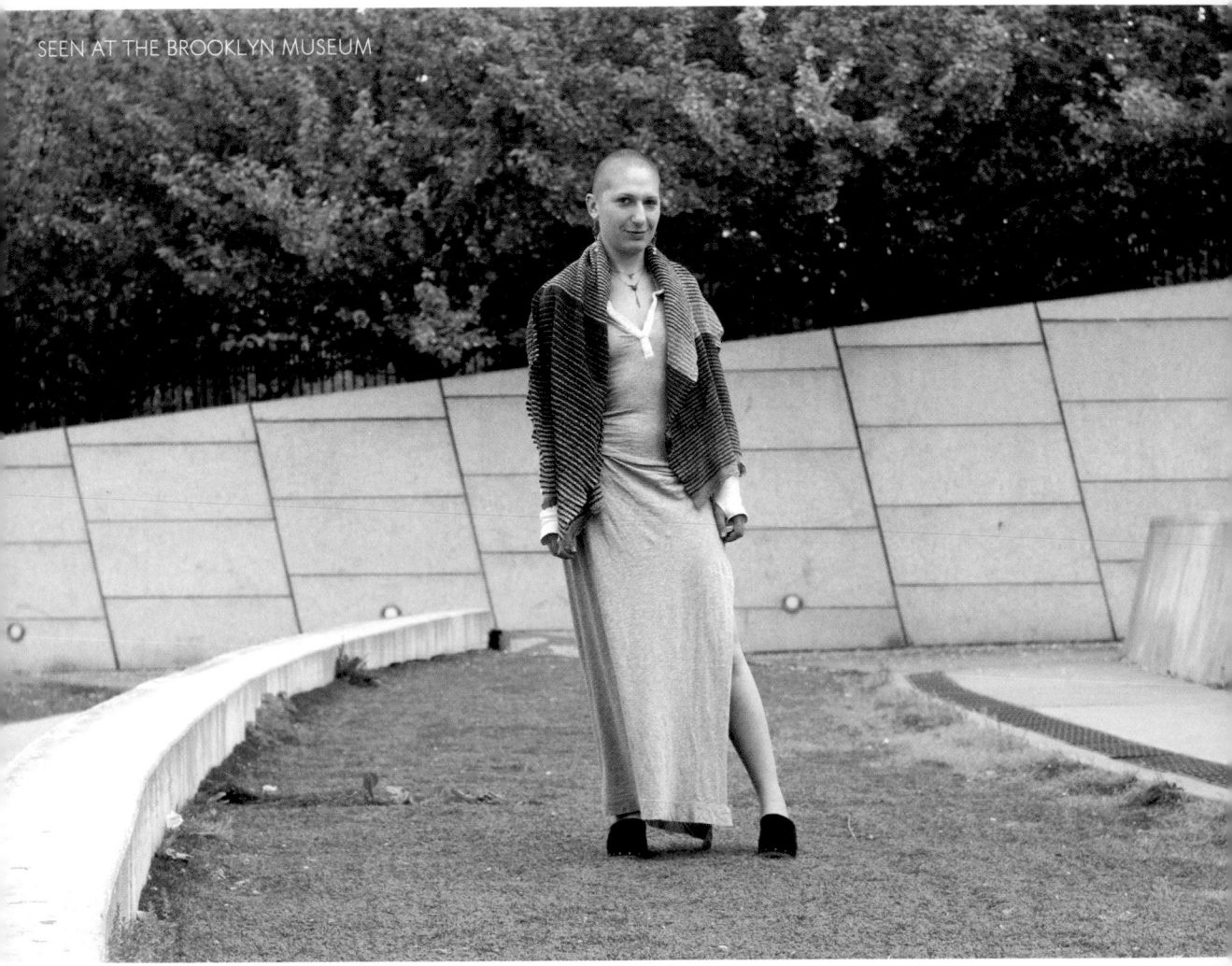
SEEN AT THE BROOKLYN MUSEUM

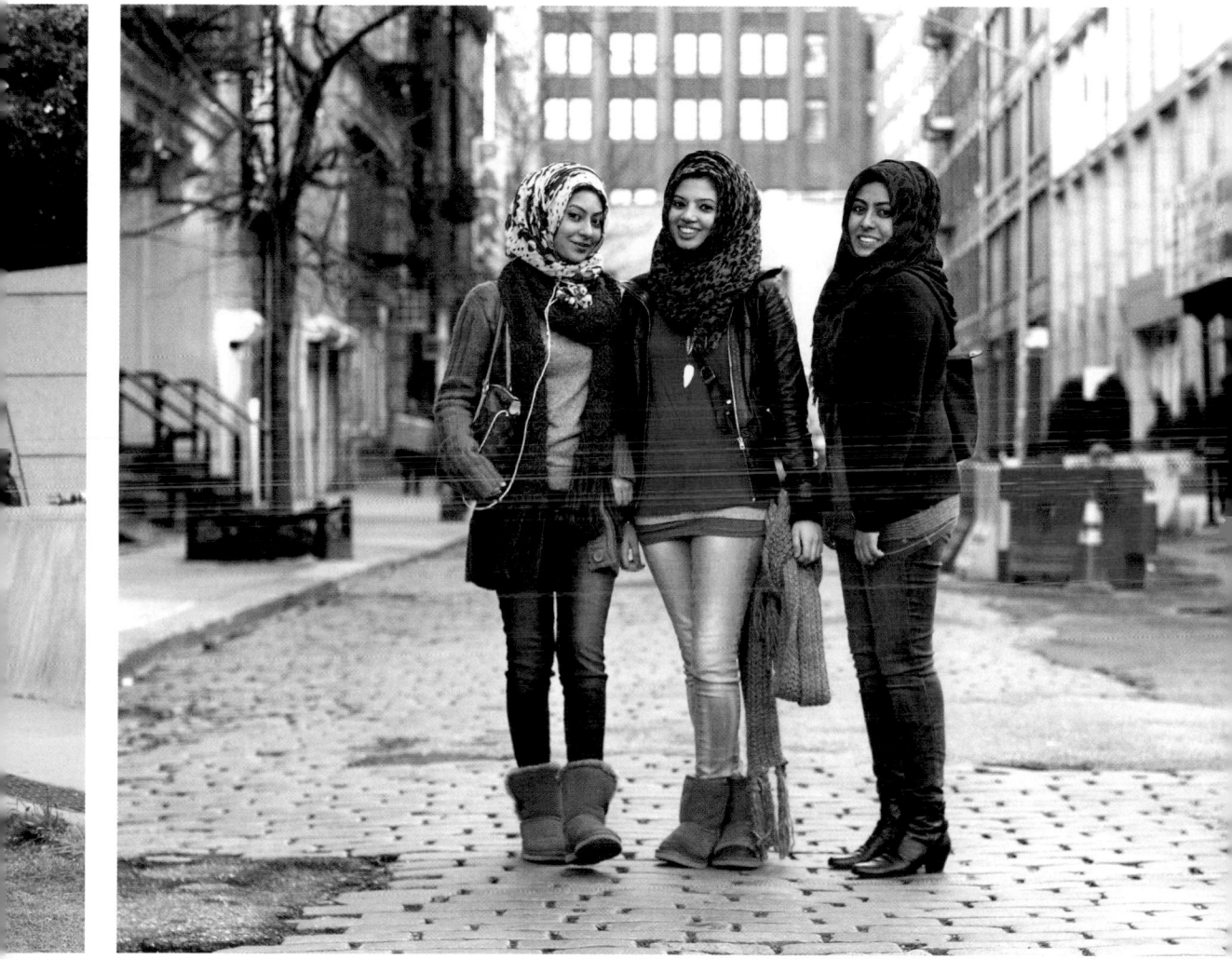

THE WILDFLOWERS

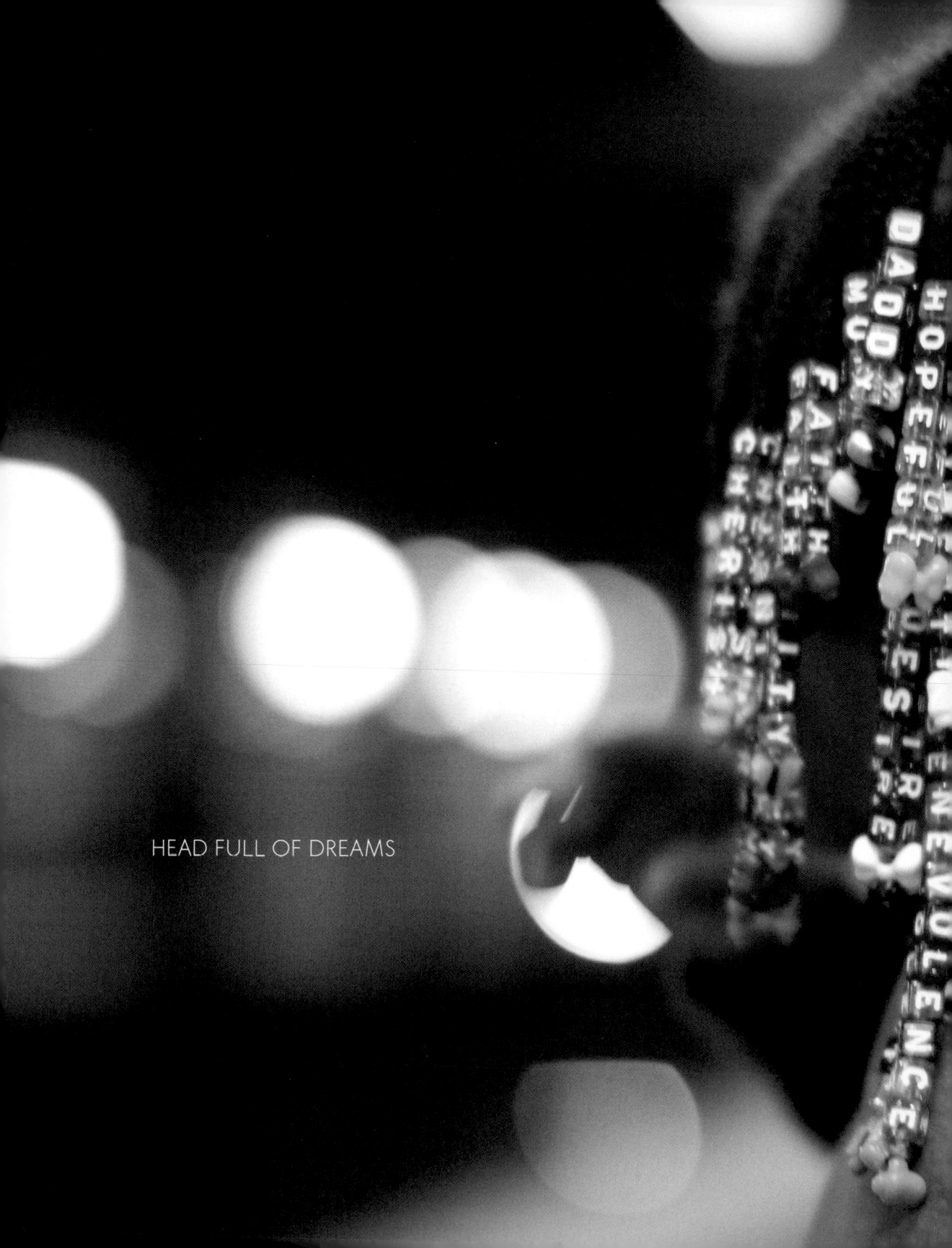
HEAD FULL OF DREAMS

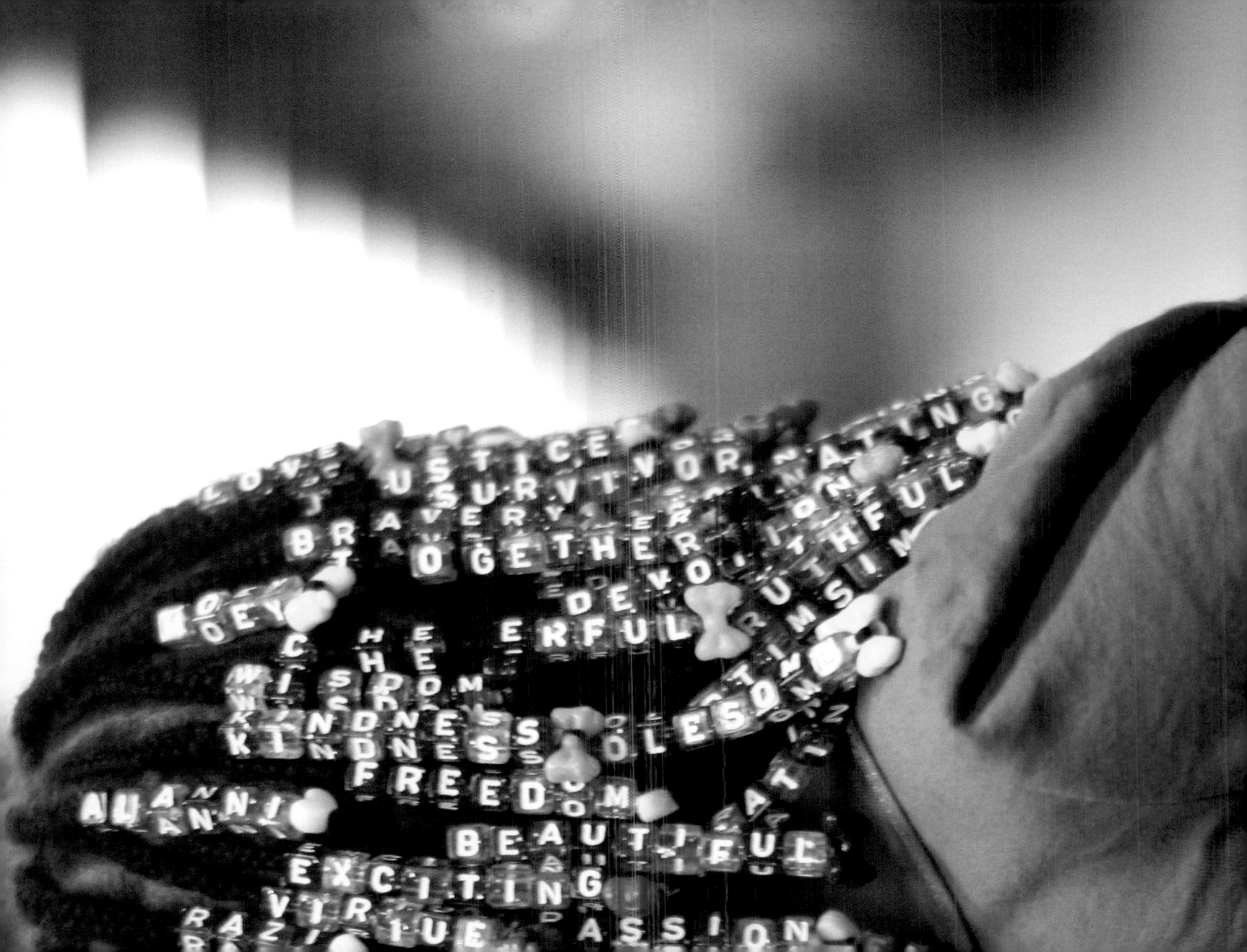
JUSTICE
SURVIVOR
BRAVERY
TOGETHER
DEVOTION
CHEERFUL
WISDOM
KINDNESS
FREEDOM
BEAUTIFUL
EXCITING
VIRTUE
PASSION

"I'M NINETY YEARS OLD AND I RIDE THIS THING AROUND EVERYWHERE. I DON'T SEE WHY MORE PEOPLE DON'T USE THEM. I CARRY MY CANE IN THE BASKET, I GET ALL MY SHOPPING DONE, I CAN GO EVERYWHERE. I'VE NEVER HIT ANYONE AND NEVER BEEN HIT. OF COURSE, I RIDE ON THE SIDEWALK, WHICH I DON'T THINK I'M SUPPOSED TO DO, BUT STILL . . ."

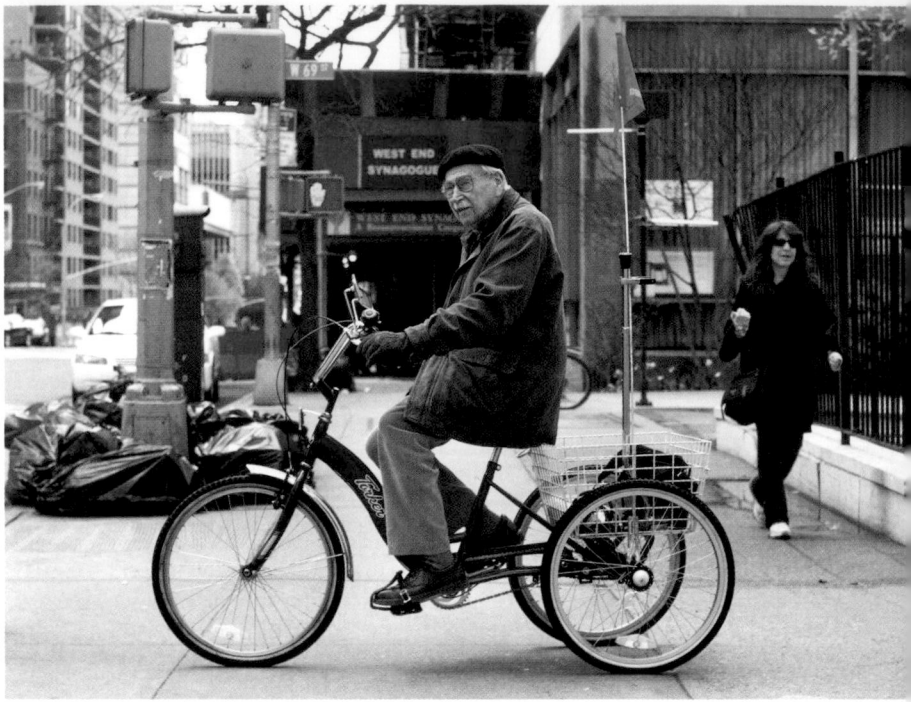


"I'M HOMELESS, AND I'M AN ALCOHOLIC. BUT I HAVE A DREAM."

"WHAT'S THAT?"

"I WANNA GO FISHING."

THIS BOY WAS PART OF A ZOMBIE FAMILY. WHEN I ASKED FOR A GROUP PORTRAIT, THE OTHER THREE ZOMBIES SEEMED RELUCTANT, BUT THIS GUY HIT THE FLOOR.

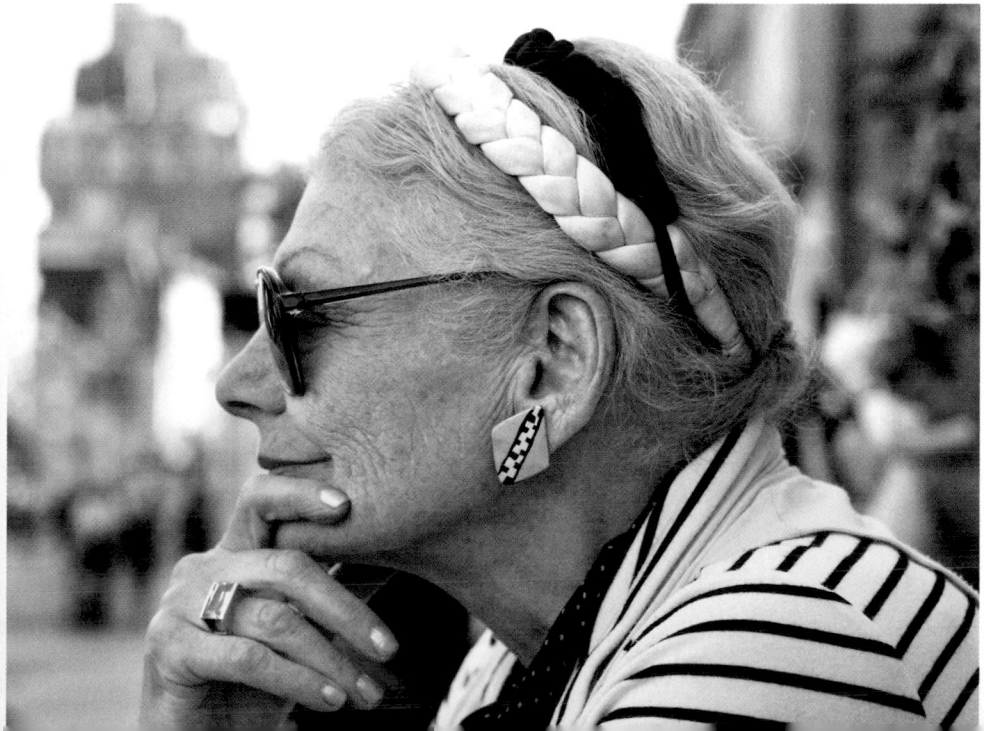

"I'M EIGHTY YEARS OLD. AN EIGHTY-SIX-YEAR-OLD MAN WAS JUST SPEAKING TO ME IN A FLIRTATIOUS MANNER, I BELIEVE. BUT HIS DAUGHTER PULLED HIM AWAY."

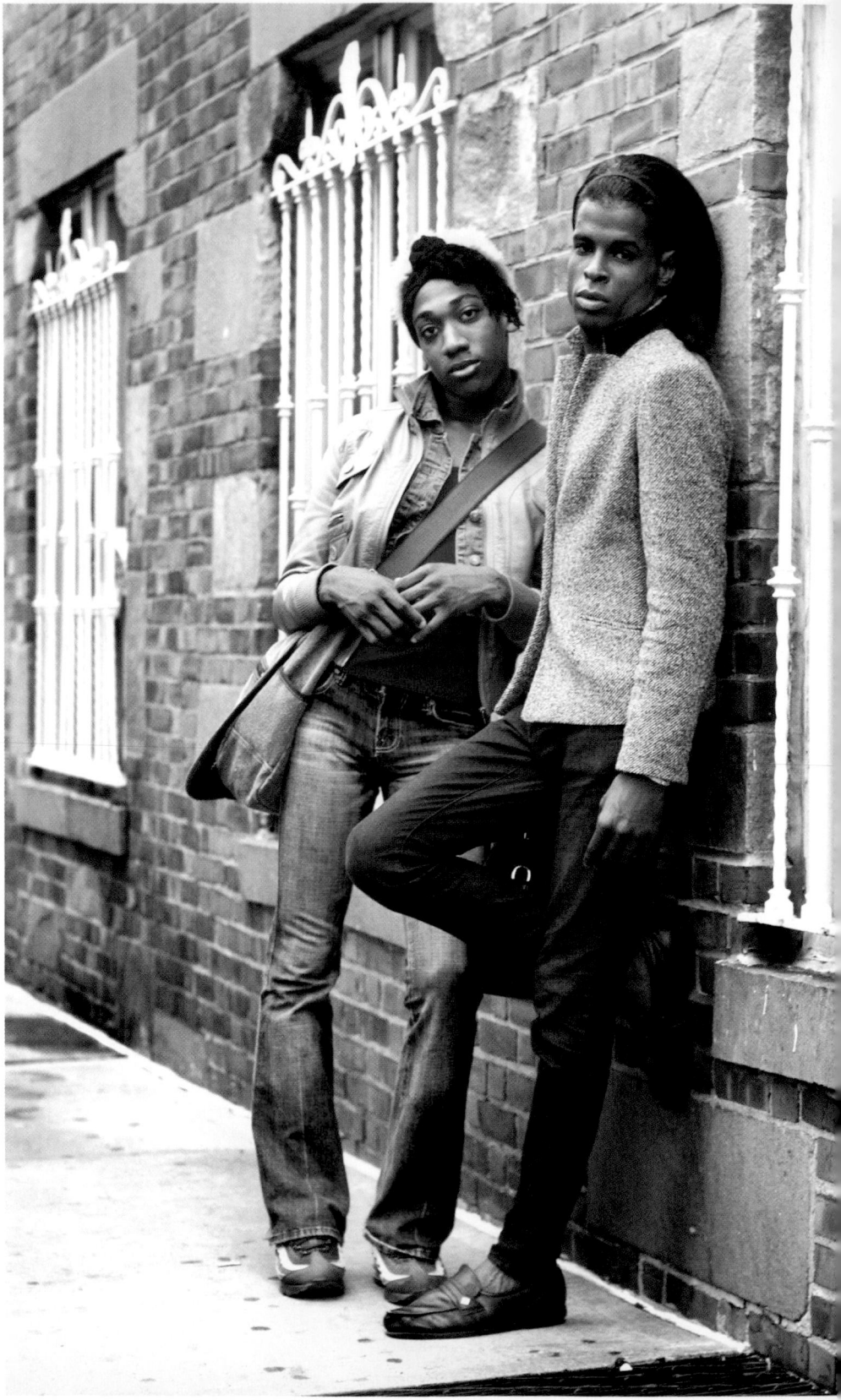

THEY WERE HAPPY WITH HOW THE PHOTO CAME OUT, IF THE SHRIEKING WAS ANY INDICATION.

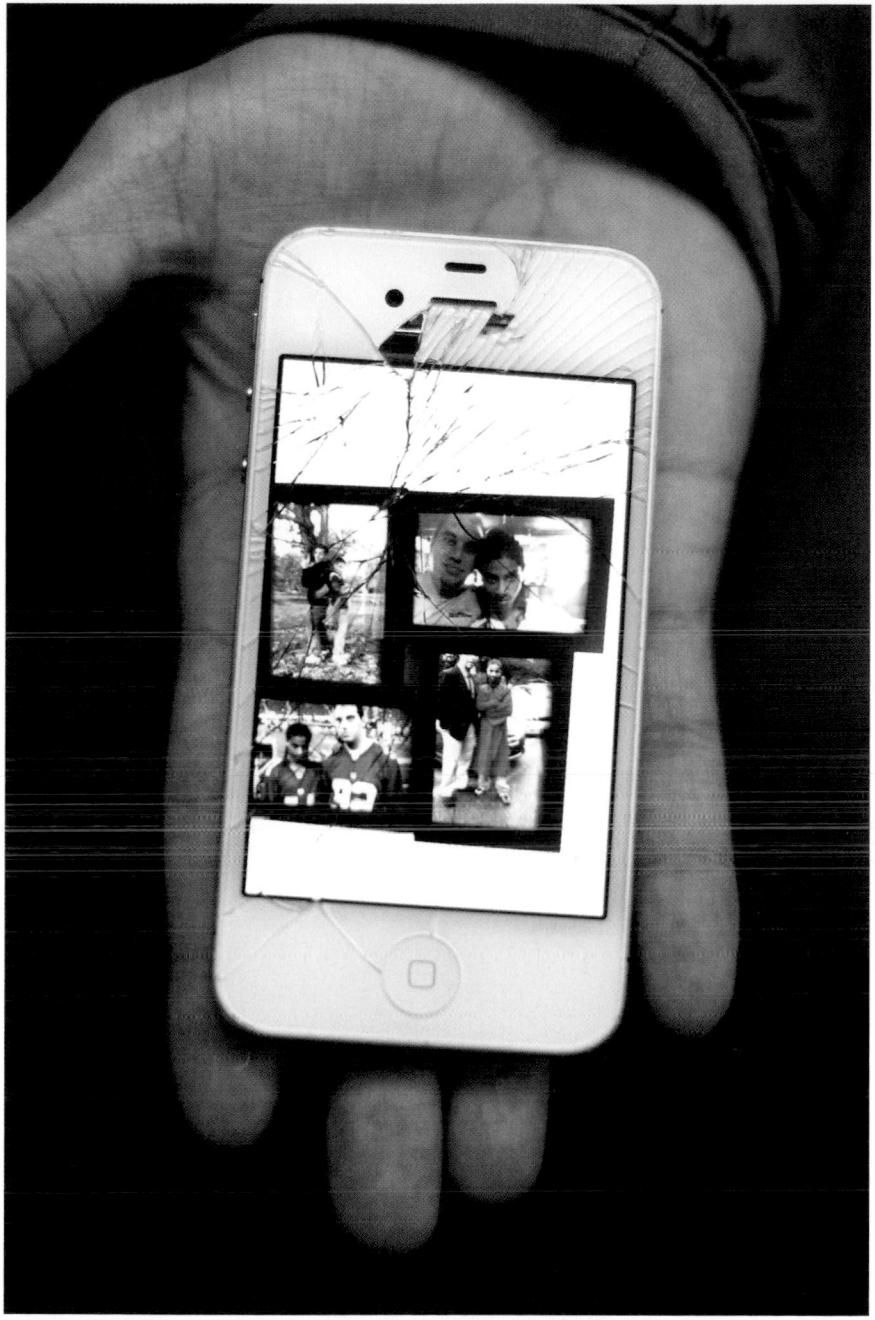

"I NEVER HAD ANY FAMILY GROWING UP. BUT I STILL WENT TO SCHOOL EVERY DAY. ONE DAY, WHEN I WAS IN ELEVENTH GRADE, MY ENGLISH TEACHER CAME UP TO ME AND SAID: 'IF YOU GRADUATE, I'LL ADOPT YOU. I'LL SHOW YOU THE LIFE. YOU'LL DO THINGS YOU NEVER DREAMED OF.' AND HE KEPT HIS PROMISE. HE MADE IT LEGAL AND EVERYTHING. ON THE DAY I GRADUATED, HE WAS THE ONLY FAMILY I HAD THERE. HE'S TAKEN ME EVERYWHERE SINCE THEN. I'VE DONE ALL KINDS OF THINGS."

"I'M GOING TO BE IN A BOOK!"

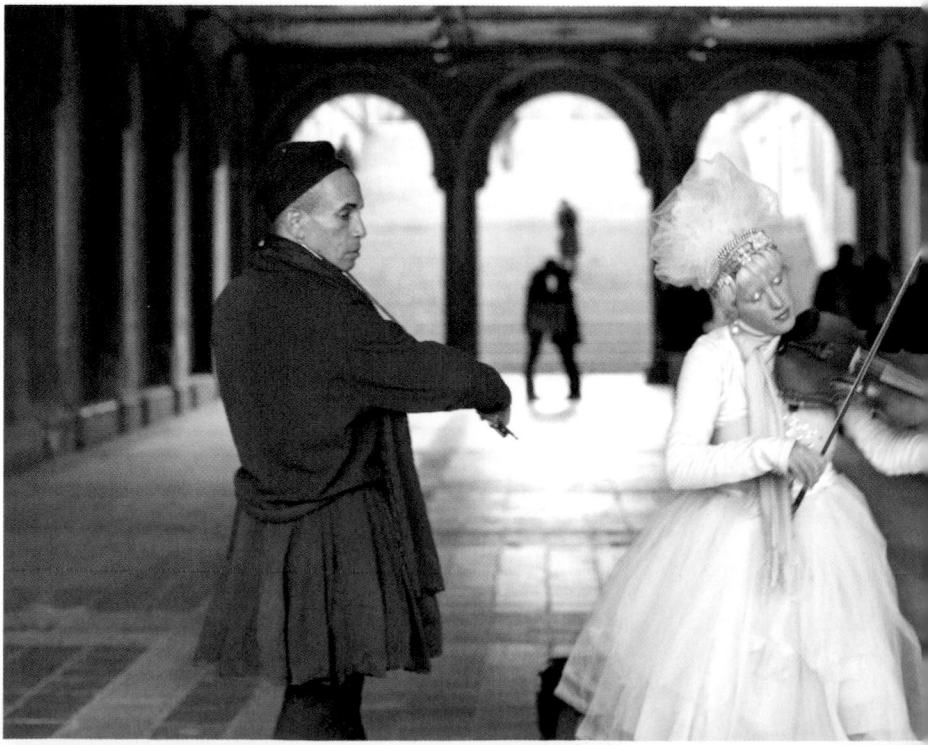

THESE TWO PERFORM A VERY UNCONVENTIONAL "PRAYERFORMANCE," WHICH INVOLVES CHANTING IN A MADE-UP LANGUAGE.

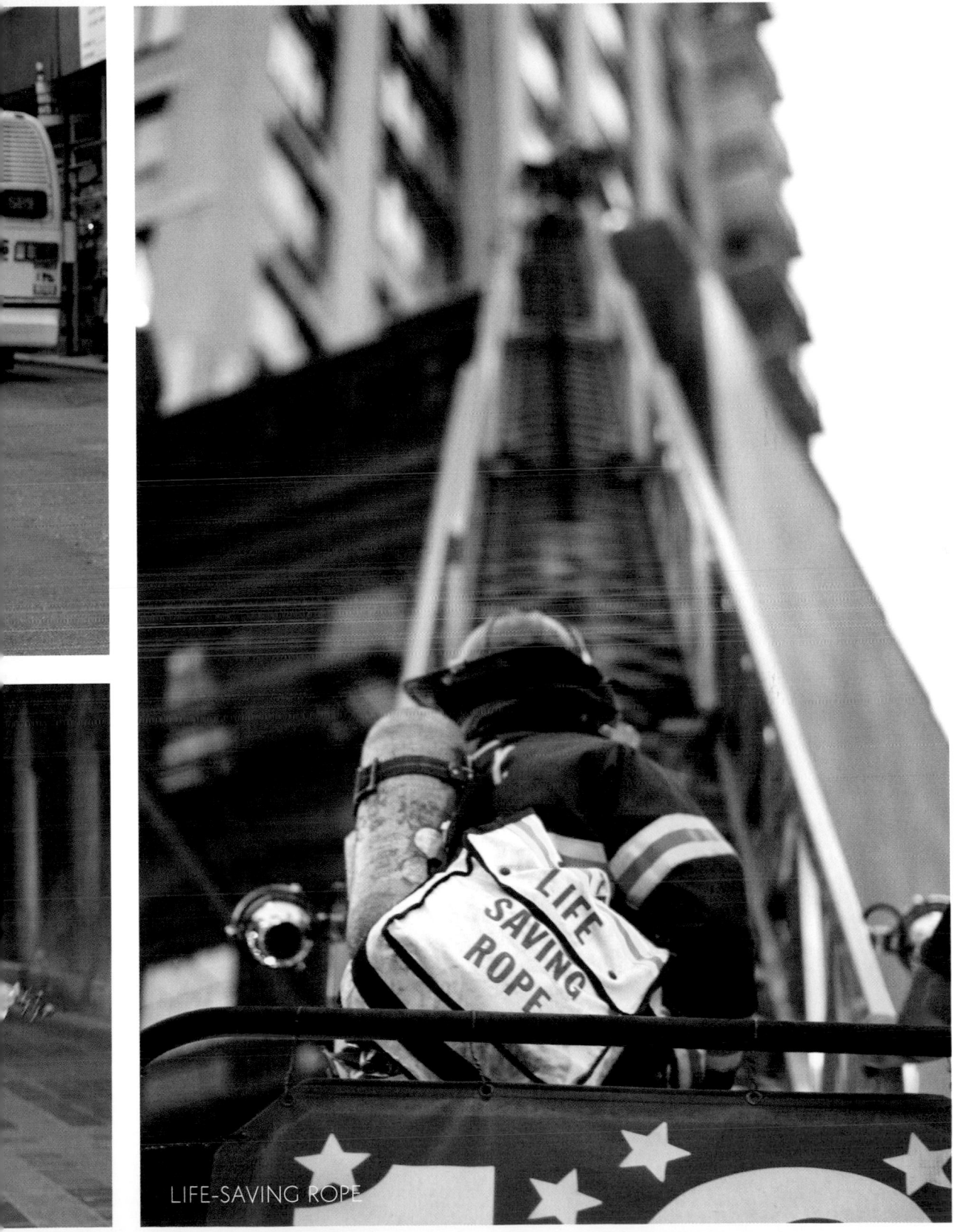


LIFE-SAVING ROPE

GARTH VADER DISAPPOINTS HIS FATHER BY SHUNNING THE THRONE AND PURSUING A FASHION CAREER.

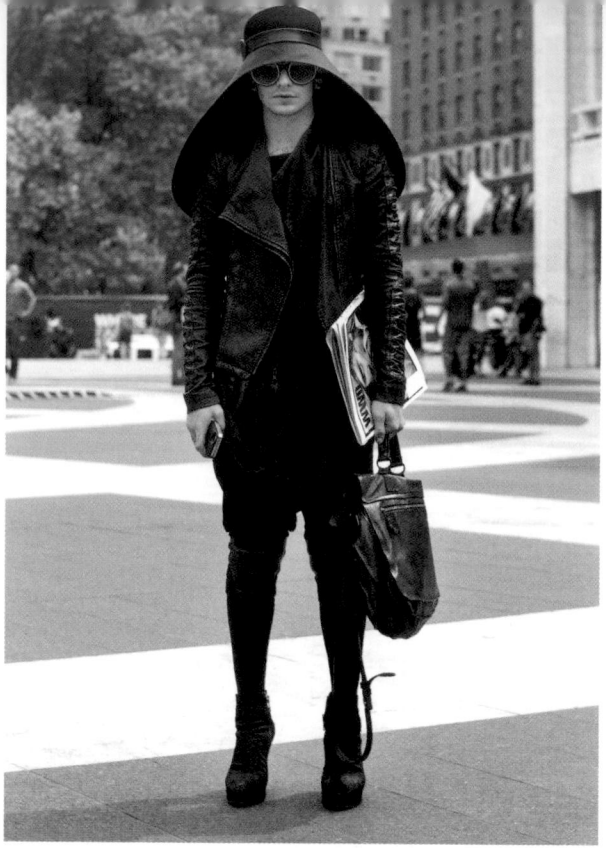

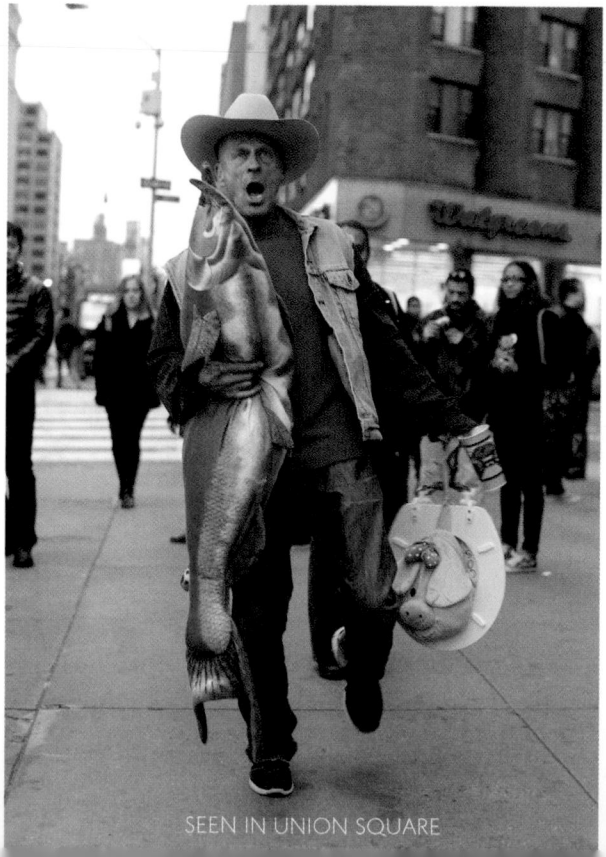

SEEN IN UNION SQUARE

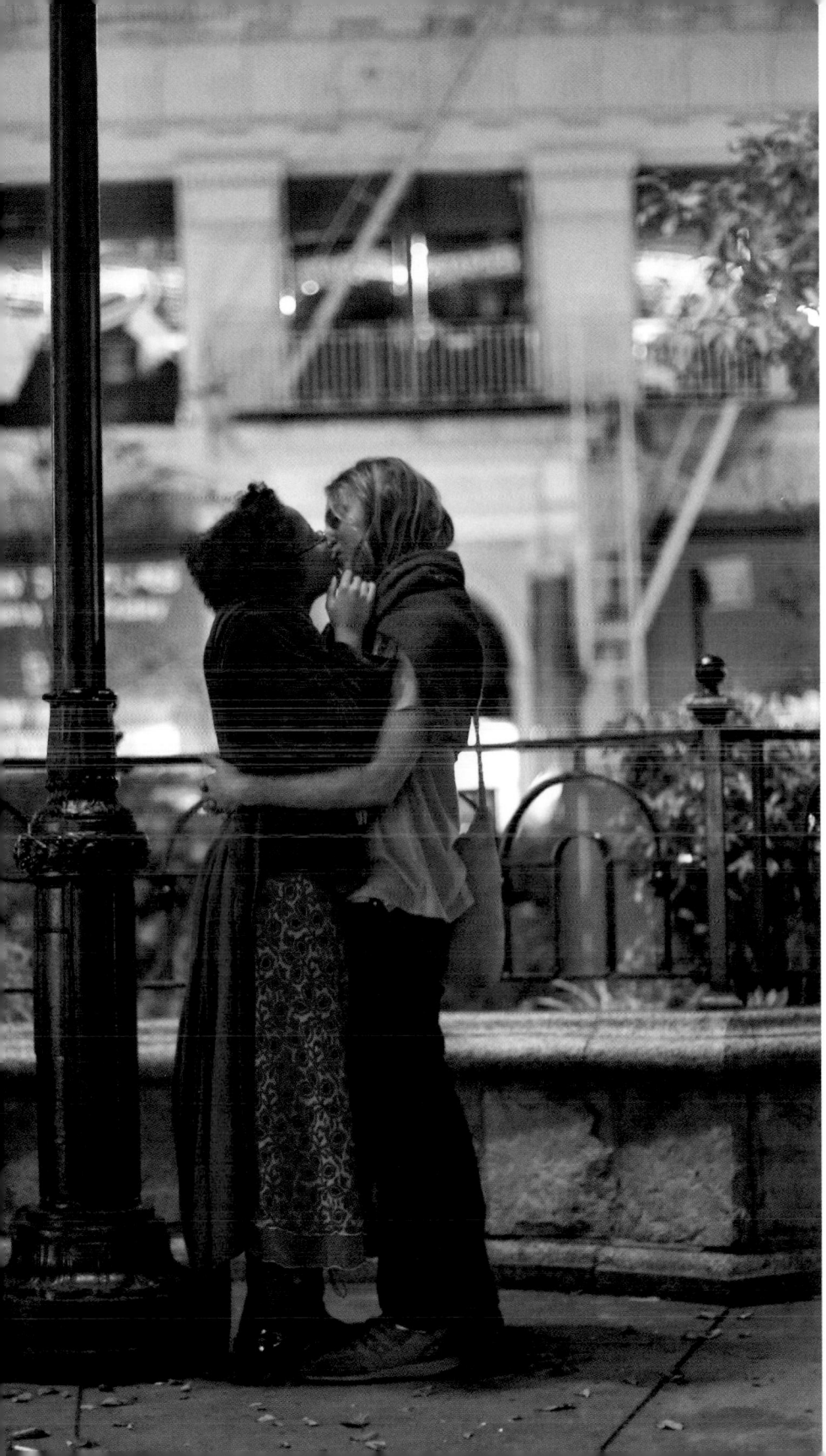

AFTER THEY FINISHED KISSING, SHE TOOK OFF HER BLUE CAPE AND LAID IT OVER A WOMAN SLEEPING ON A NEARBY BENCH. IT WAS SUCH A POETIC MOMENT, I ACTUALLY CHASED THEM DOWN TO FACT-CHECK MY OWN EYES.

"EXCUSE ME. WAS THAT YOUR BLUE BLANKET?"

"YES."

"AND YOU JUST GAVE IT TO HER?"

"YES, WHY?"

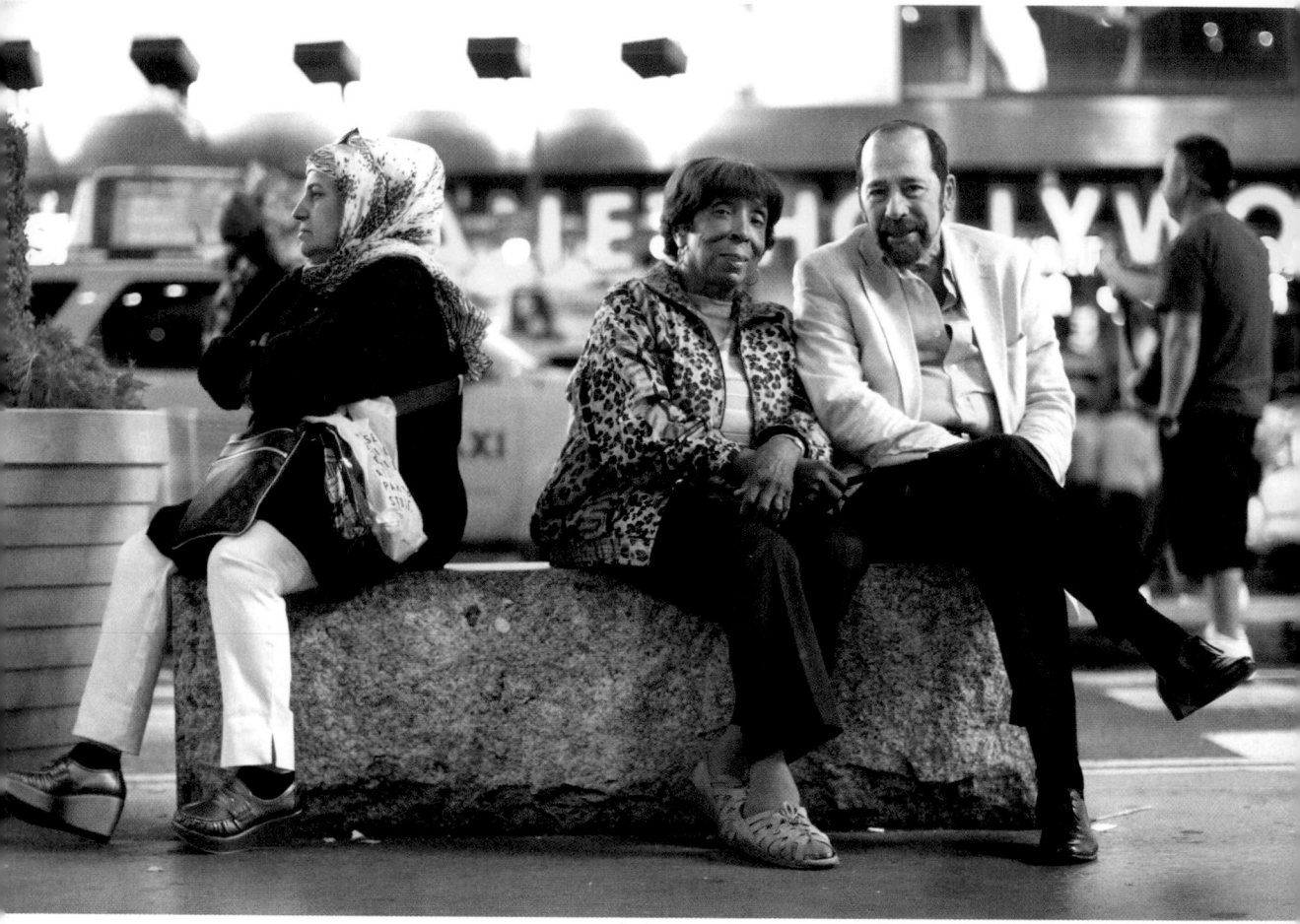

"HE DOES ABSOLUTELY EVERYTHING FOR ME. I'M COMPLETELY SPOILED."

"I USED TO BE A BUTCHER. SHE USED TO COME INTO MY STORE. EVERY WEEK I WOULD SET APART THE BEST PIECE OF MEAT FOR HER. AND LOOK HOW IT TURNED OUT—I ENDED UP WITH THE BEST PIECE OF MEAT OF THEM ALL."

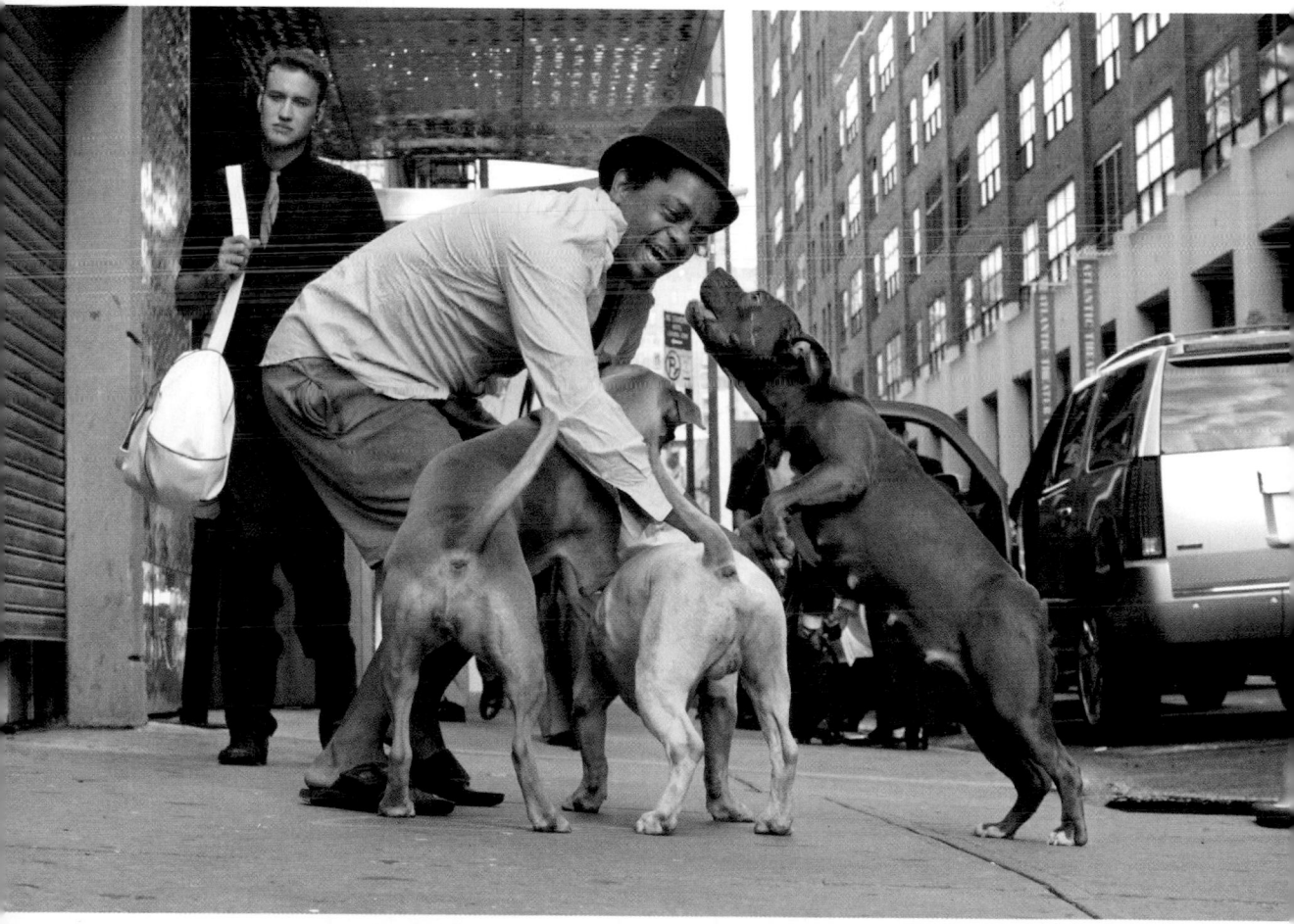

ONE NANOSECOND LATER, AN UNFORTUNATE HEAD-BUTT BROUGHT THIS PHOTO SHOOT TO A SCREECHING HALT.

"I'VE BEEN CRITICIZED FOR A LOT MORE THAN MY FURS."

THIS MAN NEEDED A BREAK FROM THE MUSEUM EXHIBITS, SO HE TURNED TO SOMETHING MORE AMUSING.

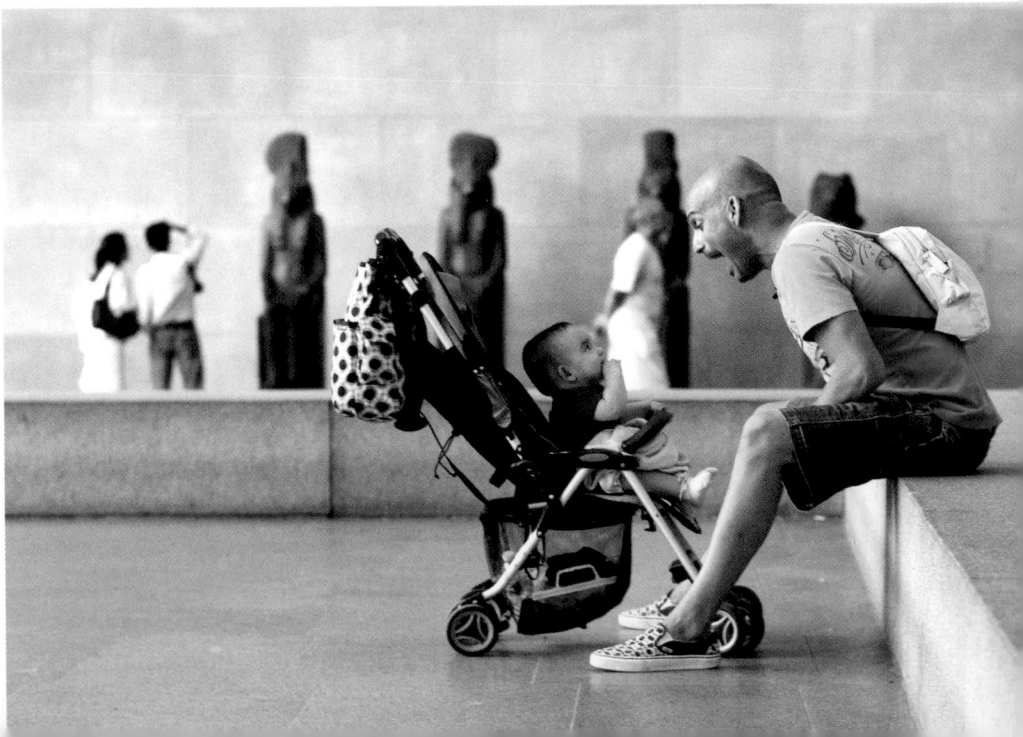

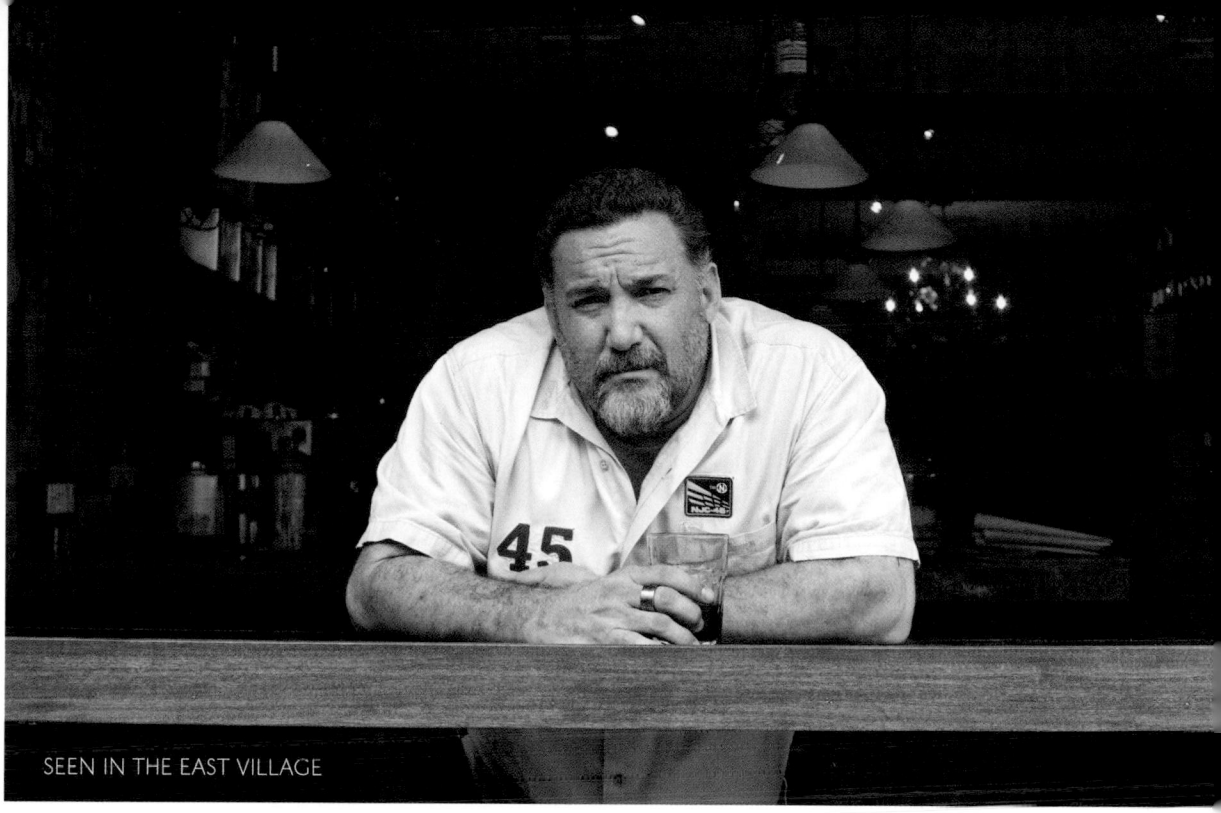


SEEN IN THE EAST VILLAGE

"IF THERE ISN'T A CROOKED FINGERPRINT ON THE BACK, YOU KNOW IT ISN'T MINE."

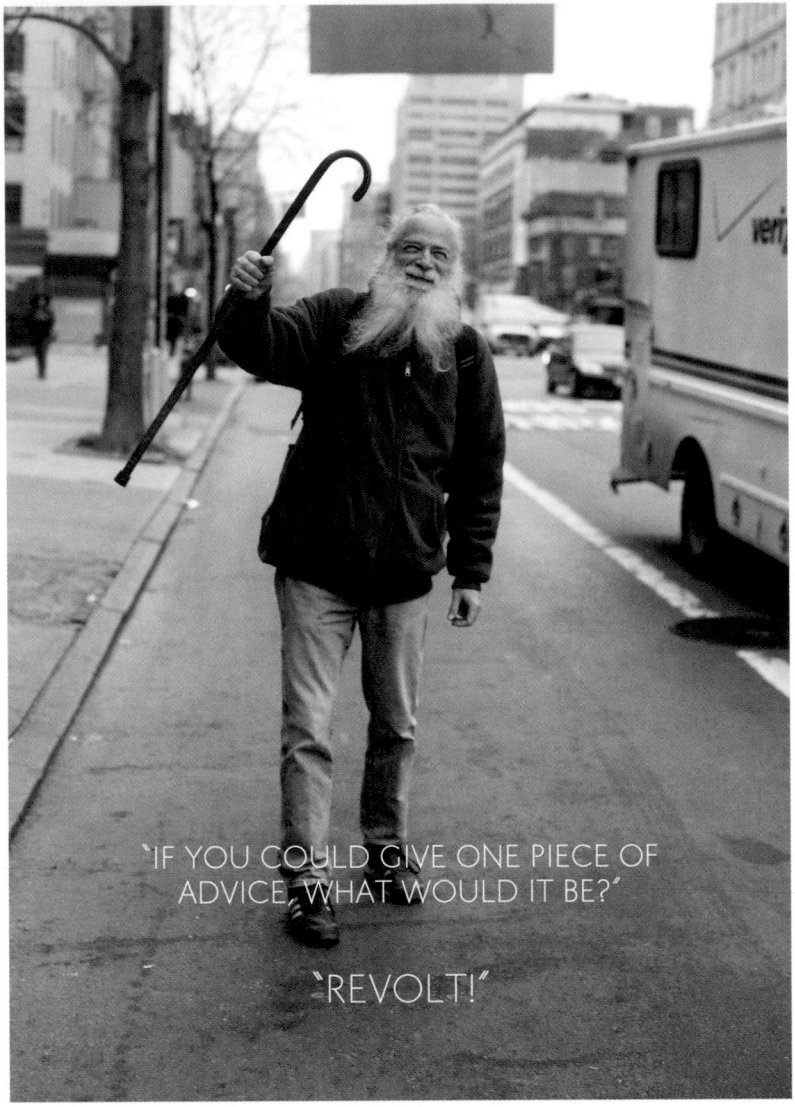

"IF YOU COULD GIVE ONE PIECE OF ADVICE, WHAT WOULD IT BE?"

"REVOLT!"

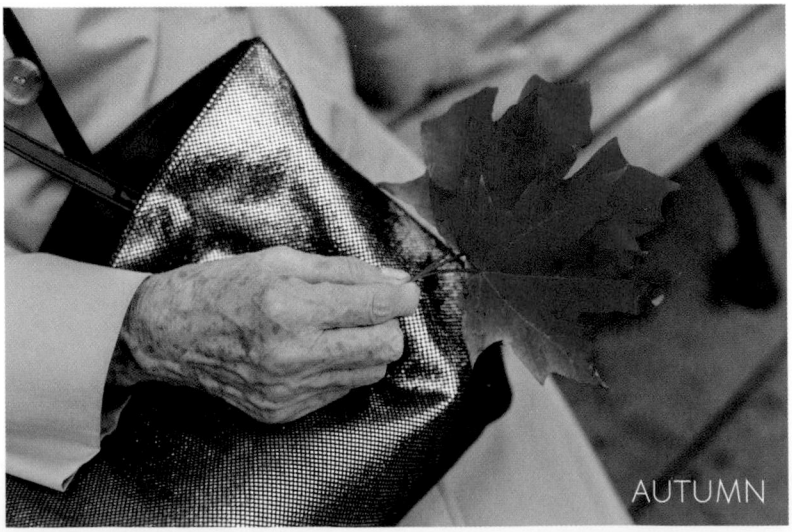

AUTUMN

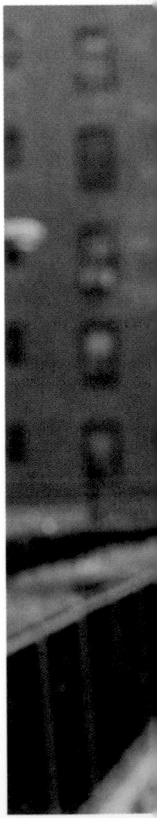

"IF WE PUT THEM AT THE END OF THE SLIDE, WILL THEY SIT STILL?"

"FOR ABOUT FIVE SECONDS."

THIS LITTLE GUY STARTED POINTING AT ME LIKE I WAS KING KONG.

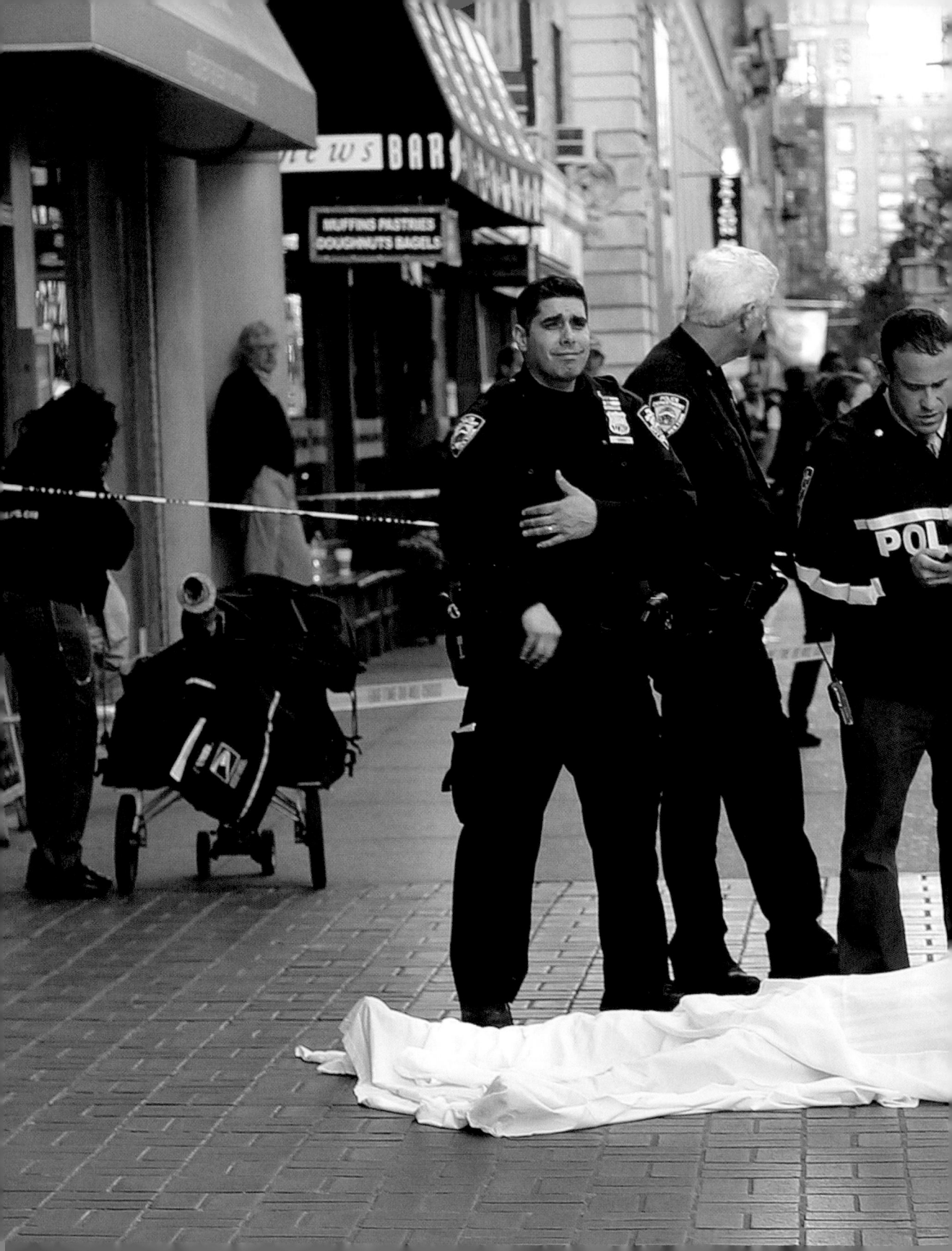
MUFFINS PASTRIES
DOUGHNUTS BAGELS

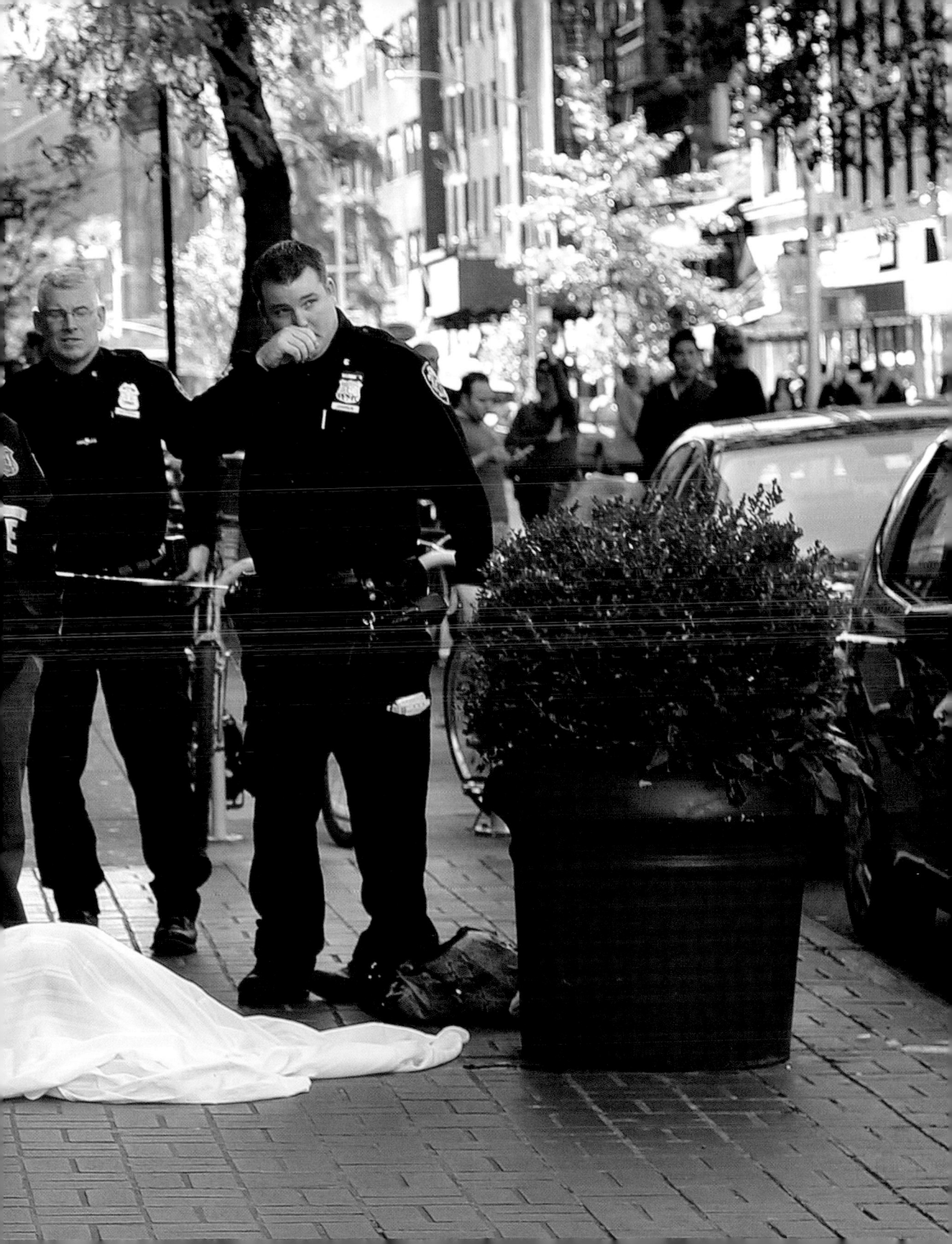

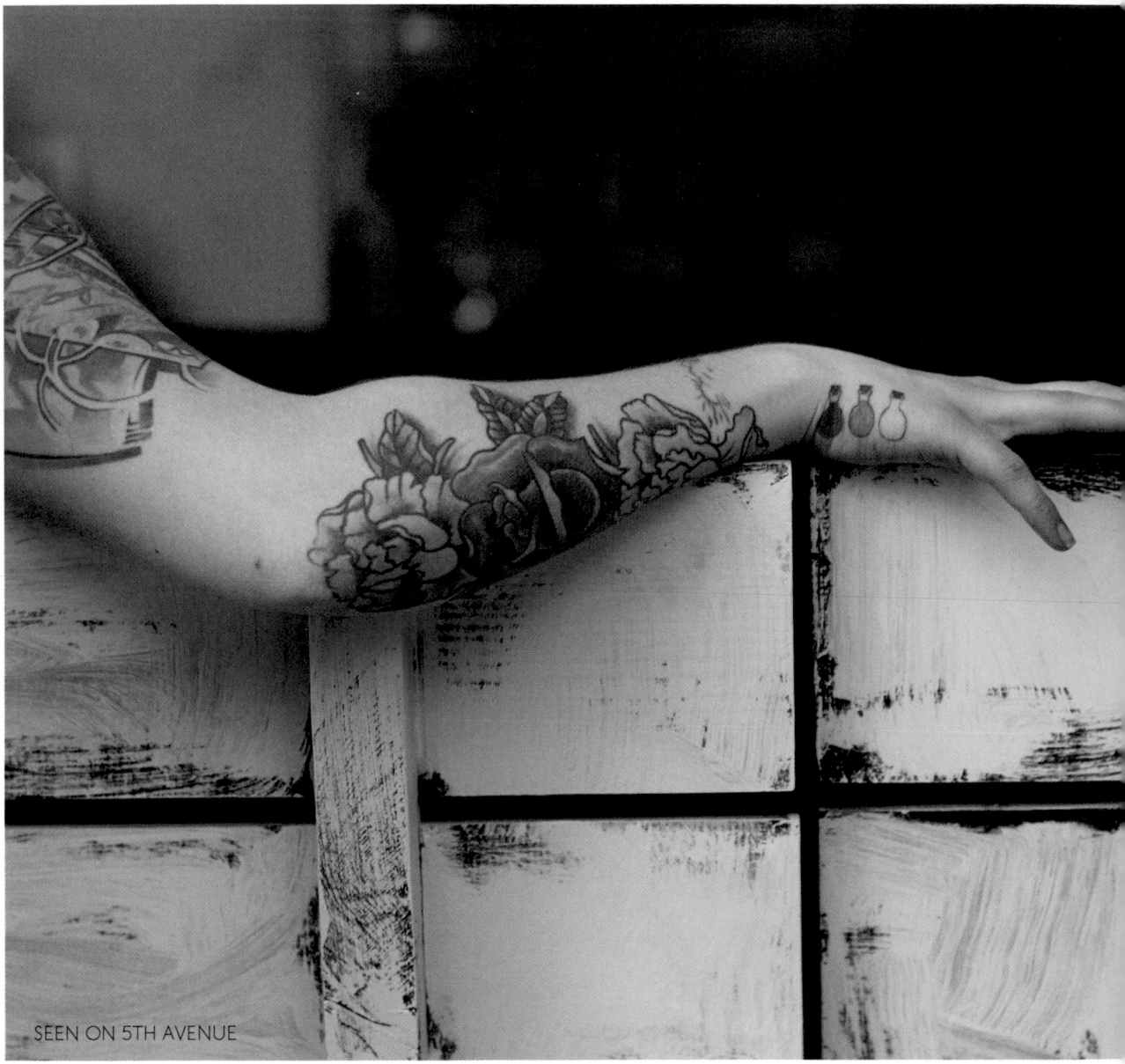
SEEN ON 5TH AVENUE

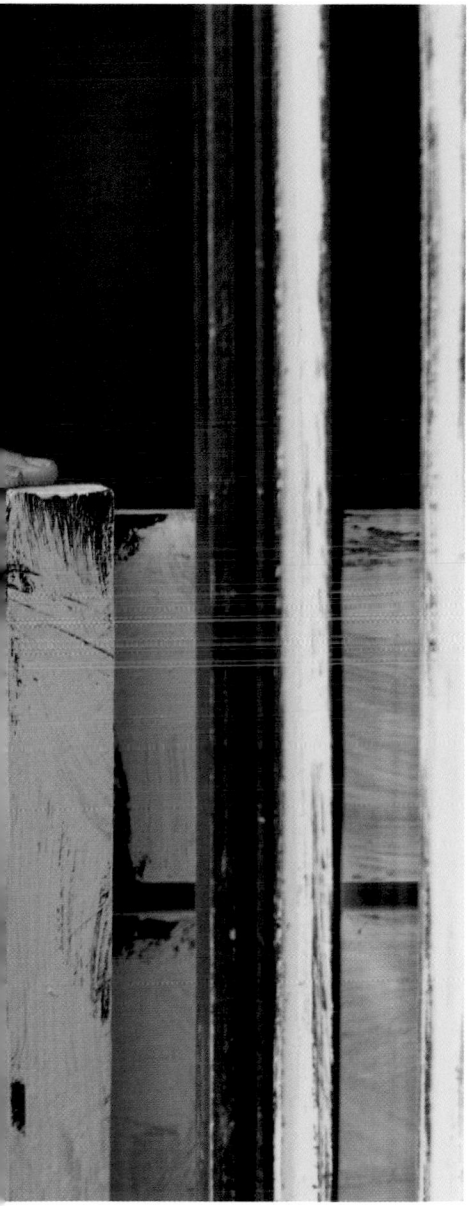

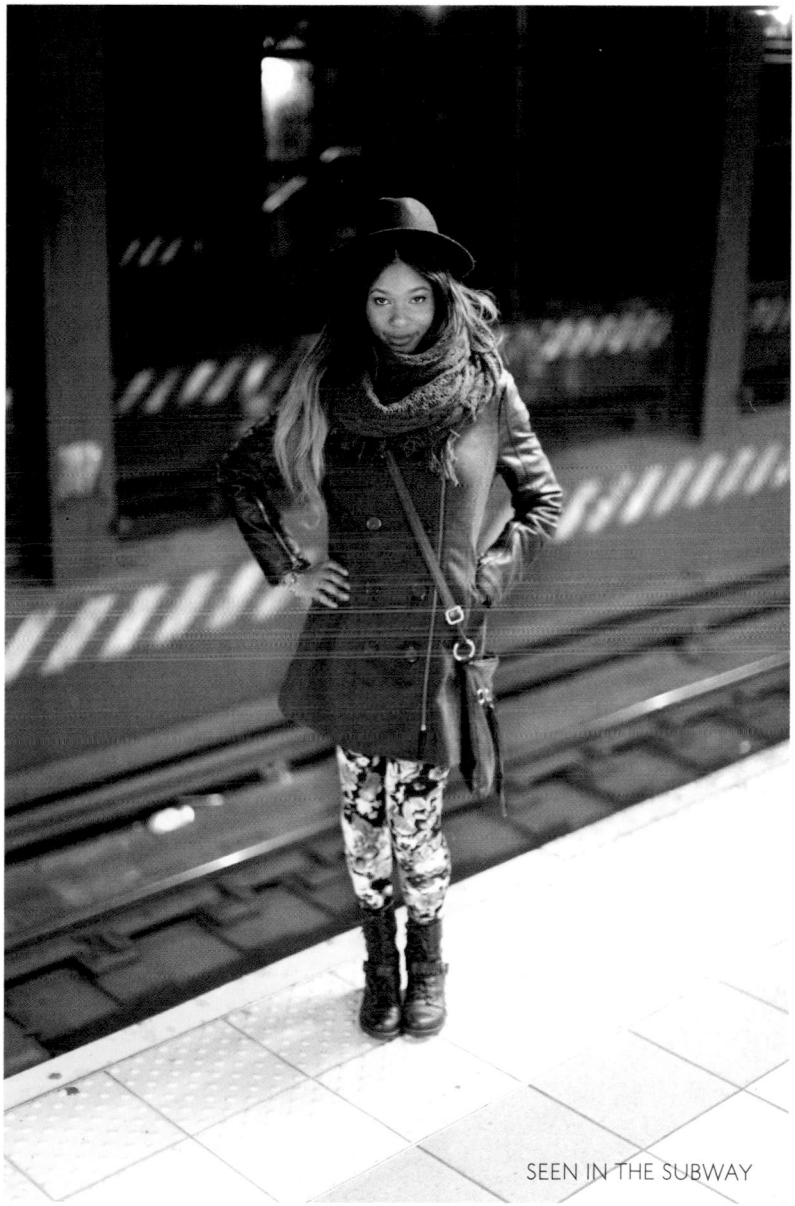

SEEN IN THE SUBWAY

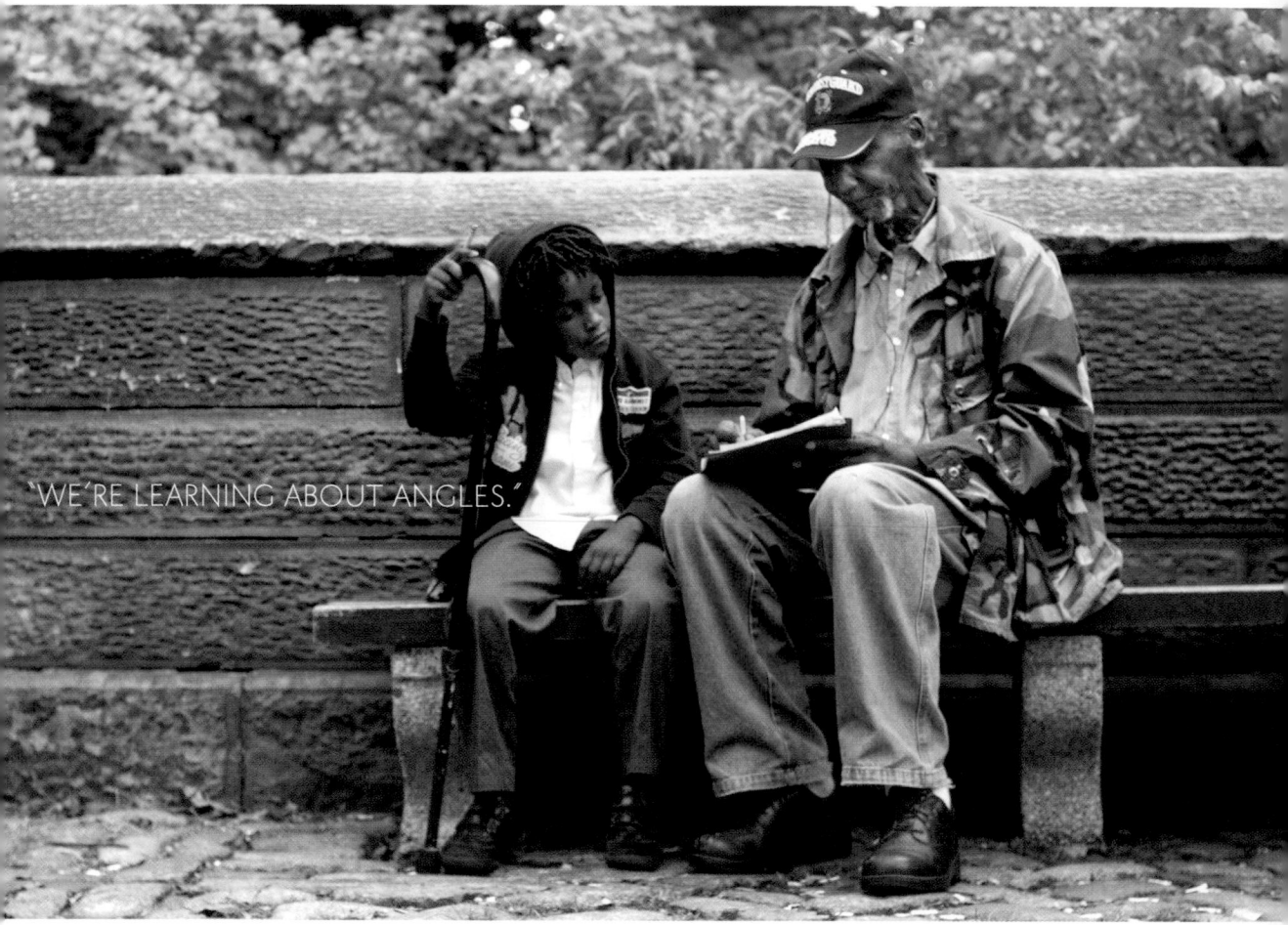

'WE'RE LEARNING ABOUT ANGLES.'

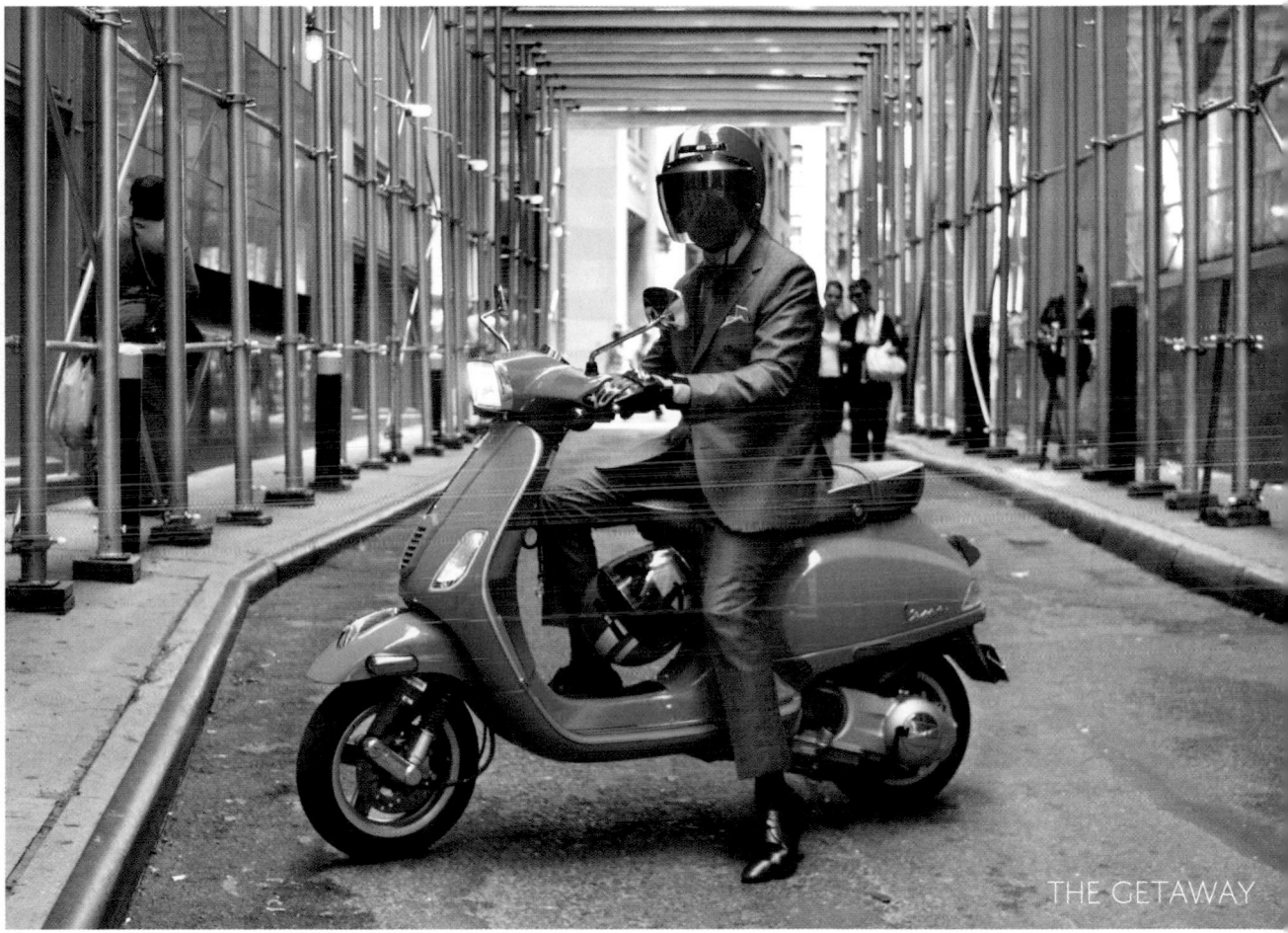
THE GETAWAY

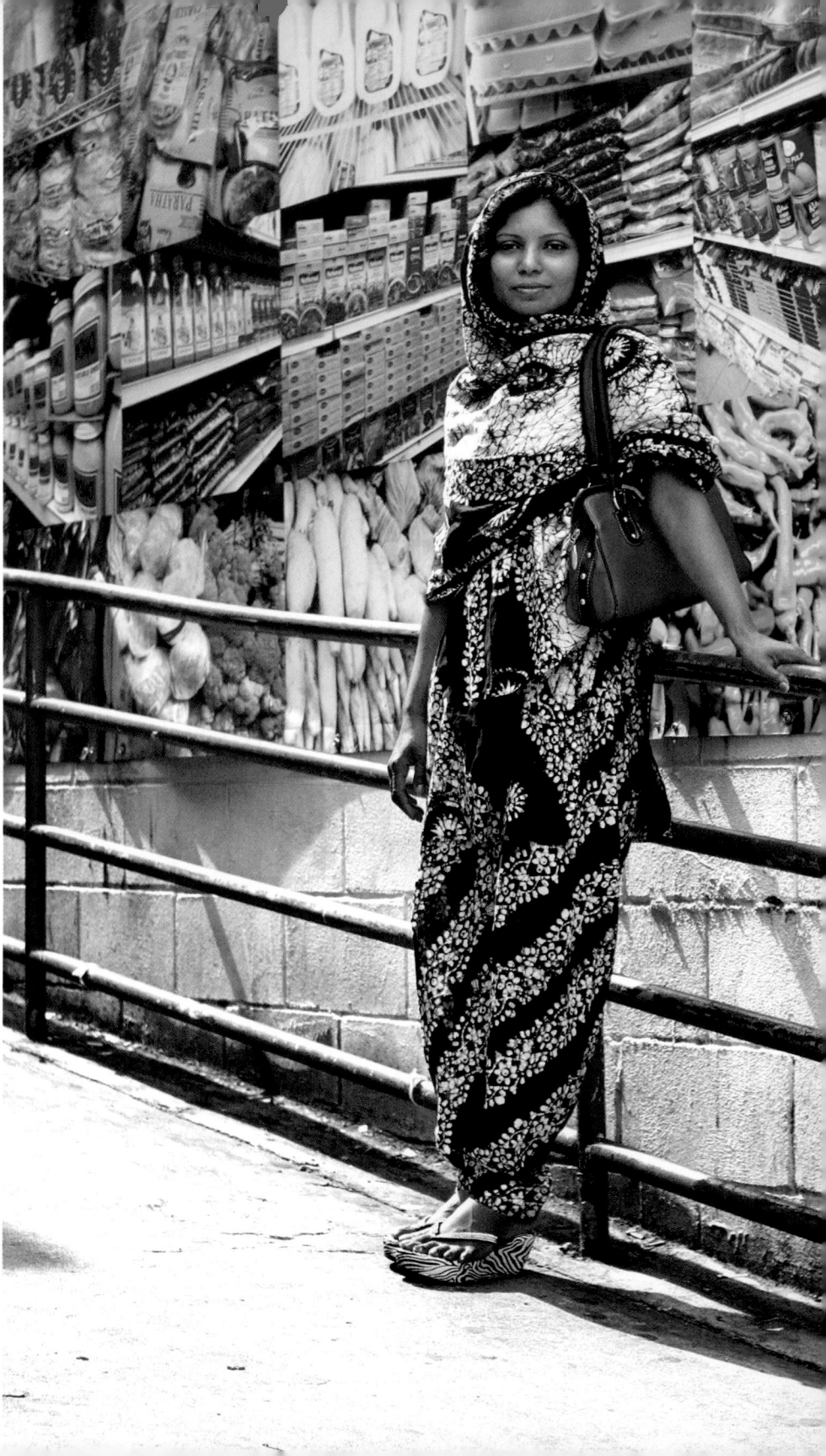

SHE WAS GUIDING HER TWO CHILDREN DOWN A SIDEWALK IN JACKSON HEIGHTS, QUEENS. NORMALLY I'D HAVE ASKED FOR A GROUP PORTRAIT, BUT THIS TIME I THOUGHT MOM DESERVED A STANDALONE.

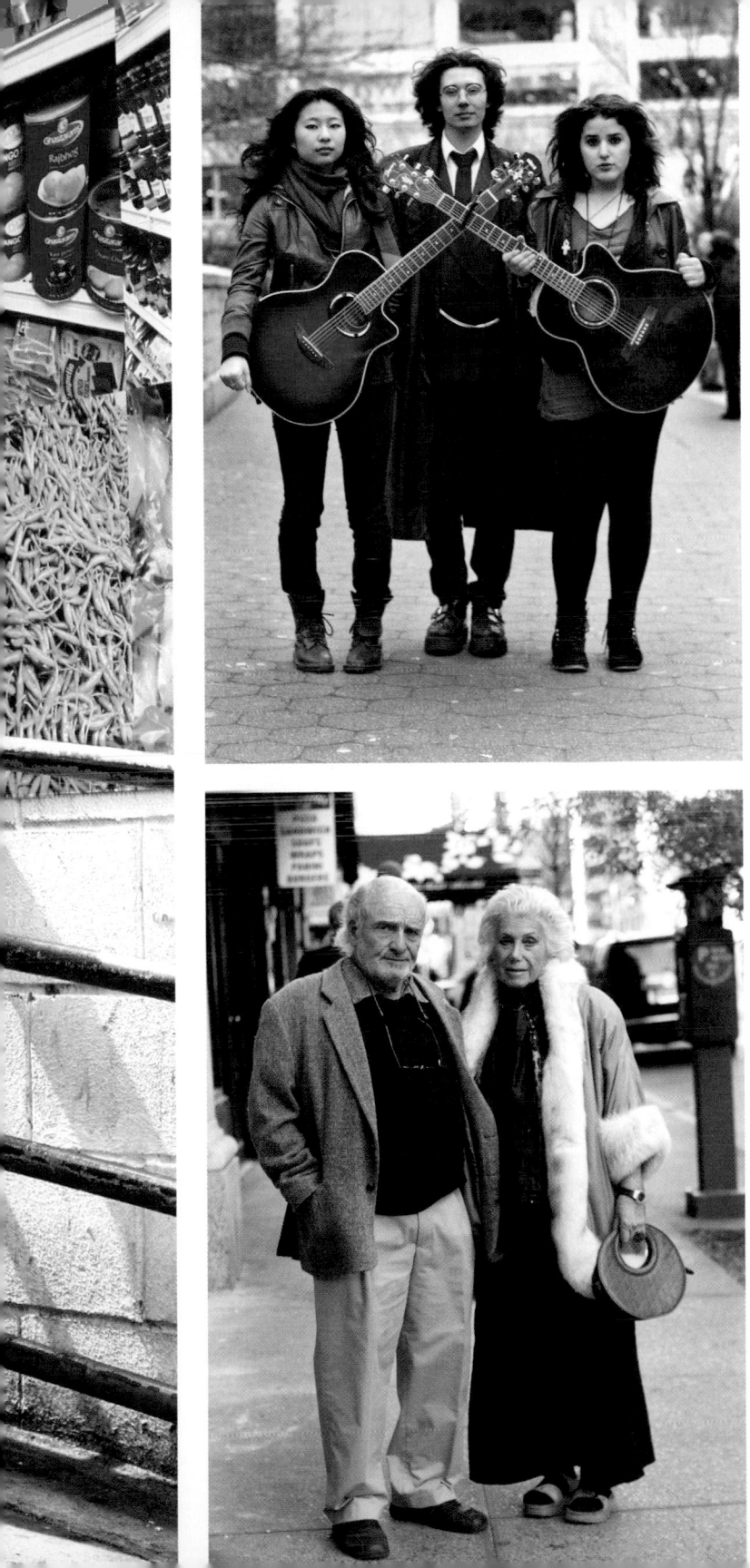

AFTER THE PHOTO WAS TAKEN, THE GUY LOOKED AT IT AND SAID: "I'VE NEVER FELT LIKE MORE OF A MAN."

"ARE YOU MARRIED?"

"WE'RE PRACTICING."

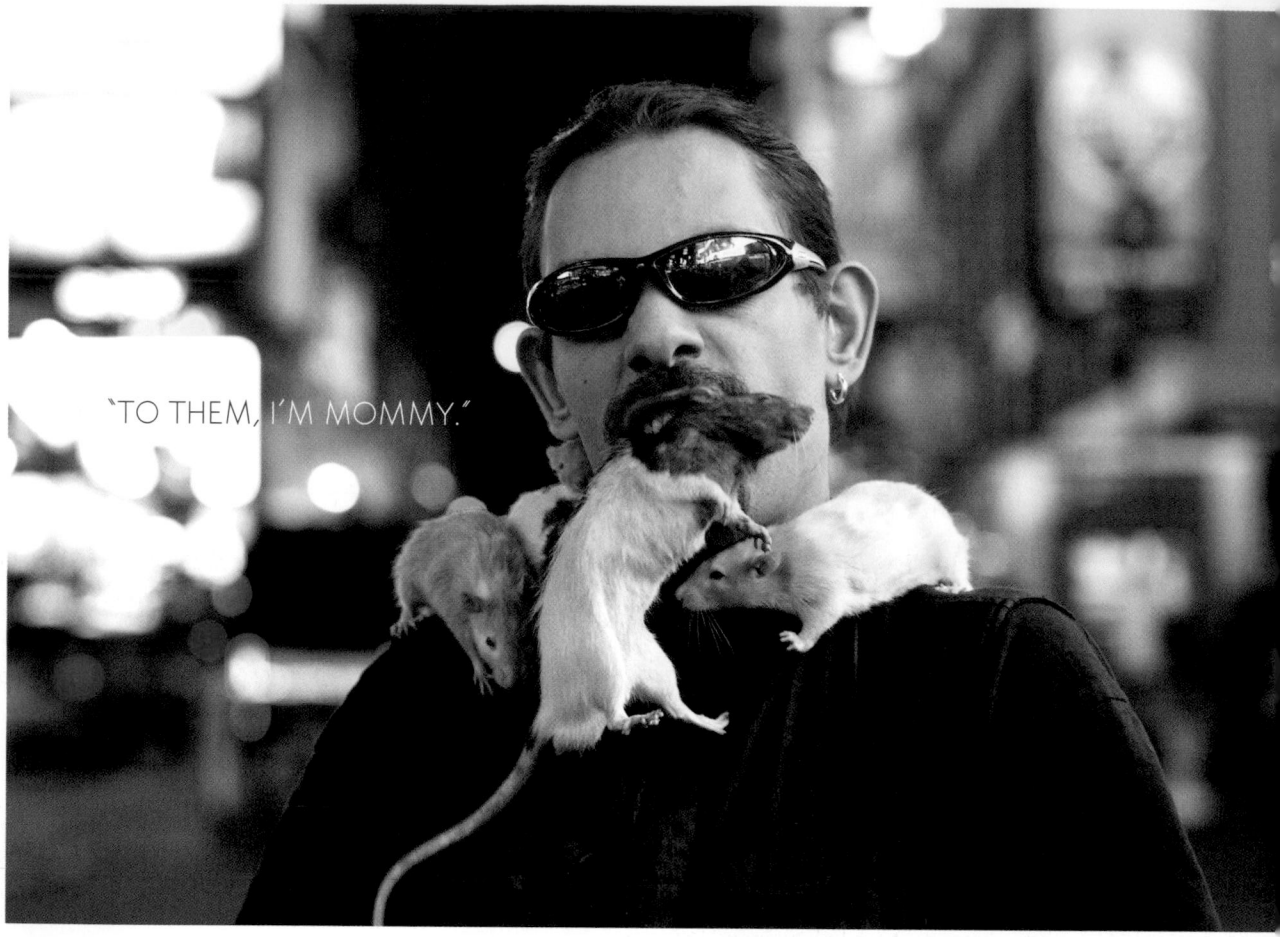
"TO THEM, I'M MOMMY."

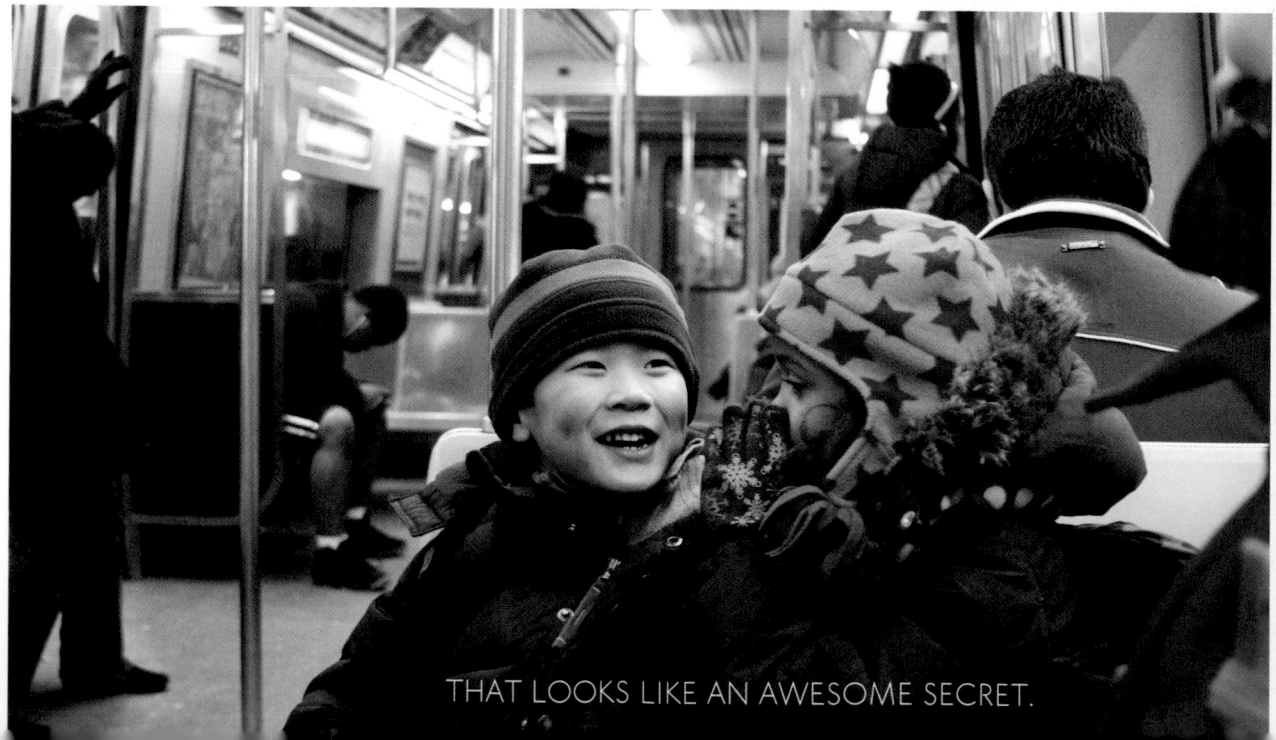
THAT LOOKS LIKE AN AWESOME SECRET.

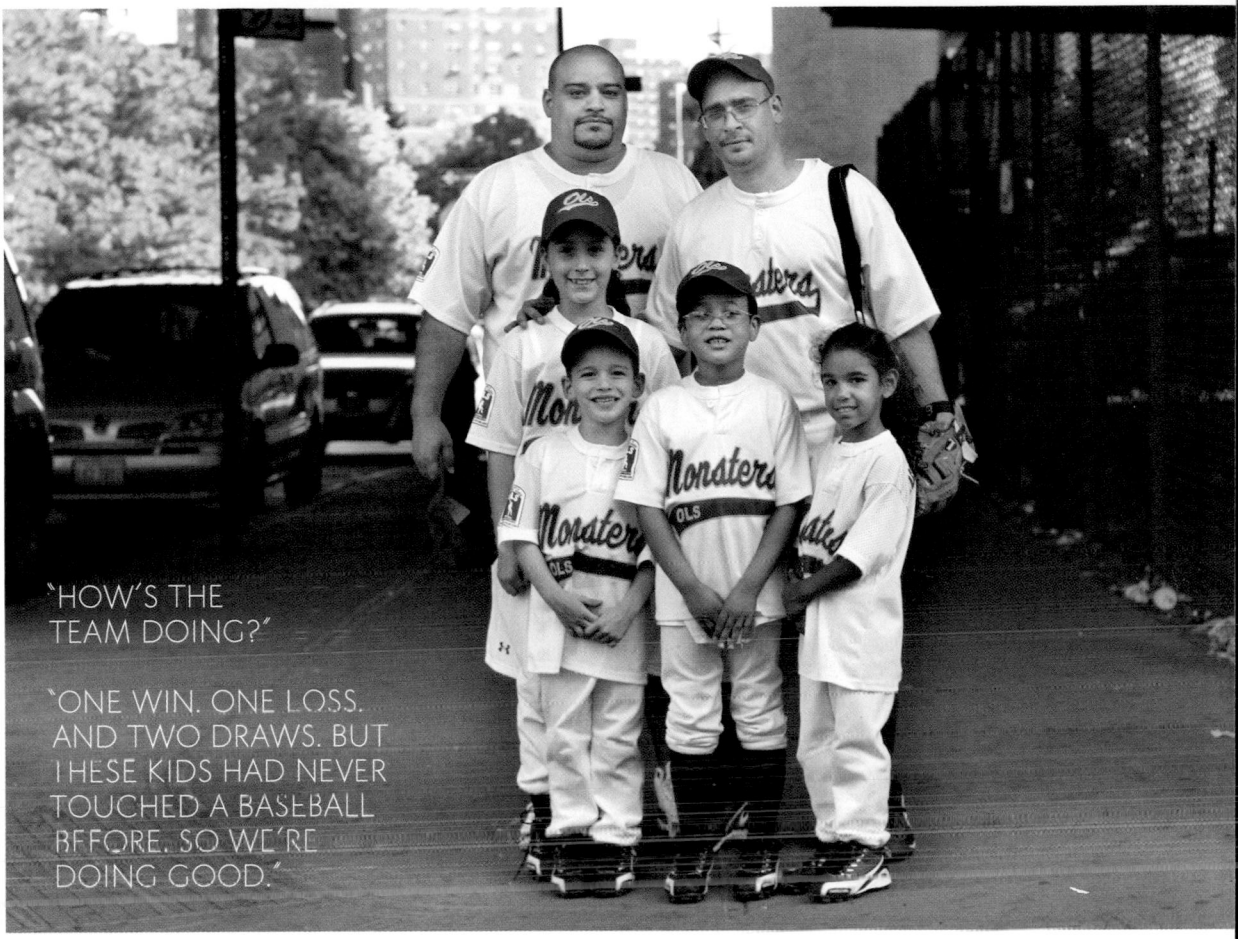


"HOW'S THE TEAM DOING?"

"ONE WIN. ONE LOSS. AND TWO DRAWS. BUT THESE KIDS HAD NEVER TOUCHED A BASEBALL BEFORE. SO WE'RE DOING GOOD."

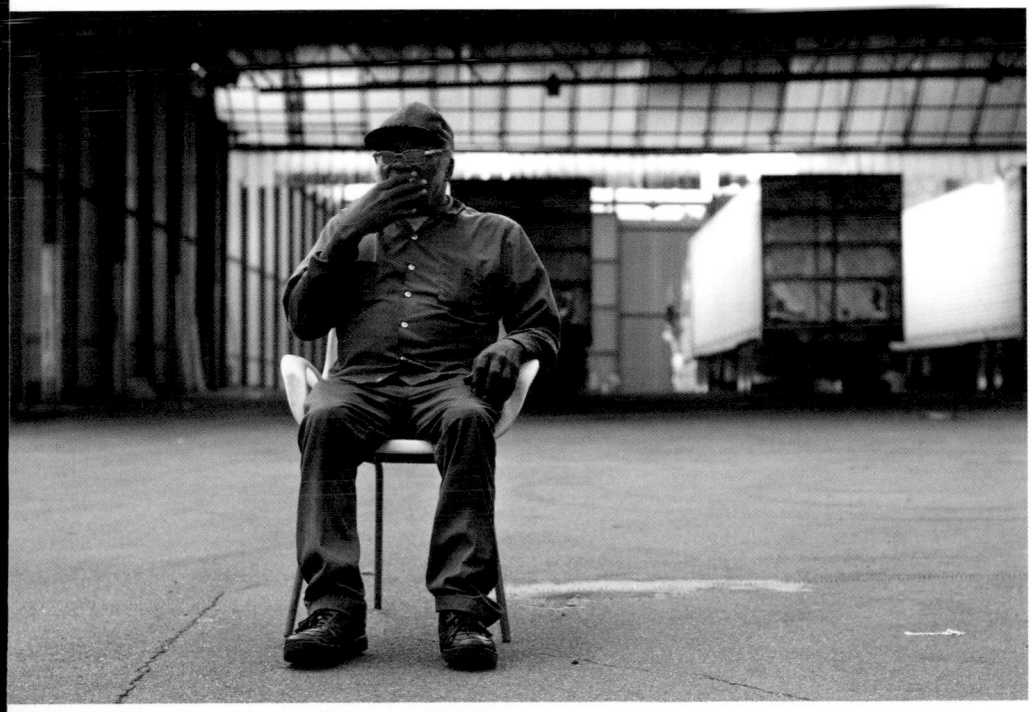

JUDGING BY EVERYONE'S EXCITEMENT, THIS DAY WILL ALWAYS BE REMEMBERED AT THE LOADING DOCK AS THE DAY "LARRY MADE IT ON THE INTERNET."

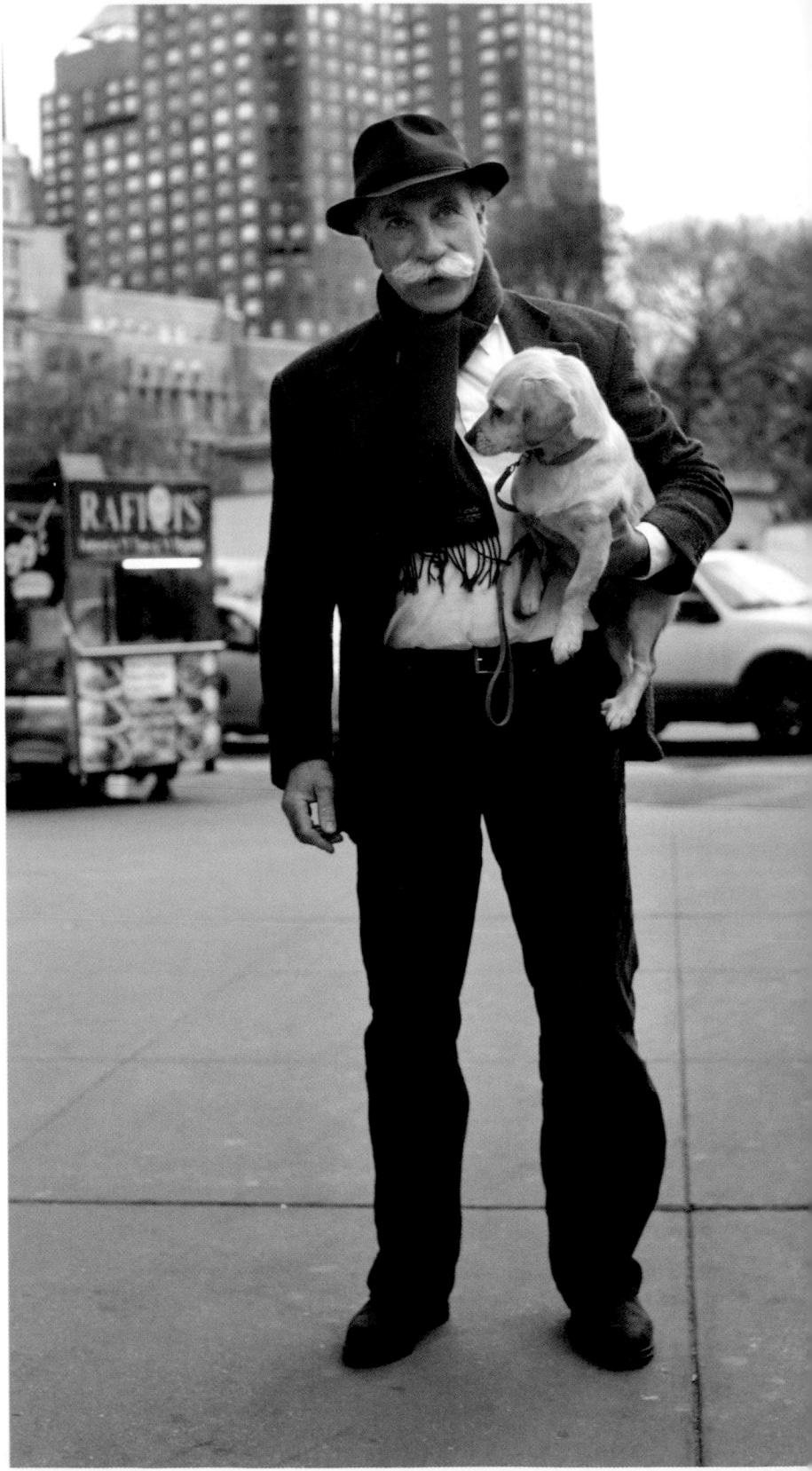


HYPERMASCULINE MYSTERY MAN COMPLEMENTS EPIC MUSTACHE WITH NEW PUPPY.

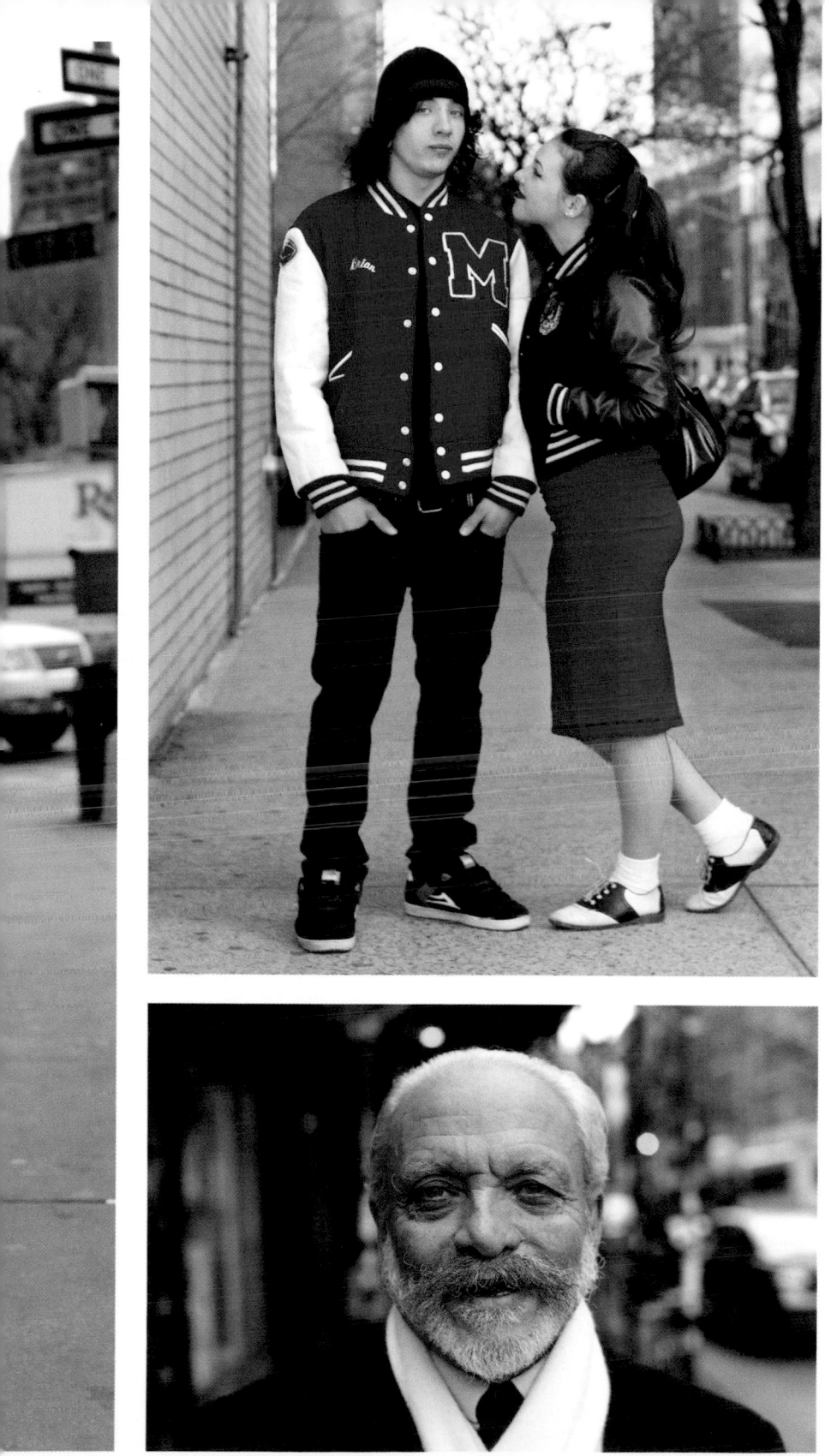

"WELL, I ALWAYS DRESS LIKE THIS—THEN I BOUGHT HIM THE JACKET AND MADE HIM WEAR IT."

"IF YOU COULD GIVE ONE PIECE OF ADVICE, WHAT WOULD IT BE?"

"PREPARE FOR THE WORST."

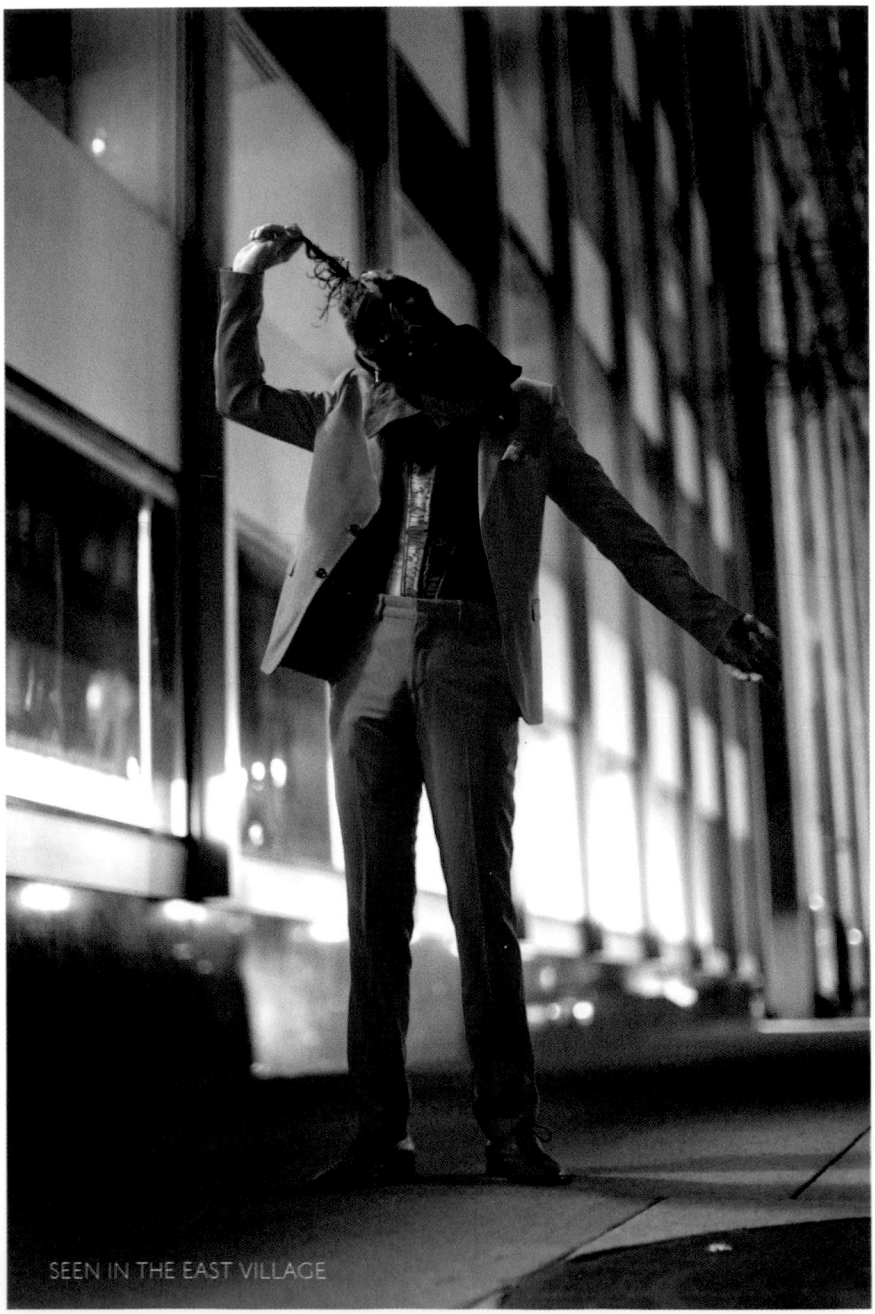

SEEN IN THE EAST VILLAGE

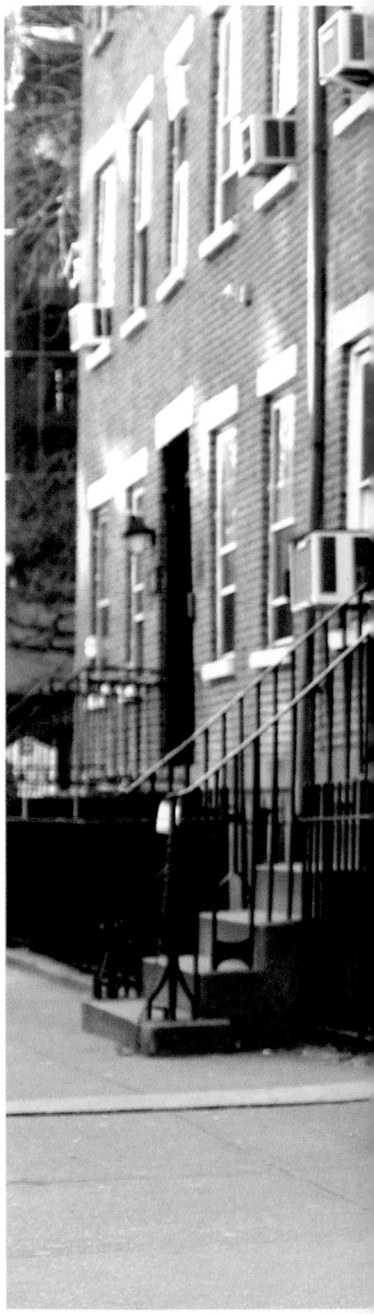

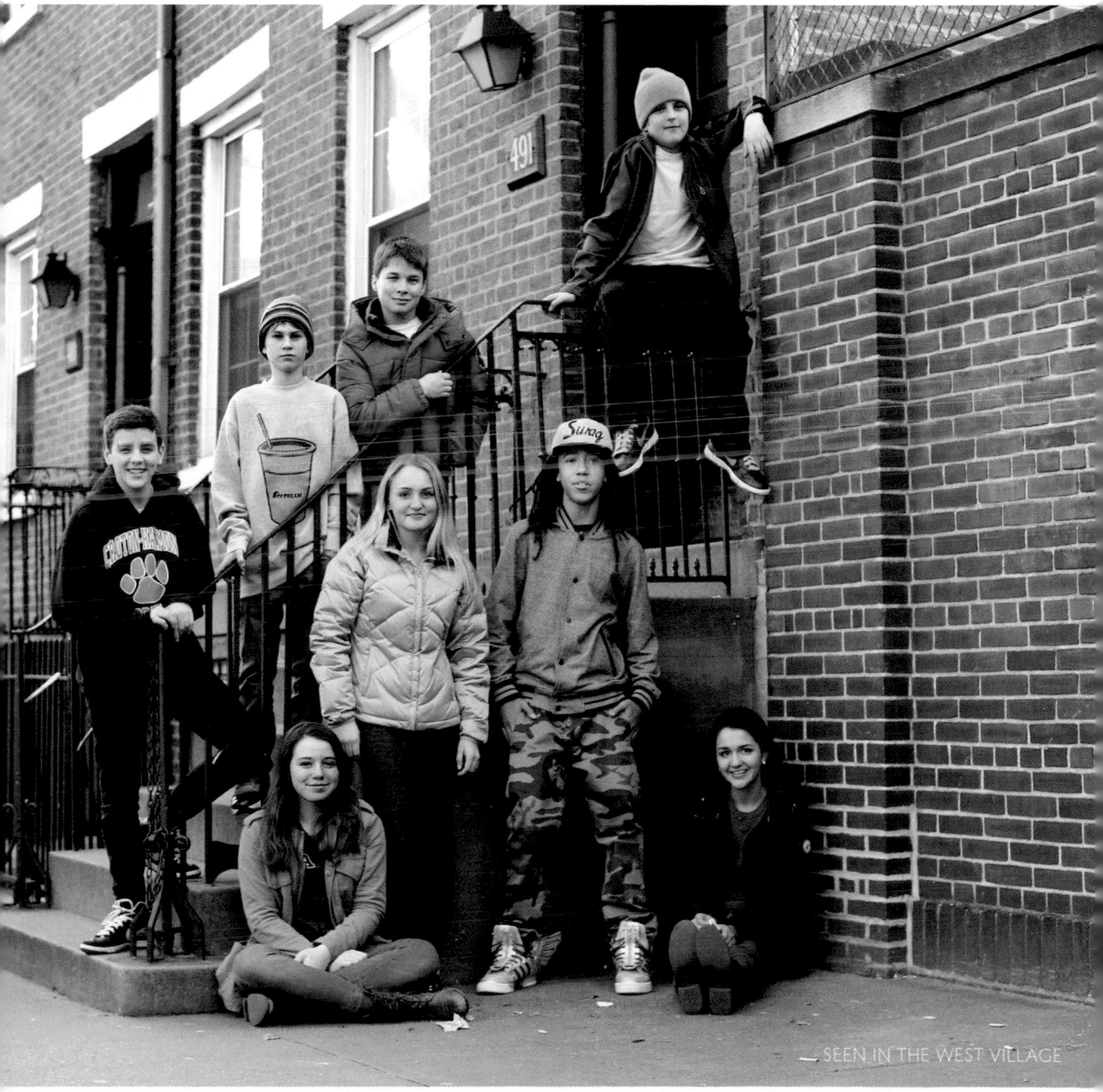


SEEN IN THE WEST VILLAGE

SOME DAYS I WORRY THAT I WON'T FIND ANYONE TO PHOTOGRAPH. THEN I TURN THE CORNER AND SEE A GIANT TREE MAN.

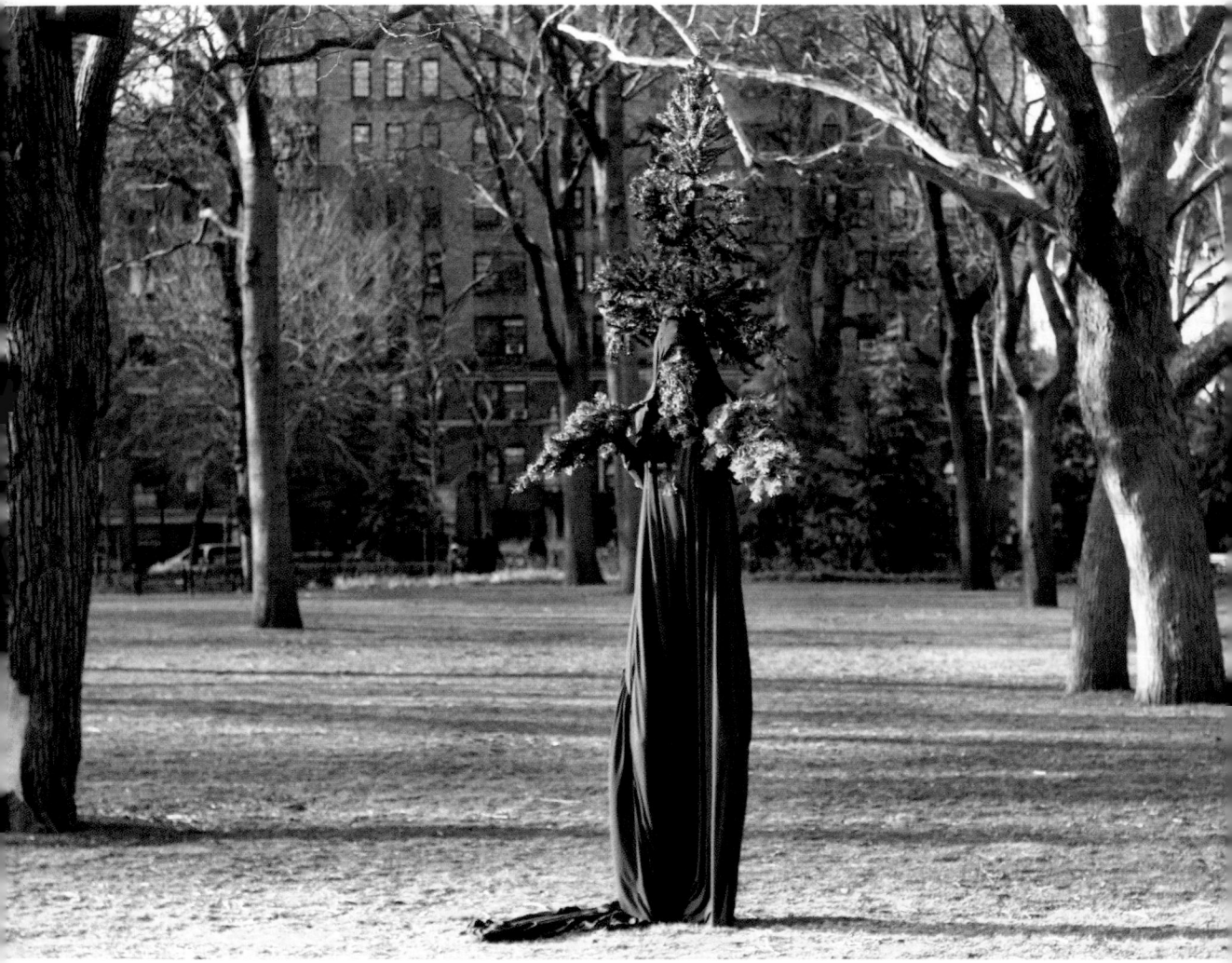

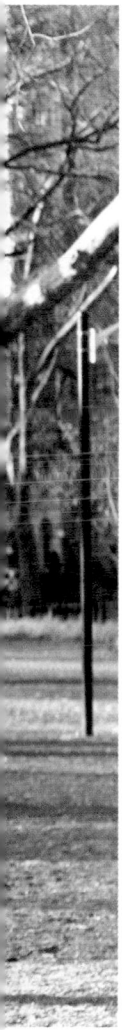

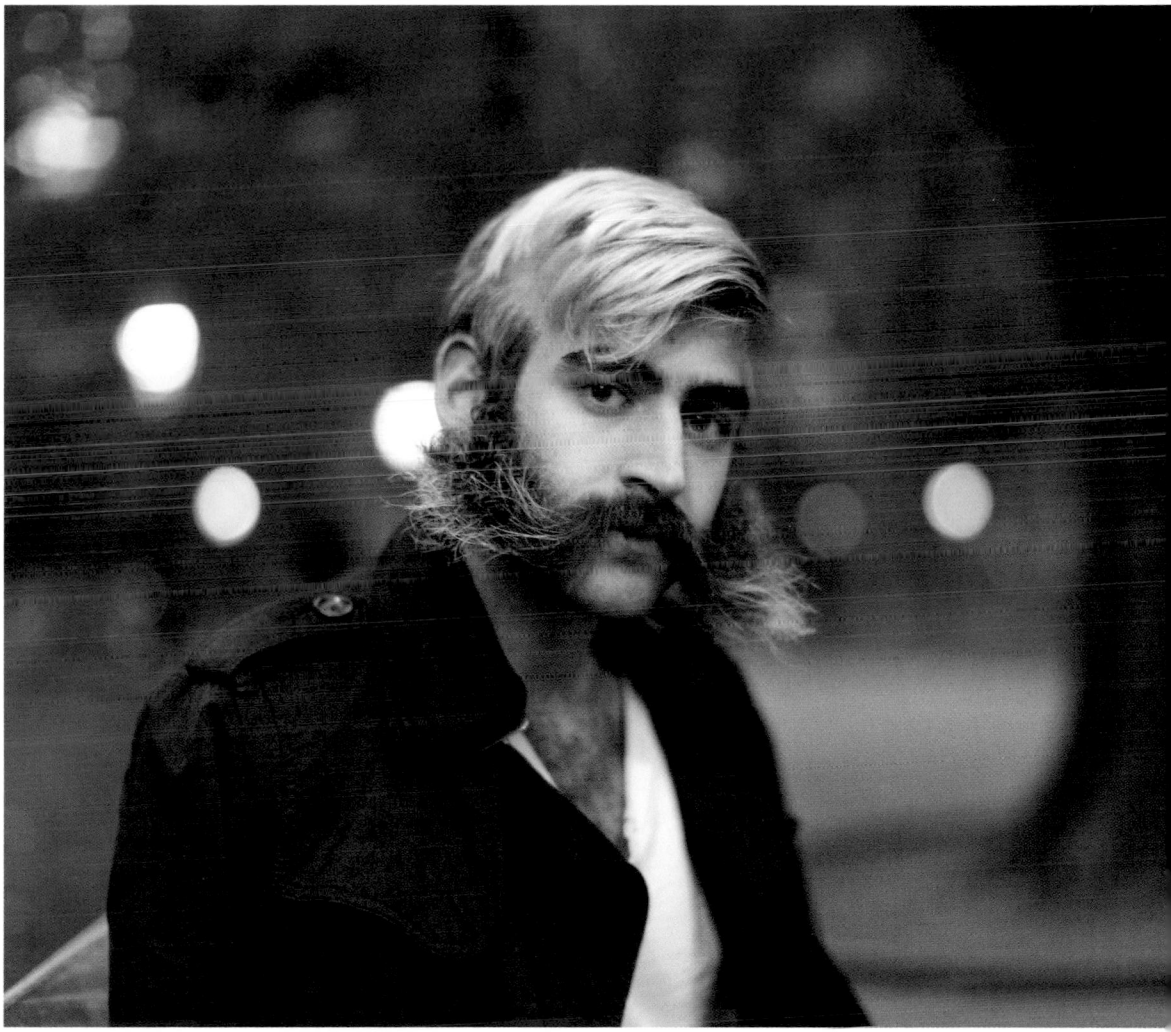

"I'M STUDYING TO GET A PH.D. IN NEUROSCIENCE, BUT IN MY FREE TIME I LIKE TO PERFORM IN BURLESQUE SHOWS."

"EVERYONE ON THE SUBWAY IS ALWAYS ABSORBED BY THEIR PHONE OR A BOOK. I'M A SOCIAL PERSON, SO THIS IS MY WAY OF INTERACTING WITHOUT BOTHERING ANYONE."

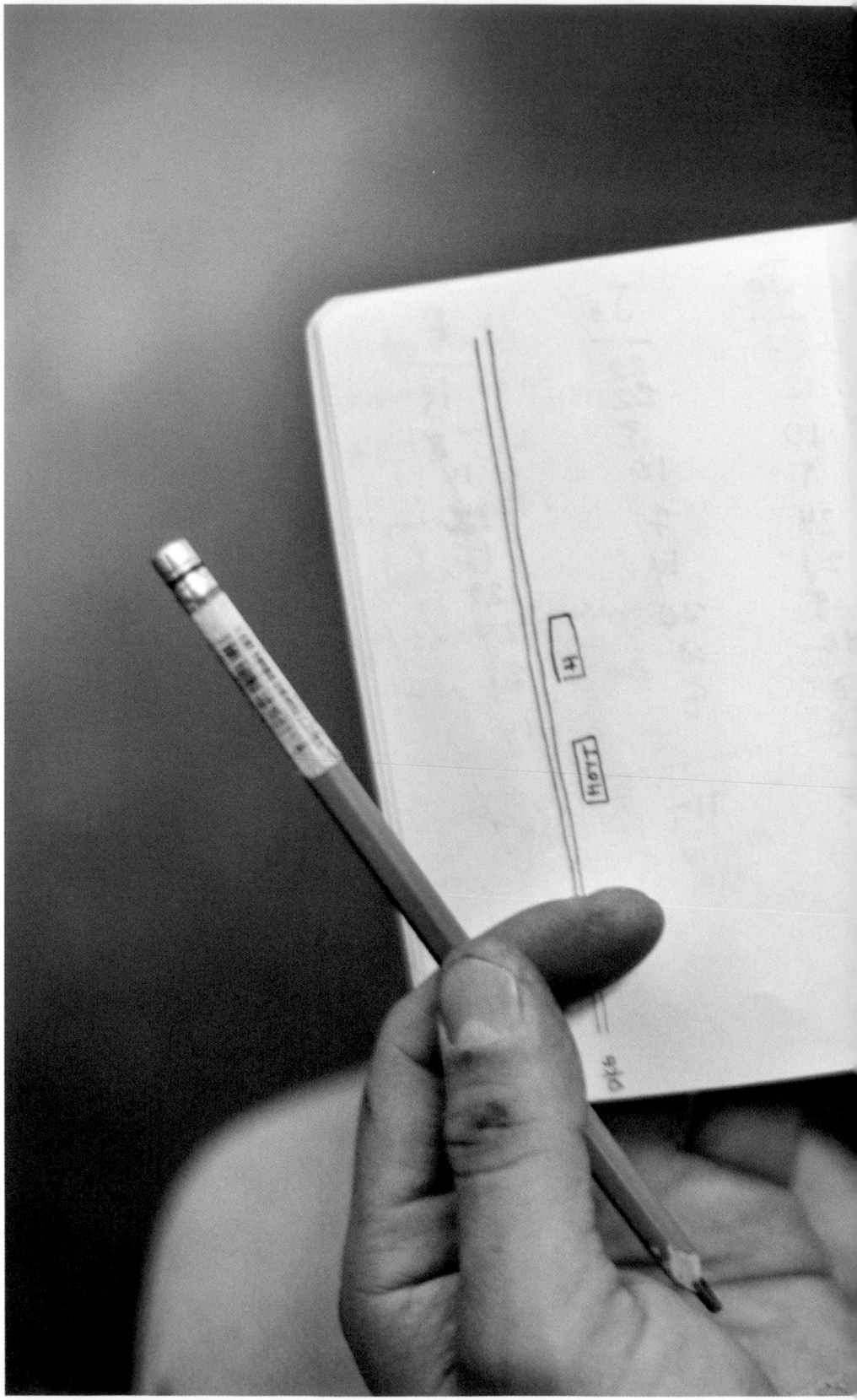

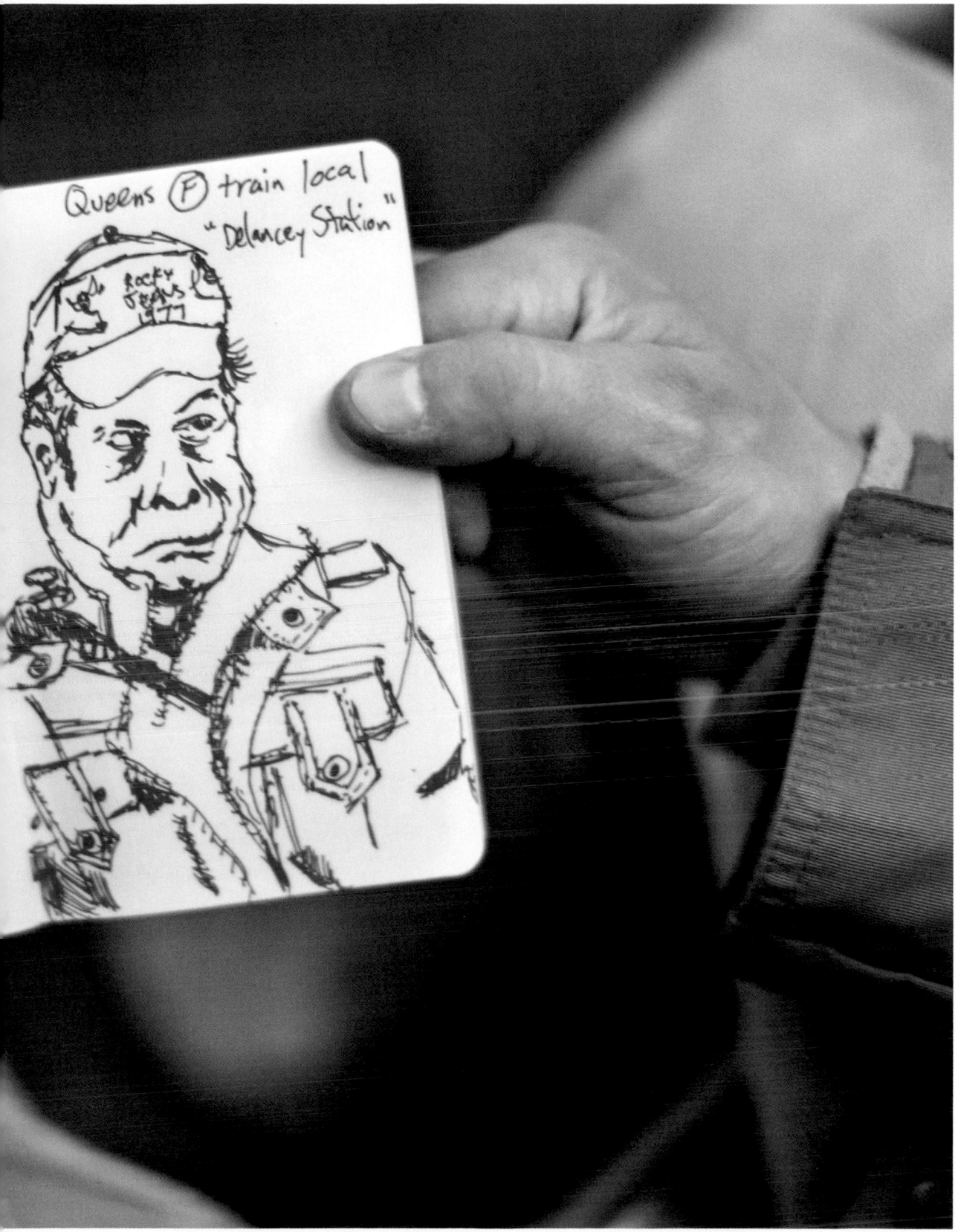
Queens (F) train local
"Delancey Station"
Rocky Jones 1977

"WHAT'S YOUR STORY?"

"JUST RUNNING FOR PRESIDENT."

HE THEN HANDED ME A PIECE OF LITERATURE THAT OUTLINED HIS PLATFORM. AMONG OTHER THINGS, HE PLANNED TO FIGHT FOR MANDATORY TOOTH-BRUSHING LAWS. HE ALSO HOPED TO PROVIDE "A FREE PONY FOR EVERY AMERICAN."

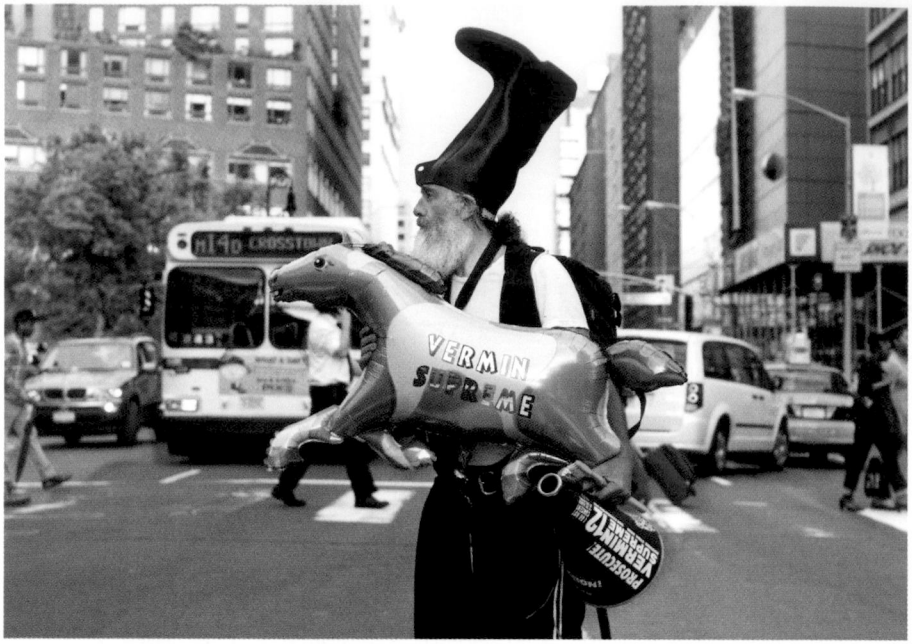


"WE ORDERED A BUNCH OF PIZZAS FOR THE FIREFIGHTERS, AND WHEN WE CAME TO PICK THEM UP, THEY REFUSED TO LET US PAY FOR THEM."

A TRAFFIC CONE WAS KNOCKED OVER ON THE SIDEWALK DIRECTLY IN FRONT OF THESE MEN. I PICKED IT UP AND CASUALLY TOSSED IT ASIDE. THE MAN ON THE LEFT GOT REALLY STERN AND SAID: "I KNOW YOU DIDN'T JUST DO THAT TO MY CONE." I LOOKED AT HIM, WAITING FOR HIM TO LAUGH. A FEW SECONDS PASSED AND HIS FACE DIDN'T CHANGE. HE SEEMED GENUINELY UPSET. "I KNOW YOU DIDN'T JUST DO THAT," HE REPEATED.

THEN HE BURST OUT LAUGHING.

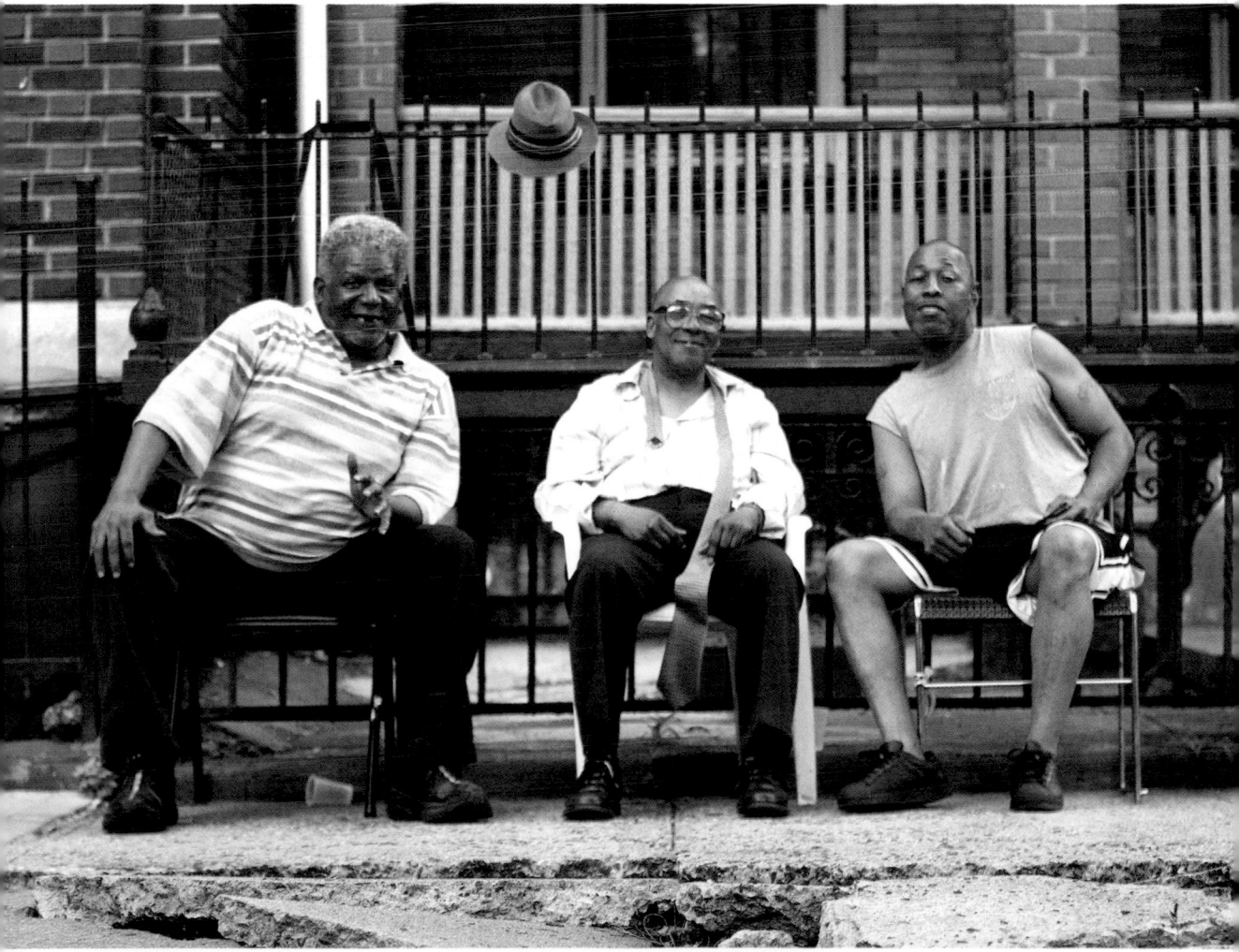

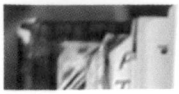

A GLIMPSE INTO THE JOURNAL OF A (QUITE INTELLIGENT) SIXTEEN-YEAR-OLD GIRL. PHOTOGRAPHED, WITH PERMISSION, IN CENTRAL PARK.

what day is it, & in what month? these clocks never seemed (alive
i can't keep up, & i can't back down, i've been losing so much time.
"BLAH BLAH BLAH. You feel trapped in your life. What i'm hearing is this; happ
isn't worth any inconvenience
growing up isn't very helpful, when it comes down to it.
when i was really little, i loved staring up at the night sky. it alwa
fascinated me, the way the darker it got, the more stars would come o
they'd almost always be there, every time i woke from a bad drea
& ran to the window, everytime the daytime sunshine just wasn't enough, ~~I needed a little extra light~~, every
time i just ~~wanted~~ needed reassurance that they hadn't gone anywhere -
odd, but before the age of eight i don't have ~~any~~ a single memory o
a cloudy night.* / ** seven years later, i'm still just a girl, looking ~~to~~ ho
~~for~~ for comfort, for sleep, for respect. ~~for you~~ for this
~~teenage~~ you. for someone to jump with, our arms outstretched,
fingertips reaching to the heavens without the slightest idea what'
out there. grasping for who-knows-what ~~the~~ our wishes have bee
enveloped by balls of fire light years away, & yet there's the feelin
that there is, there always will be, something more, something
bigger, something we want but are so so terrified to have. i live
with the constant ~~sensation~~ feeling of having something (very very importan
to say without
slightest idea of what it ~~was~~ is or who it's meant for. maybe that's w
i started writing — in hopes that someday it'll finally come out, ~~or the~~
~~documenting themself on paper~~, & i'll ~~[illegible]~~ finally know
a real epiphany feels like. ** standing there, head tilted up, taking it all in, to an audience in deep spa
really. the only difference now is far more rainy nights.
((i just really want a chick-flick romance.))
every once in a while, you meet these people that make you thi
~~you~~ that just maybe you've been doing something right after all,
deserve them in your life.

yes, i do stupid thing
make up words. i don
enough. i let my hea
my brain. i keep w
letters that i woul
send in a million

for life's not a paragraph
& death i think is no parentheses

something about you ~~[illegible]~~ now ... i can't quite figure out ... everyt
she does is beautiful ... & everything she does is right

...es right
...ight now)
...taphors
that ou... I make
editors & red pens
cringe

[* that was a time before i'd quite learned how to lose myself in words (leave myself to be found) & so i tried to let the little pinpoints of light be a replacement for something i had yet to discover.] ** i would get the strangest feeling that there was something (inside ...me, waiting ...ne to give it ...ance to ...e out, it ⊕ ...i knew ...how, & ...omehow whispering this to a twinkling dark space made me feel better. just looking at them gave me a sense of peace. sleeping right now might be a good idea... maybe...

this talking kinda wears me out

REMEMBER TO TELL NILO:
well, a friend of mine has a "proud to be a david tennant fangirl" t-shirt... it's a pity i couldn't find one for you...

"so you remember french boy?" "YES?!?!" "oh, well, nothing happened with him..."

useful phrases from "the book thief": smiles like salt. ruptured veins. waxy yellows. stood & played with the quietness. mistakes, mistakes - it's all i seem capable of at times. wooden teardrops. oaky smiles. DER.P.

what if she doesn't like, me

i don't even really know what to say; ~~putting~~ & i am fairly good at putting feelings on paper, so that's new. i dunno - i really dunno. i'm just putting syllables down on the page now with no real direction. & i haven't even really mentioned anything yet, no detail that would let ~~so~~ any one other than myself to understand, but that's just it, the "other than myself" bit. i can look at this tomorrow or next week or next month or possibly next year & most likely know what i'm talking about, & that in itself is worrying.

well that's just life i suppose

you pick them up in the unlikeliest places

i love you

insomnia is quite a beautiful thing, really - at least then i can control my dreams

I THINK I LOVE YOU.

i'm yours, eternally.
love, love, lovelovelove
loooove...

what is there to tell you about brutality & beauty that you don't already know? - the callouses on my right hand from playing the pen too - the lines on my fingers from gripping the pen too

amelia pond - the g... who wo...

if frodo can get the ring to Mordor, you can get out of bed.

sometimes i just stop & look back at the ~~last~~ fifteen ~~yr~~ & a bit years th... up my life & think about all the things i wish i hadn't ~~done~~ done - & trust... that's a pretty long list. people tell me that i'm too cautious, sometimes. & may... but i really can't help it; i just don't want you to turn into just another mistake, jus... more regret to add to my mental drama. maybe being careful is the way to happily... after - i mean, if we want fairytale simplicity, it'd be pretty helpful ~~to~~ to create it ou...

maturity?

you pick up ~~feelings~~ in the unlikeliest places - desk drawers, the cracks in cobblestone paths, for example, or in creaky desk drawers, or ~~la~~ la lie stuck in the knots of your shoelaces

listen, okay? i'm not perfect - i don't want to be. i want to stay lost & awkward & quirky & merdy & me. but then there's the matter of you... ~~we~~ it really shouldn't be this hard of a choice, giving up ~~[illegible]~~ you or giving up myself..... hmmmmm.

even

but i don't mean kind of silly th... that you look ba... & laugh at, like... weird kid you adore... for a while or wastin... time worrying about... the popular kids. i think i mean reat... regrets, although perhaps i'm not mature enough to know what exactly that even means.

"if i fuck it up, it's cool. that's art." ~ matt nathanson

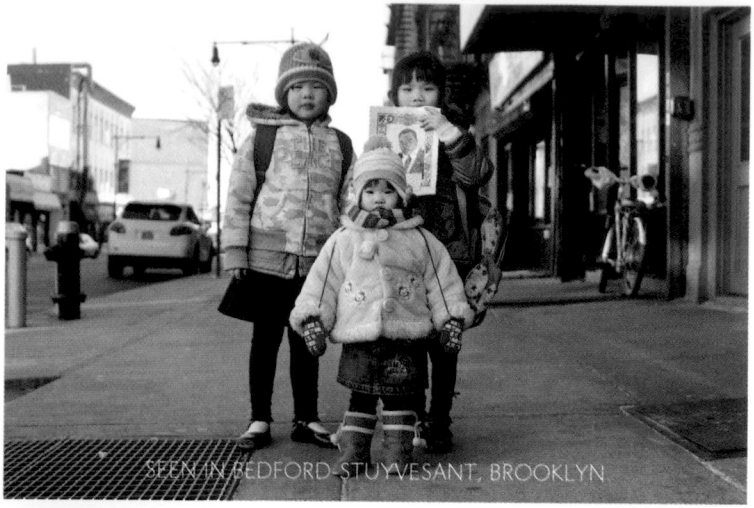

SEEN IN BEDFORD-STUYVESANT, BROOKLYN

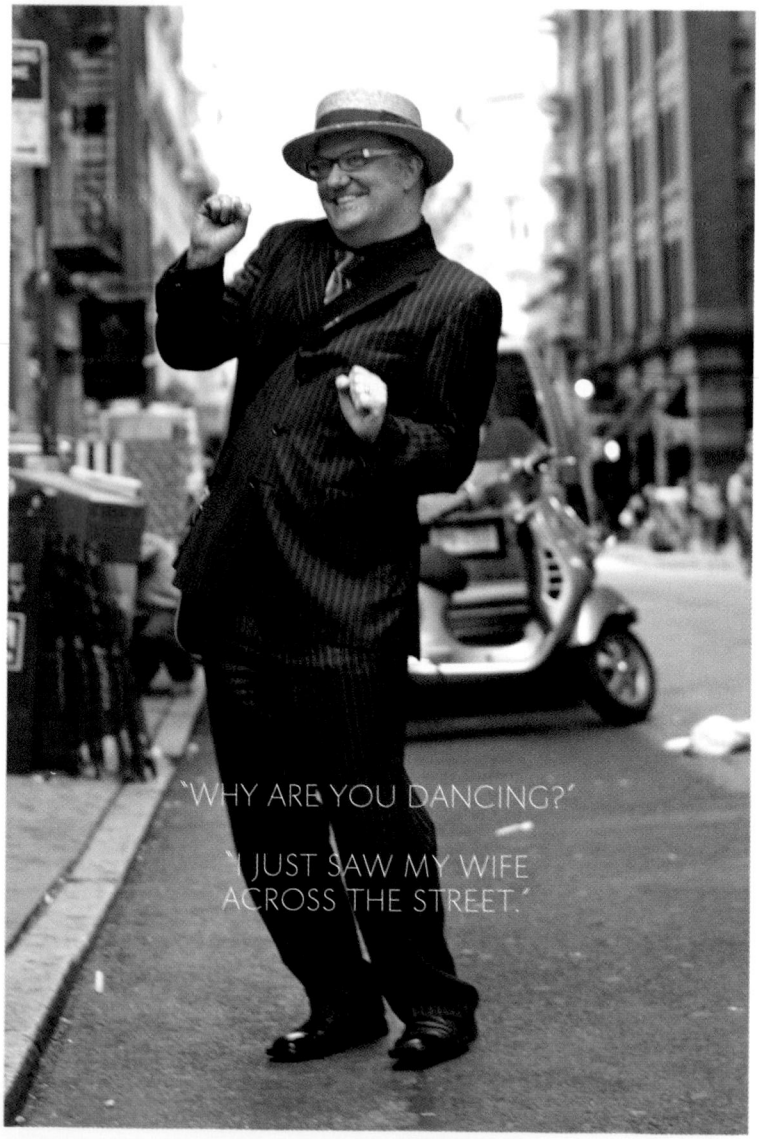

'WHY ARE YOU DANCING?'

'I JUST SAW MY WIFE ACROSS THE STREET.'

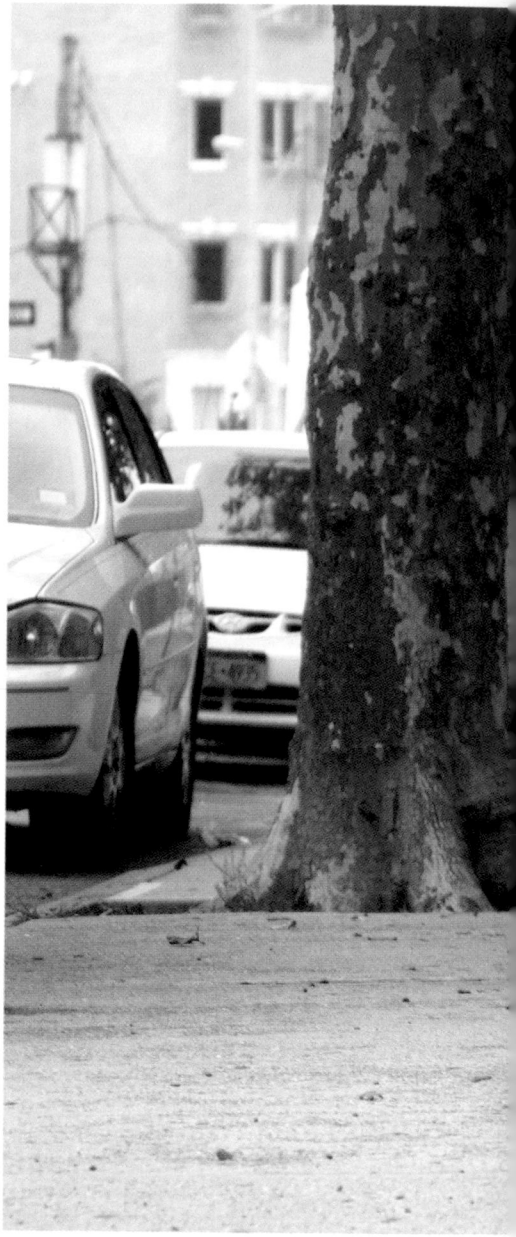

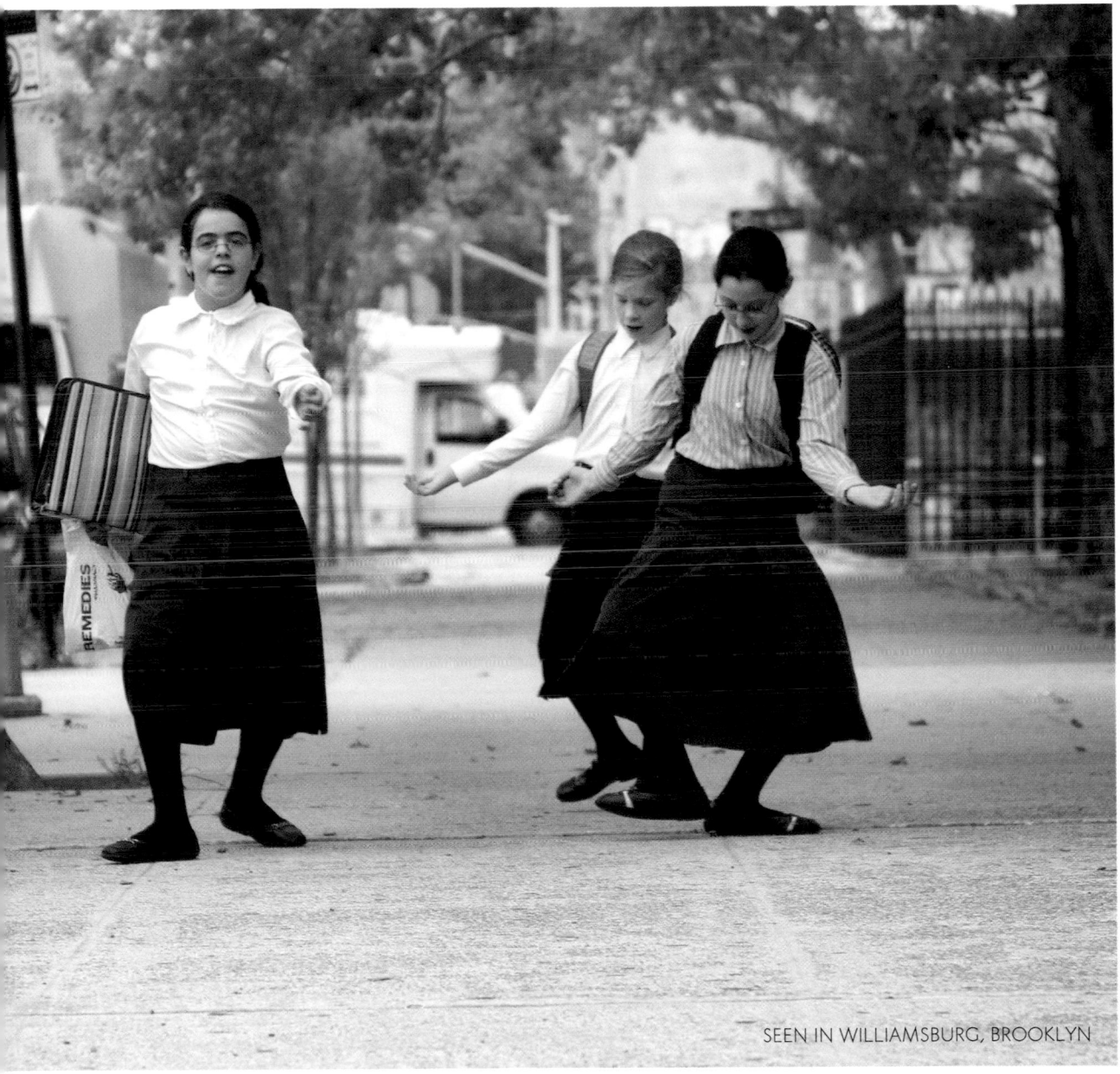


SEEN IN WILLIAMSBURG, BROOKLYN

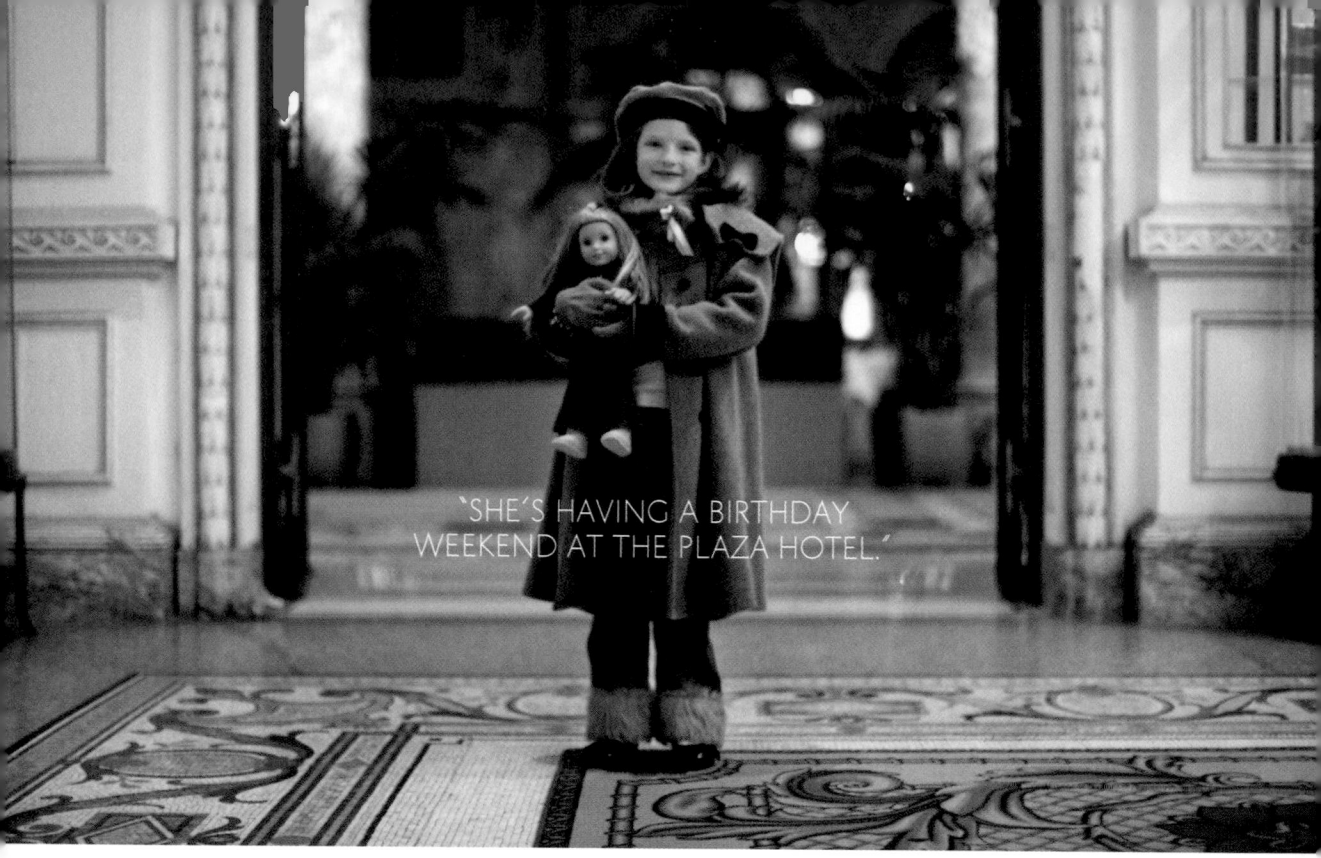

'SHE'S HAVING A BIRTHDAY WEEKEND AT THE PLAZA HOTEL.'

CHESS, LIKE SOCCER, IS A COMMON THREAD AMONG MANY CULTURES.

"MY ULTIMATE GOAL IS TO REACH A CERTAIN LEVEL OF ADULTHOOD WHERE I CAN AFFORD TO BE A CHILD."

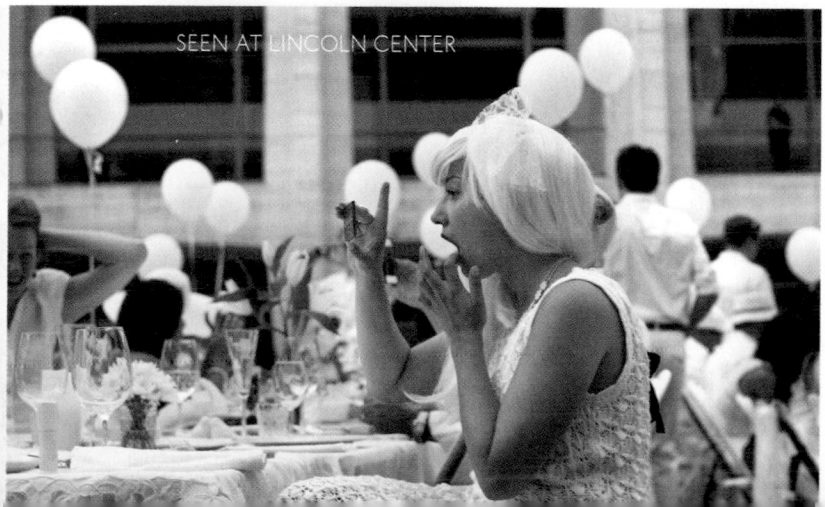

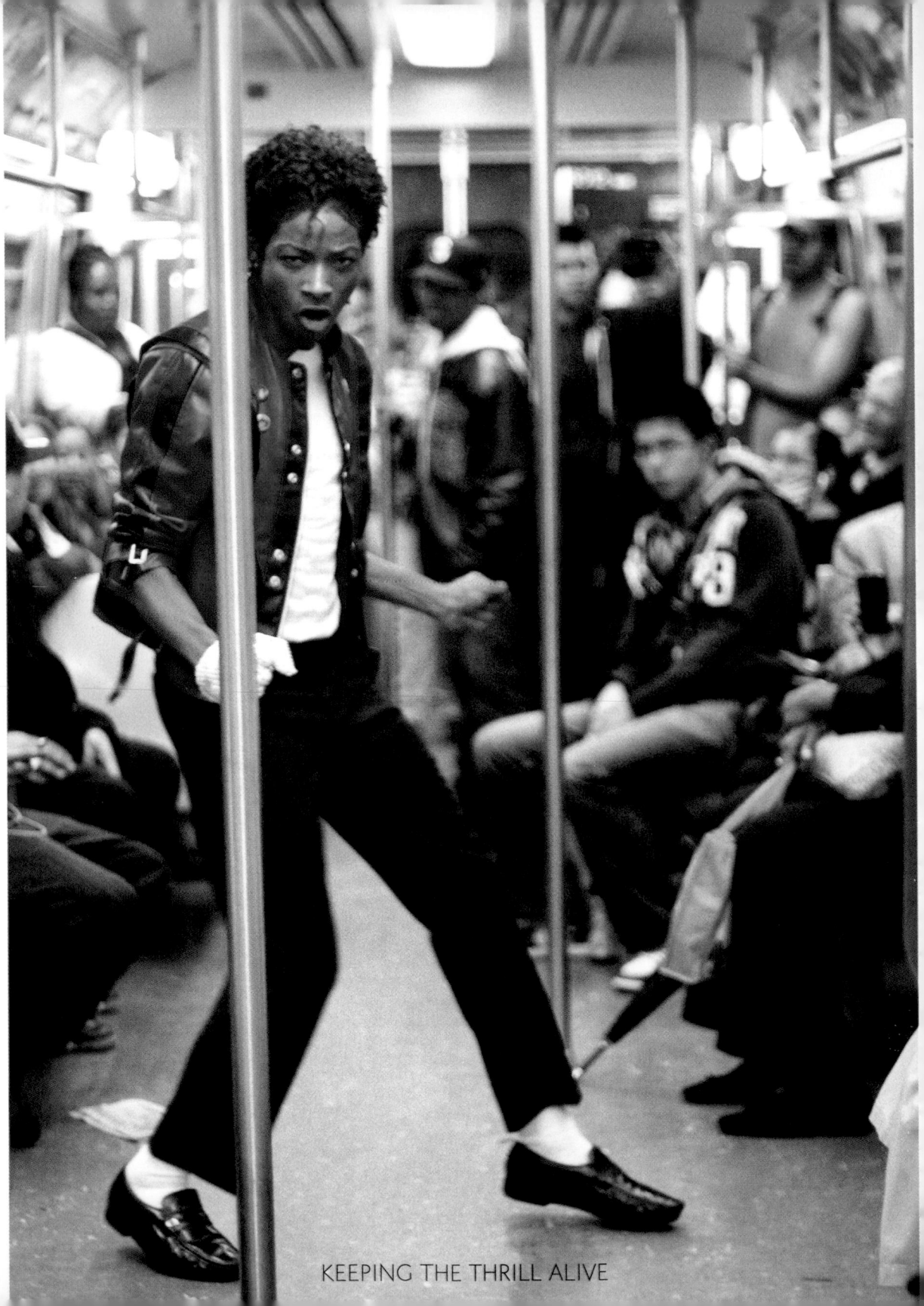

KEEPING THE THRILL ALIVE

OLD FRIENDS

SOMETIMES SPRING NEEDS A KICK START.

"I'M GOING TO LET YOU TAKE MY PHOTO BECAUSE YOU SEEM LIKE A GENUINE PERSON. BUT JUST SO YOU KNOW—I DON'T NORMALLY LET PEOPLE STEAL MY SWAG."

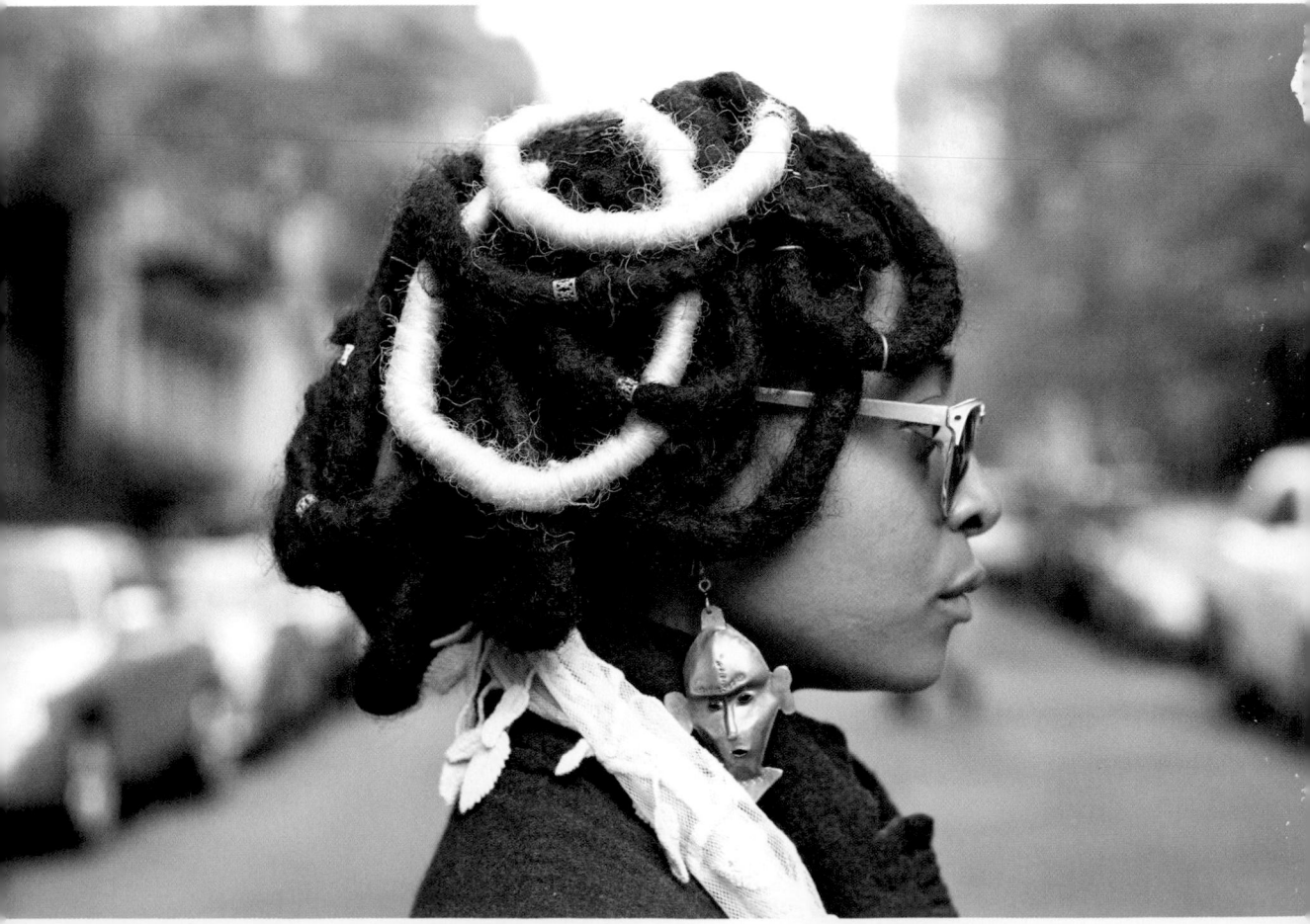

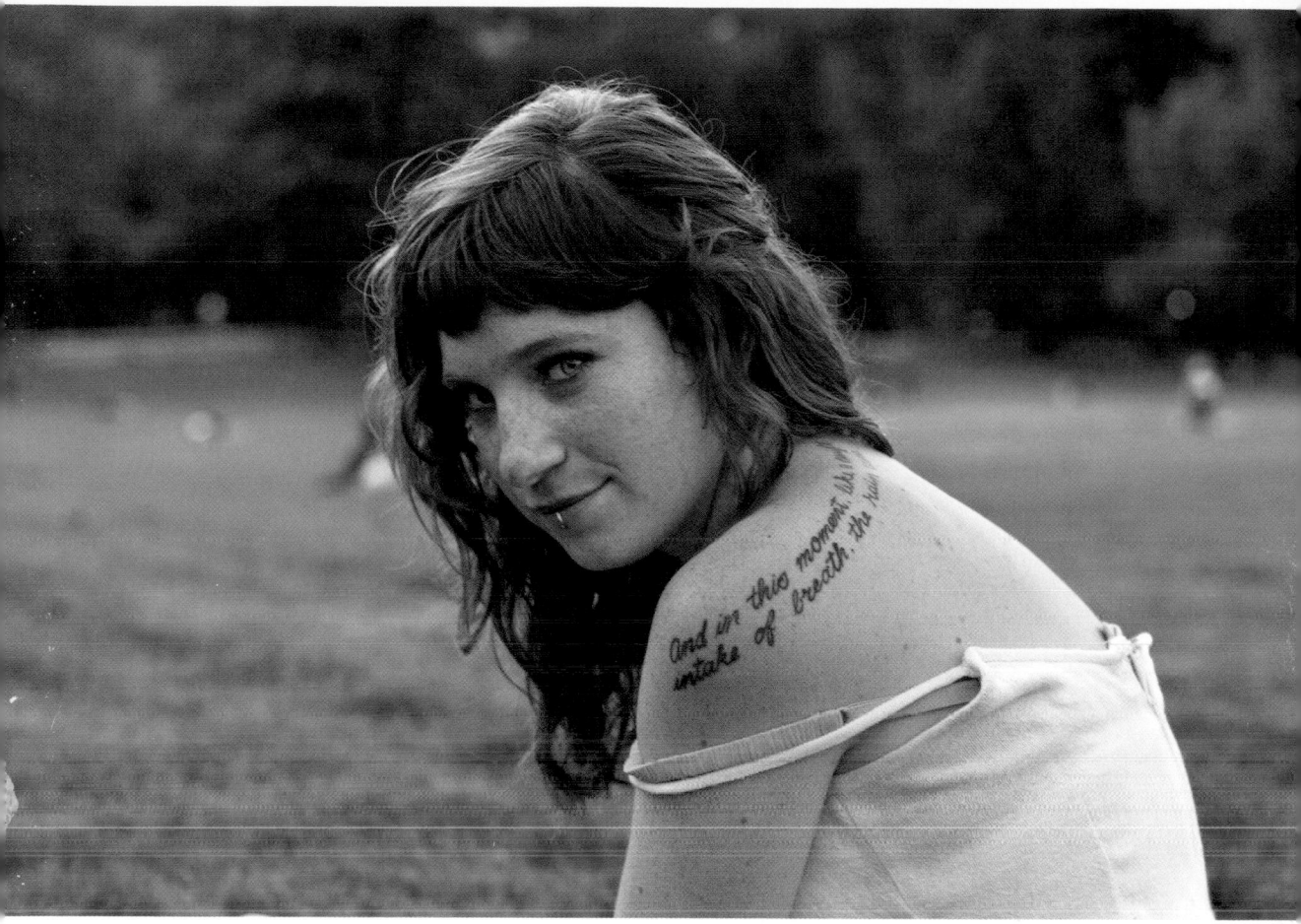


"MY FATHER HAS ASPERGER'S, SO IT'S ALWAYS BEEN VERY DIFFICULT TO CONNECT WITH HIM EMOTIONALLY. THEN, A FEW YEARS AGO, I WAS READING TRUMAN CAPOTE'S *OTHER VOICES, OTHER ROOMS*, AND THERE'S THIS SCENE WHERE THE MAIN CHARACTER PRAYS TO KNOW HIS FATHER. AND WHEN HE'S DONE PRAYING, THE CHAPTER ENDS: 'AND IN THIS MOMENT, LIKE A SWIFT INTAKE OF BREATH, THE RAIN CAME.' "

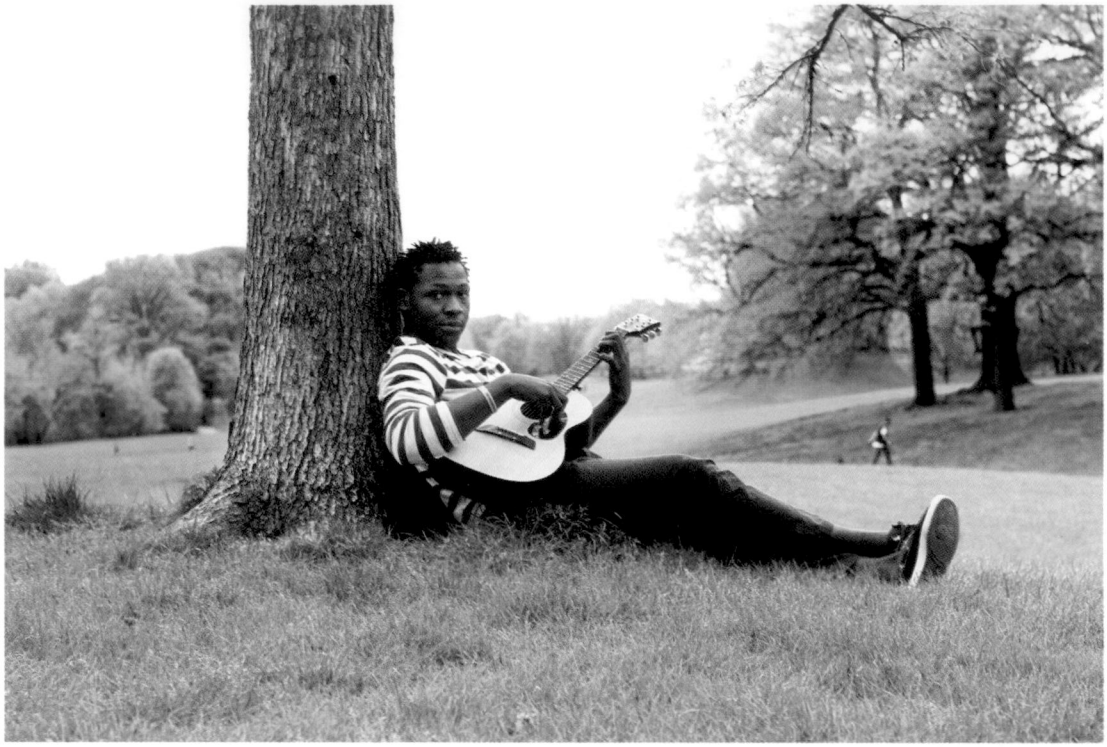

'I'M LEARNING A SONG.'

'ARE YOU LEARNING IT FOR A GIRL?'

'. . . YEAH.'

I ASKED HIS SISTER TO TELL ME SOMETHING ABOUT HER BROTHER. SHE SAID:

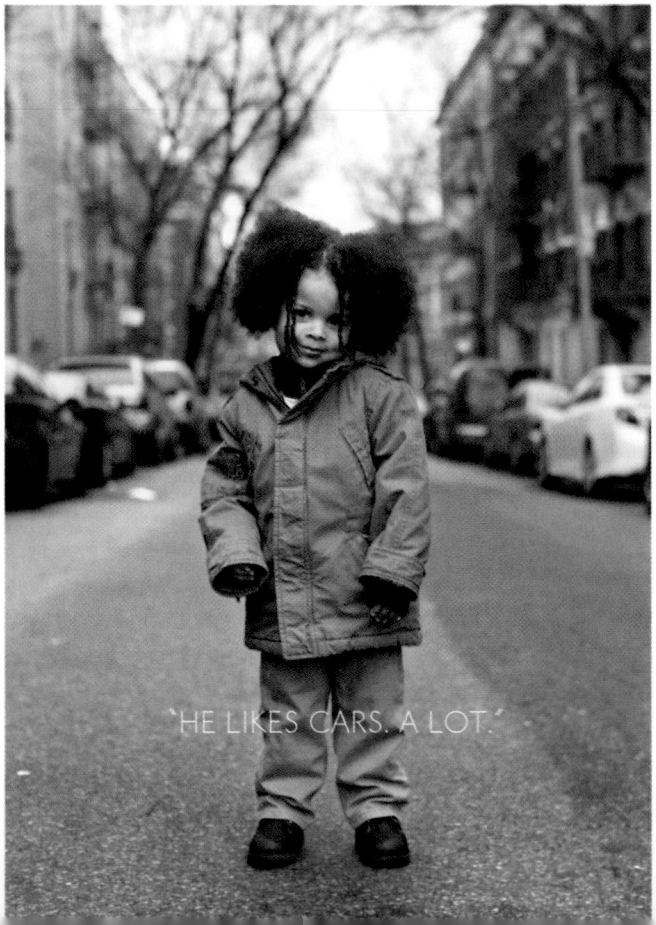

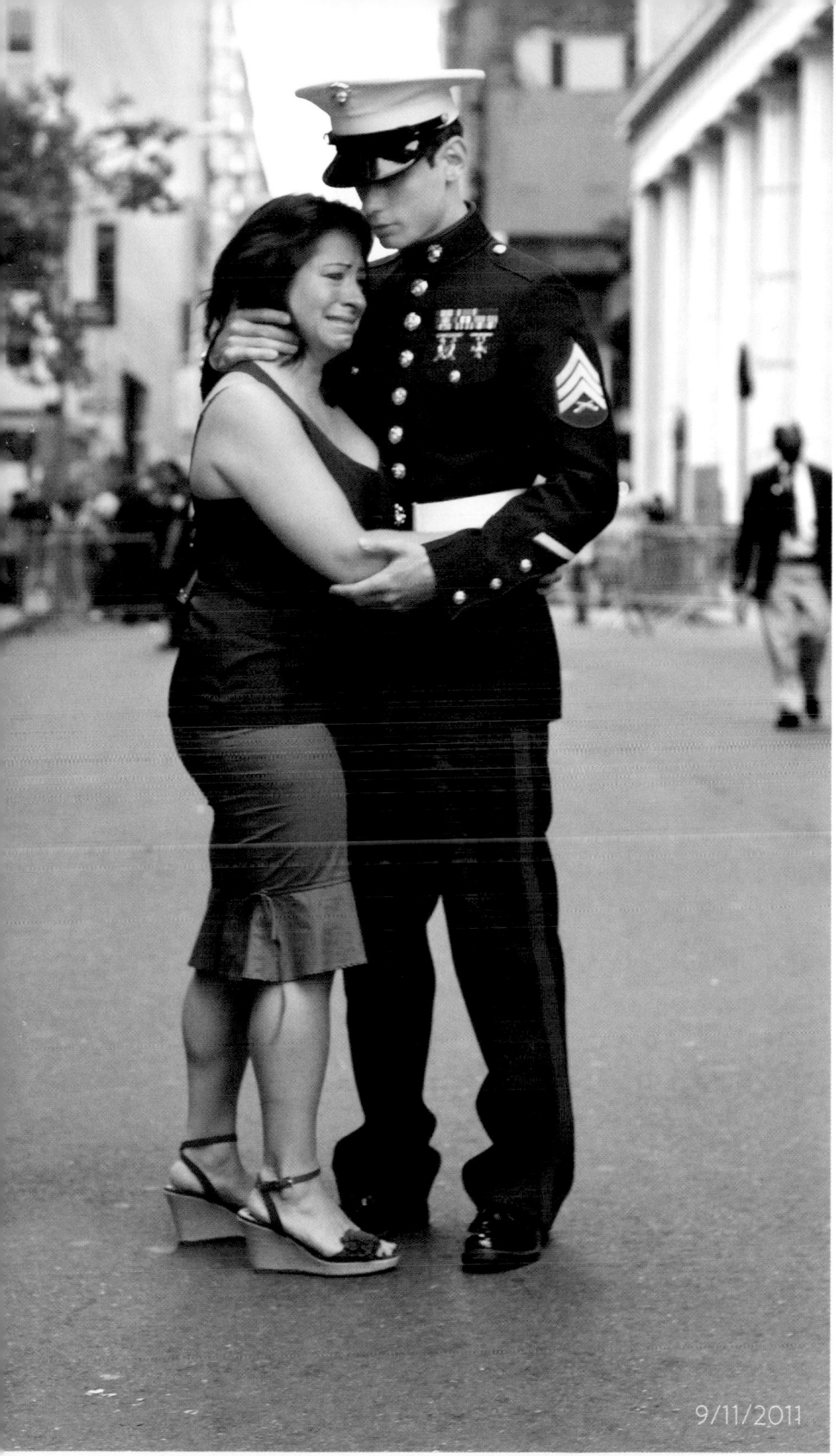
9/11/2011

SEEN IN HARLEM

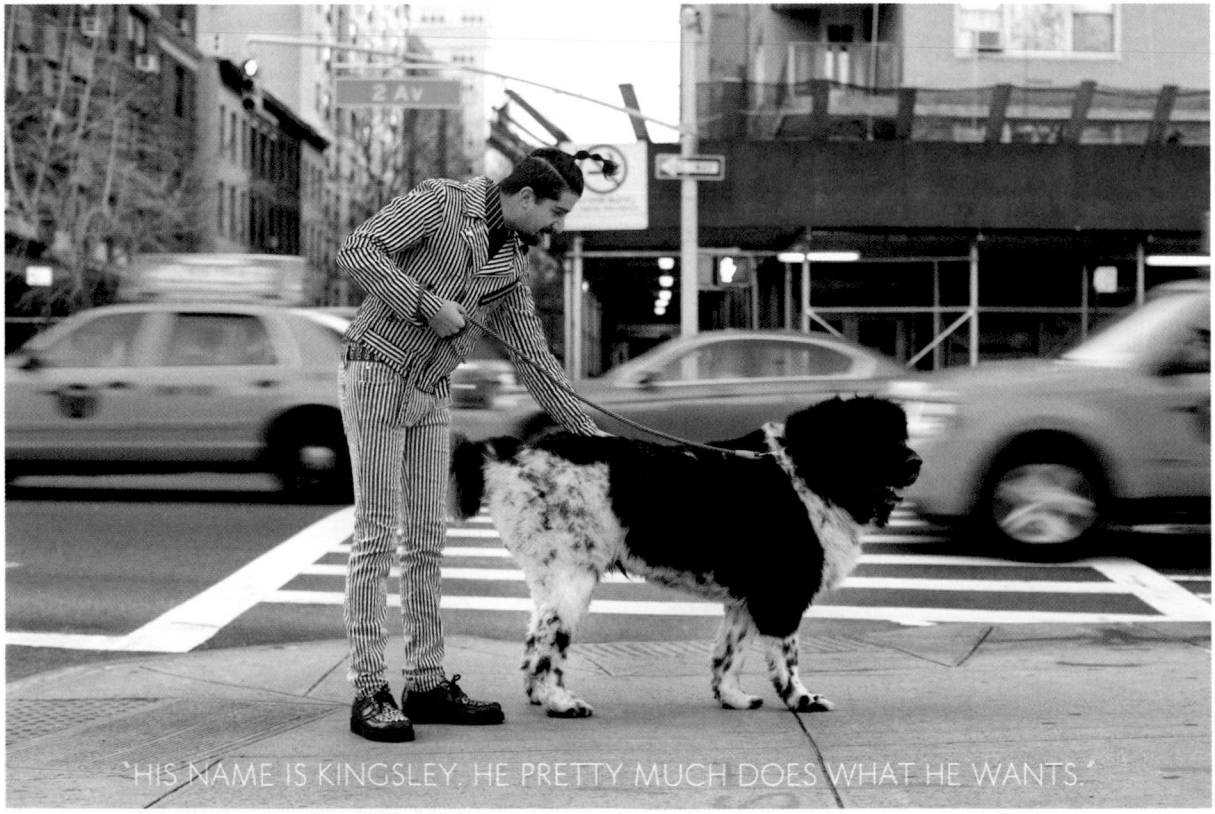


'HIS NAME IS KINGSLEY. HE PRETTY MUCH DOES WHAT HE WANTS.'

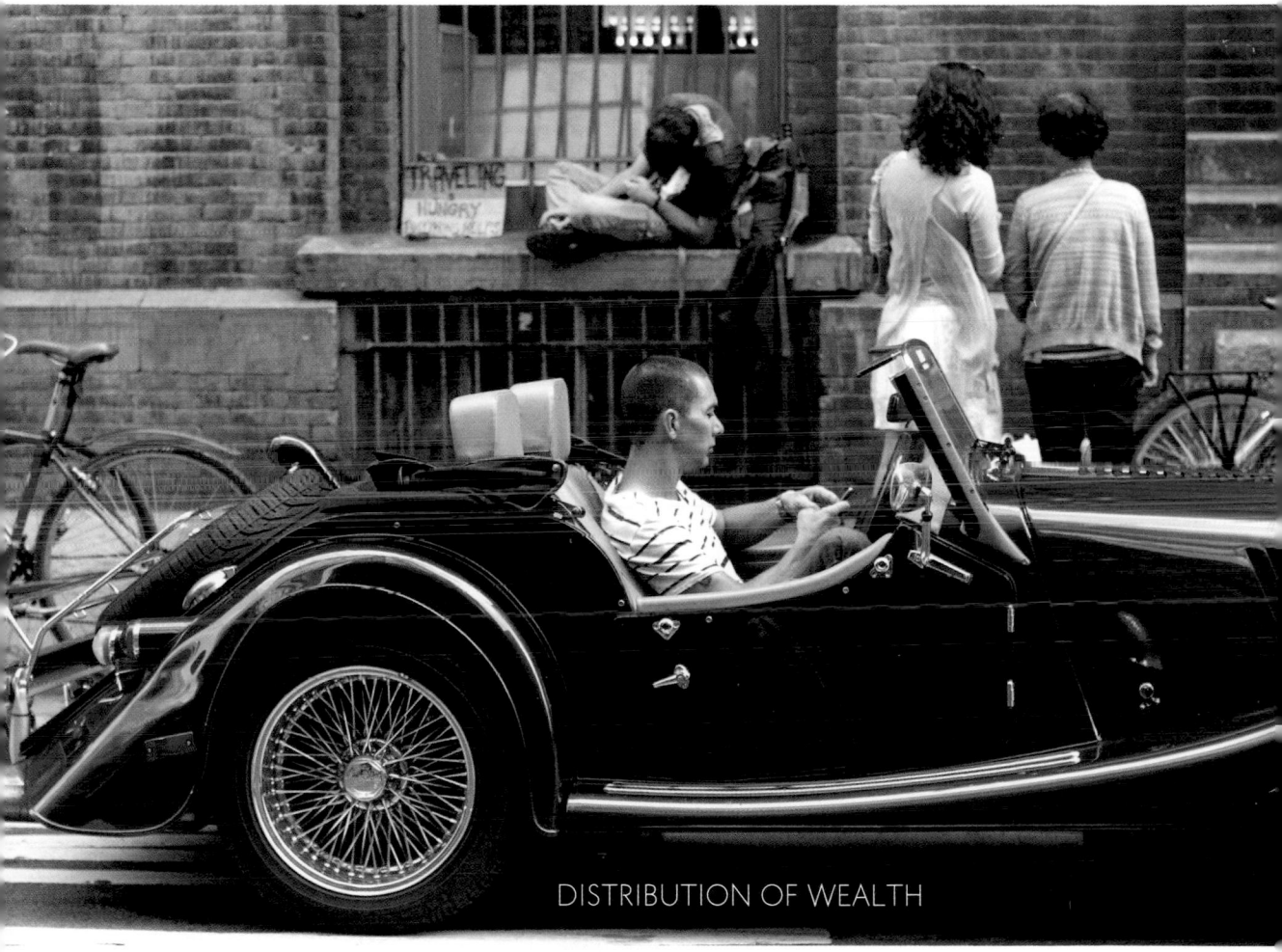


DISTRIBUTION OF WEALTH

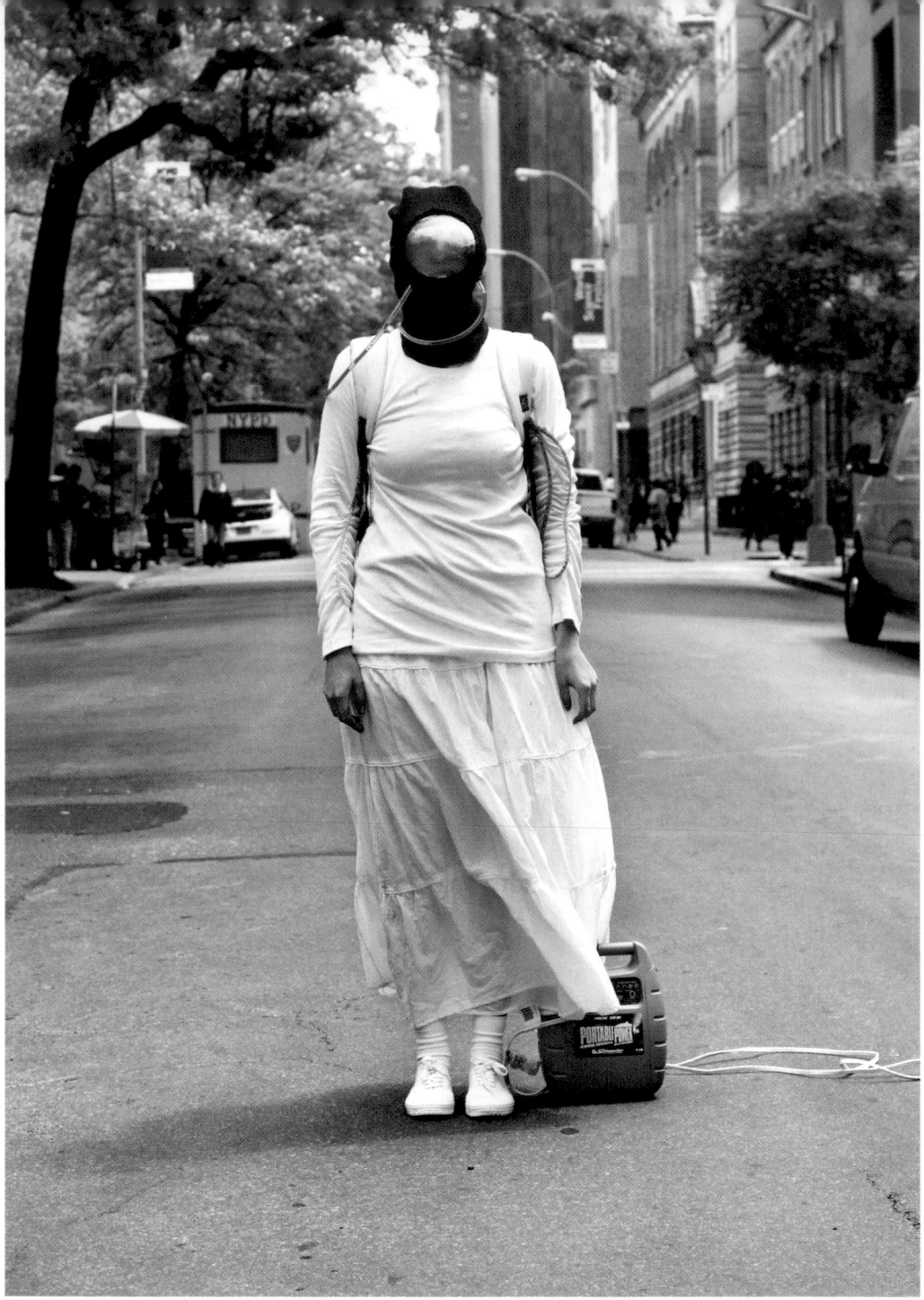


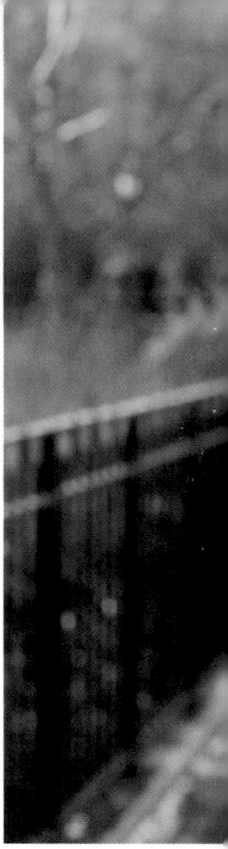

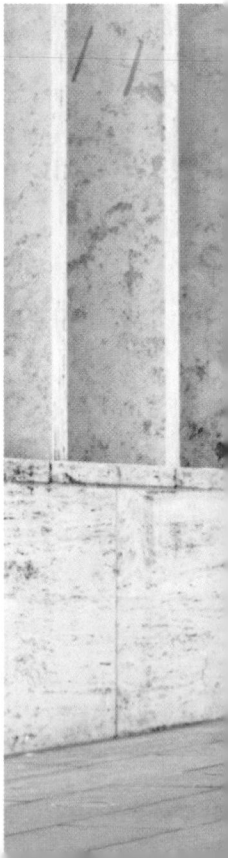

"WHEN YOUR PULSE DROPS BELOW SEVENTY-SIX, IT FUNNELS BLOOD OUT OF THE MASK AND YOUR VISION IS CLEARED. WHEN YOUR PULSE RISES ABOVE SEVENTY-SIX, THE BLOOD IS FUNNELED BACK INTO THE MASK AND YOUR VISION IS OBSCURED. IT'S DESIGNED TO TEACH THE USER TO BE SENSITIVE TO ENVIRONMENTAL STRESSORS, AND TO LEARN HOW THESE STRESSORS AFFECT THE BODY."

"I USED TO LIVE IN A PLASTIC BUBBLE. I DON'T MEAN FIGURATIVELY. I MEAN, I USED TO LIVE IN AN ACTUAL PLASTIC BUBBLE."

"I'M AN ARTIST, AND DRESSING IS MY ART."

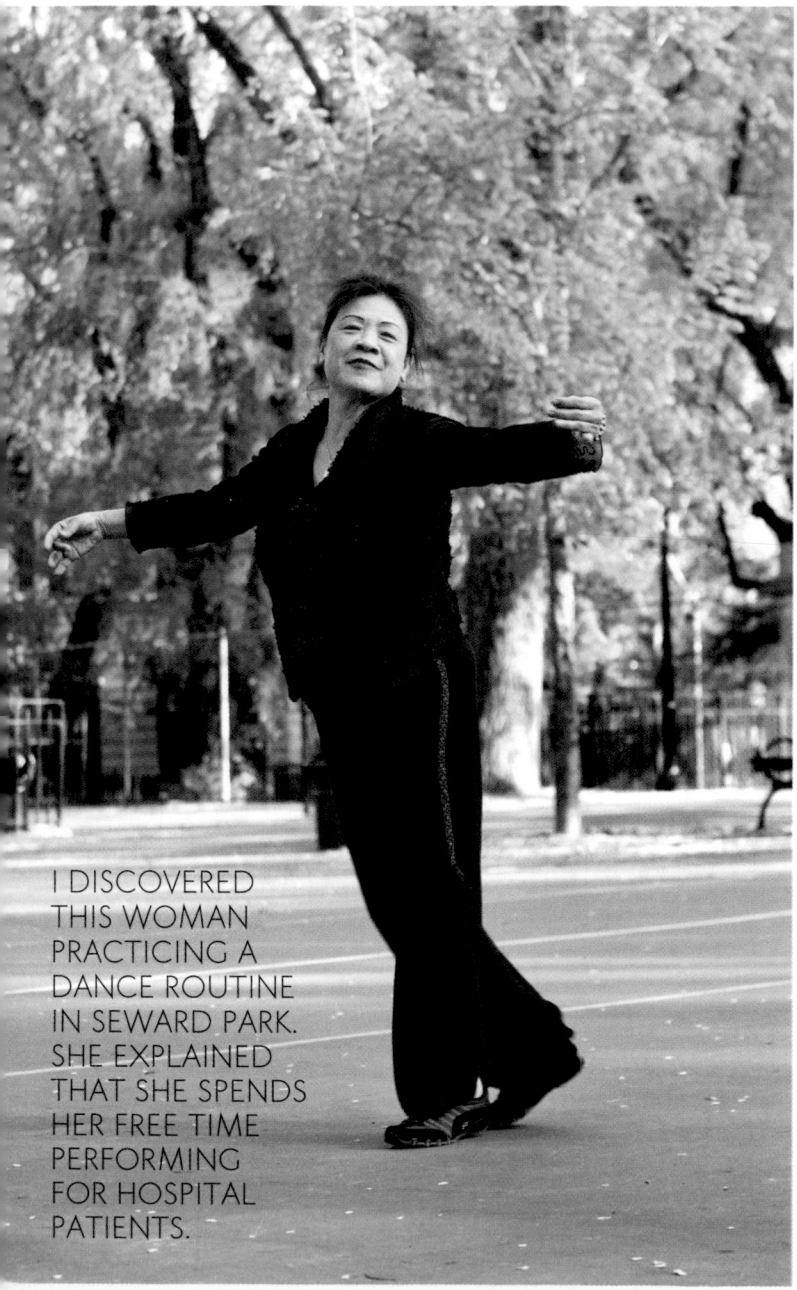

I DISCOVERED THIS WOMAN PRACTICING A DANCE ROUTINE IN SEWARD PARK. SHE EXPLAINED THAT SHE SPENDS HER FREE TIME PERFORMING FOR HOSPITAL PATIENTS.

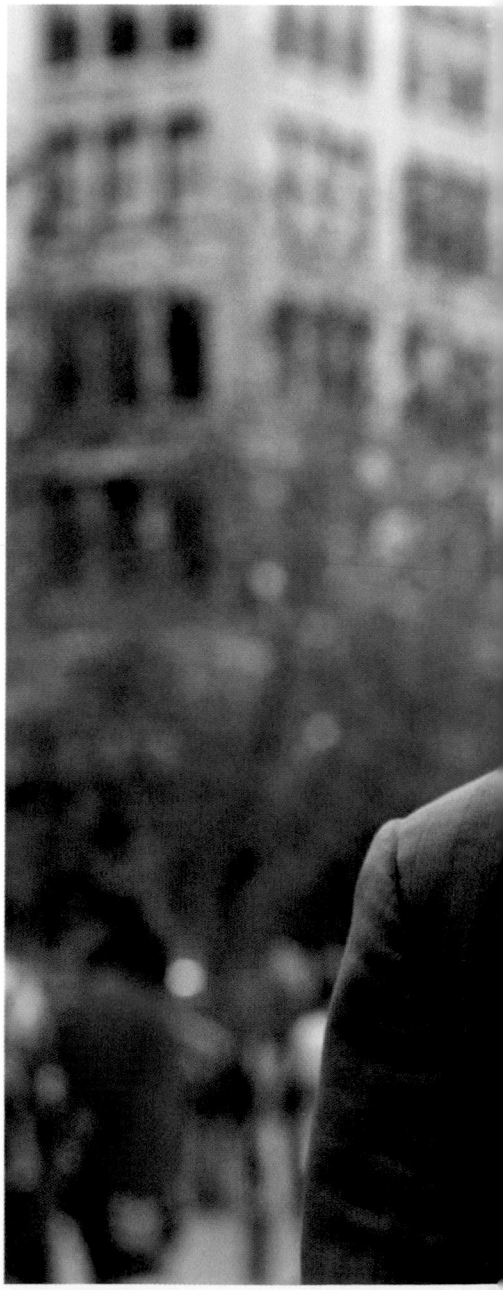

THIS MAN WAS PERFORMING PUPPET SHOWS BASED ON THE SHORT STORIES OF FRANZ KAFKA. DURING PIVOTAL SCENES, HIS YOUNG ASSISTANT WOULD BLOW WILDLY INTO A SAXOPHONE.

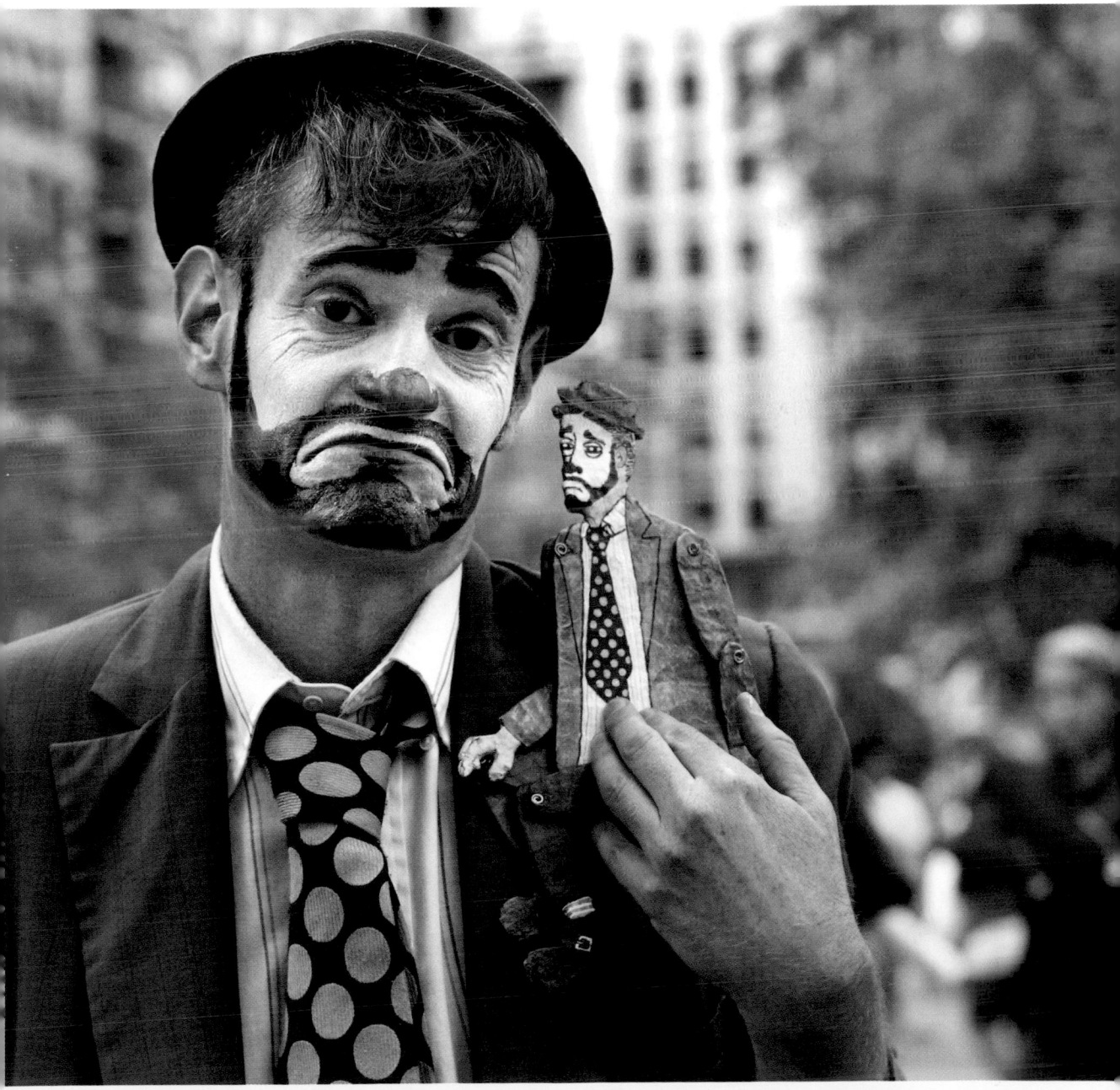

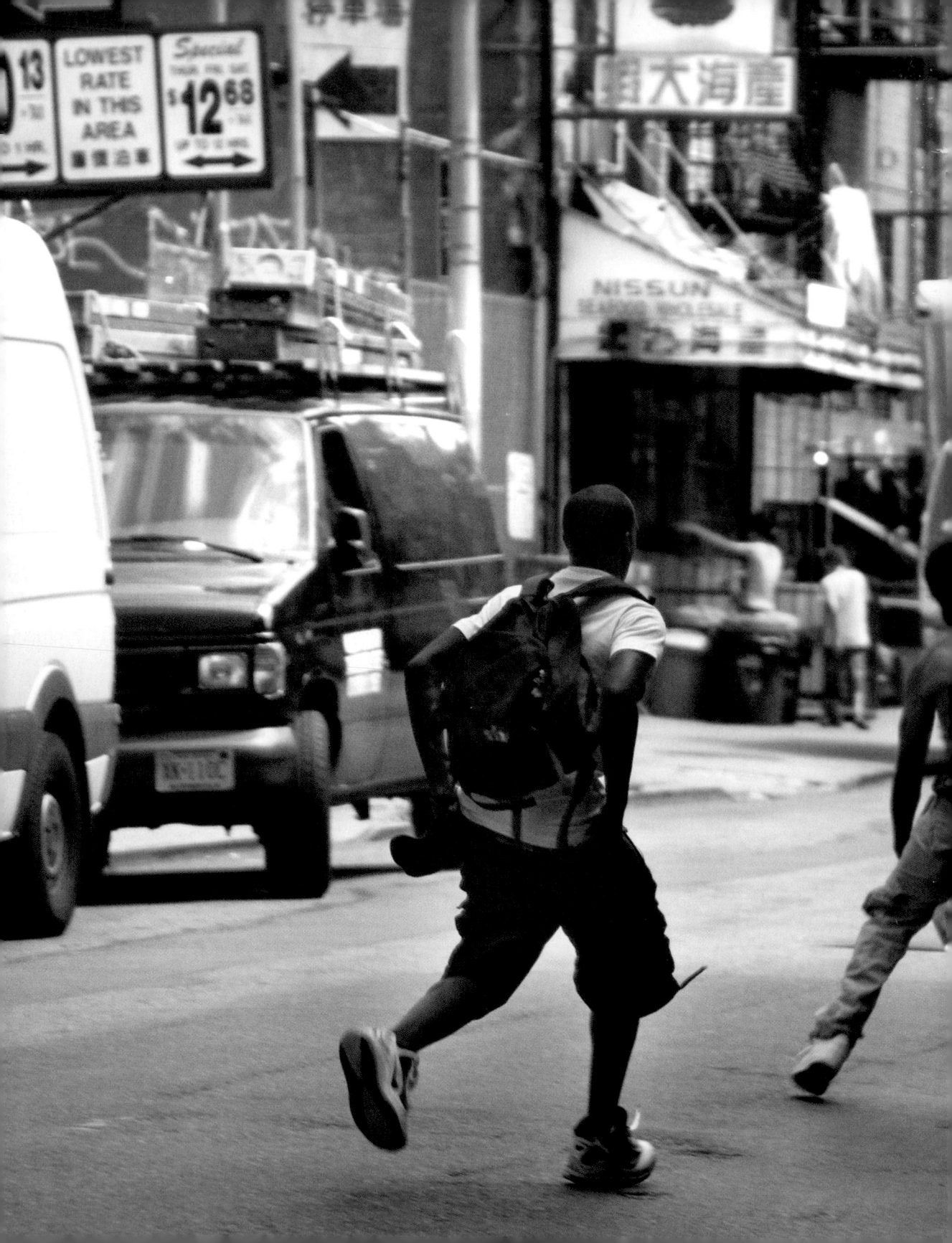
LOWEST
RATE
IN THIS
AREA
Special
$12.68
NISSUN

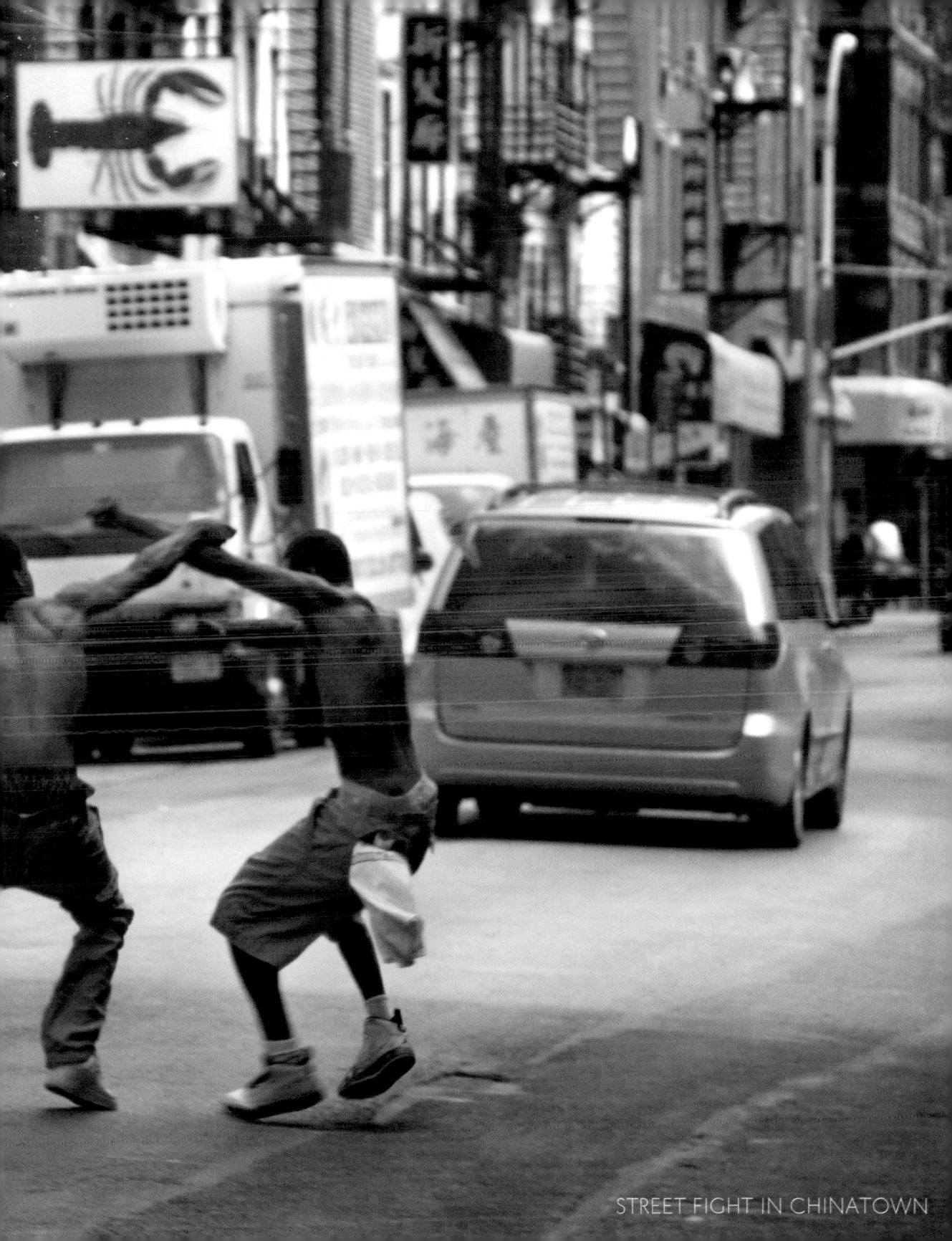

STREET FIGHT IN CHINATOWN

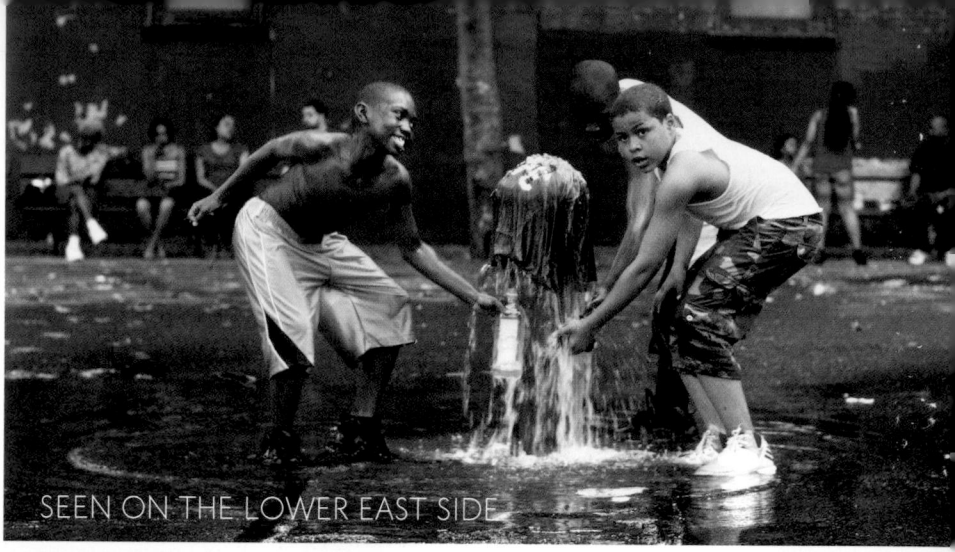

SEEN ON THE LOWER EAST SIDE

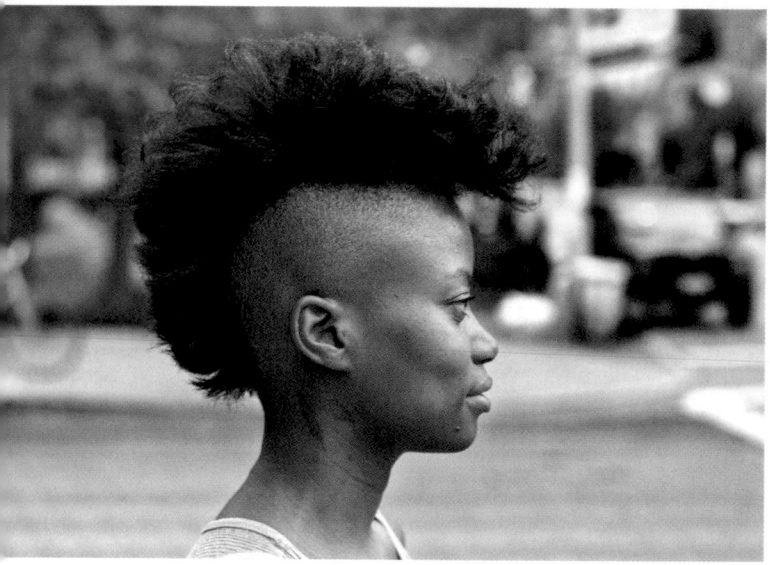

"I GREW UP IN SOUTH AFRICA, THEN I MOVED TO THAILAND FOR A FEW YEARS. NOW I'M HERE WORKING AS A PERSONAL CHEF. I SPECIALIZE IN FRENCH CUISINE, WITH A SOUTH AFRICAN AND ASIAN TWIST."

"YOU SHOULD NEVER SAY: 'I'M POOR.' INSTEAD YOU SHOULD ALWAYS SAY: 'I LIVE IN ABUNDANCE.' GIVE IT A TRY. I DID IT FOR A WHOLE MONTH ONCE. PEOPLE WERE BUYING ME LUNCHES, THEATER TICKETS—IT WAS GREAT."

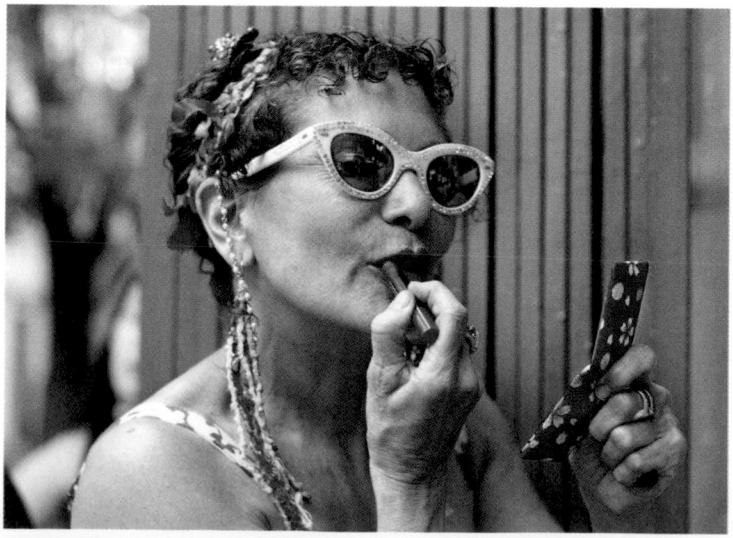

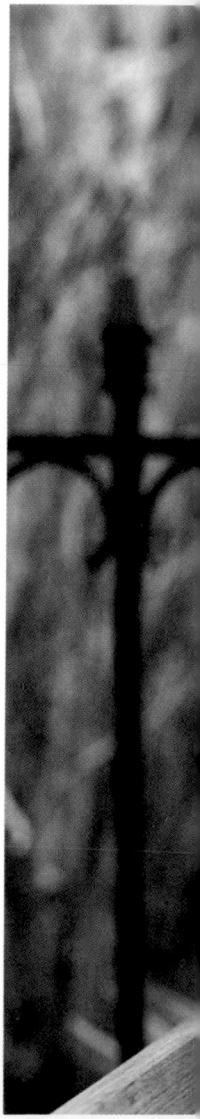

"JUST BECAUSE YOU'RE AN ADULT DOESN'T MEAN YOU'RE GROWN UP. GROWING UP MEANS BEING PATIENT, HOLDING YOUR TEMPER, CUTTING OUT THE SELF-PITY, AND QUITTING WITH THE RIGHTEOUS INDIGNATION."

"WHY DO SO MANY PEOPLE SEEM TO LOVE RIGHTEOUS INDIGNATION?"

"BECAUSE IF YOU CAN PROVE YOU'RE A VICTIM, ALL RULES ARE OFF. YOU CAN LASH OUT AT PEOPLE. YOU DON'T HAVE TO BE ACCOUNTABLE FOR ANYTHING."

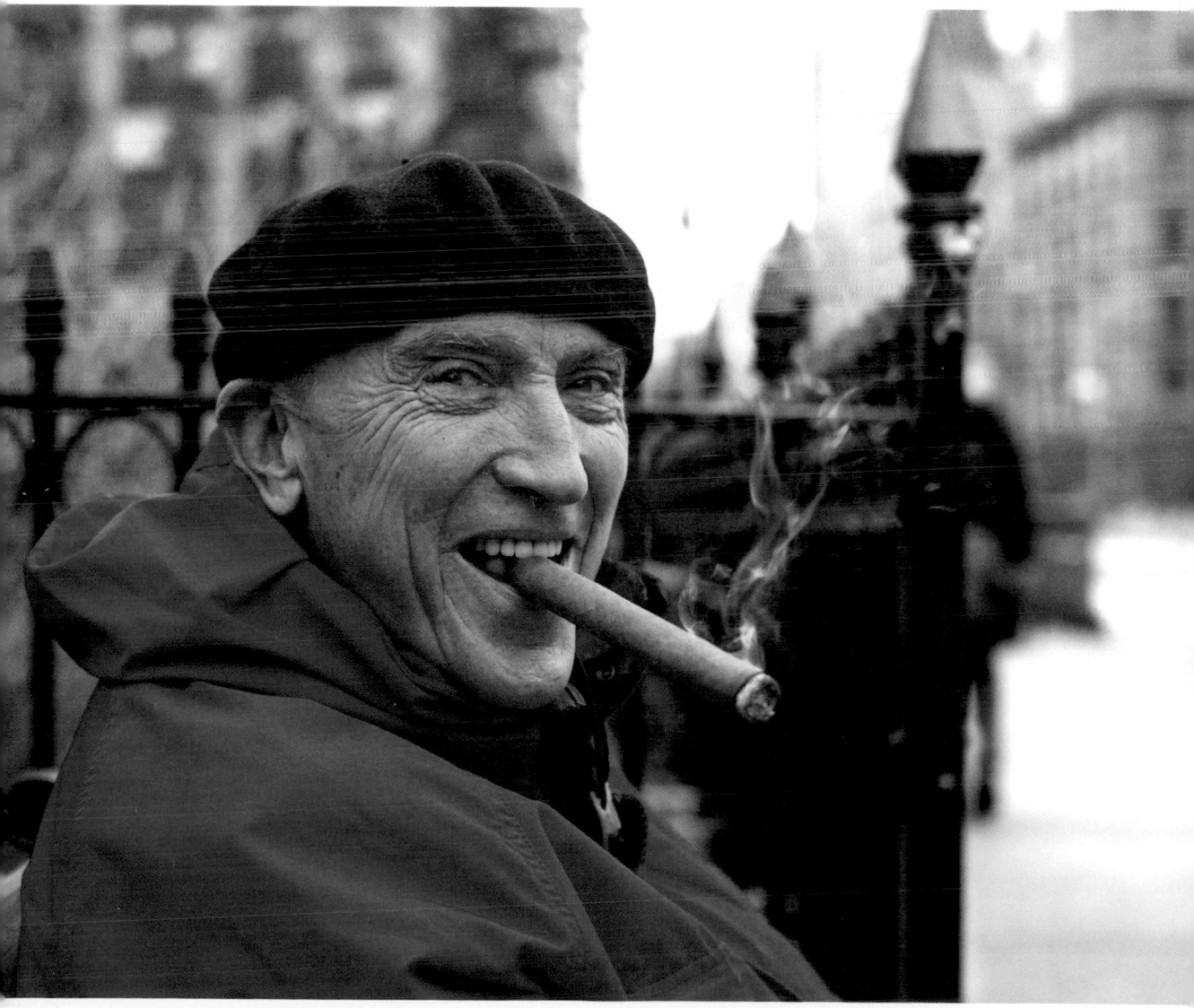

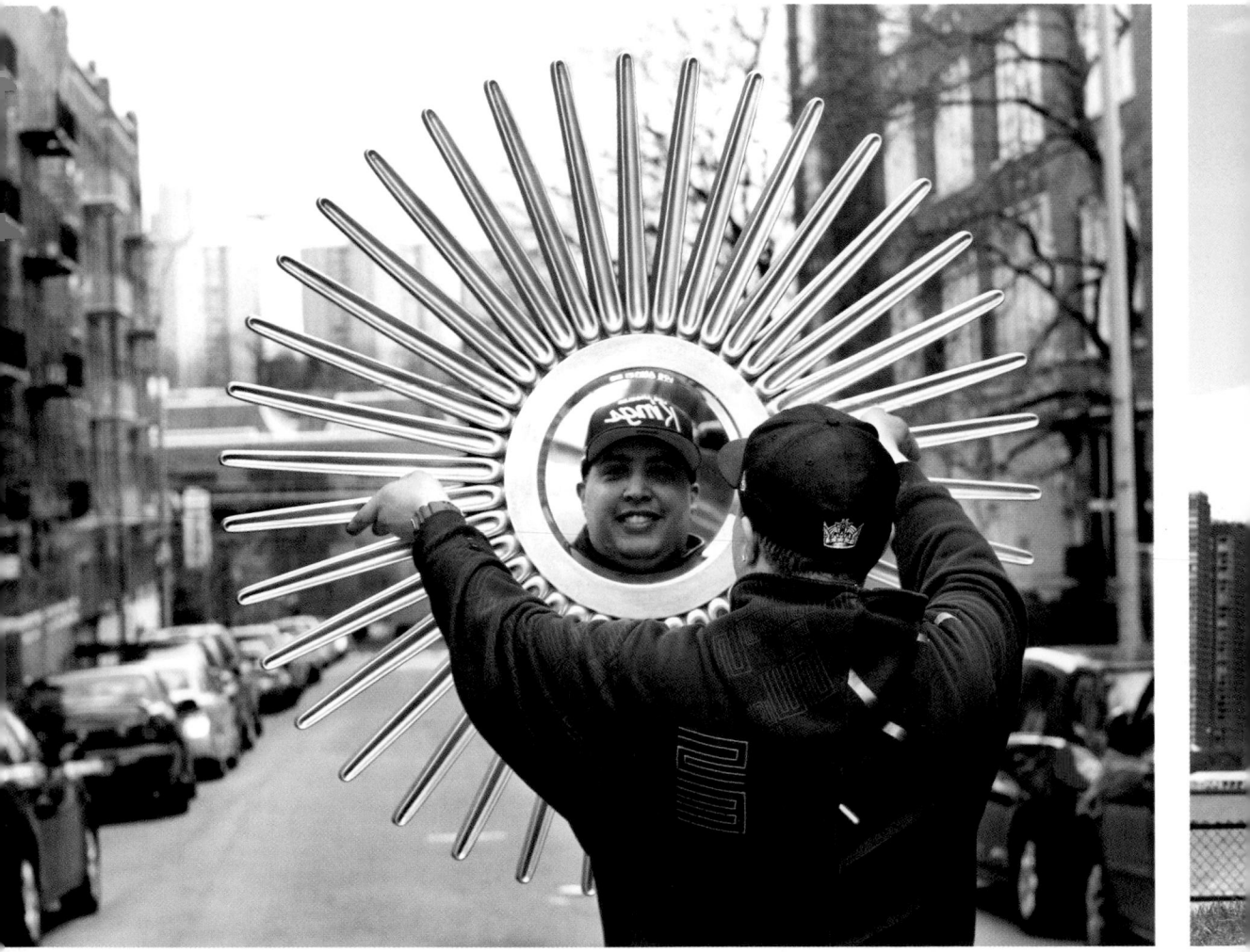

WHEN I EAT AT CAFÉS, I TRY TO GET A TABLE BY THE WINDOW.
JUST IN CASE SOMEONE WALKS BY WITH A GIANT SUN MIRROR.

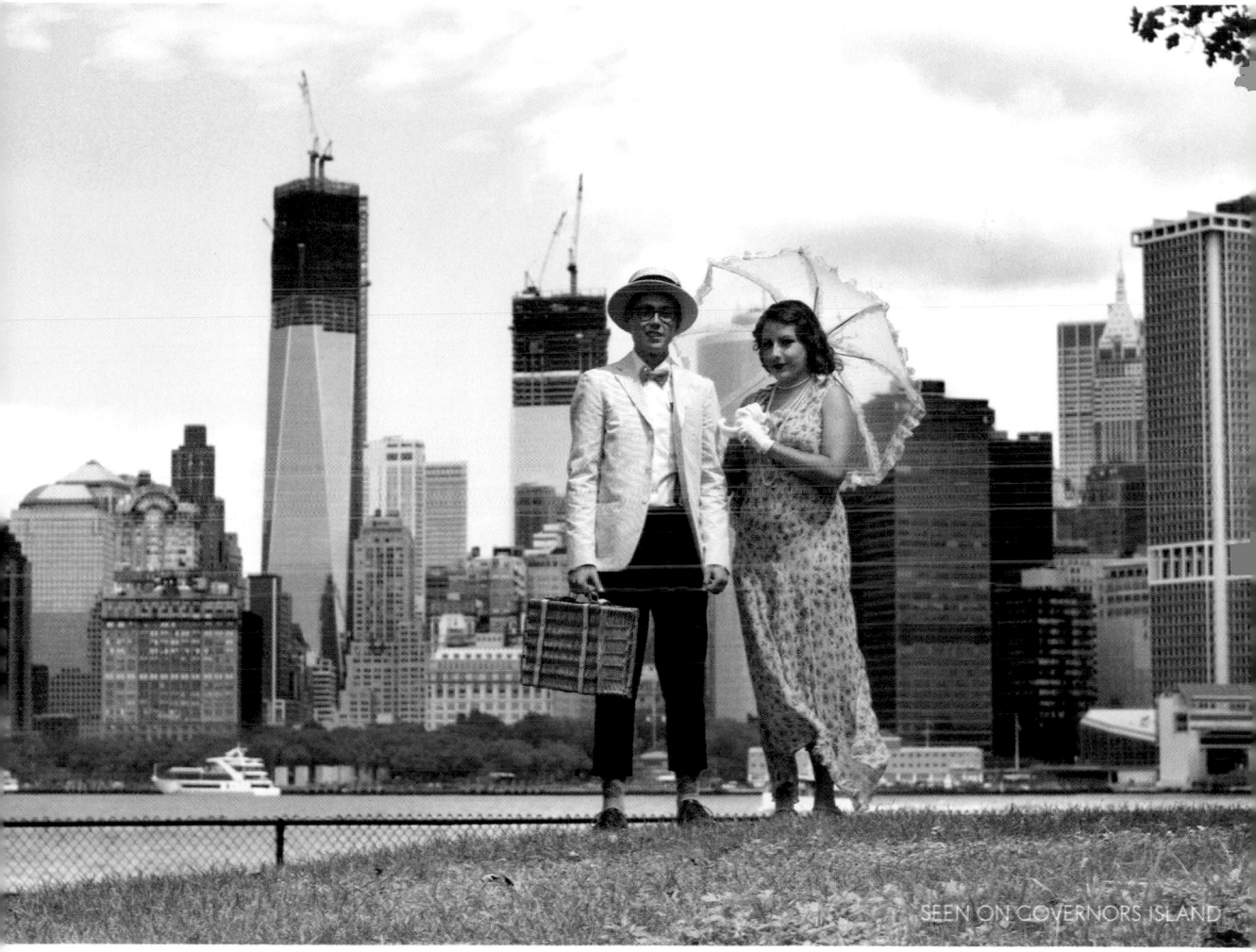
SEEN ON GOVERNORS ISLAND

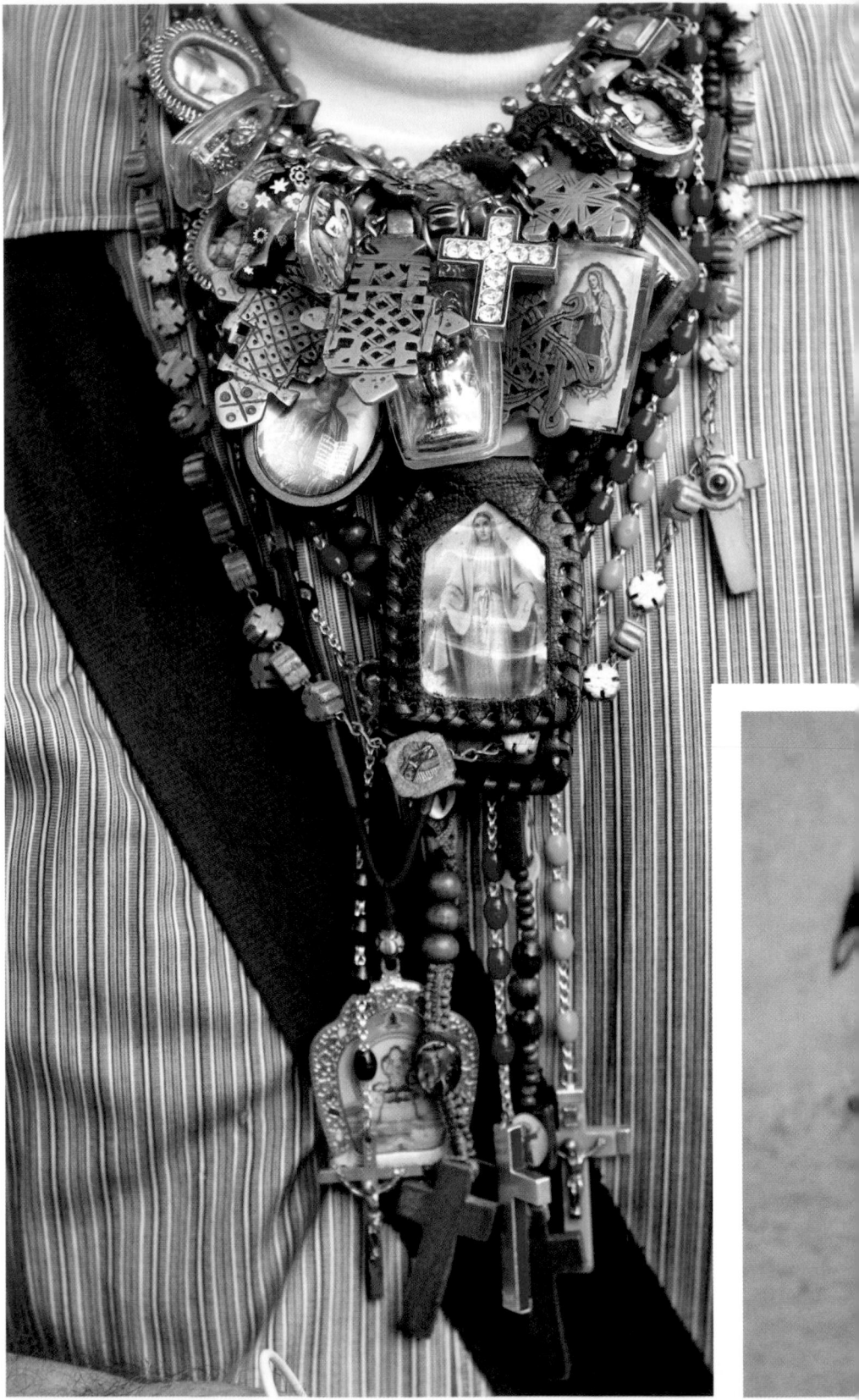

"I BELIEVE IN A LITTLE BIT OF EVERYTHING."

SEEN ON PROSPECT AVENUE, THE BRONX

THIS MURAL WAS HOUSED IN A VACANT LOT SURROUNDED BY A HUGE CHAIN-LINK FENCE. I ASKED SEVERAL YOUNG MEN TO FOLLOW ME THROUGH A HOLE IN THE FENCE, BUT NOBODY WAS WILLING TO TAKE THE RISK. AFTER SEVERAL MINUTES, I FINALLY FOUND TWO PEOPLE WITH THE BALLS TO DO IT.

THE 1 PERCENT

"I WANT TO CHANGE THE WORLD, BUT I DON'T KNOW HOW."

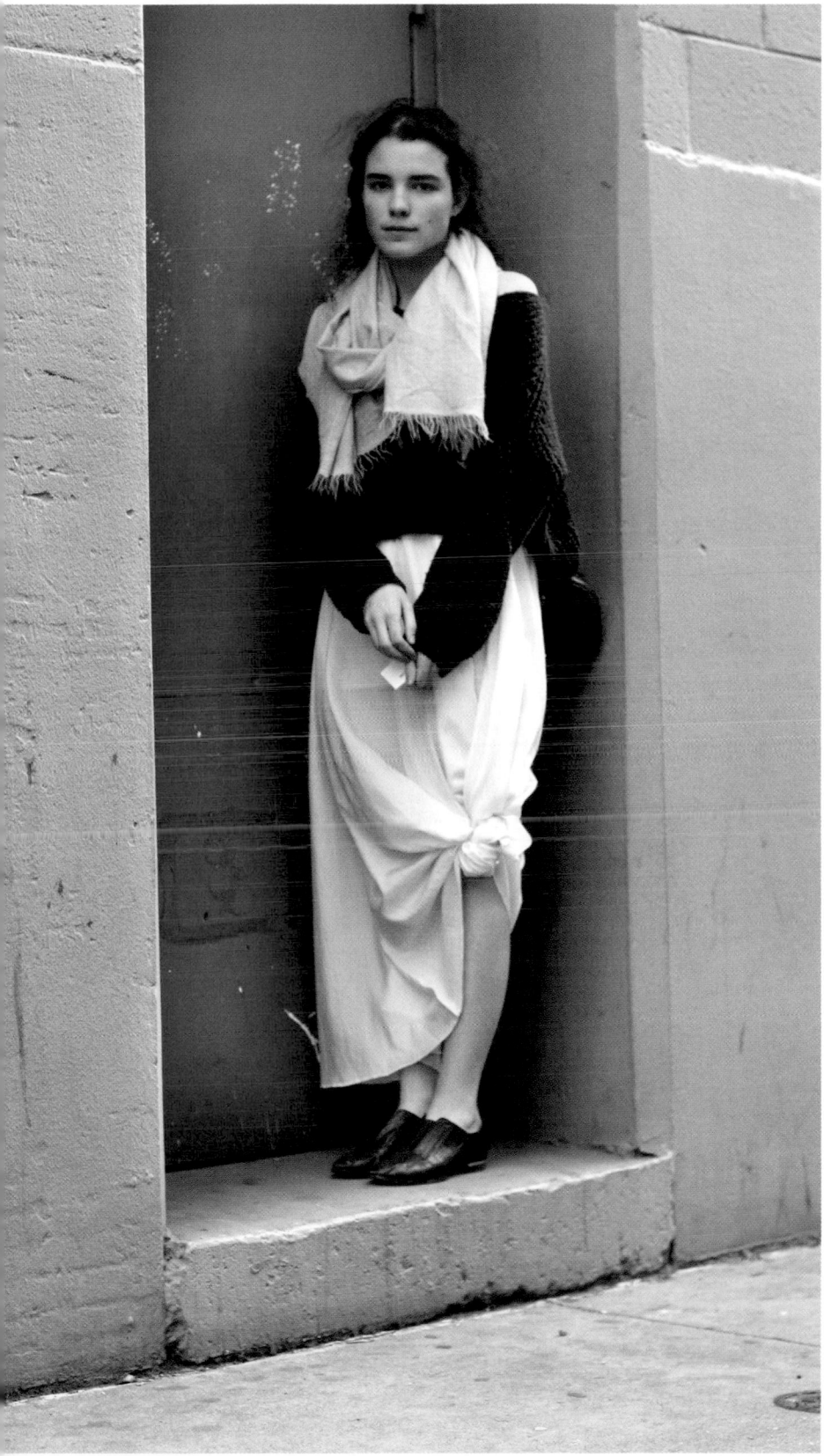

I DON'T THINK SHE WAS FULLY COMFORTABLE WITH THE PROCESS, BUT HER APPREHENSIVENESS CAME THROUGH BEAUTIFULLY.

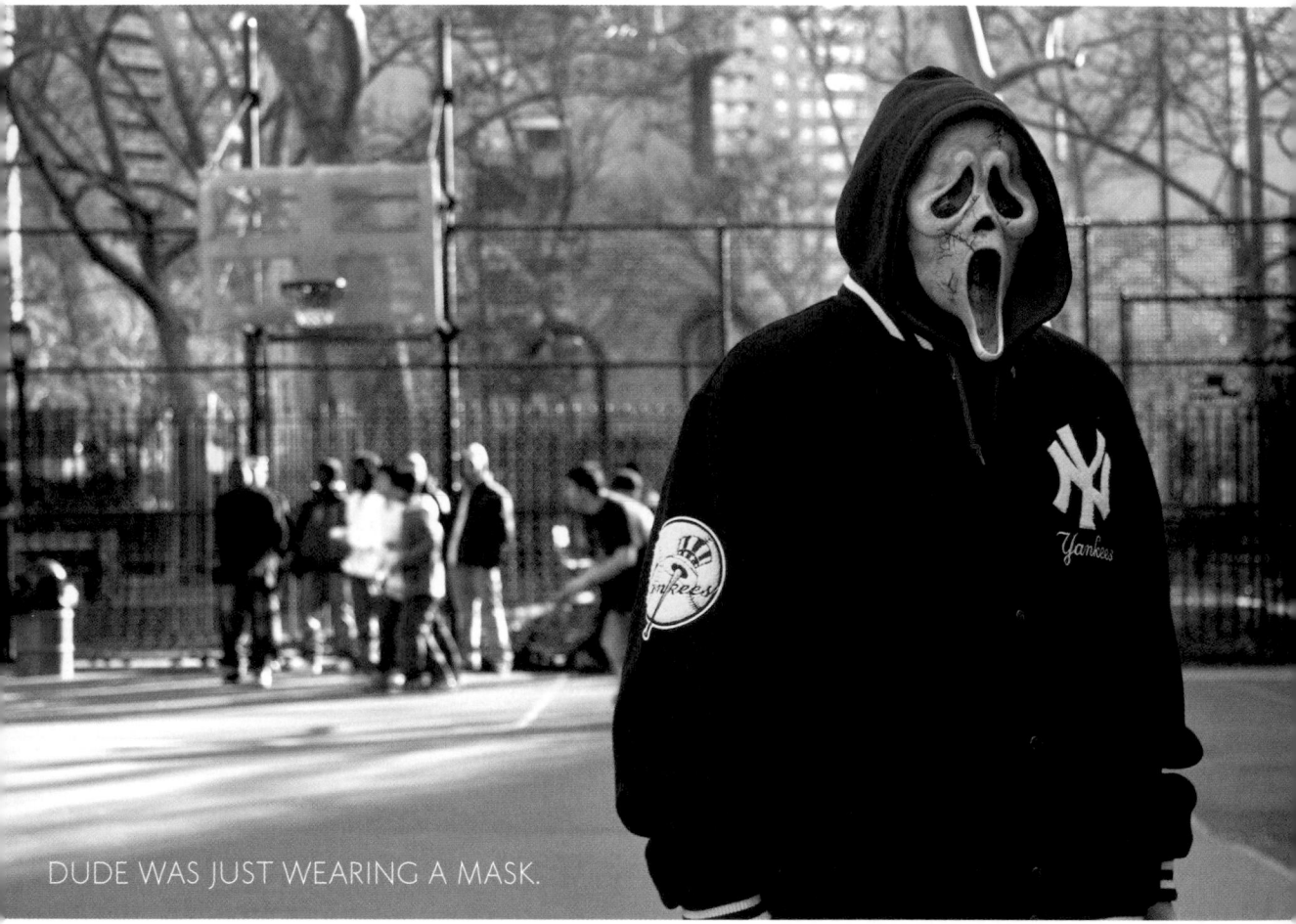


DUDE WAS JUST WEARING A MASK.

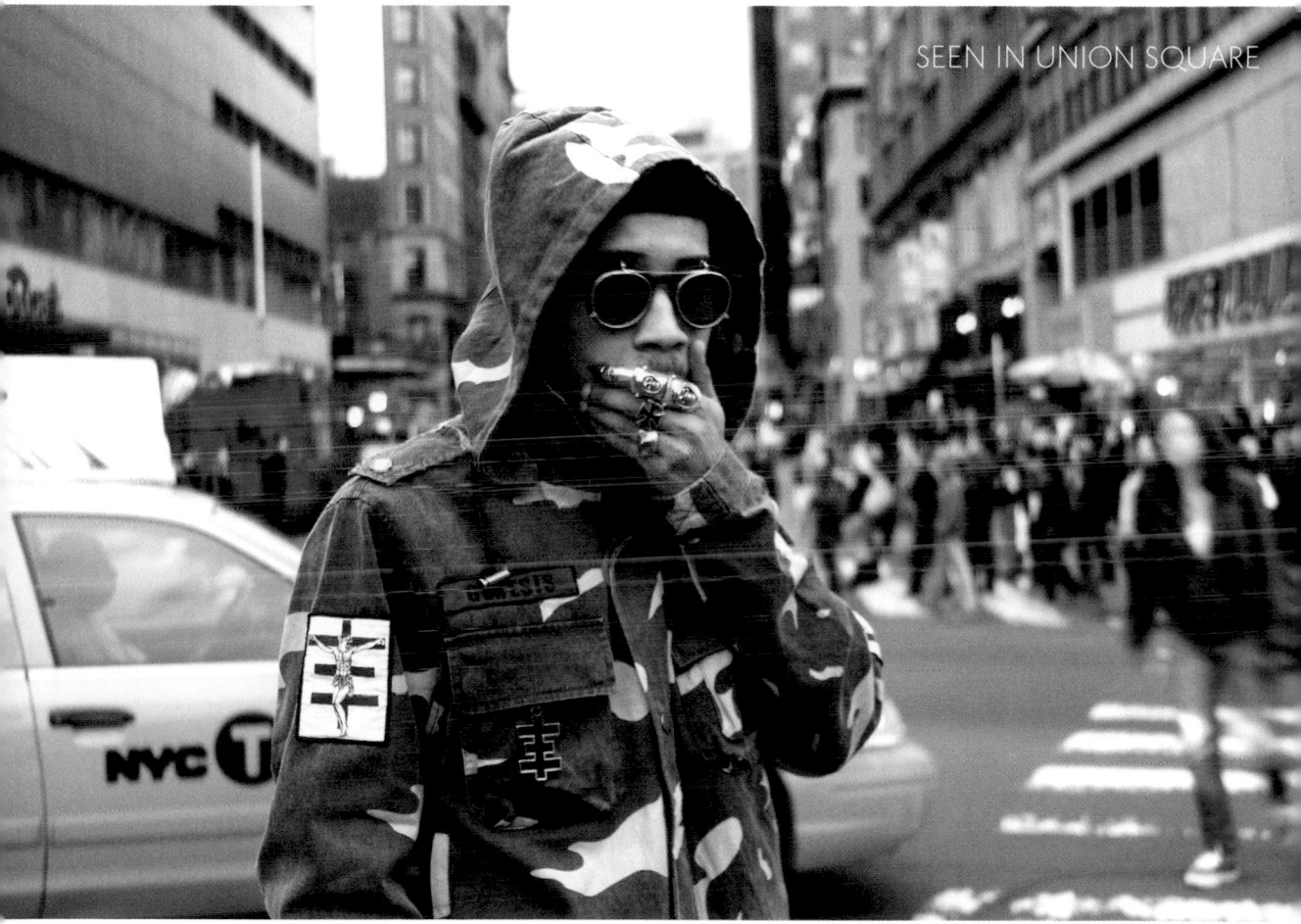


SEEN IN UNION SQUARE

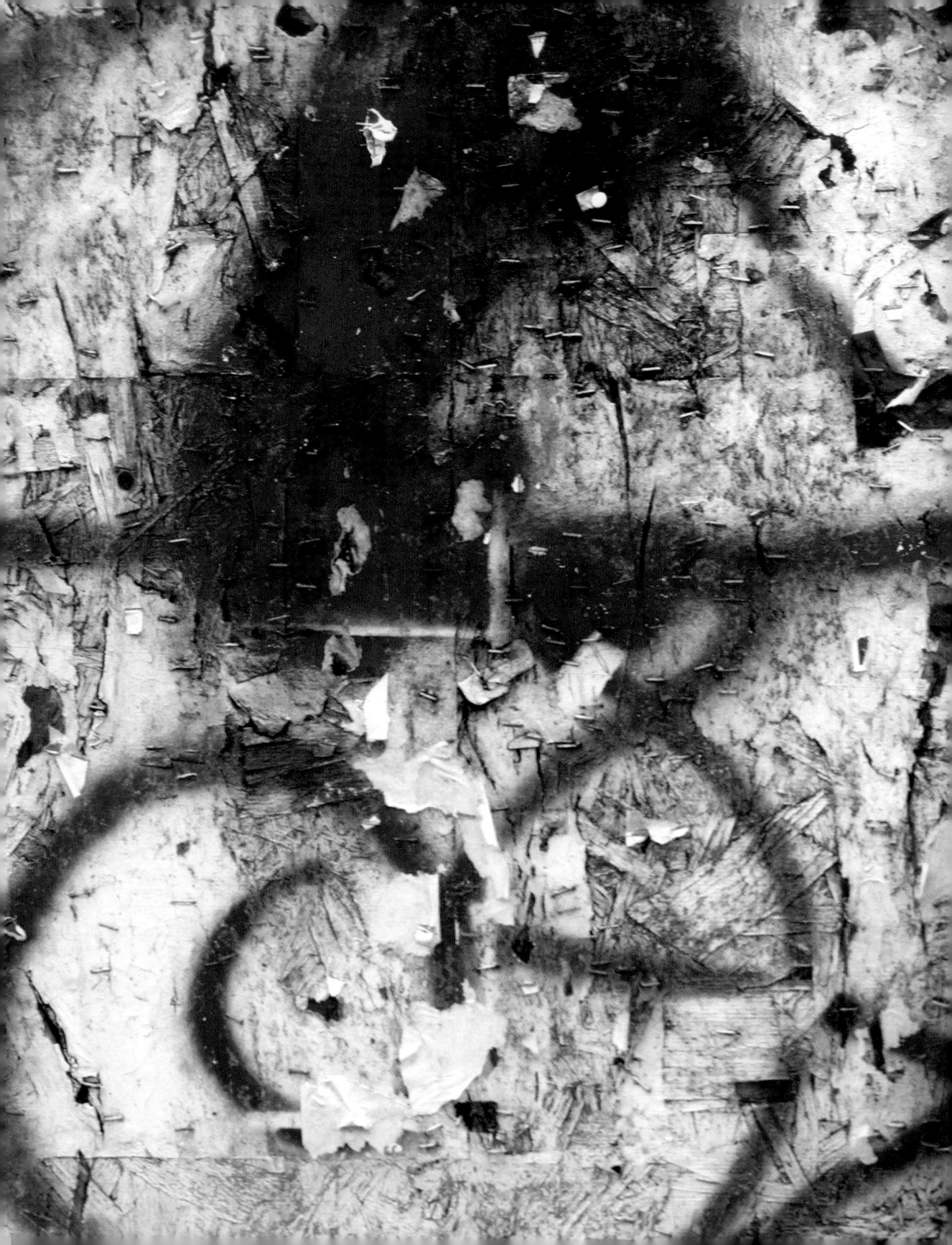

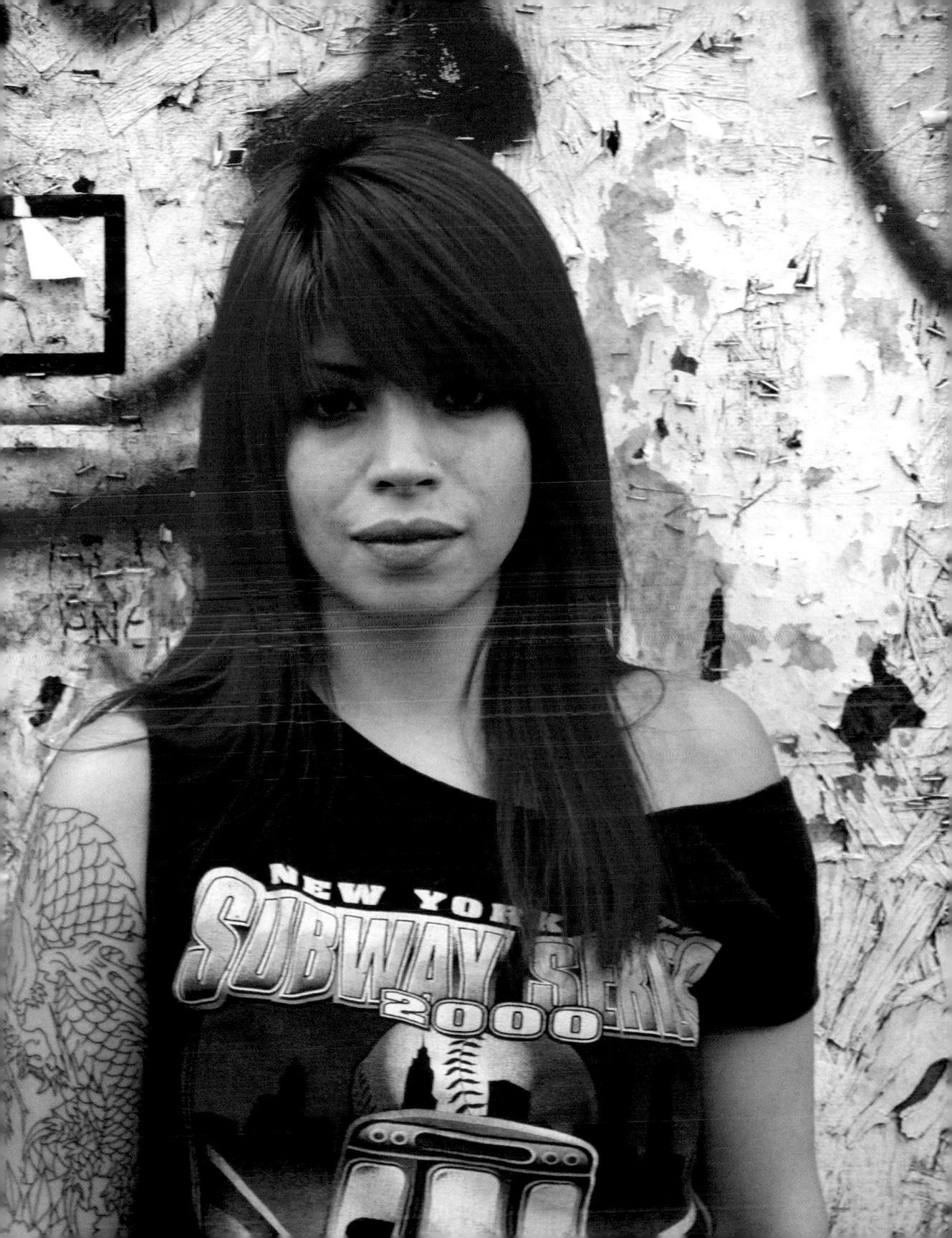
NEW YORK
SUBWAY SERIES
2000

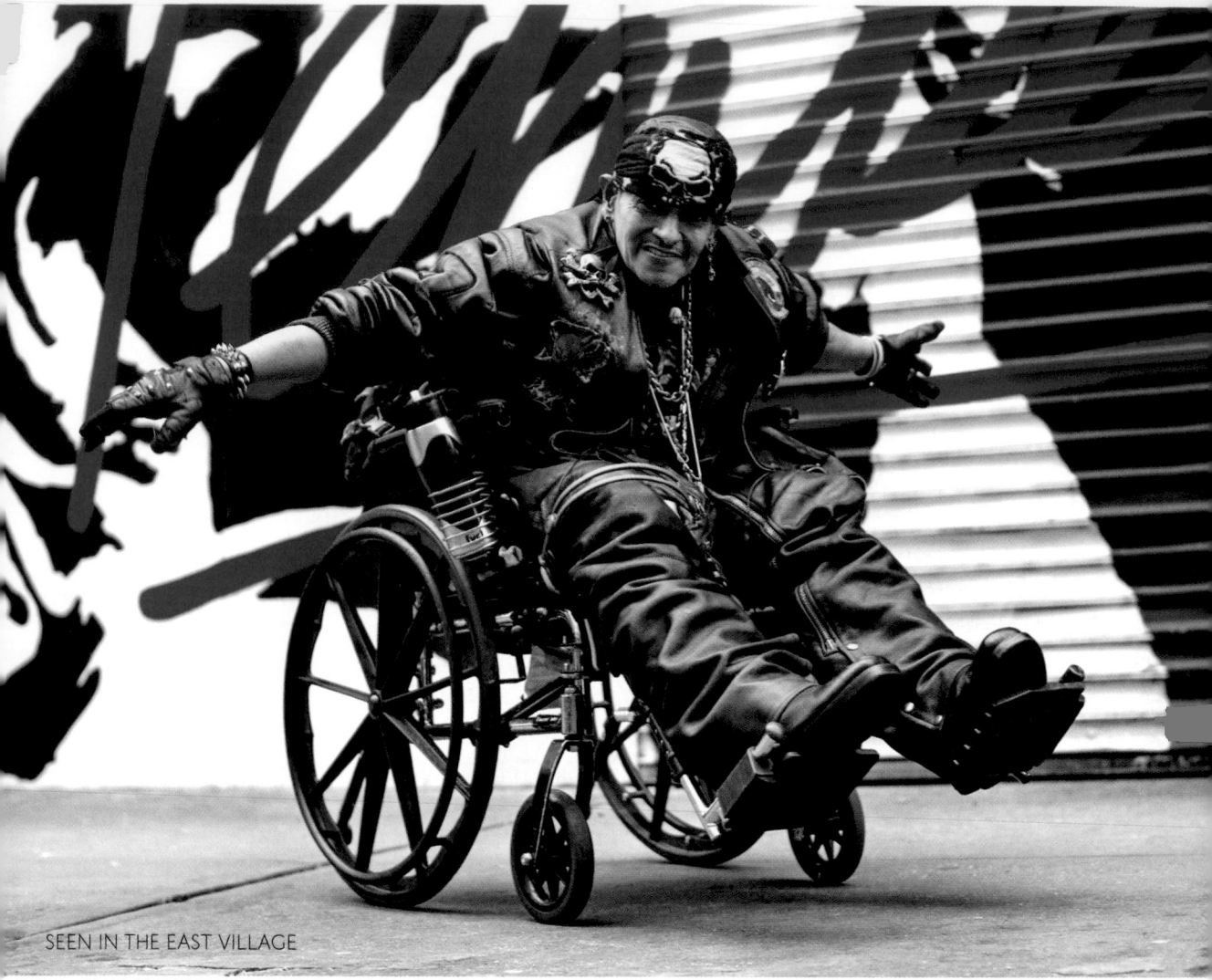

SEEN IN THE EAST VILLAGE

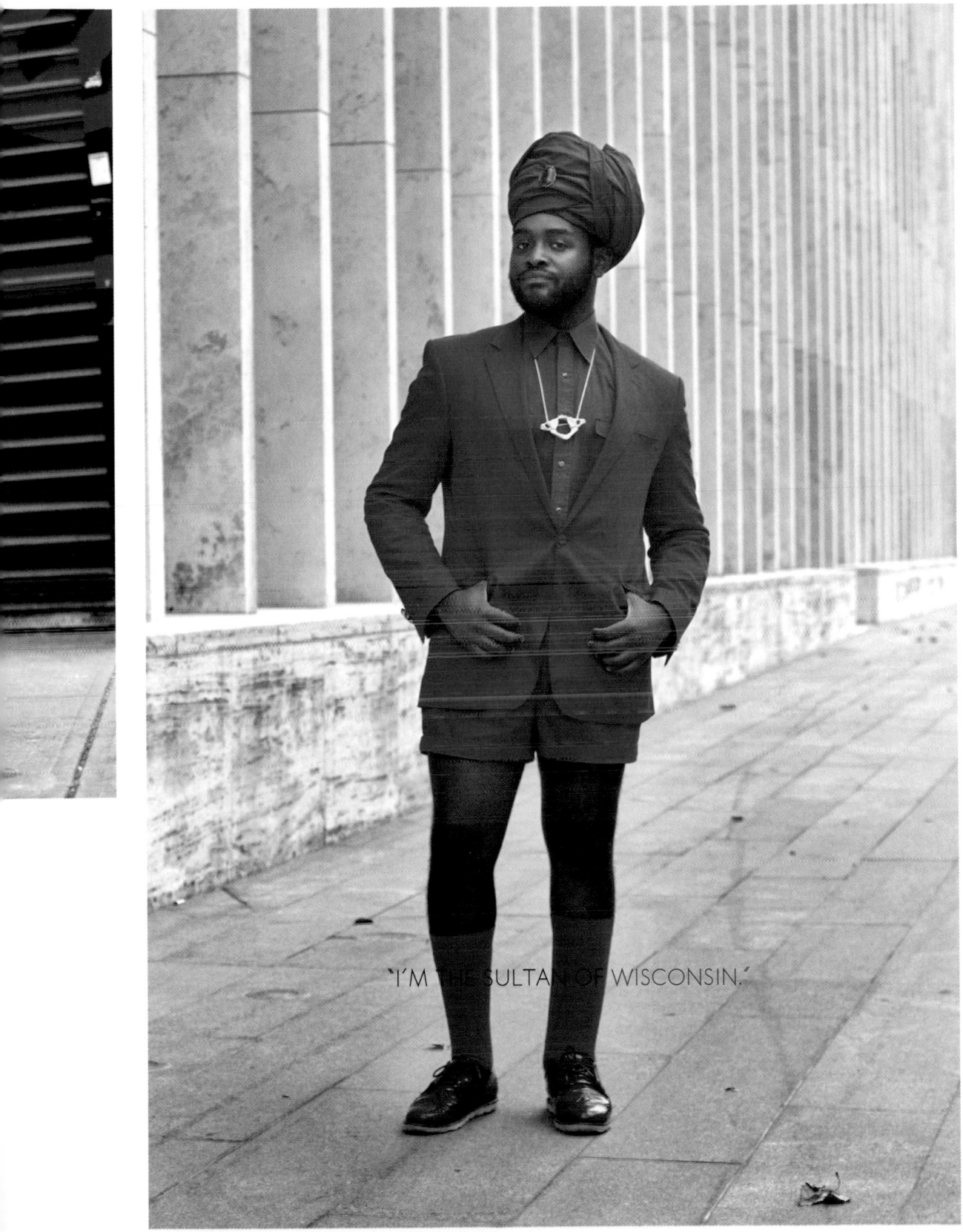
"I'M THE SULTAN OF WISCONSIN."

# ACKNOWLEDGMENTS

These days I get tons of mail from people offering advice, help, and support. I appreciate all of it, of course. But I'd like to begin by thanking the people who provided these things back when HONY was just a crazy idea. Thanks to Sam Ward for telling me that I was going to be remembered for my "people pictures"—after my very first day of shooting. Thanks to Casey and Erin, Catherine, David, and everyone else who let me sleep on their couch during my first summer in New York. Thanks to Nathan Hicks for being the first true believer. Thanks to Eric Engdahl for all the counseling. Thanks to Jessie Canon for building an awesome Web site for some guy you didn't know, for free. Who does that!?!? You do. Because you're an awesome guy.

Thanks to Brian Lighthiser, Andy Anaszewicz, and Adam Schaefer. Emotional support is great—but you guys helped pay the rent. At some point, each of you dropped a ladder when I was absolutely convinced that I'd hit a wall. You made this possible. Thanks also to Steve Churchill, for being a dick. (You know I love you.) Thanks to my assistants, Olivia and Christina, for all the work you've taken off my back, for keeping me organized, and for taking my emo phone calls when I get hate mail. Thanks also to my roommate Dave for all the cynicism, skepticism, and pessimism. It kept me grounded. Thanks to everyone at Tumblr for letting me hang out at the office and feel like a cool kid.

Thanks to my agent, Brian DeFiore. Late in the game, a lot of agents wanted to meet because of my audience. In the beginning, Brian wanted to meet because of my photos. Very grateful for his early and continued support. Brian—sorry about all the text messages on weekends. Thanks to everyone at St. Martin's Press for buying in to something new. Thanks to Yaniv Soha for all your helpful suggestions, and Jon Bennett for your mad skills.

Thanks to Tim Chia, Alex Rojas, and Keith Fiantago for teaching me how to trade bonds. You're three of the greatest guys I've ever known. You taught me that there were bighearted, honest people in every industry. You also taught me to take losses and keep swinging. And that I'll use forever. Thanks to Joe Coconate and Charles Okoye for being such great friends in Chicago.

Thanks to my parents for putting up with all the false starts and wild curves. Sorry about the scares. Thanks to Ryan for being a great brother. And lastly, thanks to my wonderful girlfriend, Erin—you have a heart of absolute gold and make me eat vegetables.

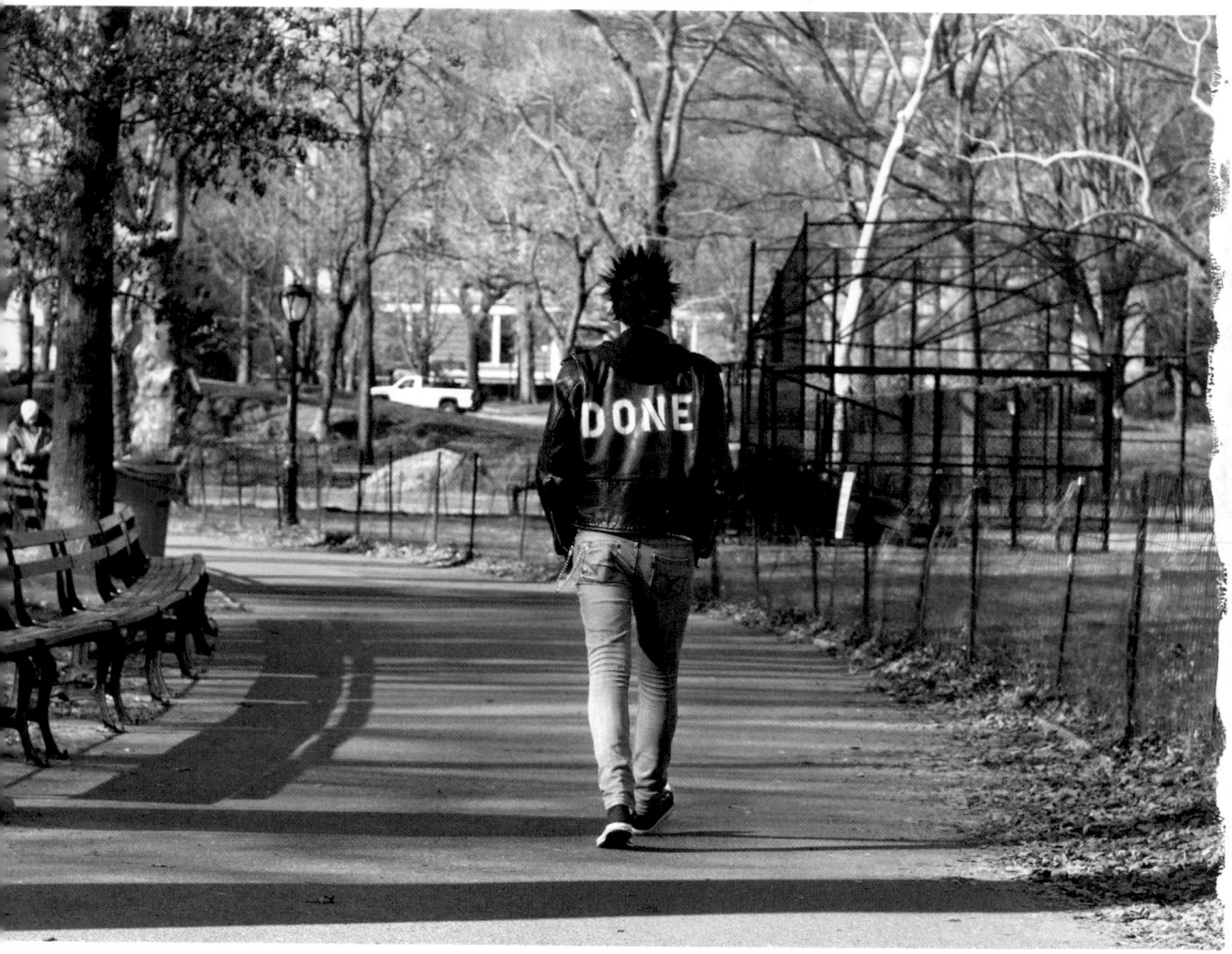
DONE